EARLY HISTORY OF THE CREEK INDIANS AND THEIR NEIGHBORS

Southeastern Classics in Archaeology, Anthropology, and History

Southeastern Classics in Archaeology, Anthropology, and History
Edited by Jerald T. Milanich

Archeology of the Florida Gulf Coast, by Gordon R. Willey
Early History of the Creek Indians and Their Neighbors, by John R. Swanton
Space and Time Perspective in Northern St. Johns Archeology, Florida, by John M. Goggin

EARLY HISTORY OF THE CREEK INDIANS AND THEIR NEIGHBORS

JOHN R. SWANTON

FOREWORD BY JERALD T. MILANICH, SERIES EDITOR

UNIVERSITY PRESS OF FLORIDA

GAINESVILLE · TALLAHASSEE · TAMPA · BOCA RATON

PENSACOLA · ORLANDO · MIAMI · JACKSONVILLE

Originally published in 1922 by the Smithsonian Institution
(Bureau of American Ethnology, Bulletin 73)
Printed in the United States of America on acid-free paper

03 02 01 00 99 98 6 5 4 3 2 1

LIBRARY OF CONGRESS CATALOGING-IN-PUBLICATION DATA

Swanton, John Reed, 1873–1958.
Early history of the Creek Indians and their neighbors /
by John R. Swanton.
p. cm. – (Southeastern classics in archaeology, anthropology, and history)
Includes bibliographical references (p.) and index.
Originally published: Washington, D.C.: Smithsonian Institution, 1922.
ISBN 0-8130-1635-5 (pbk.)
1. Creek Indians–History. 2. Creek Indians–Social life and customs. 3. Indians of North America–Southern States–History. I. Title. II. Series.
E99.C9S9 1998
975'004973–dc21

The University Press of Florida is the scholarly publishing agency for the State University System of Florida, comprising Florida A&M University, Florida Atlantic University, Florida International University, Florida State University, University of Central Florida, University of Florida, University of North Florida, University of South Florida, and University of West Florida.

University Press of Florida
15 Northwest 15th Street
Gainesville, FL 32611
http://nersp.nerdc.ufl.edu/~upf

FOREWORD

What makes a classic? Why are some books and articles as useful today as when they were first written? For archaeologists, anthropologists, and historians interested in the Native American cultures of the southeastern United States and the events of the colonial period, classics are references that contain ideas and knowledge essential to research. Some classics helped to shape a field of study, others developed the fundamental taxonomies used today, and still others offer basic building blocks of information that can be used to fuel theoretical models. Many classics exhibit all these characteristics. All are publications that active researchers cannot live without.

In my own personal research library I have a number of southeastern classics and I consult them frequently. They are the books my students covet and which I guard zealously, for scholarly as well as financial reasons. Classics—if one can still find them at all—can cost a pretty penny!

The knowledge published in classics continues to endure. Regrettably, many of the books themselves have been less fortunate. Originally published in paperback with non-acid-free pages and bindings, in limited printings, or in hard-to-find journals, some of them have become rare indeed.

The Southeastern Classics Series is putting back into print books and articles deemed by scholars to be timeless treasures, resources we all use, but which are difficult to find or, in some cases, have literally disappeared. As someone who loves books and could not wait for the Bookmobile to visit my neighborhood during the summers of my youth, I am very pleased to be a part of this project.

John Reed Swanton has authored more classics on North American Indians than any other individual. Written during his forty-four-year career as an anthropologist with the Smithsonian Institution's Bureau of American Ethnology, his more than two hundred articles and twenty books and monographs remain ageless studies of American Indian linguistics, ethnology, and ethnohistory. When he died at age eighty-five on May 2, 1958, he left an academic legacy that will never be surpassed.

Some of Swanton's very best research was on the Indians of the southeastern United States. His *Early History of the Creek Indians and Their Neighbors,* first published in 1922, is basic to any study of the Creek Indians and the formation of the Creek confederacy. The volume also provides important ethnohistorical information on many other southeastern Indians who were adjacent to the Creek Indians and their ancestors from the sixteenth century into the early nineteenth century. It is a classic by any standard.

Jerald T. Milanich
Series Editor

CONTENTS

Page.

ILLUSTRATIONS

(IN POCKET OF BACK COVER)

EARLY HISTORY OF THE CREEK INDIANS AND THEIR NEIGHBORS

By John R. Swanton

INTRODUCTION

The present paper originated in an attempt to prepare a report on the Indians of the Creek Confederacy similar to that made in Bulletin 43 for those along the lower course of the Mississippi River.[1] In this study, however, it is still possible to add information obtained from living Indians, about 9,000 of whom were enumerated in 1910.[2] But when material from all sources had been tentatively brought together the amount was found to be so great that it was thought advisable to divide the work into two or three different sections for separate publication. As our account of the distribution, interrelationship, and history of these people is to be gathered rather from documentary sources than from field investigations it is naturally the first to be ready for presentation. Since it has been compiled primarily for ethnological purposes, no attempt has been made to give a complete account of the later fortunes of the tribes under consideration, such important chapters in their career as the Creek and Seminole wars and the westward emigration belonging within the province of the historian strictly so considered. The writer's main endeavor has been to trace their movements from earliest times until they are caught up into the broad stream of later history in which concealment is practically impossible. Although not pretending that this work is as yet by any means complete, he has aimed to furnish something in the nature of an encyclopedia of information regarding the history of the southeastern Indians for the period covered, and hence has usually included direct quotations instead of attempting to recast the material in his own words.

It was found that a satisfactory study of the Creek Indians would make it necessary to extend the scope of this work so as to consider all of the eastern tribes of the Muskhogean stock as well as the Indians of Florida. The Yuchi, on the ethnological side, have been made a

[1] Swanton, Indian Tribes of the Lower Mississippi Valley, Bull. 43, Bur. Amer. Ethn., 1911.

[2] This includes the Creek and Seminole Indians of Oklahoma, the Seminole of Florida, and the Alabama and Koasati of Texas and Louisiana. (Ind. Pop. in the U. S. and Alaska, 1910. Wash., 1915.)

special subject of inquiry by Dr. Frank G. Speck,[1] but so many new facts have presented themselves in the course of this investigation regarding the early history of these Indians that they have been treated at length. Some new information is also given regarding the Natchez and those Shawnee who were for a long period incorporated with the Creeks. The Siouan tribes of the east have been made the subject of a special study by Mr. James Mooney,[2] and all that we know regarding two other southern Siouan tribes, the Biloxi and Ofo, has been given by the writer in another publication.[3] The ramifications of the Creek Confederacy extended so far that even the Chickasaw are found to be involved, and they have in consequence been considered in this paper. The Choctaw, however, form a distinct problem and the principal attention paid them has been to incorporate a statement regarding their population so that it may be compared with that of the other Muskhogean tribes.

Sections have been included on the ethnology of the Cusabo Indians and the Florida tribes, for which we are dependent entirely on documentary sources.

To illustrate this work several of the more significant of the older maps have been reproduced, and two from data compiled by the author. It must be understood that the main object has been to trace historical movements and give the relative positions of the various tribes and bands, so that few of the locations may be considered final. It is hoped that eventually intensive work in the Southeast, and in other parts of the country as well, will take form in a series of large-scale maps in which the historical as well as the prehistoric village sites of our Indians will be recorded with a high degree of accuracy. So far as the Southeast is concerned, an excellent beginning has been made by the Alabama Anthropological Society. The handbook of this society for 1920, which comes to hand as the present work is going through the press, contains a catalogue of "Aboriginal Towns in Alabama" (pp. 42–54), which marks an advance over anything which has so far appeared and should be consulted by the student desirous of more precise information regarding the locations of many of the towns dealt with in this volume. In two points only I venture a criticism of this catalogue. First, I am entirely unable to embrace that interpretation of De Soto's route which would bring him to the headwaters of Coosa River below the northern boundary of Georgia; and secondly, it seems to me a little risky to attempt an exact identification of the towns at which that explorer stopped in the neighborhood of the upper Alabama. At the same time I grant that such identifications are highly desirable and have no personal theories in conflict with the ones attempted.

[1] Ethnology of the Yuchi Indians, Anthrop. Pubs. Univ. Mus., Univ. Pa., I, No. 1, 1909.

[2] Siouan Tribes of the East, Bull. 22, Bur. Amer. Ethn., 1894.

[3] Dorsey and Swanton, Dictionary of the Biloxi and Ofo Languages, Bull. 47, Bur. Amer. Ethn., 1912. Introduction.

CLASSIFICATION OF THE SOUTHEASTERN TRIBES

Below is a classification of the linguistic groups in the southeastern part of the United States considered in whole or in part in this bulletin:

- Muskhogean stock.
  - Muskhogean branch.
    - Southern division.
      - Apalachee.
      - Hitchiti group.
        - Hitchiti.
        - Apalachicola.
        - Sawokli.
        - Okmulgee.
        - Oconee.
        - Tamałi.[1]
        - Chiaha.
        - Mikasuki.
      - Alabama group.
        - Alabama.
        - Koasati.
        - Tawasa.
        - Pawokti.
        - Muklasa.
      - Choctaw group.
        - Choctaw.
        - Chickasaw.
        - Chakchiuma.
        - Houma.
        - Mobile.
        - Tohome.
        - Pensacola.
        - Taposa.
        - Ibitoupa.
        - Quinipissa or Mugulasha.
        - Bayogoula.
        - Acolapissa.
        - Tangipahoa.
        - Okelusa.
        - Nabochi or Napissa.
      - Tuskegee.

- Muskhogean stock—Continued.
  - Muskhogean branch—Continued.
    - Southern division—Continued.
      - Guale Indians and Yamasee.
      - Cusabo.
      - Chatot.
      - Osochi.
    - Northern division.
      - Muskogee branch.
        - Kasihta.
        - Coweta.
        - Coosa.
        - Abihka.
        - Hołiwahali.[1]
        - Eufaula.
        - Hilibi.
        - Wakokai.
        - Tukabahchee.
        - Okchai.
        - Pakana.
        - Seminole.
  - Natchez branch.
    - Natchez.
    - Taensa.
    - Avoyel.
- Uchean stock.
  - Yuchi.
- Timuquanan stock.
  - Timucua.
- South Florida Indians.
  - Calusa.
  - Tekesta.
  - Ais.
  - Jeaga.
- Tamahita.

As above intimated, some consideration has also been given to a part of the Shawnee Indians of the Algonquian stock, who were for a time incorporated into the Creek Confederacy.

Of course no claim of infallibility is made for this classification. The connection of some of the tribes thus brought together is well known, while others are placed with them on rather slender circumstantial evidence. The strength of the argument for each I will now consider.

---

[1] Here and throughout the present work the Polish crossed ł stands for a surd l common to nearly all of the southeastern languages and sometimes represented in English, though inadequately, by thl or hl.

In the first place it may be stated that sufficient linguistic material is preserved from the Apalachee,[1] Hitchiti, Mikasuki, Alabama, Koasati, Choctaw, Chickasaw, the leading tribes of the Muskogee branch, Natchez, Yuchi, and Timucua, to establish their positions beyond question. The connection of all of the other tribes of the Choctaw group except Pensacola, that of the Chatot, and the tribes of the Natchez branch has been examined by the author in his Indian Tribes of the Lower Mississippi Valley, to which the reader is referred.[2]

That Hitchiti with but slight variations was spoken by the Apalachicola, Sawokli, and Okmulgee is known to all well-informed Creek Indians to-day, and some of the people of those tribes can use it or know some words of it. The town names themselves are in Hitchiti.

Oconee is placed by Bartram among those towns speaking the "Stinkard" language,[3] and all of the other towns so denominated, so far as we have positive information, spoke Muskhogean dialects belonging to either the Hitchiti or Alabama groups. Oconee, being a lower Creek town, would naturally belong to the first. Further evidence is furnished by the later associations of the Oconee people with the Mikasuki.[4]

The Tamałi, so far as our knowledge of them extends, lived in southern Georgia near towns known to have belonged to the Hitchiti group, and they were among the first to move to Florida and lay the foundations of the Seminole Nation. In Spanish documents a tribe called Tama is mentioned which is almost certainly identical with this,[5] and it may be inferred that the last syllable represents the Hitchiti plural *-ałi*. These facts all point to a Hitchiti connection for the tribe.

Bartram tells us that in his time the language of the Chiaha was entirely different from that of the Kasihta, which we know to have been Muskogee, and in his list of Creek towns he includes it among those speaking Stinkard.[3] As explained above, this latter fact suggests that Chiaha was a Muskhogean dialect, although not Muskogee. By some of the best-informed Creeks in Oklahoma I was told it was a dialect of Hitchiti, and that on account of the common language the Chiaha would not play against the Hitchiti in the tribal ball games, although they belonged to different fire clans, which ordinarily opposed each other at such times. The chief of the Mikasuki told me that Chiaha was the "foundation" of the towns called Osochi, Mikasuki, and Hotalgihuyana, and that anciently all spoke the same language.

---

[1] Almost confined to one letter published in facsimile, accompanied by its Spanish translation, by Buckingham Smith, in 1860.

[2] Bulletin 43, Bur. Amer. Ethn. The Washa and Chawasha have, however, since been identified as Chitimachan. (See Amer. Jour. Ling., I, no. 1, p. 49.)

[3] Bartram, Travels in North America, p. 462.

[4] See p. 401.

[5] See p. 181 et seq.

The Tawasa Indians ultimately united with the Alabama, and the living Alabama Indians recall no differences between the languages of the two peoples. Moreover, Stiggins, writing early in the eighteenth century, gives certain episodes in the history of the Tawasa as if he were speaking of the whole of the Alabama.[1] Still more ancient evidence is furnished by Lamhatty, a Tawasa, who was taken captive by the Creeks and made his way into the Virginia settlements in 1707. There the historian Robert Beverly met him and obtained from him an account of his travels and a rude map of the region which he had crossed in order to reach Virginia.[2] While the ending of most river names, *-oubab*, is identical with that which appears in Apalachee, the name of the Gulf of Mexico, *Ouquodky*, is plainly the *Oki hatki*, "white water," of the Hitchiti, and is the name still applied by them to the ocean. Since the present Alabama term is *Oki hatká* we may perhaps infer that Tawasa speech was anciently closer to Hitchiti than to Alabama. Later, however, it was entirely assimilated by Alabama, and therefore it is more convenient and less hazardous to place it in the Alabama group. In either case the Muskhogean connection of the language is assured.

It is probable that the "Poúhka" of Lamhatty[3] were the Pawokti later found living with the Alabama, and if so it is a fair assumption that their history was the same as that of the Tawasa.

Muklasa is set down by Bartram as a Stinkard town.[4] It was located in the upper Creek country, near the Alabama and Koasati towns, and it has a name taken from either the Alabama or the Koasati language. Gatschet states with positiveness[5] that the Muklasa people were Alabama, and he may have learned that such was the case from some well-informed Indian now dead, for to-day the Creeks have well-nigh forgotten even the name.

The Pensacola disappear from history shortly after their appearance in it, and nothing of their language has been preserved. Their name, however, is plainly Choctaw and signifies "hair people." It may have been given to them because they wore their hair in a manner different from that of most of their neighbors, and Cabeza de Vaca mentions as a curious fact that several chiefs in a party of Indians he and his companions encountered near Pensacola Bay wore their hair long.[6] When we recall Adair's statement to the effect that the Choctaw were called *Pa^{n}sfalaya*, "long hair,"[7] because of this very peculiarity a connection is at once suggested between the two peoples.

---

[1] See p. 140.

[2] D. I. Bushnell, Jr., in Amer. Anthrop., n. s. vol. x, no. 4, pp. 568–574.

[3] Ibid., map.

[4] Bartram, Travels in North America, p. 461.

[5] Gatschet, Creek Mig. Leg., I, p. 138.

[6] Bandelier, Journey of Alvar Nuñez Cabeza de Vaca, p. 48; also present work, p. 145.

[7] Adair, Hist. Am. Inds., p. 192. He spells the word Pas' Pharáàh.

The Tuskegee have spoken Muskogee for more than a hundred years, but from Taitt (1772) and Hawkins (1799) it appears that they once had a language of their own.[1] This statement was confirmed to me by some of the old people and they furnished several words which they affirmed belonged to it.[2] Perhaps these are nothing more than archaic Creek, but in any case the long association of the tribe with the Creeks, Hitchiti, and Alabama points to a Muskhogean connection as the most probable.[3]

The Muskhogean affinities of Yamasee have long been assumed by ethnologists, largely on the authority of Dr. Gatschet, but it can not be said that the evidence which he gives is satisfying.[4] One of the words cited by him as proving this, *Olataraca*, is Timucua; another, *yatiqui*, is both Creek and Timucua; and most of the others are not certainly from Yamasee. The traditions of the Creeks are divided, some holding that the Yamasee language was related to theirs, others that it was entirely distinct. This last contention need not have much weight with us, however, because to a Creek Hitchiti is an "altogether different" language. From the statements of Spanish writers it is certain that the language spoken in their territories and those of the adjoining coast tribes, northward of Cumberland Island, was distinct from the Timucua of Cumberland Island and more southern regions. One province is called the "lengua de Guale," the other the "lengua de Timucua."[5] More specific evidence as to the nature of that former language is not wanting. In 1604 Pedro de Ibarra, governor of Florida, journeyed from St. Augustine northward along the coast as far as St. Catherines Island, stopping at the important mission stations and posts, and holding councils with the Indians at each place.[6] Until he left San Pedro (Cumberland) Island he employed as interpreter a single Indian named Juan de Junco, but as soon as he passed northward of that point another interpreter named Santiago was added. Moreover, the chiefs met previously were all called "cacique," but afterwards the name "*mico*" is often appended, the chief of the very first town encountered being called the "cacique and mico mayor don Domingo." It appears in letters written both before and after the one quoted above, as in three by Governor de Canço in 1597, 1598, and 1603, and the report of a pastoral visit to the Florida missions by the Bishop of Cuba in 1606. The earliest of all is in the narrative of an expedition sent from Havana in search of Ribault's Port Royal Colony.

---

[1] Mereness, Trav. in Amer. Col., p. 541; Hawkins, Sketch of the Creek Country, Ga. Hist. Soc. Colls., III, p. 39.

[2] See p. 208.

[3] See also the Alabama tradition (p. 192) in which Tuskegee, under the name Hatcafaski, seems to be enumerated among the Alabama towns.

[4] Gatschet, op. cit., pp. 62–63.

[5] Serrano y Sanz, Doc. Hist., pp. 171, 177.

[6] Ibid., pp. 169–193.

The captain of the vessel "landed near the town of Guale and went there, where was the lord micoo (*el señor* micoo)." A little later "the micoo of a town called Yanahume"[1] came to see him. This word is nothing other than the Creek term for chief.

In 1598 the confessions of Guale Indians, whose testimony was being taken with reference to the revolt of 1597, were communicated by them to a Timucua who understood the language of Guale, and by him to another Timucua who could speak Spanish. In a letter describing his missionary work Fray Baltazar Lopez, who was stationed at San Pedro, states that, while he is himself familiar with the language of his own Indians, he employs interpreters in speaking to the Guale people passing back and forth between their own country and St. Augustine.[1]

Some supplementary evidence is furnished also by the place and personal names recorded from the Indians in this area, which will be found in the section on the Guale Indians and the Yamasee. The difference between these and Timucua names is apparent when they are compared with the list of names on pages 323–330. The phonetic *r* does not appear, except in one case where it is plainly not an original sound, while *f* and *l*, which are foreign to the eastern Siouan dialects, are much in evidence. So far as Yuchi is concerned the history of that tribe, as will be seen later, tends to discount the idea of any connection there. Besides, *m* appears to occur in the Guale language at least—Tumaque, Altamahaw, Tolomato, Tamufa, Ymunapa—while it is wanting in Yuchi. To these arguments may be added the positive resemblances to Muskhogean forms in such names as Talaxe (pronounced Talashe), Hinafasque, Ytohulo, Fuloplata, Tapala, Çapala (Sapala), Culupala, Otapalas, Pocotalligo, Dawfuskee.

Finally, the relationship is indicated by the speeches of various Creek chiefs at the time of their historic conference with Governor Oglethorpe in 1733.[2] Tomochichi, chief of the Yamacraw, a small band of Indians living near Savannah at that time, says "I was a banished man; I came here poor and helpless to look for good land near the tombs of my ancestors." The Oconee chief declares that he is related to Tomochichi, and on behalf of the Creek Nation claims all of the lands southward of the river Savannah. Finally the mico of Coweta thus expresses himself:

> I rejoice that I have lived to see this day, and to see our friends that have long been gone from among us. Our nation was once strong, and had ten towns, but we are now weak and have but eight towns. You [Oglethorpe] have comforted the banished, and have gathered them that were scattered like little birds before the eagle. We desire, therefore, to be reconciled to our brethren who are here amongst you, and we give leave to Tomo-chi-chi, Stimoiche, and Illispelle to call their kindred that love

[1] Lowery, MSS.

[2] A True and Hist. Narr. of the Colony of Ga. in Am., &c., Charles Town, S. C., 1741, pp. 31-39.

them out of each of the Creek towns that they may come together and make one town. We must pray you to recall the Yamasees that they may be buried in peace amongst their ancestors, and that they may see their graves before they die; and their own nation shall be restored again to its ten towns.

Here the Yamacraw and the Yamasee seem to be treated as former members of the Creek Confederacy. Unless the Yamasee and the Guale Indians had been so considered the Creeks at this council would not have claimed all of the land on the Georgia coast south of the Savannah River and at the same time have asked that the Yamasee be recalled to inhabit it. It is as guardians of these tribes that they ceded to Oglethorpe the coast between Savannah River and St. Simons Island, with the exception of the islands of Ossabaw, Sapello, and St. Catherines, and a small strip of land near Savannah city.

The particular Muskhogean dialect which these Indians spoke is, however, more difficult to ascertain. Ranjel indicates a connection between the Yamasee and Hitchiti,[1] and this impression appears to have been shared generally by the Muskogee Indians of later times. On the other hand, the word for chief among the Guale Indians was, as we have seen, *miko*,[2] the form which it has in Muskogee, whereas the proper Hitchiti term is *miki*. This means either that Muskogee was already the *lingua franca* upon the coast of Georgia or else that the languages of the Guale Indians and the Yamasee belonged to distinct groups. According to several traditions the Muskogee at one time lived upon this very coast, and I am inclined to accept the second explanation, but it is not put forward with overmuch confidence.

The name of the Cusabo first appears in the form "Coçapoy" in a letter of Governor Pedro Menendez Marques dated January 3, 1580. It is there given as the name of a big town occupied by hostile Indians and strongly placed in a swamp, about 15 leagues from the Spanish fort at Santa Elena.[3] The tribe appears later as one of those accused of fomenting an uprising against the Guale missionaries in 1597, and afterwards among those appealed to for help in putting it down.[4] There is every reason to believe that its appellation was connected in some way with that of the Coosa Indians of South Carolina, but how is not certain.

By the English the name is sometimes used to designate all of the coast tribes of South Carolina from Savannah River to Charleston and two on the lower course of the Santee. On the other hand, not only are the latter sometimes excluded, but at least one of the tribes of the neighborhood of Charleston Inlet. Mooney suggests a still more restricted use of the word.[5] In its most extended application

[1] See p. 95.

[2] Or *mico;* c indicates precisely the same as k.

[3] Lowery, MSS.

[4] See p. 60.

[5] Siouan Tribes of the East, Bull. 22, Bur. Amer. Ethn., p. 86.

it included the Santee, Sewee, Etiwaw, Wando, Stono, Kiawa, Edisto, Ashepoo, Combahee, Indians of St. Helena, Wimbee, Witcheau, and Coosa. However, there is good reason to reject the Santee and Sewee from this association and to place them with the Siouan tribes of the east, to which the Catawba and other tribes of northeastern South Carolina and eastern North Carolina belonged. This is the conclusion of Mooney, and it is confirmed by the following arguments.

On his second expedition toward the north, in 1609, Francisco Fernandez de Ecija had as interpreter, "for all that coast," Maria de Miranda, a woman from the neighborhood of Santa Elena, named presumably from the former governor of Santa Elena, Gutierrez de Miranda. In Cayagua entrance (Charleston Harbor) he met a Christian Indian, Alonso, with whom he had previously had dealings and who is spoken of as "interpreter (lengua) of the River Jordan," the Santee, upon which stream his own town was located. Ecija states that Alonso and Maria de Miranda understood one another and even goes so far as to state that "they spoke the same language." From what follows, however, it is evident that we are to understand only that they understood and could use the same languages, for just below Ecija says of another Indian whom he calls "mandador of the River Jordan" that he spoke through the said Maria de Miranda, "because the said Indian understood something of the language of Escamaqu." This indicates that the language of the Santee River people was distinct from that of "Escamaqu" or Santa Elena. While he was on the Santee, Ecija secured the surrender of a Frenchman living among the "Sati" (Santee) Indians. This man declared that he had obtained news of the English colony to the northward from three Indians, and when the explorers were in Charleston Harbor on their return an Indian came down the river who he said was one of those who had informed him. Ecija questioned this Indian, but "understanding that he (the Indian) understood the language of Santa Elena, the said captain (Ecija) commanded that the said Maria de Miranda should speak with him. Then he asked him through her the same questions that the Frenchman had asked him in the language of Sati."[1] These facts show plainly that the language spoken on Santee River and that of Santa Elena were not mutually intelligible.

In 1700–1701 John Lawson traveled northeastward from Charleston to the Tuscarora country, thus passing through the very heart of the eastern Siouan territory. He visited and described both the Santee and Sewee and hence must have had opportunities to hear their speech. It is significant, therefore, that he states of the languages

[1] Lowery, MSS.

of all the people through whose territories he had passed that none of them had the sounds *f* or *l*.[1] This is true of Catawba, the sole representative of the Siouan languages of the east from which we have much material. It is therefore probable that Lawson was correct for the other languages to which he refers.[2] Santee and Sewee would thus share this dialectic peculiarity and be associated by it with the other eastern Siouan tribes. On the other hand, several town or tribal and personal names from the Cusabo country contain *l* and one an *f*.[3] It is perhaps significant that in forming companies of his Indian allies before marching against the Tuscarora, Capt. Barnwell placed the "Corsaboy" in one company with the Yamasee, Yuchi, and Apalachee, while the "Congerees and Sattees," the last of whom must be the Santee, were with the "Watterees, Sagarees, Catabas, Suterees, and Waxaws." The composition of his other companies shows clearly that neighboring and related tribes were purposely placed together.[4] On the other hand, there are certain linguistic considerations which seem to indicate an alliance between the Cusabo tribes proper and the Indians of the Muskhogean stock. It is to be noted that the French Huguenots established among the Cusabo in 1562 visited the Guale chief to obtain corn, accompanied by Cusabo guides, and had no difficulty in communicating with him.[5] When Spanish missionaries were sent to the Province of Guale, south of the Savannah, they composed a grammar in the language of the people among whom they lived, and this grammar subsequently fell into the hands of missionaries among the Cusabo.[6] It would naturally be supposed that if any radical difference existed between the languages of the two provinces some comment would have been made, but neither the missionaries at this time nor the Spanish explorers then or later so much as hint that any such difference existed, though they do indeed recognize the country north of the Savannah River as constituting a distinct province from that to the southward.

In 1600, when testimony was taken from a number of Guale chiefs, it is stated in a letter detailing the proceedings that "the notary who had been eight years in the Province of Santa Elena, although he did not speak the language, understood much of the languages of those provinces, and attested that the Guale Indians

---

[1] Lawson, Hist. Carolina, p. 378.

[2] In his vocabulary of Woccon, another Siouan dialect, there is no *f* and but one *l*, in the word for "duck."

[3] See pp. 20-24.

[4] South Carolina Hist. and Genealogical Mag., ix, pp. 30-31.

[5] Since their guides belonged to the Maccou or Escamacu tribe, which there is some reason to think may have been identical with that later known as Yamacraw, this fact might not in itself be conclusive, but these Maccou were found to be associating intimately with the other Cusabo tribes in their neighborhood without any suggestion of a difference in language, and a little later the Spaniards applied their name to the entire district or "province" otherwise designated Orista or Santa Elena, the southern part of the Cusabo territory (see p. 60).

[6] Ruidiaz, La Florida, II, p. 307; Barcia, La Florida, pp. 138-139.

spoke the truth."[1] Somewhat more equivocal is a reference to an interpreter named Diego de Cardenas, who is said to have "understood the language of Santa Elena and also that of the Province of Guale." He himself testifies, in 1601, that he "has been many times in the lengua de Guale and is lengua of that (province) and of Escamacu."[1] Most important of all is, of course, the flat statement by Gov. Pedro Menendez Marques, when, in writing in 1580 of the Indians of Santa Elena, among whom he then was, he says "they speak the Guale language." A more nearly literal translation of the words he uses would perhaps be, "It (Santa Elena) pertains to the linguistic Province of Guale (viene á la lengua de Guale)."[2]

In his expedition north on the Atlantic coast, to which reference has already been made,[3] Governor Ibarra went no farther than Guale (St. Catherines Island), but one of the chiefs who came to see him at this place was named Oya, in all probability the same as the Oya or Hoya mentioned by French and Spaniards as living near the present Beaufort, S. C.[4] While Ibarra was at St. Catherines we also learn that "the chief of Aluete said that the chief of Talapo and the chief of Ufalague and the chief of Orista, his nephew and heirs, were his vassals and had left him and gone to live with the mico of Asao" (St. Simons Island);[4] and when the governor came to Asao on his return he met them there and had a conference with them.[5] Orista was certainly a Cusabo chief, and there is every reason to suppose that the others mentioned with him were also Cusabo. As we have already stated, in his dealings with the Indians north of Cumberland Island, Governor Ibarra employed two interpreters, Juan de Junco and Santiago. There is no hint that any change was made after that time, and not the slightest indication that the Cusabo employed a language different from that of the Guale Indians, among whom Ibarra met them. The chief of Oya is referred to as a "mico" along with the chief of Guale, while the chiefs Talapo, Ufalague, and Orista seemed to have moved down the coast to Asao as the result of some slight disagreement with their neighbors and to have settled there as if they were perfectly at home.

Again, as has already been remarked, while *f* and *l* are absent from the Siouan dialects to the north, *r* is a conspicuous sound, appearing in such names as Congaree, Sugeree, Wateree, Shakori, etc. It also appears in one form of the name Santee given by Lawson—Seretee. On the other hand, it is wanting in all Cusabo names that have come down to us—with one or two exceptions which need cause no disturbance. Thus, the name Orista, given above, appears persistently in

---

1 Lowery, MSS.
2 Lowery and Brooks, MSS.
3 See p. 14.
4 Serrano y Sanz, Doc. Hist., p. 188.
5 Ibid., p. 191.

Spanish documents, but it is evidently the Edisto of the English and the Audusta of the French. The Edisto are in one place called Edistare, but it is probable that this form was after the analogy of the Siouan names, and it may, in fact, have been obtained through a Siouan interpreter. Moreover, Laudonnière, on inquiring of the Cusabo Indians about the great chief Chicora, of whom he had learned through Spanish writings, was told instead of a chief Chiquola living toward the north.[1] The *l*, it is to be seen, is substituted for *r*.

Spanish attempts to record the Cusabo language were cut short by the unfriendliness of the natives and the abandonment of the missions. Linguistic material may yet be discovered, however, among the unpublished documents of Spain. At all events the Spaniards had a very much better excuse than our own South Carolina colonists for their almost complete failure to make any permanent record of the language of the people among whom their first settlements were made. A few detached phrases and the following place, personal, and other names are practically all that is left of Cusabo:

ABLANDOLES. Mentioned together with the "Chiluques" as a tribe of Santa Elena. As the latter probably refers to a non-Cusabo tribe, the Cherokee, the former may not be a Cusabo tribe either.[2]

AHOYABI, AOBI (?). A small town near Ahoya, or Hoya.

ALUSH. A chief of Edisto.[3]

ALUSTE, ALUESTE, ALIESTE, ALUETE. A chief and village probably located near Beaufort, South Carolina.[4] This may be only a form of Edisto (see p. 60).

APPEE-BEE. The Indian name of Foster Creek, S. C.[5]

ASHEPOO, ASHIPOO, ASSHEPOO, ASHA-PO, ISHPOW. A tribe and a river named from it still so called; in one place this is made a synonym for Edisto.

AWENDAW, OWENDAW, AU-EN-DAU-BOO-E. An old town, perhaps Sewee.[6] The name is preserved to the present day.

BABICKOCK. A creek flowing into Edisto River, near its mouth.

BACKBOOKS, BACKHOOKS. Coast people at war with the Santee; they may have been Siouan instead of Cusabo.[7]

BARCHO AMINI. An Indian of Santa Elena of the town of Cambe, perhaps a Spanish name.[2]

BLUACACAY. A Santa Elena Indian.[2]

BOHICKET. An Indian village near Rockville, S. C.; a creek and a modern place are still so called.[8]

BOO-SHOO-EE, BOO-CHAW-EE. A name for the land about the peninsula between Dorchester Creek and Ashley River. There are a number of variants of this name.[9]

CALLAWASSIE. An island on one side of Colleton River.[10]

CAMBE. A town in the province of Santa Elena.[2]

CATUCO. Name given in one place to the fort at Santa Elena. It seems to be an Indian word.[11]

---

1 Laudonnière, Hist. Not. de la Floride, pp. 29–31.
2 Copy of MS. in Ayer Coll., Newberry Lib.
3 S. Car. Hist. Soc. Colls., v, pp. 20, 170.
4 Serrano y Sanz, Doc. Hist., pp. 187–188.
5 S. Car. Hist. and Gen. Mag., VI, p. 64.
6 Lawson, Hist. Carolina, p. 24.
7 Ibid., p. 45.
8 S. Car. Hist. Soc. Colls., v, pp. 63, 334.
9 S. Car. Hist. and Gen. Mag., VI, p. 63 et seq.
10 Modern name.
11 Brooks, MSS.

CHATUACHE, SATUACHE, SATOACHE. A town and mission station 6 to 10 leagues north of the Spanish fort of Santa Elena.[1]

CHEHAW. A river; the name probably refers to the Chiaha tribe, to be discussed later.[2]

CHICHESSEE, CHECHESSA. A river flowing into Port Royal Sound, and also a creek, otherwise known as Deer Creek.[2]

CLOWTER. Head warrior of the "Ittuans." It appears from certain writers that he took his name from a white family of the name Crowder, therefore it is not really an Indian name.[3]

COMBAHEE, COMBOHE, COMBEHE, COMBEE, COMBAHE. A tribe on a river which still bears their name; they were bounded by the Coosa, who were said to live northeast of Combahee River.

COOSA, KUSSO, CAUSA, CUSSOES, KUSSOES, KUSSO, COOSOE, CUSSOE, COOSAW, KUSIAH, CUSSAH, KISSAH, CASOR, COCAOYO, COCAO, COZAO. A tribe sometimes reckoned among the Cusabo and sometimes excluded from them. They lived on the upper reaches of the rivers from the Ashley to the Coosawhatchie.[4]

CUSABO, CUSABES, CORSABOY, CUSABEES, CUSABOE, COOSABOYS, KORSABOI, CUSSOBOS, COÇAPOY, COSAHUE, COSAPUE, COSSAPUE. Collective name for the tribes, or part of the tribes, now under discussion.[5] Originally it seems to have been applied to a town (see p. 58).

COTEBAS. A place.[6]

DATHA, DATHAW. An island on the coast. This is south of Port Royal Sound; and although it is in South Carolina it may have been in the Yamasee territory. It is also given as the name of a chief.[7]

DAWHO. A modern river name.

EDISTO, EDISTAH, EDISTA, EDISTOE, EDISTOH, EDISTOW, EDISLOH, EDISTARE, ODISTASH, ORISTA, ORISTANUM (Latinized), AUDUSTA, ADUSTA, USTA. One of the Cusabo tribes.[8]

ESCAMACU, EESCAMAQU, ESCAMAQU, ESCAMAQUU, ESCAMATU, USCAMACU, CAMACU, CAMAQU, MACCOU. One of the most important of the tribes near Port Royal in Spanish times; it frequently gave its name to the province (see p. 60).

ETIWAW, ETEWAUS, ETIWANS, ITTAWANS, ITUAN, ITWAN, ITTAVANS, ETTIWAN, ITAWANS, ETWANS, ITAWANS, ILWANS, EUTAW (?). A tribe on Wando River, sometimes included with the Cusabo and sometimes excluded from them.[9]

GUALDAPE. Name of the region where Ayllón made his last settlement, in 1526 (see pp. 38–41).

HEMALO. A Cusabo chief who visited Madrid and was killed by a Spanish captain in 1576.

HOBCAW POINT. The extreme south termination of land lying between the Waccamaw River and the sea; also a point on the south bank of Wando River where it debouches into Cooper River, now Remley's Point. The name Hobcaw Neck was applied anciently to all land between Shem-ee Creek and Wando River.[10]

---

1 Serrano y Sanz, Doc. Hist., p. 132; Lowery, MSS.

2 Modern name.

3 South Carolina Pub. Docs., MS.

4 The name occurs in numerous places. See p. 68 et seq.

5 Occurs in numerous places. See pp. 31–80 following; also Mooney, Bull. 22, Bur. Amer. Ethn., pp. 82, 86.

6 S. Car. Hist. Soc. Colls., v, p. 332.

7 See p. 42.

8 Modern geographical name.

9 See pp. 24–25.

10 S. Car. Hist. and Gen. Mag., XIV, p. 61.

Hooks. Given with the Backbooks as a tribe at war with the Santee; they may have been Siouan instead of Cusabo [1] (see p. 20).

Hoya, Ahoya, Oya. A town mentioned by both Frenchmen and Spaniards, on or near Broad River.

Ickabee, Ickerby, Accabee. Peronneau's Point on Ashley River.[2]

Icosans. According to Bartram, a tribe near South Carolina hostile to the colonists and driven away by the Creeks; probably the Coosa.[3]

Inna. A Santa Elena Indian.[4]

Johassa. An island.[5]

Kiawa, Cayagua, Cayagna, Cayegua, Kiwaha, Kywaha, Kywaws, Cayawah, Cayawash, Kyawaw, Kiawhas, Keywaw, Keyawah, Kayawah, Kaaway, Kiawah, Keywahah, Kiaway, Kiawaws, Kiawas, Keawaw, Kayawagh, Kyewaw, Chyawhaw. A Cusabo tribe living on Ashley River.[6]

Mayon. A town, apparently on Broad River, in 1562 (see pp. 49, 50).

Palawana, Polawak (?). An island near St. Helena Island, which was granted to the remnant of the Cusabo in 1712.[7]

Patica. Given by Bartram as a tribe formerly living near South Carolina and driven off by the Creeks; they were probably one of the Yamasee bands.[8]

Oketee, Okeetee, Okatie, Oketeet. A river flowing into Colleton River, near Port Royal.[5]

Oni-se-cau. Indian name of Bull's Island, perhaps Siouan.

Santhiacho Huanucase. An Indian of Santa Elena.[4]

Shadoo, Sheedou. A chief of Edisto.[9]

Shem-ee. A creek near Charleston now called Shem.[10]

Stono, Stonah, Stonoe, Stoanoes, Stonoh, Stonoes, Ostano, Ostanum (Latinized), Stalame (?). One of the Cusabo tribes, on Stono Inlet.[6]

Sufalate. Probably Cusabo because associated with Ufalague (see p. 82).

Talapo, Talapuz, Ytalapo. A chief and town probably near Beaufort, S. C.[11]

Tibwen. A plantation.[12]

Tipicop Haw, Tippycutlaw, Tippycop Law, Tibbekudlaw. Indian name of a hill in Wadboo barony.[13]

Touppa, Toupa. A town and chief, located apparently on Broad River in 1562 (see p. 49).

Ufalague, Ufalegue. A chief, probably from the neighborhood of Beaufort, S. C.[14]

Wadboo, Watboo, Watroo. A creek flowing into Cooper River; a Wadboo Bridge appears later.[15]

Wambaw. A creek and swamp, perhaps in the Siouan territory instead of in that of the Cusabo.[16]

---

1 Lawson, Hist. Carolina, p. 45.
2 S. Car. Hist. Soc. Colls., v, p. 396.
3 Bartram, Travels, p. 54.
4 Copy of MS. in Ayer Coll., Newberry Lib.
5 Modern geographical name.
6 Modern geographical name; also see pp. 24–25, 61.
7 Thomas in 18th Ann. Rept. Bur. Amer. Ethn., pt. 2, p. 633.
8 Bartram, op. cit., p. 54.
9 S. Car. Hist. Soc. Colls., v, pp. 19, 20, 23, 64–65, 68, 70
10 S. Car. Hist. and Gen. Mag., vi, p. 64.
11 Serrano y Sanz, Doc. Hist., p. 188; also see p. 82.
12 S. Car. Hist. Soc. Colls., v, p. 175.
13 S. Car. Hist. and Gen. Mag., xi, p. 171; xii, pp. 47–48.
14 Serrano y Sanz, Doc. Hist., pp. 188, 190.
15 S. Car. Hist. Soc. Colls., v, p. 332; S. Car. Hist. and Gen. Mag. v, pp. 32, 119.
16 Modern name.

WAMPI, WAMPEE. The name of a plant which grows in the lowlands of South Carolina; also called pickerel weed (*Pontederia cordata*).[1]

WANDO, WANDOE. A tribe on Cooper River usually included with the Cusabo; Wando River is named for them but the name has been transferred from the stream to which it properly belongs.[2]

WANTOOT. A plantation in the low country of South Carolina.[3]

WAPENSAW. Lands near Charleston, S. C.[4]

WAPPETAW BRIDGE. A place name.

WAPPOO, WAPPO, WAPOO. A creek on the landward side of Edisto Island; also given by Bartram as the name of a tribe formerly living near South Carolina, which the Creeks had driven away.[5]

WASHISHOE. A plantation.[6]

WASHUA. An island.[7]

WESTO, WESTOE, WESTOH, WESTA, WESTRAS. A name which appears to have been given to the Yuchi by the Cusabo and is evidently in the Cusabo language.[8]

WESTOBOO, WESTOEBOU, WESTOE BOU, WESTOE BOO, WESTOE BOU. The name of the Savannah River in the Cusabo language, said to mean "River of the Westo" and in one place interpreted as "the Enemies' River."[9]

WIMBEE, WIMBEHE, GUIOMAEZ (?). A Cusabo tribe which seems to have been located between the Combahee and Broad Rivers.[10]

WINA. Mentioned as an Indian met near Port Royal in 1681 along with another named Antonio. It may be merely the Spanish Juan.

WISKINBOO. A swamp in Berkeley County, between Cooper and Santee Rivers.[11]

WITCHEAU, WICHCAUH, WATCHETSAU (?). A Cusabo tribe mentioned only two or three times; location unknown.[12]

WOMMONY. The son of a chief of St. Helena.[13]

YESHOE. The name of certain lands in South Carolina near Charleston.[14]

YANAHUME. A town on the south side of "the river of Santa Elena," reported by a Spanish expedition of 1564.[15]

Following are the few words and phrases to be found in early works dealing with this region:

APPADA. The [Sewee?] Indians called out this word to the English and it is probably corrupt Spanish.[16]

HIDDESKEH. This is said to mean "sickly."[17]

HIDDIE DOD. Described as "a word of great kindness among them"; the Indians who used this, however, also referred to the English as "comraro," evidently an attempt at the Spanish *camarada*, so we can not feel sure that *hiddie dod* is not a corrupt Spanish expression as well.[18]

HIDDY DODDY COMORADO ANGLES WESTOE SKORRYE, "English very good friends, Westoes are nought."[19] The words here are under the same suspicion as the one just mentioned and must therefore be handled carefully; moreover, Indian words contained in old documents are so often transcribed wrongly that we can never be certain of the exact form where we have but one example to which to refer.

---

1 Modern name.
2 See p. 61.
3 S. Car. Hist. and Gen. Mag., III, p. 192.
4 Ibid., VI, p. 64.
5 Bartram, Travels, p. 54.
6 S. Car. Hist. Soc. Colls., V, p. 175.
7 A modern place name.
8 See pp. 288–291.
9 S. Car. Hist. Soc. Colls., V, 76–77, 166, 378, 386–387, 428, 459–460.
10 Ibid., pp. 65, 334; also see p. 55.
11 S. Car. Hist. and Gen. Mag., XIII, p. 12.
12 See p. 70.
13 S. Car. Hist. Soc. Colls., V, pp. 21, 75.
14 S. Car. Hist. and Gen. Mag., VI, p. 64.
15 Lowery, MSS.
16 S. Car. Hist. Soc. Colls., V, p. 166.
17 Ibid., p. 201.
18 Ibid., p. 199.
19 Ibid., p. 459.

One among the above names, Ufalague, has an *f* and an *l*; six others an *l*, Aluete, Alush, Callawassie, Palawana, Stalame, Talapo; and seven an *m*, Combahee, Shemee, Stalame, Wambaw, Wampi, Wimbee, Wommony. As in the case of the Guale and Yamasee languages (see p. 15), these argue a Muskhogean connection.

The only other fact that seems to promise assistance is the translation of the word Westoboo as "river of the Westo," from which it would seem that *boo* signifies "river."[1] So far as I have been able to find, nothing like this occurs in either Yuchi or Catawba, the closest resemblance being with the Choctaw *bok*,[2] with which perhaps the Alabama *pa'ni*, the Timucua *ibi*(*ne*), and the Apalachee *ubab* are connected. The little evidence this one word gives us, therefore, points toward Muskhogean relationship. It is possible that the same word occurs in certain of the names given above, such as Ashepoo, Bohicket, Boo-shoo-ee, Backbooks, Cusabo, Wadboo, Wappoo, Wiskinboo, and perhaps also in Combahee (also spelled Combohe). If this explanation holds good for Cusabo the term would probably mean "Coosa River people," though it is difficult to see how such a name came to be applied generally, in some cases to the exclusion of the Coosa Indians themselves. We must suppose it to have been adopted as the name of a town near the mouth of the Coosawhatchie, or some other river on which Coosa lived, and the usage to have extended from that place along the coast. It should be noted as a rather remarkable fact, and one probably based on some feature of the Cusabo tongue, that of the place and personal names given above, 16, or more than one-fourth, begin with *w*. This is a common initial in stream names from the Creek language, owing to the fact that many of them begin with *wi*, which is almost the same as *oi*, an abbreviation of *oiwa*, water; but in the names under consideration *wa* initial is more common than *wi* and *we* together.

The evidence so far adduced applies particularly to that group of Cusabo tribes living near Beaufort, to which the term is sometimes confined. There was a second group, farther to the north, about Charleston Harbor, consisting of the Kiawa, Etiwaw, Wando, and perhaps the Stono. In both the English and Spanish narratives the chief of Kiawa appears on intimate terms with those of Edisto and St. Helena, and their solidarity is emphasized on more than one occasion by the early writers, they being classed as coast Indians, and contrasted with the Westo inland upon the Savannah River and the tribes living in the "sickly" country northward of them.[3] In later times the Etiwaw assisted the English in destroying the Siouan Santee and Congaree.[4] Henry Woodward, upon whom the English

[1] S. Car. Hist. Soc. Colls., v, p. 167.

[2] It should be noted that final -k in many Choctaw words is barely distinguishable as pronounced.

[3] See p. 67; also Lowery, MSS.

[4] S. Car. Pub. Docs., MS.

settlers of South Carolina relied in all of their communications with the natives, calls the Kiawa "Chyawhaw," [1] and although he is unsupported in this, his information should have been the most reliable. If he is correct, the Kiawa were probably a branch of those Chiaha Indians noted elsewhere, some of whom are known to have lived near the Yamasee at an early period. It is also to be observed that the chief of Kiawa accompanied Woodward on his expedition to visit the chief of "Chufytachyque" and acted as his interpreter.[2] If the latter were the Kasihta Creeks, as I shall try to show,[3] this fact would indicate some similarity between the languages of the two peoples. The following statement of the explorer Sanford may be added:

> All along I observed a kinde of Emulacon amongst the three principall Indians of this Country (viz[t]) Those of Keywaha, Eddistowe and Port Royall concerning us and our Friendshipp, contending to assure it to themselves and jealous of the other though all be allyed and this Notw[th]standing that they knewe wee were in actuall warre with the Natives att Clarendon and had killed and sent away many of them, ffor they frequently discoursed with us concerning the warre, told us that the Natives were noughts they land Sandy and barren, their Country sickly, but if wee would come amongst them Wee whould finde the Contrary to all their Evills, and never any occasion of dischargeing our Gunns but in merryment and for pastime.[4]

Clarendon County was in the North Carolina settlement between Cape Fear and Pamlico Sound, mainly in Siouan territory. In 1727 the Kiawa chief was given a grant of land south of the Combahee River, which probably means that his people removed about that time to the south to be near the other Cusabo Indians.[5]

Besides these two coastal groups of Cusabo the Coosa tribe is to be distinguished in some degree from the rest because, instead of occupying a section of coast, it was in the hinterland of South Carolina along the upper courses of the Ashley, Edisto, Ashepoo, Combahee, and Coosawhatchie Rivers. From this difference in position and on the strength of the name I suggest that it may possibly have been a branch of the Coosa of Coosa River, Alabama, and hence may have belonged to the true Muskogee group. On the basis of our present information this can not be definitely affirmed or denied.

By nearly all of the living Creeks the Osochi are supposed to be a Muskogee tribe of long standing, and Bartram classifies them with those who in his time spoke the Muskogee tongue.[6] Nevertheless Adair gives them as one of the "nations" which had settled among the Lower Creeks.[7] In very early times they came to be associated very closely with the Chiaha and when they gave up their own square ground the two combined. An old Osochi whom

---

1 S. Car. Hist. Soc. Colls., v, p. 186.
2 Ibid, p. 191.
3 See pp. 216–218.
4 S. Car. Hist. Soc. Colls., v, pp. 79–80.
5 S. Car. Docs. (Pub. Records of S. Car., x, p. 24.)
6 Bartram, Travels, p. 462.
7 Adair, Hist. Am. Inds., p. 257.

I met in Oklahoma stated that his mother knew how to speak Hitchiti and he believed that many more of his people had known how to speak that language in earlier times. This would naturally be the case if, as seems to be indicated, the Chiaha were a Hitchiti speaking people, but of course it is possible that the Osochi anciently belonged to the Hitchiti group also. However, whether they ever spoke Hitchiti as a tribe or not, I am strongly of the opinion that they are the descendants of the people known to De Soto and his companions as the Uçachile,[1] Uzachil,[2] Veachile,[3] or Ossachile.[4] Veachile is probably a misprint for Uçachile. If this identification is correct the Osochi were evidently a Timucua tribe, which gradually migrated north until absorbed by the Lower Creeks. Confirmatory evidence appears to be furnished by a Spanish official map of the eighteenth century[5] on which at the junction of the Chattahoochee and Flint Rivers a tribe or post is located with the legend, "Apalache ó Sachile." Apparently the compiler of the map supposed that the ó in this name was the Spanish conjunction instead of an integral part of the word. The position assigned to them by him agrees exactly with that of the Apalachicola Indians at that period, and if "ó Sachile" really refers to the Osochi we must suppose either that they had united with some of the Apalachicola or that they were classified with and considered a branch of them. Since the word Timucua often appears as Tomoco or Tomoka in English writings this hypothesis would also explain the Tomoóka town westward of the Apalachicola on the map of Lamhatty[6] and the Tommahees referred to by Coxe in the same region.[7] These particular Timucua would be none other than the Osochi.

The Kasihta, Coweta, Coosa, Abihka, Hołiwahali, Eufaula, Hilibi, and Wakokai, with their branches, have always, so far as our information goes, been considered genuine Muskogee people. The only suspicion to the contrary is in the case of the Coosa, whose name looks very much like a common corruption of the Choctaw word *konshak*, meaning "cane." By this name the Muskogee were known to the Mobile Indians. In Padilla's history of the De Luna expedition we read that, when the Spaniards accompanied the Coosa in an attack upon their western neighbors, they came to a wide river known as "Oke chiton," or "great river." If this name was in the Coosa language it would prove that at that time they spoke Choctaw, but more likely it was in the language of their enemies.

[1] Bourne, Narr. of De Soto, II, p. 73.
[2] Ibid. I, p. 41.
[3] Ibid, II, p. 6.
[4] Garcilasso de La Vega, in Shipp, Hist. of De Soto and Florida, p. 330.
[5] Reproduced in Hamilton, Colonial Mobile, p. 210.
[6] Amer. Anthrop., n. s. vol. X, p. 569
[7] French, Hist. Colls. La., 1850, p. 234. On his map he has "Tomachees" (Descr. Prov. Car., 1741).

About one-sixth of all Creeks are probably of Coosa descent, and it is unlikely that a tribe of such size should have given up its language while much smaller bodies retained theirs almost or quite down to the present time.

The Tukabahchee are considered by most Creek Indians at the present day as the leaders of the nation. Nevertheless Milfort,[1] and also Adair,[2] on the authority of a Tukabahchee chief of his time, declare that they had formerly been a distinct people. This question will be considered again when we come to take up Tukabahchee history, but it may be said that, even though the tribe were once distinct, it would not necessarily follow that its language was also different. There is, at all events, little reason to suppose it was anything other than some Muskhogean dialect. A foreign origin is also attributed to the Okchai Indians by the same writers. Some of the living Okchai appear to remember a tradition to this effect, but while it is probably correct there is no further proof, and there is no likelihood that their ancient speech was anything other than Muskogee.[3]

Still another people, the Pakana, who now speak pure Muskogee, are reported to have been at one time distinct, both by Adair[4] and by Stiggins.[5] Since they settled near Fort Toulouse, they have sometimes been spoken of as if they were a branch of the Alabama, but this is probably due merely to association, just as the Okchai have occasionally been classed with the Alabama because an Alabama town was known as Little Okchai. In the absence of more assured information it will be best to class them with the Muskogee.

Northern Florida was occupied by the Timucua Indians, but south of them were several tribes, which were reckoned as distinct by the Spaniards, though next to nothing has been preserved of their languages and very few hints regarding their affinities are to be found.

The Calusa of the western side of the peninsula were the most important South Florida people, and they were the last to disappear, some of them remaining in their old seats until the close of the last Seminole war. The chief centers of their population were Charlotte Harbor and the mouth of the Caloosahatchee River, and this is of importance in connection with the following facts. In a letter written by Capt. John H. Bell, agent for the Indians in Florida, addressed

---

1 Milfort, Mémoire, pp. 265–266.

2 Adair, Hist. Am. Inds., p. 179.

3 Milfort and Adair, Ibid. There is one direct statement to the effect that Okchai was a distinct language (Coll. Mass. Hist. Soc., 1st ser., II, p. 48), but the language of the Little Okchai (Alabama) may be meant (see next paragraph).

4 Adair, ibid., p. 257.

5 See p. 272.

to a committee of Congress, February, 1821, a list of Seminole towns is given.[1] The names of the first 22 are "extracted from a talk held by Gen. Jackson, with three chiefs of the Florida Indians, at Pensacola, September 19, 1821," and to them Captain Bell adds 13 towns on his own authority. The particular tribe of Seminole represented in each town is not always given, but it is appended in italics to the names of the last five. Thus there is a town of the Mikasuki, a town of the Coweta, a town of the Chiaha, a town of the Yuchi, and last of all we read "35. South of Tampa, near Charlotte's Bay, *Choctaws*." Later still, in a census of the Florida Indians taken in 1847, there were 120 warriors reported, among whom were 70 Seminole, 30 Mikasuki, 12 Creeks, 4 Yuchi, and 4 Choctaw.[2] The only Mississippi Choctaw actually known to have been brought into Florida were taken there along with some Delaware Indians as scouts for the American Army, and at a much later date than the letter of Captain Bell. Moreover, from both Bell's account and the census of 1847 the Choctaw enumerated would appear to have formed a considerable band, and it may well be asked why it is, if the scouts were brought in in such quantities, we do not hear of a Delaware band as well? These references therefore introduce the question of a possible connection between the Calusa and Choctaw.

All that is now known of the Calusa language is a considerable number of place names, for a few of which translations are given, and a single expression, also translated. Practically all of these come from the Memoir of Hernando de Escalante Fontaneda, a Spaniard held captive among the Calusa Indians for 17 years, somewhere between 1550 and 1570.[3] Attempts to find equivalents in known Indian tongues have been made by Buckingham Smith (1854) and A. S. Gatschet (1884).[4] Although better equipped for this task, the latter was handicapped, as always, by a lack of critical acumen in the treatment of etymologies, and unfortunately he chose for comparison Spanish, Timucua, and Creek, the two last because they were the Indian languages of the region with which he was most familiar. Smith, on the other hand, without a tithe of Gatschet's philological ability, was favored by fortune in happening to depend for his interpretations on several Choctaw Indians, including the famous chief, Peter Pichlynn. Smith seems not to have had any true appreciation of the differences between Indian languages and to have assumed that the authority of an Indian of almost any southeastern tribe was equally good. By mere luck, however, he

[1] Morse, Rep. to Sec. of War., pp. 306, 308, 311; also see pp. 406–407.

[2] Schoolcraft, Ind. Tribes, I, p. 522.

[3] Col. Doc. Ined., v, pp. 532–546; Smith, Letter of Hernando de Soto and Memoir of Hernando de Escalante Fontaneda. The translation in French, Hist. Colls. La., 1875, pp. 235–265, is badly disarranged.

[4] Smith, op. cit.; Gatschet, Creek Mig. Leg., I, p. 14.

chose a representative of that tribe with which we have since discovered grounds for believing the Calusa stood in a particularly close relation. But even so, he was unable to obtain interpretations for most of Fontaneda's Calusa names, and most of the remaining etymologies suggested to him must be rejected as improbable. Yet it is interesting to note that the impression made upon his informants by these names was similar to that certain to be impressed upon anyone familiar with the Muskhogean tongues. He says: "My monitors say that all these words are eminently Chahta in their sounds, but that sometimes they are too imperfectly preserved to be understood, or that their sense can be detected only in part." Of the translations obtained by Smith of names not furnished with interpretations by Fontaneda only that of Calaobe (from kåli hofobi, "deep spring") and perhaps that of Soco (from su'ko, "muscadine") seem to have some probability in their favor. Translations are, however, furnished for a few by Fontaneda himself, and while the literal correctness of these must not be assumed, they present a somewhat more promising field of investigation. These words are Guaragunve, a town on the Florida keys, the name of which is said to mean in Spanish *Pueblo de Llanto,* i. e., "the town of weeping;" Cuchiyaga, a second town on these islands, the name signifying "the place where there has been suffering;" Calos or Calusa, "in the language of which the word signifies a fierce people, as they are called for being brave and skilled in war;" the Lake of Mayaimi, so called "because it is very large;" Zertepe, "chief and great lord" (though possibly this is a specific title); Guasaca-esgui, a name of the Suwanee, "the river of canes;" Ño or Non, "town beloved;" Cañogacola, or Cañegacola, "a crafty people, skillful with the bow;" se-le-te-ga, "run to the lookout, see if there be any people coming!"

The first of the above is almost the only one in which an *r* appears—though Carlos is used for Calos occasionally—and it is possible that this town may be one which Fontaneda informs us to have been occupied by Cuban Arawaks. In English the name would be pronounced nearly as Waragunwe, and if we assume the *r* has been substituted for an original *l*, we might find a cognate for the first part of it in Choctaw *wilanli,* to weep, while the second part might be compared with Choctaw *kowi* or *ko^{n}wi,* woods, a desert, but I do not feel sure that this order is permissible, and little confidence can be placed in the rendering. For Cuchiyaga Smith's informants suggested *ku-chi* (*cha*) *ya-ya,* "going out to wail," though he remarks that the interpretations of the names of this town and the preceding may have become transposed. Calos was explained to Smith as an abbreviation of the Choctaw words *ka-la* and *lu-sa,* "strong (and) black," but the form without a terminal *a* seems to be nearer the original, and I would suggest *kållo*, strong, powerful, or violent, followed by an article pronoun such as *ash*, the aforesaid, or *osh*. In case the final *a* were original the second word in the compound might be *a*ⁿ*sha*, to sit, to be. Mayaimi recalls Choctaw *maiha*, wide, and *mih*, it is so, it is like that, although *mih* is usually initial in position. I can do nothing with Zertepe, but, as suggested, this may not be a generic word. Guasaca-esgui should probably be pronounced Wasaka-esgi, and both parts bear a strong resemblance to the Choctaw *uski* or *oski*, cane, though of course, in any case, only one would represent that word; the Choctaw word for river is *hàcha*. In explanation of Ño, Gatschet cites Creek *anokítcha*, "lover," *anukídshäs*, "I love," the Choctaw equivalent of which is *anushkunna*, *no* or *nu* being assumed as the radix, but *anoa*, "famous," "noted," "illustrious," may also be mentioned in this connection. Perhaps the most suggestive of all of these words is Cañogacola, because the ending looks suspiciously like Choctaw *okla*, people, which we often find written by early travelers *ogala* or *okala*. The first part might be explained by Alabama *kàñgo*, not good, bad, or as a shortened form of Choctaw *i*ⁿ*kana keyu*, unfriendly. Finally, *se-le-te-ga* may contain *cheli*, you fly, you go rapidly, followed by *-t*, used in connecting several verbs, and possibly *haiaka*, to appear, to peep, though I am not certain that this particular combination is admissible.

Romans is the only writer to attempt an interpretation of names along the southeastern Florida coast. He gives the name of Indian River as Aisa hatcha and interprets this as meaning "Deer River." [1] The word hatcha, however, was probably given by himself or else obtained from the Seminole Indians and there is no proof that it belonged to the ancient language of Ais, while the first was probably translated arbitrarily in terms of the Choctaw language with which Romans was to some extent familiar.

Upon the whole more resemblances between these words and Choctaw seem to occur than would be expected if the languages had nothing in common, and those which we find in Guasaca-esgui and Cañogacola are almost too striking to be merely accidental. In connection with the first of these reference should be made to the name of a province mentioned only once by Fontaneda and seemingly located near Tampa Bay. This is Osiquevede, in which it is possible we again have *oski*. The latter part of the word might be interpreted by means of Choctaw *fitiha*, to whirl or veer about.

Putting all of the above evidence together, we may fairly conclude that a connection with Choctaw, or at all events some Muskhogean dialect, is indicated, but we must equally admit that it is not proved.

---

[1] Romans, Concise Nat. Hist. of E. and W. Fla., p. 273.

In the interior of the country, about Lake Okeechobee, were many towns said to be allied with the Calusa chief, and from the names of these towns given us by Fontaneda they would appear to have been allied in language also.[1]

On the east coast of Florida were a number of small tribes settled in the various inlets. From south to north the most important were the Tekesta, Jeaga, and Ais. The name Tekesta resembles those of the Calusa towns in appearance, and so do the names of several smaller places in the same locality, one town, Janar, even having a designation absolutely identical with that of a Calusa settlement.[2]

We know little more of the Jeaga[3] and Ais. They had many cultural features in common with the Calusa—including a uniform hostility to Christian missions—and their languages were at least markedly different from Timucua. In 1605 the governor of Florida, in commenting on the visit of some Ais Indians to St. Augustine, says that the language spoken in that province was "very different from this" (i. e., Timucua). He conversed with them by means of Juan de Junco, an Indian of the Timucua mission of Nombre de Dios, who spoke to the interpreter of the Surruque, a tribe living about Cape Canaveral. We might assume from this that the Surruque spoke the same language as the people of Ais, but many of them were familiar with Ais on account of the proximity of the two peoples, and I am inclined to regard the Surruque as the southernmost band of Timuqua upon the Atlantic coast.

The linguistic position of the Tamahita Indians is uncertain, but there is some reason to think that their name will prove to be another synonym for Yuchi. This possibility will be discussed at length when we come to consider the history of that tribe.

THE CUSABO

History

Little as we know about these people, it is a curious fact that their territory was one of the first in North America on which European settlements were attempted, and these were of historical importance and even celebrity. They were made, moreover, by three different nations, the Spaniards, French, and English.

The first visitors were the Spaniards, who made a landing here in 1521, only eight years after Ponce de Leon's assumed[2] discovery of Florida. Accounts of this voyage, more or less complete, have

[1] Fontaneda in Col. Doc. Ined., v., p. 539; see pp. 331–333.

[2] See p. 333.

[3] The Spanish orthography of this word is retained; it was pronounced something like Heaga.

been given by Peter Marytr,[1] Gomara,[2] Oviedo,[3] and Herrera,[4] and in more recent times by Navarrete,[5] Henry Harrisse,[6] John Gilmary Shea,[7] and Woodbury Lowery.[8] That of Shea is based largely on original manuscripts, and, as it contains all of the essential facts, I will quote it in full.

In 1520 Lucas Vasquez de Ayllon, one of the auditors of the Island of St. Domingo, though possessed of wealth, honors, and domestic felicity, aspired to the glory of discovering some new land, and making it the seat of a prosperous colony. Having secured the necessary license, he despatched a caravel under the command of Francisco Gordillo, with directions to sail northward through the Bahamas, and thence strike the shore of the continent. Gordillo set out on his exploration, and near the Island of Lucayoneque, one of the Lucayuelos, descried another caravel. His pilot, Alonzo Fernandez Sotil, proceeded toward it in a boat, and soon recognized it as a caravel commanded by a kinsman of his, Pedro de Quexos, fitted out in part, though not avowedly, by Juan Ortiz de Matienzo, an auditor associated with Ayllon in the judiciary. This caravel was returning from an unsuccessful cruise among the Bahamas for Caribs—the object of the expedition being to capture Indians in order to sell them as slaves. On ascertaining the object of Gordillo's voyage, Quexos proposed that they should continue the exploration together. After a sail of eight or nine days, in which they ran little more than a hundred leagues, they reached the coast of the continent at the mouth of a considerable river, to which they gave the name of St. John the Baptist, from the fact that they touched the coast on the day set apart to honor the Precursor of Christ. The year was 1521, and the point reached was, according to the estimate of the explorers, in latitude 33° 30′.

Boats put off from the caravels and landed some twenty men on the shore; and while the ships endeavored to enter the river, these men were surrounded by Indians, whose good-will they gained by presents.

Some days later, Gordillo formally took possession of the country in the name of Ayllon, and of his associate Diego Caballero, and of the King, as Quexos did also in the name of his employers on Sunday, June 30, 1521. Crosses were cut on the trunks of trees to mark the Spanish occupancy.

Although Ayllon had charged Gordillo to cultivate friendly relations with the Indians of any new land he might discover, Gordillo joined with Quexos in seizing some seventy of the natives, with whom they sailed away, without any attempt to make an exploration of the coast.

On the return of the vessel to Santo Domingo, Ayllon condemned his captain's act; and the matter was brought before a commission, presided over by Diego Columbus, for the consideration of some important affairs. The Indians were declared free, and it was ordered that they should be restored to their native land at the earliest possible moment. Meanwhile they were to remain in the hands of Ayllon and Matienzo.[7]

Another account of this expedition is given by Peter Martyr,[1] from whom Gomara and nearly all subsequent writers copied it.

---

1 Peter Martyr, De Orbe Novo, II, pp. 255–271.
2 Gomara, Hist. de las Indias, p. 32
3 Oviedo, Hist. Gen., III, pp. 624–633.
4 Herrera, Hist. Gen., I, pp. 259–261.
5 Navarrete, Col., III, pp. 69–74.
6 Harrisse, Disc. of N. Amer., pp. 198–213
7 In Winsor, Narr. and Crit. Hist. Amer., II, pp. 238–241.
8 Lowery, Span. Settl., 1513–1561, pp. 153–157, 160–168.

While it is not fortified with official documents like that of Shea it comes from a contemporary and one intimately acquainted with all of the principals and therefore deserves to be placed beside the other as an original source of information.

Some Spaniards, anxious as hunters pursuing wild beasts through the mountains and swamps to capture the Indians of that archipelago [the Bahamas], embarked on two ships built at the cost of seven of them. They sailed from Puerto de Plata situated on the north coast of Hispaniola, and laid their course towards the Lucayas. Three years have passed since then, and it is only now, in obedience to Camillo Gallino, who wishes me to acquaint Your Excellency with some still unknown particulars concerning these discoveries, that I speak of this expedition. These Spaniards visited all the Lucayas but without finding the plunder, for their neighbors had already explored the archipelago and systematically depopulated it. Not wishing to expose themselves to ridicule by returning to Hispaniola empty-handed, they continued their course towards the north. Many people said they lied when they declared they had purposely chosen that direction.

They were driven by a sudden tempest which lasted two days, to within sight of a lofty promontory which we will later describe. When they landed on this coast, the natives, amazed at the unexpected sight, regarded it as a miracle, for they had never seen ships. At first they rushed in crowds to the beach, eager to see; but when the Spaniards took to their shallops, the natives fled with the swiftness of the wind, leaving the coast deserted. Our compatriots pursued them and some of the more agile and swift-footed young men got ahead and captured a man and a woman, whose flight had been less rapid. They took them on board their ships and after giving them clothing, released them. Touched by this generosity, serried masses of natives again appeared on the beach.

When their sovereign heard of this generosity, and beheld for the first time these unknown and precious garments—for they only wear the skins of lions and other wild beasts—he sent fifty of his servants to the Spaniards, carrying such provisions as they eat. When the Spaniards landed, he received them respectfully and cordially, and when they exhibited a wish to visit the neighborhood, he provided them with guide and an escort. Wherever they showed themselves the natives, full of admiration, advanced to meet them with presents, as though they were divinities to be worshipped. What impressed them most was the sight of the beards and the woolen and silk clothing.

But what then! The Spaniards ended by violating this hospitality. For when they had finished their explorations, they enticed numerous natives by lies and tricks to visit their ships, and when the vessels were quickly crowded with men and women they raised anchor, set sail, and carried these despairing unfortunates into slavery. By such means they sowed hatred and warfare throughout that peaceful and friendly region, separating children from their parents and wives from their husbands. Nor is this all. Only one of the two ships returned, and of the other there has been no news. As the vessel was old, it is probable that she went down with all on board, innocent and guilty. This spoliation occasioned the Royal council at Hispaniola much vexation, but it remained unpunished. It was first thought to send the prisoners back, but nothing was done, because the plan would have been difficult to realise, and besides one of the ships was lost.

These details were furnished me by a virtuous priest, learned in law, called the bachelor Alvares de Castro. His learning and his virtues caused him to be named Dean of the Cathedral of Concepcion, in Hispaniola, and simultaneously vicar and inquisitor.

Thus his testimony may be confidently accepted. . . . It is from Castro's report and after several enquiries into this seizure that we have learned that the women brought from that region wear lions' skins and the men wear skins of all other wild beasts. He says these people are white and larger than the generality of men. When they were landed some of them searched among the rubbish heaps along the town ditches for decaying bodies of dogs and asses with which to satisfy their hunger. Most of them died of misery, while those who survived were divided among the colonists of Hispaniola, who disposed of them as they pleased, either in their houses, the gold-mines, or their fields.

Farther on Peter Martyr gives Ayllon, "one of those at whose expense the two ships had been equipped," and his Indian servant, Francisco of Chicora, as additional informants, and states that he had sometimes invited them to his table.

In 1523 Ayllon obtained a royal cédula securing to him exclusive right of settlement within the limits of a strip of coast on either side of the place where his subordinate had come to land. In 1525, being unable to visit the new land himself, in order to secure his rights he sent two caravels to explore his territory under Pedro de Quexos. "They regained the good will of the natives," says Shea, "and explored the coast for 250 leagues, setting up stone crosses with the name of Charles V and the date of the act of taking possession. They returned to Santo Domingo in July, 1525, bringing one or two Indians from each province, who might be trained to act as interpreters." [1] After considerable delay Ayllon himself sailed for his new government early in June, 1526, with three large vessels, 600 persons of both sexes, including priests and physicians, and 100 horses. They reached the North American coast at the mouth of a river calculated by them to be in north latitude 33° 40′, and they called it the Jordan—from the name of one of Ayllon's captains, it is said. Here, however, Ayllon lost one of his vessels, and his interpreters, including Francisco of Chicora, deserted him. Dissatisfied with the region in which he had landed and obtaining news of one better from a party he had sent along the shore, Ayllon determined to remove, and he seems to have followed the coast. The explorers are said to have continued for 40 or 45 leagues until they came to a river called Gualdape, where they began a settlement, which was called San Miguel de Gualdape. The land hereabout was flat and full of marshes. The river was large and well stocked with fish, but the entrance was shallow and passable only at high tide. The colony did not prosper, the weather became severe, many sickened and died, and on October 18, 1526, Ayllon died also. Trouble soon broke out among the surviving colonists and finally, in the middle of a severe winter, those that were left sailed back to Hispaniola.[2]

---

[1] Shea, op. cit., p. 240

[2] Ibid., p. 241.

Such are the principal facts concerning the first Spanish explorations and attempts at colonization upon the coast of the Carolinas. Before giving the information obtained through them regarding the aborigines of the country and their customs it will be necessary to determine as nearly as possible the location of the three rivers mentioned in the relations, the River of St. John the Baptist, the River Jordan, and the River Gualdape, an undertaking which has been attempted already in the most painstaking manner, by the historians Harrisse, Shea, and Lowery.[1]

So far as the River Jordan is concerned, there is scarcely the shadow of a doubt that it was the Santee. The identification is indicated by evidence drawn from a great many early writers, and practically demonstrated by the statements of two or three of the more careful navigators. Ecija, for instance, places its mouth in N. lat. 33° 11′, which is almost exactly correct.[2] A very careful pilot's description appended to the account of his second voyage puts it only a little higher.[2] Furthermore, tribes that can be identified readily as the Sewee and Santee are mentioned by him and they are on this river in the positions they later occupied. He states also, on the authority of the Indians, that a trail led from the mouth of it to a town near the mountains called Xoada, which is readily recognizable as the Siouan Cheraw tribe.[2] Now, as Mr. Mooney has shown,[3] and as all evidence indicates, the Cheraw were at this time at the head of Broad River. The Pedee or the Cape Fear would have carried travelers to the Cheraw miles out of their way. Finally it must be remembered that the name Jordan was applied to a certain river during the entire Spanish period in the Southeast. It had a definite meaning, and when the English settled the country Spanish cartographers were at no loss to identify their Jordan under its new English name, so that Navarrete says that "on some ancient maps there is a river at thirty-three degrees North, which they name Jordan or Santée." [4] One of the reasons for uncertainty regarding it is the fact that the ancient Cape San Roman, from which the Jordan is frequently located, is not the present Cape Romain, but apparently Cape Fear, and is thus universally represented as north of the Jordan instead of south of it. The argument could be elaborated at length, but it is unnecessary. The burden of proof is rather on him who would deny the identification.

With regard to the other two rivers we have no such certain evidence, and their exact positions will probably always remain in doubt.

---

[1] Op. cit.

[2] Lowery, MSS., Lib. Cong.

[3] Bull. 22, Bur. Amer. Ethn., p. 57.

[4] Navarrete, Col., III, p. 70.

The cédula issued to Ayllon places the newly discovered land in which was the River of St. John the Baptist in N. lat. 35°–37°,[1] but for anything like an exact statement we must depend entirely on the testimony of the pilot Quexos, who estimated that it lay considerably farther south, in N. lat. 33° 30′.[2] It would therefore be somewhere in the immediate neighborhood of the Jordan, possibly that very stream. However, immediately after the statement of Navarrete quoted above, he adds, "to the northeast of that which they name Santee, at a distance of 48 miles, there is another river, which they call Chico."[3] This would at once suggest an identification of that stream with the Pedee, or with Winyah Bay, though of course where they enter the ocean the Santee and Pedee are much nearer together than 48 miles. I am, however, inclined to suspect that "the river Chico" represented simply some cartographer's guess as to the location of Chicora, and was not, as Navarrete seems to assume farther on, itself the original of the term Chicora.

The general position is, however, indicated by another line of evidence. It will be remembered that among the Indians carried off by Gordillo and Quexos from the River of St. John the Baptist in 1521 was one who received the name Francisco of Chicora, who related such wonderful tales of the new country that many Spaniards, including the historian Oviedo, believed that no confidence could be reposed in him.[4] His remarkable story of tailed men, however, Mr. Mooney and the writer have been able to establish as an element in the mythology of the southern Indians, and enough of the "provinces" which he mentioned are identifiable to show that the names are not the pure fabrication which Oviedo supposed.

So far as I am aware there are but three original sources for the complete list of provinces—two in the Documentos Ineditos[5] and the third in Oviedo.[6] An equally ancient authority for part of them, however, is Peter Martyr.[7] I give these in the following comparative table, and in addition the lists from Navarrete,[8] and Barcia,[9] who had access to the original documents.

---

[1] Navarrete, Col., III, p. 153; Doc. Ined., XXII, p. 79.
[2] Shea in Winsor, Narr. and Crit. Hist., II, p. 239.
[3] Navarrete, Col., III, p. 70.
[4] Oviedo, Hist. Gen., p. 628.
[5] Vols. XIV, p. 506, and XXII, p. 82.
[6] Hist. Gen., III, 628.
[7] Peter Martyr, De Orbe Novo, II, pp. 259–261.
[8] Navarrete, Col., III, p. 154.
[9] Barcia, La Florida, pp. 4–5.

No.	Doc. Ined. XIV.	Doc Ined. XXII.	Oviedo.	Peter Martyr.	Navarrete.	Barcia.
1	Duaché	Duache	Duahe	Duhâre or Duharhe.	Suache	Duaarhe.
2	Chicora	Clricora	Chicora	Chicora	Chicora	Chicora.
3	Xapira		Xapira	Xapira	Xapira	Xapira.
		Xapiracta				
4			Yta	Hitha		Ytha.
	Tatancal				y Tatancal	
5		Taucal	Tancac			
6			Anica			
	Anicatiya	Auricatuye			Anicatiye	
7				Tihe		Tihie.
			Tiveçocayo			
8	Cocayo	Cayo			Cocayo	
9				Quohathe		Cohoth.
10	Guacaya	Quacaya	Guacaya	Guacaia	Guacaya	Xuacaya.
11	Xoxi	Xoxi	Xoxi		Xoxi	
12	Sona	Sonapasqui	Sona		Sona	
13	Pasqui		Pasqui		Pasqui	
14	Arambe	Arambe	Aranui	Arambe	Arambe	Arambe.
15	Xamunambe	Xaminambe	Xamunanuc	Xamunambe	Xamunambe	Xumunaunbe.
16	Chuaque	Nuaq	Huaque		Huaq	
17	Tanzaca	Tancaca	Tanaca	Tanzacca	Tanzaca	Tamceca.
18	Yenyochol	Ymgo	Yenyohol		Yenyohol	
19	Paor	Holpaos	Pahoc	Pahor	Paor	Paor.
20	Amiscaron	Aunicoon	Yamiscaron		Yamiscaron	
21	Orix	Ouxa	Orixa			
					Corixayn-siguanin.	
	Aymi					
22		Ynsiquanin	Inisiguanin	Inzignanin		Ynsignavin.
	Guanin					
23	Anoxa	Anoxa	y Noxa		Anoxa	

The variants of these names enable us, by comparing them with one another, to determine the originals with considerable certainty in most cases, though some still remain in question. As reconstructed, the list would be something like this: Duhare or Duache, Chicora, Xapira or Xapida, Yta or Hitha, Tancal or Tancac, Anica, Tiye or Tihe, Cocayo, Quohathe, Guacaya, Xoxi, Sona, Pasqui, Arambe, Xamunambe, Huaque, Tanzaca, Yenyohol, Pahoc or Paor, Yamiscaron, Orixa, Insiguanin or Inziguanin, Anoxa.

Yamiscaron without doubt refers to the Yamasee Indians, the ending probably being a Siouan suffix, and the whole possibly the original of the name Yamacraw applied at a much later date to a body of Indians at the mouth of the Savannah. There can be little question also that Orixa is the later Spanish Orista, and English Edisto, Coçayo the Coosa Indians of the upper courses of the rivers of lower South Carolina, or perhaps the town of "Coçapoy"[1]

[1] See p. 58.

and Xapira, or rather Xapida, Sampit. Pasqui is evidently the Pasque of Ecija, which seems to have been inland near the Waxaw Indians. The remaining names can not be identified with such probability, but plausible suggestions may be made regarding some of them. Thus Yta is perhaps the later Etiwaw or Itwan, Sona may be Stono, which sometimes appears in the form "Stonah," and Guacaya is perhaps Waccamaw, *gua* in Spanish being frequently employed for the English syllable *wa*. If Pahoc is the correct form of the name of province 19 it may contain an explanation of the "Backbooks" mentioned by Lawson,[1] supposing the form of the latter which Rivers gives, "Back Hooks," is the correct one.[2]

Two facts regarding this list have particular importance for us in this investigation, first, the appearance of the phonetic *r* (in Duhare, Chicora, Xapira, Arambe, Yamiscaron, Orixa), and, second, that all of the provinces identified, all in fact for which an identification is even suggested, are in the Cusabo country or the regions in close contact with it. The first of these points indicates that Francisco came from one of the eastern Siouan tribes, while the second would show that he had considerable knowledge of the tribes south of them, and thus points to some Siouan area not far removed. Since this was also on the coast, the mouths of the Santee and Pedee are the nearest points satisfying the requirements. It is true that there is no *l* in Catawba, while two words ending in *l*—Tancal and Yenyohol—occur in the list; but these may have been taken over intact from Cusabo, or they may have been incorrectly copied, since Oviedo has Tancac for the first of them. Winyah Bay or the Pedee River would be indicated more definitely if Daxe, a town which the Indians told Ecija was four days journey north, or rather northeast, of the Santee, were identical with the Duache of the Ayllon colonists. But, however interesting it might be to establish the location of the river of John the Baptist with precision, it makes no practical difference in the present investigation whether it was the Santee or one of those streams flowing into Winyah Bay. That it was one of them can hardly be doubted.

The third river to be identified, Gualdape, is the most difficult of all. This is due in the first place to an uncertainty as to which way the settlers moved when they left the River Jordan. Oviedo, who is our only authority on this point, says: "Despues que estovieron allí algunos dias, descontentos de la tierra é ydas las lenguas ó guias que llevaron, acordaron de yrse á poblar la costa adelante háçia la costa occçidental, é fueron á un grand rio (quarenta ó quarenta é çinco leguas de allí, pocas más ó menos) que se diçe Gualdape; é allí

[1] Lawson, Hist. Carolina, p. 45.

[2] Rivers, Hist. S. Car., p. 35.

assentaron su campo ó real en la costa dél." ("After they had been there for some days, being dissatisfied with the country and the interpreters or guides having left them, they decided to go and settle on the coast beyond, in the direction of the west coast; and they went to a large river, 40 or 45 leagues from that place, more or less, called Gualdape; and there they established their camp or settlement on the coast.")[1] Navarrete interprets this to mean that they traveled north,[2] and he has been followed by both Harrisse[3] and Shea.[4] The last is confirmed in his opinion by the narrative of Ecija, which states that "Guandape" was near where the English had established their settlement;[5] consequently he carries Ayllon from the River Jordan all the way to Jamestown, in Virginia. It seems to the writer, however, that the "English settlement" to which Ecija refers and which he places on an island must have been the Roanoke colony, although in Ecija's time it had been abandoned 20 years. But in either case the distance from the mouth of the Pedee or Santee was too great to be described as "40 or 45 leagues."

On the other hand, there are good reasons for believing that Ayllon did not move north after abandoning the River Jordan, but southwest. It is unfortunate that Oviedo's words are not clearer, but it seems to the writer that the most natural interpretation of them is that the settlers followed the coast westward, which would actually be in this case toward the southwest. Lowery also comes to this conclusion, but since he starts them from a different point—the mouth of the Cape Fear River—he brings them no farther than the Pedee, our starting point.[6] To what Oviedo tells us of this movement Navarrete adds the information, that the women and the sick were transported thither in boats while the remainder of the company made their way by land.[7] Lowery accepts this statement without question,[8] but Navarrete is not an absolutely reliable authority. His information on this point can only have been drawn from unpublished manuscripts, and unless we have some means of substantiating it, it seems unsafe to assume a march of so many leagues when no reason is presented why the Spaniards should not have taken to their vessels. My belief is that they did so. But how much of the coast is embraced in these 40 or 45 leagues it is impossible to say, for often the "leagues" of these old relations are equivalent only to the same number of miles. Thus Gualdape might be anywhere from 40 to 135 miles away, somewhere between Charleston Harbor and the mouth of Savannah River.

Charleston Harbor itself seems to be excluded by the description of the bar at the mouth of the river of Gualdape which the vessels

[1] Oviedo, Hist. Gen., III, p. 628.
[2] Navarrete, Col., III, p. 723.
[3] Harrisse, Disc. of N. Amer., p. 213.
[4] Shea in Winsor, Narr. and Crit. Hist. Amer., II, p. 240.
[5] Ibid., p. 285.
[6] Lowery, Span. Settl., I, pp. 165-166.
[7] Navarrete, Col., III, p. 72.
[8] Lowery, op. cit.

could cross only at high tide—"la tierra toda muy llana é de muchas çiénegas, pero el rio muy poderoso é de muchos é buenos pescados; é á la entrada dél era baxo, si con la cresçiente no entraban los navios." ("The land very flat and with many swamps, but the river very powerful and with many good fish, and at its entrance was a bar, so that the vessels could enter only at flood tide.")[1] If Navarrete is right in stating that the able-bodied men reached Gualdape by land I think we must make a very conservative interpretation of the 40 or 45 leagues and assume miles rather than leagues. This would not bring us farther than the neighborhood of Charleston Harbor. If, however, we take the distance given by Oviedo at its face value it carries us to the mouth of the Savannah. As a matter of fact we can not know absolutely where this river lay. It might have been the Stono, the North or South Edisto, the Coosawhatchie, the Broad, or some less conspicuous stream. All of these have offshore bars, and the channels into most are so narrow that they might not have been discovered by the explorers, who therefore supposed that the Gualdape River could be entered only at high tide. But taking Oviedo's two statements, regarding the distance covered and the size of the river, which was apparently of fresh water, I am inclined to believe the Savannah to have been the river in question, because there are two independent facts which tend to bear out this theory. In the first place the companions of De Soto when at Cofitachequi discovered glass beads, rosaries, and Biscayan axes, "from which they recognized that they were in the government or territory where the lawyer Lucas Vazquez de Ayllon came to his ruin." So Ranjel.[2] Biedma says in substance the same,[3] but what the Fidalgo of Elvas tells us is more to the point: "In the town were found a dirk and beads that had belonged to Christians, who, the Indians said, had many years before been in the port, distant two day's journey."[4]

Now Cofitachequi has usually been placed upon the Savannah River, and "the port" might naturally refer to that at its mouth. At all events two days' journey would not take the traveler very far to the north or south of that river, nor is it likely that these European articles had gotten many miles from the place where they had been obtained. They might indeed have been secured from the navigators who conducted the first or the second expedition or from Ayllon when he was at "the River Jordan," but on the first voyage the dealings with the natives were very brief, and no relations with them seem to have been entered into while Ayllon and his companions were at the Jordan on their last voyage. It is also rather unlikely that so many Spanish articles should have reached the Savannah from the mouth of the Pedee. In fact this is pre-

[1] Oviedo, Hist. Gen., III, p. 628.
[2] Bourne, Narr. of De Soto, II, p. 100.
[3] Ibid., p. 14.
[4] Ibid., I, p. 67.

cluded if the statement of the Indians quoted by Elvas is to be relied upon. The second expedition was a mere reconnoissance and the explorers do not seem to have stopped long in any one place. The most natural conclusion is that Cofitachequi was not far from the point where Ayllon had made his final and disastrous attempt at colonization, and, as I have said, Cofitachequi is not usually placed by modern students eastward of the Savannah. Secondly, the name Gualdape, containing as it does the phonetic *l*, would seem not to have been in Siouan territory, but instead suggests a name or set of names very common in Spanish accounts of the Georgia coast. Thus Jekyl Island was known as Gualdaquini, and St. Catherines Island was called Guale, a name adopted by the Spaniards to designate the entire province. True, Oviedo seems to place Gualdape in N. lat. 33° or even higher,[1] but this was evidently an inference from the latitude given for the first landfall at the River Jordan and his supposition that the coast ran east and west. All things considered, it would seem most likely that the attempted settlement of San Miguel de Gualdape was at or near the mouth of Savannah River.

To sum up, then, if my identification of these places is absolutely, or only approximately, correct the River of St. John the Baptist and the River Jordan would be near the mouths of the Pedee and Santee, and any ethnological information reported by the Spaniards from this neighborhood would concern principally the eastern Siouan tribes, while Gualdape would be near the mouth of the Savannah, and any ethnological information from that neighborhood would apply either to the Guale Indians or to the Cusabo.

Regarding the Indians of Chicora and Duhare a very interesting and important account is preserved by Peter Martyr, who obtained a large part of it directly from Francisco of Chicora himself and the rest from Ayllon and his companions. This account has received less credence than it deserves because the original has seldom been consulted, but instead Gomara's narrative, an abridged and to some extent distorted copy of that of Peter Martyr, and still worse reproductions by later writers.[2] Thus in the French translation of Gomara we read that the priests of Chicora abstained from eating human flesh ("Ils ne mangent point de la chair humaine comme les autres"),[3] while the original simply says "they do not eat flesh (no comen carne)."[4] The translation also informs us that the Chicoranos made cheese from the milk of their women ("Ils font du fromage du laict de leurs femmes"), while the original states that they made

[1] Oviedo, Hist. Gen., III, p. 628.
[2] Gomara, Hist. de las Indias, chap. XLIII, pp. 32-33.
[3] Hist. Gen., Paris, 1606, p. 53.
[4] Gomara, op. cit., p. 32.

it from the milk of does.[1] But even in his original narrative Gomara has "improved upon" Peter Martyr, since he tells us that deer were kept in inclosures and sent out with shepherds, while Peter Martyr merely states that the young were kept in the houses and their mothers allowed to go out to pasture, coming back at night to their fawns (see below). Out of a not altogether impossible fact we thus have a quite improbable story and utterly impossible accessories developed. Although, as I have endeavored to show, these people were probably Siouan, they were so near the Cusabo that influences could readily pass from one to the other, and for that reason and because the material has hitherto escaped ethnological investigators I will append it.

Leaving the coast of Chicorana on one hand, the Spaniards landed in another country called "Duharhe."[2] Ayllon says the natives are white men,[3] and his testimony is confirmed by Francisco Chicorana. Their hair is brown and hangs to their heels. They are governed by a king of gigantic size, called Datha, whose wife is as large as himself. They have five children. In place of horses the king is carried on the shoulders of strong young men, who run with him to the different places he wishes to visit. At this point I must confess that the different accounts cause me to hesitate. The Dean and Ayllon do not agree; for what one asserts concerning these young men acting as horses, the other denies. The Dean said: "I have never spoken to anybody who has seen these horses," to which Ayllon answered, "I have heard it told by many people," while Francisco Chicorana, although he was present, was unable to settle this dispute. Could I act as arbitrator I would say that, according to the investigations I have made, these people were too barbarous and uncivilized to have horses.[4] Another country near Duhare is called Xapida. Pearls are found there, and also a kind of stone resembling pearls which is much prized by the Indians.

In all these regions they visited the Spaniards noticed herds of deer similar to our herds of cattle. These deer bring forth and nourish their young in the houses of the natives. During the daytime they wander freely through the woods in search of their food, and in the evening they come back to their little ones, who have been cared for, allowing themselves to be shut up in the courtyards and even to be milked, when they have suckled their fawns. The only milk the natives know is that of the does, from which they make cheese. They also keep a great variety of chickens, ducks, geese, and other similar fowls.[5] They eat maize bread, similar to that of the islanders, but they do not know the yucca root, from which cassabi, the food of the nobles, is made. The maize grains are very like our Genoese millet, and in size are as large as our peas. The natives cultivate another cereal called xathi. This is believed to be millet but it is not certain, for very few Castilians know millet, as it is nowhere grown in Castile. This country produces various kinds of potatoes, but of small varieties. . . .

The Spaniards speak of still other regions—Hitha, Xamunambe, and Tihe—all of which are believed to be governed by the same king. In the last named the inhabit-

---

[1] Gomara, op. cit., p. 33; Fr. trans., p. 53.

[2] The reader will observe in this narrative that the many wonderful things widely reported of Chicora really apply to Duhare.

[3] Evidently Indians of lighter color.

[4] Peter Martyr makes the simple difficult. The custom was universal among southern tribes of carrying chiefs and leading personages about in litters borne on the shoulders of several men.

[5] Of course these statements are erroneous, but there may have been individual cases of domestication which furnished some foundation for such reports.

ants wear a distinctive priestly costume, and they are regarded as priests and venerated as such by their neighbors. They cut their hair, leaving only two locks growing on their temples, which are bound under the chin. When the natives make war against their neighbors, according to the regrettable custom of mankind, these priests are invited by both sides to be present, not as actors, but as witnesses of the conflict. When the battle is about to open, they circulate among the warriors who are seated or lying on the ground, and sprinkle them with the juice of certain herbs they have chewed with their teeth; just as our priests at the beginning of the Mass sprinkle the worshippers with a branch dipped in holy water. When this ceremony is finished, the opposing sides fall upon one another. While the battle rages, the priests are left in charge of the camp, and when it is finished they look after the wounded, making no distinction between friends and enemies, and busy themselves in burying the dead.[1] The inhabitants of this country do not eat human flesh; the prisoners of war are enslaved by the victors.

The Spaniards have visited several regions of that vast country; they are called Arambe, Guacaia, Quohathe, Tanzacca, and Pahor. The color of the inhabitants is dark brown. None of them have any system of writing, but they preserve traditions of great antiquity in rhymes and chants. Dancing and physical exercises are held in honor, and they are passionately fond of ball games, in which they exhibit the greatest skill. The women know how to spin and sew. Although they are partially clothed with skins of wild beasts, they use cotton such as the Milanese call bombasio,[2] and they make nets of the fiber of certain tough grasses, just as hemp and flax are used for the same purposes in Europe.

There is another country called Inzignanin, whose inhabitants declare that, according to the tradition of their ancestors, there once arrived amongst them men with tails a meter long and as thick as a man's arm. This tail was not movable like those of the quadrupeds, but formed one mass as we see is the case with fish and crocodiles, and was as hard as a bone. When these men wished to sit down, they had consequently to have a seat with an open bottom; and if there was none, they had to dig a hole more than a cubit deep to hold their tails and allow them to rest. Their fingers were as long as they were broad, and their skin was rough, almost scaly. They ate nothing but raw fish, and when the fish gave out they all perished, leaving no descendants.[3] These fables and other similar nonsense have been handed down to the natives by their parents. Let us now notice their rites and ceremonies.

The natives have no temples, but use the dwellings of their sovereigns as such. As a proof of this we have said that a gigantic sovereign called Datha ruled in the province of Duhare, whose palace was built of stone, while all the other houses were built of lumber covered with thatch or grasses. In the courtyard of this palace, the Spaniards found two idols as large as a three-year-old child, one male and one female. These idols are both called Inamahari, and had their residence in the palace. Twice each year they are exhibited, the first time at the sowing season, when they are invoked to obtain successful result for their labors. We will later speak of the harvest. Thanksgivings are offered to them if the crops are good; in the contrary case they are implored to show themselves more favorable the following year.

The idols are carried in procession amidst pomp, accompanied by the entire people. It will not be useless to describe this ceremony. On the eve of the festival the king has his bed made in the room where the idols stand, and sleeps in their presence. At daybreak the people assemble, and the king himself carries these idols, hugging them

---

1 There is some confusion here. Evidently the reference is to a class of doctors or shamans who performed such offices, not to an entire tribe.

2 Probably this is a reference to the use of mulberry bark common among all southern tribes.

3 This is a native myth which Mr. Mooney has collected from the Cherokee, and I from the Alabama. Possibly it is a myth regarding the alligator from people who had only heard of that reptile.

to his breast, to the top of his palace, where he exhibits them to the people. He and they are saluted with respect and fear by the people, who fall upon their knees or throw themselves on the ground with loud shouts. The king then descends and hangs the idols, draped in artistically worked cotton stuffs, upon the breasts of two venerable men of authority. They are, moreover, adorned with feather mantles of various colors, and are thus carried escorted with hymns and songs into the country, while the girls and young men dance and leap. Anyone who stopped in his house or absented himself during the procession would be suspected of heresy; and not only the absent, but likewise any who took part in the ceremony carelessly and without observing the ritual. The men escort the idols during the day, while during the night the women watch over them, lavishing upon them demonstrations of joy and respect. The next day they were carried back to the palace with the same ceremonies with which they were taken out. If the sacrifice is accomplished with devotion and in conformity with the ritual, the Indians believe they will obtain rich crops, bodily health, peace, or if they are about to fight, victory, from these idols. Thick cakes, similar to those the ancients made from flour, are offered to them. The natives are convinced that their prayers for harvests will be heard, especially if the cakes are mixed with tears.[1]

Another feast is celebrated every year when a roughly carved wooden statue is carried into the country and fixed upon a high pole planted in the ground. This first pole is surrounded by similar ones, upon which people hang gifts for the gods, each one according to his means. At nightfall the principal citizens divide these offerings among themselves, just as the priests do with the cakes and other offerings given them by the women. Whoever offers the divinity the most valuable presents is the most honored. Witnesses are present when the gifts are offered, who announce after the ceremony what every one has given, just as notaries might do in Europe. Each one is thus stimulated by a spirit of rivalry to outdo his neighbor. From sunrise till evening the people dance round this statue, clapping their hands, and when nightfall has barely set in, the image and the pole on which it was fixed are carried away and thrown into the sea, if the country is on the coast, or into the river, if it is along a river's bank. Nothing more is seen of it, and each year a new statue is made.

The natives celebrate a third festival, during which, after exhuming a long-buried skeleton, they erect a black tent out in the country, leaving one end open so that the sky is visible; upon a blanket placed in the center of the tent they then spread out the bones. Only women surround the tent, all of them weeping, and each of them offers such gifts as she can afford. The following day the bones are carried to the tomb and are henceforth considered sacred. As soon as they are buried, or everything is ready for their burial, the chief priest addresses the surrounding people from the summit of a mound, upon which he fulfills the functions of orator. Ordinarily he pronounces a eulogy on the deceased, or on the immortality of the soul, or the future life. He says that souls originally came from the icy regions of the north, where perpetual snow prevails. They therefore expiate their sins under the master of that region who is called Mateczungua, but they return to the southern regions, where another great sovereign, Quexuga, governs. Quexuga is lame and is of a sweet and generous disposition. He surrounds the newly arrived souls with numberless attentions, and with him they enjoy a thousand delights; young girls sing and dance, parents are reunited to children, and everything one formerly loved is enjoyed. The old grow young and everybody is of the same age, occupied only in giving himself up to joy and pleasure.[2]

---

[1] This ceremony seems to correspond in intention to the Creek busk, but the form of it is quite different.

[2] Compare with this the Chickasaw belief in a western quarter peopled by malevolent beings through which the soul passes to the world of the sky deity above.

Such are the verbal traditions handed down to them from their ancestors. They are regarded as sacred and considered authentic. Whoever dared to believe differently would be ostracised. These natives also believe that we live under the vault of heaven; they do not suspect the existence of the antipodes. They think the sea has its gods, and believe quite as many foolish things about them as Greece, the friend of lies, talked about Nereids and other marine gods—Glaucus, Phorcus, and the rest of them.

When the priest has finshed his speech he inhales the smoke of certain herbs, puffing it in and out, pretending to thus purge and absolve the people from their sins. After this ceremony the natives return home, convinced that the inventions of this impostor not only soothe the spirits, but contribute to the health of their bodies.

Another fraud of the priests is as follows: When the chief is at death's door and about to give up his soul they send away all witnesses, and then surrounding his bed they perform some secret jugglery which makes him appear to vomit sparks and ashes. It looks like sparks jumping from a bright fire, or those sulphured papers, which people throw into the air to amuse themselves. These sparks, rushing through the air and quickly disappearing, look like those shooting stars which people call leaping wild goats. The moment the dying man expires a cloud of those sparks shoots up 3 cubits high with a noise and quickly vanishes. They hail this flame as the dead man's soul, bidding it a last farewell and accompanying its flight with their wailings, tears, and funereal cries, absolutely convinced that it has taken its flight to heaven. Lamenting and weeping they escort the body to the tomb.

Widows are forbidden to marry again if the husband has died a natural death;[1] but if he has been executed they may remarry. The natives like their women to be chaste. They detest immodesty and are careful to put aside suspicious women. The lords have the right to have two women, but the common people have only one. The men engage in mechanical occupations, especially carpenter work and tanning skins of wild beasts, while the women busy themselves with distaff, spindle, and needle.

Their year is divided into 12 moons. Justice is administered by magistrates, criminals and the guilty being severely punished, especially thieves. Their kings are of gigantic size, as we have already mentioned. All the provinces we have named pay them tributes and these tributes are paid in kind; for they are free from the pest of money, and trade is carried on by exchanging goods. They love games, especially tennis;[2] they also like metal circles turned with movable rings, which they spin on a table, and they shoot arrows at a mark. They use torches and oil made from different fruits for illumination at night. They likewise have olive-trees.[3] They invite one another to dinner. Their longevity is great and their old age is robust.

They easily cure fevers with the juice of plants, as they also do their wounds, unless the latter are mortal. They employ simples, of which they are acquainted with a great many. When any of them suffers from a bilious stomach he drinks a draught composed of a common plant called Guahi,[4] or eats the herb itself; after which he immediately vomits his bile and feels better. This is the only medicament they use, and they never consult doctors except experienced old women, or priests acquainted with the secret virtues of herbs. They have none of our delicacies, and as they have neither the perfumes of Araby nor fumigations nor foreign spices at their disposition, they content themselves with what their country produces and live happily in better health to a more robust old age. Various dishes and different foods are not required to satisfy their appetites, for they are contented with little.

---

1 Probably with a time limitation like the Muskhogeans.

2 This, of course, refers to the great southern ball game.

3 Oil was extracted from acorns and several kinds of nuts. One of these is evidently intended.

4 Perhaps the *Ilex vomitoria* from which the "black drink" was brewed.

It is quite laughable to hear how the people salute the lords and how the king responds, especially to his nobles. As a sign of respect the one who salutes puts his hands to his nostrils and gives a bellow like a bull, after which he extends his hands toward the forehead and in front of the face. The king does not bother to return the salutes of his people, and responds to the nobles by half bending his head toward the left shoulder without saying anything.

I now come to a fact which will appear incredible to your excellency. You already know that the ruler of this region is a tyrant of gigantic size. How does it happen that only he and his wife have attained this extraordinary size? No one of their subjects has explained this to me, but I have questioned the above-mentioned licenciate Ayllon, a serious and responsible man, who had his information from those who had shared with him the cost of the expedition. I likewise questioned the servant Francisco, to whom the neighbors had spoken. Neither nature nor birth has given these princes the advantage of size as an hereditary gift; they have acquired it by artifice. While they are still in their cradles and in charge of their nurses, experts in the matter are called, who by the application of certain herbs, soften their young bones. During a period of several days they rub the limbs of the child with these herbs, until the bones become as soft as wax. They then rapidly bend them in such wise that the infant is almost killed. Afterwards they feed the nurse on foods of a special virtue. The child is wrapped in warm covers, the nurse gives it her breast and revives it with her milk, thus gifted with strengthening properties. After some days of rest the lamentable task of stretching the bones is begun anew. Such is the explanation given by the servant, Francisco Chicorana.

The Dean of La Concepcion, whom I have mentioned, received from the Indians stolen on the vessel that was saved explanations differing from those furnished to Ayllon and his associates. These explanations dealt with medicaments and other means used for increasing the size. There was no torturing of the bones, but a very stimulating diet composed of crushed herbs was used. This diet was given principally at the age of puberty, when it is nature's tendency to develop, and sustenance is converted into flesh and bones. Certainly it is an extraordinary fact, but we must remember what is told about these herbs, and if their hidden virtues could be learned I would willingly believe in their efficacy. We understand that only the kings are allowed to use them, for if anyone else dared to taste them, or to obtain the recipe of this diet, he would be guilty of treason, for he would appear to equal the king. It is considered, after a fashion, that the king should not be the size of everybody else, for he should look down upon and dominate those who approach him. Such is the story told to me, and I repeat it for what it is worth. Your excellency may believe it or not.

I have already sufficiently described the ceremonies and customs of these natives. Let us now turn our attention to the study of nature. Bread and meat have been considered; let us devote our attention to trees.

There are in this country virgin forests of oak, pine, cypress, nut and almond trees, amongst the branches of which riot wild vines, whose white and black grapes are not used for wine-making, for the people manufacture their drinks from other fruits. There are likewise fig-trees and other kinds of spice-plants. The trees are improved by grafting, just as with us; though without cultivation they would continue in a wild state. The natives cultivate gardens in which grows an abundance of vegetables, and they take an interest in growing their orchards. They even have trees in their gardens. One of these trees is called the corito, of which the fruit resembles a small melon in size and flavor. Another called guacomine bears fruit a little larger than a quince of a delicate and remarkable odor, and which is very wholesome. They plant and cultivate many other trees and plants, of which I shall not speak further, lest by telling everything at one breath I become monotonous.[1]

[1] Peter Martyr, De Orbe Novo, II, pp. 259–269.

In this narrative there appears to be very little not based on fact. The sharp-tailed people are, as noted, still believed in by the southern Indians, from which we may infer that the story regarding them was known throughout the South. As to the receipts for making giants they are such as any Indian might believe efficacious and where great stature happened to follow assume that his treatment had been the efficient cause, and when it did not that the fault did not lie with the medicines. The notion that deer were herded and milked might very well have originated in the fact that the Spaniards encountered pet animals in certain of the villages they visited. The ceremonials described are the reverse of improbable. The reverence for a male and a female deity connected with sowing and harvesting would seem to be the result of a natural association of sexual processes with germination in the vegetable world; and the ceremonies over the bones of the dead recall what Lawson tells us of the separation of the flesh from the bones among the Santee and interment in mounds. It is a curious and interesting fact that, although the name Chicora appears most prominently in subsequent histories and charts, so as to give its name to a large part of the Carolinas, Peter Martyr, the original authority for most that has been said about that country, assigns it a very subordinate position. As already noted, the greater part of what he has to tell applies to Duhare, the second province visited by the Spaniards, and he seems to say that all of the provinces which he mentions[1] were subject to the king of Duhare and paid him tribute. At least he says as much for Hitha, Xamunambe, and Tihe. Of course no reliance can be placed upon tales of subjection and the exaction of tribute, but at least Duhare was plainly a very important country at that time, distinctly overshadowing Chicora. What is said about the people of Tihe being, as it were, a race of priests is interesting, and may mean that they were of a different stock. It is probable that Inzignanin (or rather Inziguanin), the inhabitants of which told about the race of sharp-tails, was a province farther south than the others, perhaps in the Cusabo or Guale country, but so far it has been impossible to identify it. Chicora and Duhare were evidently upon the coast, but how far apart we do not know. Unfortunately Peter Martyr does not tell us whether the Spaniards turned north or south from Chicora in going to the latter province. We may feel pretty certain that both were in Siouan territory, but more than that we can not say with any degree of assurance.

For information regarding the people of Gualdape we must consult Oviedo. While, as we have said, the quotations made from Peter Martyr evidently apply to some of the eastern Siouan tribes, we now

---

[1] See p. 43.

come to Indians almost certainly of Muskhogean stock. The following is Oviedo's description:

> The country of Gualdape, as well as from the river of Santa Elena toward the west, is all level. The Spaniards who came with the licentiate Ayllon did not see the villages; they only met with a few isolated houses or cabins forming little hamlets, at great distances one from the other. On some of the small islands on the coast there are certain mosques or temples of those idolatrous people and many remains [bones] of their dead, those of the elders apart from those of the young people or children. They look like the ossuaries or burying places of the common people; the bodies of their principal people are in temples by themselves or in little chapels in another community and also on little islands. And those houses or temples have walls of stone and mortar (which mortar they make of oyster shells) and they are about one estado and a half in height,[1] the rest of the building above this wall being made of wood (pine). There are many pines there. There are several principal [2] houses all along the coast and each one of them must be considered by those people to be a village, for they are very big and they are constructed of very tall and beautiful pines, leaving the crown of leaves at the top. After having set up one row of trees to form one wall, they set up the opposite side, leaving a space between the two sides of from 15 to 30 feet, the length of the walls being 300 or more feet. As they intertwine the branches at the top and so in this manner there is no need for a tiled roof or other covering, they cover it all with matting interwoven between the logs where there may be hollows or open places. Furthermore they can cross those beams with other [pines] placed lengthwise on the inside, thus increasing the thickness of their walls. In this way the wall is thick and strong, because the beams are very close together. In each one of those houses there is easily room enough for 200 men and in Indian fashion they can live in them, placing the opening for the door where it is most convenient.[3]

Lower down Oviedo mentions "blackberries, which, being dried, the Indians keep to eat in the winter."[4] This is practically all the ethnological information which the historians of the Ayllon expeditions furnish. It is interesting to find the mat communal house, which does not appear to have been used by the Creeks, in existence so far south, but Oviedo is probably in error in representing the walls as constructed of living trees. The ossuaries described show that the custom of erecting them, so common along the lower Mississippi, extended eastward as far as the Atlantic.

Our next information regarding the Cusabo and their neighbors comes from the chroniclers of the French Huguenot expeditions to Carolina and Florida. The first of these left France February 18, 1562, under Jean Ribault, and after a voyage of two months made land at about 30° N. lat., in what is now the State of Florida. The explorers then turned north and after having some intercourse with the Indians at the mouth of the present St. Johns River, which they named the River May from the month in which it had been discovered, resumed their voyage northward along the coast. They observed the mouths of eight rivers, which they named in succession the Seine, Somme, Loire, Charente, Garonne, Gironde, Belle, and Grande, and

---

[1] An estado is 1.85 yards.

[2] In this case "principal" means great or large.

[3] Oviedo, Hist. Gen., III, pp. 630–631.

[4] Ibid., p. 631.

finally they entered the mouth of a broad river which "by reason of its beauty and grandeur" they called Port Royal. This was the inlet in South Carolina which still bears the name of Port Royal Sound, and here, before he returned to France, Ribault left a colony of 28 men, constructing for them a small fort near the modern Port Royal, South Carolina. Ribault himself then continued northeast along the coast for a short distance, but becoming alarmed at the numerous bars and shallows which he encountered and believing he had accomplished sufficient for one voyage, he returned to France. Meanwhile the settlers whom he had left finished their fort and then set out to explore the country. Very fortunately they placed themselves on the best of terms with their Indian neighbors, from whom they obtained provisions sufficient for their sustenance, giving the Indians in exchange articles of iron and other sorts of merchandise. The building in which most of their provisions were kept was, however, destroyed by fire, troubles broke out among them, and finally the survivors built a small vessel and left the country. On the voyage they ran short of provisions and some of them starved to death, but the survivors were at length rescued by an English vessel, and part of them ultimately reached France.

From the story of these survivors recorded by Laudonnière[1] and the data on Le Moyne's map[2] we are enabled to get an interesting glimpse of the number, names, and disposition of the tribes of this section in the year 1562, as also some important information regarding their ceremonies. From these sources it appears that on the west side of Broad River, opposite Port Royal Island, were four small tribes. The first encountered in going up is called by the French Audusta[3] or Adusta[4], the second Touppa[3] or Toupa.[4] Beyond this Le Moyne places Mayon,[4] omitting Hoya,[3] the fourth, from his map entirely. From the order in which Laudonnière enumerates the tribes, however, it would seem probable that Hoya lay between Touppa and Mayon; at any rate it was in the immediate neighborhood. Farther toward the north, apparently on the channel between Port Royal Island and the mainland, was Stalame.[4] These five, according to the chief, Audusta, were in alliance, or rather on terms of friendship, with each other.[5] Farther along in the narrative we learn of a chief called Maccou living on the channels southwest of Port Royal Sound.[6] It should be noted that, following the feudal custom then prevalent in Europe, the chiefs in this narrative are given the names of their tribes. Yet more toward the south, beyond Maccou, lived two chiefs, said to be brothers. The

---

[1] Hist. Not. de la Floride, pp. 15-59.
[2] Narr. of Le Moyne, map.
[3] Laudonnière, op. cit., p. 42.
[4] Le Moyne, op. cit.
[5] Laudonnière, op. cit., p. 41.
[6] Ibid., p. 47.

nearer was named Ouadé, the more distant Couexis (Covexis).[1] According to the narrative of Laudonnière they found Ouadé on the river they had named "Belle," and, since messengers sent by Ouadé to Couexis for a quantity of provisions, returned with it very early the next day, it is evident that Couexis was only a short distance beyond.[2] From what has already been said and from other parts of Laudonnière's narrative it is evident that all these tribes except the two last mentioned were close friends, and we may suspect that they were related. Ouadé and Couexis, though not hostile to the others, seem to have stood apart from them, but there is no internal evidence that the languages of any of them differed in the slightest degree.[3] Of the first group there seems little doubt that Audusta or Adusta was the tribe afterwards known as Edisto, although they were some distance from the river which now bears their name, the shores of which were apparently occupied by them at a later period.

The name Hoya does not occur in Carolina documents, but it is given by Ibarra, Vandera, and the missionary Juan Rogel in the forms Oya, Hoya, or Ahoya.[4] Vandera mentions another place near Ahoya called Ahoyabe, "a little town subject to Ahoya."[5] Maccou is the tribe which appears in these Spanish accounts as Escamacu or Uscamacu, "an island surrounded by rivers."[6] Touppa and Mayon can not be found in Spanish narratives, nor are we able to identify them with any names in the documents of South Carolina. Even in Laudonnière's history they seem to occupy a subordinate position, and it is probable that in Pardo's time they had become united with the Orista, Escamacu, or Hoya. Very likely one of them is the Ahoyabe above noted. The failure of the Spaniards to mention Stalame may have a different meaning. This tribe lay somewhat apart from the others; away from the trail followed by Pardo in his various expeditions into the interior. Since we find in later times that the Audusta or Orista had affixed their name to Edisto River farther east it is possible that the Stalame had then moved still farther east, and I venture a guess, following a conjecture of Mooney, that they are the Stono of later colonial history. Of the two tribes lying southward a complete continuity of information shows that Ouadé was the Guale of the Spaniards and the Wallie of the English, and therefore that their home was near and gave its name to St. Catherines Island on the Georgia coast. Couexis would then apply to one of the Guale tribes or towns unless we are to discern in it an ancient form of the name Coosa.

---

1 Laudonnière, Hist. Not. de la Floride, p. 47.

2 Ibid., pp. 48, 51–52.

3 See p. 18.

4 Serrano y Sanz, Doc. Hist., p. 188; Ruidiaz, La Florida, II, pp. 304, 481.

5 Ruidiaz, La Florida, II, p. 481.

6 Ibid., pp. 304, 481. Also spelled Escamaqu, Eescamaqu, Escamaquu, Escamatu, Camacu, and Camaqu (see p. 21).

This identification of Ouadé is important because it enables us to fix with something approaching certainty the location of the rivers and islands named by Ribault. Researches among documents from Spanish sources have enabled the writer to determine with even greater accuracy the equivalent names applied by the Spaniards, and as this information will be of some value both to future ethnologists and future historians, as well as of immediate utility in the present bulletin, it is incorporated in the subjoined table. The names in this table run from south to north, beginning with the coast north of St. Augustine, Fla. The French "rivers" are practically identical with the bays, sounds, and entrances of Spanish, English, and American writers, although, indeed, one or more rivers falls into each of these.

GEOGRAPHICAL NAMES FROM ST. AUGUSTINE TO CAPE FEAR

FRENCH.	SPANISH.	ENGLISH.
....	Isla de Santa Cruz.	Coast land north of St. Augustine.
Rivière de May.	Rio de San Mateo.	River St. Johns.
....	Isla de San Juan.	Talbot Island.
R. de Sarauahi (or Serranay), called R. Halimacani and (mistakenly?) R. Somme in the Gourgues narrative.	Bahia de Santa Maria (or B. de Sarauahi).	Nassau Sound.
Ile de May.	Isla de Santa Maria.	Amelia Island.
Rivière Seine.	Bahia de San Pedro (or Tacatacuru).	St. Marys River.
Ile de la Seine.	Isla de San Pedro (or Tacatacuru).	Cumberland Island.
Rivière Somme (called Aine by Le Moyne).	Bahia de Ballenas ("Bay of whales").	St. Andrews Sound.
Ile de la Somme.	Isla de Gualequini (or Obaldaquini).	Jekyl Island.
Rivière Loire.	Bahia de Gualequini.	St. Simon Sound.
Ile de la Loire.	Isla de Asao (or Talaxe).	St. Simon Island.
Rivière Charente.	Bahia de Asao (or Talaxe).	Altamaha Sound.
Ile de la Charente.	....	Wolf Island.
Rivière Garonne.	Bahia de Espogue.	Doboy Sound.
Ile de la Garonne.	Isla de Sapala.	Sapelo Island.
Rivière Gironde.	Bahia de Sapala.	Sapelo River.
Ile de la Gironde.	Isla de Santa Catarina (or Guale).	St. Catherines Island.
Rivière Belle.	Bahia de Santa Catarina (or Cofonufo).	St. Catherines Sound.
Ile de la Rivière Belle.	Isla de Asopo.	Ossabaw Island.
Rivière Grande.	Bahia de Asopo.	Ossabaw Sound.
Ile de la Rivière Grande.	....	Great Wassaw Island (or Hilton Head Island).
....	Bahia de la Cruz (or de las Cruces).	Wassaw Sound.
Rivière Dulce.	Rio Dulce.	Savannah River.
....	Bahia de los Baxos ("Bay of shoals").	Tybee Roads.
(See Ile de la Rivière Grande above.)	Isla de los Osos ("Island of bears").	Hilton Head Island.
Rivière de Port Royal.	Bahia de Santa Elena.	Port Royal Sound.
Ile de Port Royal.	Isla de Santa Elena.	St. Helena Island.
Rivière de Belle Voir (?).	Bahia de Orista.	St. Helena Sound.
Ile de Belle Voir (?).	....	Edisto Island.
....	Bahia de Ostano.	North Edisto River.
....	Bahia de Cayagua.	Charleston Harbor.
Rivière Jordan.	Rio Jordan.	Santee River.
....	Rio de San Lorenzo (also Rio de Chico, perhaps also Rio de San Juan Bautista).[1]	Winyaw Bay (and Pedee River).
Cap Roman.	Cabo Romano.	Cape Fear.

[1] See pp. 35–36.

The French names of the coast islands are for the most part inferred from a statement by Ribault to the effect that the island (or the land assumed by him to be an island) was given the same name as the river immediately south of it.[1] Not having access to his chart, I have been unable to check up the identification of these islands. In his narrative, or the translations of it available, the Garonne is omitted from the list of rivers,[1] but I am inclined to believe this is accidental. Le Moyne makes another innovation by substituting the name Aine [Aisne] for Somme.[2] The writer would have attributed this to a mere blunder were it not that in the narrative of the Gourgues expedition the name Somme is applied to a stream between the "Seine" (St. Marys) and the "May" (St. Johns), probably the Sarauahi of other French writers, the present Nassau.[3] Therefore it is possible that some change in nomenclature was made by certain of the French explorers.

Just north of the River Grande Ribault and his companions encountered bad weather which made it necessary for them to put out to sea. When they came shoreward again the vessel in which Laudonnière sailed discovered another river, which they named Belle à Veoir, or Belle Voir. Le Moyne gives this as a river encountered south of Port Royal, but his text is based on Laudonnière and on a misunderstanding of that, so that it may be discarded as authority. For instance, where Laudonnière says that from the River Grande they explored northward *toward* the River Jordan, Le Moyne has it that they *reached* that river, and he places it between the Grande and "Belle Voir."[4] On his map, however, the Belle Voir does not appear, the Grande being next to Port Royal, and the Jordan is correctly located north of the latter place. The fact of the matter appears to be this. After leaving Ossabaw Sound and having been forced to sea by stormy weather, Ribault's vessel passed northward of Broad River, discovered one of the rivers flowing into St. Helena Sound and named it Belle Voir. But in the meantime one of his other ships had gotten into Broad River, and when it rejoined the rest informed Ribault of the great advantages of that inlet, with the result that they turned back and made their settlement there. Therefore in Ribault's narrative the River Belle Voir is placed north of Port Royal. Later, when the colonists sent men to Ouadé asking for food, they came upon a river of fresh water 10 leagues from their fort. This is the

---

[1] French, Hist. Colls. La., 1875, 2d ser., II, p. 183.

[2] Le Moyne, Narr., descr. of illus., p. 2.

[3] Laudonnière, Hist. Not. de la Floride, p. 211; French, Hist. Colls. La., 1869, 2d ser., I, pp. 350–351; Ibid., 1875, 2d ser., II, p. 279. The Gourgues narratives give the native name of this stream as Halimacani, after a Timucua chief whose town was near the mouth of the St. Johns on the north side, while St. George Inlet, or a stream flowing into it, is called Sarabay, the Sarrauahi of earlier French writers. As indicated above, I believe the last-mentioned name was originally applied to Nassau Inlet.

[4] Narr. of Le Moyne, desc. of illus., p. 2.

River Dulce of Le Moyne—on his map erroneously inserted between the Rivers Grande and Belle—and in all probability is identical with Savannah River.

The only remaining tribal name mentioned by Laudonnière is Chiquola,[1] but the circumstances under which it was obtained render its ethnographical value very slight. Being familiar with some of the narratives of the Aylion expedition in which Chicora is given considerable prominence, Laudonnière inquired of the Indians whom he met regarding it. He was entirely unacquainted with their language but understood that they were trying to tell him that Chiquola was the greatest lord of all that country, that he surpassed themselves in height by a foot and a half, and that he lived to the north in a large palisaded town. Later he tells us that the fact of the existence of such a chief and his great power were confirmed by those who were left to form a settlement. If there is any truth in this story and the Indians were not simply telling what they thought the explorers would like to hear, the great town was probably that of the Kasihta.[2]

In 1564 a Spanish vessel was sent from Habana to find the French and root them out, and the narrative of this expedition states that there were said to be 17 towns around the Bay of Santa Elena. A town called Usta is mentioned, evidently identical with Audusta, and another town, not elsewhere recorded, called Yanahume.[3] In the former was a Frenchman who had remained in the country rather than take chances in the small vessel in which his companions had ventured forth.

The same year Laudonnière again sailed for America, but this time the Frenchmen decided to settle upon St. Johns River, Florida, and they did not return to Port Royal. The year following their new settlement was destroyed by the Spaniards under Menéndez, and French attempts to colonize the Carolinas and Florida came to an end.

In a letter written shortly after his conquest, Menéndez states that he had heard that the elder brother of Ribault with the survivors from the French garrison "had gone 25 leagues away, toward the north, to a very good port called Guale, because the Indians of that place were his friends, and that there were within 3 or 4 leagues 40 villages of Indians belonging to two brothers, one of whom was named Cansin and the other Guale."[4] In Cansin and Guale we of course recognize, in spite of changes and corruptions in orthography, Couexis and Ouadé. In the spring of 1566 Menéndez sailed northward himself and reached Guale, where he was informed by a French refugee that Guale and Orista were at war with each other and that

[1] Laudonnière, Hist. Not. de la Floride, pp. 29-31.

[2] See p. 219.

[3] Lowery, MSS. in Lib. Cong.

[4] Ruidiaz, La Florida, II, p. 145.

the people of Guale had captured two men belonging to those of Orista. Menéndez prevailed upon the Guale chief to make peace with his northern neighbor, who is said to have been the more powerful of the two—the advantage which had been gained over him having been due to the French refugees at Guale. Then, taking the two Orista captives with him, and leaving two Spaniards as hostages, Menéndez kept on toward the north and finally entered Broad River. There he found that the town of Orista, which is of course identical with the French Audusta, had been burned and the inhabitants were starting to rebuild it. The Indians met him at first in no friendly spirit, but through the mediation of his two captives he soon placed himself upon good terms with them, and they sent to all the surrounding villages to summon the chiefs and people to come to see him. "They lighted great fires, brought many shellfish, and a great multitude of Indians came that night, and three chiefs who were subject to Orista; they counselled him that he should go to another village a league from Orista, where many other chiefs would come to see him." The next day Orista himself and two more chiefs came, along with other Indians. "Many Indians came laden with corn, cooked and roasted fish, oysters, and many acorns," and the Spanish leader on his side brought out biscuits, wine, and honey. After the feast "they placed the Adelantado in the seat of the chief, and Orista approached him with various ceremonies, and took his hands; afterwards the other chiefs and Indians did the same thing—the mother and relatives of the two slaves whom they had brought from Guale wept for joy. Afterwards they began to sing and dance, the chiefs and some of the principal Indians remaining with the Adelantado; and the celebration and rejoicing lasted until midnight, when they retired." Later the Spaniards returned to the village of Orista itself, where they were again hospitably entertained. "In the morning the chief took the Adelantado to a very large house, and placed him in his seat, going over with him the same ceremony that had been performed in the first village." The Spaniards were presented with well-tanned deerskins and some pearls, although these were of little value, because they had been burned. At Menéndez's request the chief showed him a site suitable for a fort, which was begun forthwith and received the name of San Felipe. On his way back Menéndez was able to make such an impression on the Indians of Guale, who believed that the cross he had set up in their town had been instrumental in breaking a long drought, that they desired to have Christians left with them and inside of the islands along the Georgia coast many Indians came down to the shore to beg for crosses. Barcia states that a bolt of lightning having fallen on a tree near the cross which had been set up at Guale "the Indians, men and women, all ran to the place and picked up the splinters in order to keep them in their houses as relics."[1] The island of Guale, as already stated, was St. Catherines Island. It is described in the narrative which we have just quoted as "about 4 or 5 leagues in diameter." In August Menéndez again visited Fort San Felipe and Guale, but his stay was short. Finding the garrison at the former place in serious straits for food, he directed Juan Pardo to take 150 soldiers inland and quarter them at intervals upon the natives. While there are several accounts of this and subsequent expeditions undertaken by Pardo into the interior, the only one that concerns us here is a Relation by Juan de la Vandera, in command of the post at San Felipe, which sets forth "the places and what sort of land is to be found at each place among the provinces of Florida, through which Captain Juan Pardo, at the command of Pero Menéndez de Avilés, entered to discover a road to New Spain, from the point of Santa Elena of the said provinces, during the years 1566 and 1567."[2] The first part of this is of considerable importance for our study of the Cusabo tribe. It runs as follows:

He started from Santa Elena with his company in obedience to orders received and on that day they went to sleep at a place called Uscamacu, which is an island surrounded by rivers. Its soil is sandy and makes very good clay for pottery, tiles, and other necessary things of the kind; there is good ground here for planting maize and grapevines, of which there is an abundance.

From Uscamacu he went straight to another place called Ahoya, where they stopped and spent the night. This Ahoya is an island; some parts of it are surrounded by rivers, others look like mainland. It is good or at least reasonably good soil where maize grows and also big vine stocks with runners.

From Ahoya he went to Ahoyabe, a small village, subject to Ahoya and in about the same kind of country.

From Ahoyabe he went to another place, which is called Cozao, which belongs to a rather great cacique and has a lot of good land like the others, and many strips of stony ground, and where maize, wheat, oats, grapevines, all kinds of fruit and vegetables, can be grown, because it has rivers and brooks of sweet water and reasonably good soil for all.

From Cozao he went to another small place which belongs to a chieftain (cacique) of the same Cozao; the land of this place is good, but there is little of it.

From here he went to Enfrenado,[3] which is a miserable place, although it has many corners of rich soil like the others.

From Enfrenado he went to Guiomaez from where to the cape of Santà Elena there are forty leagues. The road by which he went is somewhat difficult, but the land or soil is good and everything that is grown in Cozao can be cultivated here and even more and better; there are great swamps, which are deep, caused by the great flatness of the country.[4]

Uscamacu, where Pardo spent the first night, is certainly identical with the Maccou of the French, and would thus be somewhere to the southwest of Broad River. Pardo and his company were probably set across to the neighborhood of this place in boats from Fort

[1] Barcia, La Florida, pp. 104–110.

[2] Ruidiaz, La Florida, II, pp. 451–486.

[3] This word would mean "bridled" in Spanish. It may be a native term but does not look like one.

[4] Translation by Mrs. F. Bandelier.

San Felipe, unless the site ordinarily assigned to the fort is erroneous.[1] From Uscamacu they marched northwest along Broad River and then up the Coosawhatchie. The first stopping place after leaving Uscamacu was Ahoya, the Hoya of the French, one of those tribes or villages allied with Audusta. Ahoyabe would probably be an out settlement from Ahoya and hence belong to the same group. In the name of the next place, Cozao, we have the second historical mention [2] of the Coosa tribe of South Carolina, which occupied the upper reaches of the Coosawhatchie, Combahee, Ashepoo, Edisto, and Ashley Rivers, the first notice having been in the list of provinces given by Francisco of Chicora. The greater power ascribed to this chief agrees with our later information regarding the prominence of his people. From the narrative it is evident that the next place where the Spaniards stopped was also a Coosa village. The last two places may have been Coosa towns also, but there is no means of knowing. It has been suggested that Guiomaez was perhaps the later Wimbee, but, if so, the tribe must have moved nearer the coast before the period of English colonization, when they were between Combahee and Broad Rivers. The next place, Canos, 10 leagues from Guiomaez, was identical with the Cofitachequi of De Soto and probably with the later Kasihta town among the Creeks.[3]

Barcia mentions as one result of the Florida settlements the discovery of an herb of wonderful medicinal qualities, which was in all probability the nut grass (*Cyperus rotundus*). He says:

> The Spaniards discovered in this land some long roots, marked like strings of beads, so that each portion cut off remains rounded; outside they are black and within white and dry, hard like bones; the bark is so hard that one can scarcely remove it. The taste is aromatic, so that it appears to be a specific; the *galanga* is like it. The plant which produces it throws out short shoots, and spreads its branches along the ground; its leaves are very broad, and very green; it is warm (or heated) at the limit of the second degree, dries at the beginning of the first; it grows in moist situations: The Indians use the plant, crushed between two stones, to rub over their entire bodies, when they bathe themselves, because they say that it tightens and strengthens the flesh, with the good odor, which it has, and that they feel much improved on account of it. They also use it in the form of a powder, for pains in the stomach.
>
> The Spaniards learned of this from the Indians, and they used it for the same purposes, and afterwards they discovered that it was an admirable specific for colic (or pain in the side), and urinary trouble, since it causes the stones to be driven out, even though they are very large. Other virtues were discovered, its estimation growing so much among the soldiers, that they all carried rosaries of these beads, which they called "of Santa Elena" on account of the great abundance of these which there are in the marshy places at the Cape of Santa Elena and province of Orista and the neighboring parts.[4]

---

[1] Lowery, Span. Settl., II, pp. 438–440.

[2] If Couexis be excepted.

[3] See pp. 216–218.

[4] Barcia, La Florida, p. 133. See Lowery, Span. Settl., II, p. 381.

In 1569 the Jesuit missionary Juan Rogel arrived at Santa Elena, and at the same time Antonio Sedeño and Father Baez proceeded to Guale. In a letter written by Rogel to Menéndez, December 9, 1570, he relates the fortunes, or rather misfortunes, of his work among the people of the province of Orista.

In the beginning of my relations with those Indians [he says], they grew very much in my eyes, for seeing them in their customs and order of life far superior to those of Carlos, I lauded God, seeing each Indian married to only one woman, take care of and cultivate his land, maintain his house and educate his children with great care, seeing that they were not contaminated by the most abominable of sins, not incestuous, not cruel, nor thieves, seeing them speak the truth with each other, and enjoy much peace and righteousness. Thus it seemed to me we were quite sure of them and that probably I would take a longer time in learning their language in order to explain to them the mysteries of our Holy Faith than they would need to accept them and become Christians. Therefore I myself and three more of the fathers of our company studied with great diligence and haste to learn it and within six months I spoke to them and preached in their tongue.

But after two and a half months the time for gathering acorns arrived, and all left him and "scattered through those forests, each one to his own place, and came together only at certain feasts, which they held every two months, and this was not always in one place, but at one time here and at another in another place, etc." In fact they lived scattered in this manner for nine months out of the year.

And there are two reasons for this [he says]: First because they have been accustomed to live in this manner for many thousands of years, and to try to get them away from it looks to them equal to death; the second, that even if they wished to live thus the land itself does not allow it—for being so very poor and miserable and its strength very soon sapped out—and therefore they themselves state that this is the reason why they are living so disseminated and changing their abode so often.

Rogel endeavored to continue his work, attending the infrequent gatherings mentioned above whenever he was able. At one time he spoke to the greater part of "the vassals of Orista" who had come together at the Rio Dulce, presumably the Savannah, and in the spring he proposed that they plant enough ground so that they could remain in one place, where he could approach them more easily. This was done, but all except two families soon left, and later Vandera, commander of the fort of San Felipe, was compelled to exact several canoe loads of corn from the Indians and to quarter some of his troops among them. This, as Rogel anticipated and as the event proved, incensed the Indians so much that further missionary efforts on his part were out of the question, and on July 13, 1570, he left them to return to San Felipe, which he soon afterwards abandoned for Habana. One main cause of Rogel's failure to impress these people was evidently a misapprehension on his part, for he says that when he began to preach against the devil they were highly offended, declaring that he was good, and afterwards they all left him. Presumably they understood that an attack had been made on one of their own deities, and very likely Rogel was perfectly willing on his side to identify the prince of evil with any or all of them. Among the chiefs upon whom Vandera levied the above-mentioned tribute of corn Rogel mentions Escamacu, Orista, and Hoya, the first of whom is of course the Uscamacu of Vandera and Pardo.[1]

In 1576 the Indian policy which had caused Rogel's withdrawal brought on a rebellion. Most narratives attribute this to an attempt to levy a contribution of provisions on Indians near Fort San Felipe, but from one very trustworthy document it appears that it was at least brought to a head by the arbitrary conduct of a Capt. Solis, left temporarily in charge of the above-mentioned post by Hernando de Miranda. This man killed two Indians, seemingly without sufficient cause, one a chief named Hemalo, who had been in Madrid. In July of that year, the garrison of Fort San Felipe being short of provisions, and the Indians having refused to give them any, the Alférez Moyano was sent at the head of 22 men to take some by force. The Indians, however, persuaded Moyano to have his men extinguish the matches with which their guns were fired, on the ground that their women and children were afraid they were going to be killed, and as soon as they had done so the Indians fell upon them and killed all except a soldier named Andrés Calderón. This took place July 22. Testimony taken in St. Augustine in 1600 gives the name of the tribe concerned as Camacu (i. e., Escamacu)[2] but contemporary letters, which are probably correct, call it "Oristau" or "Oristan." Calderón reached the fort in three days and gave the alarm. Meanwhile "the Provinces of Guale, Uscamacu, and Oristau" had risen in revolt. News reached Hernando de Miranda and he returned at once to Santa Elena. Capt. Solis was then dispatched against the Indians, but he was ambushed and killed along with eight soldiers. The Indians to the number, according to one Spanish narrative, of 2,000 then besieged the fort, and they killed several Spaniards besides, including an interpreter named Aguilar. One account says that 32 men were slain, but it does not appear whether this included Moyano's force or not. Among those lost were the factor, auditor (contador), and treasurer. Finally the Spaniards were withdrawn to St. Augustine and the Indians entered the fort and burned it. It was restored shortly under the name of Fort San Marcos, and in 1579 Governor Pedro Menéndez Marqués visited the place to pay the troops and incidentally to take revenge on the neighboring hostiles. He attacked a fortified town named Coçapoy, 20 leagues from Fort San Marcos, strongly placed in a swamp and occupied by Indians said never to have been willing to make peace with the Spaniards. The town was severely handled, a number of Indians, including a

[1] Ruidiaz, La Florida, II, pp. 301-308.

[2] Serrano y Sanz, Doc. Hist., p. 147.

sister of the chief, his mother, a son, and the son's wife, were captured, and 40 Indians were burned in their houses. Menéndez liberated most of his male captives and exchanged the women for some Frenchmen, who were largely blamed for the uprising, and most of whom were subsequently executed.

In 1580 a new uprising occurred, again attributed to the French. In fact, shortly before, a French vessel was captured near the mouth of the St. Johns and two others belonging to the same fleet were known to have entered the bay of Gualequini and to have opened communication with the natives. Indian witnesses also testified that they had been promised assistance from a new French armada shortly to appear. Fort San Marcos was evidently abandoned, or captured by the Indians, at this time and was not reestablished until late in 1582 or early in 1583. A letter dated July 19, 1582, says that the Indians of the Province of Santa Elena had rebelled and "there was no remedy for it." In 1583, however, Governor Menéndez writes that all of the Indians—both inland and on the coast—had come to see him and to yield obedience and that the chief of Santa Elena "has done a great deal, as he was the first to embrace the faith." Fort San Marcos may have received still another name, for a document of the period refers to it as "Fort Catuco." In 1586 Gutiérrez de Miranda, who was prominent in a war against the Potano Indians of Florida, was in command of the Santa Elena fort. Late in 1587, however, or very early in 1588, it was finally abandoned and the garrison withdrawn.[1]

In a letter written to the king, February 23, 1598, Gonçalo Mendez de Canço, Governor of Florida, states that the chief of Kiawa had accompanied the chief of Escamacu to war against the Indians of Guale and they had taken seven scalps.[2] In another, written the day following, he mentions, among the chiefs who had come to St. Augustine "to give their submission" to him, "the chief of Aluste" and "the chief of Aobi."[3] I have not found a later mention of Aobi, but the name Aluste occurs several times in Spanish documents, spelled Alieste, Alueste, and Aluete. That it was to the north is shown by a statement to the effect that in the massacre of monks, which had taken place the preceding year, all of those between Aluste and Asao had been killed.[4] More specific information is contained in the relation of a visit which Governor Pedro de Ibarra made to the Indians along the Georgia coast in November and December, 1604. The northernmost point reached by him was Guale (St. Catherines Island), where, besides calling together the Guale chiefs,

---

[1] The information contained in this paragraph, except as otherwise noted, is principally from the Lowery, Brooks, and Wright manuscripts in the Library of Congress.

[2] Lowery and Brooks, MSS., Lib. Cong.

[3] Serrano y Sanz, Doc. Hist., p. 135.

[4] Ibid., p. 186.

"he commanded that within two days should assemble all the micos of Oya and Alueste and other chiefs from the country around."[1] In Oya we recognize the Cusabo town already mentioned, and we learn just below that Alueste was in the same province; for, when Ibarra inquired of the assembled chiefs if any of them had any complaints to make, "the chief of Aluete said that the chief of Talapo and the chief of Ufalague and the chief of Orista, his nephew and heirs, were his vassals and had risen and gone to live with the mico of Asao."[2]

When Ibarra returned to Asao he interviewed these chiefs, and he states that they admitted the truth of what Alueste had said, adding that they had done so "because he was a bad Indian and had a bad heart, and he gave them many bad words, and for that reason they had withdrawn and were obeying the chief of Orista, who was the heir of the said Alueste, and was a good Indian and treated them well, and gave them good words." The governor, however, exacted a promise from them that they would "return to their obedience," to which they agreed.[3] It is sufficiently evident from this that all of the tribes mentioned were Cusabo, whether Alueste and Orista are or are not variants of the later Edisto. Responsibility for the murder of the missionaries in 1597 was laid by one of the captured Indians on the Indians of Cosahue (Cosapue), the Salchiches (an unidentified tribe living inland), the Indians of Tulufina (a Guale town), and those of Santa Elena. The chiefs of Ufalague and Sufalete are said to have killed Fray Pedro de Corpa, and the Ufalague and Alueste assisted in disposing of Fray Blas, but, on the other hand, the chief of Talapo saved the life of Fray Davila, the only missionary to escape. At a later date, by a comfortable volte-face not unusual with Indians, those of Cosapue and Ufalague, together with those of Talapo, helped punish the murderers.[4]

From about the time of this massacre we begin to find the name Escamacu used for the Indians of Santa Elena in preference to Orista. In the report of his expedition of 1605, Ecija speaks of the chief of Escamacu as "the principal of that land" (i. e., the land of Santa Elena), and he places "the bar of Orista" 6 leagues north of that of Santa Elena, where is the River Edisto. Nevertheless the name had become fixed upon it at a much earlier period for in a letter of Bartólome de Arguelles, of date 1586, the bay of Orista is said to be beyond that of Santa Elena to the north, 5 leagues.[4] It is evident, therefore, that whatever temporary changes had taken place in the residence of portions of the Edisto tribe, changes such as are indicated in Ibarra's letter, a part of them, probably the main

[1] Serrano y Sanz, Doc. Hist., p. 186.

[2] Ibid., pp. 188–189.

[3] Ibid., p. 191.

[4] Lowery and Brooks, MSS., Lib. Cong.

body, had become settled upon the stream which still bears their name by the date last given.

The first clear notice of the Stono seems to be in the narrative of Ecija's second voyage, 1609. When he was in the port of Cayagua (Charleston Harbor) on his return he encountered a canoe, in which were the chiefs of Cayagua, Escamacu, and "Ostano." In the pilot's description at the end of this narrative we read, "From the bar of Orista to that of Ostano are 4 leagues." The opening was narrow and the distance to the bar of Cayagua 8 leagues.[1] From the figures it seems clear that this was not the present Stono Inlet, but North Edisto River. The possibility that this tribe was the Stalame of Laudonnière and that it moved eastward in later times has already been indicated.

A letter written June 17, 1617, by the Florida friars, complaining of conditions, mentions Santa Elena among those provinces where there were then no missions.[1] In another from the governor of Florida, dated November 15, 1633, we learn that the chief of Satuache, "more than 70 leagues" from St. Augustine, had brought to the capital three Englishmen who had been shipwrecked on his coast. This place lay from 6 to 10 leagues north of Santa Elena and seems from the context to have been newly missionized.[2] The position given would place it near the mouth of Edisto River. From a letter written in 1647 it appears that the Indians of "Satoache" had entirely abandoned their town,[1] yet they are mentioned, under the name Chatuache, in a list of missions dated 1655, in which San Felipe also appears.[3] However, the fort seems never to have been rebuilt, and the missions were nothing more than outstations served at long intervals.

In 1670, when the English colony of South Carolina was established, there was no Spanish post east of the Savannah and no mission station nearer than St. Catherines Island, although traces of former Spanish occupancy were evident at Port Royal (Santa Elena). The Edisto were still on Edisto River and the Stono near the place occupied by them at the beginning of the century. The term "Indians of St. Helens" probably includes the Escamacu and related tribes. The Coosa were on the upper courses of the Cusabo rivers, where they seem to have lived throughout the Spanish period. The Kiawa of Ashley River are of course the "Cayagua" of the Spaniards, and are in precisely the same location; the neighboring Wando on Cooper River and Etiwaw or Itwan on Wando River—particularly about Daniels Island[4]—are perhaps referred to in one or two Spanish docu-

[1] Lowery and Brooks, MSS., Lib. Cong.

[2] Lowery, MSS., Lib. Cong.

[3] P. 322; Serrano y Sanz, Doc. Hist., p. 132.

[4] S. Car. Hist. Soc. Colls., v, p. 386.

ments, but this is doubtful. As already suggested, the Wimbee, between Broad and Combahee Rivers, may be the Guiomaez or Guiomae of Pardo. The Combahee and Ashepoo on the rivers bearing those names, and the Witcheau or Wichcauh, mentioned in a sale of land, are entirely new to us.

Again we are dependent for specific information regarding these peoples on the narratives of voyages. The first which yields anything of value is "A True Relation of a Voyage upon discovery of part of the Coast of Florida, from Lat. of 31 Deg. to 33 Deg. 45 m. North Lat. in the ship *Adventure, William Hilton* Commander," etc.[1] The *Adventure* sailed from Spikes Bay, Barbados, August 10, 1663, and on September 3 entered St. Helena Sound.

> On *Saturday* the fifth of *September* [runs the narrative], two Indians came on Board us, and said they were of St. Ellens; being very bold and familiar; speaking many Spanish words, as *Cappitan*, *Commarado*, and *Adeus*. They know the use of Guns and are as little startled at the fireing of a Piece of Ordnance, as he that hath been used to them many years: They told us the nearest *Spaniards* were at *St. Augustins*, and several of them had been there, which as they said was but ten days' journey and that the *Spaniards* used to come to them at Saint *Ellens* sometimes in Conoas within Land, at other times in Small Vessels by Sea, which the Indians describe to have but two Masts.

At the invitation of the Indians the longboat with 12 hands was sent to St. Helena but the actions of the Indians appeared to its occupants so threatening that they returned without remaining overnight.

> That which we noted there [the narrative says] was a fair house builded in the shape of a dovehouse, round, two hundred foot at least, compleatly covered with *Palmeta*-leaves, the wal-plate being twelve foot high, or thereabouts, within lodging rooms and forms; two pillars at the entrance of a high Seat above all the rest; Also another house like a Sentinel-house, floored ten foot high with planks, fastened with Spikes and Nayls, standing upon Substantial Posts, with several other small houses round about. Also we saw many planks, to the quantity of three thousand foot or thereabouts, with other Timber squared, and a Cross before the great house. Likewise we saw the Ruines of an old Fort, compassing more than half an acre of land within the Trenches, which we supposed to be *Charls's* Fort, built, and so called by the *French* in 1562, &c.

In the meantime the vessel was visited by the chief of Edisto from the other side of the sound, who invited Hilton to come to his town and told him of some English castaways upon that coast, some of whom were in his custody and some at St. Helena. He informed them that three had been killed by the Stono. Those English who were with the Edisto were released, and the explorers then started to make their way to St. Helena through the inside channels in order to recover the rest. On the way "came many canoes about us with corn, pompions, and venison, deerskins, and a sort of sweet wood." Ultimately after exchanging letters with a Spanish captain who had

---

[1] S. Car. Hist. Soc. Colls., v, pp. 18–26.

been sent to St. Helena from St. Augustine to recover the English castaways, Hilton gave up his attempt, and having explored the entrance to Port Royal and ranged the coast to the northward almost to Cape Hatteras he got back to Barbados on January 6, 1664. In their general description of the land between Port Royal and Edisto River the explorers say:

The *Indians* plant in the worst Land because they cannot cut down the Timber in the best, and yet have plenty of Corn, Pompions, Water-Mellons, Musk-mellons: although the Land be over grown with weeds through their lasinesse, yet they have two or three crops of Corn a year, as the Indians themselves inform us. The Country abounds with Grapes, large Figs, and Peaches; the Woods with Deer, Conies, Turkeys, Quails, Curlues, Plovers, Teile, Herons; and as the Indians say, in Winter with Swans, Geese, Cranes, Duck and Mallard, and innumerable of other water-Fowls, whose names we know not, which lie in the Rivers, Marshes, and on the Sands: Oysters in abundance, with great store of Muscles: a sort of fair Crabs, and a round Shel-fish called *Horse-feet;* The Rivers stored plentifully with Fish that we saw play and leap. There are great Marshes, but most as far as we saw little worth, except for a Root that grows in them the *Indians* make good Bread of . . . The Natives are very healthful; we saw many very Aged amongst them.[1]

The next voyage that concerns us is entitled: "The Port Royall Discovery. Being the Relation of a voyage on the Coast of the Province of Carolina formerly called Florida in the Continent of the Northerne America from Charles River neere Cape Feare in the County of Clarendon and the Lat: of 34: deg: to Port Royall in the North Lat: of 32 d. begun 14th June 1666. Performed by Robert Sandford Esqr Secretary and Cheife Register for the Right Hon[ble] the Lords Proprietors of their County of Clarendon in the Province aforesaid."[2]

On the date mentioned Sandford sailed with a vessel of "scarce 17 tons" and a shallop "of some 3 tons." On the night of the 19th the larger vessel became separated from the shallop, and on the 22d the former sighted and entered what is now called North Edisto River. Sandford explored this for some distance and found many Indian cornfields and houses scattered among them, besides numerous heaps of oyster shells. From the Indians he learned that the chief town of the Edisto tribe was some distance inland, on what is now Edisto Island, at a place which Langdon Cheves, the editor of "The Shaftsbury Papers," suggests was "probably near cross roads, by Eding's 'Spanish mount' place." Having gone beyond the nearest landing place for this village he stopped there on his return to accommodate the Indians who were desirous to trade with him.

When we were here [he says] a Cap[t] of the Nation named Shadoo (one of them w[ch] Hilton had carryed to Barbados) was very earnest with some of our Company to goe with him and lye a night att their Towne w[ch] hee told us was but a smale distance thence I being equally desirous to knowe the forme manner and populousnesse of the place as alsoe what state the Casique held (fame in all theire things preferring this place

[1] S. Car. Hist. Soc. Colls., v, p. 24. [2] Ibid., pp. 57–82.

to all the rest of the Coast, and foure of my Company (vizt.) Lt.: Harvey, Lt: Woory, Mr Thomas Giles and mr Henry Woodward forwardly offring themselves to the service haveing alsoe some Indians aboard mee who constantly resided there night & day I permitted them to goe with Shadoo they retorned to mee the next morning wth great Comendacons of their entertainment but especially of the goodness of the land they marcht through and the delightfull situation of the Towne. Telling mee withall that the Cassique himselfe appeared not (pretending some indisposition, but that his state was supplyed by a Female who received them with gladness and Courtesy placeing my Lt: Harvey on the seat by her their relation gave myselfe a Curiosity (they alsoe assureing mee that it was not above foure Miles off) to goe and see that Towne and takeing with mee Capt. George Cary and a file of men I marched thitherward followed by a long traine of Indians of whome some or other always presented yimselfe to carry mee on his shoulders over any the branches of Creekes or plashy corners of Marshes in our Way. This walke though it tend to the Southward of the West and consequently leads neere alongst the Sea Coast Yett it opened to our Viewe soe excellent a Country both for Wood land and Meadowes as gave singular satisfaction to all my Company. We crossed one Meadowe of not lesse than a thousand Acres all firme good land and as rich a Soyle as any clothed wth a ffine grasse not passing knee deepe, but very thick sett & fully adorned with yeallow flowers. A pasture not inferiour to any I have seene in England the wood land were all of the same sort both for timber and mould with the best of those wee had ranged otherwhere and wthout alteration or abatement from their goodnes all the way of our March. Being entered the Towne wee were conducted into a large house of a Circular forme (their generall house of State) right against the entrance way a high seate of sufficient breadth for half a dozen persons on which sate the Cassique himselfe (vouchsafeing mee that favour) wth his wife on his right hand (shee who had received those whome I had sent the evening before) hee was an old man of a large stature and bone. Round the house from each side the throne quite to the Entrance were lower benches filled with the whole rabble of men Women and children in the center of this house is kept a constant fire mounted on a great heape of Ashes and surrounded with little lowe foormes Capt: Cary and my selfe were placed on the higher seate on each side of the Cassique and presented with skinns accompanied with their Ceremonyes of Welcome and freindshipp (by stroaking our shoulders with their palmes and sucking in theire breath the whilst) The Towne is scituate on the side or rather in the skirts of a faire forrest in wch at severall distances are diverse feilds of Maiz with many little houses straglingly amongst them for the habitations of the particular families. On the East side and part of the South It hath a large prospect over meadows very spatious and delightfull, before the Doore of their Statehouse is a spatious walke rowed wth trees on both sides tall & full branched, not much unlike to Elms wch serves for the Exercise and recreation of the men who by Couples runn after a marble bowle troled out alternately by themselves with six foote staves in their hands wch they tosse after the bowle in their race and according to the laying of their staves wine or loose the beeds they contend for an Exercise approveable enough in the winter but some what too violent (mee thought) for that season and noone time of the day from this walke is another lesse aside from the round house for the children to sport in. After a fewe houres stay I retorned to my Vessell wth a greate troope of Indians att my heeles. The old Cassique himselfe in the number, who lay aboard mee that night without the society of any of his people, some scores of wch lay in boothes of their own immediate ereccon on the beach.

After this Sandford passed around through Dawho River and out by the South Edisto. Soon after he fell in with the shallop from which he had been separated and then made south to the entrance of Port Royal, where he anchored in front of the principal Indian town.

I had not ridd long [he says] ere the Cassique himselfe came aboard mee wth a Canoa full of Indians presenting mee with skinns and bidding mee welcome after their manner, I went a shoare with him to see their Towne w[ch] stood in sight of our Vessell, Found as to the forme of building in every respect like that of Eddistowe with a plaine place before the great round house for their bowling recreation att th'end of w[ch] stood a faire wooden Crosse of the Spaniards ereccon. But I could not observe that the Indians performed any adoracon before itt. All round the Towne for a great space are severall feilds of Maiz of a very large growth The soyle nothing inferior to the best wee had seene att Eddistowe apparently more loose and light and the trees in the woods much larger and rangd att a greater distance all the ground under them burthened exceedingly and amongst it a great variety of choice pasturage I sawe here besides the great number of peaches w[ch] the more Northerly places doe alsoe abound in some store of figge trees very large and faire both fruite and plants and diverse grape vines w[ch] though growing without Culture in the very throng of weedes and bushes were yett filled with bunches of grapes to admiracon. . . . The Towne is scited on an Island made by a branch w[ch] cometh out of Brayne Sound and falleth into Port Royall about a mile above where wee landed a cituacon not extraordinary here.

Here the shallop rejoined him after sailing through from St. Helena Sound by the inside channel. Wommony, son of the chief of Port Royal, and one of those whom Hilton had carried to Barbados, acted as its guide. Before his departure from this place Sandford left a surgeon named Henry Woodward to learn the language and in exchange took an Indian of the town with him. He says:

I called the Cassique & another old man (His second in Authority) and their wives And in sight and heareing of the whole Towne, delivered Woodward into their charge telling them that when I retorned I would require him att their hands, They received him with such high Testimonys of Joy and thankfullnes as hughely confirmed to mee their great desire of our friendshipp & society, The Cassique placed Woodward by him uppon the Throne and after lead him forth and shewed him a large feild of Maiz w[ch] hee told him should bee his, then hee brought him the Sister of the Indian that I had with mee telling him that shee should tend him & dresse his victualls and be careful of him that soe her Brother might be the better used amongst us.

An Indian of Edisto also desired to accompany him, and thinking that soe hee should be the more acceptable hee caused himselfe to be shoaren on the Crowne after ye manner of the Port Royall Indians, a fashion w[ch] I guesse they have taken from the Spanish Fryers. Thereby to ingratiate themselves wth that Nation and indeed all along I observed a kinde of Emulacon amongst the three principall Indians of this Country (viz[t]) Those of Keywaha Edistowe and Port Royall concerning us and our Freindshipp, Each contending to assure it to themselves and jealous of the other though all be allyed and this Notw[th]standing that they knewe wee were in actuall warre with the Natives att Clarendon and had killled and sent away many of them, ffor they frequently discoursed with us concerning the warre, told us that the Natives were noughts they land Sandy and barren, their Country sickly, but if wee would come amongst them Wee should finde the Contrary to all their Evills, and never any occasion of dischargeing our Gunns but in merryment and for pastime.

Sandford now returned toward the north and, having failed to make Kiawa (Charleston Harbor), landed at Charles Town on the Cape Fear River, July 12, 1666.

The expedition that was to result in the permanent settlement of the colony of South Carolina made a landfall at Sewee (now Bull's) Bay on the 15th or 16th of March, 1670, and anchored at the south end of Oni-see-cau (now Bull's) Island. The longboat was sent ashore.

Vpon its approach to ye Land few were ye natiues who vpon ye Strand made fires & came towards vs whooping in theire own tone & manner making signes also where we should best Land & when we came a shoare they stroked vs on ye shoulders with their hands saying Bony Conraro Angles. knowing us to be English by our Collours (as wee supposed) we then gave them Brass rings & tobacco at which they seemed well pleased, & into ye boats after halfe an howre spent with ye Indians we betooke our selues, they liked our Company soe well that they would haue come a board with us. we found a pretty handsome channell about 3 fathoms & a halfe from ye place we Landed to ye Shippe, through which the next day we brought ye shipp to Anchor feareing a contrary winde & to gett in for some fresh watter. A day or two after ye Gouerno^{r} whom we tooke in at Bermuda with seuerall others went a shoare to view ye Land here. Some 3 Leagues distant from the shipp, carrying along with us one of ye Eldest Indians who accosted us ye other day, & as we drew to ye shore A good number of Indians appeared clad with deare skins hauing with them their bows & Arrows, but our Indian calling out Appada they withdrew & lodged theire bows & returning ran up to ye middle in mire & watter to carry us a shoare where when we came they gaue us ye stroaking Complim^{t} of ye country and brought deare skins some raw some drest to trade with us for which we gaue them kniues beads & tobacco and glad they were of ye Market. by & by came theire women clad in their Mosse roabs bringing their potts to boyle a kinde of thickening which they pound & make food of, & as they order it being dryed makes a pretty sort of bread, they brought also plenty of Hickery nutts, a wall nut in shape, & taste onely differing in ye thicknees of the shell & smallness of ye kernell. the Gouerno^{r} & seu'all others walking a little distance from ye water side came to ye Hutt Pallace of his Ma^{ty} of ye place, who meeteing vs tooke ye Gouerno^{r} on his shoulders & carryed him into ye house in token of his chearfull Entertainement. here we had nutts & root cakes such as their women useily make as before & watter to drink for they use no other lickquor as I can Learne in this Countrey, while we were here his Ma^{tyes} three daughters entred the Pallace all in new roabs of new mosse which they are neuer beholding to ye Taylor to trim up, with plenty of beads of diuers Collours about their necks: I could not imagine that ye sauages would so well deport themselues who coming in according to their age & all to sallute the strangers, stroaking of them. these Indians understanding our business to St Hellena told us that ye Westoes a rangeing sort of people reputed to be the Man eaters had ruinated y^{t} place killed seu'all of those Indians destroyed & burnt their Habitations & that they had come as far as Kayawah doeing the like there, ye Casseeka of which place was within one sleep of us (which is 24 howrs for they reckon after that rate) with most of his people whome in two days after came aboard of us.[1]

These people were probably of Siouan stock, but they bordered directly upon the Cusabo tribes and this account of them will give us a slight opportunity to compare the two peoples. This and the short notice that appears in Lawson embrace practically all of the information we have regarding the Sewee Indians, if such indeed they were.

Taking the chief of Kayawah, "a uery Ingenious Indian & a great Linguist in this Maine," with them the prospective settlers now sailed to Port Royal, where they anchored, but it was two days before they could speak with an Indian, when what had been told

[1] S. Car. Hist. Soc. Colls. v, pp. 165-166.

them at Sewee regarding the irruption of the Westo was confirmed. Weighing anchor from Port Royal River they then

ran in between St Hellena & Combohe where we lay at Anchor all ye time we staide neare ye Place where ye distressed Indian soiourned, who were glad & crying Hiddy doddy Comorado Angles Westoe Skorrye (which is as much as to say) English uery good friends Westoes are nought, they hoped by our Arriuall to be protected from ye Westoes, often making signes they would ingage them with their bowes & arrows, & wee should with our guns they often brought vs veneson & some deare skins wch wee bought of them for beads. many of us went ashore at St Hellena & brought back word that ye Land was good Land supplyed with many Peach trees, & a Competence of timber a few figg trees & some Cedar here & theire & that there was a mile & a half of Cleare Land fitt & ready to Plante. Oysters in great plenty all ye Islands being rounded wth bankes of ye kinde, in shape longer & scarcely see any one round, yet good fish though not altogether of soe pleasant taste as yor wall fleet oysters. here is also wilde turke which ye Indian brought but is not soe pleasant to eate of as ye tame but uery fleshy & farr bigger.

A sloop which had been sent to Kiawa to examine that place now returned with a favorable report and the colonists sailed thither and made the first permanent settlement in South Carolina.[1] At this time we learn that that section of the province watered by the Stono River was full of Indian settlements.[2]

In May of the same year a sloop called *The Three Brothers* anchored off Edisto Island—"Odistash" as they call it—and two chiefs, named Sheedou and Alush, who had been taken to Barbados by Hilton, came out to them and directed them to Kiawa.[3]

In a letter written to Lord Ashley from this colony by William Owen on September 15, 1670, he says, referring to the coast Indians:

We haue them in a pound, for to ye Southward they will not goe fearing the Yamases Spanish Comeraro as ye Indians termes it. ye Westoes are behind them a mortall enemie of theires whom they say are ye man eaters of them they are more afraid then ye little children are of ye Bull beggers in England. to ye Northward they will not goe for their they cry y^{t} is Hiddeskeh, y^{t} is to say sickly, soe y^{t} they reckon themselves safe when they haue vs amongst them, from them there cann be noe danger ap^{r}hended, they haue exprest vs vnexpected kindness for when ye ship went to and dureing her stay att Virginia provision was att the scarcest with us yet they daylie supplied vs y^{t} we were better stored att her return than when she went haueing 25 days provision in stoe beside 3 tunn of corne more wch they promised to procuer when we pleased to com for it att Seweh.[4]

In a letter written to Lord Ashley on August 30, 1671, Maurice Mathews says:

The Indians all About vs are our friends; all y^{t} we haue knowledge of by theyre Appearance and traid with vs are as followeth:

St Helena ye Southermost; Ishpow, Wimbee, Edista, Stono, Keyawah, where we now liue, Kussoo to ye westward of vs, Sampa, wando Ituan, Gt Pa;[5] Sewee, Santee,

[1] S. Car. Hist. Soc. Colls., v, pp. 166–168.

[2] Carroll, Hist. Colls. S. Car., II, p. 452.

[3] Ibid., p. 170.

[4] Ibid., pp. 200–201.

[5] In a note the editor of the Shaftesbury Papers gives an alternative rendering S^{t} Pa, and queries whether this tribe is the Sampa or Sampit repeated. There does not seem to be sufficient data for determining this point.

Wanniah, Elasie, Isaw, Cotachicach, some of these haue 4 or 5 Cassikaes more, or Less Truly to define the power of these Cassukaes I must say thus; it is noe more (scarce as much) as we owne to ye Topakin in England, or A grauer person then our selues; I finde noe tributaries among them, butt intermariages & pouerty causeth them to visitt one Another; neuer quarrelling who is ye better man; they are generally poore & Spanish; Affraid of ye very foot step of a Westoe; A sort of people y[t] liue vp to the westward [which these say eat people and are great warriors].[1]

Elsewhere in the same letter Mathews mentions an expedition inland in which "About 30 miles or more vpwards wee came Among the Cussoo Indians our friends; with whome I had been twice before." This was on Ashley River.

In September, 1671, a war broke out with the Coosa Indians. The occasion of this is given in the Council Journal under date of September 27 as follows:

At a meeting of the Governour and Councill September 27th sitting and present (the same [as given above]). The Governour and Councill taking into their serious consideration the languishing condition that this Collony is brought into by reason of the great quantity of corne from time to time taken out of the plantations by the Kussoe and other Southward Indians and for as much as the said Indians will not comply with any faire entreaties to live peaceably and quietly but instead thereof upon every light occasion have and doe threaten the lives of all or any of our people whom they will sufore (?) to them and doe dayly persist and increase in their insolencyes soe as to disturb and invade some of our plantation in the night time but that the evill of their intentions have hitherto been prevented by diligent watchings. And for as much as the said Indians have given out that they intend for and with the Spaniards to cutt off the English people in this place &c Ordered ordeyned by the said Governuor &c Councill (nemine contra dicente) that an open Warr shall be forthwith prosecuted against the said Kussoe Indians and their co-adjutors & for the better effecting thereof that Commissions be granted to Capt. John Godfrey and Capt. Thomas Gray to prosecute the same effectually. And that Mr. Stephen Bull doe take into his custody two Kussoe Indians now in Towne and them to keepe with the best security he may till he receive firther orders from this Board.[2]

As, in a letter written to Lord Ashley by Joseph West on September 3 preceding, the murder of an Indian by an Irish colonist is referred to,[3] probably the provocation was not all on one side. This war seems to have been pushed with exceeding vigor, since in the Council Journal for October 2 we read:

Upon consideration had of the disposing of the Indian prisoners now brought in for their better security and maintenance. It is resolved and ordered by the Grand Councill that every Company which went out upon that expedition shall secure and maintaine the Indians they have taken till they can transport the said Indians, but if the remaining Kussoe Indians doe in the meanetime come in and make peace and desire the Indians now prisoners then the said Indians shall be sett at Liberty having first paid such a ransom as shall be thought reasonable by the Grand Council to be shared equally among the Company of men that tooke the Indians aforesaid.[4]

---

[1] S. Car. Hist. Soc. Colls., v, p. 334. The editor of the Shaftesbury Papers gives two other lists of these Cusabo tribes. The first is dated in 1695–6 and mentions "the natives of Sainte Helena, Causa, Wimbehe, Combehe, Edistoe, Stonoe, Kiaway, Itwan, Seewee, Santee, Cussoes." Causa does not appear again; Causa and Cussoe may refer to two sections of the Coosa. The second list is dated in 1707 and refers to "those called Cusabes, viz: Santees, Ittavans, Seawees, Stoanoes, Kiawaws, Kussoes, St. Helena &c. and Bohicotts."

[2] S. Car. Hist. Soc. Colls., v, pp. 341–242.

[3] Ibid., p. 338.

[4] Ibid., v, pp. 344–345. See also Rivers, Hist. S. Car., pp. 105–106.

The transporting of the Indians meant transport to the West Indies as slaves, that being one of the amiable ways of civilizing redskins to which our ancestors were addicted. The fate of these unfortunate Coosa is uncertain, but evidently the war came to an end after the aforesaid expedition. From a note based on information obtained from Governor West we learn that the—

> Cossoes [were] to pay a dear skin monthly as an acknowledgm[t] or else to loose our amitie.[1]

This must have been one of the agreements when peace was made. In 1674, in some instructions to Henry Woodward, the Earl of Shaftesbury says: "You are to treate with the Indians of Edisto for the Island and buy it of them and make a Friendship with them."[2]

Whether the order was carried out at that time does not appear. Meantime the Coosa Indians were again restless. The Council Journals for August 3, 1674, contain the following:

> And forasmuch as it is credibly informed that the Kussoe Indians have secretly murdered 3 Englishmen and as these Indians have noe certaine abode Resolved that Capt. Mau: Mathews, M[r] W[m] Owen, capt[t] Rich[d] Conant & M[r] Ra: Marshall doe inquire where the s[d] Indians may be taken then to raise a party of men as they shall think conven[t] under command of the s[d] capt[t] Conant or any other parties under other commanders to use all meanes to come up with the s[d] Indians wheresoever to take or destroy all or any of them, the whole matter being left to their advisem[t].[3]

Still earlier the colonists had begun to experience difficulties with the Stono, as this entry under date of July 25 attests:

> For as &c it is credibly informed that the Indian Stonoe Casseca hath endeavored to confederate certaine other Indians to murder some of the English nation & to rise in Rebellion ag[t] this Settem[t] Resolved that capt. Mau: Mathews doe require & command nine men of the Inhabi[ts] of this Settlem[t] to attend him in this exped[n] to take the s[d] Indian and him cause to be brought to Charlestowne to answer to these things but if any opposition happen the s[d] capt. Mathews is to use his discret[n] in the managm[t] thereof for the security of himself & the s[d] party of men whether by killing & destroying the s[d] Indian & his confederates or otherwise.[3]

According to the Council Journals of January 15, 1675, "some neighbor Indians" had expressed a desire to be settled into a town near Charleston.[4]

To carry out the terms of the constitution drawn up for Carolina by John Locke a number of "baronies" were created in South Carolina, many of them by purchase of land from the Indian proprietors. Thus the land constituting Ashley barony on Ashley River was obtained from the Coosa Indians who surrendered it in the following terms:

> To all menner of People, &c., know ye that wee, the Cassiques naturell Born Hears & Sole owners & proprietors of great & lesser Cussoe, lying on the river of Kyewah, the

---

[1] S. Car. Hist. Soc. Colls., v, p. 388.
[2] Ibid., p. 445.
[3] Ibid., p. 451.
[4] Ibid., p. 475.

River of Stonoe, & the freshes of the River of Edistah, doe for us ourselves, our subjects & vassals, grant, &c., whole part & parcell called great & lesser Cussoe unto the Right Honble Anthony Earl of Shaftsbury, Lord Baron Ashly of Wimborne St. Gyles, Lord Cooper of Pawlet, &c., 10 March, 1675. *Marks of* The Great Cassiq, &c., an Indian Captain, a hill Captain, &c.[1]

To this are appended the signatures of several witnesses. What appears to have been a still more sweeping cession was made to Maurice Mathews in 1682 by the "chief of Stonah, chieftainess of Edisloh, chief of Asshepoo, chieftainess of St. Hellena, chief of Combahe, chief of Cussah, chief of Wichcauh, chief of Wimbee."[2] In 1693 there was a short war with the Stono, a tribe which had already showed itself hostile on more than one occasion.[3] The same year we read that the Chihaw King complained of the cruel treatment he had received from John Palmer, who had barbarously beaten and cut him with his broadsword. These "Chihaw" were perhaps in South Carolina and not representatives of that much better known band among the Creeks.[4] A body of Cusabo were in Col. John Barnwell's army raised to attack the Tuscarora in 1711–12.[5] In 1712 was passed an act for "settling the Island called Palawana, upon the Cusaboe Indians now living in Granville County and upon their Posterity forever." From the terms of this act it appears that "most of the Plantations of the said Cusaboes" were already situated upon that island which is described as "near the Island of *St. Helena*," but that it had fallen into private hands.

The act reads as follows:

Whereas the *Cusaboe* Indians of *Granville* County, are the native and ancient inhabitants of the Sea Coasts of this Province, and kindly entertained the first *English* who arrived in the same, and are useful to the Government for Watching and Discovering Enemies, and finding Shipwreck'd People; And whereas the Island called *Palawana* near the Island of *St. Helena*, upon which most of the Plantations of the said *Cusaboes* now are, was formerly by Inadvertancy granted by the Right Honorable the Lords Proprietors of this Province, to *Matthew Smallwood*, and by him sold and transferred to *James Cockram*, whose Property and Possession it is at present; Be it Enacted by the most noble Prince *Henry* Duke of Beauford, Palatine, and the Rest of the Right Honorable the true and absolute Lords and Proprietors of *Carolina*, together with the Advice and Consent of the Members of the General Assembly now met at *Charles-Town* for the South West Part of this Province, That from and after the Ratification of this Act, the Island of *Palawana*, lying nigh the Island of *St. Helena*, in *Granville* County, containing between Four and Five Hundred Acres of Land, be it more or less, now in the Possession of *James Cockram* as aforesaid, shall be and is hereby declared to be invested in the aforesaid *Cusaboe* Indians, and in their Heirs forever.[6]

---

1 S. Car. Hist. Soc. Colls., v, pp. 456–457.

2 Rivers, Hist. S. Car., p. 38, 1856; Public Records of S. C., 36, p. 125.

3 Logan, a Hist. of the Upper Country of S. C., pp. 191–192; Carroll, Hist. Colls. S. Car., I, p. 74. By later writers this disturbance was in some way associated with the Westo war and the Stono and Westo were coupled together on this account and because of a superficial resemblance between their names.

4 Carroll, op. cit., p. 116.

5 S. Car. Hist. and Gen. Mag., 9, pp. 30–31, 1908.

6 Laws of the Province of South Carolina, by Nicholas Trott (1763), No. 338, p. 277, quoted by Thomas in 18th Ann. Rept. Bur. Amer. Ethn., pt. 2, p. 633.

In 1715 the Yamasee war broke out and it is commonly supposed to have nearly exterminated the ancient tribes of South Carolina, one early authority stating that "some of the Corsaboys" along with the Congarees, Santees, Seawees, Pedees, and Waxaws were "utterly extirpated,"[1] but I quote this statement merely to refute it. As a matter of fact, remnants of nearly all the ancient tribes persisted for a considerable period afterwards. In 1716 there was a short war between the colonists and the Santee and Congaree Indians. The Etiwaw took part in this contest on the side of the whites. Over half of the offending tribes were taken prisoners and sent as slaves to the West Indies.[2] In the same year we find a note to the effect that the colony had been presented with six dressed deerskins by the "Coosoe" Indians and twelve dressed and eight raw deerskins by the "Itawans."[3] In 1717 there is a note of a present made by the "Kiawah" Indians.[4] In a letter written by Barnwell, April, 1720, there is mention of the "Coosaboys."[5] In 1727 we learn that "the King of the Kywaws" desired recompense for some service, and, apparently the same year, he was given a grant of land south of the "Combee" River.[6] About 1743 Adair mentions "Coosah" as a dialect spoken in the Catawba nation, but it is not probable that all of the Coosa removed there.[7] Some time after the founding of Georgia an old man among the Creek Indians stated that the first whites were met with at the mouth of the Coosawhatchie,[8] and it appears that this report was current among the Creeks, although sometimes the name of Savannah River is substituted. The tradition is, of course, correct, and it would seem probable that it was due not merely to hearsay information but to the actual presence among the Creeks of families or bands of Indians of Cusabo origin. Apart from those who joined the Catawba, Creeks, and other tribes, the last glimpse we have of the coast Indians shows the remnant of the Kiawa and Cusabo in the neighborhood of Beaufort. We do not know whether the Etiwaw and Wando were included among the Kiawa, but it is probable that a part at least of all of these tribes remained near their ancestral seats and were gradually merged in the surrounding population.

The following remarks of Adair may well be inserted as the valedictory of these people, although it applies also to the small Siouan tribes northward of them and to some others:

---

[1] Rivers, Hist. S. Car., pp. 93–94.

[2] Pub. Rec. of S. C., MS.

[3] Proc. of Board dealing with Indian trade, MS., p. 62.

[4] Ibid., p. 186.

[5] Pub. Rec. of S. C., MS. VIII, p. 4.

[6] Journal of the Council, S. C. docs., X, p. 24.

[7] Adair, Hist. Am. Inds., p. 225.

[8] Carroll, Hist. Colls. S. Car., I, XXXVII.

In most of our American colonies, there yet remain a few of the natives, who formerly inhabited those extensive countries; and as they were friendly to us, and serviceable to our interests, the wisdom and virtue of our legislature secured them from being injured by the neighboring nations. The French strictly pursued the same method, deeming such to be more useful than any others on alarming occasions. We called them "Parched-corn-Indians," because they chiefly use it for bread, are civilized, and live mostly by planting. As they had no connection with the Indian nations [i. e., the Catawba, Cherokee, Muskogee, Chickasaw, and Choctaw], and were desirous of living peaceable under the British protection, none could have any just plea to kill or inslave them."[1]

Ethnological Information Regarding the Cusabo

Ethnological information regarding the Cusabo is scanty and unsatisfactory, the interest of the colonists having been quickly attracted to those great tribes lying inland which they called "nations." Such material as is to be had must be interpreted in the light of the fuller information to be gathered from larger southern tribes like the Creeks, Cherokee, Choctaw, and Chickasaw. Nevertheless it is of interest to know that certain features of the lives of these peoples were or were not shared by the ones better known.

The material gathered by the Spaniards as a result of the Ayllon expedition has been given in connection with the account of that venture, and will not be considered again. The region to which it applies is too uncertain to consider it definitely under this head. From the time of the French settlement in 1562, however, we have a sufficiently clear localization, from the French, Spanish, and English narratives successively. The greater part of our information comes, however, from the French and English, the Spaniards not having been interested in the people among whom they came or not having published those papers which contained accounts of them.

The following general description of the appearance of the natives, and their mental and moral characteristics, is from Alexander Hewat. It does not apply to the Cusabo alone, but Hewat was probably better acquainted with them than with any other Indians.

In stature they are of a middle size, neither so tall nor yet so low as some Europeans. To appearance they are strong and well made; yet they are totally unqualified for that heavy burden or tedious labour which the vigorous and firm nerves of Europeans enable them to undergo. None of them are deformed, deformities of nature being confined to the ages of art and refinement. Their colour is brown, and their skin shines, being varnished with bears fat and paint. To appearance the men have no beards, nor hair on their head, except a round tuft on its crown; but this defect is not natural, as many people are given to believe, but the effect of art, it being customary among them to tear out such hair by the root. They go naked, except those parts which natural decency teaches the most barbarous nations to cover. The huts in which they live are foul, mean and offensive; and their manner of life is poor,

[1] Adair, Hist. Am. Inds., p. 343.

nasty, and disgustful. In the hunting season they are eager and indefatigable in pursuit of their prey; when that is over, they indulge themselves in a kind of brutal slumber, indolence, and ease. In their distant excursions they can endure hunger long, and carry little with them for their subsistence; but in days of plenty they are voracious as vultures. While dining in company with their chieftains we were astonished at the vast quantity of meat they devoured. Agriculture they leave to women, and consider it as an employment unworthy of a man: indeed they seem amazingly dead to tender passions, and treat their women like slaves, or beings of inferior rank. Scolding, insults, quarrels, and complaints are seldom heard among them; on solemn occasions they are thoughtful, serious, and grave; yet I have seen them free, open, and merry at feasts and entertainments. In their common deportment towards each other they are respectful, peaceable, and inoffensive. Sudden anger is looked upon as ignominious and unbecoming, and, except in liquor, they seldom differ with their neighbour, or even do him any harm or injury. As for riches they have none, nor covet any; and while they have plenty of provisions, they allow none to suffer through want; if they are successful in hunting, all their unfortunate or distressed friends share with them the common blessings of life.[1]

This description has importance, not as a moral evaluation of these people but as a set of impressions to be interpreted with due regard to the standards and ideals in the mind of the observer himself. Another writer says that bear grease was used on the hair to make it grow and at the same time kill the vermin.[2] Another says of their head hair that it was "tied in various ways, sometimes oyl'd and painted, stuck through with Feathers for Ornament or Gallantry," and he adds that they painted their faces "with different Figures of a red or Sanguine Colour."[3] Their clothing consisted of bear or deer skins dressed, it is said, "rather softer, though not so durable as ours in England."[4] They were sometimes ornamented with black and red checks.[5] Locke notes that they "dye their deer skins of excellent colours."[6] Pearls were obtained from the rivers, and they knew how to pierce them, but the process spoiled their value for European trade. They made little baskets of painted reeds,[7] and the French found the house of Ouadé, which was, it is true, in the Guale country, "hung with feathers (plumasserie) of different colors, to the height of a pike." "Moreover upon the place where the king slept were white coverings woven in panels with clever artifice and edged about with a scarlet fringe."[8] These must have been either cane mats or else textiles made of mulberry bark or some similar material, like those fabricated throughout the south. The "panels" were probably the typical diagonal designs still to be seen on southern baskets. The French add that Ouadé presented them with six pieces of his hangings made like little coverings.[9]

---

1 Hewat in Carroll, Hist. Colls. S. Car., I, pp. 65–66.
2 Carroll, op. cit., II, pp. 723.
3 Ibid., p. 73.
4 Ibid., p. 80.
5 Ibid., pp. 80–81.
6 S. Car. Hist. Soc. Colls., V, p. 462.
7 Carroll, op. cit., II, pp. 80–81.
8 Laudonnière, Hist. Not. de la Floride, p. 48.
9 Ibid., p. 49.

What Oviedo records about the large communal house said to have been found on this coast by the Spaniards early in the sixteenth century has been given already.[1] That they could build houses of considerable size without much labor is clearly shown by the experience of the French at Port Royal. One of their buildings described as "the large house" having been destroyed, the Indians of Maccou and Audusta built another in less than 12 hours "scarcely smaller than the one which had been burned." [2] As we have seen, Hewat speaks of their houses as "foul, mean, and offensive,"[3] but the structures seen by Hilton and Sandford certainly did not deserve the censure of meanness. Some of those noted by the former captain as having been seen at St. Helena were evidently put up by Spaniards, but he mentions one which was probably of native construction. At least some of the features connected with it were native. This was "a fair house builded in the shape of a Dove-house, round, two hundred foot at least, compleatly covered with *Palmeta*-leaves, the wal-plate being twelve foot high, or thereabouts, & within lodging rooms and forms; two pillars at the entrance of a high Seat above all the rest." [4] This "high seat" was perhaps a chief's seat such as were seen elsewhere on the Cusabo coast. When Capt. Sandford visited the chief Edisto town in 1666 he was "conducted into a large house of a Circular forme (their generall house of State)." Over against the entrance was "a high seate of sufficient breadth for half a dozen persons," for the chief, his wife, eminent persons, and distinguished visitors. Lower benches for the common people extended from the ends of this on each side all the way to the door, and about the fire, which was in the center of the building, were "little lowe foormes." The town house of St. Helena is said to have been of the same pattern, and was probably identical with that described by Hilton, as quoted above.[5]

In hunting, their principal weapons were bows and arrows, the latter made of reeds pointed with sharp stones or fishbones. The Cusabo country abounded with game, its rivers and inlets with fish; shellfish were also abundant along the coast. The deer was, as usual, the chief game animal, the bear being hunted more for its fat than for its flesh. According to Samuel Wilson, whose account was published in 1682, deer were so plentiful "that an Indian hunter hath killed Nine fat Deere in a day all shot by himself, and all the considerable Planters have an Indian Hunter which they hire for less than Twenty shillings a year, and one hunter will very well find a Family of Thirty people, with as much venison and foul as they can well eat." [6] What

[1] See p. 48.

[2] Laudonnière, Hist. Not. de la Floride, p. 50.

[3] See p. 72.

[4] See p. 62.

[5] See p. 64.

[6] Carroll, op. cit., II, p. 28.

the explorers in Hilton's party have to say regarding native agriculture has been given but may be requoted:

The *Indians* plant in the worst Land because they cannot cut down the Timber in the best, and yet have plenty of Corn, Pompions, Water-Mellons, Musk-mellons: although the land be overgrown with weeds through their lasinesse, yet they have two or three crops of Corn a year, as the Indians themselves inform us.[1]

Their treatment of corn was probably identical with that among the other southern tribes. Mention is made by one writer of the "cold meal" made by parching ripe corn and pounding it into a powder and of the convenience of this in traveling.[2] Sandford found extensive cornfields surrounding both Edisto and St. Helena, but in Laudonnière's time, at any rate, the Guale country seems to have been superior agriculturally. Couexis, a Guale chief, is reported as having "such a quantity of millet (*mil*), flour, and beans that through his assistance alone they [the French] might have provision for a very long time." [3] If the "mil" and "farine" are supposed to refer to two different cereals one may have been wild rice or something of the sort. Probably, however, both refer to corn—one to the unground, the other to the ground or pounded corn. Acorns and nuts were used, especially when other provisions had given out. From the hickory nut, and probably from acorns also, they expressed an oil of which it is said the English colonists also availed themselves.[4]

It is interesting to observe that in the time of Hilton and Sandford the Cusabo already had peaches and figs, and we must therefore assign to these a Spanish origin. Laudonnière also mentions the use of roots as food,[5] and the explorers under Hilton speak of a root which grew in the marshes and of which the Indians made good bread.[6] This was perhaps the "marsh potato," but more likely the kunti of the Creeks, a kind of smilax, for we know that bread was made from this throughout the south.

The Cusabo used dugout canoes extensively and were expert canoe men and good swimmers.[7] Regarding their methods of catching fish no word has been preserved. From the rapidity with which they supplied the Frenchmen with cords for rigging it may be inferred that fishing lines and nets were much in use.[8]

Regarding their government and social organization next to nothing is known. Hewat says:

Although the Indians lived much dispersed, yet they united under one chief, and formed towns, all the lands around which they claimed as their property. The bound-

---

[1] See p. 63.
[2] Carroll, op. cit., p. 68.
[3] Laudonnière, op. cit., p. 47.
[4] Carroll, op. cit., p. 64.
[5] Laudonnière, op. cit., p. 46.
[6] See p. 63.
[7] Laudonnière, op. cit., p. 27.
[8] Ibid., p. 55.

aries of their hunting grounds being carefully fixed, each tribe was tenacious of its possessions, and fired with resentment at the least encroachment on them. Every individual looked on himself as a proprietor of all the lands claimed by the whole tribe, and bound in honor to defend them.[1]

And farther on:

With respect to internal government, these savages have also several customs and regulations to which the individuals of the same tribe conform. Personal wisdom and courage are the chief sources of distinction among them, and individuals obtain rank and influence in proportion as they excel in these qualifications. Natural reason suggests, that the man of the greatest abilities ought to be the leader of all possessed of inferior endowments; in him they place the greatest confidence, and follow him to war without envy or murmur. As this warrior arrives at honour and distinction by the general consent, so, when chosen, he must be very circumspect in his conduct, and gentle in the exercise of his power. By the first unlucky or unpopular step he forfeits the goodwill and confidence of his countrymen, upon which all his power is founded. Besides the head warrior, they have judges and conjurers, whom they call Beloved Men, who have great weight among them; none of whom have indeed any coercive authority, yet all are tolerably well obeyed. In this commonwealth every man's voice is heard, and at their public demonstrations the best speakers generally prevail. When they consult together about important affairs, such as war or peace, they are serious and grave, and examine all the advantages and disadvantages of their situation with great coolness and deliberation, and nothing is determined but by the general consent.[2]

From the narratives of Hilton and Sandford we know that they had town houses, corresponding evidently to the tcokofas of the Creeks, and that there was an open space next to them in which the chunky game was played,[3] but they do not appear to have had the outdoor council ground or "square."

The manner in which strangers of distinction were received is well illustrated by the entertainment accorded Capt. Sandford at Edisto.[4] When the chiefs encountered strangers at a distance from their towns they had arbors constructed in the manner of the Florida Indians in which the conference could take place and in which the conferees could be screened from the sun.[5] When Captain Albert, the French officer in charge of Charlesfort, visited the chief Stalame the latter presented him on his arrival with a bow and arrows, "which is a sign and confirmation of alliance among them." He also presented him with deerskins.[6]

Regarding their customs in general and that relating to war in particular Hewat says:

Although in some particular customs the separate tribes of Indians differ from each other, yet in their general principles and mode of government they are very similar. All have general rules with respect to other independent tribes around them, which they carefully observe. The great concerns relating to war or peace are canvassed in assemblies of deputies from all the different towns. When injuries are committed, and Indians of one tribe happen to be killed by those of another, then

---

[1] Carroll, Hist. Colls. S. Car., I, pp. 64-65.
[2] Ibid., pp. 68-69.
[3] See pp. 62-65.
[4] See p. 64.
[5] Laudonnière, op. cit., p. 25.
[6] Ibid., p. 43.

such a meeting is commonly called. If no person appears on the side of the aggressors, the injured nation deputes one of their warriors to go to them, and, in [the] name of the whole tribe, to demand satisfactions. If this is refused, and they think themselves able to undertake a war against the aggressors, then a number of warriors, commonly the relations of the deceased, take the field for revenge, and look upon it as a point of honor never to leave it till they have killed the same number of the enemy that had been slain of their kinsmen. Having accomplished this, they return home with their scalps, and by some token let their enemy know that they are satisfied. But when the nation to whom the aggressors belong happen to be disposed to peace, they search for the murderer, and they are, by the general judgment of the nation, capitally punished, to prevent involving others in their quarrel, which act of justice is performed often by the aggressor's nearest relations. The criminal never knows of his condemnation until the moment the sentence is put into execution, which often happens while he is dancing the war dance in the midst of his neighbors, and bragging of the same exploit for which he is condemned to die. . . .

The American savages almost universally claim the right of private revenge. It is considered by them as a point of honor to avenge the injuries done to friends, particularly the death of a relation. Scalp for scalp, blood for blood, and death for death, can only satisfy the surviving friends of the injured party. . . . But should the wife and aged men of weight and influence among the Indians interpose, on account of the aggressor, perhaps satisfaction may be made by way of compensation. In this case some present made to the party aggrieved serves to gratify their passion of revenge, by the loss the aggressor sustains, and the acquisition of property the injured receives. Should the injured friends refuse this kind of satisfaction, which they are entirely at liberty to do, then the murderer, however high his rank may be, must be delivered up to torture and death, to prevent the quarrel spreading wider through the nation ... When war is the result of their councils, and the great leader takes the field, any one may refuse to follow him, or may desert him without incurring any punishment; but by such ignominious conduct he loses his reputation, and forfeits the hopes of distinction and preferment. To honor and glory from warlike exploits the views of every man are directed, and therefore they are extremely cautious and watchful against doing any action for which they may incur public censure and disgrace.[1]

Regarding marriage, another writer says:

Polygamy is permitted among them, yet few have more than one wife at a time, possibly on account of the expense of supporting them, for he is accounted a good gunsman that provides well for one; besides the Indians are not of an amorous complexion. It is common with them, however, to repudiate their wives, if disobliged by them or tired of them; the rejected woman, if with child, generally revenges herself for the affront by taking herbs to procure an abortion—an operation that destroys many of them, and greatly contributes to depopulate them.[2]

The Spanish missionary Rogel remarks on the monogamous condition of the Cusabo of his time as presenting a pleasing contrast to the state of the Calusa of southern Florida, from whom he had just come.[3]

Regarding adultery, Hewat says:

In case of adultery among Indians, the injured husband considers himself as under an obligation to revenge the crime, and he attempts to cut off the ears of the adulterer,

---

[1] Carroll, op. cit., I, pp. 66–68, 69.

[2] Ibid., pp. 517–518. Locke notes, however, that they were "kind to their women."—(S. Car. Hist. Soc. Colls., v, p. 462.)

[3] See p. 57.

provided he be able to effect it; if not, he may embrace the first opportunity that offers of killing him without any danger to his tribe. Then the debt is paid, and the courage of the husband proved.[1]

No mention being made of punishment inflicted on the wife, it may be concluded that the custom of punishing only the male offender existed as it did among the Siouan tribes to the north.[2]

The comparative absence of theft among our southeastern Indians is attested in this section also by the circumstance that when two Indians whom Ribault had retained on board his vessel by force escaped they left behind all of the presents the Frenchmen had made them, although some of these were articles of high value in their eyes.[3]

A relation published in 1682 says of their religious beliefs:

Their religion chiefly consists in the adoration of the sun and moon. At the appearance of the new moon I have observed them with open extended arms, then folded, with inclined bodies, to make their adorations with much ardency and passion.[4]

The personal observation is of some value, but little or none can be attached to the first statement, which seems to be made by explorers in all parts of the world for want of any definite information. Laudonnière notes of the two Cusabo Indians kept overnight on Ribault's vessel that they "made us to understand that before eating they were accustomed to wash their faces and wait until the sun was set,"[5] from which it may be inferred that they were fasting. The fullest account of the religious beliefs of these people is the following from Hewat:

The Indians, like all ignorant and rude nations, are very superstitious. They believe that superior beings interfere in, and direct, human affairs, and invoke all spirits, both good and evil, in hazardous undertakings. Each tribe have their conjurers and magicians, on whose prophetic declarations they place much confidence, in all matters relating to health, hunting, and war. They are fond of prying into future events, and therefore pay particular regard to signs, omens, and dreams. They look upon fire as sacred, and pay the author of it a kind of worship. At the time of harvest and at full moon they observe several feasts and ceremonies, which it would seem were derived from some religious origin. As their success, both in warlike enterprises and in procuring subsistence depends greatly on fortune, they have a number of ceremonious observances before they enter on them. They offer in sacrifice a part of the first deer or bear they kill, and from this they flatter themselves with the hopes of future success. When taken sick they are particularly prone to superstition, and their physicians administer their simple and secret cures with a variety of strange ceremonies and magic arts, which fill the patients with courage and confidence, and are sometimes attended with happy effects.[6]

Among the Carolina notes in the Shaftesbury Papers is this by Locke: "Kill servants to wait on them in the other world."[7] This would be interesting if we could feel sure that it applied to the Indians

[1] Carroll, op. cit., I, p. 68.

[2] Lawson, Hist. Carolina, p. 306.

[3] Laudonnière, op. cit., p. 31.

[4] Carroll, op. cit., II, pp. 80–81.

[5] Laudonnière, op. cit., p. 28.

[6] Carroll, op. cit., I, pp. 69–70.

[7] S. Car. Hist. Soc. Colls., V, p. 462.

of Carolina, and had not been picked up by Locke in the course of his general reading.

In the matter of medicine another writer says:

In Medicine, or the Nature of Simples, some have an exquisite knowledge; and in the cure of Scorbutick, Venereal, and Malignant Distempers are admirable: In all External Diseases they suck the part affected with many Incantations, Philtres and Charms: In Amorous Intrigues they are excellent either to procure Love or Hatred; They are not very forward in Discovery of their secrets, which by long Experience are religiously transmitted and conveyed in a continued Line from one Generation to another, for which those skill'd in this Faculty are held in great Veneration and Esteem.[1]

Rogel refers to the Cusabo feasts, but only in a general way.[2] It appears, however, that they had a festival of the first fruits like other southern tribes. The only description of one of their ceremonies, of any length, is given by Laudonnière. He calls this ceremony "the feast of Toya," and says that they kept it "as strictly as we do Sunday."[3] It is probable that this corresponded to the Creek busk, although agreeing with it in few formal particulars. Laudonnière's account runs as follows:

Since the time was near for celebrating their feasts of Toya, ceremonies strange to recount, he [Audusta] sent ambassadors to the French to beg them on his part to be present, which they agreed to very willingly, on account of the desire they had of knowing what these were. They embarked then and proceeded toward the dwelling of the king, who was already come out on the road before them in order to receive them kindly, to caress them and conduct them into his house, where he exerted himself to treat them in the best manner of which he was capable.

However, the Indians prepared to celebrate the feast the next day, when the king led them in order to see the place where the feast was to take place, and there they saw many women about who were laboring with all their might to make the place pure and clean. This place was a great compass of well leveled land of a round shape. The next day then, very early in the morning, all those who were chosen to celebrate the feast, being ornamented with paints and feathers of many different colors, betook their way, on leaving the house of the king, toward the place of Toya. Having arrived there they ranged themselves in order and followed three Indians, who in paintings and manner of dress were different from the others. Each one of them carried a little drum (tabourasse) on his fist, with which they began to go into the middle of the round space, dancing and singing mournfully, being followed by the others, who responded to them. After they had sung, danced, and wheeled around three times they began running like unbridled horses through the midst of the thickest forests. And the Indian women continued all the rest of the day in tears so sad and lamentable that nothing more was possible, and in such fury they clutched the arms of the young girls which they cut cruelly with well sharpened mussel shells, so deep that the blood ran down from them, which they sprinkled in the air crying "he Toya" about three times. The king Audusta had withdrawn all of our Frenchmen into his house during the ceremony, and was as grieved as possible when he saw them laugh. He had done that all the more because the Indians are very angry when one watches them during their ceremonies. However, one of our Frenchmen managed so well that by stealth he got out of Audusta's house and stealth-

---

[1] Carroll, op. cit., II, pp. 80–81.

[2] See p. 57.

[3] Laudonnière, op. cit., p. 29.

ily went to hide himself behind a thick bush, where at his pleasure he could easily reconnoiter the ceremonies of the feast. The three who began the feast are called joanas,[1] and are like priests or sacrificers according to the Indian law, to whom they give faith and credence in part because as a class[2] they are devoted to the sacrifices and in part also because everything lost is recovered by their means. And not only are they revered on account of these things but also because by I do not know what science and knowledge that they have of herbs they cure sicknesses. Those who had thus gone away among the woods returned two days later. Then, having arrived, they began to dance with a courageous gayety in the very middle of the open space, and to cheer their good Indian fathers, who on account of advanced age, or else their natural indisposition, had not been called to the feast. All these dances having been brought to an end they began to eat with an avidity so great that they seemed rather to devour the food than to eat it. For neither on the feast day nor on the two following days had they drunk or eaten. Our Frenchmen were not forgotten in this good cheer, for the Indians went to invite them all, showing themselves very happy at their presence. Having remained some time with the Indians a Frenchman gained a young boy by presents and inquired of him what the Indians had done during their absence in the woods, who gave him to understand by signs that the joanas had made invocations to Toya, and that by magic characters they had made him come so that they could speak to him and ask him many strange things, which for fear of the joanas he did not dare to make known. They have besides many other ceremonies which I will not recount here for fear of wearying the readers over matters of such small consequence.[3]

Which shows that matters of small consequence to one generation may become of great interest to later ones. Although the feast is represented as of three days' duration it is evident that this is only one case of the common substitution by early writers of the European sacred number 3 for the Indian sacred number 4. In this particular, therefore, and in the careful clearing of the dance ground before the ceremony, this feast recalls the Creek busk. The rest of it seems to be entirely different, though the idea of retiring into the deep forest to commune with deity is shared by all primitive peoples.

For any suggestions regarding the mortuary customs of the Cusabo we must go back to the first attempt at settlement by the Spaniards and Oviedo's comments upon the country of Gualdape already given.[4]

THE GUALE INDIANS AND THE YAMASEE

The coast of what is now the State of Georgia, from Savannah River as far as St. Andrews Sound, was anciently occupied by a tribe or related tribes which, whatever doubts may remain regarding the people just considered, undoubtedly belonged to the Muskhogean stock.[5] This region was known to the Spaniards as "the province of Guale (pronounced Wallie)," but most of the Indians living there finally became merged with a tribe known as the Yamasee, and it

---

1 Hakluyt has "Iawas"; see French, Hist. Colls. La., 1869, p. 204.

2 Or perhaps "by birth."

3 Laudonnière, op. cit., pp. 43–46.

4 See p. 48.

5 See pp. 14–16.

will be well to consider the two together. From a letter of one of the Timucua missionaries we learn that the Guale province was called Ybaha by the Timucua Indians,[1] and this is evidently the Yupaha of which De Soto was in search when he left the Apalachee. "Of the Indians taken in Napetuca," says Elvas, "the treasurer, Juan Gaytan, brought a youth with him, who stated that he did not belong to that country, but to one afar in the direction of the sun's rising, from which he had been a long time absent visiting other lands; that its name was Yupaha, and was governed by a woman, the town she lived in being of astonishing size, and many neighboring lords her tributaries, some of whom gave her clothing, others gold in quantity."[2] As the description of the town and its queen corresponds somewhat with Cofitachequi, perhaps Ybaha or Yubaha was a general name for the Muskhogean peoples rather than a specific designation of Guale.

The towns of Guale lay almost entirely between St. Catherines and St. Andrews Sounds. An early Spanish document refers to "the 22 chiefs of Guale." Menéndez says there were "40 villages of Indians" within 3 or 4 leagues. Between St. Catherines Sound and the Savannah, where the province of Orista or Escamacu, the later Cusabo, began, there appear to have been few permanent settlements. South of St. Andrews Sound began the Timucua province. When Governor Pedro de Ibarra visited the tribes of this coast he made three stops at or near the islands of St. Simons, Sapello, and St. Catherines, respectively, and at each place the chiefs assembled to hold councils with him. It may reasonably be assumed that the chiefs mentioned at each of these councils were those living nearer that particular point than either of the others. In this way we are able to make a rough division of the towns into three groups—northern, central, and southern. Other towns are sometimes referred to with reference to these, so that we may add them to one or the other.

Thus the following towns appear as belonging to the northern group, synonymous terms being placed in parentheses: Asopo (Ahopo); Chatufo, Couexis (Cansin); Culapala (Culopaba); Guale (Goale, Gale); Otapalas; Otaxe (Otax, Otafe); Posache; Tolomato (Tonomato); Uchilape; Uculegue (Oculeygue, Oculeya); Unallapa (Unalcapa); Yfusinique; Yoa (Yua).

Asopo, Culupala, Guale, Otapalas, Otaxe, Uculegue, Unallapa, and Yoa are given by Ibarra. Guale was the name of St. Catherines Island, but the town was "on an arm of a river which goes out of another which is on the north bank of the aforesaid port in Santa

[1] Lowery, MSS.

[2] Bourne, Narr. of De Soto, I, pp. 50-51.

Elena in 32° N. lat."[1] Chatufo is mentioned in the narrative of a visit to the Florida missions by the Bishop of Cuba. Couexis is given in the French narratives; Menéndez changing it to Cansin.[2] Posache is located "in the island of Guale." Tolomato is described in one place as "2 leagues from Guale," and in another as on the mainland near the bar of Capala (Sapello), and it is said to have been a place from which one could go to the Tama Indians on the Altamaha River. Uchilape is located "near Tolomato." Yfusinique was the name of the town to which the chief Juanillo of Tolomato retired after the massacre of the friars and where the other Indians besieged him. Yoa is said to have been 2 leagues by a river behind an arm of the sea back of the bars of Çapala and Cofonufo (Sapello and St. Catherines Sounds). Large vessels could come within 1 league of it and small vessels could reach the town.[3] In the account of the massacre of the missionaries in 1597 Asopo (or Assopo) is described as "in the island of Guale."[4]

Aluste (Alieste, Alueste, Aluete), Oya, Orista, Talapo (Talapuz or Ytalapo), Ufalague (also spelled Ufalegue), Aobi, and Sufalate must be classed as belonging properly to the Cusabo, the first five on the basis of the information quoted above from Ibarra, and the last from its association with Ufalague. Aobi may be intended, as already suggested, for Ahoyabi.[5] Although mentioned in connection with the northern group of towns, they left the Cusabo country and settled in the southern group, where Talapo and Ufalague are frequently referred to.

The central towns were Aleguifa; Chucalagaite (Chucaletgate, Chucalate, Chucalae); Espogache (Aspoache); Espogue (Hespogue, Ospogue, Espo, Ospo, Espoque); Fosquiche (Fasque); Sapala (Çapala, Capala); Sotequa; Tapala; Tulufina (Tolufina, Tolofina); Tupiqui (Topiqui, Tuxiqui, Tupica); Utine (Atinehe).

Chiefs called Fuel, Tafecauca, Tumaque, and Tunague are also mentioned, the last two distinct persons in spite of the close resemblance between their names. All of these towns and chiefs, except Espogache, Tulufina, Aleguifa, and Chucalagaite, are given by Ibarra. Fasquiche and Espogache were evidently not far from Espogue. The last mentioned was on the mainland not more than 6 leagues from Talaxe.[6] Fasquiche is given in the account of a visit to the Florida missions by the Bishop of Cuba. Tulufina appears to have been a place or tribe of importance intimately connected with the interior Indians; the other two are placed "near Tulufina."

---

[1] This is about a third of a degree too far north. From this statement it appears that the town of Guale was on Ossabaw Island, and this agrees with the position given it on Le Moyne's map, on an island between the mouths of the rivers Grande and Belle.

[2] If we follow Le Moyne we must place this on St. Catherines Island. (See preceding note.)

[3] The material in this paragraph is drawn from the Lowery MSS., except that regarding Couexis, for which see p. 50.

[4] See p. 86.

[5] See p. 20.

[6] See p. 243.

An inland people known as Salchiches were represented at the council which Ibarra held in this country. They appear to have been Muskhogeans and seem to have had numerous relatives in the province of Guale. In one place mention is made of "a chief of the Salchiches in Tulufina." In another we are told that the Timucua chief of San Pedro laid the blame for the uprising of 1597 on the people of Tulufina and the Salchiches. An Indian prisoner stated that "the Indians of Cosahue (Cusabo) and the Salchiches, and those of Tulufina and of Santa Elena had said that they would kill them (the friars) and that each chief should kill his own friar." Elsewhere the chief of Chucalagaite and the chief of the Salchiches are mentioned, together with the statement that they were not Christians. It is said that the heir of Tolomato joined with "the other Salchiches" to kill Fray de Corpa. In another place Tulufina and the Salchiches are both referred to as if they were provinces of Tama. The Tama were, as we have seen, an inland people who probably spoke Hitchiti.[1]

The southern group of towns consisted of Aluque (Alaje); Asao (Assaho); Cascangue (Oscangue, Lascangue); Falquiche (Falque); Fuloplata (possibly a man's name); Hinafasque; Hocaesle; Talaxe (Talax, Talaje); Tufulo; Tuque (or Suque); Yfulo (Fulo, Yfielo, Ofulo).

All of these names except Tuque are from Ibarra's letter. Cascangue presents a puzzling problem, for it is referred to several times as a Guale province, but identified by the Franciscan missionaries with the province of Icafi, which was certainly Timucua. Until further light is thrown upon the matter I prefer to consider the two as distinct. The name has a Muskhogean rather than a Timucua aspect. Tuque is given in an account of a visit which the Bishop of Cuba made to Florida in 1606 to confirm the Indians.

In addition to the towns which can be classified in this manner, albeit a rough one, several towns and town chiefs are mentioned which are known to belong to the Guale province, but can not be located more accurately. They are the following:

Ahongate, an Indian of Tupiqui. Ahongate "count!" might be an appropriate Creek personal name.

Alpatopo.

Aytochuco, Ytoçuço.

Ayula.

Lonoche (or Donoche), an Indian of Ospo. Lonoche, "Little Lone," is still used as a Creek name.

Olatachahane (perhaps a chief's name).

Olatapotoque, Olata Potoque (given as a town, but perhaps a chief's name). It was near Aytochuco.

Olataylitaba (or two towns, Olata and Litabi).

---

[1] See p. 12.

Olocalpa.
Sulopacaques.
Tamufa.
Ymunapa.

The chief of each Guale town bore the title of mico, a circumstance which, as has been shown, has important bearings in classifying the people in the Muskhogean linguistic group. It appears also that there was a head mico or "mico mayor" for the whole Guale province. In 1596 a chief whom the Spaniards called Don Juan laid claim to the title of head mico of Guale. There is some confusion regarding him, for the text seems to identify him with a Timucua chief. However, this claim elicited from the Spanish Crown a request for an explanation of the term, to which Governor Mendez de Canço replied:

> In regard to your majesty's instructions to report about the pretension of the cacique Don Juan to become head mico, and to explain what that title or dignity is, he informs me himself that the title of head mico means a kind of king of the land, recognized and respected as such by all the caciques in their towns, and whenever he visits one of them, they all turn out to receive him and feast him, and every year they pay him a certain tribute of pearls and other articles made of shells according to the land.

Guale was thus a kind of confederacy with a head chief, more closely centralized in that particular than the Creek confederacy. It does not appear from the Spanish records whether the position of head mico was hereditary or elective, but the latter is indicated. When the Spaniards first came to Guale the head mico seems to have lived in Tolomato, and mention is made of one Don Juanillo, "whose turn it was to be head mico of that province."[1] The friars are said to have brought on the massacre of 1597 by depriving him of this office, but they appear to have conferred it upon one of the same town.[2] There were, however, three or four chiefs of particular estimation, which are spoken of sometimes as lords of different parts of the country, and when the Spaniards organized a native army to punish those who had killed the friars, it was placed in charge of the chief of Asao, who was head of the southern group of towns. In the narrative which tells of a visit made to the missions in 1606 by the Bishop of Cuba, Don Diego, chief of Talaxe and Asao, is represented as overlord or "head mico" of the entire province.

Gualdape may perhaps be a form of Guale and the information obtained regarding the people there by the Ayllon colonists applicable rather to the Guale Indians than the Cusabo.[2] In the narratives of the French Huguenot colony of 1562, as we have seen, Guale appears as Ouadé and a neighboring town or tribe is mentioned called Couexis.[3] All that the French have to tell us about these

[1] One Spanish document registers the primacy of Tolomato in these words: "La lengua de Guale de que es mico y cabeça Tolomato."
[2] See p. 41.
[3] See p. 50.

two I have given and I have recorded Menéndez's visit to Guale and the settlement of Jesuit missionaries there and at St. Helena. In his letter to Menéndez, quoted above, Rogel says:

Brother Domingo Augustin was in Guale more than a year, and he learned that language so well that he even wrote a grammar, and he died; and Father Sedeño was there 14 months, and the father vice provincial 6, Brother Francisco 10, and Father Alamo 4; and all of them have not accomplished anything.[1]

Had the grammar of Augustin been preserved we would not to-day consider the labors of these early missionaries by any means fruitless; and it may yet come to light.

In 1573 a Spanish officer named Aguilar and fourteen or fifteen soldiers were killed in the province of Guale. In 1578 Captain Otalona and other officials were killed in the Guale town of Ospogue or Espogue.[2]

After this field had been abandoned by the Society of Jesus it was entered by the Franciscans. According to Barcia, missions were opened in Guale by them in 1594, but unpublished documents seem to set a still earlier date. One of these would place the beginning of the work as far back as 1587. In 1597 there were five missionaries in this province and the work seemed to be of the utmost promise, when a rebellion broke out against the innovators, the mission stations were burned, and all but one of the friars killed. The following account contained in Barcia's Florida is from clerical sources:

The friars of San Francisco busied themselves for two years in preaching to the Indians of Florida, separated into various provinces. In the town of Tolemaro or Tolemato lived the friar Pedro de Corpa, a notable preacher, and deputy of that doctrina, against whom rose the elder son and heir of the chief of the island of Guale, who was exceedingly vexed at the reproaches which Father Corpa made to him, because although a Christian, he lived worse than a Gentile, and he fled from the town because he was not able to endure them. He returned to it within a few days, at the end of September [1597], bringing many Indian warriors, with bows and arrows, their heads ornamented with great plumes, and entering in the night, in profound silence, they went to the house where the father lived; they broke down the feeble doors, found him on his knees, and killed him with an axe. This unheard-of atrocity was proclaimed in the town; and although some showed signs of regret, most, who were as little disturbed, apparently, as the son of the chief, joined him, and he said to them the day following: "Although the friar is dead he would not have been if he had not prevented us from living as before we were Christians: let us return to our ancient customs, and let us prepare to defend ourselves against the punishment which the governor of Florida will attempt to inflict upon us, and if this happens it will be as rigorous for this friar alone as if we had finished all; because he will pursue us in the same manner on account of the friar whom we have killed as for all."

Those who followed him in the newly executed deed approved; and they said that it could not be doubted that he would want to take vengeance for one as he would take it for all. Then the barbarian continued: "Since the punishment on account of one is not going to be greater than for all, let us restore the liberty of which these friars

---

[1] Ruidiaz, La Florida, II, p. 307; Barcia, La Florida, pp. 138–139.

[2] Lowery, MSS.

have robbed us, with promises of benefits which we have not seen, in hope of which they wish that those of us who call ourselves Christians experience at once the losses and discomforts: they take from us women, leaving us only one and that in perpetuity, prohibiting us from changing her; they obstruct our dances, banquets, feasts, celebrations, fires, and wars, so that by failing to use them we lose the ancient valor and dexterity inherited from our ancestors; they persecute our old people calling them witches; even our labor disturbs them, since they want to command us to avoid it on some days, and be prepared to execute all that they say, although they are not satisfied; they always reprimand us, injure us, oppress us, preach to us, call us bad Christians, and deprive us of all happiness, which our ancestors enjoyed, with the hope that they will give us heaven. These are deceptions in order to subject us, in holding us disposed after their manner; already what can we expect, except to be slaves? If now we kill all of them, we will remove such a heavy yoke immediately, and our valor will make the governor treat us well, if it happens that he does not come out badly." The multitude was convinced by his speech; and as a sign of their victory, they cut off Father Corpa's head, and they put it in the port[1] on a lance, as a trophy of their victory, and the body they threw into a forest, where it was never found.

They passed to the town of Topiqui, where lived Fr. Blàs Rodriguez (Torquemada gives him the appelation of de Montes), they went in suddenly, telling him they came to kill him. Fr. Blàs asked them to let him say mass first, and they suspended their ferocity for that brief time; but as soon as he had finished saying it, they gave him so many blows, that they finished him, and they threw his body outside, so that the birds and beasts might eat it, but none came to it except a dog, which ventured to touch it, and fell dead. An old Christian Indian took it up and gave it burial in the woods.

From there they went to the town of Assopo, in the island of Guale, where were Fr. Miguél de Auñon, and Fr. Antonio Badajoz; they knew beforehand of their coming, and seeing that flight was impossible, Fr. Miguél began to say mass, and administered the sacrament to Fr. Antonio, and both began to pray. Four hours afterward the Indians entered, killed friar Antonio instantly with a club (*macana*); and afterward gave friar Miguél two blows with it, and, leaving the bodies in the same place, some Christain Indians buried them at the foot of a very high cross, which the same friar Miguél had set up in the country.

The Indians, continuing their cruelty, set out with great speed for the town of Asao where lived friar Francisco de Velascola, native of Castro-Urdiales, a very poor and humble monk, but with such forcefulness that he caused the Indians great fear: he was at that time in the city of St. Agustine. Great was the disappointment of the Indians, because it appeared to them that they had done nothing if they left the friar Francisco alive. They learned in the town the day when he would return to it, went to the place where he was to disembark, and some awaited him hidden in a clump of rushes, near the bank. Friar Francisco arrived in a canoe, and, dissimulating, they surrounded him and took him by the shoulders, giving him many blows, with clubs (*macanas*) and axes, until his soul was restored to God.

They passed to the town of Ospo, where lived friar Franciso Davila,[2] who as soon as he heard the noise at the doors was able under cover of night to go out into the country; the Indians followed him, and although he had hidden himself in some rushes, by the light of the moon they pierced his shoulders with three arrows; and wishing to continue until they had finished him, an Indian interposed, in order to possess himself of his poor clothing, which he had to do in order that they might leave him, who took him bare and well bound, and he was carried to a town of infidel Indians to serve as a slave. These cruelties did not fail to receive the punishment of God; for many of those who were concerned in these martyrdoms hung themselves with their bow-

[1] This word, puerto, may be a misprint of puerta, gate.

[2] This name is given farther on as de Avila or Avila. See p. 87.

strings, and others died wretchedly; and upon that province God sent a great famine of which many perished, as will be related.

The good success of these Indians caused others to unite with them, and they undertook to attack the island of San Pedro with more than 40 canoes, in order to put an end to the monks who were there, and destroy the chief, who was their enemy. They embarked, provided with bows, arrows, and clubs; and, considering the victory theirs, they discovered, near the island, a brigantine, which was in the harbor where they were to disembark, and they assumed that it had many people and began to debate about returning. The brigantine had arrived within sight of the island 30 days before with succor of bread and other things, which the monks needed; but they had not been able to reach the port, although those who came in it tried it many times, nor to pass beyond, on account of a bar (caño) which formed itself from the mainland (?) a thing which had never happened before in that sea. It carried only one soldier, and the other people were sailors, and even less than the number needed for navigation.

Finding the Indian rebels in this confusion the chief of the island went out to defend himself with a great number of canoes.[1] He attacked them with great resolution; and although they tried to defend themselves, their attempt was in vain, they fled, and those who were unable to jumped ashore; and the chief, collecting some of his enemies' canoes, returned triumphantly to his island, and the friars gave him many presents, with which he remained as satisfied as with his victory.

Of the others who had sprung to land none escaped, because they had no canoes in which they might return; some hung themselves with their bowstrings, and others died of hunger in the woods.

Nor were those exempt who escaped, because the governor of Florida, learning of the atrocities of the Indians, went forth to punish the evildoers; but he was only able to burn the cornfields, because the aggressors retired to the marshes, and the highlands prevented him from punishing them, except with the famine which followed immediately the burning of the harvests, of which many Indians died. . . .

The Indians kept the friar Francisco de Avila in strict confinement, ill-treating him much; afterwards they left him more liberty in order to bring water and wood, and watch the fields. They turned him over to the boys so that they might shoot arrows at him; and although the wounds were small, they drained him of blood, because he was not able to stop the blood; this apostolic man suffering these outrages with great patience and serenity. . . .

Wearied of the sufferings of Father Avila the Indians determined to burn him alive. They tied him to a post, and put much wood under him. When about to burn him, there came to the chief one of the principal Indian women, whose son the Spaniards held captive in the city of St. Agustine without her having been able to find any way to rescue him although she had tried it. This moved her to beg the chief earnestly that he should give friar Francisco to her to exchange him for her son. Other Indians, who desired to see him free, begged the same thing; and although it cost them much urging to appease the hatred of the chief for the father, he granted what the Indian woman asked, giving him to her so badly treated, that he arrived at St. Agustine in such a condition that they did not recognize him: he had endured such great and such continuous labors. He accomplished the exchange, and the people of the city expressed a great deal of sympathy for friar Francisco.

God wished to give a greater punishment to the Indians of Florida, who killed the missionaries so unjustly; and, refusing water to the earth, upon the burning of the crops, there began such a great famine in Florida that the conspirators died miserably themselves, confessing the cause of their misfortune to have been the barbarity, which they exercised against the Franciscan monks.[2]

---

[1] It appears from unpublished Spanish documents that he sent two canoes against two which the enemy had dispatched in advance.

[2] Barcia, La Florida, pp. 170–172.

Davila was liberated in 1599, and Barcia speaks as if the famine occurred the year following.

A letter containing an account of this uprising and accompanied by testimony taken from several witnesses is preserved among the Spanish archives and a copy of this is in the Lowery collection. While less dramatic, naturally, than the narrative given, it differs in no essential particulars. The governor's punitive expedition was in 1597 or very early in 1598. He burned the principal Guale towns, including their granaries, and quickly reduced the greater part of the people to submission. In a letter of date 1600 he says:

> No harm, not even death, that I have inflicted upon them has had as much weight in bringing them to obedience as the act of depriving them of their means of subsistence.

In the same letter he has some additional information regarding the causes of the war which do not appear in the communications of the missionaries. He states that it was Don Juanillo's turn to be head mico of Guale, but—

> owing to his being a quarrelsome and warlike young man, he was deprived of that dignity by the Rev. Friars Pedro de Corpa and Blas Rodriguez, who conferred it upon Don Francisco, a man of age and of good and humble habits. And this caused the massacre of the friars, among whom were the two mentioned. Although in the depositions that I took from several Indians in regard to that massacre they all affirmed that to have been the direct cause for the commission of that crime, yet I never allowed it to be written, as I could not consent to have anything derogatory to the priests made public, and besides I look upon the Indians as being very little truthful and to cover their treachery would invent many lies.

Yet it is strange that Don Juanillo and Don Francisco were both leaders of the hostile Indians, and were irreconcilable to the last.[1]

The chief of Espogache was among the first to surrender and he was quickly followed by others. In a letter written April 24, 1601, Gov. de Canço states that the chief of Asao and 40 Indians had just come to tender their submission and that all had given in except the chief of Tolomato, his nephew, and two other chiefs.[2] Later the same year the governor induced the chief of Asao to head an expedition against this refractory element, he being one of the chiefs of most consideration in the province. This mico solicited assistance from the chiefs of Tulufina, Guale, Espogache, Yoa, Ufalague, Talapo, Olata Potoque, Ytoçuço, the chiefs of the Salchiches, the Tama, and the Cusabo. Don Juanillo and his partisans had established themselves in a stockaded town called Yfusinique and met the first attack of their more numerous foes so valiantly that many of them were killed. The allied chiefs then decided that a general assault would be necessary, and this was successful. Don Juanillo and Don Francisco were killed and their scalps taken and with them fell great

[1] The above material is from the Brooks and Lowery MSS. in the Library of Congress.

[2] Serrano y Sanz, Doc. Hist., p. 161.

numbers of their warriors, including 24 principal men. The remainder were taken back to Tamufa, from which the expedition had started.[1]

In a report on his missionary work dated September 15, 1602, Fray Baltazar Lopez, who was stationed at San Pedro, says that there were then no missionaries in the province of Guale, but more than 1,200 Christian Indians.[2]

In 1604, as we have seen, in November, Gov. Pedro de Ibarra visited San Simon, Sapelo, and Guale. One of his objects was to listen to complaints and compose differences, but he represented as almost equally important his desire to see the province Christianized. By that time a church had been built at Asao, on or near San Simon, and another in Guale, while a third was to be constructed at Espogache near Sapelo. Ibarra was accompanied on this expedition by Fray Pedro Ruiz, then in charge of the doctrina at San Pedro, who said mass in each place.[3] When the Bishop of Cuba visited Florida in 1606 Ruiz was in immediate charge of the doctrina of Guale, and Fray Diego Delgado was located at the doctrina of Talaxe, close to Asao, from which he occasionally visited Espogache. The province of Guale was soon thoroughly missionized and work there continued until the practical destruction of the province in the latter part of the century. In a letter of 1608 we find a note to the effect that five Guale chiefs had rebelled, but nothing more is said about the disturbance, which must have been of small consequence. Another letter, dated April 16, 1645, states that the Indians of Guale were then in insurrection, but could be readily reduced.[2] The list of Florida missions, made in 1655, mentions four or five belonging to the province of Guale, San Buenaventura de Boadalquivi [Guadalquini] on Jekyl Island, Santo Domingo de Talaje on or near the present St. Simons, San Josef de Zapala on or near Sapelo, Santa Catarina de Guale on St. Catherines Island, and perhaps Santiago de Ocone, which is said to have been on an island 30 leagues from St. Augustine, and therefore perhaps near Jekyl Island.[4] It is evident that the attacks of the northern Indians, which were soon to put an end to the missions entirely, had begun at this date, because we find Santiago, mico of Tolomato, and his people located 3 leagues from St. Augustine, between two creeks, evidently those called San Diego Tolomato, or North River, and Guana. This was the mission station of Nuestra Señora de Guadalupe de Tolomato, which appears again in the list of 1680. In 1661, as we learn by letters from Gov. D. Alonso de Aranguiz y Cotes to the king, Guale was invaded by Indians, "said to be Chichumecos," but probably, as we shall see, Yuchi. From the letter of a soldier setting forth his

[1] Lowery and Brooks, MSS., Lib. Cong.

[2] Lowery, MSS.

[3] Serrano y Sanz, Doc. Hist., pp. 164–193.

[4] See p. 322; and Serrano y Sanz, Doc. Hist., p. 132.

past services it appears that these strangers sacked the churches and convents and killed many Christian Indians, but were driven off by a force sent from St. Augustine.[1]

When South Carolina was settled, in the year 1670, the English found the post and missions about Port Royal abandoned, but those in Guale still flourishing. In a letter to Lord Ashley, dated the same year, William Owen says:

There are only foure [Spanish missionaries] betweene us and St. Augustines. Our next neighbour is he of Wallie wch ye Spaniard calls St Katarina who hath about 300? Indians att his devoir. With him joyne ye rest of ye Brotherhood and cann muster upp from 700 hundred Indians besides those of ye main they vpon any vrgent occasions shall call to their assistance, they by these Indians make warr with any other people yt disoblige them and yet seem not to be concerned in ye matter.[2]

In addition to Nuestra Señora de Guadalupe de Tolomato, four Guale missions appear in the mission list of 1680, viz, San Buenaventura de Ovadalquini, Santo Domingo de Assaho, San Joseph de Capala, and Santa Cathalina de Guale. They were placed in one province with two Timucua missions, the whole being called the Provincia de Guale y Mocama.[1] Mocama means "on the sea" in Timucua, the Timucua towns in this province being on and near the Atlantic.

Through a letter written to the court of Spain May 14, 1680, we learn that the "Chichumecos, Uchizes, and Chiluques (i. e., the Yuchi, Creeks, and Cherokee) had made friends with the English and had jointly attacked two of the Guale missions. The writer says that (apparently in the year preceding):

They entered all together, first that on the island of Guadalquini, belonging to said province [of Guale]. There they caused several deaths, but when the natives appeared led by my lieutenant, to defend themselves, they retired and within a few days they entered the island of Santa Catalina, capital and frontier post, against these enemies. They were over three hundred men strong, and killed the guard of six men, with the exception of one man who escaped and gave the alarm, thus enabling the inhabitants of that village to gather for their defense. They consisted of about 40 natives and five Spaniards of this garrison, who occupied the convent of the friar of that doctrina, where a few days previously captain Francisco Fuentes, my lieutenant of that province had arrived. He planned their defense so well and with such great courage that he kept it up from dawn until 4 p. m. with sixteen Indians who had joined him with their firearms (on this occasion I considered it important that the Indians should carry firearms). As soon as I was advised of what had occurred I sent assistance, the first three days ahead. Then I sent a body of about thirty men and a boat with thirteen people, including the sailors, but when they arrived the enemy had retreated. . I am assured that among them [the enemies] there came several Englishmen who instructed them, all armed with long shotguns, which caused much horror to those natives, who abandoned the island of Santa Catalina. I am told that they might return to live there if the garrison be doubled. As I have heard that they had eight men there from this garrison, I have resolved to send as many as

[1] Lowery, MSS. [2] S. Car. Hist. Soc. Colls., v, p. 198.

twenty, because it is very important to support the province of Guale for the sake of this garrison, as well for its safety and conservation as for its subsistence and protection against invasion as it is the provider of this garrison on account of its abundance and richness compared with this place which is so poor. I am always afraid that they might penetrate by the sandbar of Zapata [Zapala].[1]

That the friars were not in all cases protectors of the Indians appears from a letter written to Governor Cabrera by "the casique of the province of Guale," dated May 5, 1681, complaining of their arbitrary and overbearing attitude. Cabrera was, however, no lover of friars. Meantime the pressure of the northern Indians continued. Cabrera, in a letter dated December 8, 1680, speaks of what appears to have been a second invasion of Guale by the English and "Chuchumecos," and in one of June 14, 1681, he states that some Guale Indians had taken to the woods, while others had assembled in the Florida towns farther south, the town of Carlos, "40 leagues from St. Augustine," being particularly mentioned. Several invasions appear to have taken place at about this time and a letter, written March 20, 1683, states that Guale had been totally ruined by them.[2]

In 1682 the South Carolina Documents refer to "the nations of Spanish Indians, which they call Sapalla, Soho [Asaho], and Sapicbay," and from the identity of the first two it is probable that all were Guale tribes.[3]

We now come to the final abandonment of Guale, both by Spaniards and Indians; and here our authorities do not agree. Barcia, presumably relying upon documents to which no one else has had access, states that the governor of Florida wished to remove the Indians forcibly to islands nearer St. Augustine, whereupon they rebelled and took to the woods or passed over to the English. Certain manuscript authorities, however, represent the removal as having been at the request of the Indians themselves, and the raid upon St. Catherines mentioned above doubtless had something to do with it. Barcia's account runs thus:

[Don Juan Marquez] had occasioned a rebellion of the Indians of the towns of San Felipe, San Simon, Santa Catalina, Sapala, Tupichihasao, Obaldaquini, and others, because he wanted to move them to the islands of Santa Maria, San Juan, and Santa Cruz, and in order to escape this transplantation many fled to the forests, and others passed to the province of S. Jorge, or Carolina, a colony made shortly before by the English in the country of the Spaniards, upon which Virginia joins, and bordering upon Apalachicolo, Caveta, and Casica . . . [4]

The name Tupichihasao seems to combine the names of the towns Topiqui and Asao (or Hasao), which were probably run together in copying. The latter was on or near St. Simons Island and may be

[1] Serrano y Sanz, Doc. Hist., pp. 216–219.

[2] Lowery, MSS., Lib. Cong.

[3] MS., Pub. Rec. of S. C., II, 8.

[4] Barcia, La Florida, p. 287.

merely the Indian name of the St. Simons mission. The San Felipe mission must have been a comparatively new one; it evidently had nothing to do with the former Fort Felipe at St. Helena, which had been long abandoned.

An entirely different view of this Indian movement is given in a letter from the King of Spain, dated September 9, 1688, from which it appears that the chiefs and natives of Guale had asked to be settled where they could enjoy more quiet and had chosen the islands of San Pedro, Santa Maria, and San Juan. It was, however, decided to assign them the last two of these, and instead of San Pedro a third nearer St. Augustine, called Santa Cruz.[1]

An interesting glimpse of these missions is furnished us by the Quaker Dickenson in 1699, when he and his companions who had been shipwrecked on the southeast coast of Florida passed north from St. Augustine on their way to Carolina. He says:

Taking our departure from Augustine [Sept. 29] we had about 2 or 3 leagues to an Indian town called St. a Cruce, where, being landed, we were directed to the Indian warehouse [town house]. It was built round, having 16 squares,[2] and on each square a cabin [3] built and painted, which would hold two people, the house being about 50 feet diameter; and in the middle of the top was a square opening about 15 feet. This house was very clean; and fires being ready made nigh our cabin, the Spanish captain made choice of cabins for him and his soldiers and appointed us our cabins. In this town they have a friar and a large house to worship in, with three bells; and the Indians go as constantly to their devotions at all times and seasons, as any of the Spaniards. Night being come and the time of their devotion over, the friar came in, and many of the Indians, both men and women, and they had a dance according to their way and custom. We had plenty of Casseena drink, and such victuals as the Indians had provided for us, some bringing corn boiled, others pease; some one thing, some another; of all which we made a good supper, and slept till morning.

This morning early [Sept. 30] we left this town, having about 2 leagues to go with the canoes, and then we were to travel by land; but a cart was provided to carry our provisions and necessaries, in which those that could not travel were carried. We had about 5 leagues to a sentinel's house, where we lay all night, and next morning travelled along the sea shore about 4 leagues to an inlet. Here we waited for canoes to come for us, to carry us about 2 miles to an Indian town called St. Wan's [San Juan's], being on an island. We went through a skirt of wood into the plantations, for a mile. In the middle of this island is the town, St. Wan's, a large town and many people; they have a friar and worship house. The people are very industrious, having plenty of hogs, fowls, and large crops of corn, as we could tell by their corn houses. The Indians brought us victuals as at the last town, and we lay in their warehouse, which was larger than at the other town.

This morning [Oct. 2] the Indians brought us victuals for breakfast, and the friar gave my wife some loaves of bread made of Indian corn which was somewhat extraordinary; also a parcel of fowls.

About 10 o'clock in the forenoon we left St. Wan's walking about a mile to the sound; here were canoes and Indians ready to transport us to the next town. We did

[1] Brooks, MSS. Miss Brooks has given the name of this king as Philip IV, but he was long dead and Charles II was on the throne. For the location of these islands see p. 51 and plate 1.

[2] This term seems to be applied to the spaces between the vertical wall timbers.

[3] Old name for a bed raised on posts close to the wall of an Indian house.

believe we might have come all the way along the sound, but the Spaniards were not willing to discover the place to us.

An hour before sun set we got to the town call'd St. Mary's. This was a frontier and garrison town; the inhabitants are Indians with some Spanish soldiers. We were conducted to the ware house, as the custom is, every town having one: we understood these houses were either for their times of mirth and dancing, or to lodge and entertain strangers. The house was about 31 feet diameter,[1] built round, with 32 squares; in each square a cabin about 8 feet long, of good height, painted and well matted. The centre of the building is a quadrangle of 20 feet, being open at the top, against which the house is built. In this quadrangle is the place they dance, having a great fire in the middle. In one of the squares is the gate way or passage. The women natives of these towns clothe themselves with the moss of trees, making gowns and petticoats thereof, which at a distance, or in the night, looks very neat. The Indian boys we saw were kept to school in the church, the friar being their schoolmaster. This was the largest town of all, and about a mile from it was another called St. Philip's. At St. Mary's we were to stay till the 5th or 6th inst. Here we were to receive our 60 roves of corn and 10 of pease. While we staid we had one half of our corn beaten into meal by the Indians, the other we kept whole, not knowing what weather we should have. . . . We got of the Indians plenty of garlick and long pepper, to season our corn and pease, both of which are griping and windy, and we made wooden trays and spoons to eat with. We got rushes and made a sort of plaited rope thereof; the use we intended it for, was to be serviceable to help us in building huts or tents with, at such times as we should meet with hard weather . . .

We departed this place [Oct. 6] and put into the town of St. Philip's, where the Spanish Captain invited us on shore to drink Casseena, which we did: the Spaniards, having left something behind, we staid here about an hour, and then set forward.

About 2 or 3 leagues from hence we came in sight of an Indian town called Sappataw."[2]

"Sappataw" is probably a misprint for Sappalaw, i. e., Sapelo. Some, and probably all, of these missions were on the sites of former missions occupied by Timucua, but most of the latter Indians must have died out or been removed. At least, Dickenson says in two places that the Indians living there were "related" to the Yamasee then in Carolina.[3]

If Barcia may be trusted, a considerable number of Guale Indians fled to South Carolina at the time when the remainder of the tribe was removed to Florida. In 1702 a second outbreak occurred, resulting, apparently, in the reunion of all of the Guale natives on Savannah River, in the edge of the English colony and under the lead of the Yamasee. These two rebellions are indicated in the legend on an early Spanish map which states that the Spaniards occupied San Felipe, Guale, and Sapelo until 1686, when they withdrew to St. Simons, and that in 1702 St. Simons was also abandoned. It is clear, however, from Dickenson's narrative that the Georgia coast had been practically given up in his time, so that the "withdrawal"

---

[1] This figure is too small, perhaps due to a misprint; 32 squares 8 feet long would mean a circumference of 256 feet and a diameter of 70–80 feet. The figure 3 in 31 is probably a misprint for 8 as suggested by Bushnell (see below).

[2] Dickenson, Narrative, pp. 90–94. See D. I. Bushnell, Jr., in Bull. 69, Bur. Amer. Ethn., pp. 84–85, who gives diagrammatic plans of the town houses.

[3] Dickenson, Narrative, pp. 94, 96.

from St. Simons meant in reality the removal of the remaining Guale Indians from Florida. Probably most of those who fled to the English at the earlier date were from the northern part of the Georgia coast, while those who went to Florida were principally from St. Simons and other southern missions. Even in 1702 a few probably remained under the Spanish government until their kinsmen shifted their allegiance once more in 1715. The only specific reference to this second outbreak that has come to my attention is contained in a letter written from London, about 1715, by Juan de Ayala, who says:

> In the year 1702 the native Indians of all the provinces of San Agustin, who since its discovery had been converted to the Catholic faith, and maintained as subjects of his Majesty, revolted, and, forsaking that religion, sought the protection of the English of Carolina, with whom they have remained ever since, continually harassing the Catholic Indians.[1]

This revolt was due, in part, to compulsion exercised by the English and their allies, in part it was an unavoidable "taking to the woods," through the failure of the Spaniards to protect their proteges, and in part it came from the prestige which success brought the victorious English. The underlying cause was the unwillingness on the part of the Spaniards to allow their Indians the use of firearms and a niggardly home policy, which left Florida insufficiently defended. It is doubtful how far the Timucua tribes engaged in this secession. At any rate they did not go in such numbers as to attract the attention of the English. The Apalachee and the people of Guale remained distinct. The fortunes of those Guale Indians who remained in Florida from the time of the rebellion until they were rejoined by their kinsmen who had gone to Carolina will be considered when we come to speak of the Timucua, probably constituting the largest portion of the Indians who were true to Spain.

From this time on the name Guale practically disappears, and the people who formerly bore it are almost invariably known as Yamasee. It has been thought by recent investigators that the people of Guale and the Yamasee were identical, but facts contained in the Spanish archives show that this is incorrect. They make it plain that the Yamasee were an independent tribe from very early times, belonging, as Barcia states, to the province of Guale, or perhaps rather to its outskirts, but not originally a dominant tribe of the province. It was only in later years that by taking the lead among the hostile Indians their name came to supersede that of Guale and of every band of Guale Indians. They are not mentioned frequently until late, and it is only by piecing together bits of information from various quarters that we can get any idea of their history.

---

[1] Brooks, MSS.

For our first notice we must go back to the very beginning of Spanish exploration on the Atlantic coast of North America, to the list of "provinces" for which Francisco of Chicora was responsible. In this list, as previously noted,[1] we find one province called "Yamiscaron," which there is every reason to believe refers to the tribe we have under discussion. The peculiar ending suggests a form which appears again in Yamacraw and which it is difficult to account for in a tribe supposed to be Muskhogean and without a true phonetic *r* in the language. I can explain it only by supposing that it was originally taken from the speech of the Siouan neighbors of these people to the northeast.[2]

April 4, 1540, De Soto's army came to a province called by Biedma "the Province of Altapaha." Elvas gives it as "the town of Altamaca," but Ranjel has the correct form Altamaha. The last mentioned speaks as if the Spaniards did not pass through the main town, but they received messengers from the chief, who furnished them with food and had them transported across a river. This was probably the river which Biedma says encouraged them because it flowed east instead of south. Ranjel seems to imply that Altamaha, like a neighboring chief called Çamumo, was the subject of "a great chief whose name was Ocute" (the Hitchiti).[3] The significance in this encounter is due to the fact that Altamaha afterwards appears as the head town of the Lower Yamasee. From Ranjel's statement it would seem that the Yamasee were at this time connected with the Hitchiti, whereas the language of the Guale people proper was somewhat different.

The next reference comes in a letter dated November 15, 1633, and is as follows: "The Amacanos Indians have approached the Province of Apalache and desire missionaries." [4] August 22, 1639, Gov. Damian de la Vega Castro y Pardo writes that he has made peace between the Apalachee on one side and the "Chacatos [Chatot], Apalachocolos [Lower Creeks], and Amacanos." [5] These last references indicate that while the Yamasee may have been theoretically in the Province of Guale, they rather belonged to its hinterland and, as presently appears, were not missionized or affected much by European influences. In 1670 William Owen speaks of them as allies of the Spaniards living south of the Cusabo.[6] They come to light next in Spanish documents, this time unequivocally, in a letter of Gov. Don Pablo de Hita Salazar, dated March 8, 1680. He says:

It has come to the notice of his honor that some Yamasee Indians, infidels (unos yndios Yamasis ynfieles), who are in the town which was that of San Antonio de Anacape, have asked for a minister to teach them our holy Catholic faith.[7]

[1] See p. 37.

[2] But see p. 108.

[3] Bourne, Narr. of De Soto, I, p. 56; II, pp. 10, 89-90.

[4] Lowery, MSS.

[5] Ibid.; also Serrano y Sanz, Doc. Hist., pp. 198-199.

[6] See p. 67.

[7] Lowery, MSS.

This mission was 20 leagues from St. Augustine, evidently that called Antonico in the Fresh Water district, and the governor entrusted these Yamasee at first to the care of Fray Bartholome de Quiñones, Padre and Doctrinero del Pueblo de Maiaca, which was 16 leagues beyond. These Yamasee explain why the station of San Antonio is called a "new conversion" in the mission list of 1680, although it existed at a very much earlier period as a Timucua mission.[1] The application of the term "infidels" to them is significant; had they been from the coast district of Guale they would in all probability have been Christianized by this time. The name Nombre de Dios de Amacarisse, which also occurs in the mission list of 1680, indicates still another body of Yamasee in that old station.[1] Fairbanks calls it Macarisqui and speaks of it as the principal town.[2] Barcia [3] spells it Mascarasi and says it was within 600 yards (varas) of St. Augustine, which would agree with the known situation of Nombre de Dios. The next we hear of them the Yamasee have taken the lead among those Indians which sought refuge near the English colony of Carolina and they became so prominent that the English do not appear to have been aware that any other Indians accompanied them.

In a letter to the Spanish monarch, dated London, October 20, 1734, Fray Joseph Ramos Escudero seems to attribute their primacy to encouragement given the Yamasee by the English and the supplies of clothing and arms with which they provided them.[4]

In the copy of this letter made by Miss Brooks the name of the tribe is consistently spelled Llamapas, but there can be no question regarding its identity. The original *Y* has been transposed into a double *l* and the old style *ss* into *p*. Escudero explains their removal from the Spanish colony by saying that these Yamasee "had a grudge against a certain governor of Florida on account of having ill treated their chief by words and deeds, because the latter, owing to the sickness of his superior, had failed one year to send to the city of St. Augustine, Florida, a certain number of men for the cultivation of the lands as he was obliged to do."

Another account of the rebellion is given by Barcia. Referring to the colony of South Carolina, he says:

Some Indians fled to this province because the English who occupied it had persuaded them to give them obedience, instead of to the king; especially the chief of the Iamacos, a nation which lived in the province of Guale, becoming offended at the governor, without being placated by the strong persuasions and repeated kindnesses which the Franciscan missionaries showed to him in the year 1684, for despising all

[1] Lowery, MSS.

[2] G. R. Fairbanks, Hist. of St. Augustine, p. 125. The name of this town helps explain the later "Yamacraw." (See p. 108.)

[3] Barcia, La Florida, p. 240.

[4] Brooks, MSS.

he withdrew to his country and afterwards gave obedience to the English settled in Santa Elena and San Jorge, other Indians following him; and not satisfied with this lapse of faith, he returned the following year to the province of Timuqua or Timagoa to make war, plundered the Doctrina of Santa Catalina, carried off the furnishings of the church and convent of San Francisco, burned the town, inflicted grievous death on many Indians, and carried back other prisoners to Santa Elena, where he made slaves of them, which invasion was so unexpected that it could not be foreseen nor prevented . . .[1]

Early South Carolina documents speak of 10 Yamasee towns there, 5 upper towns headed by Pocotaligo, and 5 lower towns headed by Altamahaw or Aratomahaw.[2] The new settlers were given a strip of land back of Port Royal on the northeast side of the Savannah River, which, long after they had vacated it, was still known as "the Indian land." The following names of chiefs or "kings" are given in the South Carolina documents and these evidently refer to their towns: The Pocotalligo king, the Altamahaw king, the Yewhaw king, the Huspaw king, the Chasee king, the Pocolabo king, the Ilcombe king, and the Dawfuskee king,[3] though the identity of this last is a little uncertain. The "Peterba king" mentioned among those killed in the Tuscarora war in 1712 was also probably a Yamasee, though he may have been an Apalachee. There were 87 Yamasee among Col. Barnwell's Indian allies in the Tuscarora expedition.[4]

In 1715 the Yamasee war broke out, the most disastrous of all those which the two Carolina settlements had to face. The documents of South Carolina show clearly that the immediate cause of this uprising was the misconduct of some English traders, but it is evident that the enslavement of Indians, carried on by Carolina traders in an ever more open and unscrupulous manner, was bound to produce such an explosion sooner or later. The best contemporary narratives of this revolt are to be found in "An Account of Missionaries Sent to South Carolina, the Places to Which They Were Appointed, Their Labours and Success, etc.," and in "An Account of the Breaking Out of the Yamassee War, in South Carolina, extracted from the Boston News, of the 13th of June, 1715," both contained in Carroll's Historical Collections of South Carolina.[5] The following is from the first of these documents:

In the year 1715, the Indians adjoining to this colony, all round from the borders of Fort St. Augistino to Cape Fear, had formed a conspiracy to extirpate the white people. This war broke out the week before Easter [actually on April 15]. The parish of St. Helen's had some apprehensions of a rising among the adjoining Indians, called the Yammosees. On Wednesday before Easter, Captain Nairn, agent among the Indians,

[1] Barcia, La Florida, p. 287.
[2] Proc. Board dealing with Indian Trade, MS., pp. 46 and 47.
[3] Ibid., pp. 55, 58, 81, 102; Council Records, MS., VI, p. 159; VII, p. 186; X, p. 177.
[4] S. Car. Hist. and Gen. Mag., 9, pp. 30–31.
[5] Vol. II, pp. 538–576.

went, with some others, to them [and it appears by direct commission of Governor Craven who had rumors of trouble], desiring to know the reason of their uneasiness, that if any injury had been done them, they might have satisfaction made them. The Indians pretended to be well content, and not to have any designs against the English. Mr. Nairn therefore and the other traders continued in the Pocotaligat-Town, one of the chief of the Yammosee nations. At night they went to sleep in the round-house, with the King and chief War-Captains, in seeming perfect friendship; but next morning, at break of day, they were all killed with a volley of shot, excepting one man and a boy, who providentially escaped (the man much wounded) to Port-Royal, and gave notice of the rising of the Indians to the inhabitants of St. Helen's. Upon this short warning, a ship happening to be in the river, a great number of the inhabitants, about 300 souls, made their escape on board her to Charles-Town, and among the rest, Mr. Guy, the society's missionary; having abandoned all their effects to the savages: some few families fell into their hands, who were barbarously tortured and murdered.

The Indians had divided themselves into two parties; one fell upon Port-Royal, the other upon St. Bartholomew's parish; about 100 Christians fell into their hands, the rest fled, among which [was] the Reverend Mr. Osborn, the society's missionary there. The women and children, with some of the best of their effects, were conveyed to Charles-Town; most of the houses and heavy goods in the parish were burnt or spoil'd. The Yammosees gave the first stroke in this war, but were presently joined by the Appellachee Indians.[1] On the north side of the province, the English had at first, some hopes in the faithfulness of the Calabaws [Catawbas] and Creek Indians, but they soon after declared for the Yammosees.

Upon news of this rising, the governor (the Honourable Charles Craven, Esq.), with all expedition, raised the forces in Colleton county, and with what assistance more could be got presently, put himself at their head, and marched directly to the Indians, and the week after Easter came up with them and attacked them at the head of the river Cambahee; and after a sharp engagement put them to flight, and stopped all farther incursions on that side.[2]

The narrative in the Boston News is as follows:

On Tuesday last arrived here His Majesty's ship *Success*, Captain Meade, Commander, about 12 days' passage from South Carolina, by whom his excellency, our Governor, had a letter from the Honourable Gov. Craven, of South Carolina, acquainting him that all their Indians, made up of many various Nations, consisting of between 1000 to 1200 men, (lately paid obedience to that Government) had shaken off their fidelity, treacherously murdering many of His Majesty's subjects.

Gov. Craven hearing of this rupture, immediately despatched Captain Nairn and Mr. John Cockran, gentlemen well acquainted with the Indians, to know the cause of their discontent, who accordingly on the 15th of April, met the principal part of them at the Yamassee Town, about 130 miles from Charlestown, and after several debates, pro and con, the Indians seemed very ready to come to a good agreement and reconciliation, and having prepared a good supper for our Messengers, all went quietly to rest; but early next morning their lodging was beset with a great number of Indians, who barbarously murdered Captain Nairn and Messieurs John Wright, and Thomas Ruffly, Mr. Cockran and his wife they kept prisoners, whom they afterwards slew. One Seaman Burroughs, a strong robust man, seeing the Indians' cruel barbarity on the other gentlemen, made his way good through the middle of the enemy, they pursuing and firing many shot at him. One took him through the cheek (which is since cured) and coming to a river, he swam through, and alarmed the plantations; so that by his escape, and a merchantman that lay in Port Royal River, that fired some great guns on the Enemy, several Hundreds of English lives were saved.

---

[1] That part of the Apalachee settled near Augusta by Governor Moore in 1703. See p. 124.

[2] Carroll, op. cit., pp. 548-549.

At the same time that Governour Craven despatched Captain Nairn and Mr. Cockran to make enquiry of the rupture between us and the Indians, he got himself a party of horse, and being accompanied with several gentlemen volunteers, intended for the Yamassee Town, in order to have an impartial account of their complaints and grievances, to redress the same, and to rectify any misunderstanding or disorders that might have happened. And on his journey meeting with certain information of the above Murder, and the Rebellion of the Enemy, he got as many men ready as could be got, to the Number of about TWO HUNDRED AND FORTY, designing to march to the Enemies' Head Quarters, and engage them.

At the same time the Governour despatched a Courier to Colonel Mackay, with orders forthwith to raise what forces he could, to go by water and meet him at Yamassee Town. The Governour marched within SIXTEEN miles of said town, and encamped at night in a large Savanna or Plain, by a Wood-side, and was early next morning by break of day saluted with a volley of shot from about FIVE HUNDRED of the enemy; that lay ambuscaded in the Woods, who notwithstanding of the surprise, soon put his men in order, and engaged them so gallantly three quarters of an hour, that he soon routed the enemy; killed and wounded several of them; among whom some of their chief Commanders fell, with the loss on our side of several men wounded, and only John Snow, sentinel, killed. The Governour seeing the great numbers of the enemy, and wanting pilots to guide him over the river, and then having vast woods and swamps to pass through, thought best to return back.

Captain Mackay, in pursuit of his orders, gathered what force he could, and embarked by water, and landing marched to the Indian Yamassee town; and though he was disappointed in meeting the Governour there, yet he surprised and attacked the enemy, and routed them out of their town, where he got vast quantities of provision that they stored up, and what plunder they had taken from the English. Colonel Mackay kept possession of the Town; and soon after hearing that the enemy had got into another fort, where were upwards of 200 Men, he detached out of his Camp about 140 Men, to attack it and engaged them. At which time a young Strippling, named Palmer, with about SIXTEEN Men, who had been out upon a Scout, came to Colonel Mackay's assistance, who, at once, with his men, scaled their walls, and attacked them in their trenches, killed several, but meeting with so warm a reception from the enemy that he was necessitated to make his retreat; yet on a second re-entry with men, he so manfully engaged the enemy as to make them fly their fort. Colonel Mackay being without, engaged them on their flight, where he slew many of them. He has since had many skirmishes with them.

The Governour has placed garrisons in all convenient places that may be, in order to defend the country from depredations and incursions of the enemy, till better can be made. We had about a hundred traders among the Indians, whereof we apprehend they have murdered and destroyed about NINETY Men, and about FORTY more Men we have lost in several skirmishes.[1]

Meanwhile the Indians to the north of the colony had not been idle, and the missionary account already quoted has the following regarding their activities:

In the mean time, on the northern side, the savages made an inroad as far as the plantation of Mr. John Herne, distant 30 miles from Goosecreek; and treacherously killed that gentleman, after he had (upon their pretending peace) presented them with provisions. Upon news of this disaster, a worthy gentleman, Captain Thomas Barker, was sent thither with 90 men on horseback; but by the treachery of an Indian whom he trusted, fell into an ambuscade, in some thick woods, which they must necessarily pass. The Indians fired upon them from behind trees and bushes. The

[1] Carroll, op. cit., pp. 570-572.

English dismounted, and attacked the savages, and repulsed them; but having lost their brave commanding officer, Mr. Barker, and being themselves in some disorder, made their retreat.

Upon this advantage, the Indians came farther on toward Goosecreek, at news of which, the whole parish of Goosecreek became deserted, except two fortified plantations: and the Reverend Dr. Le Jeau, the society's missionary there, fled to Charles-Town.

These northern Indians, being a body of near 400 men, after attacking a small fort in vain, made proposals of peace, which the garrison unwarily hearkening to, admitted several of them into the fort, which they surprised and cut to pieces the garrison, consisting of 70 white people and 40 blacks; a very few escaped. After this they advanced farther, but on the 13th of June, Mr. Chicken, the Captain of the Goosecreek Company, met and attacked them, and after a long action, defeated them, and secured the province on that side from farther ravages.[1]

The northern hostiles probably consisted principally of the Indians of the small Siouan tribes, the Cheraw in particular having been long at odds with the settlers.

In a letter to the Spanish king, already quoted, the monk Escudero says regarding this war:

About seventeen or eighteen years ago the said Indians Llamapas [Yamassas], while being settled at their towns, living quietly and feared by all around these provinces, four English Captains with a body of soldiers descended upon the towns of the said Llamapas, and wanted to count the number of Indians that each town contained. Which upon being noticed by the said Indians they judged that the object of the English was to make slaves of them and one night they revolted against the English, and after having killed them all, captains and soldiers, they went to other English settlements and killed everyone of them, sparing only the women that could be of service to them and the negroes to sell to the Spaniards. Their fury and cruelty was such that they did not even spare the children.[2]

Escudero then passes over the specific events of the war and refers to the removal of the Yamasee to Florida and the reception given them. He is not accurate in all of his statements by any means, but it is interesting to note that a census of all of the Indian tribes, including among them the Yamasee, was actually made a few months before the outbreak. It is to be feared, from the general conduct of the settlers of our Southern States toward the Indians during that period, that their inference from this was only too well justified.

This grand conspiracy of Indian tribes has never been given enough attention by our historians. It was a movement of the same order as the conspiracies of Opechancanough in Virginia, King Philip in New England, the Natchez in Louisiana, and, although on a smaller scale, of Pontiac and Tecumseh, individualism's tribute to cooperation in time of adversity, inspired by a broader insight into the movement of events for the time being, and failing because the unifying tendency is too late, the individualistic instinct too normal and too deep-seated. From what we learn of this particular uprising, from both French and English sources, we know that it

[1] Carroll, op. cit., pp. 549–550.

[2] Brooks, MSS.

was the result of a conspiracy shared by the Creeks, the Choctaw, the Catawba and other Siouan tribes, and probably by the Cherokee. Apparently the only exceptions were the Chickasaw and a few small bands of Indians within the colony of South Carolina itself. Fortunately the greater tribes were at a distance and rested satisfied when they had killed the traders among them and plundered their stores. Fortunately too, the governor of South Carolina and his subordinates acted with promptness and complete success. The Yamasee were handled so severely that they left the country and settled for the most part in Florida, whither their women and children had preceded them. The Indians attacking from the north, probably small tribes only, were driven back. This removed the first line of Indian attack on the colony in short order, and either the more remote hostiles must be prepared to bear the brunt of the fighting if the original project was to be carried out or they must get out of danger. It was one thing to take the part of passive conspirators behind the backs of the Yamasee, but quite another to be the principal performers, especially after the impressive and rapid manner in which their allies had been routed. As a result the more distant tribes immediately quieted down. The Catawba ever after remained staunch friends of the colonists, and the Cherokee resumed peaceful relations with them. To secure themselves against possible reprisals many of the other tribes moved farther from the borders of Carolina, the Apalachee, Oconee, Apalachicola, and part of the Yuchi and Savannah falling back to the Ocmulgee and thence to the Chattahoochee, while the great body of Lower Creeks, who were then living on the Ocmulgee and its branches, also fell back to the Chattahoochee, some of them, apparently, removing as far as the Tallapoosa. Aside from its immediate effects on the colony of South Carolina the Yamasee war is thus of great importance in tracing the history of the Indian tribes of the Southeast, marking as it does a great step in their progressive decline and fall.

From what Escudero says it may be inferred that another cause of the lukewarmness of the Creeks was jealousy of the Yamasee, and, as we shall see when we come to consider the part played in this disturbance by the Apalachee, there was an English as well as a Spanish faction in the Creek Nation. The former apparently obtained control shortly after the beginning of the war.

The part played by the Spaniards in all this was perhaps nothing more than that of passive sympathizers. They may or may not have been aware that a massacre was coming when they received the women and children of the Yamasee, for it was a natural measure of precaution preceding the change of allegiance. Some light is thrown on the events of the time by Juan de Ayala's letter to the Spanish ambassador. He says:

The Governor and Captain General of these provinces [of Florida] at that time reported to H. M. that on the 27th of May of last year [1715?], there had appeared before him, four Indian Caciques of the revolted towns [i. e., those which had previously revolted from the Spaniards], soliciting pardon and permission to return under the dominion of H. M., and to become his subjects, representing one hundred and sixty of their towns [!!]. And that the Governor had granted them pardon in the name of H. M., designating to them the territory they should occupy in order that they might resume the cultivation of their lands in peace and quietness, as they had lived before.[1]

Of their reception in Florida after they had been driven from Carolina, Escudero says:

They came to the provinces of Florida occupied by us, asking to be admitted into the service of our King, which was granted them by that Governor, amidst great rejoicing by the people of that city [St. Augustine]. They founded their towns at a distance of ten and twelve leagues from the said city and were maintained by Y. E. that first year with an abundance of everything, and afterwards by allowing them whatever they asked for to the present day [1734].[1]

Escudero thus sketches the history of these returned Yamasee during the first few years:

Of these Indians, seven or eight of their caciques, not having sufficient confidence in the Spaniards, remained in the depopulated province of Apalache, about a hundred and fifty leagues from St. Augustine, but having heard of the good reception and kind treatment that their companions had received from the Spaniards, asked the governor to send to their towns a few missionary fathers, as they desired to become Christians and subjects of our king.

Missionaries were asked from Spain, and about thirteen years ago, twelve of them were sent to that province of Florida. Upon their arrival in St. Augustine, I was selected, together with ten other clergymen, for that mission. I remained among them, in those deserts, during three years, at which time they had all become Christians.

Just then the Vehipes[2] [Creek] Indians, instigated by the English, came down upon us, but after the loss of some men, I succeeded with my Indians in withdrawing from those woods and falling back upon St. Augustine, where we joined the other Indians of the same nation, so that united we could resist the attacks of the enemy. We formed our towns in that province of Florida, but about seven or eight years ago the enemy again hunted us up and killed many Indians.[3]

A few Yamasee may have gone to live with their northern allies, since Adair mentions their language as one of those spoken in the Catawba confederacy in 1743.[4] Just after the Yamasee war we also hear of Yamasee on "Sapola River,"[5] but we do not know whether this settlement was one of long standing or whether it was a position occupied by some of these people during their retreat to Florida. At any rate, all of those who continued in the Spanish interest were soon united near St. Augustine. Immediately after their removal the English colonists learned that the Huspaw king, a Yamasee chief, had been made general in chief by the Spaniards over 500

[1] Brooks, MSS.

[2] Probably misread from Ochisses.

[3] Brooks, MSS. The attack referred to in the last sentence must have been that by Palmer, detailed farther on.

[4] Adair, Hist. Am. Inds., p. 225.

[5] Pub. Rec. S. C., MS., VI, p. 119.

Indians who were to be sent against Carolina.[1] In 1719 a captive taken by the English testified that there were 60 Yamasee near St. Augustine.[2] In 1722 it is said that they were expelled from St. Augustine because they would not work in the way the Spaniards wished.

From Tobias Fitch's journal we learn that the head chief of the Lower Creeks, whom he calls "Old Brinins," "Old Brunins," or "Old Brmins," sent an expedition against the Yamasee in Florida in 1725. While Fitch was still with him two runners came back and gave the following account of this expedition:

The Pilot that we had, Carried us to a Fort in a Town Where we thought the Yamases were, and we fired at the Said Fort, Which alarmed ten Men that was Placed To Discover us which we past when they were asleep. Our fireing awaked them and they Ran round us and gave Notice to the Yamasees Who was Removed from this town Nigher the Sea and had there Build a new fort which we found and Attacked but with litle Success through it happen'd the Huspaw Kings Family was not all got in the fort and we took three of them and fired Several Shott at the Huspaw king and are in hopes have killed him. There Came out a party of the Yamases who fought us and we took the Capt. We waited three days about there Fort, Expecting to get ane oppertunity to take Some More but to no purpose. We then Came away and the Yamases pursued us. We fought them and gained the Batle. We drove the Yamases unto a pond and was Just Runing in after them where we Should a had a great advantage of them but we discover'd about fourty Spanyards armed on horse Back Who made Toward us wt a White Cloth before them and as they advanced toward us They made Signes that we Should fforbear fireing. Some of our head men gave Out orders not to fire, But Steyamasiechie or Gogel Eys Told them it was spoilt and to fire away. According we did, and the Spanyards fled. After that the Yamases pursued us [and] gave us ane other Batle in which they did us the most Damnadge. We have killed Eight of the Yamases, on of which is the huspaw kings head Warriour and have Brought off all their Scalps. We have likewise Taken nine of them a Live, Together with Several Guns, Some Cloth, and Some plunder Out of there Churches, Which you will See When the Warriours Come in.[3]

Fitch adds that the Creeks lost on their side five men killed and six wounded.[4] In the "Introduction to the Report on General Oglethorpe's Expedition to St. Augustine," we read that in 1727—

A Party of Yamasee Indians, headed by Spaniards from St. Augustine, having murdered our *Out-Scouts*, made an incursion into our Settlements, within *Ten* Miles of *Ponpon*, where they cut off one Mr. *Micheau*, with another *White-man* on the same *plantation*, and carried off a *Third* Prisoner, with all the *Slaves*, *Horses*, *&c.* But being briskly pursued by the Neighbours, who had Notice of it, they were overtaken, routed, and obliged to quit their Booty.

The Government [the narrative goes on to say], judged it Necessary to chastise (at least) those *Indians*, commissioned Col. *Palmer* for that Purpose instantly; who with about *One Hundred Whites*, and the like Number of our *Indians*, landed at St. Juan's, and having left a sufficient Number to take care of the Craft, *marched undiscovered* to the *Yamasee Town*, within a Mile of St. *Augustine*. He attack'd it *at once*, killed several of those *Indians*, took several Prisoners, and drove the Rest into the very Gates

[1] Pub. Rec. S. C., MS., VII, p. 186.

[2] Ibid., VIII, p. 7.

[3] Mereness, Travels in the American Colonies, pp. 204–205.

[4] Ibid., p. 205.

of St. *Augustine* Castle; where they were sheltered. And having *Destroyed their Town*, he returned.

In the beginning of 1728, a Party of those *Yamasees* having landed at *Daffuskee* surprised one of our *Scout-Boats*, and killed every Man but Capt. *Gilbert*, who commanded her. One of the *Indians*, seizing him as his Property, saved his Life. In their Return back to St. *Augustine* a debate arose that it was necessary to kill him, *for that the Governor would not have them to bring any one Alive.* But Capt. *Gilbert*, pleading with the *Indian* that claim'd him was protected by him; and upon coming to St. *Augustine* was after some Time released by the Governor.[1]

In a letter dated Habana, August 27, 1728, Gov. Dionisio de la Vega gives an account of the decline of the Florida missions from the time of the first English invasions. He states that before the English raid under Palmer there were four Indian settlements near St. Augustine, named Nombre de Dios, Tolemato, Palica [probably Patica], and Carapuyas, but the occupants of these spoke several different languages and it is impossible to say which were occupied by Yamasee. Tolemato was, of course, named from the old Guale town, but in the changes that had taken place there is no certainty that any of the original population remained. The Patica are referred to by Bartram as a former Carolina tribe, but again no certain connection can be established between the name and the later population. Nombre de Dios, or Chiquito as it is also called, was originally a Timucua settlement and may have remained such in part; but as we have seen,[2] it had now received a new name from the Yamasee who constituted at least the larger part of the population. De la Vega says of the above mentioned attack:

A body of two hundred English having penetrated into that town on the aforesaid day, the 20th of March, (1728), together with as many Indians, they plundered and pillaged it and set the whole town on fire. They robbed the church and the convent and profaned the images, killing six and wounding eight Indians, a lieutenant and a soldier of infantry. They also took several prisoners with them and withdrew without further action. In view of this the governor had the church blown up by means of powder, withdrawing the Indians who had remained there to the shelter of this city [St. Augustine], leaving only the town of Pocotabaco under the protection of the guns of this Fort.

It would appear, then, that after this raid the four towns were reduced to one close to St. Augustine, and the fact that its name preserves that of the leading upper Yamasee town shows the primacy of that tribe among the remnants gathered there. This name should be Pocotalaco; the *l* has been miscopied *b*. However, the town certainly embraced several villages, as appears from a number of documents. One speaks of a Yamasee village called Tachumite existing about 1734,[3] and another gives an enumeration, not only of the villages but the names and ages of the warriors as well. This latter, a copy of which is in the Ayer collection, is entitled: "List of Indians capable of bearing arms divided according to their towns who are

[1] Carroll, S. Car. Hist. Soc. Colls., II, pp. 355–356. De la Vega seems to date this attack a year later (see below).

[2] See p. 96.

[3] MS. in Ayer Collection, Newberry Library.

at the service of the Presidio of San Agustin de la Florida."[1] It is as follows:

PUEBLO DE POTALACA

	Años.
El Cacique Clospo	60
El Cacique Antonio	20
Juan Sanchez	30
Francisco	60
Pedro Huse	60
Ygnacio	60
Asencio Arapa	20
Chislada	30
Francisco el Largo	30
Pedro Tusque	30
Antonio Rimendo	30
Bernardo de la Cruz	20
Francisco Sarqueno	30
Manuel	20
Antonio Yinquichate	25
Juan Chislada	15
Juan Solana	20
Francisco Arlana	19
Juan Ygnacio	35
Juanillo	12
Sanchez	12
Antonio Yuta	25
Antonio Benavides	14

PUEBLO DE CHIQUITO[2]

El Cacique Yuta	40
El Cacique Juan Sanchez	30
Yfallasquita	30
Marcos Rendon	30
Juan Gregorio	25
Lorenzo Santiago	25
Baltasar	20
Diego de Asuela	65
Antonio Clara	16
Luis Santa Fee	16
Joseph su cuñado	12
Esteban	19
Juan Pasqua	25
Miguel	60
Felipe	25

PUEBLO DE SAN NICOLAS

El Cacique Manuel	60
El Cacique Domingo Gacho	60
Juan Joseph	55
Geronimo	20

PUEBLO DE SAN NICOLAS—continued

	Años.
Agustin Nicolas	30
Miguel	14
Rafael	14
Joseph Antonio	30
Dionisio	20
Bentura	15

PUEBLO DE TOLOMATO

El Cacique Bernardo	40
Domingo	45
Luis Gabriel	45
Lorenzo	20
Felipe	30
Antonio Cagelate	25
Lasaro	16
Martin	16
Diego el Mestiro	40

MAS DENTRO DEL LUGAR

El Cacique Fuentes	60
Juan Sanchez	30
Tomás	25
Juan	17

PUEBLO DE LA COSTA

El Cacique Costa	45
Luis	20
Juan Sanchez	20
Pablo	25
Juan Joseph	30
Lorenzo Nieto	25
Romualdo	25
Antonio	14
Vicente	20
Antonio Puchero	20

PALICA

El Cacique Lorenzo	80
El Cacique Juan Ximenez	60
Ygnacio	80
Joseph	80
Andres	45
Juan Bautista	18
Lorenzo	20
Juan Savina	25
Miguel	20
Manuel	12

PALICA—continued

	Años.
Juan Pufe	14
Tomas	40
Juan	11
Pedro de la Cruz	35
El Cacique Marcos	60
Juan Melchor	11
Juan el Apalachino	80
Francisco del Maral	50

LA PUNTA

El Cacique Juan	80
Francisco	70
Pedro del Sastre	60
Antonio el Mison	35
Francisco Luis	35
Crisostomo	25
Joseph Atase	20
Joseph	20
Juan del Costa	25
Juan Joseph	14
Sanchez	12
Joseph Satagane	30
Joseph el Apalachino	19
Antonio Cachimbo	19
Agustin	25
Arguelles	60
Juan Casapueva	50

PUEBLO DE TIMUCUA

"El Cacique Alucatesa"	80
Riso	60
Crisostomo	50
Juan Bautista	50
Gaspar	25
Santiago Baquero	40
Juan Alonso	20
Bartolo	40
Miguel Mototo	60
Manuel Mototo	60
Miguel	12
Benito	12
Antonio	12
Juan Chirico	50
Santiago	30
Solana	20
Miguel	25

Total number, 122.[3]

[1] MS. in Ayer Collection, Newberry Library.
[2] Also known as Nombre de Dios.
[3] This should be 123 if there is no error in the lists on which it is based.

So that the eight towns contain in all a hundred and twenty-two men[1] capable of bearing arms, having in all of women and children two hundred and ninety-five, which added to the hundred and twenty-two make four hundred and seventeen, the remains of about thirty thousand which were formerly at the service of Spain within the jurisdiction of Florida.

This was written November 27, 1736, at Habana. The "Pueblo de Timucua" probably contained the remnants of the Timucua people, the rest the descendants of the Yamasee proper and the old people of Guale. Apalachee do not appear to have settled near St. Augustine in any number, although two individuals in the above list bear the name of that tribe.

In a letter written at St. Augustine, August 30, 1738, and preserved among the Spanish Archives of the Indies,[2] is an interesting relation of the adventures of "the Indian Juan Ignacio de los Reyes, of the Yguaja Nation, one of the villages which compose the town of Pocotalaca, in the neighborhood of this place." This man, under orders from the governor of Florida, Don Manuel de Montiano, visited the English posts on Cumberland Island and in St. Andrews and St. Simons Sounds during the months of July and August, 1738, and brought back valuable information regarding their condition and regarding the English projects with reference to St. Augustine.

Some Yamasee evidently accompanied the Apalachee to Pensacola and Mobile. Under date of 1714 Barcia notes that the chief of the Yamasee and some of his people, along with the chief of the Apalachee, visited the commandant of Pensacola, and we find the legend "Yamase Land," on the northeast shore of Pensacola Bay, in Jefferys' map of Florida which stands opposite the title page of John Bartram's Description of East Florida.[3] From the parish registers of Mobile we learn of the baptism in 1728 of a "Hiamase" Indian, Francois, and a map of 1744 shows, at the mouth of Deer River, near Mobile, a settlement of "Yamane," the name evidently intended for this tribe.[4]

Under date of July, 1754, the Colonial Records of Georgia speak of the Yamasee as still allied with the Spaniards,[5] and about the year 1761 we hear of "a few Yamasees, about 20 men, near St. Augustine."[6]

Meantime, however, they were being harrassed continually by the Creek Indians in alliance with the English, and presently some Creeks began to move into the peninsula and make permanent homes there. Bartram, who visited Florida in 1777–78, speaks of the Yamasee Nation as entirely destroyed as a distinct body, and he

---

[1] This should be 123 if there is no error in the lists on which it is based.
[2] Serrano y Sanz, Doc. Hist., pp. 260–264.
[3] John Bartram, quoted by Gatschet, Creek Mig. Leg., I, p. 65.
[4] Hamilton, Col. Mobile, p. 113.
[5] Col. Rec. Ga., VII, p. 441.
[6] Description of South Carolina, p. 63.

thus describes the site on St. Johns River of what he terms "the last decisive battle":

In the morning I found I had taken up my lodging on the border of an ancient burying ground, containing sepulchres or tumuli of the Yamasees, who were here slain by the Creeks in the last decisive battle, the Creeks having driven them into the point, between the doubling of the river, where few of them escaped the fury of the conquerors. These graves occupied the whole grove, consisting of two or three acres of ground. There were nearly thirty of these cemeteries of the dead, nearly of an equal size and form, being oblong, twenty feet in length, ten or twelve feet in width, and three or four feet high, now overgrown with orange trees, live oaks, laurel magnolias, red bays, and other trees and shrubs, composing dark and solemn shades.[1]

He saw Yamasee slaves living among the Seminole;[2] but from other data it is evident that free bands, in whole or in part Yamasee, still existed. One of these will be mentioned later. Several writers on the Seminole state that the Oklawaha band was said to be descended from this tribe,[3] and it appears probable since that band occupied the region in which most maps of the period immediately preceding place the Yamasee. According to the same writers their complexion was somewhat darker than that of the other Seminole. The noted leader Jumper is said by some to have been of Yamasee descent,[4] but Cohen sets him down as a refugee from the Creeks.[5] In the long war with the Americans which followed, whatever remained of the tribe became fused with one of the larger bodies, very likely with the Mikasuki, whose language is supposed to have been nearest to their own. We do not know whether those Yamasee who went to Pensacola and Mobile with the Apalachee remained with them or returned to east Florida, but the former supposition is the more likely.

Another part of the Yamasee evidently settled among the Creeks, though for our knowledge of this fact we are almost entirely dependent upon maps. The late Mr. H. S. Halbert was the first to call my attention to the evidence pointing to such a conclusion. On the Covens and Mortier map compiled shortly after the Yamasee war the name appears in the form "Asassi" among the Upper Creeks. An anonymous French writer, of the middle of the eighteenth century or earlier, adds to his enumeration of the Creek villages this statement:

There are besides, ten leagues from this last village [a Sawokli town], two villages of the ïamasé nation where there may be a hundred men, but this nation is attached to the Spaniards of St. Augustine.[6]

On the Mitchell map of 1755 we find "Massi," probably intended for the same tribe, placed on the southeast bank of the Tallapoosa River between Tukabahchee and Hoiiwahali.[7] The name appears also

[1] Bartram, Travels, p. 137.
[2] Ibid., pp. 183–184, 390.
[3] See Cohen, Notices of Florida, p. 33.
[4] Williams, Terr. of Florida, p. 272, 1837.
[5] Cohen, Notices of Florida, p. 237.
[6] MS., Ayer Lib.
[7] See plate 6.

on several later maps, such as those of Evans, 1771, and D'Anville, 1790, but it was probably copied into them from Mitchell. Without giving any authority Gatschet quotes a statement to the effect "that the Yemasi band of Creeks refused to fight in the British-American war of 1813."[1]

There is reason to think that this band subsequently moved down among the Lower Creeks and thence into Florida. Into his report of 1822 Morse copies a list of "Seminole" bands from the manuscript journal of a certain Captain Young, and among these we find the "Emusas," consisting of only 20 men and located 8 miles above the Florida boundary.[2] Their name is probably preserved in that of Omusee Creek, in Henry and Houston Counties, Alabama. What is evidently the same band appears again in a list of Seminole towns made in 1823, where it has the more correct form "Yumersee." They had then moved into Florida and were located at the "head of the Sumulga Hatchee River, 20 miles north of St. Mark's." The chief man was "Alac Hajo," whose name is Creek, properly Ahalâk hadjo, "Potato hadjo."[3] It may be surmised that these people were subsequently absorbed into the Mikasuki band of Seminole.

Connected intimately with the Yamasee were a small tribe found on the site of what is now Savannah by Governor Oglethorpe in 1733, when he founded the colony of Georgia. They are called Yamacraw by the historians of the period, and their town was on a bluff, which still bears their name, in what is now the western suburb of the city. This name is a puzzle, since no *r* occurs in the Muskhogean tongues. It suggests Yamiscaron, the form in which the tribal name of the Yamasee first appears in history through Francisco of Chicora, but as I have shown elsewhere there is every reason to believe that the ending *-ron* is Siouan.[4] Its first definite appearance is in the later (1680) name of the Florida mission Nombre de Dios de Amacarisse, also given as Macarisqui or Macarizqui. We may safely assume that the leaders of the later Georgia Yamacraw came from this place, but the name itself remains as much of a mystery as before. They seem to be mentioned in the Public Records of South Carolina a few years before the Yamasee war as the "Amecario," or "Amercaraio," "above Westoe [i. e., Savannah] River."[5] From the conference which Oglethorpe held with these people and the Creeks and the speeches delivered at that conference we obtain some further information regarding the history of the town. It was settled in 1730 by a body of Indians from among the Lower Creeks, numbering 17 or 18 families and 30 or 40 men, under the

[1] Gatschet, Creek Mig. Leg., I, p. 65.
[2] Morse, Rept. on Indian Affairs, p. 364; see p. 409.
[3] Amer. State Papers, Ind. Affairs, II, p. 439; see p. 411.
[4] See p. 37 et seq.
[5] Pub. Rec. S. C., II, pp. 8-9, MS.

leadership of a chief named Tomochichi. These are said to have been banished from their own country for some crimes and misdemeanors. Tomochichi himself had "tarried for a season with the Palla-Chucolas" before settling there, and it must be remembered that before the Yamasee war the Apalachicola tribe had been located upon Savannah River some 50 miles higher up. It is therefore likely that he belonged to some refugee Yamasee among the Apalachicola, and his occasion for settling in this place may have been as much because it was the land of his ancestors as because he had been "outlawed." Indeed he says as much in his speech to Oglethorpe. In 1732 the Yamacraw asked permission of the government of South Carolina to remain in their new settlement and it was accorded them. When Oglethorpe arrived they are said to have been the only tribe for 50 miles around. They received the settlers in a friendly manner and acted as intermediaries between them and the Creeks. From the negotiations then undertaken it would seem that both the Yamacraw and the Yamasee were reckoned as former members of the Creek confederacy. At least the confederacy arrogated to itself at that time the right to dispose of their lands, all of which, except the site of Yamacraw, a strip of land between Pipemakers Bluff and Pally-Chuckola Creek, and the three islands, Ossabaw, Sapello, and St. Catherines, were ceded to Oglethorpe. Tomochichi, his wife, nephew, and a few of his warriors went to England in 1734, where they received much attention. A painting of Tomochichi and his nephew, Tonahowi, was made by Verelst, and from this engravings were afterwards made by Faber and Kleinschmidt.[1] Tomochichi died October 5, 1739,[2] and the Yamacraw population declined rather than increased. After a time they moved to another situation later known as New Yamacraw,[3] but ultimately those that were left probably retired among their kindred in the Creek Nation, and we may conjecture that they united with the Creek band of Yamasee mentioned above.

The Yamasee made a considerable impression on Creek imagination and are still remembered by a few of the older Creek Indians. According to one of my informants, a Hitchiti, they lived north of the Creeks, which was in any sense true of them only when they were located in South Carolina. It was from this tribe, according to the same informant, that many of the Creek charms known as *sabia* came.

THE APALACHEE

The third Muskhogean group to be considered is known to history under the name Apalachee, a word which in Hitchiti, a related dialect, seems to signify "on the other side." The Apalachee proper

---

[1] See Jones, Hist. Sketch of Tomo-chi-chi; Tailfer, A true and hist. narr. of the colony of Georgia.
[2] Jones, Ibid., p. 121.
[3] Tailfer, op. cit., p. 74.

occupied, when first discovered, a portion of what is now western Florida, between Ocilla River on the east and the Ocklocknee and its branches on the west. They probably extended into what is now the State of Georgia for a short distance, but their center was in the region indicated, northward of Apalachee Bay. Tallahassee, the present State capital of Florida, is nearly in the center of their ancient domain.

A fair idea of the number and names of their towns may be obtained from the lists of missions made in the years 1655[1] and 1680.[2] The first of these contains the following Apalachee missions, together with their distances in leagues from St. Augustine:

San Lorenzo de Apalache..........	75	San Pedro y San Pablo de Kpal [Kpal evidently for Apal].........	87
San Francisco de Apalache.........	77	San Cosme y San Damián..........	90
La Concepción de Apalache........	77	San Luis de Apalache..............	88
San Josef de Apalache.............	84	San Martín de Apalache...........	87
San Juan de Apalache.............	86		

Fortunately the second list gives native names also. In this the missions are classified by provinces, but no distances appear. The following are enumerated in the "Provincia de Apalache," the order having been altered to agree as far as possible with that in the first mission list:

San Lorenço de Ybithachucu.
Nuestra Señora de La Purissima Conçepçión de Ajubali.
San Françisco de Oconi.
San Joseph de Ocuia.
San Joan de Ospalaga.
San Pedro y San Pablo de Patali.
San Antonio de Bacuqua.
San Cosme y San Damian de Yecambi.
San Carlos de los Chacatos, conversion nueva.
San Luis de Talimali.
Nuestra Señora de la Candelaria de la Tama, conversion nueva.
San Pedro de los Chines, conversion nueva.
San Martin de Tomoli.
Santa Cruz y San Pedro de Alcantara de Ychutafun.

There is little doubt that the missions of this second list corresponding with those of the former are pure Apalachee—i. e., the first six, the eighth, the tenth, and the thirteenth. The omission of the name Apalachee after San Cosme and San Damián in the first is probably due to lack of space in the original text. After the preceding name it is abbreviated. San Antonio de Bacuqua was also in all probability Apalachee, a town missionized later than the others. San Carlos de los Chacatos was of course the mission among the neighboring Chatot Indians, and

[1] Serrano y Sanz, Doc. Hist., pp. 132-133; also Lowery, MSS., Lib. Cong. Reproduced on p. 323.
[2] Lowery, MSS. Reproduced on p. 323.

Nuestra Señora de la Candelaria de la Tama that among the Tama or Tamali. The Chines appear to have been another foreign tribe, though, like the rest, of Muskhogean origin. There are few references to them. The last mission on the list, Santa Cruz y San Pedro de Alcantara de Ychutafun, seems from other evidence to have been located in a true Apalachee town established in later times on the banks of the Apalachicola River and thus to the westward of the original Apalachee country. Since *tafa* was a name for "town" peculiar to the Apalachee dialect, of which *tafun* would be the objective form, and *ichu*, *itcu*, or *itco* a common Muskhogean word for "deer," it is probable that the native name signifies "Deer town." The settlement may have been made at this place because deer were plentiful there.

In addition to the above we have notice in two or three places of a mission called Santa Maria. The Van Loon map of 1705 has a legend stating that this mission had been destroyed by the Alabama in the year in which the map was published. About the same time (1702) we hear of a town called Santa Fe.[1] In 1677 there existed a mission called San Damian de Cupayca. The town is mentioned in a letter of 1639.[2] San Marcos belongs to a later period.

We have, besides, the native names of some towns not identified with the mission stations. They are Iniahica, Calahuchi, Uzela, Ochete, Aute, Yapalaga, Bacica, Talpatqui, Capola, and Ilcombe. The first four appear only in the De Soto narratives. Iniahica is spelled Iviahica by Ranjel, Iniahico by Biedma, and is given as Anhayca Apalache by Elvas.[3] It can not be identified in later documents and the name may be in Timucua. Calahuchi is mentioned by Ranjel[4] and Uzela by Elvas.[5] Ochete is located by Elvas 8 leagues south of Iniahica.[5] Aute was a town visited by Narvaez, eight or nine days journey south, or probably rather southwest, of the main Apalachee towns.[6] Garcilasso gives this appellation to the town of Ochete, but the distance of the latter from the main Apalachee towns does not at all agree with that given for the Aute of Narvaez. Yapalaga is entered on most of the more detailed maps of the eighteenth century. Bacica, as well as Bacuqua, already given in the mission lists, seems to have been somewhat removed from the other Apalachee towns, yet probably belonged to them. Its name is perpetuated in Wacissa River and town. Talpatqui appears in the Apalachee letter of 1688.[7] Possibly it was identical with Talimali and therefore with San Luis. Capola and Ilcombe appear as Apalachee towns on the Popple map of 1733 (pl. 4). As the first of

[1] See p. 120.
[2] Serrano y Sanz, Doc. Hist., pp. 200, 208.
[3] Bourne, Narr. of De Soto, I, p. 47; II, pp. 7, 79.
[4] Ibid., II, p. 79.
[5] Ibid., I, p. 47.
[6] Bandelier, Journey of Cabeza de Vaca, p. 29.
[7] Buckingham Smith, Two Docs.

these resembles Sapello and the second is given in South Carolina documents as the name of a Yamasee chief, "the Ilcombe king,"[1] it is probable that they had moved from the Guale coast in later times. The Apalachee town of Oconi, although missionized as early as 1655, may also have been an adopted town, part of the Oconee tribe to be mentioned later. A town called Machaba, which is located on many maps not far from the Apalachee settlements, was really Timucua. Although perhaps not as prominent toward the close of Apalachee history as San Luis de Talimali Ibitachuco, the San Lorenço de Ybithachucu of the missionaries, has the longest traceable history. It appears as far back as the De Soto narratives in the forms Ivitachuco, Uitachuco, and Vitachuco, although Garcilasso, our authority for the last form, bestows it upon a Timucua chief instead of an Apalachee town.[2] In a letter of 1677 it appears as Huiståchuco,[3] in the mission list above given Ybithachuco, and in the Apalachee letter written to Charles II in 1688 Ybitachuco.[4] Finally, Colonel Moore, who destroyed it, writes the name Ibitachka.[5] Ajubali is noted more often under the forms Ayaville or Ayubale.

Very little has been preserved regarding the ethnology of the Apalachee. Their culture was midway between that of the Florida tribes and their own Muskhogean relatives to the north. Writing in 1673 one of the governors of Florida says of their dress:

> The men wear only bark and skin clothing and the women small cloaks (goaipiles), which they make of the roots of trees.

These last must have been similar to, if not identical with, the mulberry bark garments. From what the De Soto chroniclers say of the change in domestic architecture which they encountered in south-central Georgia it is evident that the Apalachee were associated in this feature rather with the southern than with the northern tribes.

Fontaneda makes a few brief remarks regarding the customs of the Apalachee,[6] but it is secondhand information obtained through the south Florida Indians and of little value.

The first historical reference to the Apalachee is in Cabeza de Vaca's narrative of the Narvaez expedition. On their way north through the central part of the Florida Peninsula in the spring of 1528 the explorers met some Indians who led them to their village, and "there," says Cabeza de Vaca, "we found many boxes for merchandize from Castilla. In every one of them was a corpse covered with painted deer hides. The commissary thought this to be some

---

[1] See p. 97.
[2] Bourne, Narr. of De Soto, I, p. 47; II, pp. 7, 79; Shipp's Garcilasso, p. 283.
[3] Serrano y Sanz, Doc. Hist., p. 207.
[4] Buckingham Smith, Two Docs.
[5] See p. 121.
[6] Buckingham Smith, Letter of De Soto and Mem. of Fontaneda, pp. 27–28.

idolatrous practice, so he burnt the boxes with the corpses. We also found pieces of linen and cloth, and feather headdresses that seemed to be from New Spain, and samples of gold."

The narrative continues as follows:

We inquired of the Indians (by signs) whence they had obtained these things and they gave us to understand that very far from there, was a province called Apalachen, in which there was much gold. They also signified to us that in that province we would find everything we held in esteem. They said that in Apalachen there was plenty.[1]

The form "Apalachen" here given seems to contain the Muskhogean objective ending *-n*, which by a stranger would often be taken over as a necessary part of the word. The people among whom the Spaniards then were, were Timucua, therefore the mistake was perhaps on the part of the Indians, but more likely it is the form as heard by the Spaniards afterwards from the Apalachee themselves. The Spaniards continued their journey in search of this province and "came in sight of Apalachen without having been noticed by the Indians of the land" on the day after St. John's Day.[2]

Cabeza continues thus:

Once in sight of Apalachen, the governor commanded me to enter the village with nine horsemen and fifty foot. So the inspector and I undertook this. Upon penetrating into the village we found only women and boys. The men were not there at the time, but soon, while we were walking about they came and began to fight, shooting arrows at us. They killed the inspector's horse, but finally fled and left us. We found there plenty of ripe maize ready to be gathered and much dry corn already housed. We also found many deer skins and among them mantles made of thread and of poor quality, with which the women cover parts of their bodies. They had many vessels [mortars] for grinding [or rather pounding] maize. The village contained forty small and low houses, reared in sheltered places, out of fear of the great storms that continuously occur in the country. The buildings are of straw, and they are surrounded by dense timber, tall trees and numerous water-pools, where there were so many fallen trees and of such size as to greatly obstruct and impede circulation.[3]

Below he adds:

In the province of Apalachen the lagunes are much larger than those we found previously. There is much maize in this province and the houses are scattered all over the country as much as those of the Gelves.[4]

Following is the account of the rest of their dealings with the Apalachee:

Two hours after we arrived at Apalachen the Indians that had fled came back peaceably, begging us to give back to them their women and children, which we did. The governor, however, kept with him one of their caciques, at which they became so angry as to attack us the following day. They did it so swiftly and with so much audacity as to set fire to the lodges we occupied, but when we sallied forth they fled to

[1] Bandelier, Journey of Cabeza de Vaca, pp. 12-13.
[2] Ibid., p. 24.
[3] Ibid., pp. 25-26.
Ibid., p. 27.

the lagunes nearby, on account of which and of the big corn patches we could not do them any harm beyond killing one Indian. The day after Indians from a village on the other side came and attacked us in the same manner, escaping in the same way, with the loss of a single man.

We remained at this village for 25 days, making three excursions during the time. We found the country very thinly inhabited and difficult to march through, owing to bad places, timber, and lagunes. We inquired of the cacique whom we had retained and of the other Indians with us (who were neighbors and enemies of them) about the condition and settlements of the land, the quality of its people, about supplies, and everything else. They answered, each one for himself, that Apalachen was the largest town of all; that further in less people were met with who were very much poorer than those here, and that the country was thinly settled, the inhabitants greatly scattered, and also that further inland big lakes, dense forests, great deserts, and wastes were met with.

Then we asked about the land to the south, its villages and resources. They said that in that direction and nine days' march toward the sea was a village called Aute, where the Indians had plenty of corn and also beans and melons, and that, being so near the sea, they obtained fish and that those were their friends. Seeing how poor the country was, taking into account the unfavorable reports about its population and everything else, and that the Indians made constant war upon us, wounding men and horses whenever they went for water (which they could do from the lagunes where we could not reach them) by shooting arrows at us; that they had killed a chief of Tuzcuco called Don Pedro, whom the commissary had taken along with him, we agreed to depart and go in search of the sea, and of the village of Aute, which they had mentioned. And so we left, arriving there five days after. The first day we traveled across lagunes and trails without seeing a single Indian.

On the second day, however, we reached a lake very difficult to cross, the water reaching to the chest, and there were a great many fallen trees. Once in the middle of it, a number of Indians assailed us from behind trees that concealed them from our sight, while others were on fallen trees, and they began to shower arrows upon us, so that many men and horses were wounded, and before we could get out of the lagune our guide was captured by them. After we had got out, they pressed us very hard, intending to cut us off, and it was useless to turn upon them, for they would hide in the lake and from there wound both men and horses.

So the Governor ordered the horsemen to dismount and attack them on foot. The purser dismounted also, and our people attacked them. Again they fled to a lagune, and we succeeded in holding the trail. In this fight some of our people were wounded in spite of their good armor. There were men that day who swore they had seen two oak trees, each as thick as the calf of a leg, shot through and through by arrows, which is not surprising if we consider the force and dexterity with which they shoot. I myself saw an arrow that had penetrated the base of a poplar tree for half a foot in length. All the many Indians from Florida we saw were archers, and, being very tall and naked, at a distance they appeared giants.

Those people are wonderfully built, very gaunt and of great strength and agility. Their bows are as thick as an arm, from eleven to twelve spans long, shooting an arrow at 200 paces with unerring aim. From that crossing we went to another similar one, a league away, but while it was half a league in length it was also much more difficult. There we crossed without opposition, for the Indians, having spent all their arrows at the first place, had nothing wherewith they would dare attack us. The next day, while crossing a similar place, I saw the tracks of people who went ahead of us, and I notified the Governor, who was in the rear, so that, although the Indians turned upon us, as we were on our guard, they could do us no harm. Once on open ground they pursued us still. We attacked them twice, killing two, while they wounded me and two or three other Christians, and entered the forest again, where we could no longer injure them.

In this manner we marched for eight days, without meeting any more natives, until one league from the site to which I said we were going. There, as we were marching along, Indians crept up unseen and fell upon our rear. A boy belonging to a nobleman, called Avellaneda, who was in the rear guard, gave the alarm. Avellaneda turned back to assist, and the Indians hit him with an arrow on the edge of the cuirass, piercing his neck nearly through, so that he died on the spot, and we carried him to Aute. It took us nine days from Apalachen to the place where we stopped. And then we found that all the people had left and the lodges were burnt. But there was plenty of maize, squash, and beans, all nearly ripe and ready for harvest. We rested there for two days.

After this the governor entreated me to go in search of the sea, as the Indians said it was so near by, and we had, on this march, already suspected its proximity from a great river to which we had given the name of the *Rio de la Magdalena*. I left on the following day in search of it, accompanied by the commissary, the captain Castillo, Andrés Dorantes, 7 horsemen, and 50 foot. We marched until sunset, reaching an inlet or arm of the sea, where we found plenty of oysters on which the people feasted, and we gave many thanks to God for bringing us there.

The next day I sent 20 men to reconnoiter the coast and explore it, who returned on the day following at nightfall, saying that these inlets and bays were very large and went so far inland as greatly to impede our investigations, and that the coast was still at a great distance. Hearing this and considering how ill-prepared we were for the task, I returned to where the governor was. We found him sick, together with many others. The night before Indians had made an attack, putting them in great stress, owing to their enfeebled condition. The Indians had also killed one of their horses.[1]

The next day they left Aute and, with great exertion, reached the spot where Cabeza de Vaca had come out on the Gulf. It was determined to build boats and leave the country, but meanwhile, in order to provide themselves with sufficient provisions, they made four raids upon Aute "and they brought as many as 400 fanegas of maize, although not without armed opposition from the Indians." [2] Our author adds that "during that time some of the party went to the coves and inlets for sea food, and the Indians surprised them twice, killing ten of our men in plain view of the camp without our being able to prevent it. We found them shot through and through with arrows, for, although several wore good armor, it was not sufficient to protect them, since, as I said before, they shot their arrows with such force and precision." [3] Near the end of September, 1528, they embarked in five barges and left the country, coasting along toward the west, and having nothing further to do with Apalachee or its inhabitants. The narrative given by Oviedo[4] is practically the same; that in the "Relacion" published in the Documentos Ineditos[5] is even briefer.

The next we learn of the Province of Apalachee is from the chroniclers of the great expedition of De Soto. Ranjel, who is generally the most reliable, gives the following account:

On Wednesday, the first of October, [1539] the Governor Hernando de Soto, started from Agile and came with his soldiers to the river or swamp of Ivitachuco, and they

[1] Bandelier, op. cit., pp. 28–34.

[2] Ibid., p. 38. A fanega is about equal to a bushel.

[3] Bandelier, op. cit., p. 39.

[4] Oviedo, Hist. Gen., III, pp. 578–582.

[5] Doc. Ined., XIV, pp. 265–279.

made a bridge; and in the high swamp grass on the other side there was an ambuscade of Indians, and they shot three Christians with arrows. They finished crossing this swamp on the Friday following at noon and a horse was drowned there. At nightfall they reached Ivitachuco and found the village in flames, for the Indians had set fire to it. Sunday, October 5, they came to Calahuchi, and two Indians and one Indian woman were taken and a large amount of dried venison. There the guide whom they had ran away. The next day they went on, taking for a guide an old Indian who led them at random, and an Indian woman took them to Iviahica, and they found all the people gone. And the next day two captains went on further and found all the people gone.

Johan de Añasco started out from that village and eight leagues from it he found the port where Pamphilo de Narvaez had set sail in the vessels which he made. He recognized it by the headpieces of the horses and the place where the forge was set up and the mangers and the mortars that they used to grind corn and by the crosses cut in the trees.

They spent the winter there, and remained until the 4th of March, 1540, in which time many notable things befell them with the Indians, who are the bravest of men and whose great courage and boldness the discerning reader may imagine from what follows. For example, two Indians once rushed out against eight men on horseback; twice they set the village on fire; and with ambuscades they repeatedly killed many Christians, and although the Spaniards pursued them and burned them they were never willing to make peace. If their hands and noses were cut off they made no more account of it than if each one of them had been a Mucius Scaevola of Rome. Not one of them, for fear of death, denied that he belonged to Apalache; and when they were taken and were asked from whence they were they replied proudly: "From whence am I? I am an Indian of Apalache." And they gave one to understand that they would be insulted if they were thought to be of any other tribe than the Apalaches.[1]

Farther on we read:

The Province of Apalache is very fertile and abundantly provided with supplies with much corn, kidney beans, pumpkins, various fruits, much venison, many varieties of birds and excellent fishing near the sea; and it is a pleasant country, though there are swamps, but these have a hard sandy bottom.[2]

The account in Elvas is as follows:

The next day, the first of October, the Governor took his departure in the morning, and ordered a bridge to be made over a river, which he had to cross. The depth there, for a stone's throw, was over the head, and afterward the water came to the waist, for the distance of a crossbow-shot, where was a growth of tall and dense forest, into which the Indians came, to ascertain if they could assail the men at work and prevent a passage; but they were dispersed by the arrival of crossbow-men, and some timbers being thrown in, the men gained the opposite side and secured the way. On the fourth day of the week, Wednesday of St. Francis, the Governor crossed over and reached Uitachuco, a town subject to Apalache, where he slept. He found it burning, the Indians having set it on fire.

Thenceforward the country was well inhabited, producing much corn, the way leading by many habitations like villages. Sunday, the twenty-fifth of October, he arrived at the town of Uzela, and on Monday at Anhayca Apalache, where the lord of all that country and Province resided. The Camp-master, whose duty it is to divide and lodge the men, quartered them about the town, at the distance of half a

[1] Bourne, Narr. of De Soto, II, pp. 78–80.
[2] Ibid., p. 82.

league to a league apart. There were other towns which had much maize, pumpkins, beans, and dried plums of the country, whence were brought together at Anhayca Apalache what appeared to be sufficient provision for the winter.[1] These *ameixas* [persimmons] are better than those of Spain, and come from trees that grow in the fields without being planted.

Below we read:

The Governor ordered planks and spikes to be taken to the coast for building a piragua, into which thirty men entered well armed from the bay, going to and coming from sea, waiting the arrival of the brigantines, and sometimes fighting with the natives, who went up and down the estuary in canoes. On Saturday, the twenty-ninth of November, in a high wind, an Indian passed through the sentries undiscovered, and set fire to the town, two portions of which, in consequence, were instantly consumed.

On Sunday, the twenty-eighth of December, Juan de Añasco arrived; and the Governor directed Francisco Maldonado, Captain of Infantry, to run the coast to the westward with fifty men, and look for an entrance; proposing to go himself in that direction by land on discoveries. The same day, eight men rode two leagues about the town in pursuit of Indians, who had become so bold that they would venture up within crossbow-shot of the camp to kill our people. Two were discovered engaged in picking beans, and might have escaped, but a woman being present, the wife of one of them, they stood to fight. Before they could be killed, three horses were wounded, one of which died in a few days.[2]

The balance of the narrative is practically the same as that of Ranjel.

The following is from Biedma:

Across this stream [on the confines of Apalache] we made a bridge, by lashing many pines together, upon which we went over with much danger, as there were Indians on the opposite side who disputed our passage; when they found, however, that we had landed, they went to the nearest town, called Ivitachuco, and there remained until we came in sight, when as we appeared they set all the place on fire and took to flight.

There are many towns in this Province of Apalache, and it is a land abundant in substance. They call all that other country we were travelling through, the Province of Yustaga.

We went to another town, called Iniahico.[3]

In Garcilasso's Florida we have some additional information regarding the Apalachee Indians:

Alonso de Carmona, in his *Peregrinacion*, remarks in particular upon the fierceness of the Indians of the Province of Apalache, of whom he writes as follows, his words being exactly quoted: Those Indians of Apalache are very tall, very valiant and full of spirit; since, just as they showed themselves and fought with those who were with Pamphilo de Narvaez, and drove them out of the country in spite of themselves, they kept flying in our faces every day and we had daily brushes with them; and as they failed to make any headway with us, because our Governor was very brave, energetic, and experienced in Indian warfare, they concluded to withdraw to the woods in small bands, and as the Spaniards were going out for wood and were cutting it in the forest the Indians would come up at the sound of the axe and would kill the Spaniards and

[1] A mistake has probably been made here in the division of sentences, which must have read: "The Camp-master, whose duty it is to divide and lodge the men, quartered them about the town. At the distance of half a league to a league apart there were other towns which had much maize," etc.

[2] Bourne, Narr. of De Soto, I, pp. 46–49.

[3] Ibid., II, pp. 6–7.

loose the chains of the Indians whom they brought to carry back the cut wood and take the Spaniards' scalps, which was what they most prized, to hang upon the arm of their bows with which they fought; and at the sound of the voices and of arms we would immediately repair thither, and we found the consequences of a lack of precaution. In that way they killed for us more than twenty soldiers, and this happened frequently. And I remember that one day seven horsemen went out from the camp to forage for food and to kill a little dog to eat; which we were used to do in that land, and a day that we got something we thought ourselves lucky; and not even pheasants ever tasted better to us. And going in search of these things they fell in with five Indians who were waiting for them with bows and arrows, and they drew a line on the ground and told them not to cross that or they would all die. And the Spaniards who would not take any fooling, attacked them, and the Indians shot off their bows and killed two horses and wounded two others, and also a Spaniard severely; and the Spaniards killed one of the Indians and the rest took to their heels and got away, for they are truly very nimble and are not impeded by the adornments of clothes, but rather are much helped by going bare.[1]

After leaving Iviahica, De Soto came to the River Guacuca and later reached a province called Capachequi. It is uncertain what relation this and the subsequent places into which he came bore to the Apalachee. Probably most of them belonged to the people we now know as Hitchiti.

Pareja, the well-known missionary to the Timucua Indians, and another friar, Alonso de Peñaranda, state in letters, written in 1607, that the Apalachee had asked for missionaries that same year through the friars in Potano. Their statement that the Apalachee towns numbered 107 is, of course, a gross exaggeration.[2] We read that in 1609 more than 28 Timucua and Apalachee chiefs were begging for baptism.[2] In 1622 an Englishman named Brigstock claims to have visited the "Apalachites" and to have discovered near them a colony of English refugees. He published his narrative in 1644. It has received some credence from as noted a student as D. G. Brinton, but may now be dismissed as essentially a fabrication.[3] The need of missionaries to begin converting the Apalachee is frequently dwelt upon in documents written between 1607 and 1633, but it was not until the latter date that work was actually begun. A letter dated November 15, 1633, states that two monks had gone to the Province of Apalachee on October 16. It adds that these people had desired conversion for more than 20 years, that their country was 12 leagues in extent and contained 15,000 to 16,000 Indians, which last statement is of course another gross exaggeration, though indeed more moderate than one of 30,000 made in 1618 and another of 34,000 made in 1635.[2] This last placed the number of Christian converts in the province at 5,000, probably more than the total Apalachee population. By a letter of September 12, 1638, we learn that conversions of Apalachee

[1] Trans. by Bourne, op. cit., II, pp. 151–152.

[2] Lowery, MSS.

[3] John Davies, Hist. Carribbee Islands, pp. 228–249.

were greatly on the increase,[1] and Gov. Damian de Vega Castro y Pardo writes, August 22, 1639, that there had been more than a thousand conversions there, although there were still only two friars. He also states that he had made peace between the Apalachee and three tribes called Chacatos, Apalochocolos, and Amacanos, evidently the Chatot, Lower Creeks, and Yamasee.[2] Barcia informs us that the Apalachee made war upon the Spaniards in 1638, but were driven back into their own country, which was in turn invaded.[3] The documents of the time make no mention of this struggle and I think Barcia is in error, or more likely the notice is out of place. In 1647 a war did break out, however, attributed to the fact that the Spaniards were not giving the Indians as much as formerly, and also to the influence of some Chisca (Yuchi) Indians. At that time there were eight friars in the province and seven churches and convents. Eight of the chiefs, of whom there were said to be more than 40, had accepted the new faith. In the revolt three missionaries were killed and all of the churches and convents, with the sacred objects which they contained, were destroyed, and among the slain were the lieutenant of the province and his family. Capt. Don Martin de Cuera was sent against the rebels with a troop of soldiers, but his party was surrounded by a multitude of Indians and after a battle which lasted all day he was forced to return to St. Augustine for reinforcements.

And then a strange thing happened, well illustrating the fickleness of the Indian nature. Francisco Menendez Marques, acting on advices privately received from the enemy's country, went there in person secretly and put down the rebellion with comparative ease, assisted almost entirely, it would seem, by friendly Apalachee. Twelve of the ringleaders were killed, and 26 others condemned to labor on the fortifications of St. Augustine. The rest were pardoned, but with the understanding that they should send additional men to work on the fortifications of the capital. After this most of the Apalachee sought baptism.[4] The obligation to labor in St. Augustine is a constant source of complaint from this time on—sometimes by the Indians themselves; sometimes by the friars on their behalf. In 1656 there was an uprising among the Timucua Indians, which spread to the Apalachee, but it seems to have died out there without necessitating drastic measures, although we learn that a captain and 12 soldiers were placed in San Luis.[1] In a letter written just after this war we are told that there were then six monks in the province,[2] and by the mission list of two years earlier we find that

---

[1] Lowery, MSS.

[2] Serrano y Sanz, Doc. Hist., p. 198; also Lowery, MSS.

[3] Barcia, La Florida, p. 203.

[4] Lowery, MSS.; also see Serrano y Sanz, Doc. Hist., pp. 204–205.

they had nine missions to serve. In the memorial of a missionary named Fray Alonso de Moral, dated November 5, 1676, it is said that there had been 16,000 Apalachee Indians in 1638, and that at the date of writing they were reduced to 5,000,[1] but it may be considered doubtful whether they ever numbered more than the latter figure. In 1677 a body of Apalachee undertook a successful expedition against some Chisca (Yuchi) Indians living to the westward who had committed depredations upon their settlements. The full account of it is given elsewhere.[2] In 1681 Gov. Cabrera notes that he had stopped the ball game among the Apalachee Indians as a heathenish practice inimical to their well being. January 21, 1688, is noteworthy as the date on which a letter in the Spanish and Apalachee languages was written for transmission to King Charles II. This has fortunately been preserved, and it contains practically all of the Apalachee language known to be in existence.[3] The chiefs of the Apalachee express their pleasure at having missionaries among them and at being relieved from the former burdensome labors they were compelled to undergo in St. Augustine. That this relief was only temporary, however, is shown by an appeal, dated Vitachuco, February 28, 1701, made by "Nanhula Chuba, Don Patricio, chief of the [Apalachee] Indians" to Gov. Qiroga y Losada, in the name of all of the Apalachee chiefs, begging to be relieved from work on the fortifications of St. Augustine.[4] From an entry in Barcia's history it would seem that final relief was not granted before 1703,[5] and as the Apalachee Nation was nearly destroyed at about the same period, few were benefited by it. The attacks of northern Indians, instigated by English in Carolina, were increasing in frequency and violence. March 20, 1702, Gov. Zuñiga writes that infidel Indians had attacked the town of Santa Fe in the Apalachee province and, though driven off, had burned the church.[4]

The first encounter on a large scale between the English and their allies on the one hand and the Apalachee and Spaniards took place in the following manner, as related by an English chronicler:

In 1702, before Queen ANNE's Declaration of War was known in these Parts, the *Spaniards* formed another Design to fall upon our Settlements by Land, at the Head of *Nine Hundred Apalachee Indians* from thence. The *Creek Indians*, in Friendship with this Province, coming at a Knowledge of it, and sensible of the Dangers approaching, acquainted our Traders, then in the Nation with it, when this Army was actually on their March coming down that way. The Traders having thereupon encourag'd the *Creeks* to get together an Army of *Five Hundred* Men, headed the same, and went out to meet the other. Both Armies met in an Evening on the Side of *Flint-River*, a

---

[1] Lowery, MSS.

[2] See pp. 299-304.

[3] See p. 12.

[4] Brooks, MSS., Lib. Cong.

[5] Barcia, La Florida, p. 323.

Branch of the *Chatabooche* [Chattahoochee]. In the Morning, just before Break of Day (when *Indians* are accustomed to make their Attacks) the *Creeks* stirring up their Fires drew back at a Little Distance leaving their Blankets by the Fires in the very same Order as they had slept. Immediately after the *Spaniards* and *Apalatchees* (as was expected) coming on to attack them, fired and run in upon the Blankets. Thereupon the *Creeks* rushing forth fell on them, killed and took the greatest Part, and entirely routed them. To this *Stratagem* was owing the Defeat of the then intended Design.[1]

Shortly after this affair, in the winter of 1703–4, occurred the great Apalachee disaster, the invasion of Apalachia by Col. Moore with a body of 50 volunteers from South Carolina and 1,000 Creek auxiliaries, and the almost complete breaking up of the Apalachee Nation. The best account of this is printed in the second volume of Carroll's Historical Collections of South Carolina[2] under the following heading: "An Account of What the Army Did, under the Command of Col. Moore, in His Expedition Last Winter, against the Spaniards and Spanish Indians in a Letter from the Said Col. Moore to the Governor of Carolina. Printed in the Boston News, May 1, 1704." It runs as follows:

To the Governor of Carolina:

May it please your honour to accept of this short narrative of what I, with the army under my command, have been doing since my departure from the Ockomulgee, on the 19th[3] of December [1703].

On the 14th of December we came to a town, and strong and almost regular fort, about Sun rising called *Ayaville*. At our first approach the Indians in it fired and shot arrows at us briskly; from which we sheltered ourselves under the side of a great Mud-walled house, till we could take a view of the fort, and consider of the best way of assaulting it: which we concluded to be, by breaking the church door, which made a part of the fort, with axes. I no sooner proposed this, but my men readily undertook it: ran up to it briskly (the enemy at the same time shooting at them), were beaten off without effecting it, and fourteen white men wounded. Two hours after that we thought fit to attempt the burning of the church, which we did, three or four Indians assisting us. The Indians obstinately defending themselves, killed us two men, viz. Francis Plowden and Thomas Dale. After we were in their fort, a fryar, the only white in it, came forth and begged mercy. In this we took about twenty-six men alive, and fifty-eight women and children. The Indians took about as many more of each sort. The fryar told us we killed, in the two storms of the fort, twenty-five men.

The next morning the captain of St. Lewis Fort, with twenty-three men and four hundred Indians, came to fight us, which we did; beat him; took him and eight of his men prisoners; and, as the Indians, which say it, told us, killed five or six whites. We have a particular account from our Indians of one hundred and sixty-eight Indian men killed and taken in the fight; but the Apalatchia Indians say they lost two hundred, which we have reason to believe to be the least. Capt. John Bellinger, fighting bravely at the head of our men was killed at my foot. Capt. Fox dyed of a wound given him at the first storming of the fort. Two days after, I sent to the cassique of the Ibitachka,

[1] As set forth in "Statements Made in the Introduction to the Report on General Oglethorpe's Expedition to St. Augustine" (printed in Carroll's Historical Collections of South Carolina, vol. II, p. 351).

[2] Pp. 570–576.

[3] There is evidently a mistake in this date, which should be the 9th instead of the 19th.

who, with one hundred and thirty men, was in his strong and well made fort, to come and make his peace with me, the which he did, and compounded for it with his church's plate, and ten horses laden with provisions. After this, I marched through five towns, which had all strong forts, and defences against small arms. They all submitted and surrendered their forts to me without condition. I have now in my company all the whole people of three towns, and the greatest part of four more. We have totally destroyed all the people of four towns; so that we have left the Apalatchia but that one town which compounded with one part of St. Lewis; and the people of one town, which run away altogether: their town, church and fort, we burnt. The people of St. Lewis come to me every night. I expect and have advice that the town which compounded with me are coming after me. The waiting for these people make my marches slow; for I am willing to bring away with me, free, as many of the Indians as I can, this being the address of the commons to your honour to order it so. This will make my men's part of plunder (which otherwise might have been 100£ to a man) but small. But I hope with your honour's assistance to find a way to gratifie them for their loss of blood. I never see or hear of a stouter or braver thing done, than the storming of the fort. It hath regained the reputation we seemed to have lost under the conduct of Robert Macken, the Indians now having a mighty value for the whites. Apalatchia is now reduced to so feeble and low a condition, that it can neither support St. Augustine with provisions, nor distrust, endamage or frighten us: our Indians living between the Apalatchia and the French. In short, we have made Carolina as safe as the conquest of Apalatchia can make it.

If I had not so many men wounded in our first attempt, I had assaulted St. Lewis fort, in which is about 28 or 30 men, and 20 of these came thither from Pensacola to buy provisions the first night after I took the first fort.

On Sabbath, the 23d instant, I came out of Apalatchia settle, and am now about 30 miles on my way home; but do not expect to reach it before the middle of March, notwithstanding my horses will not be able to carry me to the Cheeraque's Mountain. I have had a tedious duty, and uneasy journey; and though I have no reason to fear any harm from the enemy, through the difference between the whites, and between Indians and Indians, bad way and false alarms, I do labour under hourly uneasiness. The number of free Apalatchia Indians that are now under my protection, and bound with me to Carolina, are 1300, and 100 slaves. The Indians under my command killed and took prisoners on the plantations, whilst we stormed the fort, as many Indians as we and they took and killed in the fort.

Dated in the woods 50 miles north and east of Apalatchia.

An account of this from the Spanish side is contained in a letter to the king written by Governor Don José de Zuñiga, March 30, 1704, though there is a discrepancy in the dates, which differences in calendar do not seem fully to account for. The mention of Guale is evidently a mistake; probably Ayaville is intended. He says:

After the late siege of St. Augustine the enemy invaded San Jose and San Francisco, destroying everything in their path, killing many Indians and carrying with them over 500 prisoners.

They returned afterward, accompanied by the English who laid siege to this fort and invaded the province of Apalachee, destroying all the lands. They then assaulted Guale, on the 25th of January of the present year, which was vigorously defended by the Indians and the clergyman, Fray Angel de Miranda, who bravely defended the position, fighting from early in the morning until two o'clock in the afternoon, when their ammunition was exhausted. The enemy then advanced through the passage adjoining the church, which they set on fire, gaining possession of the passage.

On the 26th I sent my lieutenant, Juan Ruiz, with thirty Spanish soldiers mounted and four hundred Indians. They attacked the enemy, inflicting a loss upon them of seven Englishmen and about one hundred Indians killed, besides others that were killed by Fray Miranda and his Indians. But our men having run out of ammunition they were in their turn finally defeated. My lieutenant was wounded by a shot that knocked him down from his horse, and the clergyman, Fray Juan de Parga, together with two soldiers, were killed. The rest of the force withdrew, leaving in the hands of the enemy, my lieutenant, eight soldiers, and a few Indians as prisoners, whom the infidels treated in the most cruel and barbarous manner. After having bound the unfortunate Indian prisoners, by the hands and feet to a stake, they set fire to them, when they were burned up alive. This horrible sight was witnessed by my lieutenant and soldiers, who, naked, were tied up in the stocks. Only Fray Angel de Miranda was free....

The affliction of the clergymen is great, and they have written to me and to their prelate urging that they be moved away from the danger that threatens them....

The enemy released the clergyman, the lieutenant, and four soldiers, but with the understanding that each one was to pay a ransom of four hundred dollars, five cows, and five horses. But the captain whom my lieutenant had left in his place, in charge of the defence of the strong house at San Luis, sent word to the English governor that he would not send him anything. Finally, sir, the governor withdrew with his forces without attacking the Strong House, but not before he had succeeded in destroying five settlements, carrying with him the Indians of two of them, together with all the cattle, horses, and everything else that they could carry. The Indians that abandoned their settlements and went away with the enemy numbered about six hundred.

The enemy carried away the arms, shotguns, pistols, and horses, and with flags of peace marched upon the Strong House at old San Luis in order to ill treat the captain that was stationed there.[1]

The only satisfactory French account is contained in a letter written by Bienville to his Government. This also contains the best statement relative to the settlement of a part of the Apalachee refugees near Mobile. I venture to translate it as follows:

The Apalachee have been entirely destroyed by the English and the savages. They made prisoners thirty-two Spaniards, who formed a garrison there, besides which they had seventeen burned, including three Franciscan fathers (Peres Cordelliers), and have killed and made prisoner six or seven thousand Apalachee, the tribe which inhabited this country, and have killed more than six thousand head of cattle and other domestic animals such as horses and sheep. The Spaniards have burned the little fortress which they had there and have all retired to St. Augustine. Of all the Apalachee savages there have escaped only four hundred persons who have taken refuge in our river and have asked my permission to sow there and establish a village. Another nation, named Chaqueto, which was established near Pansacola, has also come to settle in our river. They number about two hundred persons. I asked them why they left the Spaniards. They told me that they did not give them any guns, but that the French gave them to all of their allies. The English have drawn over to themselves all of the savages who were near the castle of St. Augustine, among whom there were Spanish missionaries. There remain to them [the Spaniards] at present only two or three allied villages of the savages. The English intend to return to besiege the castle of St. Augustine, according to information which I have received from the governor of the said castle, and they also threaten to make the French withdraw from Mobille. If they come here, which I do not believe, they will not make us withdraw easily.[2]

---

[1] Brooks, MSS., Miss Brooks's translation.

[2] Louisiane: Correspondence Générale, MS. vol. in Library Louisiana Historical Society, pp. 567-568. The "Chaqueto" are the Chatot.

Farther on we learn that the Spanish governor had offered the chiefs of the Apalachee and Chatot very considerable presents to return to Florida, but they refused,[1] stating that the French protected them better. This was written July 28, 1706, which tends to confirm Pénicaut's statement that the removal occurred toward the end of 1705.[2] He adds that Bienville furnished them with corn with which to plant their first crop. The first mention of Apalachee in the register of the old Catholic church in Mobile records the baptism of a little Apalachee boy on September 6, 1706.[3]

Pénicaut has the following to say regarding these Apalachee:

> The Apalaches perform divine service like the Catholics in France. Their grand feast is on the day of St. Louis;[4] they come the evening before to ask the officers of the fort to come to the fete in their village, and they extend great good cheer on that day to all who come there, especially to the French.
>
> The priests of our fort go there to perform high mass, which they listen to with much devotion, singing the psalms in Latin, as is done in France, and, after dinner, vespers and the benediction of the Holy Sacrament. Men and women are there that day very well dressed. The men have a kind of cloth overcoat and the women cloaks, skirts of silk stuff after the French manner, except that they do not have head coverings, their heads being uncovered; their hair, long and very black, is braided and hangs in one or two plaits behind after the manner of the Spanish women. Those who have too long hair bend it back as far as the middle of the back and tie it with a ribbon.
>
> They have a church, where one of our French priests goes to say mass Sundays and feast days; they have a baptismal font, in which to baptize their infants, and a cemetery side of the church, in which there is a cross, where they are buried.
>
> Toward evening, on St. Louis's day, after the service is finished, men, women, and children dress in masks; they dance the rest of the day with the French who are there, and the other savages who come that day to their village; they have quantities of food cooked with which to regale them. They love the French very much, and it must be confessed that they have nothing of the savage except their language, which is a mixture of the language of the Spaniards and of the Alibamons.[5]

Meantime the Apalachee carried away by Moore had been settled near New Windsor, South Carolina, below what is now Augusta, Georgia, where they remained until 1715, the year of the Yamasee uprising. When that outbreak occurred, the Apalachee, as might have been anticipated, joined the hostiles, and from then on they disappear from English colonial history.

However, the greater part of these revolted Apalachee evidently settled first near the Lower Creeks, a faction of whom opposed the English. In the following letter to the crown from Gov. Juan de Ayala of Florida we get a view of the struggle between these two factions, and the apparent victory of that in the English interest,

---

[1] Louisiane: Correspondence Générale, MS. vol. in Library Louisiana Historical Society, pp. 621–622.

[2] Margry, Déc., v, pp. 460–461.

[3] Hamilton, Colonial Mobile, 1910, p. 109.

[4] It will be remembered that St. Louis was one of the leading Apalachee towns and one of those which escaped destruction.

[5] Pénicaut, in Margry, v, pp. 486–487.

and in that fact we have an evident reason for the return of the Apalachee to Florida which soon took place. He says:

I beg to report to Y. M. that on the 10th of July of the present year [1717] there came to pledge obedience to Y. M., Osingulo, son and heir of the Emperor of Caveta, accompanied by Talialicha,[1] the great general and captain of war, and the cacique Adrian [the Apalachee chief], who is a Christian, together with fifty-seven Indians their subjects. They asked me for arms and ammunition for themselves and their people as there were many who were in need of them.

Their entrance having been made with great public ostentation, I ordered a salute to be fired by the guns of the royal fort. They reached the government houses amidst great rejoicings and their usual dance and song, "La Paloma," escorted by a body of infantry which I had sent out to meet them. Myself, together with all the ministers and the officers of this garrison, received them at the door of my residence. All of which will more extensively appear in the written testimony which I herewith enclose.

They were splendidly treated and feasted during the time they remained here, not only on account of Y. M., but also on my own and that of the city, I giving over my own residence to the caciques, in order to please them and to induce them to return satisfied. These attentions proved to be of great importance, as I will mention further. They left here on the 26th of the same month of July,[2] and I sent with them, to go as far as their provinces, a retired officer, lieutenant of cavalry, named Diego Pena, with twelve soldiers, in order that they might procure, either by purchase or exchange, some horses for the company of this garrison, for which purpose they carried with them sufficient silver and goods and a very gorgeous and costly dress for the Emperor as a present, together with a cane and a fine hat with plumes. When they arrived at a place called Caveta, situated 160 leagues from this city, which is the residence of the Emperor, they found there twelve Englishmen and a negro from Carolina, of those who had been previously engaged in destroying the country, who were on horseback. They were there with presents for the Emperor in order to draw him to their side and turn him from this government and from the obedience pledged to Y. M. But when his son, the cacique, who had left here so much gratified, saw that his father, the Emperor, was consenting to the presence of the Englishmen there, he attempted to take up arms against his father. At the same time the dissatisfied Indians, those in favor of the English, were getting ready to fire on our aforesaid soldiers, which they would have done had not the said Osingulo and the great general of war, Talichaliche, together with the Christian cacique Adrian and the subjects of his towns, who were many, taken the part of the Spaniards and accompanied them back to this city, with the exception of the said Osingulo, who started hence for Pensacola in quest of arms and ammunition and men in order to drive the English away and punish those dissatisfied Indians who obeyed his father.[3]

To all intents and purposes, then, the English faction, which included the head chief of Coweta, remained masters of the situation. Shortly afterwards we hear of bands of Apalachee asking permission to establish themselves near the Spanish settlements.

In 1717 a Spanish officer reports Apalachee dispersed in west Florida, near their former country.[4] A part of them removed, however, to Pensacola, probably to be near their congeners at Mobile.

[1] Spelled Talichaliche below.

[2] Barcia (La Florida, p. 329) says the 26th of August.

[3] Brooks, MSS., Miss Brooks's translation with some emendations: also see Barcia, La Florida, p. 329.

[4] Serrano y Sanz, Doc. Hist., p. 228.

Their chief, or their principal chief, was a certain Juan Marcos, and Barcia says that in 1718—

He began to form a town of Apalachee Indians, the people of his own nation, in the place which they call the Rio de los Chiscas, 5 leagues from Santa Maria de Galve [Pensacola], which was named Nuestra Señora de la Soledad, and San Luis; for its peopling he sent the Apalache Indians who were in Santa Maria de Galve with the same rations that they had in the presidio; there came together in it more than a hundred persons; the number was increased every day; with many of the Apalache subject to Movila, who abandoned their lands and came to the new town, causing the post great expense, because, as they did not have crops, it was necessary to give them daily rations of maize until the following year when they could gather fruits; Juan Marcos assured his governor that others would come who were waiting to harvest their crops to return to the authority of the king, from which the French had drawn them. . . . Friar Joseph del Castillo, one of the chaplains of the post, counseled Don Juan Pedro that he should ask the Provincial of Santa Elena for two curates who understood the language of Apalache well in order to teach the Indians in the new town of la Soledad.[1]

Farther on we find the following among the items for the same year:

July 13 two Topocapa Indians came to Santa Maria de Galve, who had fled from Movila on account of the bad treatment of the French. Don Juan Pedro sent them to the new town of the Indians of their nation, which had been formed near the port of San Marcos de Apalache, because they were of a nation subject to the king, who had in their towns curates of the order of St. Francis of the province of Santa Elena, and all those who came in this manner he sent to the people of their own nation, entertained in accordance with their quality, from which they experienced great satisfaction.[2]

It would seem from this that Topocapa was an Apalachee town or else a tribe supposed to be connected with the Apalachee. The new settlement near the port of San Marcos de Apalache seems to have been founded after La Soledad, partly in order to cover a new Spanish post. It was close to Apalachee Bay and therefore on the skirts of the old Apalachee country. Further information regarding the settlement of this place is given in the following words:

April 10 [1719] there arrived at Santa Maria de Galve the chief, Juan Marcos, governor of the new town of la Soledad, who returned from the city of St. Augustine, stating that he had come from founding another town of Apalaches, near the port of San Marcos. Don Juan Pedro gave him a garment and [he gave] another to the captain of the Yamaces, who arrived at the same time with some of his nation; the Indians left very well satisfied, and on the 17th the chief, Juan Marcos, took away to the new town many of the Indians of the town of la Soledad. Those who remained there, seeing that their governor was going, although he assured them he would soon return, discussed the election of a chief, but they did not agree further, and in order to avoid disturbances came to Don Juan Pedro that he might pacify them, and he commended them to their guardian Father that he should persuade them and that they should cease these disputes, cautioning them that he would not entrust to them ornaments of the church until a curate should be named for that particular town.[3]

The new Apalachee settlements in Florida show their influence in the baptismal records of the old church at Mobile, for while there are

[1] Barcia, La Florida, pp. 341-342. [2] Ibid., p. 344. [3] Ibid., pp. 347-348.

many entries between 1704 and 1717, after that date there is a considerable falling off.[1] When Fort Toulouse was founded, about 1715, the Tawasa Indians, formerly neighbors of the Apalachee, settled near it among the Alabama. It is probable that some Apalachee accompanied them. At any rate a few known to be of Apalachee descent are still living among the Alabama near Weleetka, Oklahoma.

At a considerably later date we find two Apalachee towns in the territory which the tribe formerly occupied. Gov. Dionisio de la Vega, to whom we are indebted for information regarding these, represents them as Apalachee which had been left after the destruction of the province. Writing August 27, 1728, he says:

> The entire province of Apalache became reduced to two towns. The one called Hamaste, distant two leagues from the fort [of San Marcos], had about sixty men, forty women, and about the same number of children who were being taught the doctrine. The other one, named San Juan de Guacara, which was its old name, had about ten men, six women, and four children, all Christians.[2]

San Juan de Guacara was, however, originally a Timucua town, and the above settlement may have been Timucua miscalled "Apalache" by the governor, or they may have been Apalachee settled on the site of a former Timucua town. Hamaste was very likely the town established by Juan Marcos. De la Vega adds that these towns had revolted March 20, 1727, but he had learned that some of the Indians had "returned to their obedience," while those still hostile had apparently withdrawn from the neighborhood of the fort.[2] Most of those Apalachee who remained in Florida evidently gravitated at last to the vicinity of Pensacola, where they could also be near the Mobile band. We will now revert to these last.

As already stated, Bienville placed those Apalachee who sought his protection near the Mobile Indians, but their settlement was broken up by the Alabama and they took refuge near the new Fort Louis. Afterward Bienville assigned them lands on the River St. Martin, a league from the fort. "This," says Hamilton, "would be at our Three Mile Creek, probably extending to Chickasabogue, the St. Louis." He adds that "The cellar of the priest's house still exists behind a sawmill near Magazine Point."[3] Some time before 1733 they made another change, perhaps because so many had gone to Pensacola. Says Hamilton:

> We know that at some time they moved over across the bay from the city, where the eastern mouth of the Tensaw River still preserves their name. They seem to have lived in part on an island there, for in Spanish times it is mentioned as only recently abandoned. . . . Their main seat was at and above what we now know as Blakely. Bayou Solimé probably commemorates Salome, so often named in the baptisma.[4]

---

1 Hamilton, Colonial Mobile, pp. 109–111.

2 Brooks, MSS.

3 Hamilton, op. cit., p. 109.

4 Ibid., p. 111.

The last Apalachee baptismal notice in the registers of the parish church at Mobile is under date of 1751.[1]

In his report of 1758 De Kerlerec says under the heading "Apataches," which is of course a misprint for Apalaches:

This nation of about 30 warriors is situated on the other (i. e., east) side of Mobile Bay. They are reduced to this small number on account of the quantity of drink which has been sold to them in trade at all times; they are Christians and have a curacy established among them administered by a Capuchin, who acquits himself of it very poorly.

This nation has been attached to us for a long time. It is divided into two bands, one of which is on Spanish territory, a dependence of Pensacola. The warriors who are allied with us (*dependent de nous*) are equally of great use in conveying the dispatches of Tombigbee and the Alabamas, especially this latter, where we send soldiers as little as possible on account of the too great ease with which they can desert and pass to the English.[2]

In 1763 all Spanish and French possessions east of the Mississippi passed under the government of Great Britain. This change was not at all to the liking of most of the small tribes settled about Mobile Bay, and a letter of M. d'Abbadie, governor of Louisiana, dated April 10, 1764, informs us that the Taensas, Apalachee and the Pakana tribe of the Creeks had already come over to Red River in his province, or were about to do so.[3] We know that such a movement did actually take place. Probably the emigrant Apalachee included both the Mobile and the Pensacola bands. Sibley, in his "Historical sketches of several Indian Tribes in Louisiana, south of the Arkansas River, and between the Mississippi and River Grand," written in 1806, has the following to say regarding this tribe:

Appalaches, are likewise emigrants from West Florida, from off the river whose name they bear; came over to Red River about the same time the Boluxas did, and have, ever since, lived on the river, above Bayau Rapide. No nation have been more highly esteemed by the French inhabitants; no complaints against them are ever heard; there are only fourteen men remaining; have their own language, but speak French and Mobilian.[4]

From the papers on public lands among the American State Papers we know that they and the Taensa Indians settled together on a strip of land on Red River between Bayou d'Arro and Bayou Jean de Jean. This land was sold in 1803 to Miller and Fulton, but only a portion of it was allowed them by the United States commissioners in 1812 on the ground that the sale had not been agreed to by the Apalachee.[5] Nevertheless it is probable that the Apalachee did not remain in possession of their lands for a much longer period, though they appear to have lived in the same general region and to have

[1] Hamilton, op. cit., p. 112.

[2] Internat. Congress Am., Compte Rendu, xv sess., I, p. 86.

[3] Am. Antiq., XIII, 252–253, Sept., 1891.

[4] Sibley in Ann. of Cong., 9th Cong., 2d sess., 1085.

[5] Am. State Papers, Ind. Aff., II, pp. 796–797.

died out there or gradually lost their identity. At the present time there are said to be two or three persons of Apalachee blood still living in Louisiana, but they have forgotten their language and of course all of their aboriginal culture.[1]

THE APALACHICOLA

There has been considerable confusion regarding this tribe, because the name was applied by the Spaniards from a very early period to the Lower Creeks generally, Coweta and Kasihta in one account being mentioned as Apalachicola towns.[2] It is used in its general sense in the very earliest place in the Spanish records in which the name occurs, a letter dated August 22, 1639, and in the same way in letters of 1686 and 1688.[3]

On the other hand, in the letter of 1686 the name "Apalachicoli" is distinctly applied also to a particular town,[4] and inasmuch as it is clearly the name of a tribe and town in later times it is probable that its original application was to such a tribe among or near the Lower Creeks. From this the Spaniards evidently extended it over the whole of the latter. That the town was considered important is shown by the Creek name which it bears, Tålwa łåko, "Big Town," and from Bartram's statement that it was the leading White or Peace town.[5] In one Spanish document we read that Oconee was "under Apalachicolo," and at a council between the Lower Creeks and Spaniards at San Marcos about 1738 Quilate, the chief of this town, spoke for all.[6] Replying to a speech of John Stuart, the British Indian agent, delivered in the Chiaha Square, September 18, 1768, a Lower Creek speaker says: "There are four head men of us have signed our Names in the presence of the whole lower Creeks as you will see: Two of us out of the Pallachicolas which is reckoned the Head Town of upper & lower Creeks and two out of the Cussitaw Town, which are friend Towns, which two towns stand for in behalf of the upper and lower Creeks." It is probable that this speaker wishes to exaggerate the representative character of the chiefs of these two towns, but the important position assigned to Apalachicola was not a mere invention on his part. Ten years later we find John Stuart writing, without the same bias as that which the speaker quoted above may be supposed to have had,

---

1 Information from Dr. Milton Dunn, Colfax, La.

2 It appears in two forms, Apalachicoli and Apachicolo, the first of which is evidently in the Hitchiti dialect, the second in Muskogee. Apalachicola is a compromise term.

3 Lowery, MSS.; Serrano y Sanz, Doc. Hist., pp. 199–201, 219–221. The latter has made an unfortunate blunder in dating the letter of 1686 as if it were 1606.

4 Serrano y Sanz, op. cit., pp. 193, 195.

5 Bartram, Travels, p. 387.

6 Copy of MS. in Ayer Coll., Newberry Library.

148061°—22——9

that this town "is considered as the Mother & Governing Town of the whole Nation."[1]

It is quite probable, as we shall see later, that it was a tribe of considerable size, often scattered among several settlements. In spite of the resemblance which its name bears to that of the Apalachee I am inclined to think that there was only a remote relationship between the two peoples, although the meanings of the two words may have been something alike. The ending of the name resembles *okli*, the Hitchiti word for "people." Judge G. W. Stidham told Dr. Gatschet that he had heard the name was derived from the ridge of earth around the edge of the square ground made in sweeping it.[2] In recent times Apalachicola has always been classed by the Creeks as a Hitchiti-speaking town, while the fragment of Apalachee that has come down to us shows that language to have been an independent dialect.

According to Creek legend the Apalachicola were found in possession of southwestern Georgia when the Muskogee invaded that section.[3] In 1680 two Franciscans were sent into the Province of Apalachicola to begin missionary work, but the Coweta chief would not allow them to remain, and the effort was soon abandoned.[4]

A great deal of light has been thrown upon the ethnographical complexion of the region along Apalachicola River by the discovery by Mr. D. I. Bushnell, Jr., of an old manuscript already alluded to (p. 13), preserved among the Ludwell papers in the archives of the Virginia Historical Society.[5] This gives the account of an Indian named Lamhatty, who was captured by a band of "Tusckaroras," in reality probably Creeks, and who, after having been taken through various Creek towns, was sold to the Shawnee. Later he came northward with a hunting party of Shawnee, escaped from them, and reached the Virginia settlements. As much of his story as he was able to communicate was taken down by Robert Beverly, the historian, and on the reverse side of the sheet containing it was traced a map of the region through which Lamhatty had come, as Lamhatty himself understood it. In his narrative this Indian represents himself as belonging to the Tawasa, or, as he spells it, "Towasa," people, which he says consisted of 10 "nations." In the year 1706, however, the "Tusckaroras" (or Creeks?) made a descent upon them and carried off three of the "nations." In the spring of 1707 they carried off four more, and two fled. The narrative says "the other two fled," but that would leave one still to be accounted for. It is difficult to know just what Lamhatty means by the 10 "nations." On his map there are indeed 10 towns laid down on and near the

---

[1] English Transcriptions, Lib. Cong.

[2] Creek Mig. Leg., I, p. 127.

[3] Ibid., p. 250.

[4] Lowery, MSS.

[5] Published in Amer. Anthrop., n. s. vol. x, pp. 568–574.

lower Apalachicola, but only one is marked "Towasa." Nevertheless it appears likely that the 10 towns are the "nations" to which Lamhatty refers, especially as what he says regarding their fate may be made to fit in very well with other information concerning them. The names of these 10 towns are given as: Towasa, Poúhka, Sowólla, Choctóuh, Ogolaúghoos, Tomoóka, Ephippick, Aulédly, Socsósky, and Sunepâh. Towasa is of course the well-known Tawasa tribe. The five following may probably be identified with the Pawokti, Sawokli, Chatot, Yuchi, and a band of Timucua. This last and the Poúhka are the only ones the identification of which is uncertain. With the remaining four nothing can be done. Of the first six, the Tawasa and Chatot are known to have taken refuge with the French and may have been the two that Lamhatty says fled on the occasion of the second attack.[1] The band of Yuchi evidently remained in this country much longer and may have been the "nation" left out of consideration. The three others identified always remained separate, and we are reduced to the conclusion that the four unidentified towns represented the people afterwards called Apalachicola. They were perhaps those carried off on the last raid.

Be that as it may, the next we hear of the Apalachicola they were settled upon Savannah River at a place known for a long time as Palachocolas or Parachocolas Fort, on the east or southeast side, almost opposite Mount Pleasant, and about 50 miles from the river's mouth. In 1716, after the Yamasee war, the Apalachicola, and part of the Yuchi and Shawnee, abandoned their settlements on the Savannah and moved over to the Chattahoochee. The Apalachicola chief at that time was named Cherokee Leechee.[2] The date is fixed by a manuscript map preserved in South Carolina. They settled first at the junction of the Flint and Chattahoochee Rivers, at a place known long afterwards as Apalachicola Fort. Later they abandoned this site and went higher up; in fact, they probably moved several times.

Some early Spanish documents treat Apalachicola and Cherokee Leechee as distinct towns. Thus in the directions given to a Spanish emissary about to set out for the Lower Creek towns he is informed that he would encounter these towns in the following order: "Tamaxle, Chalaquilicha, Yufala, Sabacola, Ocone, Apalachicalo, Ocmulque, Osuche, Chiaja, Casista, Caveta." This was evidently due to the removal of a large part of the Apalachicola Indians from the forks of Chattahoochee River to the position later occupied by the entire tribe, while some still remained with their chief in the district first settled.

---

1 Later information shows, however, that the Chatot must have fled after the first attack, for they had gone to Mobile before July 28, 1706 (see pp. 123–124).

2 "Cherokee killer" in Creek. Brinton, Floridian Peninsula, p. 141.

Tobias Fitch, in the journal narrating his proceedings among the Creeks in 1725, relates, under date of September 28, that Cherokee Leechee had, indeed, intended to move north as well, but had been frightened out of his purpose by a Spanish emissary who represented that the English were trying to draw away his people in order to send them all across the ocean.[1] He, too, mentions Apalachicola as a distinct town.

A Spanish document gives the name of the Apalachicola chief in 1734 as Sanachiche.[2] Bartram visited them in 1777 and has the following account:

After a little refreshment at this beautiful town [Yuchi] we repacked and set off again for the Apalachucla town, where we arrived after riding over a level plain, consisting of ancient Indian plantations, a beautiful landscape diversified with groves and lawns.

This is esteemed the mother town or capital of the Creek or Muscogulge confederacy; sacred to peace; no captives are put to death or human blood spilt here. And when a general peace is proposed, deputies from all the towns in the confederacy assemble at this capital, in order to deliberate upon a subject of so high importance for the prosperity of the commonwealth.

And on the contrary the great Coweta town, about twelve miles higher up this river, is called the bloody town, where the Micos, chiefs, and warriors assemble when a general war is proposed; and here captives and state malefactors are put to death.

The time of my continuance here, which was about a week, was employed in excursions round about this settlement. One day the chief trader of Apalachucla obliged me with his company on a walk of about a mile and a half down the river, to view the ruins and site of the ancient Apalachucla; it had been situated on a peninsula formed by a doubling of the river, and indeed appears to have been a very famous capital by the artificial mounds or terraces, and a very populous settlement, from its extent and expansive old fields, stretching beyond the scope of the sight along the low grounds of the river. We viewed the mounds or terraces, on which formerly stood their round house or rotunda and square or areopagus, and a little behind these, on a level height or natural step, above the low grounds, is a vast artificial terrace or four square mound, now seven or eight feet higher than the common surface of the ground; in front of one square or side of this mound adjoins a very extensive oblong square yard or artificial level plain, sunk a little below the common surface, and surrounded with a bank or narrow terrace, formed with the earth thrown out of this yard at the time of its formation; the Creeks or present inhabitants have a tradition that this was the work of the ancients, many ages prior to their arrival and possessing this country.

The old town was evacuated about twenty years ago by the general consent of the inhabitants, on account of its unhealthy situation, owing to the frequent inundations of the great river over the low grounds; and moreover they grew timorous and dejected, apprehending themselves to be haunted and possessed with vengeful spirits, on account of human blood that had been undeservedly spilt in this old town, having been repeatedly warned by apparitions and dreams to leave it.

At the time of their leaving this old town, like the ruin or dispersion of the ancient Babel, the inhabitants separated from each other, forming several bands under the conduct or auspices of the chief of each family or tribe. The greatest number, however, chose to sit down and build the present new Apalachucla town, upon a high

[1] Tobias Fitch's Journal, in Mereness, Travels, p. 193.

[2] Copy of a MS. in Ayer Coll., Newberry Library. This name may, however, be intended for that of Tomochichi, the Yamacraw chief.

bank of the river above the inundations. The other bands pursued different routes, as their inclinations led them, settling villages lower down the river; some continued their migration towards the sea coast, seeking their kindred and countrymen amongst the Lower Creeks in East Florida, where they settled themselves.[1]

While this account apparently throws a great deal of light upon the history of the Apalachicola, it actually introduces many perplexities. At the present time Coweta is indeed recognized as the head war town of the Lower Creeks, but the head peace town among them, so far as anyone can now recall, is and always was Kasihta. Still, the name by which this Apalachicola town is now known to the Creeks proper is, as stated above, Tålwa łåko, or Big Town, from which a former prominence may be inferred. Moreover, in the migration legend told to Oglethorpe the priority of Apalachicola as a peace town seems to be taught, Kasihta having acquired the "white" character later.[2] Therefore it is probable that this town did anciently have a sort of precedence among the peace towns of the Lower Creeks. Again it is perplexing to find that Bartram appears to have been entirely unaware of the former residence of the Apalachicola on Savannah River, though their removal had not taken place much over 60 years earlier. In the light of other facts brought out this seems still more confusing. He explains the reference to "human blood undeservedly spilt in this old town" in a footnote, which runs as follows:

About fifty or sixty years ago almost all the white traders then in the nation were massacred in this town, whither they had repaired from the different towns, in hopes of an asylum or refuge, in consequence of the alarm, having been timely apprised of the hostile intentions of the Indians by their temporary wives. They all met together in one house, under the avowed protection of the chiefs of the town, waiting the event; but whilst the chiefs were assembled in council, deliberating on ways and means to protect them, the Indians in multitudes surrounded the house and set fire to it; they all, to the number of eighteen or twenty, perished with the house in the flames. The trader showed me the ruins of the house where they were burnt.[3]

This wholesale massacre reminds us so strongly of the sweeping character of the Yamasee rebellion, which the fact itself can not have followed by many years, that one is at first tempted to think reference is made to that uprising. But at that time the Apalachicola were upon Savannah River, and, since the trader was able to show Bartram the ruins of the house in which the unfortunate victims were burned, it is evident that the massacre could not have taken place there. Another suggestion is that only part of the Apalachicola were on Savannah River, but of this we have not the slightest evidence. It is surprising, to say the least, that Bartram's trading acquaintance could not or would not tell him about the comparatively recent immigration of this tribe among the Lower Creeks. The

[1] Bartram, Travels, pp. 386-390.

[2] Gatschet, Creek Mig. Leg., I, pp. 244-251.

[3] Bartram, Travels, pp. 388-389, note.

extensive mounds which Bartram notes must have owed their origin for the most part to some other of the Lower Creek tribes. It should be observed also that the people whom Bartram calls Lower Creeks were really Seminole, and it is to the Seminole that most of the scattered bands of Apalachicola went.

We find through a list of trading assignments made in 1761 that the "Pallachocolas" were then assigned to Macartan and Campbell.[1] In 1797 the trader was Benjamin Steadham.[2]

Hawkins, in 1799, has the following to say regarding Apalachicola:

> Pā-lā-chooc-le is on the right bank of Chat-to-ho-che, one and a half miles below Au-he-gee creek on a poor, pine barren flat; the land back from it is poor, broken, pine land; their fields are on the left side of the river, on poor land.
>
> This was formerly the first among the Lower Creek towns; a peace town, averse to war, and called by the nation, Tal-lo-wau thluc-co (big town). The Indians are poor, the town has lost its former consequence, and is not now much in estimation.[3]

This confirms Bartram and Tchikilli regarding the former importance of the town, and also shows a rather early fall of the tribe from its high estate.

The census of 1832, taken just before the removal of the Creeks west of the Mississippi, gives 77 "Palochokolo" Indians, and 162 "Tolowarthlocko" Indians, besides 7 slaves.[4] While there were no doubt two settlements of these people at the time, the enumerator has made an evident error in giving the Hitchiti name to one and the Creek name, Tålwa łåko, to the other.

The remnant are to be found principally in the neighborhood of Okmulgee, Okla., a former capital of the Creek Nation in the west.

THE CHATOT

The only one of all of the Apalachicola River tribes which maintained an existence apart from the Creek confederacy was the Chatot—or Chateaux as it is sometimes called. It is probable that this was anciently very important, for La Harpe calls the Apalachicola River "la rivière du Saint-Esprit, a présent des Châteaux, ou Cahouitas." [5] On the Lamhatty map an eastern affluent of the principal river delineated, perhaps the Flint, is called Chouctoúbab, apparently after this tribe.[6] When we first get a clear view of them in the Spanish documents, however, they were living west of Apalachicola River, somewhere near the middle course of the Chipola.

The first mention appears to be in a letter of August 22, 1639, already quoted, in which the governor of Florida states that he has

---

[1] Ga. Col. Docs., VIII, pp. 522–524.
[2] Ga. Hist. Soc. Colls., IX, p. 171.
[3] Ibid., III, p. 65.
[4] Sen. Doc. 512, 23d Cong., 1st sess., IV, pp. 345–347.
[5] La Harpe, Jour. Hist., p. 2.
[6] Amer. Anthrop., n. s. vol. X, p. 569.

made peace between the "Chacatos, Apalachocolos, and Amacanos" and the Apalachee. He adds:

It is an extraordinary thing, because the aforesaid Chacatos never had peace with anybody.[1]

In 1674 two missions were established among the Chatot Indians—San Carlos de los Chacatos and San Nicolas de Tolentino. The same year the friars were threatened by three Chiskas (Yuchi) and appealed to the Apalachee commandant, Capt. Juan Hernandez de Florencia, who proceeded to the Chatot country with 25 soldiers. In the certification which these friars, Fray Miguel de Valverde and Fray Rodrigo de la Barreda, give regarding his conduct they state that they had converted the Chatot chiefs and more than 300 of the common people.[2] In 1675, as appears from a letter from the Spanish governor of Florida to the crown, the Chatot rebelled, incited, as he claims, by the Chiska, wounded Fray Rodrigo de la Barreda, and drove him to Santa Cruz, the new Apalachee mission station on Apalachicola River.[2] There he was protected by Florencia, who put an end to the disturbances,[2] but soon afterwards the Chatot abandoned their country and withdrew among the Apalachee, where they settled in "the land of San Luis."[3] This withdrawal was probably due to hostilities on the part of the Chiska. At the same time the two missions appear to have been combined into one called San Carlos de los Chacatos given in the mission list of 1680 as a "new conversion."[4] In 1695 the governor of Florida writes that shortly before the Lower Creeks, whom he calls "Apalachecole," had entered San Carlos de los Chacatos "and carried off forty two Christians, despoiling and plundering the church."[5] This attack was only a foretaste of what was to come, but for specific information regarding the subsequent troubles of these people we are obliged to turn to French and English sources.

Unfortunately the similarity between the words Chatot and Chacta, or Choctaw, has resulted in some confusion regarding the history of this tribe. Thus the following account in La Harpe, which is made to apply to the Choctaw, probably refers in reality to another English and Creek attack upon the Chatot:

Jan. 7, 1706, M. Lambert brought a Chacta chief; he brought the news that this nation had been attacked by four thousand savages, at the head of whom were many English, who had carried away more than three hundred women and children.[6]

The following items should also be added:

Aug. 25 news was received that two hundred savages allied with the English had gone to Pensacola, and that they had burned the houses which were outside of the

[1] Serrano y Sanz, Doc. Hist., p. 196; also Lowery, MSS.
[2] Lowery, MSS.
[3] Serrano y Sanz, Doc. Hist., p. 208.
[4] See p. 323.
[5] Serrano y Sanz, Doc. Hist., p. 224.
[6] La Harpe, Jour. Hist., pp. 94–95.

fort; that they had killed ten Spaniards and a Frenchman, and made twelve slaves of [Indians of] the Apalache and Chacta Nations.[1]

On the 20th [of November] two hundred Chacta arrived with four slaves and thirteen scalps of Cahouitas and Hiltatamahans.[1]

Bienville's account of the Chatot migration to the neighborhood of Mobile and its causes has already been given.[2] It seems strange that La Harpe nowhere mentions it, but from what Bienville tells us, it is apparent that it followed upon the attack of which news had reached Mobile January 7, 1706. The Lamhatty narrative merely says that three "nations" of the Tawasa were destroyed first, and that in a second expedition in the spring of 1707 four more were swept away.[3] Pénicaut, usually much inferior to La Harpe in his record of events, describes the removal at some length, though he places it in the year 1708, at least two years too late. He says:

Some days afterward, the Chactas, who were a nation repelled from the domination of the Spaniards, arrived at Mobile with their women and children and begged MM. d'Artaguiette and de Bienville to give them a place in which to make their dwelling. Lands were assigned them at a place lower down on the right, on the shore of the bay, in a great arm about a league in circuit. It is still called to-day l'Anse des Chactas.[4]

Hamilton says that this Anse des Chactas extended "from our Choctaw Point west around Garrow's Bend." He adds:

They occupied the site of the present city of Mobile and were its first inhabitants. . . . When Bienville selected this very ground for new Mobile he had to recompense these Choctaws with land on Dog River. Maps of 1717 and later show them on the south side of that stream, sometimes near the bay, sometimes several miles up.

He notes that their name seems to survive in the Choctaw Point just mentioned and in an adjacent swamp known as Choctaw Swamp. Hamilton also cites several entries referring to members of this tribe in the baptismal registers between 1708 and 1729, but one or two of these may be true Mississippi Choctaw, since Hamilton fails to distinguish the two peoples.[5]

In speaking of the tribes about Mobile Bay Du Pratz says:

Nearest the sea on Mobile River is the little Chatot Nation, consisting of about forty cabins; they are friends of the French, to whom they render all the services which can be paid for. They are Catholics or reputed to be such.[6]

He adds that the French post, Fort Louis, was just to the north of them. His information would apply to about the year 1738. According to the late H. S. Halbert, of the Alabama State Department of Archives and History, the Choctaw of Mississippi until lately remembered this tribe, and stated that the Chatot language was dis-

[1] La Harpe, Jour. Hist., p. 103.

[2] Amer. Anthrop. n. s. vol. x, p. 568. See p. 138.

[3] See p. 123.

[4] Margry, v, p. 479.

[5] Colonial Mobile, pp. 113–114.

[6] Du Pratz, Hist. de La Louisiane, II, pp. 212–213.

tinct from their own. Du Pratz, however, in speaking of the small tribes of Mobile Bay, says:

The Chickasaws moreover, regard them as their brothers, because they have almost the same language, as well as those to the east of Mobile who are their neighbors.[1]

This matter has already been considered in full.[2]

About the time when the other Mobile tribes left to settle in Louisiana the Chatot departed also, as we know by Sibley's entry regarding them, though he is wrong in speaking of them as "aborigines" of the part of Louisiana they then inhabited. His statement probably means that they had been one of the first tribes to settle on Bayou Beauf. The entry is as follows:

Chactoos live on Bayau Beauf, about ten miles to the southward of Bayau Rapide, on Red River, toward Appalousa; a small, honest people; are aborigines of the country where they live; of men about thirty; diminishing; have their own peculiar tongue; speak Mobilian. The lands they claim on Bayau Beauf are inferior to no part of Louisiana in depth and richness of soil, growth of timber, pleasantness of surface, and goodness of water.[3]

Their last appearance in history is in the enumeration of Indian tribes contained in Jedidiah Morse's Report to the Secretary of War regarding the Indians, where they are referred to as the "Chatteau," and are located on Sabine River, 50 miles above its mouth.[4] This report was published in 1822, but the information applies to the year 1817. What happened to them later we do not know, but it is probable that they are represented by or in a Choctaw band in the neighborhood of Kinder, Louisiana.

THE TAWASA AND PAWOKTI

The first reference to the Tawasa is by Ranjel and the Fidalgo of Elvas. Tawasa is mentioned as one of the towns at which the De Soto expedition stopped and is placed between Ulibahali (Hołiwahali) and Talisi (Tulsa). It is called by Ranjel Tuasi, by Elvas Toasi.[5] From this location it is evident that the tribe, or part of it, was at that time among the Upper Creeks, but from Lamhatty's narrative it appears they had moved southeast before 1706 and settled somewhere between Apalachicola and Choctawhatchee Rivers. A Spanish letter of 1686 refers to the tribe in one place as "Tauasa," whose chief was "a very great scoundrel," in another as Tabara, the last evidently a misprint.[6] It is impossible to tell from this letter whether the tribe was where De Soto found it or not. In 1706 and 1707, as

[1] Du Pratz, Hist. de la Louisiane, II, p. 214.

[2] See Bull. 43, Bur. Amer. Ethn., pp. 27, 33.

[3] Sibley in Annals of Congress, 9th Cong., 2d sess. (1806–7), 1087.

[4] Morse, Rept. to Sec. of War, p. 373.

[5] Bourne, Narr. of De Soto, I, p. 85; II, p. 114. On plates 2 accompanying, Tawasa (1) and Tulsa (1) should be transposed.

[6] Serrano y Sanz, Doc. Hist., p. 196; also Lowery, MSS.

we know by the Lamhatty document, they were partly destroyed and partly driven away by other Indians. As Lamhatty was himself a Tawasa, and since he represents all of the ten towns to have been Tawasa as well, it will be best to give his statement in this place in the form in which it was recorded by Robert Beverley:

> The foregoing year ye Tusckaroras made war on ye Towasas & destroyed 3 of theyr nations (the whole consisting of ten) haveing disposed of theyr prisoners they returned again & in ye Spring of ye year 1707 they swept away 4 nations more, the other 2 fled, not to be heard of.[1]

The rest consists of an account of the personal fortunes of Lamhatty himself which do not concern us. If the dates given are correct that set by Pénicaut for the appearance of the Tawasa at Mobile, 1705, would seem to be an error. At any rate we know that the Tawasa, or a part of them, did seek refuge with the French. Pénicaut's account of their coming is as follows:

> In the beginning of this year [1705] a nation of savages, named the Toüachas, came to find M. de Bienville at Mobile in order to ask of him a place in which to establish itself; he indicated to them a piece of land a league and a half below the fort, where they remained while we were established at Mobile. These savages are good hunters, and they bring to us every day all kinds of game. They brought in addition to their movables, much corn with which to sow the lands which M. de Bienville had given them. They had left the Spaniards to come to live on the French soil, because they were every day exposed to the incursions of the Alibamons, and they were not supported by the Spaniards.[2]

In 1710, according to the same authority, the year in which the position of the post of Mobile was changed, the Indians were relocated also, or at least some of them, and he says:

> The Taouachas were also placed on the river [Mobile], adjoining the Apalaches and one league above them. They had also left the Spaniards on account of wars with the Alibamons; they are not Christians like the Apalaches, the only Christian nation which has come from the neighborhood of the Spaniards.[3]

Whether due to persistent tradition regarding the early home of this tribe or to the fact that some individuals belonging to it did remain in their old country, we find a Tawasa town laid down among the Lower Creeks on several maps, as, for instance, the Purcell map (pl. 7).

It is strange that, as in the case of the Chatot, La Harpe is silent regarding the time when these people came to Mobile or the circumstances attending their coming, but there are notes in his work which attest that they were certainly there. Thus he says that "in the month of March [1707] the Parcagoules [Pascagoula] declared war on the Touacha Nation. M. de Bienville reconciled them."[4] The 16th of the following November he notes that "some Touachas came to the fort with four scalps and a young slave of the Albika [Abihka]

[1] Amer. Anthrop., n. s. vol. x, p. 568.
[2] Pénicaut in Margry, v, p. 457.
[3] Ibid., p. 486.
[4] La Harpe, Jour. Hist., p. 101.

Nation." [1] Neither La Harpe nor Pénicaut, however, drops a hint about the time or manner of their leaving Mobile. Hamilton has the following to say of them in addition to what Pénicaut tells us:

The only mention of them noticed in the church registers is where, in 1716, Huvé baptized Marguerite, daughter of a savage, slave of Commissary Duclos, and a free Taouache woman. The godmother was Marguerite Le Sueur. What became of them we do not certainly know, but it would seem probable that as early as 1713 they had made some change of residence. The creek Toucha, emptying into Bayou Sara some distance east of Cleveland's Station on the M. & B. R. R., or, according to some, into Mobile River at Twelve Mile Island, would seem even yet to perpetuate this location, which corresponds nearly with Delisle's map, and one of 1744. As Touacha, it occurs a number of times in Spanish documents.[2]

Hamilton's belief that the tribe had made some change of residence as early as 1713 is evidently founded on Pénicaut's statement that the Taënsa were brought to Mobile that year and given "the plantation [habitation] where the Chaouachas [Tawasa] had formerly been located, within two leagues of our fort." [3] However, we know that this event must have taken place in the year 1715.[4]

The removal of the Tawasa I believe to have been due to the establishment of Fort Toulouse, or the Alabama Fort as it is also called, at the junction of the Coosa and Tallapoosa. Pénicaut sets this down among the events of the year 1713,[5] but some of the other happenings recorded by him for the same year, such as the removal of the Taënsa noted above and the outbreak of the Yamasee war, belong properly to 1715. I can not avoid the conclusion that the establishment of this post took place in the year 1715, Bienville having taken advantage of the Yamasee uprising to strengthen himself in that quarter. At any rate it must have been between 1713 and 1715, and it is an important point that just at this time the Tawasa disappear. The mention of a Tawasa in the baptismal records of 1716 need not trouble us,[2] for the woman there referred to, although free, had married a slave and probably remained behind when her people migrated to their new settlement. Their name occurs again in the French census of 1760, when two bodies are given, one settled with the Fus-hatchee Indians on the Tallapoosa, 4 leagues from Fort Toulouse, the other forming an independent body 7 leagues from that post.[6] When next we hear of them it is from Hawkins in 1799, and they are on Alabama River below the old French post, and are reckoned as one of the four towns of the Alabama Indians.[7]

---

[1] La Harpe, Jour. Hist., p. 103.

[2] Hamilton, Col. Mobile, pp. 112–113.

[3] Margry, Déc., v, p. 509.

[4] La Harpe, op. cit., pp. 118–119.

[5] Margry, op. cit., p. 511.

[6] Miss. Prov. Arch., I, pp. 94–95.

[7] Hawkins's description of the Tawasa town as it existed in 1799 is given, along with descriptions of the other Alabama towns, on pp. 197–198.

The fact of this removal from Mobile Bay to the upper Alabama is confirmed from the Indian side by Stiggins in giving what he supposes to be the history of all of the Alabama Indians. He says:

The first settlement we find in tracing the Alabamas (a branch of the Creek or Ispocoga tribe) is at the confluence of the Alabama River and Tensaw Lake, near the town of Stockton, in Baldwin County. Their settlements extended up the lake and river as far as Fort Mimbs; their town sites and other settlements they called Towassee, and at this time they call that extent of country Towassee Talahassee, which is Towassee Old Town. The white settlers of the place call it the Tensaw settlement. The Indians say traditionally that at the time of their residence there that they were a very rude, barbarous set of people and in a frightful state of ignorance; their missile weapons for both war and subsistence were bows and arrows made of cane and pointed with flint or bone sharpened to a point. With the same weapons they repelled their foe in time of war; in the wintertime they got their subsistence in the forest, and they made use of them to kill their fish in the shallow parts of the lakes in the summer season. They say very jocosely they consider that at this time were they to meet one of their ancestors armed in ancient manner, and dressed in full habiliment with buckskin of his own manufacture that it would inspire them with dread to behold his savage appearance. They very often make mention of their forefathers of that age calling it the time when their ancestors made an inhuman appearance, by which we may judge that the then state of their forefathers has been handed down to them as a very rude and frightful state almost beyond conception. They do not pretend to any traditional account, when or for what they emigrated to this distance. They have a tradition that many of the inhabitants of ancient Towassee for some reason unknown to them were carried off on shipboard by the French or some other white people many years since. It must have been in consequence of said interruption when the Towassee settlement was depopulated and carried off on shipboard that the remaining part of the tribe removed up the river and made the settlements and towns Autauga and Towassee in the bend of the river below the city of Montgomery, where they resided to the close of their hostile movements in the year of eighteen hundred and thirteen.[1]

From this it appears that Autauga, the Alabama town farthest downstream, was settled by the same people.[2] From the records available we learn nothing regarding the supposed deportation of part of the tribe, but it is quite likely that some members embarked on sailing vessels, or Stiggins may have confused the Natchez story with this. I have already given my own explanation of the Tawasa removal to the upper Alabama.[3] There is nothing to indicate any break in the amicable relations existing between this tribe and the French.

We may infer that their ancient occupancy of this region, as evidenced by the De Soto narratives, had something to do in determining them to return to it when Fort Toulouse was founded. And it is also probable that their language was not very distantly related to Alabama. At any rate, from this time on they followed the fortunes of the Alabama tribe. Not long after the time to which

[1] Stiggins, MS.

[2] Hawkins's description of Autauga in 1799 is on p. 197.

[3] See p. 139.

Hawkins's description applies the Alabama divided, part moving into Louisiana to be near the French, part remaining with the English and subsequently accompanying the rest of the Creeks into what is now Oklahoma. Some of the Tawasa evidently went to Louisiana, because the name is still remembered by the descendants of that portion of the tribe and the father of one of my most intelligent informants among them was a Tawasa. The majority, however, would seem to have remained with the Creeks, since Tawasa and Autauga are the only names of Alabama towns which appear on the census roll of 1832.[1]

In Hawkins's time Pawokti was the name of one of the four Alabama towns. From the resemblance between the name of the tribe and and Poúhka, one of those given on the Lamhatty map,[2] and from the fact that two other Alabama towns, Tawasa and Autauga, are known to have come from the same region, it may be suspected that the two were identical and that the Pawokti and Tawasa had had similar histories.

Hawkins's description of the town occupied by this tribe as it existed in 1799 is given with his account of the other Alabama towns on page 197.[3]

THE SAWOKLI

The earliest home of the Sawokli of which we have any indication was upon or near the coast of the Gulf of Mexico, probably in the neighborhood of Choctawhatchee Bay. Thus Barcia refers to "the Provinces of Pancacola, Sabacola, and others, upon the ports and bays of the Gulf of Mexico,"[4] and the position above given agrees very well with that assigned to them, under the name "Sowoolla," upon the Lamhatty map.[5]

In a letter written in the year 1680 Gov. Cabrera of Florida says:

> The Cazique Saucola, distant forty leagues from Apalache, came [to the Apalache missions] and three monks went [back] with him, but with no results.[6]

Fray Francisco Gutierrez de Vera, writing May 19, 1681, from this new province, is naturally more optimistic than Cabrera, who was by no means favorable to the missionaries. He says:

> Thirty adults have been baptized in two months, including the head chief and two sons, and his stepfather, and now, on knowing the prayers, his mother will be also, the casique governador, his wife, and three children, and a grandson who has no family, five sons of the principal *enixa*, two *henixas*, and other leading men with their wives and families.[6]

---

[1] Sen. Doc. 512, 23d Cong., 1st. sess., pp. 258–259; Schoolcraft, Ind. Tribes, IV, p. 578.

[2] Amer. Anthrop., n. s. vol. x, p. 571.

[3] Ga. Hist. Soc. Colls., III, p. 36.

[4] Barcia, La Florida, p. 324.

[5] Amer. Anthrop., n. s. vol. x, p. 571.

[6] Lowery, MSS.

The *enixa* or *henixa* was of course the heniha or "second man" of the Creeks. This reference shows that the customs of the Sawokli were even then similar to those of the Creeks proper.

The Sawokli mission was evidently stopped shortly afterwards by those influences which had brought the Apalachicola mission to a premature end, particularly the hostile attitude of the English.

I have ventured a guess that this was one of the three "nations" carried off by hostile Indians in 1706.[1] At any rate, the next we hear of them they are living among the Lower Creeks. They are mentioned, without being definitely located, in a Spanish letter of 1717.[2]

The De Crenay map of 1733 shows a town called "Chaouakale" on the west bank of the Chattahoochee, and another, "Chaogouloux," eastward of the Flint (pl. 5). It seems probable that part of the tribe at least settled first near Ocmulgee River, because on the Moll map of 1720 they are placed on the west bank of a southern affluent of that stream. The name appears in a few later maps—for instance, the Homann map of 1759—but none of these, except the De Crenay map above mentioned, shows a Sawokli town on the Chattahoochee until 1795, when it appears between the Apalachicola town and the mouth of the Flint. This is repeated on some subsequent maps. However, there is every reason to believe that they had been on Chattahoochee River ever since the Yamasee war. They appear in the Spanish enumeration of 1738 and the French estimates of 1750 and 1760.[3] In 1761 the Sawokli trading house was owned by Crook & Co.[4] Sawokli occurs also in the lists of Creek towns given by Bartram,[5] Swan,[6] and Hawkins.[7] Some of these contain a big and a little Sawokli, and Hawkins gives the following description of the two as they existed in his time:

Sau-woo-ge-lo is six miles below O-co-nee, on the right bank of the river [the Chattahoochee], a new settlement in the open pine forest. Below this, for four and a half miles, the land is flat on the river, and much of it in the bend is good for corn. Here We-lau-ne, (yellow water) a fine flowing creek, joins the river; and still lower, Co-waggee, (partridge),[8] a creek sixty yards wide at its mouth. Its source is in the ridge dividing its waters from Ko-e-ne-cuh, Choc-tan hatche and Telague hache;[9] they have some settlements in this neighborhood, on good land.

Sau-woog-e-loo-che is two miles above Sau-woo-ge-lo, on the left bank of the river, in oaky woods, which extend back one mile to the pine forest; they have about twenty families, and plant in the bends of the river; they have a few cattle.[10]

Besides the Big and Little Sawokli which Hawkins describes there was at a very early date a northern branch living in the neighborhood

---

[1] Amer. Anthrop., n. s. vol. x, p. 568.

[2] Serrano y Sanz, Doc. Hist., p. 228.

[3] MS., Ayer Coll.; Miss. Prov. Arch., I, p. 96.

[4] Ga. Col. Docs., VIII, pp. 522–524.

[5] Bartram, Travels, p. 462.

[6] Schoolcraft, Ind. Tribes, V, p. 262.

[7] Ga. Hist. Soc. Colls., III, p. 25.

[8] "Partridge" is probably a mistranslation, the name being a contraction of Okawaigi (see below).

[9] The words "Choc-tan hatche and Telague hache" are wanting in the MS. in the Library of Congress.

[10] Ga. Hist. Soc. Colls., III, pp. 65–66.

of the Kasihta and Coweta. In a Spanish document dated 1738 this seems to be called "Tamaxle Nuevo" and is represented as the northernmost of the Lower Creek towns,[1] but it is usually known by a variant of the tribal name now under discussion, although the initial consonant is sometimes *ch* rather than *s*. One of the two names given above as appearing on the De Crenay map evidently refers to this band, but which is uncertain. In the Spanish census of 1750 it occurs again in the distorted form "Couacalé," [1] and in the French census of 1760 it is spelled "Chaouaklé" and placed between Kasihta and Coweta.[2] Finally, one of my best Indian informants—a man who was born in the country of the Lower Creeks in Alabama—remembered that there were two distinct towns called Sawokli and Tcawokli, both of which he believed to belong to the Hitchiti group. This latter probably gave its name to a branch of Uphapee Creek called Chewockeleehatchee Creek, which in turn furnished the designation for a body of Tulsa who had nothing to do with the Sawokli tribe.[3] If we may trust the census of 1832, a village inhabited by Kasihta bore the same name.[4]

The towns of Okawaigi (or Kawaigi) and Okiti-yagani are said to have branched off from the Sawokli. The former is probably one of the Sawokli towns which appear in the French census. The latter is evidently the "Oeyakbe" of the same list,[2] and the "Weupkees" of the census of 1761,[5] in which the name has been translated into Muskogee, Oiyakpi, "water (or river) fork." Manuel Garcia, a Spanish officer sent against the adventurer Bowles, mentions it in the grossly distorted form "Hogue ôhotehanne."[6] Okawaigi and Okiti-yakani are both in Hitchiti, the first signifying "Place to get water," and the second "Zigzag stream land." They are in the census list of 1832 along with still another Sawokli off branch called Hatchee tcaba [Hatci tcaba] [7] which is to be distinguished carefully from an Upper Creek town of the same name, a branch of Kealedji.[8] After accompanying the other Creeks west the Sawokli soon gave up their independent busk ground and united with the Hitchiti. Their descendants are living near Okmulgee, the former capital of the Creek Nation in the west.

THE PENSACOLA

Westward of the tribes just considered, and probably immediately west of the Sawoḳli, the Spanish "Province of Sabacola," lived anciently the Pensacola. Their name, properly Paⁿshi okla, "Bread People," is Choctaw or from a closely related tongue, but we know

[1] MS. in Ayer Coll., Newberry Lib. This document incidentally serves as an additional argument for the Hitchiti connection of the Tamali Indians.

[2] Miss. Prov. Arch., I, p. 96.

[3] See p. 245.

[4] See p. 225.

[5] Ga. Col. Docs., VIII, 522.

[6] Copy of MS. in Ayer Coll., Newberry Library.

[7] Sen. Doc. 512, 23d Cong., 1st sess., pp. 342-344; Ala. Hist. Soc. Misc. Colls., 1, p. 396.

[8] See p. 272.

next to nothing regarding the people themselves. Our earliest information of value concerning any of the people of this coast is contained in the relation of Cabeza de Vaca, who encountered them in 1528 on his way westward from the Apalachee country by sea with the remains of the Narvaez expedition. Although none of the tribes which the explorers met is mentioned by name there is every reason to believe that one of them was the Pensacola. He says:

That bay from which we started is called the Bay of the Horses. We sailed seven days among those inlets, in the water waist deep, without signs of anything like the coast. At the end of this time we reached an island near the shore. My barge went ahead, and from it we saw five Indian canoes coming. The Indians abandoned them and left them in our hands, when they saw that we approached. The other barges went on and saw some lodges on the same island, where we found plenty of ruffs and their eggs, dried, and that was a very great relief in our needy condition. Having taken them, we went further, and two leagues beyond found a strait between the island and the coast, which strait we christened San Miguel, it being the day of that saint. Issuing from it we reached the coast, where by means of the five canoes I had taken from the Indians we mended somewhat the barges, making washboards and adding to them and raising the sides two hands above water.

Then we set out to sea again, coasting towards the River of Palms. Every day our thirst and hunger increased because our supplies were giving out, as well as the water supply, for the pouches we had made from the legs of our horses soon became rotten and useless. From time to time we would enter some inlet or cove that reached very far inland, but we found them all shallow and dangerous, and so we navigated through them for thirty days, meeting sometimes Indians who fished and were poor and wretched people.

At the end of these thirty days, and when we were in extreme need of water and hugging the coast, we heard one night a canoe approaching. When we saw it we stopped and waited, but it would not come to us, and, although we called out, it would neither turn back nor wait. It being night, we did not follow the canoe, but proceeded. At dawn we saw a small island, where we touched to search for water, but in vain, as there was none. While at anchor a great storm overtook us. We remained there six days without venturing to leave, and it being five days since we had drunk anything our thirst was so great as to compel us to drink salt water, and several of us took such an excess of it that we lost suddenly five men.

I tell this briefly, not thinking it necessary to relate in particular all the distress and hardships we bore. Moreover, if one takes into account the place we were in, and the slight chances of relief, he may imagine what we suffered. Seeing that our thirst was increasing and the water was killing us, while the storm did not abate, we agreed to trust to God, our Lord, and rather risk the perils of the sea than wait there for certain death from thirst. So we left in the direction we had seen the canoe going on the night we came here. During this day we found ourselves often on the verge of drowning and so forlorn that there was none in our company who did not expect to die at any moment.

It was our Lord's pleasure, who many a time shows His favor in the hour of greatest distress, that at sunset we turned a point of land and found there shelter and much improvement. Many canoes came and the Indians in them spoke to us, but turned back without waiting. They were tall and well built, and carried neither bows nor arrows. We followed them to their lodges, which were nearly along the inlet, and landed, and in front of the lodges we saw many jars with water, and great quantities of cooked fish. The chief of that land offered all to the governor and led him to his abode. The dwellings were of matting and seemed to be permanent. When we entered the home of the chief he gave us plenty of fish, while we gave him of our maize, which they ate in our presence, asking for more. So we gave more to them, and the governor presented him with some trinkets. While with the cacique at his lodge, half an hour after sunset, the Indians suddenly fell upon us and upon our sick people on the beach.

They also attacked the house of the cacique, where the governor was, wounding him in the face with a stone. Those who were with him seized the cacique, but as his people were so near he escaped, leaving in our hands a robe of marten-ermine skin, which, I believe, are the finest in the world and give out an odor like amber and musk. A single one can be smelt so far off that it seems as if there were a great many. We saw more of that kind, but none like these.

Those of us who were there, seeing the governor hurt, placed him aboard the barge and provided that most of the men should follow him to the boats. Some fifty of us remained on land to face the Indians, who attacked thrice that night, and so furiously as to drive us back every time further than a stone's throw.

Not one of us escaped unhurt. I was wounded in the face, and if they had had more arrows (for only a few were found) without any doubt they would have done us great harm. At the last onset the Captains Dorantes, Peñalosa and Tellez, with fifteen men, placed themselves in ambush and attacked them from the rear, causing them to flee and leave us. The next morning I destroyed more than thirty of their canoes, which served to protect us against a northern wind then blowing, on account of which we had to stay there, in the severe cold, not venturing out to sea on account of the heavy storm. After this we again embarked and navigated for three days, having taken along but a small supply of water, the vessels we had for it being few. So we found ourselves in the same plight as before.

Continuing onward, we entered a firth and there saw a canoe with Indians approaching. As we hailed them they came, and the governor, whose barge they neared first, asked them for water. They offered to get some, provided we gave them something in which to carry it, and a Christian Greek, called Doroteo Teodoro (who has already been mentioned), said he would go with them. The governor and others vainly tried to dissuade him, but he insisted upon going and went, taking along a negro, while the Indians left two of their number as hostages. At night the Indians returned and brought back our vessels, but without water; neither did the Christians return with them. Those that had remained as hostages, when their people spoke to them, attempted to throw themselves into the water. But our men in the barge held them back, and so the other Indians forsook their canoe, leaving us very despondent and sad for the loss of those two Christians.

In the morning many canoes of Indians came, demanding their two companions, who had remained in the barge as hostages. The governor answered that he would give them up, provided they returned the two Christians. With those people there came five or six chiefs, who seemed to us to be of better appearance, greater authority and manner of composure than any we had yet seen, although not as tall as those of whom we have before spoken. They wore the hair loose and very long, and were clothed in robes of marten, of the kind we had obtained previously, some of them done up in a very strange fashion, because they showed patterns of fawn-colored furs that looked very well.

They entreated us to go with them, and said that they would give us the Christians, water and many other things, and more canoes kept coming towards us, trying to block the mouth of that inlet, and for this reason, as well as because the land appeared very dangerous to remain in, we took again to sea, where we stayed with them till

148061°—22——10

noon. And as they would not return the Christians, and for that reason neither would we give up the Indians, they began to throw stones at us with slings, and darts, threatening to shoot arrows, although we did not see more than three or four bows. While thus engaged the wind freshened and they turned about and left us.[1]

This contains many interesting points. The Bay of Horses must have been somewhere near the mouth of Apalachicola River, and the place where they met the five Indian canoes in what the Spaniards knew later as the province of Sabacola, though the Indians need not have been of that tribe, as we know from the account of Lamhatty that there were several other peoples in the neighborhood. The poor fisher folk whom they encountered were of the same province. The inlet in which they found the first Indian settlement must have been either East Pass or the entrance to Pensacola Bay, and the second entrance where Doroteo Teodoro and the negro went after water would be either Pensacola entrance or the opening into Mobile Bay. That these points were not west of Mobile Bay at all events is shown by one circumstance. In his narrative of the De Soto expedition Ranjel says:

In this village, Piachi, it was learned that they had killed Don Teodoro and a black, who came from the ships of Pamphilo de Narvaez.[2]

Now, from a study of the narratives, we feel sure that Piachi was near the upper course of the Alabama River or between it and the Tombigbee. It thus appears that the Greek and the negro were carried, or traveled, inland, but it is not likely that they deviated much from the direct line inland, not more than the ascent of the Alabama or Tombigbee would make necessary.

We need not suppose that the place where these Indians were met was Pensacola Bay, for there is reason to believe that at least the lower portion of Mobile Bay, perhaps the upper portion also, was in times shortly before the opening of certain history occupied by tribes different from those found in possession by the French. It will be remembered that when Iberville settled at Biloxi and began to explore the coast eastward he touched at an island which he named Massacre Island, "because we found there, at the southwest end, a place where more than 60 men or women had been killed. Having found the heads and the remainder of the bones with much of their household articles, it did not appear that it was more than three or four years ago, nothing being yet rotted."[3] The journal of the second ship, *Le Marin*, confirms the statement, and adds:

The savages who are along this coast are wanderers (vagabonds); when they are satiated with meat they come to the sea to eat fish, where there is an abundance of it.[4]

---

1 Bandelier, The Journey of Alvar Nunez Cabeza de Vaca, pp. 41–49.

2 Bourne, Narr. of De Soto, II, p. 123.

3 Iberville in Margry, IV, p. 147.

4 Margry, Déc., IV, p 232.

Pénicaut, as usual, "improves upon the truth." He says:

We were very much frightened, on landing there, to find such a prodigious number of bones of the dead that they formed a mountain, so many there were. We learned afterward that it was a numerous nation, which being pursued and having retired into the country, had almost all died there of sickness, and as it is the custom of savages to collect together all the bones of the dead, they had brought them to this place. This nation is named Movila, of which there still remain a small number.[1]

Pénicaut's conclusion was probably due to his knowledge that it was customary among the Choctaw, and probably some of the neighboring nations as well, to treat the bones of the dead as he describes, but his explanation is not borne out by the descriptions of Iberville and his colleague, who are much more worthy of credence. Of course, there is no certainty to what tribe the bones in question belonged, but I make the suggestion that they were from some band of the ancient coast people of whom I am speaking. It is possible that, instead of being members of the Mobile tribe, the people killed here had been the victims of the Mobile. Perhaps these sinister relics and the mysterious disappearance of the Pensacola may have been due to causes set in motion by De Soto, 20 years after the time of Cabeza de Vaca, when he overthrew the Mobile Indians. At that period it is not improbable that they pushed down toward the coast and were instrumental in destroying the aboriginal inhabitants of the region.

In November, 1539, while De Soto was in the Province of Apalachee, Maldonado was despatched westward in the brigantines. He returned reporting that he had discovered an excellent harbor. He "brought an Indian from the province adjacent to this coast, which was called Achuse, and he brought a good blanket of sable fur. They had seen others in Apalache, but none like that." This is from Ranjel's account.[2] The Fidalgo of Elvas says that this province, which he calls "Ochus," was "sixty leagues from Apalache" and that Maldonado had "found a sheltered port with a good depth of water."[3] Biedma states that Maldonado "coasted along the country, and entered all the coves, creeks, and rivers he discovered, until he arrived at a river having a good entrance and harbour, with an Indian town on the seaboard. Some inhabitants approaching to traffic, he took one of them, and directly turned back with him to join us." He adds that he was absent on this voyage two months.[4] Later the bay in which the De Luna colonists established themselves is called the "Bay of Ichuse," or "Ychuse," but it is uncertain whether this was

[1] Margry, Déc., v, p. 383.
[2] Bourne, Narr. of De Soto, II, p. 81.
[3] Ibid., I, p. 50.
[4] Ibid., II, pp. 8-9.

Mobile or Pensacola.[1] Nevertheless, what Biedma says of the river and his later statement, when the army reached what must have been the Alabama, or a stream between it and the Tombigbee, that they considered it to be "that which empties into the Bay of Chuse,"[2] along with the further fact that they there heard of the brigantines,[3] would seem to indicate Mobile. An interesting point in connection with this expedition of Maldonado is the mention of the "good blanket of sable fur" superior to anything they had seen in Apalachee, because it will be recalled that Cabeza de Vaca noticed in the very same region "a robe of marten-ermine skin" which he believed to be "the finest in the world."[4] The blankets seen by Cabeza de Vaca and the companions of De Soto were probably of the same sort, and it is likely that the Indians of that particular region had peculiar skill in making them. The names Achuse, Ochus, Ichuse, Ychuse recall the Hitchiti word *Otcisi*, "people of a different speech," and it is not improbable that the term occurred likewise in Apalachee and was applied to this province because the Pensacola and Mobile languages were distinct from those spoken east of them.

In letters written in 1677 this tribe and the Chatot are mentioned as peoples living between the Chiska Indians and the Gulf of Mexico,[5] and from a letter dated May 19, 1686, and sent by Antonio Matheos, lieutenant among the Apalachee, to the governor of Florida, it appears that the "Panzacola" were then at war with the Mobile Indians,[6] a circumstance which would tend to bear out my theory above expressed. Shortly afterwards, however, when a Spanish post was established in their country the tribe itself had disappeared. Barcia says:

> They say that the province was called Pancacola because anciently a nation of Indians inhabited it named Pancocolos, which the neighboring nations destroyed in wars, leaving only the name in the province.[7]

Nevertheless, Barcia himself records encounters with Indians in the surrounding country by the Spaniards sent to make a reconnoissance of the harbor in 1693. His account is as follows:

> On the 11th [of September] starting from the "Punta de Gijon" and navigating in a depth of from one to two fathoms, they went along the coast, going northeast with easterly wind, and at a distance of about two leagues and a half, it looked as if the water had changed its colour. They tasted it and found it sweet, and one-quarter of a league further on it was very sweet and they were then sure it was the mouth of a river which ran east-southeast, about three-quarters of a league and its width was one fourth [of a league], being lost at the distance mentioned. On the north side there is a canal, which extends about a pistol shot. They entered the first inlet

[1] See p. 159.
[2] Bourne, Narr. of De Soto, II, p. 17.
[3] Ibid., p. 21.
[4] See p. 145.
[5] Serrano y Sanz, Doc. Hist., p. 197; Lowery, MSS.
[6] Ibid., p. 210.
[7] Barcia, La Florida, p. 316.

for about a quarter of a league and seeing some smoke rise on the south shore, they discovered three bulks which looked like tree trunks, but when these began to move towards the forest, they recognised them to be Indians. They jumped on land and although they tried to catch up with them they could not find them any more, not even their traces, for the soil was covered with dry leaves.

They found the lighted fire, and on it a badly shaped earthen pan, with lungs[1] of bison, very tastelessly prepared, stewing in it, and some pieces of meat toasting on wooden roasters. On one of them some fish was transfixed, which looked like "Chuchos." In baskets made of reed, and which the Indians call "Uzate" (Uçate) there was some corn, calabash-seeds, bison-wool and hair of other animals, put in deerskin bags, a lot of mussels (shell-fish), shells, bones and similar things. They found several feather plumes of fine turkeys,[2] cardinal birds or redbirds, and other birds and many small crosses, the sight of which delighted them, although they recognised soon that those were spindles on which the Indian women span the wool of the bison. The Spaniards put into one of the baskets cakes, into the other knives and scissors, and, after erecting a cross, they returned to their boat. They navigated half a league when they saw to starboard four or five Indians, who, in order to escape more swiftly threw away all they carried. They [the Spaniards] landed and found several skins of marten, fox, otter, and bison and a lot of meat pulverised and putrid, in wooden troughs.[3] In one of the baskets which were strewn about, they found some roots looking like iris or ginger, very sweet in taste, bison-wool done up in balls, spindles and beaver-wool or hair in bags, very soft white feathers and pulverised clay or earth apparently for painting, combs, not so badly made, leather shoes shaped more like boots, claws of birds and other animals, roots of dittany,[4] several pieces of brazil, a very much worn, large hoe and an iron adze. The Indian huts, which they saw here, were made of tree-bark and in the sea were two canoes or boats, one with bows and arrows made of very strong wood and points of bone; the other was badly used [in bad condition]. These boats showed that those Indians had probably come here by water . . .

. . . Toward the south-southeast went Don Carlos de Siguenza with captain Juan Jordan, Antonio Fernandez, carpenter, and an artillery man, and they found a hut, built on four posts and covered with palm leaves. Inside they found a deerskin, a sash made of bison wool, a piece of blue cloth of Spain, about a yard and a half long and thrown over the poles, many mother-of-pearl shells, fish-spines, animal-bones and several large locks of [human hair]. A little further on at the foot of a tall pine tree they saw in a hamper[5] a decayed body, to all appearances that of a woman; but, leaving all this as it was, they went to the spot where they had seen the two Indians and they found one, who fled, leaving in the place where he had been a gourd filled with water and a bit of roasted meat; which provisions, however, made them suppose him to be a sentinel, the more so as they soon found traces of children's and women's feet, but could find nobody.[6]

There are also three specific references to the Pensacola by French writers. Pénicaut states that in 1699 the chiefs of "five different nations, named the Pascagoulas, the Capinans, the Chicachas, the Passacolas, and the Biloxis, came with ceremony to our fort, singing,

1 Probably the whole lights, or haslet, i, e., lungs, heart, and liver.

2 Plumeras de plumas de pavos finos.

3 Pilones, probably wooden mortars.

4 Which might have been flaxinella or marjoram.

5 *Petaca* means really a leather trunk fashioned after the style of a hamper.

6 Barcia, La Florida, pp. 309–310. Translated by Mrs. F. Bandelier.

to present the calumet to M. d'Iberville."[1] La Harpe in his *Journal Historique* says that on October 1, 1702, at Mobile, "other savages were received who sang the calumet, and promised to live in peace with the Chicachas, the Pensacolas, and the Apalaches."[2] These "other savages" were probably Alabama Indians. And finally, Bienville in an unpublished account of the native tribes of Louisiana dating from about 1725 says that the villages of the Pensacola and Biloxi lay near each other on Pearl River, the two containing but 40 warriors.[3] In a letter on Indian affairs, dated Pensacola, December 1, 1764, is an estimate of the Indian population in the Gulf region, and among the entries, we read, "Beloxies, Chactoes, Capinas, Panchaculas [Pensacolas], Washaws, Chawasaws, Pascagulas, 251."[4] It is therefore probable that a remnant of the tribe continued a precarious existence, probably in close alliance with some larger one, for a long time after it was supposed to be extinct. This would be quite in line with what we find in the case of so many other small tribes.

THE MOBILE AND TOHOME

So far as our information goes, the first white men to have dealings with the Indians of Mobile Bay were probably the Spaniards under Pinedo. Pinedo was sent out by Garay, governor of Jamaica, in the year 1519, to explore toward the north, and he appears to have coasted along the northern shore of the Gulf of Mexico from the peninsula of Florida to Panuco. In the description of this voyage in the Letters Patent we read that after having covered the entire distance "they then turned back with the said ships, and entered a river which was found to be very large and very deep, at the mouth of which they say they found an extensive town, where they remained 40 days and careened their vessels. The natives treated our men in a friendly manner, trading with them, and giving what they possessed. The Spaniards ascended a distance of 6 leagues up the river, and saw on its banks, right and left, 40 villages."[5]

The river referred to is usually identified with the Mississippi, but I am entirely in accord with Mr. Hamilton in finding in it the River Mobile.[6] When first known to us the banks of the Mississippi near the ocean were not permanently occupied by even small tribes, and occupancy the year around would have been practically impossible. On the other hand, the shores of Mobile River must once have been quite thickly settled, for Iberville, on his first visit to the Indian tribes there, notes numbers of abandoned Indian settlements all along the way. There seems to be practically no other place answer-

[1] Margry, Déc., v, p. 378.
[2] La Harpe, Jour. Hist., pp. 73-74.
[3] French transcription, Lib. Cong.
[4] Amer. Hist. Rev., xx, No. 4, p. 825.
[5] Harrisse, Disc. of N. Amer., p. 168.
[6] Hamilton, Col. Mobile, p. 10.

ing to the description here given. The later depopulation can be accounted for by the wars of which Iberville speaks and by the pestilences, which seem to have moved just a little in advance of the front rank of white invasion.

Narvaez encountered some of the Indians of Mobile Bay,[1] but it is open to question whether they were the ones in possession in Iberville's time. The Province of Achuse or Ochus, discovered by Maldonado, may also have been here, and again it may have been about Pensacola.[2]

Our next historical encounter with the Mobile tribes was that famous and sanguinary meeting between De Soto and the Mobile, which has served to immortalize the Indians participating almost as much as does the city which bears their name.

According to Ranjel they first heard of the people of Mobile at "Talisi," probably the Creek town now known as Tâlsi, where messengers reached them from Tascaluça, the Mobile chief. His name is in the Choctaw language or one almost identical with Choctaw, just as we should expect, and means "Black warrior." Ranjel calls him "a powerful lord and one much feared in that land." "And soon," he adds, "one of his sons appeared and the governor ordered his men to mount and the horsemen to charge and the trumpets to be blown (more to inspire fear than to make merry at their reception). And when those Indians returned the commander sent two Christians with them instructed as to what they were to observe and to spy out, so that they might take counsel and be forewarned."

On Tuesday, October 5, 1540, the army left Talisi and, after passing through several villages, encamped the following Saturday, October 9, within a league of Tascaluça's village. "And the governor dispatched a messenger, and he returned with the reply that he would be welcome whenever he wished to come." Ranjel's narrative goes on as follows:

Sunday, October 10, the governor entered the village of Tascaluça, which is called Athahachi, a recent village. And the chief was on a kind of balcony on a mound at one side of the square, his head covered by a kind of coif like the almaizal, so that his headdress was like a Moor's, which gave him an aspect of authority; he also wore a *pelote* or mantle of feathers down to his feet, very imposing; he was seated on some high cushions, and many of the principal men among his Indians were with him. He was as tall as that Tony of the Emperor, our lord's guard, and well proportioned, a fine and comely figure of a man. He had a son, a young man as tall as himself, but more slender. Before this chief there stood always an Indian of graceful mien holding a parasol on a handle something like a round and very large fly fan, with a cross similar to that of the Knights of the Order of St. John of Rhodes, in the middle of a black field, and the cross was white. And although the governor entered the plaza and alighted from his horse and went up to him, he did not rise, but remained passive in perfect composure, and as if he had been a king.

---

[1] See pp. 144–146. [2] See pp. 147–148.

The governor remained seated with him a short time, and after a little he arose and said that they should come to eat, and he took him with him and the Indians came to dance; and they danced very well in the fashion of rustics in Spain, so that it was pleasant to see them. At night he desired to go, and the commander told him that he must sleep there. He understood it and showed that he scoffed at such an intention for him, being the lord, to receive so suddenly restraints upon his liberty, and dissembling, he immediately despatched his principal men each by himself, and he slept there notwithstanding his reluctance. The next day the governor asked him for carriers and a hundred Indian women; and the chief gave him four hundred carriers and the rest of them and the women he said he would give at Mabila, the province of one of his principal vassals. And the governor acquiesced in having the rest of that unjust request of his fulfilled in Mabila; and he ordered him to be given a horse and some buskins and a scarlet cloak for him to ride off happy.

At last, Tuesday, October 12, they departed from the village of Atahachi, taking along the chief, as has been said, and with him many principal men, and always the Indian with the sunshade attending his lord, and another with a cushion And that night they slept in the open country The next day, Wednesday, they came to Piachi, which is a village high above the gorge of a mountain stream; and the chief of this place was evil intentioned, and attempted to resist their passage; and as a result, they crossed the stream with effort, and two Christians were slain, and also the principal Indians who accompanied the chief. In this village, Piachi, it was learned that they had killed Don Teodoro and a black, who came from the ships of Pamphilo de Narvaez.[1]

Saturday, October 16, they departed thence into a mountain where they met one of the two Christians whom the governor had sent to Mabila, and he said that in Mabila there had gathered together much people in arms The next day they came to a fenced village, and there came messengers from Mabila bringing to the chief much bread made from chestnuts, which are abundant and excellent in that region.

Monday, October 18, St. Luke's day, the governor came to Mabila, having passed that day by several villages, which was the reason that the soldiers stayed behind to forage and to scatter themselves, for the region appeared populous And there went on with the governor only forty horsemen as an advance guard, and after they had tarried a little, that the governor might not show weakness, he entered into the village with the chief, and all his guard went in with him. Here the Indians immediately began an areyto,[2] which is their fashion for a ball with dancing and song. While this was going on some soldiers saw them putting bundles of bows and arrows slyly among some palm leaves, and other Christians saw that above and below the cabins were full of people concealed. The governor was informed of it, and he put his helmet on his head and ordered all to go and mount their horses and warn all the soldiers that had come up. Hardly had they gone out when the Indians took the entrances of the stockade, and there were left with the governor, Luis de Moscoso and Baltasar de Gallegos, and Espindola, the captain of the guard, and seven or eight soldiers. And the chief went into a cabin and refused to come out of it. Then they began to shoot arrows at the governor. Baltasar de Gallegos went in for the chief, he not being willing to come out. He disabled the arm of a principal Indian with the slash of a knife. Luis de Moscoso waited at the door, so as not to leave him alone, and he was fighting like a knight and did all that was possible until "not being able to endure any more, he cried, Señor Baltasar de Gallegos, come out, or I will leave you, for I cannot wait any longer for you." During this, Solis, a resident of Triana of Seville, had ridden up, and Rodrigo Ranjel, who were the first, and for his sins Solis was immediately stricken down dead; but Rodrigo Ranjel got to the gate of the town at the time when

---

[1] See p. 145. [2] A West Indian word for an Indian dance. (Note by Bourne.)

the governor went out, and two soldiers of his guard with him, and after him came more than seventy Indians who were held back for fear of Rodrigo Ranjel's horse, and the governor, desiring to charge them, a negro brought up his horse; and he told Rodrigo Ranjel to give aid to the captain of the guard, who was left behind, for he had come out quite used up, and a soldier of the guard with him; and he with a horse faced the enemy until he got out of danger, and Rodrigo Ranjel returned to the governor and had him draw out more than twenty arrows, which he bore fastened to his armour, which was a loose coat quilted with coarse cotton. And he ordered Ranjel to watch for Solis, to rescue him from the enemy, that they should not carry him inside. And the governor went to collect the soldiers. There was great valour and shame that day among all those that found themselves in this first attack and beginning of this unhappy day; for they fought to admiration and each Christian did his duty as a most valiant soldier. Luis de Moscoso and Baltasar de Gallegos came out with the rest of the soldiers by another gate.

As a result the Indians were left with the village and all the property of the Christians, and with the horses that were left tied inside, which they killed immediately. The governor collected all of the forty horse that were there and advanced to a large open place before the principal gate of Mabila. There the Indians rushed out without venturing very far from the stockade, and to draw them on the horsemen made a feint of taking flight at a gallop, withdrawing far from the walls. And the Indians believing it to be real, came away from the village and the stockade in pursuit, greedy to make use of their arrows. And when it was time the horsemen wheeled about on the enemy, and before they could recover themselves, killed many with their lances. Don Carlos wanted to go with his horse as far as the gate, and they gave the horse an arrow shot in the breast. And not being able to turn, he dismounted to draw out the arrow, and then another came which hit him in the neck above the shoulder, at which, seeking confession, he fell dead. The Indians no longer dared to withdraw from the stockade. Then the Commander invested them on every side until the whole force had come up; and they went up on three sides to set fire to it, first cutting the stockade with axes. And the fire in its course burned the two hundred odd pounds of pearls that they had, and all their clothes and ornaments, and the sacramental cups, and the moulds for making the wafers, and the wine for saying the mass; and they were left like Arabs, completely stripped, after all their hard toil. They had left in a cabin the Christian women, which were some slaves belonging to the governor; and some pages, a friar, a priest, a cook, and some soldiers defended themselves very well against the Indians, who were not able to force an entrance before the Christians came with the fire and rescued them. And all the Spaniards fought like men of great courage, and twenty-two died, and one hundred and forty-eight others received six hundred and eighty-eight arrow wounds, and seven horses were killed and twenty-nine others wounded. Women and even boys of four years of age fought with the Christians; and Indian boys hanged themselves not to fall into their hands, and others jumped into the fire of their own accord. See with what good will those carriers acted. The arrow shots were tremendous, and sent with such a will and force that the lance of one gentleman named Nuño de Tovar, made of two pieces of ash and very good, was pierced by an arrow in the middle, as by an auger, without being split, and the arrow made a cross with the lance.

On that day there died Don Carlos, and Francis de Soto, the nephew of the Governor, and Johan de Gamez de Jaen, and Men Rodriguez, a fine Portugues gentleman, and Espinosa, a fine gentleman, and another named Velez, and one Blasco de Barcarrota, and many other honoured soldiers; and the wounded comprised all the men of most worth and honour in the army. They killed three thousand of the vagabonds without counting many others who were wounded and whom they afterwards found dead in the cabins and along the roads. Whether the chief was dead or alive was never known. The son they found thrust through with a lance.

After the end of the battle as described, they rested there until the 14th of November, caring for their wounds and their horses, and they burned over much of the country.[1]

Biedma's account of this affair is as follows:

From this point (Coça) we went south, drawing towards the coast of New Spain, and passed through several towns, before coming to another province, called Taszaluza, of which an Indian of such size was chief that we all considered him a giant. He awaited us quietly at his town, and on our arrival we made much ado for him, with joust at reeds, and great running of horses, although he appeared to regard it all as a small matter. Afterward we asked him for Indians to carry our burdens; he answered that he was not accustomed to serving any one, but it was rather for others all to serve *him*. The governor ordered that he should not be allowed to return to his house, but be kept where he was. This detention among us he felt—whence sprang the ruin that he afterwards wrought us, and it was why he told us that he could there give us nothing, and that we must go to another town of his, called Mavila, where he would bestow on us whatever we might ask. We took up our march in that direction, and came to a river, a copious flood, which we considered to be that which empties into the Bay of Chuse. Here we got news of the manner in which the boats of Narvaez had arrived in want of water, and of a Christian, named Don Teodoro, who had stopped among these Indians, with a negro, and we were shown a dagger that he had worn. We were here two days, making rafts for crossing the river. In this time the Indians killed one of the guard of the governor, who, thereupon, being angry, threatened the cacique, and told him that he should burn him if he did not give up to him those who had slain the Christian. He replied that he would deliver them to us in that town of his, Mavila. The cacique had many in attendance. An Indian, was always behind him with a fly brush of plumes, so large as to afford his person shelter from the sun.

At nine o'clock one morning we arrived at Mavila, a small town very strongly stockaded, situated on a plain. We found the Indians had demolished some habitations about it, to present a clear field. A number of the chiefs came out to receive us as soon as we were in sight, and they asked the governor, through the interpreter, if he would like to stop on that plain or preferred to enter the town, and said that in the evening they would give us the Indians to carry burdens. It appeared to our chief better to go thither with them, and he commanded that all should enter the town, which we did.

Having come within the enclosure, we walked about, talking with the Indians, supposing them to be friendly, there being not over three or four hundred in sight, though full five thousand were in the town, whom we did not see, nor did they show themselves at all. Apparently rejoicing, they began their customary songs and dances; and some fifteen or twenty women having performed before us a little while, for dissimulation, the cacique got up and withdrew into one of the houses. The governor sent to tell him that he must come out, to which he answered that he would not; and the captain of the bodyguard entered the door to bring him forth, but seeing many Indians present, fully prepared for battle, he thought it best to withdraw and leave him. He reported that the houses were filled with men, ready with bows and arrows, bent on some mischief. The governor called to an Indian passing by, who also refusing to come, a gentleman near took him by the arm to bring him, when, receiving a push, such as to make him let go his hold, he drew his sword and dealt a stroke in return that cleaved away an arm.

---

[1] Ranjel, Trans. in Bourne, Narr. of De Soto, II, pp. 120–128.

With the blow they all began to shoot arrows at us, some from within the houses. through the many loopholes they had arranged, and some from without. As we were so wholly unprepared, having considered ourselves on a footing of peace, we were obliged, from the great injuries we were sustaining, to flee from the town, leaving behind all that the carriers had brought for us, as they had there set down their burdens. When the Indians saw that we had gone out, they closed the gates, and beating their drums, they raised flags, with great shouting; then, emptying our knapsacks and bundles, showed up above the palisades all we had brought, as much as to say that they had those things in possession. Directly as we retired, we bestrode our horses and completely encircled the town, that none might thence anywhere escape. The governor directed that sixty of us should dismount, and that eighty of the best accoutred should form in four parties, to assail the place on as many sides, and the first of us getting in should set fire to the houses, that no more harm should come to us; so we handed over our horses to other soldiers who were not in armour, that if any of the Indians should come running out of the town they might overtake them.

We entered the town and set it on fire, whereby a number of Indians were burned, and all that we had was consumed, so that there remained not a thing. We fought that day until nightfall, without a single Indian having surrendered to us, they fighting bravely on like lions. We killed them all, either with fire or the sword, or, such of them as came out, with the lance, so that when it was nearly dark there remained only three alive; and these, taking the women that had been brought to dance, placed the twenty in front, who, crossing their hands, made signs to us that we should come for them. The Christians advancing toward the women, these turned aside, and the three men behind them shot their arrows at us, when we killed two of them. The last Indian, not to surrender, climbed a tree that was in the fence, and taking the cord from his bow, tied it about his neck, and from a limb hanged himself.

This day the Indians slew more than twenty of our men, and those of us who escaped only hurt were two hundred and fifty, bearing upon our bodies seven hundred and sixty injuries from their shafts. At night we dressed our wounds with the fat of the dead Indians, as there was no medicine left, all that belonged to us having been burned. We tarried twenty-seven or twenty-eight days to take care of ourselves, and God be praised that we were all relieved. The women were divided as servants among those who were suffering most. We learned from the Indians that we were as many as forty leagues from the sea. It was much the desire that the governor should go to the coast, for we had tidings of the brigantines; but he dared not venture thither, as it was already the middle of November, the season very cold; and he found it necessary to go in quest of a country where subsistence might be had for the winter; here there was none, the region being one of little food.[1]

The Elvas narrative parallels that of Ranjel in most particulars but adds interesting details. It confirms the Ranjel narrative in stating that the first messenger from Tascaluça reached De Soto at the Tålsi town. From what he tells us a little farther on it would seem that the village called Caxa by Ranjel was the first belonging to the Province of Tascaluça, or Tastaluça as Elvas has it. "The following night," he goes on to say, "he [De Soto] rested in a wood, two leagues from the town where the cacique resided, and where he was then present. He sent the field marshal, Luis de Moscoso, with fifteen cavalry, to inform him of his approach."

---

[1] Bourne, Narr. of De Soto, II, pp. 16–21.

From this point we will follow the narrative consecutively:

The cacique was at home, in a piazza. Before his dwelling, on a high place, was spread a mat for him, upon which two cushions were placed, one above another, to which he went and sat down, his men placing themselves around, some way removed, so that an open circle was formed about him, the Indians of the highest rank being nearest to his person. One of them shaded him from the sun with a circular umbrella, spread wide, the size of a target, with a small stem, and having a deerskin extended over cross-sticks, quartered with red and white, which at a distance made it look of taffeta, the colours were so very perfect. It formed the standard of the chief, which he carried into battle. His appearance was full of dignity: he was tall of person, muscular, lean, and symmetrical. He was the suzerain of many territories and of a numerous people, being equally feared by his vassals and the neighboring nations. The field marshal, after he had spoken to him, advanced with his company, their steeds leaping from side to side, and at times towards the chief, when he, with great gravity, and seemingly with indifference, now and then would raise his eyes and look on as in contempt.

The governor approached him, but he made no movement to rise; he took him by the hand, and they went together to seat themselves on the bench that was in the piazza.

Here follows the speech of the chief, real or imaginary, which we will omit.

The governor satisfied the chief with a few brief words of kindness. On leaving, he determined for certain reasons, to take him along. The second day on the road he came to a town called Piache; a great river ran near, and the governor asked for canoes. The Indians said they had none, but that they could have rafts of cane and dried wood, whereon they might readily enough go over, which they diligently set about making, and soon completed. They managed them; and the water being calm, the governor and his men easily crossed. . . .

After crossing the river of Piache, a Christian having gone to look after a woman gotten away from him, he had been either captured or killed by the natives, and the governor pressed the chief to tell what had been done; threatening, that should the man not appear, he would never release him. The cacique sent an Indian thence to Mauilla, the town of a chief, his vassal, whither they were going, stating that he sent to give him notice that he should have provisions in readiness and Indians for loads; but which, as afterwards appeared, was a message for him to get together there all the warriors in his country.

The governor marched three days, the last of them continually, through an inhabited region, arriving on Monday, the eighteenth day of October, at Mauilla. He rode forward in the vanguard, with fifteen cavalry and thirty infantry, when a Christian he had sent with a message to the cacique, three or four days before, with orders not to be gone long, and to discover the temper of the Indians, came out from the town and reported that they appeared to him to be making preparations for that while he was present many weapons were brought, and many people came into the town, and work had gone on rapidly to strengthen the palisade. Luis de Moscoso said that, since the Indians were so evil disposed, it would be better to stop in the woods; to which the governor answered, that he was impatient of sleeping out, and that he would lodge in the town.

Arriving near, the chief came out to receive him, with many Indians singing and playing on flutes, and after tendering his services, gave him three cloaks of marten skins. The governor entered the town with the caciques, seven or eight men of his guard, and three or four cavalry, who had dismounted to accompany them; and they seated themselves in a piazza. The cacique of Tastaluca asked the governor to allow him to remain there, and not to weary him any more with walking; but, finding that was not to be permitted, he changed his plan, and under pretext of speaking with some of the chiefs, he got up from where he sate, by the side of the governor, and entered a house where were many Indians with their bows and arrows. The governor, finding that he did not return, called to him; to which the cacique answered that he would not come out, nor would he leave that town; that if the governor wished to go in peace, he should quit at once, and not persist in carrying him away by force from his country and its dependencies.

The governor, in view of the determination and furious answer of the cacique, thought to soothe him with soft words; to which he made no answer, but with great haughtiness and contempt withdrew to where Soto could not see nor speak to him. The governor, that he might send word for the cacique for him to remain in the country at his will, and to be pleased to give him a guide, and persons to carry burdens, that he might see if he could pacify him with gentle words, called to a chief who was passing by. The Indian replied loftily that he would not listen to him. Baltasar de Gallegos, who was near, seized him by the cloak of marten skins that he had on, drew it off over his head, and left it in his hands; whereupon the Indians all beginning to rise he gave him a stroke with a cutlass, that laid open his back, when they, with loud yells, came out of their houses, discharging their bows.

The governor, discovering that if he remained there they could not escape, and if he should order his men, who were outside of the town, to come in, the horses might be killed by the Indians from the houses and great injury done, he ran out; but before he could get away he fell two or three times, and was helped to rise by those with him. He and they were all badly wounded: within the town five Christians were instantly killed. Coming forth, he called out to all his men to get farther off, because there was much harm doing from the palisade. The natives discovering that the Christians were retiring, and some, if not the greater number, at more than a walk, the Indians followed with great boldness, shooting at them, or striking down, such as they could overtake. Those in chains having set down their burdens near the fence while the Christians were retiring, the people of Mauilla lifted the loads on to their backs, and, bringing them into the town, took off their irons, putting bows and arms in their hands, with which to fight. Thus did the foe come into possession of all the clothing, pearls, and whatsoever else the Christians had beside, which was what their Indians carried. Since the natives had been at peace to that place, some of us, putting our arms in the luggage, went without any; and two, who were in the town, had their swords and halberds taken from them and put to use.

The governor, presently as he found himself in the field, called for a horse, and, with some followers, returned and lanced two or three of the Indians; the rest, going back into the town, shot arrows from the palisade. Those who would venture on their nimbleness came out a stone's throw from behind it, to fight, retiring from time to time, when they were set upon.

At the time of the affray there was a friar, a clergyman, a servant of the governor, and a female slave in the town, who, having no time in which to get away, took to a house, and there remained until after the Indians became masters of the place. They closed the entrance with a lattice door; and there being a sword among them, which the servant had, he put himself behind the door, striking at the Indians that would have come in; while, on the other side, stood the friar and the priest, each with a club in hand, to strike down the first that should enter. The Indians, finding that they could not get in by the door, began to unroof the house; at this moment the cavalry were all arrived at Mauilla, with the infantry that had been on the march, when a difference of opinion arose as to whether the Indians should be attacked, in order to enter the town; for the result was held doubtful, but finally it was concluded to make the assault.

So soon as the advance and the rear of the force were come up the governor commanded that all the best armed should dismount, of which he made four squadrons of footmen. The Indians, observing how he was going on arranging his men, urged the cacique to leave, telling him, as was afterwards made known by some women who were taken in the town, that as he was but one man, and could fight but as one only, there being many chiefs present very skilful and experienced in matters of war, any one of whom was able to command the rest, and as things in war were so subject to fortune, that it was never certain which side would overcome the other, they wished him to put his person in safety; for if they should conclude their lives there, on which they had resolved rather than surrender, he would remain to govern the land; but for all that they said, he did not wish to go, until, from being continually urged, with fifteen or twenty of his own people he went out of the town, taking with him a scarlet cloak and other articles of the Christians' clothing, being whatever he could carry and that seemed best to him.

The governor, informed that the Indians were leaving the town, commanded the cavalry to surround it; and into each squadron of foot he put a soldier, with a brand, to set fire to the houses, that the Indians might have no shelter. His men being placed in full concert, he ordered an arquebuse to be shot off; at the signal the four squadrons, at their proper points, commenced a furious onset, and, both sides severely suffering the Christians entered the town. The friar, the priest, and the rest who were with them in the house, were all saved, though at the cost of the lives of two brave and very able men who went thither to their rescue. The Indians fought with so great spirit that they many times drove our people back out of the town. The struggle lasted so long that many Christians, weary and very thirsty, went to drink at a pond near by, tinged with the blood of the killed, and returned to the combat. The governor, witnessing this, with those who followed him in the returning charge of the footmen, entered the town on horseback, which gave opportunity to fire the dwellings; then breaking in upon the Indians and beating them down, they fled out of the place, the cavalry and infantry driving them back through the gates, where, losing the hope of escape, they fought valiantly; and the Christians getting among them with cutlasses, they found themselves met on all sides by their strokes, when many, dashing headlong into the flaming houses, were smothered, and heaped one upon another, burned to death.

They who perished there were in all two thousand five hundred, a few more or less; of the Christians there fell eighteen, among whom was Don Carlos, brother-in-law of the governor; one Juan de Gamez, a nephew; Men Rodriguez, a Portuguese; and Juan Vazquez, of Villanueva de Barcarota, men of condition and courage; the rest were infantry. Of the living, one hundred and fifty Christians had received seven hundred wounds from the arrows; and God was pleased that they should be healed in little time of very dangerous injuries. Twelve horses died, and seventy were hurt. The clothing the Christians carried with them, the ornaments for saying mass, and the pearls, were all burned there; they having set the fire themselves, because they considered the loss less than the injury they might receive of the Indians from within the houses, where they had brought the things together.[1]

The chronicler adds that De Soto learned here that Maldonado "was waiting for him in the port of Ochuse, six days' travel distant." Fearing, however, that the barrenness of his accomplishment up to that time would discourage future settlements in his new province, he remained in that place twenty-eight days and then moved on toward the northwest. He says of this land of Mauilla:

[1] Bourne, Narr. of De Soto, I, pp. 87–97.

The country was a rich soil, and well inhabited; some towns were very large, and were picketed about. The people were numerous everywhere; the dwellings standing a crossbow-shot or two apart.[1]

In 1559 a colony consisting of 1,500 persons left Mexico under Don Tristan de Luna and landed in a port on the north coast of the Gulf of Mexico. If this was in the Bay of Ichuse or Ychuse, as some say, it was probably Mobile Bay, and yet there are difficulties, for the environs of Mobile Bay appear to have been well populated in early times, while the explorers found few inhabitants. Falling short of provisions, a detachment of four companies of soldiers was sent inland, and 40 leagues from the port they came upon a village called Nanipacna, which the few Indians they met gave them to understand had been formerly a large place, but it had been almost destroyed by people like themselves. The impression is given that this event had happened a very short time before, but, if there was any truth in the assertion, it could have occurred only during De Soto's invasion; and this is probably the event to which reference was made, because the distance of this place from the port is about the same as that given by the De Soto chroniclers as the distance of Mabila from the port where Maldonado was expecting them.[2] Another point of resemblance is shown by the name, which is pure Choctaw, meaning "Hill top."[3]

In Vandera's enumeration of the provinces visited by Juan Pardo in 1566 and 1567 "Trascaluza" is mentioned as "the last of the peopled places of Florida" and seven days' journey from "Cossa."[4] It was not, however, reached by that explorer. In the letter of May 19, 1686, so often quoted, there is a reference to the tribe, bay, and river of "Mobila" or "Mouila." When it was written the people so called were at war with the Pensacola.[5] A bare notice of the Mobile occurs also in a letter of 1688.[6]

After this no more is heard of the Mobile tribes until Iberville established a post in Biloxi Bay which was to grow into the great French colony of Louisiana. There were then two principal tribes in the region, the Mobile and the Tohome or Thomez, the former on Mobile River, about 2 leagues below the junction of the Alabama and the Tombigbee, while the main settlement of the latter was about McIntosh's Bluff, on the west bank of the latter stream.[7] Pénicaut distinguishes a third tribe, already referred to, which he calls Naniaba and also People of the Forks.[8] This last name was given to them be-

---

[1] Bourne, Narr. of De Soto, I, p. 98.

[2] See Biedma in Bourne's De Soto, II, p. 21.

[3] Mr. H. S. Halbert believed that Nanipacna was at Gees Bend on the Alabama River and was that town afterwards indicated as an old site of the Mobile Indians. (See pl. 5.)

[4] Ruidiaz, La Florida, II, p. 486.

[5] Serrano y Sanz, Doc. Hist., p. 197.

[6] Ibid., p. 219.

[7] Hamilton, Col. Mobile, p. 106.

[8] Margry, Déc., V, pp. 425, 427.

cause they lived at the junction of the Alabama and Tombigbee Rivers, the former evidently because their settlement was on a bluff or hill. It is still retained in the form Nanna Hubba and in the same locality.[1] Since Iberville does not mention this tribe and speaks of encountering the Tohome at the very same place,[2] it is probable that they were sometimes considered a part of the latter.

The Mobile are, of course, the identical tribe with which De Soto had such a sanguinary encounter. The meaning of the name, properly pronounced Mowil, is uncertain; Mr. Halbert suggests that it is from the Choctaw *moeli*, to skim, and also to paddle. Since De Soto's time the tribe had moved much nearer the sea, probably in consequence of that encounter and as a result of later wars with the Alabama. On the French map of De Crenay there is a place marked "Vieux Mobiliens" on the south side of the Alabama, apparently close to Pine Barren Creek, between Wilcox and Dallas Counties, Alabama.[3] This was probably a station occupied by the Mobile tribe between the time of De Soto and the period of Iberville.

Nothing positive is known regarding the history of the Tohome before they appear in the French narratives. On the De Crenay map above alluded to, however, there is a short affluent of the Alabama below where Montgomery now stands called "Auke Thomé," evidently identical with the creek now known as Catoma, the name of which is probably corrupted from Auke Thomé. *Auke* is evidently *oke*, the Alabama word for "water" or "stream", and the Thomé is the spelling for the Tohome tribe used on the same map. The natural conclusion is that the creek was named for the tribe and marked a site which they had formerly occupied.[4] Thus they, like the Mobile, would appear to have come from the neighborhood of the Alabama country.

Iberville says that Tohome means "Little Chief," but he is evidently mistaken.[5] "Little Chief" would require an entirely distinct combination in Choctaw or any related language; the nearest Choctaw word is perhaps *tomi*, *tommi*, or *tombi*, which signifies "to shine," or "radiant," or "sunshine," but we really know nothing about the meaning of the tribal name.

In April, 1700, Iberville ascended Pascagoula River to visit the tribes upon it, and there he learned that the village of the Mobile was three days' journey farther on toward the northeast and that they numbered 300 men. The Tohome were said to be one day's journey beyond on the same river of the Mobile and they also were said to have 300 men.

---

1 Hamilton, Col. Mobile, p. 107.

2 Margry, Déc., IV, p. 514.

3 Hamilton, Col. Mobile, p. 190 and plate 5; see footnote, page 159.

4 Ibid. Mr. Halbert has suggested that Thomé may be from a Choctaw word referred to just below and may have nothing to do with the tribe, but I believe he is in error.

5 Margry, Déc. IV, p. 514.

On leaving Pascagoula, Iberville selected two of his men to go, with the chief of that nation and his brother, to the Choctaw, Tohome, and Mobile, sending the chief of each nation a present and inviting them to come and enter into relations of friendship with him.[1] His people returned in May, having gone as far as the village of the Tohome, but they had turned back there on account of the high waters.[2] In the winter of 1700–1701 Bienville sent to the Mobile Indians for corn.[3] In January, 1702, after Iberville had reached Louisiana on his third voyage, he sent Bienville to begin work upon a fort on Mobile River, and soon afterwards followed him in person. This fort, as Hamilton informs us, was located at what is now known as Twenty-seven Mile Bluff.[4] On March 4 he sent his brother "to visit many abandoned settlements of the savages, in the islands which are in the neighborhood of this place." He continues as follows:

My brother returned in the evening. He noted many places formerly occupied by the savages, which the war against the Conchaque and Alibamons has forced them to abandon. The greater number of these settlements are inundated about half a foot when the waters are high. These habitations are in the islands, with which this river is full for thirteen leagues. He made a savage show him the place where their gods are, of which all the nations in the neighborhood tell so many stories, and where the Mobilians come to offer sacrifices. They pretend that one can not touch them without dying immediately; that they are descended from heaven. It was necessary to give a gun to the savage who showed the place to them. He approached them only stealthily and to within ten paces. They found them by searching on a little rise in the canes, near an ancient village which was destroyed, in one of these islands. They brought them out. They are five figures: of a man, a woman, a child, a bear, and an owl, made in plaster so as to look like the savages of this country. For my part I think that it was some Spaniard who, at the time of Soto made in plaster the figures of these savages. It appeared that that had been done a long time ago. We have them at the establishment; the savages, who see them there, are surprised at our hardihood and that we do not die. I am bringing them to France although they are not much of a curiosity.[5]

Five days later Iberville left to visit the Tohome, and he gives us the following account of his trip:

The 9th I left in a felucca to go to the Tohomés. I spent the night five leagues from there; one finds the end of the islands three leagues above the post. From the post I have found almost everywhere, on both sides, abandoned settlements of the savages, where it is only necessary to place settlers, who would have only canes or reeds, or roots, to cut in order to sow; the river, above the islands, is half a league wide and five to six fathoms deep.

The 10th I spent the night with the Tohomés, whom I found eight leagues distant from the post, following the windings of the river. The first settlements, called [those of the] Mobiliens, are six leagues from it. These two nations are established along the two banks of the river and in the islands and little rivers, separated by families; sometimes there are four or five and sometimes as many as twelve cabins together. They are very industrious, working the earth very much. The greater

[1] Margry, Déc., IV, p. 427.
[2] Ibid., p. 429.
[3] Ibid., p. 504.
[4] Hamilton, Col. Mobile, p. 52.
[5] Iberville, in Margry, IV, pp. 512–513.

number of their settlements are inundated during the high waters for from eight to ten days. The village of the Tohomés, that is to say of the Little Chief, where there are about eight or ten cabins together, is at about the latitude of 31 degrees 22 minutes. They have communicating trails from one to another; that place may be six and a half leagues to the north a quarter northeast from the post. Following the rising grounds one comes easily to these villages; it would be easy to make wagon roads; one can go there and return at present on horseback. The ebb and flow come as far as the Tohomés when the waters are low. According to the number of settlements, which I have seen abandoned this river must have been well peopled. These savages speak the language of the Bayogoulas, at least there is little difference. There are in these two nations 350 men.[1]

Pénicaut mentions the arrival of the chiefs of several nations of Indians at the Mobile fort in 1702 to sing the calumet, and among them those of "the Mobiliens, the Thomez, and the people of the Forks [the Naniaba]."[2] The following further translation from Pénicaut contains some interesting information regarding the tribes with which we are dealing:

At this time five of our Frenchmen asked permission of M. de Bienville to go to trade with the Alibamons in order to have fowls or other provisions of which they had need. They took the occasion to leave with ten of these Alibamons, who were at our fort of Mobile and who wished to return. On the way they stopped five leagues from our fort in a village where were three different nations of savages assembled, who held their feast there. They are called the Mobiliens, the Tomez and the Namabas; they do not have a temple, but they have a cabin in which they perform feats of jugglery.

To juggle (*jongler*), in their language, is a kind of invocation to their great spirit. For my part, and I have seen them many times, I think that it is the devil whom they invoke, since they go out of this cabin raving like those possessed, and then they work sorceries, like causing to walk the skin of an otter, dead for more than two years, and full of straw. They work many other sorceries which would appear incredible to the reader. This is why I do not want to stop here. I would not even mention it if I, as well as many other Frenchmen who were present there with me, had not been witness of it. Those who perform such feats, whether they are magical or otherwise, are very much esteemed by the other savages. They have much confidence in their prescriptions for diseases.

They have a feast at the beginning of September, in which they assemble for a custom like that of the ancient Lacedemonians, it is that on the day of this feast they whip their children until the blood comes. The entire village is then assembled in one grand open space. It is necessary that all pass, boys and girls, old and young, to the youngest age, and when there are some children sick, the mother is whipped for the child. After that they begin dances, which last all night. The chiefs and the old men make an exhortation to those whipped, telling them that it is in order to teach them not to fear the injuries which their enemies may be able to inflict upon them, and to show themselves good warriors, and not to cry nor weep, even in the midst of the fire, supposing that they were thrown there by their enemies.[3]

Pénicaut goes on to say that four of the five prospective traders were treacherously killed by Alabama Indians when close to their

[1] Iberville, in Margry, IV, pp. 513–514. For the Bayogoulas see Bull. 43, Bur. Amer. Ethn., pp. 274–279.
[2] Margry, V, p. 425.
[3] Pénicaut, in Margry, V, pp. 427–428.

town, one barely escaping with his life, and that this was the cause of a war between the French and that tribe.[1]

La Harpe, a better authority than Pénicaut, places this event in the year 1703.[2] We learn from the same explorer that in May, 1702, eight chiefs of the Alabama had come to Mobile to ask Bienville whether or not they should continue their war with the Chickasaw, Tohome (*Tomès*), and Mobile, and that Bienville had advised them to make peace.[3] October 1 some of them came down, sang the calumet, and promised to make peace.[4] From this it appears that the alliance which Pénicaut represents as existing between the Alabama and the Mobile and Tohome was not of long standing. The act of treachery in killing four out of five French traders was, it seems, a first act of hostility after peace had been made the year before. The leader of the traders was named Labrie, and the one who escaped was a Canadian.[5] According to Pénicaut, Bienville's first attempt to obtain reparation for this hostile act had to be given up on account of the treachery of the Mobile, Tohome, People of the Forks, and other Indian allies who misled and abandoned him "because they were friends and allies of the Alibamons against whom we were leading them to war."[6] La Harpe does not mention this. Bienville led another party later on with little better success. Pénicaut places this expedition in 1702,[7] La Harpe in December, 1703, and January, 1704.[8] Two Tohome are mentioned by La Harpe as deputed along with three Canadians to bring in the Choctaw chiefs in order to make peace between them and the Chickasaw, who had come to Mobile to ask it. This was December 9, 1705.[9] On the 18th of the same month it is noted that Bienville "reconciled the Mobilian nation with that of the Thomés; they were on the point of declaring war against each other on account of the death of a Mobilian woman, killed by a Thomé."[9]

This is the only mention of any difference between these two tribes; it is enough, however, to show that there was a clear distinction between them. In January, 1706, M. de Boisbrillant set out against the Alabama with 60 Canadians and 12 Indians. According to La Harpe he returned February 21 with 2 scalps and a slave.[10] Pénicaut, who places the expedition in 1702, says that he had 40 men, killed all the men in 6 Alabama canoes, and enslaved all of the women and children. He adds that the Mobilians begged the slaves from M. de Bienville, "because they were their relations," that the

[1] Margry, Déc., v, pp. 428–429.

[2] La Harpe, Jour. Hist., pp. 76–77, 79.

[3] Ibid., p. 72.

[4] Ibid., pp. 73–74.

[5] Ibid., pp. 77, 79.

[6] Margry, Déc., v, p. 429.

[7] Ibid., pp. 429–431.

[8] La Harpe, Jour. Hist., pp. 82–83. The accounts of these two writers are given on pp. 194–195.

[9] Ibid., p. 94.

[10] Ibid., p. 96.

request was granted; and that because of this action the Mobile afterwards joined the French in all the wars which they had with the Alabama.[1] In view of the hostilities known to have existed between the tribes in question when the French first arrived in the country this last statement may well be doubted. According to Pénicaut the Alabama and their allies marched against the Mobile in 1708 with more than 4,000 men, but, owing to the forethought of D'Artaguette, who had advised his Indian allies to post sentinels, they accomplished no further damage than the burning of some cabins.[2] This incursion is not mentioned by La Harpe, but, as D'Artaguette was actually in command at the time and La Harpe passes over the years 1708 and 1709 in almost complete silence, such a raid is very probable.

From what has been said above it is apparent that the Mobile and Tohome tribes were originally distinct, but they must have united in rather early French times. The last mention of the latter in the narrative of La Harpe is in connection with the murder, in 1715, of the Englishman, Hughes, who had come overland to the Mississippi, had been captured there and sent as a prisoner to Mobile by the French, and had afterwards been liberated by Bienville. He passed on to Pensacola and started inland toward the Alabama when he was killed by a Tohome Indian.[3] Bienville, about 1725, speaks of the Little Tohome and the Big Tohome, by which he probably means the Naniaba and the Tohome respectively.[4] Although none of our authorities mentions the fact in specific terms, and indeed the map of De Crenay of 1733 still places the Tohome in their old position on the Tombigbee,[5] it is evident from what Du Pratz says regarding them, that by the third decade in the eighteenth century they had moved farther south, probably to have the protection of the new Mobile fort and partly to be near a trading post.

A little to the north of Fort Louis is the nation of the Thomez, which is as small and as serviceable as that of the Chatôts; it is said also that they are Catholics; they are friends to the point of importunity.[6]

Keeping toward the north along the bay, one finds the nation of the Mobiliens, near the point where the river of Mobile empties into the bay of the same name. The true name of this nation is *Mowill*; from this word the French have made *Mobile*, and then they have named the river and the bay Mobile, and the natives belonging to this nation Mobiliens.[7]

The Mobile church registers do not contain any references to the Tohome tribe, but the Mobile, or Mobilians, are mentioned in several

[1] Margry, Déc., v, p. 432.
[2] Ibid., p. 478.
[3] La Harpe, Jour. Hist., pp. 118–119.
[4] French transcriptions, Lib. Cong.
[5] Plate 5; Hamilton, Col. Mobile, p. 196.
[6] Du Pratz, Hist. de la Louisiane, II, p. 213.
[7] Ibid., pp. 213–214.

places, the first date being in 1715, the last in 1761.[1] The Tohome and Naniaba come to the surface still later in a French document dated some time before the cession of Mobile to Great Britain (1763)[2] and in a list of Choctaw towns and chiefs compiled by the English, 1771–72.[3] It is probable that the languages spoken by them were so close to Choctaw that they afterwards passed as Choctaw and, mingling with the true Choctaw, in time forgot their own original separateness. And this probability is strengthened by a Choctaw census made by Regis du Roullet, a French officer, in 1730, who classes the Tohome, Naniaba, and some Indians "aux mobiliens" as "Choctaw established on the river of Mobile." [4]

THE OSOCHI

On an earlier page I have registered my belief that the origin of the Osochi is to be sought in that Florida "province" through which De Soto passed shortly before reaching the Apalachee. The name is given variously as Uçachile,[5] Uzachil,[6] Veachile,[7] and Ossachile.[8] Since the Timucua chief Uriutina speaks of the Uçachile as "of our nation," [9] while the chief of Uçachile is said to be "kinsman of the chief of Caliquen," [6] it may be inferred that the tribe then spoke a Timucua dialect.[10] If this were really the case it is strange that, instead of retiring farther into Florida with the rest of the Timucua, these people chose to move northward entirely away from the old Timucua country. Nevertheless, Spanish documents do inform us of one northward movement as an aftermath of the Timucua rebellion in 1656.[11] Other evidence seeming to mark out various steps in the migration of these people has been adduced already,[12] mention being made of "Tommakees" near the mouth of Apalachicola River about 1700 by Coxe,[13] "Tomoóka" in the same region by Lamhatty in 1707,[14] and a town or tribe near the junction of the Apalachicola and Flint Rivers called "Apalache ó Sachile" at a considerably later date.[15] The *ó* in the last term has been mistaken by the cartographer for the Spanish connective *ó*, but there can be no doubt that it belongs properly with what follows. Osochi is always accented on the first syllable. The spot indicated on this map is that at which the Apalachicola Indians settled after the Yamasee war. We must suppose, then,

[1] Hamilton, Col. Mobile, p. 108.

[2] Miss. Prov. Arch., I, p. 26.

[3] Lib. Cong., MSS.

[4] French Transcriptions, Lib. Cong.

[5] Bourne, Narr. of De Soto, II, p. 73.

[6] Ibid., I, p. 41.

[7] Ibid., II, p. 6.

[8] Shipp's De Soto and Fla., p. 299.

[9] Bourne, op. cit., II, p. 75.

[10] However, it is to be noted that the tribes southeast of Ocilla River are spoken of as constituting the Yustaga province, which is sometimes distinguished from the Timucua province proper.

[11] See p. 338.

[12] See p. 26.

[13] French, Hist. Colls. La., 1850, p. 234.

[14] Amer. Anthrop., n. s. vol. X, p. 571.

[15] Hamilton, Col. Mobile, p. 210; Ruidiaz, La Florida, I, XLV.

unless we have to do with a very bad misprint, either that the Osochi were considered an Apalachicola band or that they were living with the Apalachicola midway between their old territories and the homes of the Lower Creeks. These facts do not, of course, amount to proof of a connection between the Uçachile and Osochi, but they point in that direction.

Adair, writing in the latter half of the eighteenth century, mentions the "Oosécha" as one of those nations, remains of which had settled in the lower part of the Muskogee country.[1] On the De Crenay map (1733) their name appears under the very distorted form Cochoutehy (or Cochutchy) east of Flint River, between the Sawokli and Eufaula,[2] but the French census of 1760 shows them between the Yuchi and Chiaha[3] and those of 1738 and 1750 near the Okmulgee.[4] In the assignment to the traders, July 3, 1761, we find "The Point Towns called Ouschetaws, Chehaws and Oakmulgees," given to George Mackay and James Hewitt along with the Hitchiti town.[5] Bartram spells the name "Hooseche," and says that they spoke the Muskogee tongue, but this is probably an error even for his time.[6] In 1797 their trader was Samuel Palmer.[7] Hawkins, in 1799, has the following to say about them:

> Oose-oo-che; is about two miles below Uchee, on the right bank of Chat-to-ho-chee; they formerly lived on Flint river, and settling here, they built a hot house in 1794; they cultivate with their neighbors, the Che-au-haus, below them, the land in the point.[8]

The statement regarding their origin tends to tie them a little more definitely to the tribe mentioned in the Spanish map. The census of 1832 gives two settlements as occupied by this tribe, which it spells "Oswichee," one on Chattahoochee River and one "on the waters of Opillike Hatchee (Opile'ki hå'tci).[9] In 1804 Hawkins condemns the Osochi for a reactionary outbreak which occurred there when "we were told they would adhere to old times, they preferred the old bow and arrow to the gun."[10] After their removal west of the Mississippi the Osochi were settled on the north side of the Arkansas some distance above the present city of Muskogee. Later a part of them moved over close to Council Hill to be near the Hitchiti and also, according to another authority, on account of the Green Peach war. An old man belonging to this group told me that his grandmother could speak Hitchiti, and he believed that in the past more spoke Hitchiti than Creek. This is also indicated by the close association of the Osochi and Chiaha in early days.

---

1 Adair, Hist. Am. Inds., p. 257.

2 Plate 5; Hamilton, Col. Mobile, p. 190.

3 Miss. Prov. Arch., I, p. 96.

4 MSS., Ayer Coll.

5 Ga. Col. Docs., VIII, p. 522.

6 Bartram, Travels, p. 462.

7 Ga. Hist. Soc. Colls., IX, p. 171.

8 Ibid., III, p. 63.

9 Senate Doc. 512, 23d Cong., 1st sess., pp. 353-356; Schoolcraft, Ind. Tribes, IV, p. 578.

10 Ga. Hist. Soc. Colls., IX, p. 438.

The two together settled a town known as Hotalgihuyana.[1] Their familiarity with Hitchiti may have been merely a natural result of long association with Chiaha and Apalachicola Indians. No remembrance of any language other than Hitchiti and Muskogee is preserved among them.

THE CHIAHA

The Chiaha were a more prominent tribe and evidently much larger than those last mentioned. While the significance of their name is unknown it recalls the Choctaw *chaha*, "high," "height," and this would be in harmony with the situation in which part of the tribe was first encountered northward near the mountains of Tennessee. There is also a Cherokee place name which superficially resembles this, but should not be confounded with it. It is written by Mooney Tsiyahi and signifies "Otter place." One settlement so named formerly existed on a branch of the Keowee River, near the present Cheohee, Oconee County, South Carolina; another in Cades Cove, on Cove Creek, in Blount County, Tennessee; and a third, still occupied, about Robbinsville, in Graham County, North Carolina.[2]

As a matter of fact we know from later history that there were at least two Chiahas in very early times—one as above indicated and a second among the Yamasee. In discussing the Cusabo I have already spoken of the possibility that the Kiawa of Ashley River were a third group of Chiaha, and will merely note the point again in passing.[3] That there were Chiaha among the Yamasee is proved by a passage in the manuscript volume of proceedings of the board dealing with the Indian trade of Carolina. There we find it recorded that in 1713 an agent of this board among the Lower Creeks proposed that a way be prepared that "the Cheehaws who were formerly belonging to the Yamassees and now settled among the Creeks might return."[4] This seems to be confirmed by the presence of a Chehaw River in South Carolina between the Edisto and Combahee, though it is possible that that received its name from the Kiawa. There is, however, another line of evidence. In 1566 and 1567 Juan Pardo made two expeditions inland toward the northwest, and reached among other places in the second of these the Chiaha whom De Soto had formerly encountered. Now Pardo calls them "Chihaque, que tiene por otro nombre se llama Lameco,"[5] and in another place "Lameco, que tiene por otro nombre Chiaha,"[6] while in Vandera's account we read "Solameco, y por otro nombre Chiaha."[7] Gatschet derives this last from the Creek Súli miko, "Buzzard chief,"

[1] See pp. 170, 409.
[2] Mooney in 19th Ann. Rept. Bur. Amer. Ethn., p. 538.
[3] See p. 25.
[4] MS. as above, p. 66.
[5] Ruidiaz, La Florida, II, p. 471.
[6] Ibid., p. 472.
[7] Ibid., p. 484.

but attention should be called to a similar name recorded by the De Soto chroniclers in the neighborhood of the lower Savannah. This is the Talimeco or Jalameco of Ranjel,[1] and the Talomeco of Garcilasso.[2] I venture the suggestion that all of these names are intended for the same word, Talimico or Talimiko, which again was probably from Creek Tålwa immiko, "town its chief," *-wa* being uniformly dropped in composition. The name would probably be applied to an important town. While we do not know definitely that it was applied to the Chiaha among the Yamasee, the fact that a tribe by that name is mentioned as living in the immediate neighborhood may be significant. In fact I am inclined to believe that the Talimeco, Jalameco, or Talomeco of the chroniclers of De Soto were the southern band of Chiaha. If this were the case the first appearance of both Chiaha bands in history would be in the De Soto chronicles.

The Spaniards first learned of Talimeco from "the lady of Cofitachequi," who speaks of it as "my village,"[3] but the expression as quoted by Ranjel hardly agrees with his later statement to the effect that "this Talimeco was a village holding extensive sway."[3] The relation which Cofitachequi and Talimeco bore to each other is rather perplexing, but, discounting the tendency of the Spaniards to discover kings, emperors, and ruling and subjugated provinces, we may guess that the tribes were allied and on terms of perfect equality. Later we find the Chiaha and Kawita maintaining just such an alliance. Ranjel says:

In the mosque, or house of worship, of Talimeco there were breastplates like corselets and headpieces made of rawhide, the hair stripped off; and also very good shields. This Talimeco was a village holding extensive sway; and this house of worship was on a high mound and much revered. The *caney*, or house of the chief, was very large, high, and broad, all decorated above and below with very fine, handsome mats, arranged so skilfully that all these mats appeared to be a single one; and, marvellous as it seems, there was not a cabin that was not covered with mats. This people has many very fine fields and a pretty stream and a hill covered with walnuts, oak trees, pines, live oaks, and groves of liquid amber, and many cedars.[4]

Garcilasso is the only other chronicler who has much to say of Talimeco, or who even mentions its name. He says:

Both sides of the road, from the camp to this town, were covered with trees, of which a part bore fruit, and it seemed as though they promenaded through an orchard, so that our men arrived with pleasure and without difficulty at Talomeco, which they found abandoned on account of the pest. Talomeco is a beautiful town, and quite noted, as it was the residence of the caciques. It is upon a small eminence near the river, and consists of five hundred well-built houses. That of the chief is elevated above the town, and is seen from a distance. It is also larger, stronger, and more agreeable than the others. Opposite this house is the temple, where are the coffins of the lords of the province. It is filled with riches, and built in a magnificent manner.[2]

---

1 Bourne, Narr. of De Soto, II, pp. 98, 101.

2 Garcilasso, in Shipp, De Soto and Florida, p. 362.

3 Bourne, op. cit., p. 101.

4 Ibid., pp. 101-102.

Garcilasso then devotes an entire chapter to a description of this temple, which, though evidently exaggerated, doubtless is true in outline.[1] It is questionable whether these Chiaha belonged originally to the Yamasee proper or were one of the peoples of Guale. Probably the English trader spoke only in a general way, however, and we are not justified in drawing any other than a general inference as to the ancient location of the tribe. We know nothing of the date when they settled among the Lower Creeks, except that it was before the year 1715. We find them among the Creek towns on Ocmulgee River on some of the early maps, such as the Moll map of 1720 and a map in Homann's atlas of date 1759, the information contained in which evidently antedates the Yamasee war (see also pl. 3).

In 1715, however, nearly all of the Lower Creeks moved over to the Chattahoochee, the Chiaha among them. On later maps the Chiaha appear on Chattahoochee River, sometimes under the name "Achitia," between the Okmulgee on the north and a part of the Yuchi known as the Hoglogees on the south. They seem to have been numerous, and Adair mentions "Cha-hah" among his six principal Creek towns.[2] In 1761 the "Chehaws," Osochi, and Okmulgee, called collectively "point towns," were assigned to the traders George Mackay and James Hewitt, along with the Hitchiti.[3] Bartram states that he crossed the Chattahoochee "at the point towns Chehaw and Usseta (Kasihta). "These towns," he adds, "almost join each other, yet speak two languages, as radically different perhaps as the Muscogulge and Chinese."[4]

Hawkins (1799) has the following description:

Che-au-hau, called by the traders Che-haws, is just below, and adjoining Oose-oo-che, on a flat of good land. Below the town the river winds round east, then west, making a neck or point of one thousand acres of canebrake, very fertile, but low, and subject to be overflowed; the land back of this is level for nearly three miles, with red, post, and white oak, hickory, then pine forest.

These people have villages on the waters of Flint River; there they have fine stocks of cattle, horses, and hogs, and they raise corn, rice, and potatoes in great plenty.

The following are the villages of this town:

1st. Au-muc-cul-le (pour upon me) is on a creek of that name, which joins on the right side of Flint River, forty-five miles below Timothy Barnard's. It is sixty feet wide, and the main branch of Kitch-o-foo-ne, which it joins three miles from the river; the village is nine miles up the creek;[5] the land is poor and flat, with limestone springs in the neighborhood; the swamp is cypress in hammocks, with some water oak and hickory; the pine land is poor with ponds and wire grass; they have sixty gun men in the village; it is in some places well fenced; they have cattle, hogs, and horses, and a fine range for them, and raise corn, rice, and potatoes in great plenty.

---

[1] Garcilasso, in Shipp, De Soto, and Florida, pp. 362–366.

[2] Adair, Hist. Am. Inds., p. 257.

[3] Ga. Col. Docs., VIII, p. 522.

[4] Bartram, Travels, p. 456.

[5] Elsewhere he says "15 miles up the creek."—Ga. Hist. Soc. Colls., IX, p. 172.

2d. O-tel-le-who-yau-nau (hurricane town) is six miles below Kitch-o-foo-ne, on the right bank of Flint River, with pine barren on both sides;[1] they have twenty families in the village, which is fenced; and they have hogs, cattle, and horses; they plant the small margins near the mouth of a little creek. This village is generally named as belonging to Che-au-hau, but they are mixed with Oose-oo-ches [2]

In notes taken in 1797 the same writer mentions a small Chiaha settlement on Flint River, 3 miles below "Large Creek," and 9 miles above Hotalgihuyana.[3]

Another Chiaha settlement is referred to in the following terms:

Che-au-hoo-che (little che-au-hau) is one mile and a half west from Hit-che-tee, in the pine forest, near Au-he-gee; a fine little creek, called at its junction with the river, Hit-che-tee; they begin to fence and have lately built a square.[4]

When the Creeks were removed to Oklahoma the Chiaha established themselves in the extreme northeastern corner of the new Creek territory, where they made a square ground on Adams Creek. This was later given up, but it was restored for a period after the Civil War. It is now altogether abandoned, and the Chiaha themselves are rapidly losing their identity in the mass of the population. It is said that most of the true Chiaha are gone and that those that are now so called have been brought in from outside—by marriage presumably. Even before the Creek war many Chiaha had gone to Florida, and afterwards the numbers there were very greatly augmented. At the present day there is a square ground in the northern part of the old Seminole Nation named Chiaha, but the different elements among the Seminole have fused so completely that in only a few cases can they be separated. The name is little more than a convenient term, a historical vestige applied after all substance has departed.

We have still to say a word regarding the Chiaha whom De Soto found in the mountains—those to whom the name was first applied. This seems to have been a powerful nation by itself in his time, for he learned of it while still at Cofitachequi. The Fidalgo of Elvas says:

The natives [of Cofitachequi] were asked if they had knowledge of any great lord farther on, to which they answered, that twelve days' travel thence was a province called Chiaha, subject to a chief of Coça.[5]

The statement regarding subjection may be taken to indicate some kind of alliance, nothing more. De Soto reached this place June

---

[1] In notes taken two years earlier Hawkins mentions two towns of this name, or rather two town sites 7 miles apart on Flint River, and clearly indicates that the people had occupied them in succession.—Ga. Hist. Soc. Colls., IX, p. 173.

[2] Hawkins, Sketch, in Ga. Hist. Soc. Colls., III, pt. I, pp. 63–64; IX, p. 172. The second of these branches long maintained an independent existence. It is mentioned by the Spanish officer, Manuel Garcia in 1800 (copy of Diary in Newberry Lib., Ayer Coll.), and by Young (see p. 409).

[3] Ga. Hist. Soc. Colls., IX, p. 173.

[4] Ibid., III, p. 64.

[5] Bourne, Narr. of De Soto, I, p. 68.

5, 1540, and left it on the 28th. Ranjel mentions the rather interesting fact that here the explorers first encountered fenced villages.[1] In 1566 Juan Pardo penetrated from the fort at Santa Elena as far north as the Cheraw country at the head of Broad River and built a fort there, which he named Fort San Juan. He returned to Santa Elena the same year, leaving a sergeant named Moyano in charge.[2] In 1567 Moyano, acting in accordance with instructions, set out from Fort San Juan and marched westward until he came to Chiaha, where he built another fort and awaited Pardo. Pardo left Fort San Felipe at Santa Elena September 1, reached Chiaha, and passed beyond it into the country of the Upper Creeks; but, hearing that a great army of Indians was assembling to oppose him, he returned to Chiaha, strengthened the fort which Moyano had built, and, leaving a garrison there consisting of a corporal and 30 soldiers, returned to Santa Elena.

Vandera, in his enumeration of the places which Pardo had visited, speaks of Chiaha as "a rich and extensive country, a broad land, surrounded by beautiful rivers. All around this place there are, at distances of one, two, and three leagues, more or less, many smaller places all surrounded by rivers. There are leagues and leagues of plenty (bendicion), with such great quantities of fine grapes and many medlar-trees; in short, a country for angels."[3]

Pardo also left a garrison, consisting of a corporal and 12 soldiers, at a place called Cauchi. These posts, along with the one among the Cheraw, lasted for a time but were ultimately destroyed by the people among whom they had been placed.[4] This is the last we hear of a Chiaha so far to the north. When the veil of obscurity which covered these regions for more than a hundred years after this time is again lifted they are found only in the south on the Ocmulgee and Chattahoochee. Now, since, according to the testimony of the English trader already quoted, the Chiaha among the Lower Creeks had come from the Yamasee, are we to suppose that these northern Chiaha had in the interval first joined the Yamasee and then moved back to the Ocmulgee and Chattahoochee, or did they join the Chiaha whom I have indicated as probably already existing among the Yamasee after they had retired westward? On this point our information is almost entirely wanting. There are, however, a few indications that there may have been during all this period a body of Chiaha among the Upper Creeks separate from those whose history we have already traced, in which case we must assume that they did not unite with their relatives before

[1] Bourne, Narr. of De Soto, II, p. 108.
[2] Ruidiaz, La Florida, II, pp. 465–473, 477–480.
[3] Vandera in Ruidiaz, La Florida, II, pp. 484–485
[4] Ibid.; also Lowery, Span. Settl., II, pp. 274–276, 284–286, 294–297.

they emigrated west of the Mississippi, if at all. One of these indications is the name "Chiaha" applied by Coxe to the Tallapoosa River,[1] another the name of a creek in Talladega County, Alabama, Chehawhaw Creek, known to have borne it as far back as the end of the eighteenth century,[2] and a third the enumeration of two bodies of Upper Creek Indians in the census of 1832 under names which appear to be intended to represent the name of this tribe.[3] One of these is given as "Chehaw" with 126 people and the other as "Chearhaw" with 306. This is greater than the combined population of the Chiaha and Hotalgihuyana towns among the Lower Creeks, and it is difficult to see how they could have persisted as a distinct people for such a long period without separate notice. While there are no Upper Creek Chiaha now there seems to be a tradition of such a body as having existed in former times; and if so, we may consider it almost certain that they were descendants of those whom De Soto and Pardo encountered at the very dawn of American history.

THE HITCHITI

Hitchiti among the Creeks was considered the head or "mother" of a group of Lower Creek towns which spoke closely related languages distinct from Muskogee. This group included the Sawokli, Okmulgee, Oconee, Apalachicola, and probably the Chiaha, with their branches, and all of these people called themselves *Atcik-hà'ta*, words said by Gatschet to signify "white heap (of ashes)." [4] If this interpretation could be relied upon we might suppose that the name referred to the ash heap near each square ground, but it is doubtful. Gatschet states that the name Hitchiti was derived from a creek of the name which flows into the Chattahoochee, and explains it by the Creek word *ähi'tcita*, "to look up (the stream)." [4] This interpretation would be entitled to considerable respect, since it probably came from Judge G. W. Stidham, a very intelligent Hitchiti, from whom Gatschet obtained much of his information regarding this people, were it not that history shows that the name belonged to the tribe before it settled upon the Chattahoochee. In the following origin myth, related to the writer by Jackson Lewis, another meaning is assigned to it, but it is probably an *ex post facto* explanation. It is more likely that there was some connection with the general term *Atcik-hà'ta*.

---

[1] Coxe, Carolana, map.

[2] Hawkins's Viatory MS., Lib. Cong.

[3] Senate Doc. 512, 23d Cong., 1st. sess., pp. 264-265, 307-309; these "Upper Cheehaws" are also mentioned in a volume of treaties between the U. S. A. and the Several Indian Tribes from 1778 to 1837, pp. 68-69, and, according to a letter dated June 17, 1796, their chiefs took part in a meeting at Coleraine (MS., Lib. Cong.), though there is some reason to think that part of them were Natchez.

[4] Gatschet, Creek Mig. Leg., I, p. 77.

The origin of the Hitchiti is given in various ways, but this is what I have heard regarding them. The true name of these people was A′tcik hă′ta. They claim that they came to some place where the sea was narrow and frozen over. Crossing upon the ice they traveled from place to place toward the east until they reached the Atlantic Ocean. They traveled to see from where the sun came. Now they found themselves blocked by the ocean and, being tired, they lingered along the coast for some days. The women and children went down on the beach to gather shells and other things that were beautiful to look at. They were shown to the old men who said, "These are pretty things, and we are tired and cannot proceed farther on account of the ocean, which has intercepted us. We will stop and rest here." They took the beautiful shells, pebbles, etc., which the women and children had brought up and made rattles, and the old men said, "Inasmuch as we cannot go farther we will try to find some way of enjoying ourselves and stop where we now are." They amused themselves, using those rattles as they did so, and while they were there on the shore with them people came across the water to visit them. These were the white people, and the Indians treated them hospitably, and at that time they were on very friendly terms with each other. The white people disappeared, however, and when they did so they left a keg of something which we now know was whisky. A cup was left with this, and the Indians began pouring whisky into this cup and smelling of it, all being much pleased with the odor. Some went so far as to drink a little. They became intoxicated and began to reel and stagger around and butt each other with their heads. Then the white people came back and the Indians began trading peltries, etc., for things which the white people had.

Then the Muskogees, who claim to have emerged from the navel of the earth somewhere out west near the Rocky Mountains, came to the place where the Hitchiti were living. The Muskogee were very warlike, and the Hitchiti concluded it would be best to make friends with them and become a part of them. Ever since they have been together as one people. Hitciti is the Muskogee word meaning "to see," and was given to them because they went to see from whence the sun came. So their name was changed from A′tcik-hă′ta. The two people became allied somewhere in Florida.

Gatschet says that some Hitchiti Indians claimed that their ancestors had fallen from the sky. Chicote and Judge Stidham, however, told him the following story:

Their ancestors first appeared in the country by coming out of a canebrake or reed thicket near the seacoast. They sunned and dried their children during four days, then set out; arrived at a lake and stopped there. Some thought it was the sea, but it was a lake. They set out again, traveled up a stream and settled there for a permanency.[1]

The origin on the seacoast and the migration upstream suggest that this last myth may have belonged to the Sawokli.

At one time the Hitchiti were probably the most important tribe in southern Georgia and their language the prevailing speech in that region from the Chattahoochee River to the Atlantic Ocean. Nevertheless the true Muskogee entered at such an early period that we can not say we have historical knowledge of a time when the Hitchiti were its sole inhabitants.

[1] Gatschet, Creek Mig. Leg., I, pp. 77–78.

The first appearance of the Hitchiti tribe in written history is in the De Soto chronicles, under the name Ocute[1] or Ocuti.[2] That the Ocute were identical with the later Hitchiti is strongly indicated, if not proved, by the following line of argument. The name Ocute appears in a few of the earlier Spanish authorities only, but much later there is mention of a Lower Creek tribe, called on the De Crenay map Aëquité,[3] and in the French census of 1760, Aeykite.[4] There is every reason to believe that we have here the Ocute of De Soto; certainly no name recorded from the region approximates it as closely. Now, the De Crenay map was drawn in 1733, shortly after the Yamasee war, and the data it contains would apply to the period immediately following that war. Although apparently located on the Flint, the position of Aëquité is farther downstream than any of the other Creek towns on the map. Turning to the English maps of the same epoch we find that, with the exception of the Apalachicola, who were for a time at the junction of the Chattahoochee and Flint, Hitchiti was at that period the southernmost town of all. This by itself is not conclusive, because the arrangement of towns on this particular part of the De Crenay map (pl. 5) seems unreliable. Turning to the census of 1760, however, we find the Lower Creek towns laid out in regular order from north to south, the distance of each from Fort Toulouse being marked in leagues. Now, when we compare this list with the later arrangement of towns exhibited by the Early map of 1818[5] (pl. 9) we obtain the following result:

CENSUS OF 1760	EARLY MAP
Kaouitas	Cowetau.
	Cowetau Tal-la-has-see.
Chaouaklé	
Kachetas	Kussetau.
Ouyoutchis	Uchee.
Ouchoutchis	Osachees.
Tchiahas	Che-au-choo-chee.
Aeykite	Hitch-e-tee.
Apalatchikolis	Pal-la-choo-chee.
Okonis	Oconee.
Omolquet	
Choothlo	Sau-woo-ga-loo-chee.
Choothlotchy	Sau-woo-ga-loo-chee.
Youfalas	Eu-ta-lau (properly Eu-fa-lau).
Tchoualas	
Oeyakbe	Oke-te-yo-con-ne.

The correspondences between the two, it will be noted, are very marked. They become still closer when we supplement the Early

[1] Bourne, Narr. of De Soto, I, p. 56; II, p. 90.

[2] Ibid., II, p. 11.

[3] Plate 5; Hamilton, Col. Mobile, p. 190.

[4] Miss. Prov. Arch., I, p. 96.

[5] In this I have omitted the Okfuskee settlements higher up the stream, which are not considered by the French enumerators.

map with other authorities. Che-au-choo-chee is laid down on the Early map just opposite Hitchiti town, but for some reason or other the town of Chiaha itself was overlooked, and Hawkins describes it exactly where the French census places it, just below Osochi (Ouchoutchis). Instead of the first Sau-woo-ga-loo-chee he also has Sau-woo-ge-lo, for which Choothlo is certainly intended. Tchoualas is also probably intended for Sawokli or Sawoklo, and in position it corresponds to a town called Kawaigi, said to be a Sawokli offshoot. Oeyakbe means "water (or river) fork" in Muskogee and Oke-te-yo-con-ne, "zigzag stream land," in Hitchiti. The same town is probably intended by them. In only three cases, Chaouaklé, Omolquet, and Tchoualas, does the census of 1760 contain names not represented on the Early map, and in only one case, Cowetau Tal-la-has-see, does the Early map contain a name not represented in the census of 1760. As this last was an outvillage of Cowetau its omission is readily explained. Aeykite, like Hitch-e-tee, is placed between Chiaha and Apalachicola, and with the exception of Che-au-choo-chee, which was of course only an outsettlement of Chiaha, and the Westo town, which disappeared at an early date, no town is laid down on any other map known to me between the two aforesaid places. In fact, the distance between them is not great. If Aeykite is not identical with Hitch-e-tee we must not only assume a distinct town of the name not otherwise explained, but we must assume that Hitchiti is the only important town omitted from the French census, a rather unlikely happening. To the writer the conclusion seems quite overwhelming that Aeykite refers to the Hitchiti town, and if that be the case Ocute probably does also. The latest use of this particular term seems to be by Manuel Garcia (1800) when it appears in the form "Oakjote."[1] The Spanish census of 1738 has an intermediate form "Ayjichiti."[1]

Assuming, then, that Ocute and Aeykite are synonyms for Hitchiti, we will now proceed to trace the history of this tribe.

Elvas says:

> The governor [De Soto] set out [from Achese] on the first day of April [1540] and advanced through the country of the chief, along up a river, the shores of which were very populous. On the fourth he went through the town of Altamaca, and on the tenth arrived at Ocute.[2]

And elsewhere he adds:

> The land of Ocute is more strong and fertile than the rest, the forest more open, and it has very good fields along the margins of the rivers.[3]

Ranjel says that, after passing Altamaha they met a chief named Çamumo, who, along with others, was a subject of "a great chief

[1] Copy of MS. in Ayer Coll., Newberry Lib.

[2] Bourne, Narr. of De Soto, I, p. 56.

[3] Ibid., p. 220.

whose name was Ocute." The chief of Ocute furnished bearers and provisions to the Spaniards, though apparently not without protest, and the latter set up a wooden cross in his village as an entering wedge to conversion.[1] Ocute would seem to have been the province called Cofa by Garcilasso, which he describes as "suitable for cattle, very productive in corn, and very delightful."[2]

Our next glimpse of Ocute is in the testimony given by Gaspar de Salas with respect to his expedition from St. Augustine to Tama in the year 1596.

The greater part of this testimony will be introduced in discussing the Tamałi tribe. After leaving Tama the narrative continues:

> At one day's journey from Tama they came upon the village of Ocute, where they were very well received by its cacique, who made them many presents, the women bringing their shawls, which he calls aprons, which look like painted leather.[3] Some of them say that they have been in New Spain and have or are imitating their dress. As they wished to go on farther, the cacique of Ocute tried very earnestly to dissuade them from it, weeping over it with them, as he said that if they went any farther inland the Indians there would kill them, because a long time ago, which must have been when Soto passed there, taking many people on horseback, they killed many of them; how much more would they kill them who were but few? This is the reason why they did not go ahead, but returned from there. They likewise heard the Indians of that village as well as the Salchiches say that at four days' journey from there, and after passing a very high mountain where, when the sun rose, there seemed to be a big fire, on the farther side of it lived people who wore their hair clipped (cut), and that the pine trees were cut down with hatchets, and that it seems to the witness that such signs can only apply to Spaniards. He [the witness] says that this country [Tama, etc.] seems to him to be very rich, or at least sufficiently so to produce any kind of grain, even if it be wheat, and has many meadows and pastures for cattle, and its rivers have sweet water in places, and that it seems to him that if there were anybody who knew how to find and wash gold in those rivers it could surely be found.[4]

The first appearance of the Hitchiti under the name by which we know them best is after South Carolina had been settled, when it occurs in documents as that of a Lower Creek town, and on the maps of that period it is laid down on Ocmulgee River below the town of the Coweta. From the Mitchell map this site is identifiable as the "Ocmulgee old fields" on the site of the present Macon, which is in agreement with a legend reported by Gatschet to the effect that the Hitchiti were "the first to settle at the site of Okmulgee town, an ancient capital of the confederacy."[5]

William Bartram thus describes the Ocmulgee old fields as they appeared in his time:

---

[1] Bourne, op. cit., pp. 90-91.
[2] Garcilasso in Shipp, De Soto and Florida, p. 344.
[3] He says carpeta, which in Spanish is a table cover, a portfolio, or any leather case.
[4] Serrano y Sanz, Doc. Hist., pp. 144-145. Translated by Mrs. F. Bandelier.
[5] Gatschet, Creek Mig. Leg., I, p. 78.

About seventy or eighty miles above the confluence of the Oakmulge and Ocone, the trading path, from Augusta to the Creek Nation, crosses these fine rivers, which are there forty miles apart. On the east bank of the Oakmulge this trading road runs nearly two miles through ancient Indian fields, which are called the Oakmulge fields; they are the rich low lands of the river. On the heights of these low lands are yet visible monuments, or traces, of an ancient town, such as artificial mounds or terraces, squares and banks, encircling considerable areas. Their old fields and planting land extended up and down the river, fifteen or twenty miles from this site.[1]

As Bartram states that the Creeks had stopped here after their immigration from the west, the Hitchiti may not have been in occupancy always. On the other hand, Bartram may have inferred a Creek occupancy from the tradition that the confederacy had there been founded, but this may really have had reference to a compact of some kind between the Hitchiti and the invading Creeks, irrespective of the land actually held by each tribe.

After the Yamasee war the Hitchiti moved across to Chattahoochee River with most of the other Lower Creeks, first to a point low down on that river, later higher up between the Chiaha and Apalachicola.[2] In 1761 they were assigned to the traders, George Mackay and James Hewitt, along with the Point towns.[3] Their name occurs in the lists of both Swan and Bartram.[4] In 1797 the trader there was William Grey.[5] Hawkins (1799) gives the following description of the Hitchiti town and its branch villages:

Hit-che-tee is on the left bank of Chat-to-ho-che, four miles below Che-au-hau; they have a narrow strip of good land bordering on the river, and back of this it rises into high, poor land, which spreads off flat. In approaching the town on this side there is no rise, but a great descent to the town flat; on the right bank of the river the land is level and extends out for two miles; is of thin quality; the growth is post oak, hickory, and pine, all small; then pine barren and ponds.

The appearance about this town indicates much poverty and indolence; they have no fences; they have spread out into villages, and have the character of being honest and industrious; they are attentive to the rights of their white neighbors, and no charge of horse stealing from the frontiers has been substantiated against them. The villages are:

1st. Hit-che-too-che (Little Hit-che-tee), a small village of industrious people, settled on both sides of Flint River, below Kit-cho-foo-ne; they have good fences, cattle, horses, and hogs, in a fine range, and are attentive to them.

2d. Tut-tal-lo-see (fowl), on a creek of that name, twenty miles west from Hit-che-too-che. This is a fine creek on a bed of limestone; it is a branch of Kitch-o-foo-ne; the land bordering on the creek, and for eight or nine miles[6] in the direction towards Hit-che-too-che, is level, rich, and fine for cultivation, with post and black oak, hickory, dogwood and pine. The villagers have good worm fences, appear industrious, and have large stocks of cattle, some hogs and horses; they appear decent and

---

[1] Bartram, Travels, pp. 52–53.

[2] See p. 174.

[3] Ga. Col. Docs., VIII, p. 522.

[4] Schoolcraft, Ind. Tribes, V, p. 262; Bartram, Travels, p. 462.

[5] Ga. Hist. Soc. Colls., IX, p. 171.

[6] The Lib. of Cong. MS. has "six or eight."

orderly, and are desirous of preserving a friendly intercourse with their neighbors; they have this year, 1799, built a square.[1]

Manuel Garcia calls this latter village "Totolosehache."[2] According to an anonymous writer quoted by Gatschet there were, about 1820, six "Fowl towns," Cahalli hatchi, old Tallahassi, Atap'halgi, Allik hadshi, Eetatulga, and Mikasuki.[3] Most of these will be referred to again when we come to speak of Seminole towns.[4] The census of 1832 mentions a Hitchiti village called Hihaje.

After their removal to the west the Hitchiti were placed in about the center of the Creek Nation, near what is now Hitchita station, and their descendants have remained there and about Okmulgee up to the present time. A portion migrated to Florida and after the removal maintained a square ground for a time in the northern part of the Seminole Nation, Oklahoma. Some persons in this neighborhood still preserve the language.

THE OKMULGEE

This tribe also belonged to the Hitchiti group. The name refers to the bubbling up of water in a spring, and in Creek it is called Oiki łåko, and Oikewali, signifying much the same thing. The designation is said to have come originally from a large spring in Georgia. One of my informants thought that this was near Fort Mitchell, but probably it was the same spring from which the Ocmulgee River got its name, and this would be the famous "Indian Spring" in Butts County, Georgia. As early maps consulted by me do not show a town of the name on Ocmulgee River, and as the site of the Ocmulgee old fields was occupied by Hitchiti, I believe the Okmulgee were a branch of the Hitchiti, which perhaps left the town on the Ocmulgee before the main body of the people and made an independent settlement on Chattahoochee River. There their nearest neighbors were the Chiaha and Osochi, and the three together constituted what were sometimes known as "the point towns" from a point of land made by the river at that place. Bartram does not give the tribe separate mention, perhaps because he reckoned them as part of the Chiaha or Osochi. The French enumeration of 1750 records them as "Oemoulké,"[5] the French census of about 1760 as "Omolquet,"[6] and the Georgia census of 1761 gives them as one of "the point towns."[7] Hawkins omits them from his sketch, but mentions them in his notes taken in 1797, where he says:

[1] Hawkins' Sketch, in Ga. Hist. Soc. Colls., III, pt. 1, pp. 64–65. Hitchiti were also on Chickasawhatchee Creek.—Hawkins, in Ga. Hist. Soc. Colls., IX, p. 174.

[2] Ayer. Coll., Newberry Lib.

[3] Misc. Coll., Ala. Hist. Soc., I, p. 413.

[4] See pp. 406–412.

[5] MSS., Ayer Coll.

[6] Miss. Prov. Arch., I, p. 96.

[7] Ga. Col. Docs., VIII, p. 522.

Ocmulgee Village, 7 miles [below Hotalgihuyana]. There is a few families, the remains of the Ocmulgee people who formerly resided at the Ocmulgee fields on Ocmulgee River; lands poor, pine barren on both sides; the swamp equally poor and sandy; the growth dwarf scrub brush, evergreens, among which is the Cassine."[1]

The mouth of Kinchafoonee creek was 8 miles below.

Manuel Garcia mentions their chief as one of several Lower Creek chiefs with whom he had a conference in the year 1800. He spells the name "Okomulgue."[2] Morse (1822) includes them in a list of towns copied from a manuscript by Capt. Young. They were then located east of Flint River, near the Hotalgihuyana, and numbered 220.[3] They are wanting from the census rolls of 1832, but perhaps formed one of the two Osochi towns mentioned, each of which is given a very large population. On their removal west of the Mississippi they settled in the northeastern corner of the new Creek territory, near the Chiaha. They were among the first to give up their old square ground and to adopt white manners and customs. Probably in consequence of this progress they furnished three chiefs to the Creek Nation—Joe Perryman, Legus Perryman, and Pleasant Porter—and a number of leading men besides.

THE OCONEE

In addition to two groups of Muskhogean people bearing this name[4] it should be noticed that it was popularly applied by the whites to a Cherokee town, properly called Ukwû'nû (or Ukwû'nĭ),[5] but the similarity may be merely a coincidence. Of the two Creek groups mentioned one seems to be associated exclusively with the Florida tribes, while the second, when we first hear of it, was on the Georgia river which still bears its name. The first reference to either appears to be in a report of the Timucua missionary, Pareja, dated 1602. He mentions the "Ocony," three days' journey from San Pedro, among a number of tribes among which there were Christians or which desired missionaries.[6] In a letter dated April 8, 1608, Ibarra speaks of "the chief of Ocone which marches on the province of Tama."[6] This might apply to either Oconee division. The mission lists of 1655 contain a station called Santiago de Ocone, described as an island and said to be 30 leagues from St. Augustine. As it was certainly not southward of the colonial capital it would seem to have been near the coast to the north, according to the distance given, in the neighborhood of Jekyl Island. At the very same time there was another Oconee mission among the Apalachee Indians called San Francisco de Apalache in the list of 1655; it is given in the

[1] Ga. Hist. Soc. Colls., IX, p. 173.
[2] Copy MS. in Ayer Coll., Newberry Lib.
[3] Morse, Rept. on Ind. Aff., p. 364.
[4] See p. 112.
[5] 19th Ann. Rept. Bur. Amer. Ethn., p. 541.
[6] Lowery, MSS.

list of 1680 as San Francisco de Oconi.[1] This group probably remained with the rest of the Apalachee towns and followed their fortunes.

The main body of the Oconee was located, when first known to Englishmen, on Oconee River, about 4 miles south of the present Milledgeville, Georgia, just below what was called the Rock Landing. In a letter, dated March 11, 1695, Gov. Laureano de Torres Ayala tells of an expedition consisting of 400 Indians and 7 Spaniards sent against the "Cauetta, Oconi, Cassista, and Tiquipache" in retaliation for attacks made upon the Spanish Indians. About 50 persons were captured in one of these towns, but the others were found abandoned.[2] On the Lamhatty map they appear immediately west of a river which seems to be the Flint, but the topography of this map is not to be relied on. In the text accompanying, the name is given as "Opponys." [3] Almost all that is known of later Oconee history is contained in the following extract from Bartram:

> Our encampment was fixed on the site of the old Ocone town, which, about sixty years ago, was evacuated by the Indians, who, finding their situation disagreeable from its vicinity to the white people, left it, moving upwards into the Nation or Upper Creeks,[4] and there built a town; but that situation not suiting their roving disposition, they grew sickly and tired of it, and resolved to seek an habitation more agreeable to their minds. They all arose, directing their migration southeastward towards the seacoast; and in the course of their journey, observing the delightful appearance of the extensive plains of Alachua and the fertile hills environing it, they sat down and built a town on the banks of a spacious and beautiful lake, at a small distance from the plains, naming this new town Cuscowilla; this situation pleased them, the vast deserts, forests, lake, and savannas around affording abundant range of the best hunting ground for bear and deer, their favourite game. But although this situation was healthy and delightful to the utmost degree, affording them variety and plenty of every desirable thing in their estimation, yet troubles and afflictions found them out. This territory, to the promontory of Florida, was then claimed by the Tomocas, Utinas, Caloosas, Yamases, and other remnant tribes of the ancient Floridians, and the more Northern refugees, driven away by the Carolinians, now in alliance and under the protection of the Spaniards, who, assisting them, attacked the new settlement and for many years were very troublesome; but the Alachuas or Ocones being strengthened by other emigrants and fugitive bands from the Upper Creeks [i. e., the Creeks proper], with whom they were confederated, and who gradually established other towns in this low country, stretching a line of settlements across the isthmus, extending from the Alatamaha to the bay of Apalache; these uniting were at length able to face their enemies and even attack them in their own settlements; and in the end, with the assistance of the Upper Creeks, their uncles, vanquished their enemies and destroyed them, and then fell upon the Spanish settlements, which also they entirely broke up.[5]

We know that the removal of this tribe from the Oconee River took place, like so many other removals in the region, just after the Ya-

---

[1] See p. 110.

[2] Serrano y Sanz, Doc. Hist., p. 225.

[3] Am. Anthrop., n. s. vol. x, p. 571.

[4] Bartram calls all of the Creeks, Upper Creeks, and the Seminole of Florida, Lower Creeks.

[5] Bartram, Travels, pp. 378–379.

masee outbreak of 1715, and the movement into Florida about 1750.[1] Their chief during most of this period was known to the whites as "The Cowkeeper." Although Bartram represents the tribe as having gone in a body, we know that part of them remained on the Chattahoochee much later, for they appear in the assignments to traders for 1761,[2] and in Hawkins's Sketch of 1799,[3] while Bartram himself includes the town in his list as one of those on the Apalachicola or Chattahoochee River.[4] The list of towns given in 1761 includes a big and a little Oconee town, the two having together 50 hunters. Their trader was William Frazer.[2] Hawkins describes their town as follows:

> O-co-nee is six miles below Pā-lā-chooc-le, on the left bank of Chat-to-ho-che. It is a small town, the remains of the settlers of O-co-nee; they formerly lived just below the rock landing, and gave name to that river; they are increasing in industry, making fences, attending to stock, and have some level land moderately rich; they have a few hogs, cattle, and horses.[4]

They are not represented in the census of 1832, so we must suppose either that they had all gone to Florida by that time or that they had united with some other people. Bartram's narrative gives, not merely the history of the Oconee, but a good account also of the beginnings of the Seminole as distinct from the Creeks. When we come to a discussion of Seminole history we shall find that the Oconee played a most important part in it, in fact that the history of the Seminole is to a considerable extent a continuation of the history of the Oconee.

THE TAMAŁI

It is in the highest degree probable that this town is identical with the Toa, Otoa, or Toalli of the De Soto chroniclers, the *-lli* of the last form representing presumably the Hitchiti plural *-ali*. Be that as it may, there can be little question regarding the identity of Tamałi with the town of Tama, which appears in Spanish documents of the end of the same century and the beginning of the seventeenth.[5] In 1598 Mendez de Canço, governor of Florida, writes that he plans to establish a post at a place "which is called Tama, where I have word there are mines and stones, and it is a very fertile land abounding in food and fruits, many like those of Spain." It was said to be 40 leagues from St. Augustine.[6] In a later letter, dated February, 1600, is given the testimony of a soldier named Gaspar de Salas, who had visited this town in the year 1596. He undertook this expedition in company with the Franciscan fathers, Pedro Fernandez de Chosas and Francisco de Veras. He found the

---

[1] See pp. 398–399.

[2] Ga. Col. Docs., VIII, p. 522.

[3] Ga. Hist. Soc. Colls., III, p. 65.

[4] Bartram, Travels, p. 462.

[5] See p. 12.

[6] Serrano y Sanz, Doc. Hist., p. 138.

town to be farther off than the governor had supposed—"about 50 leagues, little more or less," from St. Augustine. They reached it from Guale—that is, from St. Catherines Island. De Salas states that

> It took them eight days to go from Guale to Tama, and seven of those eight days led through deserted land, which was very poor, and on arriving at Tama they found abundance of food, like corn, beans, and much venison and turkeys [1] and other fowl, and a great abundance of fish, as, for instance sturgeon, which they call "sollo real" in Spain; and likewise much fruit, as big grapes of as nice a taste as in Spain, and[2] white plums like the "siruela de monje," and cherries and watermelons [3] and other fruit.
>
> That all around the said village of Tama and neighbouring territory there is very good brown soil, which, when it rains, clings to one's feet like marl. There are in certain regions many barren hills where he saw many kinds of minerals. In several of these parts he and the two monks gathered of those stones those which seemed to them to contain metals and which were on the surface, because they did not have anything with which they could dig, and that he, the said witness, brought some of them, pulverised, to the governor and another part to a jeweler who at that time lived in the city, but who died in those days past, and that he made assays of them and told this witness that where those had been found there existed silver for they were the slags and scum of such a mine, and if they should find the vein of this mineral it would certainly prove to be a rich mine. About all this the said governor would certainly be better informed, for he, too, was told about it and made the experiment with the said jeweler. And near those mines grew an herb which is highly treasured by the Indians as a medicinal plant and to heal wounds, and they call it "guitamo real." On those same hills and on the banks of big streams they gathered many crystalisations and even fine crystals.[4]

Ocute was one day's journey beyond this place. On their return they took a more southerly route, better and not so devoid of human habitation, since they were only two days away from settlements. They came first to places called Yufera and Cascangue, and finally reached the coast at the island of San Pedro (Cumberland Island).[5]

In 1606 the chief of Tama was among those who met Governor Ibarra at Sapelo, which we many assume to have been the most convenient place on the coast for him to present himself.[6] The name, sometimes spelled Thama, appears frequently from this time on, applied to a province of somewhat indefinite extent in southern Georgia, and one for which missionaries were needed. No earnest attempt at its conversion took place, however, until late in the seventeenth century. In the mission lists of 1680 a station known as Nuestra Señora de la Candelaria de la Tama appears among those

---

1 Gallinas de papada.

2 Sollo="pike."

3 The watermelon was introduced from Africa; perhaps these were really pumpkins. The word used is "sandias."

4 Serrano y Sanz, Doc. Hist., p. 144. Translated by Mrs. F. Bandelier.

5 Ibid., p. 145.

6 Ibid., p. 184.

in the Provincia de Apalache, and it is called a "new çonversion."[1] The missionary effort was probably instrumental in bringing this tribe nearer the Apalachee, and such an inference is confirmed by a letter of 1717 in which reference is made to "a Christian Indian named Augustin, of the nation Tama of Apalache."[2] On the De Crenay map of 1733 the name appears as Tamatlé, and the tribe is located on the west bank of the Chattahoochee River below all of the other Creek towns on that stream.[3] This position is confirmed from Spanish sources, particularly from one document in which the order of Lower Creek towns from south to north is given as "Tamaxle, Chalaquilicha, Yufala, Sabacola, Ocone, Apalachicalo, Ocomulque, Osuche, Chiaja, Casista, Caveta."[4] A Spanish enumeration of Creek towns made in 1738 gives two towns of this name, "Tamaxle el Viejo," the southernmost of all Lower Creek towns, and "Tamaxle nuevo," apparently the northernmost.[5] The enumeration of 1750 places them between the Hitchiti and the Oconee.[4] Hawkins enumerates them as one of those tribes out of which the Seminole Nation had been formed.[6] Since all of the others mentioned by him were still represented among the Lower Creeks it is probable that this tribe had emigrated in its entirety. It is wanting in the lists of Bartram and Swan, and from the census of 1832, but appears in that contained in Morse's Report to the Secretary of War (1822), and also in the diary of Manuel Garcia (1800), where it is given as a Lower Creek town. It was then on the Apalachicola River, 7 miles above the Ocheese.[7] It so appears on the Melish map of 1818–19, where it is called "Tomathlee-Seminole" (pl. 8). These are the last references to it, and it was probably swallowed up in the Mikasuki band of Seminole.

It should be observed that the name of this tribe, or a name very similar, appears twice far to the north in the Cherokee country. One town bearing it was "on Valley River, a few miles above Murphy, about the present Tomatola, in Cherokee County, North Carolina." The other was "on Little Tennessee River, about Tomotley ford, a few miles above Tellico River, in Monroe County, Tennessee." Mooney, from whom these quotations are made, adds that the name does not appear to be Cherokee.[8] This fact should be considered in connection with a similar north and south division of the Tuskegee, Koasati, and Yuchi. Gatschet states definitely that one of these Cherokee towns was settled by Creek Tamałi Indians,[9] but this appears to have been merely a guess on his part.

---

1 See pp. 110, 323.
2 Serrano y Sanz, Doc. Hist., p. 228.
3 Plate 5; also Hamilton, Col. Mobile, p. 190.
4 Copy of MS. in Ayer Coll., Newberry Lib.
5 Ibid. See p. 143.
6 Ga. Hist. Soc. Colls., III, p. 26.
7 Morse, Rept. to Sec. of War, 1822, p. 364.
8 19th Ann. Rept. Bur. Amer. Ethn., p. 534.
9 Ala. Hist. Soc., Misc. Colls., I, p. 410.

The name Tamaɬi suggests the Hitchiti form of the name of a Creek clan, the Tâmâlgi, Hitchiti Tâmaɬi, and it is possible that there is historical meaning in this resemblance, but there is just enough difference between the pronunciations of the two to render it doubtful.

THE TAMAHITA

In 1673 the Virginia pioneer Abraham Wood sent two white men, James Needham and Gabriel Arthur, the latter probably an indentured servant, in company with eight Indians, to explore western Virginia up to and beyond the mountains. They were turned back at first "by misfortune and unwillingness of ye Indians before the mountaines that they should discover beyond them"; but May 17 they were sent out again, and on June 25 they met some "Tomahitans" on their way from the mountains to the Occaneechi, a Siouan tribe. Some of these came to see Wood, and meanwhile the rest returned to their own country, along with the two white men and one Appomatox Indian. From this point the narrative proceeds as follows:

They jornied nine days from Occhonechee to Sitteree: west and by south, past nine rivers and creeks which all end in this side ye mountaines and emty themselves into ye east sea. Sitteree being the last towne of inhabitance and not any path further untill they came within two days jorney of ye Tomahitans; they travell from thence up the mountaines upon ye sun setting all ye way, and in foure dayes gett to ye toppe, some times leading thaire horses sometimes rideing. Ye ridge upon ye topp is not above-two hundred paces over; ye decent better than on this side. in halfe a day they came to ye foot, and then levell ground all ye way, many slashes upon ye heads of small runns. The slashes are full of very great canes and ye water runes to ye north west. They pass five rivers and about two hundred paces over ye fifth being ye middle most halfe a mile broad all sandy bottoms, with peble stones, all foardable and all empties themselves north west, when they travell upon ye plaines, from ye mountaines they goe downe, for severall dayes they see straged hilles on theire right hand, as they judge two days journy from them, by this time they have lost all theire horses but one; not so much by ye badness of the way as by hard travell. not haveing time to feed. when they lost sight of those hilles they see a fogg or smoke like a cloud from whence raine falls for severall days on their right hand as they travell still towards the sun setting great store of game, all along as turkes, deere, elkes, beare, woolfe and other vermin very tame, at ye end of fiftteen dayes from Sitteree they arive at ye Tomahitans river, being ye 6th river from ye mountains. this river att ye Tomahitans towne seemes to run more westerly than ye other five. This river they past in cannoos ye town being seated in ye other side about foure hundred paces broad above ye town, within sight, ye horses they had left waded only a small channell swam, they were very kindly entertained by them, even to addoration in their cerrimonies of courtesies and a stake was sett up in ye middle of ye towne to fasten ye horse to, and aboundance of corne and all manner of pulse with fish, flesh and beares oyle for ye horse to feed upon and a scaffold sett up before day for my two men and Appomattocke Indian that theire people might stand and gaze at them and not offend them by theire throng. This towne is seated on ye river side, haveing ye clefts of ye river on ye one side being very high for its defence, the other three sides trees of two foot over, pitched on end, twelve foot high, and on ye topps scafolds placed with parrapits to defend the walls and offend theire enemies which men stand on to fight, many nations of Indians inhabitt downe this river, which runes west upon ye salts which they are att waare withe and to that end keepe one hundred and fifty cannoes under ye command of theire forte. ye leaste of them will carry twenty men, and made sharpe at both ends like a wherry for swiftness, this forte is foure square; 300: paces over and ye houses sett in streets, many hornes like bulls hornes lye upon theire dunghills, store of fish they have, one sorte they have like unto stoche-fish cured after that manner. Eight dayes jorny down this river lives a white people which have long beardes and whiskers and weares clothing, and on some of ye other rivers lives a hairey people, not many yeares since ye Tomahittans sent twenty men laden with beavor to ye white people, they killed tenn of them and put ye other tenn in irons, two of which tenn escaped and one of them came with one of my men to my plantation as you will understand after a small time of rest one of my men returnes with his horse, ye Appomatock Indian and 12 Tomahittans, eight men and foure women, one of those eight is hee which hath been a prisoner with ye white people, my other man remaines with them untill ye next returne to learne ye language. the 10th of September my man with his horse and ye twelve Indians arrived at my house praise bee to God, ye Tomahitans have about sixty gunnes, not such locks as oures bee, the steeles are long and channelld where ye flints strike, ye prisoner relates that ye white people have a bell which is six foot over which they ring morning and evening and att that time a great number of people congregate togather and talkes he knowes not what. they have many blacks among them. oysters and many other shell-fish, many swine and cattle. Theire building is brick, the Tomahittans began theire jorny ye 20th of September intending, God blessing him, at ye spring of ye next yeare to returne with his companion att which time God spareing me life I hope to give you and some other friends better satisfaction.[1]

The greater part of the information contained in this report is from Needham. Not long afterwards Needham was killed by an Occaneechi Indian. Arthur, however, was among the Tomahitans. He escaped the fate of his companion and after several rather remarkable adventures, if we may trust his own statements, he returned to the home of his employer in safety and communicated to him an account of all that had happened. Wood informs us that a complete statement of everything Arthur told him would be too long to record, therefore he sets down only the principal points. The account runs thus:

Ye Tomahittans hasten home as fast as they can to tell ye newes [regarding the murder of Needham]. ye King or chife man not being att home, some of ye Tomahittans which were great lovers of ye Occheneechees went to put Indian Johns command in speedy execution and tied Gabriell Arther to a stake and laid heaps of combustible canes a bout him to burne him, but before ye fire wås put too ye King came into ye towne with a gunn upon his shoulder and heareing of ye uprore for some was with it and some a gainst it. ye King ran with great speed to ye place, and said who is that that is goeing to put fire to ye English man. a Weesock borne started up with a fire brand in his hand said that am I. Ye King forthwith cockt his gunn and shot ye wesock dead, and ran to Gabriell and with his knife cutt ye thongs that tide him and had him goe to his house and said lett me see who dares touch him and all ye wesock

[1] Alvord and Bidgood, First Explorations Trans-Allegheny Region, pp. 212–214.

children they take are brought up with them as ye Ianesaryes are a mongst ye Turkes. this king came to my house upon ye 21th of June as you will heare in ye following discouerse.

Now after ye tumult was over they make preparation for to manage ye warr for that is ye course of theire liveing to forage robb and spoyle other nations and the king commands Gabriell Arther to goe along with a party that went to robb ye Spanyarrd. promising him that in ye next spring hee him selfe would carry him home to his master, Gabriell must now bee obedient to theire commands. in ye deploreable condition hee was in was put in armes, gun, tomahauke, and targett and soe marched a way with ye company, beeing about fifty. they travelled eight days west and by south as he guest and came to a town of negroes, spatious and great, but all wooden buildings. Heare they could not take any thing without being spied. The next day they marched along by ye side of a great carte path, and about five or six miles as he judgeth came within sight of the Spanish town, walld about with brick and all brick buildings within. There he saw ye steeple where in hung ye bell which Mr. Needham gives relation of and harde it ring in ye eveing. heare they dirst not stay but drew of and ye next morning layd an ambush in a convenient place neare ye cart path before mentioned and there lay allmost seven dayes to steale for theire sustenance. Ye 7th day a Spanniard in a gentille habitt, accoutered with gunn, sword and pistoll. one of ye Tomahittans espieing him att a distance crept up to ye path side and shot him to death. In his pockett were two pieces of gold and a small gold chain. which ye Tomahittans gave to Gabriell, but hee unfortunately lost it in his venturing as you shall heare by ye sequell. Here they hasted to ye negro town where they had ye advantage to meett with a lone negro. After him runs one of the Tomahittans with a dart in his hand, made with a pice of ye blaide of Needhams sworde, and threw it after ye negro, struck him thrugh betwine his shoulders soe hee fell downe dead. They tooke from him some toys. which hung in his eares, and bracelets about his neck and soe returned as expeditiously as they could to theire owne homes.

They rested but a short time before another party was commanded out a gaine and Gabrielle Arther was commanded out a gaine, and this was to Porte Royall. Here hee refused to goe saying those were English men and he would not fight a gainst his own nation, he had rather be killd. The King tould him they intended noe hurt to ye English men, for he had promised Needham att his first coming to him that he would never doe violence a gainst any English more but theire business was to cut off a town of Indians which lived neare ye English. I but said Gabriell what if any English be att that towne, a trading, ye King sware by ye fire which they adore as theire god they would not hurt them soe they marched a way over ye mountains and came upon ye head of Portt Royall River in six days. There they made perriaugers of bark and soe past down ye streame with much swiftness, next coming to a convenient place of landing they went on shore and marched to ye eastward of ye south, one whole day and parte of ye night. At lengeth they brought him to ye sight of an English house, and Gabriell with some of the Indians crept up to ye house side and lisening what they said, they being talkeing with in ye house, Gabriell hard one say, pox take such a master that will not alow a servant a bit of meat to eate upon Christmas day, by that meanes Gabriell knew what time of ye yeare it was, soe they drew of secretly and hasten to ye Indian town, which was not above six miles thence. about breake of day stole upon ye towne. Ye first house Gabriell came too there was an English man. Hee hard him say Lord have mercy upon mee. Gabriell said to him runn for thy life. Said hee which way shall I run. Gabriell reployed, which way thou wilt they will not meddle with thee. Soe hee rann and ye Tomahittans opened and let him pas cleare there they got ye English mans snapsack with beades, knives and other petty truck, in it. They made a very great slaughter upon the Indians and a bout sun riseing they hard many great guns fired off amongst the English. Then they hastened a way with what speed they could and in less than fourteene dayes arived att ye Tomahittns with theire plunder.

Now ye king must goe to give ye monetons a visit which were his frends, mony signifing water and ton great in theire language. Gabriell must goe along with him They gett forth with sixty men and travelled tenn days due north and then arived at ye monyton towne sittuated upon a very great river att which place ye tide ebbs and flowes. Gabriell swom in ye river severall times, being fresh water, this is a great towne and a great number of Indians belong unto it, and in ye same river Mr. Batt and Fallam were upon the head of it as you read in one of my first jornalls. This river runes north west and out of ye westerly side of it goeth another very great river about a days journey lower where the inhabitance are an inumarable company of Indians, as the monytons told my man which is twenty dayes journey from one end to ye other of ye inhabitance, and all these are at warr with the Tomahitans. when they had taken theire leave of ye monytons they marched three days out of thire way to give a clap to some of that great nation, where they fell on with great courage and were as couragiously repullsed by theire enimise.

And heare Gabriell received shott with two arrows, one of them in his thigh, which stopt his runing and soe was taken prisoner, for Indian vallour consists most in theire heeles for he that can run best is accounted ye best man. These Indians thought this Gabrill to be noe Tomahittan by ye length of his haire, for ye Tomahittans keepe theire haire close cut to ye end an enime may not take an advantage to lay hold of them by it. They tooke Gabriell and scowered his skin with water and ashes, and when they perceived his skin to be white they made very much of him and admire att his knife gunn and hatchett they tooke with him. They gave those thing to him a gaine. He made signes to them the gun was ye Tomahittons which he had a disire to take with him, but ye knife and hatchet he gave to ye king. they not knowing ye use of gunns, the king receved it with great shewes of thankfullness for they had not any manner of iron instrument that hee saw amongst them whilst he was there they brought in a fatt bevor which they had newly killd and went to swrynge it. Gabriell made signes to them that those skins were good a mongst the white people toward the sun riseing. they would know by signes how many such skins they would take for such a knife. He told them foure and eight for such a hattchett and made signes that if they would lett him return, he would bring many things amongst them. they seemed to rejoyce att it and carried him to a path that carried to ye Tomahittans gave him Rokahamony for his journey and soe they departed, to be short. when he came to ye Tomahittans ye king had one short voyage more before hee could bring in Gabriell and that was downe ye river, they live upon in perriougers to kill hoggs, beares and sturgion which they did incontinent by five dayes and nights. They went down ye river and came to ye mouth of ye salts where they could not see land but the water not above three foot deepe hard sand. By this meanes wee know this is not ye river ye Spanyards live upon as Mr. Needham did thinke. Here they killed many swine, sturgin and beavers and barbicued them, soe returned and were fifteen dayes runing up a gainst ye streame but noe mountainous land to bee seene but all levell.[1]

Arthur was then sent back to Virginia by the Tamahita chief; and he reached Wood's house June 18, 1674.

This narrative leaves a great deal to be desired, and the reliability of much of that reported by Arthur is not beyond question, but the existence of a tribe of the name and its approximate location is established. The narrative is also of interest as containing the

[1] Alvord and Bidgood, op. cit., pp. 218-223.

only specific information of any sort regarding their manners and customs.

For some years after the period of this narrative we hear not a word regarding the tribe, and when they reappear it is on the De Crenay map as "Tamaitaux," on the east bank of the Chattahoochee above the Chiaha and nearly opposite a part of the Sawokli.[1] A little later Adair enumerates the "Ta-mè-tah" among those tribes which the Muskogee had induced to incorporate with them.[2] They appear among other Lower Creek towns in the enumeration of 1750, placed between the northern Sawokli town and the Kasihta.[3] On one of the D'Anville maps of early date we find "Tamaita" laid down on the west bank of the Coosa not far above its junction with the Tallapoosa. The Koasati town was just below. In the list of Creek towns given in 1761 in connection with the assignment of traderships we find this entry: "27 Coosawtee including Tomhetaws." The hunters of the two numbered 125 and they were located "close to the French barracks" where was the Koasati town from very early times.[4] Thus it appears that some at least of the Tamahita had moved over among the Upper Creeks sometime between 1733 and 1761 or perhaps earlier. Bernard Romans, on January 17, 1772, when descending the Tombigbee River, mentions passing the "Tomeehettee bluff, where formerly a tribe of that nation resided,"[5] and Hamilton identifies this bluff with McIntosh's Bluff, a former location of the Tohome tribe.[6] It is probable that some Tamahita moved over to this river at the same time as the Koasati and Okchai, a little before Romans's time, and afterwards returned with them to the upper Alabama.

Memory of them remained long among the Lower Creeks, since an aged informant of the writer, a Hitchiti Indian, born in the old country, claimed to be descended from them. According to him there was a tradition that the Tamahita burned a little trading post belonging to the English, whereupon the English called upon their Creek allies to punish the aggressors. The Tamahita were much more numerous than their opponents, but were not very warlike, and were driven south to the very point of Florida, where they escaped in boats to some islands. This tradition appears to be the result of an erroneous identification of the Tamahita with the Timucua. There is no evidence that the Creeks had a war with the former people.

After the above account had been prepared some material came under the eye of the writer tending to the conclusion that Tamahita must be added to that already long list of terms under which the

[1] See plate 5; Hamilton, Col. Mobile, p. 190.

[2] Adair, Hist. Am. Inds., p. 257.

[3] MS., Ayer Coll.

[4] Ga. Col. Docs., VIII, p. 524.

[5] Romans, Nat. Hist. E. and W. Fla., p. 332.

[6] Hamilton, op. cit., p. 106. See pp. 160–165.

Yuchi tribes appear in history. In view of the already formidable number of these Yuchi identifications—Hogologe, Tahogale, Chiska, Westo, Rickohockan—he would have preferred some other outcome, but we must be guided by facts and these facts point in one and the same direction.

The first significant circumstance is that, with one or two easily explained exceptions, wherever the name Tamahita or any of its synonyms is used none of the other terms bestowed upon the Yuchi occurs. This is true of the De Crenay map (pl. 5), of the French census of 1750,[1] and of the list of tribes incorporated into the Creek confederacy given by Adair.[2] The only exceptions are where different bands might be under consideration. Thus in the census of 1761 "Tomhetaws" are mentioned in connection with the Koasati living near the junction of the Coosa and Tallapoosa Rivers, Alabama, while the Yuchi among the Lower Creeks and those which had formerly been on the Choctawhatchee are entered under their proper names.[3] Romans, too, speaks of a town of "Euchas" among the Lower Creeks and in a different part of his work of a former tribe called "Tomeehetee" which gave its name to a bluff on the Tombigbee River.[4] These exceptions, however, are not of much consequence.

In the second place the names of almost all of the other important Creek tribal subdivisions do occur alongside of the Tamahita. On the De Crenay map and in the French census of 1750 this tribe is located among the Lower Creeks, alongside of the Coweta, Kasihta, Apalachicola, Sawokli, Osochi, Eufaula, Okmulgee, Oconee, Hitchiti, Chiaha, and Tamałi.[5] Adair gives them as one of a number of "broken tribes" said to have been incorporated with the Creeks proper, and he seems to have been familiar only with those living among the Upper Creeks, for the others mentioned in connection with them were all settled here, viz, Tuskegee, Okchai, Pakana, Witumpka, Shawnee, Natchez, and Koasati. As incorporated tribes among the Lower Creeks he notes the Osochi, Oconee, and Sawokli. In other places where Tamahita are mentioned among the Upper Creeks we find, in addition to the above, the Okchaiutci, Kan-tcati (Alabama), people of Coosa Old Town, and Muklasa, while the Tawasa are given in the census of 1750 and on the De Crenay map of 1733 as entirely distinct.[5]

Taking the Lower Creek towns by themselves we find all of the towns accounted for except the Yuchi towns and two or three which were located upon Chattahoochee River for a very brief period. These last were a Shawnee town, Tuskegee, Kolomi, Atasi, and per-

[1] MS. in Ayer Coll., Newberry Lib.
[2] Hist. Am. Inds., p. 257.
[3] Ga. Col. Docs., VIII, pp. 522–524.
[4] Romans, E. and W. Fla., pp. 280, 332.
[5] Loc. cit.

haps Kealedji. The first two, however, occur independently in Adair's list, and the others are well-known Muskogee divisions which appear alongside of the Tamahita among the Upper Creeks. The Yamasee were also here for very brief periods but at a point much farther down the river than that where the Tamahita are placed.

Thirdly, Yuchi are known to have lived at or in the neighborhood of most of the places assigned to the Tamahita. The topography of the De Crenay map is too uncertain to enable us to base any conclusions upon it, but in the census of 1750 the Tamahita are given at approximately the same distance from Fort Toulouse as Coweta and Kasihta, and 3 leagues nearer than Chiaha, very close to the position which the (unnamed) Yuchi then occupied. As we shall see when we come to discuss the Yuchi as a whole, there was at least one band of Indians belonging to this tribe among the Upper Creeks, remnants apparently of the Choctawhatchee band. The Tamahita which figure in this section of the Creek country may, therefore, have been a part of these. I believe, however, that there was a second band of Yuchi here, which had had a somewhat different history. When we come to discuss the Yuchi Indians we shall find that a section of these people, called generally Hogologe or Hog Logee, accompanied the Apalachicola Indians and part of the Shawnee to the Chattahoochee River about 1716. The Apalachicola were satisfied with this location, but some time later the Shawnee migrated to the Tallapoosa, and I think it probable that at least a part of the Hogologe Yuchi went with them. We know that relations between these two tribes must have been intimate for Bartram was led to believe that the Yuchi spoke "the Savanna or Savanuca tongue," and Speck testifies to cordial understandings between them extending down to the present time.[1] But Hawkins gives us something more definite. In a diary which he kept during his travels through the Creek Nation in 1796 he states, under date of Monday, December 19, when he was following the course of the Tallapoosa River toward its mouth and along its southern shore, "half a mile [beyond a large spring by the river bank is] the Uchee village, a remnant of those settled on the Chattahoochee; half a mile farther pass a Shawne village."[2] In his Sketch, representing conditions a few years later, he says, in the course of his description of the same Shawnee village, "Some Uchees have settled with them," and there is every reason to believe that they were the Yuchi who had formerly occupied a town of their own half a mile away.[3]

Last of all, we must not lose sight of the fact that the origin of the Tamahita, like that of the Yuchi, may be traced far north to the

[1] Bartram, Travels, p. 387; Speck, Anth. Pub., U. of Pa. Mus., I, p. 11.

[2] Ga. Hist. Soc. Colls., IX, p. 41.

[3] See p. 320; also plate 8.

Tennessee mountains. It seems rather improbable that a tribe from such a distant country could have settled among the Creeks and, after living in closest intimacy with them for so many years, have passed entirely out of existence without any further hint of their affiliations or any more information regarding them. And the fact that they and the Yuchi share so many points in common and appear in the same places, though practically never side by side, must be added to this as constituting strong circumstantial evidence that they were indeed one and the same people.

THE ALABAMA

Next to the Muskogee themselves the most conspicuous Upper Creek tribe were the Alabama, or Albamo. As shown by their language and indicated by some of their traditions they were connected more nearly with the Choctaw and Chickasaw than with the Creeks. Stiggins declares that the Choctaw, Chickasaw, Hitchiti, and Koasati languages were mutually intelligible,[1] and this was true at least of Choctaw, Chickasaw, and Koasati.

According to the older traditions the Alabama had come from the west, or perhaps, rather from the southwest, to their historic seats, but these traditions do not carry them to a great distance. Adair, referring to the seven distinct dialects reported as spoken near Fort Toulouse, said that the people claimed to have come from South America.[2]

The following account of their origin was obtained originally from Se-ko-pe-chi ("Perseverance"), who is described as "one of the oldest Creeks, . . . in their new location west of the Mississippi," about the year 1847, and was published by Schoolcraft:[3]

> The origin of the Alabama Indians as handed down by oral tradition, is that they sprang out of the ground, between the Cahawba and Alabama Rivers. . . . The earliest migration recollected, as handed down by oral tradition, is that they emigrated from the Cahawba and Alabama Rivers to the junction of the Tuscaloosa [Tombigbee ?] and Coosa [Alabama ?] Rivers.[4] Their numbers at that period were not known. The extent of the territory occupied at that time was indefinite. At the point formed by the junction of the Tuscaloosa and Coosa Rivers the tribe sojourned for the space of two years, after which their location was at the junction of the Coosa and Alabama Rivers, on the west side of what was subsequently the site of Fort Jackson. It is supposed that at this time they numbered fifty effective men. They claimed the country from Fort Jackson to New Orleans for their hunting-grounds. . . .
>
> They are of the opinion that the Great Spirit brought them from the ground, and that they are of right possessors of this soil.

[1] Stiggins, MS.

[2] Adair, Hist. Am. Inds., pp. 267-268.

[3] Ind. Tribes, I, pp. 266-267.

[4] The name Coosa was once extended over the Alabama as well as the stream which now bears the name; there is some reason to think that the Tombigbee may occasionally have been called the Tuscaloosa. At any rate this construction would reconcile the present tradition with the one following.

From Ward Coachman, an old Alabama Indian in Oklahoma, Dr. Gatschet obtained the following:

Old Alabama men used to say that the Alabama came out of the ground near the Alabama River a little up stream from its junction with the Tombigbee, close to Holsifa (Choctaw Bluff). After they had come out an owl hooted. They were scared and most of them went back into the ground. That is why the Alabama are few in number. The Alabama towns are Tawasa, Pawokti, Oktcaiyutci, Atauga, Hatcafa'ski (River Point, at the junction of the Coosa and Tallapoosa), and Wetumka.

From one of the oldest women among the Alabama living in Texas I obtained a long origin myth in which the tribe is represented as having come across the Atlantic, but this is evidently mixed up with the story of the discovery of America by the white people and is of little value in restoring the old tradition. The relationship recognized between the Alabama and Koasati is illustrated by the following story, said to have been told by an old Indian now dead:

The Alabama and Koasati came out of the earth on opposite sides of the root of a certain tree and settled there in two bodies. Consequently these differed somewhat in speech, though they always kept near each other. At first they came out of the earth only during the night time, going down again when day came. Presently a white man came to the place, saw the tracks, and wanted to find the people. He went there several times, but could discover none of them above ground. By and by he decided upon a ruse, so he left a barrel of whisky near the place where he saw the footsteps. When the Indians came out again to play they saw the barrel, and were curious about it, but at first no one would touch it. Finally, however, one man tasted of its contents, and presently he began to feel good and to sing and dance about. Then the others drank also and became so drunk that the white man was able to catch them. Afterward the Indians remained on the surface of the earth.

The tradition of a downstream origin may have been due to the former residence of the Tawasa Alabama near Mobile. This has certainly given its entire tone to the story which Stiggins relates.[1]

Finally, mention may be made of Milfort's extravagant Creek migration legend in which the Creek Indians proper are represented as having pursued the Alabama from the western prairies near Red River across the Missouri, Mississippi, and Ohio in succession until they reached their later home in central Alabama.

After De Soto and his companions had left the Chickasaw, by whom they had been severely handled, they reached a small village called Limamu[2] by Ranjel and Alimamu[3] by Elvas. This was on April 26, 1541. Biedma says nothing of the village, but states that they set out toward the northwest for a province called Alibamo.[4]

On Thursday they came to a plain where was a stockaded fort defended by many Indians. According to Biedma the Indians had built this stockade across the trail the Spaniards were to take merely

[1] See p. 140.
[2] Bourne, Narr. of De Soto, II, p. 136.
[3] Ibid., I, p. 108.
[4] Ibid., II, p. 24.

to try their strength, though having nothing whatever to defend.[1] It is evident that no women or children were there, but it is most likely that the place was a stockaded town from which the noncombatants had been removed in anticipation of the arrival of the Spaniards. Elvas gives quite a lively picture of this fort and the Indians within. He says:

> Many were armed, walking upon it, with their bodies, legs, and arms painted and ochred, red, black, white, yellow, and vermilion in stripes, so that they appeared to have on stockings and doublet. Some wore feathers and others horns on the head; the face blackened, and the eyes encircled with vermilion, to heighten their fierce aspect. So soon as they saw the Christians draw nigh they beat drums, and, with loud yells, in great fury came forth to meet them.[2]

After a sharp engagement the Spaniards drove these Indians from their position with considerable loss, but were prevented from following up their success by an unfordable river behind the stockade, across which the greater part of the Indians escaped. Garcilasso, who, as usual, passes this entire affair under a magnifying glass, calls the fort "Fort Alibamo,"[3] but it so happens that not one of the three standard authorities applies this term to it. Two of them, as we have seen, give the name to a small village in which they had camped two days earlier. Nevertheless Biedma's reference to a "Province of Alibamo" seems to indicate that the Spaniards were actually in a region occupied by Alabama Indians, although we do not know whether the entire tribe was present or only one section of it. It has been supposed by some that the Ulibahali mentioned before the great Mobile encounter were the later Alabama or constituted an Alabama town, but while it is true that the name bears some resemblance to that of a possible Alabama town, the Alabama word for village being *ola*, it is quite certain that we must seek in it the name of a true Muskogee town.[4]

After 1541 the Alabama disappear entirely from sight until the French settlement of Louisiana, when we find them located in their well-known later historic seats on the upper course of the river which bears their name. The first notice of them occurs in March, 1702, after the foundation of the first Mobile fort had been begun, where they appear together with the Conchaque—by which is evidently meant the Muskogee—as enemies of the Mobile tribes whom they had caused to abandon many of their former settlements. Pénicaut says that Iberville sent messengers from Mobile to the Choctaw and Alabama, and that their chiefs came to him to sing the calumet of peace along with the chiefs of the Mobile;[5]

---

[1] Bourne, Narr. of De Soto, II, p. 24.
[2] Ibid., I, pp. 108-109.
[3] Garcilasso, in Shipp, De Soto and Fla., pp. 401-403.
[4] See p. 254.
[5] Margry, Déc., V, p. 425.

but he is perhaps in error in placing the visit of the chiefs before Iberville's return; as Iberville himself says nothing regarding it, while La Harpe states that eight honored chiefs of the Alabama came to the Mobile fort May 12, fifteen days after Iberville's departure. These eight chiefs, La Harpe informs us, "came to ask M. de Bienville whether they should continue the war against the Chicachas, the Tomès, and the Mobiliens. He counseled them to make peace, gave them some presents, and so determined them to carry out what they had promised."[1] In the report which he drew up after his return to France from this expedition Iberville speaks of these Indians as follows:

The Conchaques and Alibamons have their first villages thirty-five or forty leagues northeast, a quarter east from the Tohomés, on the banks of a river which falls into the Mobile five leagues above the fort, toward the east. These two villages may consist of four hundred families; the greater part have guns, are friends of the English and will be shortly ours.[2]

In May, 1703, the English induced the Alabama to declare against the French, and the latter, deceived by the promise that they would find plenty of corn among them, sent into their country a man named Labrie with four Canadians. When within two days journey of the Alabama village 12 Indians came to meet them bringing a peace calumet. That night, however, they killed all of the Frenchmen but one named Charles, who escaped, although with a broken arm, and carried the news to Mobile.[3] According to Pénicaut, Bienville immediately undertook to avenge this injury, but was deserted by his Mobile and other allies who were secretly in sympathy with his enemies. This obliged him to return without having accomplished anything.[4] Such an expedition may have been undertaken, but from other information relative to the relations between the Mobile tribes and the Alabama an understanding between the two seems rather improbable. According to La Harpe it was not until December 22, 1703, that Bienville set out to punish the injury that had been received.[5] This Pénicaut represents as immediately following the abortive attempt just related.[6] La Harpe says:

He left [Fort Louis de la Mobile] with forty soldiers and Canadians in seven pirogues. January 3, 1704, he discovered the fire of a party of the enemy. A little afterward, having discovered ten pirogues, he took counsel of MM. de Tonty and de Saint-Denis, who were of the opinion, contrary to his own, that they should wait until night in order to attack them. These Alibamons were camped on a height difficult of access. The night was very dark, and they took a trail filled with brambles and vines, almost impracticable. The enemy posted in this place to the number of twelve, hearing the noise, fired a volley from their guns through the bushes; they killed two Frenchmen and wounded another; but they soon took to flight in order

[1] La Harpe, Jour. Hist., p. 72.
[2] Margry, Déc., IV, p. 594.
[3] La Harpe, Jour. Hist., pp. 76–77.
[4] Margry, Déc., V, p. 429.
[5] La Harpe, Jour. Hist., p. 82.
[6] Margry, Déc., V, pp. 429–431.

to join their party, which was hunting in the neighborhood of this place. M. de Bienville had their canoes loaded with meat and corn upset. He then returned to the fort on the 11th of the same month.[1]

Pénicaut's account of the affair is as follows:

After we had returned [from the previous abortive expedition which he describes] M. de Bienville had prepared some days afterward ten canoes, and as soon as they were ready he had us embark to the number of fifty Frenchmen with our officers, of which he was first in rank, and we left secretly at night in order to conceal our movement from the savages. At the end of some days of travel, when we were within ten leagues of the village of the Alibamons, very near the place where the four Frenchmen had been killed, we saw a fire. There was on the river within two gunshots from this fire fourteen canoes of these Alibamons, who were hunting, accompanied by their families. We went down again a quarter of a league because it was too light; we remained half a league from the savages the rest of the day, in a place where our canoes were concealed behind a height of land. We sent six men up on this height in order to reconnoiter the place where their cabins were, which we discovered easily from there. It was necessary to ascend the river to a point above in order to land opposite. When we perceived that their fire was almost out, and they were believed to be asleep, M. de Bienville had us advance. After having passed a little height, we went down into a wood, where there was a very bad trail. When we were near the cabins where the savages were asleep, one of our Frenchmen stepped on a dry cane, which made a noise in breaking. One of the savages who was not yet asleep began to cry out in their language, "Who goes there?" which obliged us to keep silence. The savage, after some time, hearing no more noise, lay down. We then advanced, but the savages, hearing us march, rising uttered the death cry and fired a volley, which killed one of our people. Immediately their old people, their women, and their children fled. Only those bearing arms retired last, letting go at us many volleys. On our side we did not know whether we had killed a single one, because we did not know in the night where we were shooting. The savages having retired, we remained in their cabins until daybreak; we burned them before leaving them in order to return to the river, where we found their canoes, which we took, along with the merchandises which were in them, to our fort of Mobile.[2]

La Harpe notes that on March 14, 1704, following, 20 Chickasaw brought to Mobile 5 Alabama scalps and received guns, powder, and ball in exchange.[3] November 18, 20 Choctaw brought in 3 more scalps of the same people.[4] January 21, 1706, many Choctaw chiefs came bringing 9 more Alabama scalps.[5] February 21, M. de Boisbrillant led a party of 60 Canadians and 12 Indians against the Alabama. He surprised a hunting party of Alabama and, according to Pénicaut, killed all of the men and carried away all of the women and children.[6] La Harpe says that he brought back 2 scalps and 1 slave.[7] The same year it was learned that the Alabama and Chickasaw together, incited by an English trader, had been instrumental in forcing the Tunica to abandon their former homes on the lower Yazoo.

[1] La Harpe, Jour. Hist., pp. 82–83.
[2] Margry, Déc. v, pp. 429–431.
[3] La Harpe, Jour. Hist., p. 83.
[4] Ibid., p. 86.
[5] Ibid., p. 95.
[6] Margry, Déc., v, pp. 431–432.
[7] La Harpe, Jour. Hist., p. 96.

According to Pénicaut, M. de Chateaugué led an expedition against the Alabama about this time, encountered a war party of that nation on its way to attack the Choctaw, and killed 15 of them.[1] He places this among the events of the year 1703, but it must have been either in 1705 or 1706. The Alabama probably took part in the English expedition against the Apalachee in 1703, already related, and in those against the Apalachicola in 1706 and 1707.[2] In November, 1707, they and the Creeks together invested Pensacola, led by 13 Englishmen, but they were obliged to withdraw.[3] Under date of 1708 Pénicaut mentions an expedition under M. de Chateaugué, consisting of 60 Frenchmen and 60 Mobile Indians, against Alabama hunting in the neighborhood, in which they killed 30, wounded 7, and carried 9 away prisoners.[4] The same year he relates an adventure on the part of two Frenchmen who were captured by Indians of this tribe, but being left with only two guards were able to kill them and escape to Mobile.[5] The Alabama and their allies marched against the Mobile "with 4,000 men," but only succeeded in burning some cabins.[6] In 1709 Pénicaut speaks of an encounter between 15 Choctaw and 50 Alabama, to the advantage of the former—who tell the story.[7] In March, 1712, La Harpe notes that Bienville "placated the Alibamons, Alibikas, and other nations of Carolina, and reconciled them with those who were allied to us; the peace was general among the savages." [8]

In 1714 English influence was so strong that it even extended over most of the Choctaw, but the next year the Yamasee war broke out and proved to be a general anti-English movement among southern Indians. Bienville seized this opportunity to renew his alliance with the Alabama and other tribes, and it was at about the same period that he established a post in the midst of the Alabama, which was known officially as Fort Toulouse, but colloquially as the Alabama Fort. Later the Tawasa came from Mobile Bay and settled near their relatives. Pénicaut mentions the Alabama among those tribes which came to "sing the calumet" before M. de l'Epinay in 1717,[9] but from the time of the founding of Fort Toulouse until the end of French domination we hear very little about these people from the French. Peace continued to subsist between them, and the greater part of the tribe was evidently devoted to the French interest. In the early Carolina documents there are few references to them, the general name Tallapoosa being used for them and their Creek neighbors on Tallapoosa River. It is curious that the name Alabama does

---

[1] Margry, Déc., v, p. 435.

[2] See pp. 121-123, 130.

[3] La Harpe, Jour. Hist., pp. 103-104.

[4] Margry, op. cit., pp. 478-479.

[5] Ibid., pp. 479-481.

[6] Ibid., p. 478.

[7] Ibid., p. 483.

[8] La Harpe, op. cit., p. 110.

[9] Margry, op. cit., p. 547.

not occur in the list of Creek towns in the census of 1761, but part of them may be included in the following: "Welonkees including red Ground, 70 hunters," the name of the principal Alabama town being "Red Ground" in Hawkins's time.[1] Another part of them are, however, represented by the "Little Oakchoys, assigned to Wm. Trewin."[2] The enumeration of 1750 seems to give Red Ground in the distorted form "Canachequi."[3] In 1777 Bartram visited a town which he calls "Alabama" situated at the junction of the Coosa and Tallapoosa Rivers, but this seems really to have been Tuskegee.[4] Hawkins enumerates four settlements which he believed to be the ancient Alabama, but in fact only the first of these appears to have consisted of true Alabama, the others being probably made up of later additions, which have already been considered (pp. 137–141). Following is his description of these four places:

1st. E-cun-chāte; from E-cun-nā, *earth*, and chāte, *red*. A small village on the left bank of Alabama, which has its fields on the right side, in the cane swamp; they are a poor people, without stock, are idle and indolent, and seldon make bread enough, but have fine melons in great abundance in their season. The land back from the settlement is of thin quality, oak, hickory, pine and ponds. Back of this, hills, or waving. Here the soil is of good quality for cultivation; that of thin quality extends nearly a mile.

2d. Too-wos-sau, is three miles below E-cun-chā-te, on the same side of the river; a small village on a high bluff, the land is good about, and back of the village; they have some lots fenced with cane, and some with rails, for potatoes and ground nuts; the corn is cultivated on the right side of the river, on rich cane swamps; these people have a few hogs, but no other stock.

3d. Pau-woc-te; a small village two miles below Too-was-sau,[5] on a high bluff, the same side of the river; the land is level and rich for five miles back; but none of it is cultivated around their houses; their fields are on the right bank of the river, on rich cane swamp; they have a few hogs and horses, but no cattle; they had, formerly, the largest and best breed of hogs in the nation, but have lost them by carelessness or inattention.[6]

4th. At-tau-gee; a small village four miles below Pau-woc-te, spread out for two miles on the right bank of the river; they have fields on both sides, but their chief dependence is on the left side; the land on the left side is rich; on the right side the pine forest extends down to At-tau-gee Creek; below this creek the land is rich.

These people have very little intercourse with white people; although they are hospitable, and offer freely any thing they have, to those who visit them. They have this singular custom, as soon as a white person has eaten of any dish and left it, the remains are thrown away, and every thing used by the guest immediately washed.

They have some hogs, horses, and cattle, in a very fine range, perhaps the best on the river; the land to the east as far as Ko-e-ne-cuh, and except the plains (Hi-yuc-

---

[1] Ga. Col. Docs., VIII, p. 524.

[2] Ibid., p. 524.

[3] MS., Ayer Coll.

[4] Bartram, Travels, pp. 445, 461.

[5] Also given as 7 miles below the junction of the Coosa and Tallapoosa.—Hawkins in Coll. Ga. Hist. Soc., IX, p. 170.

[6] In 1797 Hawkins states that the trader here was "Charles Weatherford, a man of infamous character, a dealer in stolen horses; condemned and reprieved the 28th of May."—Coll. Ga. Hist. Soc., IX, p. 170; the last clause, after "but," is wanting in the Lib. of Cong. MS.

pul-gee), is well watered, with much canebrake, a very desirable country. On the west or right side, the good land extends about five miles, and on all the creeks below At-tau-gee, it is good; some of the trees are large poplar, red oak, and hickory, walnut on the margins of the creeks, and pea-vine in the valleys

These four villages have, in all, about eighty gunmen; they do not conform to the customs of the Creeks, and the Creek law for the punishment of adultery is not known to them.[1]

At an earlier period the Alabama had a town still farther downstream which appears in many maps under the name Nitahauritz, interpreted by Mr. H. S. Halbert to mean "Bear Fort."

Hawkins mentions the fact that already a body of Koasati had gone beyond the Mississippi.[2] He does not say the same of the Alabama, yet we know that that tribe had also begun to split up. In describing the Koasati an account of one of these migrations will be given. From the papers of the British Indian agent, John Stuart, we learn that as early as 1778 bands of Kan-tcati and Tawasa had moved into northern Florida,[3] and after the Creek-American war their numbers were swollen very considerably. They did not, however, long maintain a distinct existence. The movement toward the west was of much more importance. It appears that the long association of these Indians with the French, due to the presence of a French post among them, had bred an attachment to that nation among the Alabama equally with the tribes about Mobile Bay, and part of them also decided to move across into Louisiana after the peace of 1763. A further inducement was the almost virgin hunting ground to be found in parts of that colony. That the first emigration occurred about the date indicated (1763)[4] is proved by Sibley, writing in 1806, who has the following to say of the Alabama in the State of Louisiana in his time:

Allibamis, are likewise from West Florida, off Allibami River, and came to Red River about the same time of the Boluxas and Appalaches. Part of them have lived on Red River, about sixteen miles above the Bayau Rapide, till last year, when most of this party, of about thirty men, went up Red River, and have settled themselves near the Caddoques, where, I am informed, they last year made a good crop of corn. The Caddos are friendly to them, and have no objection to their settling there. They speak the Creek and Chactaw languages, and Mobilian; most of them French, and some of them English.

There is another party of them, whose village is on a small creek, in Appelousa district, about thirty miles northwest from the church of Appelousa. They consist of about forty men. They have lived at the same place ever since they came from Florida; are said to be increasing a little in numbers, for a few years past. They raise corn, have horses, hogs, and cattle, and are harmless, quiet people.[5]

---

[1] Ga. Hist. Soc. Colls., III, pp. 36-37. Bossu's account shows clearly that the last statement is erroneous.

[2] See p. 204.

[3] Copy of MS., Lib. Cong.

[4] It may have been a few years later, for John Stuart, the British Indian agent, writes, December 2, 1766, that some of these Indians had expressed a desire to settle on the banks of the Mississippi.—English transcriptions, Lib. Cong.

[5] Sibley in Annals of Congress, 9th Cong., 2d sess., 1085 (1806-7).

In August, 1777, William Bartram visited an Alabama village on the Mississippi 2 miles above the Manchac. He describes it as "delightfully situated on several swelling green hills, gradually ascending from the verge of the river."[1] A friend accompanying him purchased some native baskets and pottery from the inhabitants. In 1784 Hutchins found them in about the same place.[2] It will be noticed that Sibley does not mention a previous sojourn of either of the parties of Alabama described by him on the Mississippi River, and we are in the dark as to whether they had separated after coming into Louisiana or before. If they came separately it would seem most likely that the Opelousas band was the one settled on the Mississippi. This at any rate was in accordance with the belief of John Scott, the late chief of the Alabama now residing in Texas and the oldest person among them. He informed the writer in 1912 that the name of the old Alabama town on the Mississippi River was Aktcabehåle. From there they moved to "Mikiwī'l" close to Opelousas, and from there to the Sabine River, where they formed a new town which received no special name. There was an Alabama village in Texas called Fenced-in-village a short distance west by south of a mill and former post office called Mobile, Tyler County, Texas. Next they settled in what is now Tyler County, Texas, at a town which they called Tak'o'sha-o'la ("Peach-tree Town"). This was about 2 miles due north of Chester or 20 miles north of Woodville, Texas. Their next town was 3 miles from Peach-tree Town and contained a "big house" (i' sa tcuba) and a dance ground, but was unnamed. After a time the Alabama chief decided to move to Pat'alā'ka (said to mean "Cane place") where the Biloxi and Pascagoula lived, and some other Indians went with him. Part, however, returned to Louisiana, where they remained three years. At the end of that time they came back to Texas and formed a village which took its name from a white man, Jim Barclay. They moved from there to the village which they now occupy, which is called Big Sandy village from the name of a creek, although it took some time for the families scattered about in Texas to come in.

According to some white informants the Alabama settled on Red River, moved to Big Sandy village, and perhaps both parties finally united there. A few families, however, still remain in Calcasieu and St. Landry Parishes, Louisiana. The language of all of the Texas Alabama is practically uniform, but the speech of some of the Tapasola clan is said to vary a little from the normal.

The Alabama who had remained in their old country took a prominent part in the Creek war. Indeed Stiggins says that "they did more murder and other mischief in the time of their hostilities in the year

[1] Bartram, Travels, p. 427.

[2] Hutchins, Narr., p. 44.

1813 than all the other tribes together."[1] After the treaty of Fort Jackson, in 1814, by which all of the old Alabama land was ceded to the whites, the same writer says that part of them settled above the mouth of Cubahatche in a town called Towassee, while the rest moved to a place on Coosa River above Wetumpka. He states that the town belonging to this latter division was Otciapofa, but he is evidently mistaken, because Otciapofa has been pure Creek as far back as we have any knowledge of it.[2] Perhaps the Coosa settlement was that called Autauga in the census of 1832, or it may have contained the Okchaiutci Indians, whose history will be given presently. I have suggested elsewhere that the names of these towns seem to show the part of the tribe which remained with the Creeks to have been the Tawasa. Speaking of the Alabama Indians in his time Stiggins says that, while their chiefs were admitted to the national councils on the same terms as the others, they seldom associated with the Creeks otherwise. After their removal the Alabama settled near the Canadian, but some years later went still farther west and located about the present town of Weleetka, Okla. A small station on the St. Louis-San Francisco Railroad just south of Weleetka bears their name. While a few of these Indians retain their old language it is rapidly giving place to Creek and English. They have the distinction of being the only non-Muskogee tribe incorporated with the Creeks, exclusive of the Yuchi, which still maintains a square ground.

As already noted, one Alabama town received the name, Okchaiutci, "Little Okchai," which suggests relationship with the Okchai people, but the origin of this the Indians explain as follows: At one time the Alabama (probably only part of the tribe) had no square ground and asked the Okchai to take them into theirs. The Okchai said, "All right; you can seat yourself on the other side of my four backsticks and I will protect you." They did so, and for some time afterwards the two tribes busked together and played on the same side in ball games. Later on, however, a dispute arose in connection with one of these games and the Alabama separated, associating themselves with the Tukabahchee and hence with the opposite fire clan. Afterwards those Alabama formed a town which they called Okchaiutci, and to this day Okchaiutci is one of the names given the Alabama Indians in set speeches at the time of the busk. According to my informant, himself an Okchai Indian, the date of this separation was as late as 1872–73, but he must be much in error since we find Okchaiutci in existence long before the removal to Oklahoma.

Okchaiutci appears first, apparently, in the census list of 1750, though the diminutive ending is not used. In 1761 the trader located

[1] Stiggins, MS.

[2] Still they may have occupied the site of Otciapofa for a time. This place and Little Tulsa were so close together that they were often confounded.

there was William Trewin.[1] It is not separately mentioned by Bartram nor certainly by Swan, but is probably intended by the town which he calls "Wacksoyochees."[2] Hawkins gives the following description:

Hook-choie-oo-che, a pretty little compact town, between O-che-au-po-fau and Tus-kee-gee, on the left bank of Coosau; the houses join those of Tus-kee-gee; the land around the town is a high, poor level, with high-land ponds; the corn fields are on the left side of Tallapoosa, on rich low grounds, on a point called Sam-bul-loh, and below the mouth of the creek of that name which joins on the right side of the river.

They have a good stock of hogs, and a few cattle and horses; they formerly lived on the right bank of Coosau, just above their present site, and removed lately, on account of the war with the Chickasaws. Their stock ranges on that side of the river; they have fenced all the small fields about their houses, where they raise their peas and potatoes; their fields at Sam-bul-loh, are under a good fence; this was made by Mrs. Durant, the oldest sister of the late General McGillivray, for her own convenience.[3]

This town does not appear in the census list of 1832, unless it is one of the two Fishpond towns there given, "Fish Pond" and "Tholl thlo coe." After the removal to Oklahoma it is said to have maintained its separate square for a short time, and, as has been said, its name is retained as a busk designation of all the Alabama.

THE KOASATI

The Koasati Indians, as shown by their language, are closely related to the Alabama. There were at one time two branches of this tribe—one close to the Alabama, near what is now Coosada station, Elmore County, Ala., the other on the Tennessee River north of Langston, Jackson County. These latter appear but a few times in history, and the name was considerably garbled by early writers. There is reason to believe, however, that it has the honor of an appearance in the De Soto chronicles, as the Coste of Ranjel,[4] the Coste or Acoste of Elvas,[5] the Costehe of Biedma,[6] and the Acosta of Garcilasso.[7] The omission of the vowel between *s* and *t* is the only difficult feature in this identification. It is evident also that it was at a somewhat different point on the river from that above indicated, since it was on an island. The form Costehe, used also by Pardo, tends to confirm our identification, since it appears to contain the Koasati and Alabama suffix *-ha* indicating collectivity. Ranjel gives the following account of the experience of the explorers among these "Costehe:"

On Thursday [July 1, 1540] the chief of Coste came out to receive them in peace, and he took the Christians to sleep in a village of his; and he was offended because some soldiers provisioned themselves from, or, rather, robbed him of, some barbacoas of corn

[1] Ga. Col. Docs., VIII, p. 524.
[2] Schoolcraft, Ind. Tribes, V, p. 262.
[3] Ga. Hist. Soc. Colls., III, p. 37.
[4] Bourne, Narr. of De Soto, II, p. 109.
[5] Ibid., I, p. 78.
[6] Ibid., II, p. 15.
[7] Garcilasso in Shipp, De Soto and Fla., p. 373.

against his will. The next day, Thursday,[1] on the road leading toward the principal village of Coste, he stole away and gave the Spaniards the slip and armed his people. Friday, the 2d of July, the governor arrived at Coste. This village was on an island in the river, which there flows large, swift, and hard to enter. And the Christians crossed the first branch with no small venture, and the governor entered into the village careless and unarmed, with some followers unarmed. And when the soldiers, as they were used to do, began to climb upon the barbacoas, in an instant the Indians began to take up clubs and seize their bows and arrows and to go to the open square.

The governor commanded that all should be patient and endure for the evident peril in which they were, and that no one should put his hand on his arms; and he began to rate his soldiers and, dissembling, to give them some blows with a cudgel; and he cajoled the chief, and said to him that he did not wish the Christians to make him any trouble; and they would like to go out to the open part of the island to encamp. And the chief and his men went with him; and when they were at some distance from the village in an open place, the governor ordered his soldiers to lay hands on the chief and ten or twelve of the principal Indians, and to put them in chains and collars; and he threatened them, and said that he would burn them all because they had laid hands on the Christians. From this place, Coste, the governor sent two soldiers to view the province of Chisca, which was reputed very rich, toward the north, and they brought good news. There in Coste they found in the trunk of a tree as good honey and even better than could be had in Spain. In that river were found some muscles that they gathered to eat, and some pearls. And they were the first these Christians saw in fresh water, although they are to be found in many parts of this land.[2]

In one of the accounts of Juan Pardo's expedition of 1567 we are told that he turned back because he learned that the Indians of Carrosa, Costehe, Chisca, and Cosa had united against him.[3] This is the last mention of such a tribe by the Spaniards, and what we hear of the northern body of Koasati at a later period is little enough. We merely know that there was a Koasati village on the Tennessee River in the latter part of the seventeenth century. The "Cochali" of Coxe is probably a misprint for the name of this town. They were said to live on an island in the river just like the Costehe,[4] and Sauvolle, who derived his information from a Canadian who had ascended the Tennessee in the summer of 1701 with four companions, says that "the Cassoty and the Casquinonpa are on an island, which the river forms, at the two extremities of which are situated these two nations."[5] They also gave their name to the Tennessee River. In the map reproduced in plate 3 we find "Cusatees 50 in 2 villages" laid down on a big island in the "Cusatees" or "Thegalegos River," just below the "Tohogalegas" (Yuchi), and between the two a French fort. According to Mr. O. D. Street, Coosada was the name of a mixed settlement of Creeks and Cherokees established about 1784 on the south bank of the Tennessee "at what is now called

[1] Probably Friday.
[2] Bourne, Narr. of De Soto, II, pp. 109-111.
[3] Ruidiaz, La Florida, II, pp. 271-272.
[4] French, Hist. Colls. La., 1850, p. 230.
[5] MS. in Lib. La. Hist. Soc., Louisiane, Correspondence Générale, pp. 403-404. Mr. W. E. Myer, the well-known student of Tennessee archeology, thinks that this was Long Island.

Larkin's Landing in Jackson County."[1] Either this was a new settlement by the people we are considering or 1784 marks the date when Cherokee came to live there. The former alternative may very well have been the true one, because the earlier settlement appears not to have been on the mainland. We do not know whether these Koasati were finally absorbed into the Cherokee or whether they emigrated.

The southern Koasati settlement seems to be mentioned first in the enumeration of 1750, where the name is spelled "Couchati," and in the census of 1760 where it appears as "Conchatys."[2] It occurs often on maps, however, and in approximately the same place. The first allusion to the tribe in literature is probably by Adair, who speaks of "two great towns of the Koo-a-sah-te" as having joined the Creek Confederacy.[3] In the list of towns made out in 1761 in order to assign them to traders "Coosawtee including Tomhetaws" is enumerated as having 125 hunters, but is not assigned to anyone on account of its proximity to the French fort.[4] Shortly after this list was made out occurred the cession of Mobile to England and the movement of so many Indian tribes across the Mississippi. This occasioned the Koasati removal thus referred to by Adair:

> Soon after West-Florida was ceded to Great Britain, two warlike towns of the Koo-a-sah te Indians removed from near the late dangerous Alabama French garrison to the Choktah country about twenty-five miles below Tombikbe—a strong wooden fortress, situated on the western side of a high and firm bank, overlooking a narrow deep point of the river of Mobille, and distant from that capital one hundred leagues. The discerning old war chieftain of this remnant perceived that the proud Muskohge, instead of reforming their conduct towards us, by our mild remonstrances, grew only more impudent by our lenity; therefore being afraid of sharing the justly deserved fate of the others, he wisely withdrew to this situation; as the French could not possibly supply them, in case we had exerted ourselves, either in defence to our properties or in revenge of the blood they had shed. But they were soon forced to return to their former place of abode, on account of the partiality of some of them to their former confederates; which proved lucky in its consequences, to the traders, and our southern colonies: for, when three hundred warriors of the Muskohge were on their way to the Choktah to join them in a war against us, two Kooasâhte horsemen, as allies, were allowed to pass through their ambuscade in the evening, and they gave notice of the impending danger. These Kooasâhte Indians annually sanctify the mulberries by a public oblation, before which they are not to be eaten; which, they say, is according to their ancient law.[5]

They were accompanied in this movement by some Alabama of Okchaiutci, and apparently by the Tamahita. In 1771 Romans passed their deserted fields on the Tombigbee, which he places 3 miles below the mouth of Sucarnochee River.[6] Not many years later the lure of the west moved them again and a portion migrated into Louisiana.

---

[1] Pub. Ala. Hist. Soc., I, p. 417.

[2] MS., Ayer Lib.; Miss. Prov. Arch. I, p. 94.

[3] Adair, Hist. Am. Inds., p. 257.

[4] Ga. Col. Docs., VIII, p. 524.

[5] Adair, Hist. Am. Inds., p. 267.

[6] Romans, Nat. Hist. of E. & W. Fla., pp. 326–327.

Sibley would place this event about 1795,[1] and this agrees well with Hawkins's statement that they had left shortly before his time. Stiggins is still more specific. He says:

About the year seventeen hundred and ninety-three there was an old Cowassada chieftain that was called Red Shoes, who was violently opposed to their makeing war on the Chickasaws, and as it was determined on contrary to his will he resolved to quit the nation, so he and a mulatto man who resided with the Alabamas named Billy Ashe headed a party of about twenty families, part Cowasadas and the rest Alabamas, and removed to the Red River and tried a settlement about sixty miles up from its mouth, but on trial they were so annoyed and infested by a small red ant that were so very numerous in that country, that they found it hardly possible to put any thing beyond their reach or destruction, so after living there a few years they removed finally from thence to the province of Texas, on the river Trinity, a few miles from the mouth of said river, where they now live.[2]

Hawkins thus describes the town occupied by those of the tribe who remained in their old territory as it existed in 1799:

Coo-sau-dee is a compact little town situated three miles below the confluence of Coosau and Tallapoosa, on the right bank of Alabama; they have fields on both sides of the river; but their chief dependence is a high, rich island, at the mouth of Coosau. They have some fences, good against cattle only, and some families have small patches fenced, near the town, for potatoes.

These Indians are not Creeks, although they conform to their ceremonies; the men work with the women and make great plenty of corn; all labor is done by the joint labor of all, called public work, except gathering in the crop. During the season for labor, none are exempted from their share of it, or suffered to go out hunting.

There is a rich flat of land nearly five miles in width, opposite the town, on the left side of the river, on which are numbers of conic mounds of earth. Back of the town it is pine barren, and continues so westward for sixty to one hundred miles.

The Coo-sau-dee generally go to market [3] by water, and some of them are good oarsmen. A part of this town moved lately beyond the Mississippi, and have settled there. The description sent back by them that the country is rich and healthy, and abounds in game, is likely to draw others after them. But as they have all tasted the sweets of civil life, in having a convenient market for their products, it is likely they will soon return to their old settlements, which are in a very desirable country well suited to the raising of cattle, hogs and horses; they have a few hogs, and seventy or eighty cattle, and some horses. It is not more than three years since they had not a hog among them. Robert Walton,[4] who was then the trader of the town, gave the women some pigs, and this is the origin of their stock.[5]

In 1832 eighty-two Koasati were enumerated in the old nation.[6] After their emigration west of the Mississippi they formed two towns—Koasati No. 1 and Koasati No. 2. But few now remain

---

1 See p. 205.

2 Stiggins, MS.

3 The Lib. of Cong. MS. has "to Mobile" inserted here.

4 He was trader there in 1797 when Hawkins describes him as "an active man, more attentive to his character now than heretofore." (Ga. Hist. Soc. Colls., IX, p. 169.) He also gives the names of two other traders, "Francis Tuzant, an idle Frenchman in debt to Mr. Panton and to the factory," and "John McLeod of bad character." (Ibid.)

5 Ga. Hist. Soc. Colls., III, pp. 35–36.

6 Senate Doc. 512, 23d Cong., 1st sess., IV, p. 267.

there who can speak the language. Some of these still remember that a part went to Texas.

Stiggins's account above given of the Koasati migration to Louisiana and Texas seems to be considerably abbreviated. There were probably several distinct movements, or at least the tribe split into several distinct bands from time to time. It is very likely that, as in the case of so many other tribes, the Koasati first settled on Red River, but that part of them soon left it. Sibley's account of their movements in Louisiana is more detailed than that of Stiggins. He says:

Conchattas are almost the same people as the Allibamis, but came over only ten years ago; first lived on Bayau Chico, in Appelousa district, but, four years ago, moved to the river Sabine, settled themselves on the east bank, where they now live, in nearly a south direction from Natchitoch, and distant about eighty miles. They call their number of men one hundred and sixty, but say, if they were altogether, they would amount to two hundred. Several families of them live in detached settlements. They are good hunters, and game is plenty about where they are. A few days ago, a small party of them were here,[1] consisting of fifteen persons, men, women, and children, who were on their return from a bear hunt up Sabine. They told me they had killed one hundred and eighteen; but this year an uncommon number of bears have come down. One man alone, on Sabine, during the Summer and Fall, hunting, killed four hundred deer, sold his skins at forty dollars a hundred. The bears, this year, are not so fat as common; they usually yield from eight to twelve gallons of oil, each of which never sells for less than a dollar a gallon, and the skin a dollar more; no great quantity of the meat is saved; what the hunters don't use when out, they generally give to their dogs. The Conchattas are friendly with all other Indians, and speak well of their neighbors the Carankouas, who, they say, live about eighty miles south of them, on the bay, which I believe, is the nearest point to the sea from Natchitoches. A few families of Chactaws have lately settled near them from Bayau Beauf. The Conchattas speak Creek, which is their native language, and Chactaw, and several of them English, and one or two of them can read it a little.[2]

They may have been on Red River previous to their settlement on Bayou Chicot. Schermerhorn[3] states that in 1812 the Koasati on the Sabine numbered 600, but most of these must have left before 1822, because Morse in his report of that year estimates 50 Koasati on the Neches River in Texas and 240 on the Trinity, while 350 are set down as living on the Red River in Louisiana.[4] These last are elsewhere referred to as a band which had obtained permission from the Caddo to locate near them. Whether they were part of the original settlers from lower down the river or had moved over from the Sabine is not apparent. By 1850 most of these had gone to Texas, where Bollaert estimated that the number of their warriors then on the lower Trinity was 500 in two villages called Colête and Batista.[5] All of the Koasati did not leave Louisiana at that time,

---

[1] He is writing from the post of Natchitoches.

[2] Sibley in Annals of Congress, 9th Cong., 2d sess., 1085–86 (1806–7).

[3] Mass. Hist. Soc. Colls., 2d ser., II, p. 26, 1814.

[4] Morse, Rept. to Sec. of War, p. 373.

[5] Bollaert, in Jour. Ethn. Soc. London, II, p. 282.

however, a considerable body continuing to occupy the wooded country in Calcasieu and St. Landry Parishes. Later the two Texas villages were reduced to one, which in turn broke up, probably on account of a pestilence, part uniting with the Alabama in Polk County, but the greater part returning to Louisiana to join their kindred there. At the present time about 10 are still living with the Alabama. Those in Louisiana are more numerous, counting between 80 and 90, and here is the only spot where the tribe still maintains itself as a distinct people. Their village is in the pine woods about 7 miles northeast of Kinder, Allen Parish, La., and 2½ miles north of a flag station called Lauderdale on the Frisco Railroad. Elsewhere very few of this tribe are now to be found who speak pure Koasati uncorrupted by either Creek or Alabama.

A band of Koasati probably joined the Seminole, since we find a place marked "Coosada Old Town" on the middle course of Choctawhatchee River in Vignoles's map of Florida, dated 1823.

Associated with the Koasati we find an Upper Creek town called Wetumpka, which means in Muskogee "tumbling or falling water." It must not be confounded with a Lower Creek settlement of the same name, an outvillage of Coweta Tallahassee. It is also claimed that Wiwohka (q. v.) was originally so called. The Wetumpka with which we have to deal was on the east bank of Coosa River, in Elmore County, Alabama, near the falls. At one time there were two towns here, known as Big Wetumpka and Little Wetumpka respectively, the former on the site of the modern town of Wetumpka, the latter above the falls in Coosa River.[1] Possibly this tribe may be identical with the Tononpa or Thomapa, which appears on French maps at the western end of the falls. (See map of De l'Isle, 1732, and De Crenay, 1733.)[2] It is probably represented by the "Welonkees" of the enumeration of 1761, classed with a town which appears to have been the principal town of the Alabama.[3] It is noted by Bartram as one of those speaking the "Stinkard" language—i. e., something other than Muskogee.[4] He places it beside that of the Koasati, and it would seem likely that this indicates the true position of its people, for when the Koasati moved to Tombigbee River Wetumpka accompanied them. On January 16, 1772, Romans passed "the remains of the old Weetumpkee settlement," 7 miles above a point which Hamilton identifies as Carneys Bluff,[5] on the Tombigbee River. The removal was probably recent, because on April 4 of the same year Taitt visited their town "about one mile E.S.E. from this [Koasati], up the Tallapuse River," and found them

[1] Swan in Schoolcraft, Ind. Tribes, v, p. 262.
[2] Plate 5; also Hamilton, Col. Mobile, p. 190.
[3] Ga. Col. Docs., VIII, p. 524.
[4] Bartram, Travels, p. 461.
[5] Hamilton, Col. Mobile, p. 284, 1910.

engaged in building a new hot house.[1] Presumably this was the first to be erected after their return from the Tombigbee.

Swan's reference, 1792, is the last we hear of the tribe.[2] They probably united with the Koasati or the Alabama.

THE MUKLASA

Still another town in this neighborhood not speaking Muskogee was Muklasa. The name means "friends" or "people of one nation" in Alabama, Koasati, or Choctaw, therefore it is probable that the town was Alabama or Koasati, the Choctaw being at a considerable distance. According to the list of 1761 it was then estimated to contain 30 hunters. William Trewin and James Germany were the traders.[3] In 1797 the trader was Michael Elhart, "an industrious, honest man; a Dutchman."[4] Bartram visited it in 1777,[5] and in 1799 Hawkins gives the following account of it:

> Mook-lau-sau is a small town one mile below Sau-va-noo-gee, on the left bank of a fine little creek, and bordering on a cypress swamp; their fields are below those of Sau-va-no-gee, bordering on the river; they have some lots about their houses fenced for potatoes; one chief has some cattle, horses, and hogs; a few others have some cattle and hogs.
>
> In the season of floods the river spreads out on this side below the town, nearly eight miles from bank to bank, and is very destructive to game and stock.[6]

After the Creek war we are informed that the Muklasa emigrated to Florida in a body. At all events we do not hear of them again, and the Creeks in Oklahoma have forgotten that such a town ever existed. Gatschet says "a town of that name is in the Indian Territory,"[7] but nobody could give the present writer any information regarding it.

THE TUSKEGEE

Many dialects were spoken anciently near the junction of the Coosa and Tallapoosa. Adair says:

> I am assured by a gentleman of character, who traded a long time near the late Alebahma garrison, that within six miles of it live the remains of seven Indian nations, who usually conversed with each other in their own different dialects, though they understood the Muskohge language; but being naturalized, they are bound to observe the laws and customs of the main original body.[8]

Some of these "nations" have already been considered. We now come to a people whose language has not been preserved to the present day, but they are known from statements made by Taitt and

[1] Mereness, Trav. Am. Col., pp. 536–537.
[2] Schoolcraft, Ind. Tribes, v, p. 262.
[3] Ga. Col. Docs., VIII, p. 523.
[4] Hawkins in Ga. Hist. Soc. Colls., IX, p. 169.
[5] Bartram, Travels, p. 444 et seq.
[6] Ga. Hist. Soc. Colls., III, p. 35.
[7] Gatschet, Creek Mig. Leg., I, p. 138.
[8] Adair, Hist. Am. Inds., p. 267.

Hawkins to have spoken a dialect distinct from Muskogee.[1] These were the Tuskegee,[2] called by Taitt northern Indians. On inquiring of some of the old Tuskegee Indians in Oklahoma regarding their ancient speech I found that they claimed to know of it, and I obtained the following words, said to have been among those employed by the ancient people. Some of these are used at the present day, and the others may be nothing more than archaic Muskogee, but they perhaps have some value for future students.

lutcu′ȧ, a mug.
ki′lȧs, to break.
aia′łito, I will be going; modern form, aibastce′.
tcibūksa′ktce′, come on and go with us! (where one person comes to a crowd of people and asks them to go with him).
ili-hu′ko-lutci, hen (-utci, little).
talu′sutci, chicken.
ilisai′dja, pot; modern form, lihai′a łȧ′ko.
apa′lȧ, on the other side; modern form, tȧpa′la.
wilikȧ′pkȧ, I am going on a visit; modern form, tcukupileidja-lani.

The town Tasqui encountered by De Soto between Tali and Coosa was perhaps occupied by Tuskegee. Ranjel is the only chronicler who mentions it, and it can not have impressed the Spaniards as a place of great importance.[3] In 1567 Vandera was informed by some Indians and a soldier that beyond Satapo, the farthest point reached by the Pardo expedition, two days' journey on the way to Coosa, was a place called Tasqui, and a little beyond another known as Tasquiqui.[4] The second of these was certainly, the other probably, a Tuskegee town. It is possible that a fission was just taking place in this tribe.

Later in the seventeenth century, when English and French began to penetrate into the region, we find the Tuskegee divided into two or more bands, the northernmost on the Tennessee River. Coxe, who gives their name under the distorted form Kakigue, places these latter upon an island in the river.[5] While they are noticed in documents and on maps at rare intervals (I find the forms Cacougai, Cattougui, Caskighi), the clearest light upon their later history and ultimate fate is thrown by Mr. Mooney in his "Myths of the Cherokee."[6] He says:

Another refugee tribe incorporated partly with the Cherokee and partly with the Creeks was that of the Taskigi, who at an early period had a large town of the same name on the south side of the Little Tennessee, just above the mouth of Tellico,

[1] Taitt in Trav. in Amer. Col., p. 541; Hawkins, see p. 210. To-day some Indians repeat a tradition to the effect that the Tuskegee are a branch of the Tulsa, but this is evidently a late fabrication based on the friendship which in later years has subsisted between these two towns.
[2] This name perhaps contains the Alabama and Choctaw word for warrior, táska.
[3] Bourne, Narr. of De Soto, II, p. 111.
[4] Ruidiaz, La Florida, II, p. 485.
[5] French, Hist. Colls. La., 1850, p. 230.
[6] 19th Ann. Rept. Bur. Amer. Ethn., pp. 388–389.

in Monroe County, Tennessee. Sequoya, the inventor of the Cherokee alphabet, lived here in his boyhood, about the time of the Revolution. The land was sold in 1819. There was another settlement of the name, and perhaps once occupied by the same people, on the north bank of Tennessee River, in a bend just below Chattanooga, Tennessee, on land sold also in 1819. Still another may have existed at one time on Tuskegee Creek, on the south bank of Little Tennessee River, north of Robbinsville, in Graham County, North Carolina, on land which was occupied until the removal in 1838. It is not a Cherokee word, and Cherokee informants state positively that the Taskigi were a foreign people, with distinct language and customs. They were not Creeks, Natchez, Uchee, or Shawano, with all of whom the Cherokee were well acquainted under other names. In the town house of their settlement at the mouth of Tellico they had an upright pole, from the top of which hung their protecting "medicine," the image of a human figure cut from a cedar log. For this reason the Cherokee in derision sometimes called the place Atsĭnăk taûñ ("Hanging-cedar place"). Before the sale of the land in 1819 they were so nearly extinct that the Cherokee had moved in and occupied the ground.

While part of these people may have removed to the south to join their friends among the Creeks, the majority were probably absorbed in the surrounding Cherokee population.

A few maps, such as one of the early Homann maps and the Seale map of the early part of the eighteenth century, place Tuskegee near the headwaters of the Coosa. This may be intended to represent the Tennessee band of Tuskegee or it may show that the migration of the Alabama Tuskegee southward was a comparatively late movement, something which took place late in the seventeenth century or very early in the eighteenth.

The Tuskegee are placed on the Coosa north of the Abihka Indians on the Couvens and Mortier map of the early part of the eighteenth century. Perhaps these were the southern band mentioned by Adair, in the badly misprinted form Tae-keo-ge, as one of those which the Muskogee had "artfully decoyed to incorporate with them." [1] He is confirmed in substance by Milfort, who states that they were a tribe who had suffered severely from their enemies and had in consequence sought refuge with the Creeks.[2] The town appears in the census estimates of 1750.[3] In the enumeration of 1761 we find "Tuskegee including Coosaw old Town" with 40 hunters.[4] The name does not occur in Bartram's list, but, as I have said elsewhere, it appears to be the town which he calls Alabama.[5] Hawkins (1799) has the following to say regarding it:

Tus-kee-gee: This little town is in the fork of the two rivers, Coo-sau and Tal-la-poo-sa, where formerly stood the French fort Toulouse. The town is on a bluff on the Coo-sau, forty-six feet above low-water mark; the rivers here approach each other within a quarter of a mile, then curve out, making a flat of low land of three thousand acres, which has been rich canebrake; and one-third under cultivation in times past; the

[1] Adair, Hist. Am. Inds., p. 257.

[2] Milfort, Mémoire, p. 267.

[3] MS., Ayer Coll.

[4] Ga. Col. Docs., VIII, p. 524.

[5] Bartram, Travels, p. 461; see also p. 197.

center of this flat is rich oak and hickory, margined on both sides with rich cane swamp; the land back of the town, for a mile, is flat, a whitish clay; small pine, oak, and dwarf hickory, then high pine forest.

There are thirty buildings in the town, compactly situated, and from the bluff a fine view of the flat lands in the fork, and on the right bank of Coosau, which river is here two hundred yards wide. In the yard of the town house there are five cannon of iron, with the trunions broke off, and on the bluff some brickbats, the only remains of the French establishment here. There is one apple tree claimed by this town now in possession of one of the chiefs of Book-choie-oo-che [Okchaiyutci].[1]

The fields are the left side of Tal-la-poo-sa, and there are some small patches well formed in the fork of the rivers, on the flat rich land below the bluff.

The Coosau extending itself a great way into the Cherokee country and mountains, gives scope for a vast accumulation of waters, at times. The Indians remark that once in fifteen or sixteen years,[2] they have a flood, which overflows the banks, and spreads itself for five miles or more[3] in width, in many parts of A-la-ba-ma. The rise is sudden, and so rapid as to drive a current up the Tal-la-poo-sa for eight miles. In January, 1796,[4] the flood rose forty-seven feet, and spread itself for three miles on the left bank of the A-la-ba-ma. The ordinary width of that river, taken at the first bluff below the fork, is one hundred and fifty yards. The bluff is on the left side, and forty-five feet high. On this bluff are five conic mounds of earth, the largest thirty yards diameter at the base, and seventeen feet high; the others are smaller.

It has been for sometime a subject of enquiry, when, and for what purpose, these mounds were raised; here it explains itself as to the purpose; unquestionably they were intended as a place of safety to the people, in the time of these floods; and this is the tradition among the old people. As these Indians came from the other side of the Mississippi, and that river spreads out on that side for a great distance, it is probable, the erection of mounds originated there; or from the custom of the Indians heretofore, of settling on rich flats bordering on the rivers, and subject to be overflowed. The name is *E-cun-li-gee*, mounds of earth, or literally, *earth placed*. But why erect these mounds in high places, incontestably out of the reach of floods? From a superstitious veneration for ancient customs.

The Alabama overflows its flat swampy margins, annually; and generally, in the month of March, but seldom in the summer season.

The people of Tuskogee have some cattle, and a fine stock of hogs, more perhaps than any town of the nation. One man, Sam Macnack [Sam Moniack], a half breed, has a fine stock of cattle. He had, in 1799, one hundred and eighty calves. They have lost their language, and speak Creek, and have adopted the customs and manners of the Creeks. They have thirty-five gun men.[5]

After their removal west the Tuskegee formed a town in the southeastern part of the nation. Later a portion, consisting largely of those who had negro blood, moved northwest and settled west of Beggs, Okla., close to the Yuchi.

Although our early histories, books of travel, and documents are well-nigh silent on the subject, it is evident from maps of the southern regions that part of the Tuskegee got very much farther east at an early date. A town of Tuskegee, spelled most frequently "Jaskages," appears on Chattahoochee River below a town of the Atasi and above a town of the Kasihta. This appears on the maps of Popple

[1] The Lib. Cong. MS. has "Hook-choie."

[2] The Lib. Cong. MS. has "fifteen or twenty years."

[3] The Lib. Cong. MS. has "five or six miles."

[4] The Lib. Cong. MS. has "1795."

[5] Ga. Hist. Soc. Colls., III, pp. 37-39.

(1733), D'Anville (1746, 1755), Bellin (1750–55), John Rocque (1754–61), Bowen and Gibson (1755), Sr Le Roque (1755), Mitchell (1755, 1777), Bowles (1763?), D'Anville altered by Bell (1768), D'Anville by Evans (1771), and Andrews (1777). Another appears on the Ocmulgee, oftenest on a small southern affluent of it, in the maps of Moll (1720), Popple (1733), Bellin (1750–55), and in Homann's Atlas (1759). This seems to mean that there was a Tuskegee village among the Lower Creeks, originally on Ocmulgee River, and after the Yamasee war on the Chattahoochee. The town is referred to in a letter of Matheos, the Apalachee lieutenant under the governor of Florida, written May 19, 1686.[1] Evidently it was then on or near the Ocmulgee. In a letter of September 20, 1717, Diego Pena in narrating his journey to the Lower Creeks says that he spent the night at "Tayquique," evidently intended for Tasquique, "within a short league" of Coweta. It must have been on the Chattahoochee, at a place given on none of the maps.[2]

TENNESSEE RIVER TRIBES OF UNCERTAIN RELATIONSHIP

We have had occasion to notice several tribes or portions of tribes in the valley of the Tennessee or even farther north whose history is in some way bound up with that of the better-known peoples of the Creek Confederacy. Thus the Tamahita came from the upper Tennessee or one of its branches, part of the Koasati and part of the Tuskegee were on the Tennessee, and there are indications that the same was true of part of the Tamałi. Perhaps another case of the kind is furnished by the Oconee.[3] Still another people divided into a northern and southern band were the Yuchi, whose principal residence was Savannah River, but part of whom were on the Tennessee. There were, however, two tribes in the north not certainly represented among the southern Muskhogeans and not certainly Muskhogean, but of sufficient importance in connection with the general problem of southern tribes to receive notice here.

One of these was the Tali, a tribe which appears first in the De Soto narratives. It is not mentioned by Biedma or Garcilasso, and Elvas gives it but scant attention,[4] but from what Ranjel says it was evidently of some importance. His account is as follows:

Friday, July 9 [1540], the commander and his army departed from Coste and crossed the other branch of the river and passed the night on its banks. And on the other side was Tali, and since the river flows near it and is large, they were not able to cross it. And the Indians, believing that they would cross, sent canoes and in them their wives

[1] Serrano y Sanz, Doc. Hist., pp. 194–195.

[2] Ibid., p. 229. For a more particular account of the later condition and ethnology of these people see Speck, The Creek Indians of Taskigi town, in Mem. Am. Anthr. Asso., II, pt. 2.

[3] See p. 179.

[4] Bourne, Narr. of De Soto, pp. 80–81.

and sons and clothes from the other side; but they were all taken suddenly, and as they were going with the current, the governor forced them all to turn back, which was the reason that this chief came in peace and took them across to the other side in his canoes, and gave the Christians what they had need of. And he did this also in his own land as they passed through it afterwards, and they set out Sunday and passed the night in the open country.

Monday they crossed a river and slept in the open country. Tuesday they crossed another river and slept at Tasqui. During all the days of their march from Tali the chief of Tali had corn and mazamorras and cooked beans, and everything that could be brought from his villages bordering the way.[1]

The Tali now disappear from sight and are not heard of again until late in the seventeenth century, when they are found in approximately the same position as 150 years earlier.[2] Daniel Coxe gives them as one of four small nations occupying as many islands in the Tennessee River.[3] He represents them as the nation farthest upstream. In the summer of 1701 five Canadians ascended the Tennessee and reached South Carolina, and from one of these Sauvolle, Iberville's brother, who had been left in command of the French fort at Biloxi, obtained considerable information regarding the tribes then settled along that river. He embodied it in an official letter dated at Biloxi, August 4, 1701. From this it appears that the Canadians first came upon a Chickasaw town "about 140 leagues" from the mouth of the Ohio, then upon the "Taougalé," a band of Yuchi, an unspecified distance higher up, and "after that the Talé, where an Englishman is established to purchase slaves, as they make war with many other nations." [4]

On the maps of the latter part of the seventeenth and early part of the eighteenth centuries this name is persistent. The tribe is generally placed above the Tahogale, now known to have been a band of Yuchi, and below the Kaskinampo and Shawnee. The name of the Tennessee band of Koasati rarely appears. In another set of maps we find a different group of towns, one of which is called Taligui, and in still another, from the French, a set in which a town Talicouet is in evidence. There can be no doubt that Talicouet is the Cherokee town Tellico, since the maps show it in the proper position, and of the three other towns one, Aiouache, is evidently Hiwassee or Ayuhwa'si; while another, Amobi, is the Cherokee town Amoye which appears on some maps. The fourth, Tongeria, is the Tahogale of other cartographers. Taligui is evidently intended for the same town as Talicouet. These two forms combined with a well-known Algonquian suffix would produce a name almost identical with that of the Talligewi of Delaware tradition. Mr. Mooney believes that the Talligewi were the Cherokee,[5] and this would tend to confirm the iden-

---

[1] Bourne, Narr. of De Soto, II, pp. 111-112.

[2] Here, as throughout the present paper, I accept that theory of De Soto's route which carries him as far north as the Tennessee.

[3] French, Hist. Colls. La., 1850, p. 230.

[4] MS. in Library of the La. Hist. Soc.; Louisiane, Correspondence Générale, 1678-1706, pp. 403-404; cf. French, Hist. Colls. La., 1851, p. 238. In French the name Talés has been miscopied "Calés."

[5] 19th Ann. Rept. Bur. Amer. Ethn., pp. 184-185.

tification, since the whole tribe may have received its name from the Tellico towns. This is a matter which does not, however, concern us here. The important question is, Were the Tali, Taligui, and Talicouet identical? If so, then the Tali are at once established as Cherokee. That the Cherokee country extended in later times as far as the great bend of the Tennessee is well known, but this fact necessarily tends to cast doubt upon any earlier tradition of such an extension, since it assumes an intervening period of abandonment. Still it is interesting to know that there was such a tradition. In an article on "The Indians of Marshall County, Alabama," by Mr. O. D. Street, of Guntersville, Alabama, we read:

> The late Gen. S. K. Rayburn, who came to this country many years before the removal of the Cherokees to the West and was intimately acquainted with many of them, told the writer that he had been informed by intelligent Cherokees that, many thousand moons before, their people had occupied all the country westward to Bear Creek and Duck River, but that on account of constant wars with the Chickasaws they had sought quiet by withdrawing into the eastern mountains, though they had never renounced their title to the country.[1]

Our investigation has now brought out the following facts. On early maps four or five small tribes appear on the middle course of Tennessee River. One of these, Tali, bears the same name as a tribe found by De Soto near the big bend of the same stream. Maps of a somewhat later date show the same number of towns, but they are not all identical. Three are, however, evidently Cherokee towns, and one, Taligui or Talicouet, is certainly the Cherokee town of Tellico (Talikwa). We also have traditional evidence that the Cherokee were in possession at an early date of that region where the Tali lived. If the Taligui and Talicouet of later maps are the same as the Tali of earlier ones the identification is complete; if there was merely a chance resemblance between the names they were, of course, distinct. The chances, in my opinion, are very much in favor of the identification.

The name of another problematical tribe is spelled variously Kaskinampo, Caskinampo, Kaskin8ba, Caskemampo, Cakinonpa, Kakinonba, Karkinonpols, Kasquinanipo. It is applied also to the Tennessee River. Coxe speaks of the Tennessee as a river "some call Kasqui, so named from a nation inhabiting a little above its mouth."[2] This spelling serves to connect the tribe with one mentioned by De Soto, and called in the writings of his expedition Casqui,[3] Icasqui,[4] or Casquin.[5] The Spaniards reached the principal town of Casqui about a week after they had crossed the Mississippi, while moving north. The Casqui were at that time engaged in war with another province or tribe known as Pacaha. In the principal town of Casqui near the

[1] Trans. Ala. Hist. Soc., IV, p. 195.
[2] Coxe in French, Hist. Colls. La., 1850, p. 229.
[3] Bourne, Narr. of De Soto, I, p. 128; II, p. 138.
[4] Ibid., II, p. 26.
[5] Shipp, De Soto and Fla., p. 408.

chief's house was an artificial mound on which De Soto had a cross set. Ranjel says, "It was Saturday when they entered his village, and it had very good cabins and in the principal one, over the door, were many heads of very fierce bulls, just as in Spain noblemen who are sportsmen mount the heads of wild boars or bears. There the Christians planted the cross on a mound, and they received it and adored it with much devotion, and the blind and lame came to seek to be healed." [1]

Afterwards De Soto went on to Pacaha and finally made peace between the two, a peace which we may surmise did not last much longer than the presence of De Soto insured it. While at Pacaha the Spaniards learned of a province to the north called Caluça[2] or Caluç.[3] This would seem to be the Choctaw or Chickasaw Oka lusa, "black water," from which we may possibly infer the Muskhogean connection of Casquin, but, on the other hand, the name may have been obtained from interpreters secured east of the Mississippi, and may be nothing more than a translation of the original into Chickasaw. After this sudden and rather dramatic appearance of the tribe we are studying upon the page of history, they disappear into the dark, and all that is preserved to us from a later period is the reference of Coxe, two or three other short notices, and the persistent clinging of their name in its ancient form to the Tennessee; but scarcely anything is known regarding them, either as to their affinities or ultimate fate. A French description of the province of Louisiana dated about 1712 states that the "Caskinanpau" were then living upon the river now called the Tennessee, but that the Cumberland was known as "the River of the Caskinanpau" because they had formerly lived there.[4] In the letter of Sauvolle, already quoted, the "Cassoty" and "Casquinonpa" are represented as "on an island which the river forms, on the two extremities of which are situated these two nations." [5] On very many maps they appear associated with the Shawnee, and on several a trail is laid down from the Tennessee to St. Augustine, with a legend to the effect that "by this trail the Shawnee and Kasquinampos go to trade with the Spaniards."

Besides these well-defined, though unidentified, tribes we find a few names on early maps which are perhaps synonyms for some of those already considered. One is "8abanghiharea," placed on Tennessee River and perhaps identical with the "Wabano" of La Salle. It contains the Algonquian word for "east." On the same map and on the same river is "Matahale," perhaps the "Matohah" of Joliet's map.

1 Bourne, Narr. of De Soto, II, pp. 138–139.
2 Ibid., I, p. 128.
3 Ibid., II, p. 30.
4 French Transcription, Lib. Cong.
5 MS. in Lib. La. Hist. Soc., Louisiane, Correspondence Générale, pp. 403–404.

THE MUSKOGEE

The dominant people of the Creek Confederacy called themselves and their language in later times by a name which has become conventionalized into Muscogee or Muskogee, but it does not appear in the Spanish narratives of the sixteenth and seventeenth centuries, and careful examination seems to show that the people themselves were complex. If we were in possession of full internal information regarding their past history I feel confident we should find that the process of aggregation which brought so many known foreign elements together had been operating through a much longer period and had brought extraneous elements in still earlier. Evidence pointing toward a foreign origin for several supposedly pure Muskogee tribes will be adduced presently. At the same time we are now no longer in a position to separate the two clearly, and will consider all under one head. We do know, however, that even though they spoke the Muskogee language, there were several distinct bands, the history of each of which must be separately traced.

The name Muskogee was of later origin, presumably, than the names of the constituent parts. What it means no Creek Indian seems to know. In fact it does not appear to be a Muskogee word at all. Several explanations have been suggested for it, but the one to which I am inclined to give most weight is that of Gatschet,[1] who affirms that it is derived from an Algonquian word signifying "swamp" or "wet ground." Gatschet devotes considerable space to a discussion of the name. It was probably first bestowed by the Shawnee, who were held in high esteem by the Creeks, especially by those of Tukabahchee, and probably came into use for want of a native term to cover all of the Muskogee tribes.

The origin of the English term "Creeks" seems to have been satisfactorily traced by Prof. V. W. Crane to a shortening of "Ocheese Creek Indians," Ocheese being an old name for the Ocmulgee River, upon which most of the Lower Creeks were living when the English first came in contact with them.[2]

A careful examination of the Muskogee bodies proper yields us about 12 whose separate existence extends back so far that we must treat them independently, although we may have a conviction that they were not all originally major divisions. On the other hand, there are a few bands not included among the 12 which may have had an independent origin, though this seems very unlikely. The 12 bodies above referred to are the Kasihta, Coweta, Coosa, Abihka, Wakokai, Eufaula, Hilibi, Atasi, Kolomi, Tukabahchee, Pakana, and Okchai. As we know, they were in later times distinguished into Upper Creeks and Lower Creeks, the former including those residing

[1] Gatschet, Creek Mig. Leg., pp. 58–62.

[2] Crane in The Miss. Val. Hist. Rev., vol. 5, no. 3, Dec., 1918.

on the Coosa, Tallapoosa, and Alabama Rivers, and in the neighboring country, and the latter those on the Chattahoochee and Flint. The "Upper Creeks" of Bartram are the Creeks proper, while his "Lower Creeks" are the Seminole. Sometimes a triple division is made into Upper Creeks, Middle Creeks, and Lower Creeks, the first including those on the Coosa River, the Middle Creeks those on and near the Tallapoosa, and the last as in the previous classification. The first are also called Coosa or Abihka, the second Tallapoosa, and the last Coweta. The traditions of nearly all, so far as information has come down to us, point to an origin in the west, but these will be taken up in a separate volume when we come to treat of Creek social organization. That the drift of population throughout most of this area had been from west to east can hardly be doubted, but it is plain that practically all of the Muskogee tribes had completed the movement before De Soto's time, though all can not be identified in the narratives of his expedition. The prime factors in the formation of the confederacy were the Kasihta and Coweta, which I will consider first.

The Kasihta

The honorary name of this tribe in the Creek Confederacy was Kasihta łako, "Big Kasihta." According to the earliest form of the Creek migration legend that is available—that related to Governor Oglethorpe by Chikilli in 1735—the Kasihta and Coweta came from the west "as one people," but in time those dwelling toward the east came to be called Kasihta and those to the west Coweta.[1] This ancient unity of origin appears to have been generally admitted down to the present time. According to John Goat, an aged Tulsa Indian, they were at first one town, and when they separated the pot of medicine which had been buried under their busk fire was dug up and its contents divided between them. He also maintained that anciently Kasihta was the larger and more important of the two, and others state the same, while on the point of numbers, they are confirmed by the census of 1832.[2] Oftener the Coweta were given precedence.

The first appearance of the Kasihta in documentary history is, I believe, in the De Soto chronicles as the famous province of Cofitachequi,[3] Cutifachiqui,[4] Cofitachyque,[4] Cofitachique,[5] or Cofaciqui.[6] Formerly it was generally held that this was Yuchi. The name has, however, a Muskhogean appearance, and Dr. F. G. Speck, our leading Yuchi authority, is unable to find any Yuchi term resembling it. In fact, with one doubtful exception, he is unable to discover

[1] Gatschet, Creek Mig. Leg., I, pp. 244–251.
[2] See p. 430.
[3] Bourne, Narr. of De Soto, II, p. 93.
[4] Ibid., I, p. 69.
[5] Ibid., II, p. 11.
[6] Garcilasso in Shipp, De Soto and Fla., p. 352.

any name in the De Soto narratives which resembles a Yuchi word even remotely.[1]

The specific identification of this place with Kasihta rests mainly upon the early documents of the colony of South Carolina. In a letter from Henry Woodward, interpreter for the colonists, to Sir John Yeamans, dated September 10, 1670, the writer states that he had visited "Chufytachyqj y^t fruitfull Provence where ye Emperour resides." "It lys," he says, "West & by Northe nearest from us 14 days trauell after ye Indian manner of marchinge."[2] He is writing from near where Charleston, S. C., was afterwards built. In a letter to the Lords Proprietors from the same place, dated September 11, 1670, the Council of the new colony mentions this expedition again, and calls the country "Chufytachyque."[3] It is also referred to in a letter written to Lord Ashley by Stephen Bull, only that the distance is given as ten days' journey.[4] In a letter from William Owen to Lord Ashley, written September 15, 1670, we read:

The Emperour of Tatchequiha, a verie fruitfull countrey som 8 days iourney to ye Northwest of vs, we expect here within 4 days, som of his people being alreadie com with whom he would haue bein had not he heard in his way y^t ye Spaniard had defeated vs. His friend^pp with us is very considerable against ye Westoes if euer they intend to Molest us. He hath often defeated them and is euer their Master. The Indian Doctor tells us y^t where he liues is exceedinge rich and fertill generally of a red mould and hillie with most pleasant vallies and springes haueing plentie of white and black Marble and abundantly stored with Mulberries of wch fruite they make cakes wch I have tasted.[5]

From the context it is evident that Tatchequiha and Chufytachyqj were the same. Mr. Thomas Colleton adds the information that this potentate had a thousand bowmen in his town.[6] In the memoranda in John Locke's handwriting we find other spellings, "Caphatachaques,"[7] and Chufytuchyque.[8] In still another place he speaks of "the Emperor Cotachico at Charles town with 100 Indians."[9] In his instructions to Henry Woodward, dated May 23, 1674, Lord Shaftesbury says:

You are to consider whether it be best to make a peace with the Westoes or Cussitaws, which are a more powerful nation said to have pearle and silver and by whose Assistance the Westoes may be rooted out, but no peace is to be made with either of them without Including our Neighbour Indians who are at amity with us.[10]

Rivers has the following:

Order for trade with the Westoes & Cussatoes Indians, 10 April 1677.

Whereas ye discovery of ye Country of ye Westoes & ye Cussatoes two powerful and warlike nations, hath bine made at ye charge of ye Earle of Shaftsbury, &c.,

[1] The exception is the name Yubaha which I have discovered to be from Timucua; see p. 81.

[2] S. C. Hist. Soc. Colls., v, p. 186.

[3] Ibid., p. 191.

[4] Ibid., p. 194.

[5] Ibid., p. 201.

[6] Ibid., p. 249.

[7] Ibid., p. 258.

[8] Ibid., p. 262.

[9] Ibid., p. 388.

[10] Ibid., p. 446.

and by the Industry & hazard of Dr. Henry Woodward, and a strict peace & amity made Betweene those said nations and our people in or province of Corolina, &c.[1]

We could wish there were more information, but this is sufficient to show that the early English colonists called the Kasihta by a name corresponding very closely with that used by De Soto's companions. They give the tribe so called the prominent position which it had in his day and which it afterwards occupied, and distinguish it clearly from the Westo, who I believe to have been Yuchi.[2] We have, therefore, a valid reason for concluding that the Cofitachequi and Kasihta were one and the same people.

That this was not the only body of Kasihta Indians in the Creek country seems to be shown by the name of a town, Casiste, which the Spaniards in De Soto's time passed through somewhere near the Tallapoosa.[3]

On Saturday, May 1, 1540, after having lost his way and spent some days floundering about among the wastes of southeastern Georgia, De Soto with the advance guard of his army came to the river on the other side of which was Cofitachequi, was met by the chieftainess of that place—or by her niece, for authorities differ—and was received into her town in peace. May 3 the rest of the army came up and they were given half of the town. On the 12th or 13th they left. They found here a temple or ossuary which the Spaniards call a "mosque and oratory," and which they opened, finding there bodies covered with pearls and a number of objects of European manufacture, from which they inferred that they were near the place in which Ayllon and his companions had come to grief.[4] Elvas says of the people of that province:

The inhabitants are brown of skin, well formed and proportioned. They are more civilized than any people seen in all the territories of Florida, wearing clothes and shoes. This country, according to what the Indians stated, had been very populous, but it had been decimated shortly before by a pestilence.[5]

The location of Cofitachequi has been discussed by many writers. Most of the older maps place it upon the upper Santee or the Saluda, in what is now South Carolina, but this is evidently too far to the east and north. Later opinion has inclined to the view that it was on the Savannah, and the point oftenest fixed upon is what is now known as Silver Bluff. The present writer in a paper published among the Proceedings of the Mississippi Valley Historical Association[6] expressed the opinion that it was on or near the Savannah but lower down than Silver Bluff, on the ground that the Yuchi, who have

---

1 Rivers, Hist. of S. C., p. 389.

2 See pp. 288–291.

3 Bourne, Narr. of De Soto, I, p. 87; II, p. 116. Elvas calls it "a large town"; Ranjel, "a small village." In later Spanish documents the name of Kasihta is spelled Casista.

4 Bourne, Narr. of De Soto, I, p. 69; II, pp. 13–15, 98–102.

5 Ibid., I, pp. 66–67.

6 Proc. Miss. Val. Hist. Asso., V, pp. 147–157.

usually been regarded as earlier occupants of this territory than the Creeks, extended down the river as far as Ebenezer Creek.

Later researches have tended to show, however, that in De Soto's time the Yuchi were not on the Savannah River at all, while the Pardo narratives indicate that the position of Cofitachequi was at least as far inland as Barnwell or Hampton Counties, S. C. Elvas says that the sea "was stated to be two days' travel" from Cofitachequi,[1] and Biedma has this: "From the information given by the Indians, the sea should be about 30 leagues distant."[2]

In Vandera's account of the Pardo expedition of 1566–67 Cofitachequi is said to be 50 leagues from Santa Elena and 20 from the mouth of the river on which it was located.[3] It is probable that the first of these figures is too high and the second too low. All things considered, Silver Bluff would seem to be too far inland; a point is indicated between Mount Pleasant and Sweet Water Creek, in Barnwell or Hampton Counties, S. C.

From the prominent position assigned to Cofitachequi by the De Soto chroniclers, by Pardo and Vandera, and by the later English settlers, it is altogether probable that this was the town which Laudonnière and the Frenchmen left at Charlesfort believed was being described to them as lying inland and ruled by a great chief called Chiquola. Laudonnière says:

Those who survived from the first voyage have assured me that the Indians have made them understand by intelligible signs that farther inland in the same northerly direction was a great inclosure, and within it many beautiful houses, in the midst of which lived Chiquola.[4]

Laudonnière evidently stumbled upon the name Chiquola from having asked about the Chicora of the Ayllon expedition, with the story of which he was familiar. The Indians, who probably had no *r* in their language, changed the sound to *l* and at the same time perhaps gave him a distorted form of one name for the Kasihta, a name which we seem to find again in the form "Tatchequiha" in Owen's letter to Lord Ashley.[5] The location indicated also agrees very well with that in which Pardo found Cofitachequi a few years later. Vandera gives the following account of the country occupied by these people in his time:

From Guiomaez he started directly for Canos, which the Indians call Canosi, and by another name Cofetazque; there are three or four rather large rivers within this province, one of them even carrying much water or rather two are that way; there are few swamps, but anybody, even a child, can pass them afoot. There are deep valleys surrounded by rocks and stones, and cliffs. The soil is reddish and fertile, very much better than all those before mentioned.

---

1 Bourne, Narr. of De Soto, I, p. 66.

2 Ibid., II, p. 14.

3 Ruidiaz, La Florida, II, p. 482.

4 Laudonnière, Hist. Not. de la Floride, p. 31.

5 See p. 217.

Canos is a country through which flows one of the two powerful rivers; it contains that and many small rivulets; it has great meadows and very good ones, and here and from here on, the maize is abundant; the grapes are plentiful, big, and very good; there are also bad ones, thick skinned and small, in fact, there are very many varieties. It is a country in which a big town can be settled. To Santa Elena there are 50 leagues and to the sea about twenty, and it is possible to reach it by way of the big river crossing the country and [to go] much further inland by the same river; and equally could one go by the other river which passes near Guiomaez.[1]

The first of these rivers can have been only the Savannah; the second probably the Coosawhatchie, the Salkehatchie, or Briar Creek. The name Canosi is perhaps perpetuated in Cannouchee River, a branch of the Ogeechee, upon which the Kasihta may once have dwelt.

In 1628 Pedro de Torres was sent inland by the governor of Florida, Luis de Rojas y Borjas. He went as far as "Cafatachiqui" (or "Cosatachiqui"), "more than two hundred leagues inland," and the governor states in his letter to the king describing this expedition that the men in his party were the first Spaniards to visit it since De Soto's time. This last statement is, of course, an error. The governor says little more except that all the chiefs in the country were under the chief of Cofitachequi, and the rivers there abounded in pearls, which the natives appear to have gathered in a manner described by Garcilasso.[2]

By the time the English came to South Carolina it is evident that the Kasihta had changed their location. This is apparent both from Henry Woodward's Westo narrative and from what we learn of his visit to them. The Westo were then on Savannah River; the Kasihta, or "Chufytachyqj" as he calls them, were 14 days' travel west by north "after ye Indian manner of marchinge."[3] The location is uncertain, but must have been near the upper Savannah. It was certainly farther away than that of the Westo and more to the north. In Elbert County, Ga., on Broad River, a few miles south of Oglesby, is an old village site which would answer very well to the probable location of the tribe at this period. At any rate, from 1670 until some time before 1686 the Kasihta were in northern Georgia, near Broad River, perhaps ranging across to the Tennessee. Maps of the period locate the Kasihta and Coweta in this area, about the heads of the Chattahoochee and Coosa. South Carolina documents place this tribe on Ocheese Creek in 1702, Ocheese Creek being an old name for the upper part of the Ocmulgee,[4] and it seems probable from an examination of the Spanish documents that they were settled there as early as 1680–1685. From the context of a letter written May 19, 1686, by Antonio Matheos, lieutenant of Apalachee, to

---

[1] Ruidiaz, La Florida, II, p. 482.

[2] Garcilasso in Shipp, De Soto and Fla., pp. 371–373.

[3] S. C. Hist. Soc. Colls., v, p. 186.

[4] Jour. of the Commons House of Assembly, MS.

Cabrera, the governor of Florida, it appears that, shortly before, the Spaniards had undertaken an expedition against the Creek Indians and had burned several of their villages. The letter states that two of four Apalachee Indians sent among the Apalachicolas [i. e., Lower Creeks] as spies had returned the day before. He continues as follows:

They report that they have visited, as I ordered them to do, all the places of said province, where they were well received, except at Casista and Caveta. The people of these two places had sent them two messengers before they reached the said villages, telling them that they did not want them to come there, because they were from Apalache and consequently their enemies. Thus they should not try to go there, for they would not have peace. Notwithstanding, the spies resolved to go there, risking whatever might happen to them, sending word with the last messenger [sent them] that they were not Apalachinos, but Thamas, and that they did not come for any other reason than to see their relatives and buy several things, and that therefore they should permit them to come. And the two spies arriving near these two places at the time when they [the inhabitants of both villages] were playing ball, they remained there until the game was ended without anybody in the meantime coming to them, although one of them had relatives there. And when they approached Casista, the cacique of that village came to meet them before they could enter it, and he asked them where they were going. Had he not told them not to come into his village? That besides there not being anything to eat in the village, nobody would speak to them; that he knew that they were sent for a certain purpose; that consequently they were his enemies and should not come to his village. Being given a canoe to cross the river, they went to Tasquique, where, as well as in Colome, they were very well received and entertained. These people told them that although the Christians had burnt their villages they were patient [forbearing], because they knew it was their own fault, although it had been mainly the fault of the caciques of Casista and Caveta, who had deceived and involved the rest of them, bringing the English in and forcing them to receive them and go into the forests, for which cause their village had been burnt down. That if another occasion should arise [that the Spaniards should come] they would not flee for they knew now how the Spaniards acted. At Caveta they received them the same way as in Casista, giving them to understand that although they were sowing, they had no intention of remaining there. The said spies say that in those two places there is not a thing done or begun, whereas at the other two, i. e. Colome and Tasquique, there are a great many [things] as well accomplished as started.[1]

From the text it is impossible to say where the four towns mentioned were located, but the reference to a river combined with our later knowledge regarding these Indians indicates the Ocmulgee.

In 1695 an expedition, composed of 7 Spaniards and 400 Indians, marched against the Lower Creeks to seek revenge for injuries inflicted upon them in numerous attacks. They reached the town sites of the "Cauetta, Oconi, Casista, and Tiquipache." In one they captured about 50 Indians; the others were found burned and abandoned.[2] After the Yamasee war the Kasihta settled on the

[1] Serrano y Sanz, Doc. Hist., pp. 193-195; also Lowery MSS. The first writer dates this letter 1606 instead of 1686.

[2] Serrano y Sanz, Doc. Hist., p. 225.

Chattahoochee. Maps representing the location of tribes at that time give the Kasihta under the name Gitasee. This is made evident when we come to compare early and late maps, which are found to agree in nearly all particulars except that some variant of the name Kasihta is substituted for Gitasee. The reason for the use of Gitasee is entirely unknown. As laid down on these maps the Kasihta were between the Okmulgee on the south and a body of Tuskegee on the north. In the census list of 1761 they were assigned to John Rae as trader.[1] In January, 1778, Bartram passed this town, which he calls "Usseta," and he says that it joined Chiaha, but that the two spoke radically different languages.[2] The traders located there in 1797 were Thomas Carr and John Anthony Sandoval, the latter a Spaniard.[3] Hawkins gives the following description of Kasihta as it was in 1799, which shows incidentally that the town had been moved once after it was located on the river:

Cus-se-tuh; this town is two and a half miles below Cow-e-tuh Tal-lau-has-see, on the left bank of the river. They claim the land above the falls on their side. In descending the river path from the falls in three miles you cross a creek running to the right, twenty feet wide; this creek joins the river a quarter of a mile above the Cowetuh town house; the land to this creek is good and level and extends back from the river from half to three-quarters of a mile to the pine forest; the growth on the level is oak, hickory, and pine; there are some ponds and slashes back next to the pine forest, bordering on a branch which runs parallel with the river; in the pine forest there is some reedy branches.

The creek has its source nearly twenty miles from the river, and runs nearly parallel with it till within one mile of its junction; there it makes a short bend round north, thence west to the river; at the second bend, about two hundred yards from the river, a fine little spring creek joins on its right bank. . . .

The flat of good land on the river continues two and a half miles below this creek, through the Cussetuh fields to Hat-che-thluc-co. At the entrance of the fields on the right there is an oblong mound of earth; one-quarter of a mile lower there is a conic mound forty-five yards in diameter at the base, twenty-five feet high, and flat on the top, with mulberry trees on the north side and evergreens on the south. From the top of this mound they have a fine view of the river above the flat land on both sides of the river, and all the field of one thousand acres;[4] the river makes a short bend round to the right opposite this mound, and there is a good ford just below the point. It is not easy to mistake the ford, as there is a flat on the left, of gravel and sand; the waters roll rapidly over the gravel, and the eye, at the first view, fixes on the most fordable part; there are two other fords below this, which communicate between the fields on both sides of the river; the river from this point comes round to the west, then to the east; the island ford is below this turn, at the lower end of a small island; from the left side, enter the river forty yards below the island, and go up to the point of it, then turn down as the ripple directs, and land sixty yards below; this is the best ford; the third is still lower, from four to six hundred yards.

The land back from the fields to the east rises twenty feet and continues flat for one mile to the pine forest; back of the fields, adjoining the rise of twenty feet, is a beaver pond of forty acres, capable of being drained at a small expense of labor; the large creek bounds the fields and the flat land to the south.

---

[1] Ga. Col. Docs., VIII, p. 522.

[2] Bartram, Travels, p. 456.

[3] Ga. Hist. Soc. Colls., IX, p. 171.

[4] The Lib. Cong. MS. has "100 acres."

Continuing on down the river from the creek, the land rises to a high flat, formerly the Cussetuh town, and afterwards a Chickasaw town. This flat is intersected with one branch. From the southern border of this flat, the Cussetuh town is seen below, on a flat, just above flood mark, surrounded with this high flat to the north and east, and the river to the west; the land about the town is poor, and much exhausted; they cultivate but little here of early corn; the principal dependence is on the rich fields above the creek; to call them rich must be understood in a limited sense; they have been so, but being cultivated beyond the memory of the oldest man in Cussetuh, they are almost exhausted; the produce is brought from the fields to the town in canoes or on horses; they make barely a sufficiency of corn for their support; they have no fences around their fields, and only a fence of three poles, tied to upright stakes, for their potatoes; the land up the river, above the fields, is fine for culture, with oak, hickory, blackjack and pine.

The people of Cussetuh associate, more than any other Indians, with their white neighbors, and without obtaining any advantage from it; they know not the season for planting, or, if they do, they never avail themselves of what they know, as they always plant a month too late.

This town with its villages is the largest in the Lower Creeks; the people are and have been friendly to white people and are fond of visiting them; the old chiefs are very orderly men and much occupied in governing their young men, who are rude and disorderly, in proportion to the intercourse they have had with white people; they frequently complain of the intercourse of their young people with the white people on the frontiers, as being very prejudicial to their morals; that they are more rude, more inclined to be tricky, and more difficult to govern, than those who do not associate with them.

The settlements belonging to the town are spread out on the right side of the river; here they appear to be industrious, have forked fences, and more land enclosed than they can cultivate. One of them desires particularly to be named Mic E-maut-lau. This old chief has, with his own labor, made a good worm fence, and built himself a comfortable house; they have but a few peach trees, in and about the town; the main trading path, from the upper towns, passes through here; they estimate their number of gun men at three hundred; but they cannot exceed one hundred and eighty.

Au-put-tau-e [Apatána, bull frog village?];[1] a village of Cussetuh, twenty miles from the river, on Hat-che thluc-co; they have good fences, and the settlers under [enjoy?] the best characters of any among the Lower Creeks; they estimate their gun men at forty-three. On a visit here the agent for Indian affairs was met by all the men, at the house of Tus-se-kiah Micco. That chief addressed him in these words: Here, I am glad to see you; this is my wife, and these are my children; they are glad to see you; these are the men of the village; we have forty of them in all; they are glad to see you; you are now among those on whom you may rely. I have been six years at this village, and we have not a man here, or belonging to our village, who ever stole a horse from, or did any injury to a white man.

The village is in the forks of Hatche thlucco, and the situation is well chosen; the land is rich, on the margins of the creeks and the cane flats; the timber is large, of poplar, white oak, and hickory; the uplands to the south are the long-leaf pine; and to the north waving oak, pine, and hickory; cane is on the creeks and reed in all the branches.

At this village, and at the house of Tus-se-ki-ah Micco, the agent for Indian affairs has introduced the plough; and a farmer was hired in 1797 to tend a crop of corn, and with so good success, as to induce several of the villagers to prepare their fields for the plough. Some of them have cattle, hogs and horses, and are attentive to them.

[1] Gatschet derives this name from apatayas, I cover, and says it means "a sheet-like covering." A native informant suggested to the writer apâtäna, bullfrog. This is probably the village which Hawkins elsewhere calls Thlonotiscauhatche, after Flint River.—Ga. Hist. Soc. Colls., IX, p. 172.

The range is a good one, but cattle and horses require salt; they have some thriving peach trees, at several of the settlements.

On Auhe-gee creek, called at its junction with the river, Hitchetee, there is one settlement which deserves a place here. It belongs to Mic-co thluc-co, called by the white people, the "Bird tail King [Fus hadji]." The plantation is on the right side of the creek, on good land, in the neighborhood of pine forest; the creek is a fine flowing one, margined with reed; the plantation is well fenced, and cultivated with the plough; this chief had been on a visit to New York, and seen much of the ways of white people, and the advantages of the plough over the slow and laborious hand hoe. Yet he had not firmness enough, till this year, to break through the old habits of the Indians. The agent paid him a visit this spring, 1799, with a plough completely fixed, and spent a day with him and showed him how to use it. He had previously, while the old man was in the woods, prevailed on the family to clear the fields for the plough. It has been used with effect, and much to the approbation of a numerous family, who have more than doubled their crop of corn and potatoes; and who begin to know how to turn their corn to account, by giving it to their hogs, cattle, and horses, and begin to be very attentive to them; he has some apple and peach trees, and grape vines, a present from the agent.

The Cussetuhs have some cattle, horses, and hogs; but they prefer roving idly through the woods, and down on the frontiers, to attending to farming or stock raising.[1]

In notes taken two years earlier Hawkins thus speaks of another Kasihta village, located on Flint River:

Salenojuh, 8 miles [below Aupiogee Creek]. Here was a compact town of Cusseta people, of 70 gunmen in 1787, and they removed the spring after Colonel Alexander killed 7 of their people near Shoulderbone. Their fields extended three miles above the town; they had a hothouse and square, water, fields well fenced; their situation fine for hogs and cattle. Just above the old fields there are two curves on each side of the river of 150 acres, rich, which have been cultivated. Just below the town the Sulenojuhnene ford, the lands level on the right bank. There is a small island to the right of the ford; on the left a ridge of rocks. The lands on the left bank high and broken. Above the town there is a good ford, level, shallow, and not rocky; the land flat on both sides.[2]

Another description of Kasihta is given by Hodgson, an English missionary who passed through the Creek country in 1820. He says:

It [Kasihta][3] appeared to consist of about 100 houses, many of them elevated on poles from two to six feet high, and built of unhewn logs, with roofs of bark, and little patches of Indian corn before the doors. The women were hard at work, digging the ground, pounding Indian corn, or carrying heavy loads of water from the river; the men were either setting out to the woods with their guns or lying idle before the doors; and the children were amusing themselves in little groups. The whole scene reminded me strongly of some of the African towns described by Mungo Park. In the centre of the town we passed a large building, with a conical roof, supported by a circular wall about three feet high; close to it was a quadrangular space, enclosed by four open buildings, with rows of benches rising above one another; the whole was appropriated, we were informed, to the Great Council of the town, who meet under shelter or in the open air, according to the weather. Near the spot was a high pole, like our may-poles, with a bird at the top, round which the Indians celebrate their Green-Corn Dance. The town or township of Cosito is said to be able to muster 700

[1] Ga. Hist. Soc. Colls., III, pp. 52-61. For some recent information regarding the site of Kasihta, see P. A. Brannon in Amer. Anthrop., n. s. vol. xi, p. 195.

[2] Ga. Hist. Soc. Colls., IX, p. 172.

[3] Hodgson spells the name Cosito.

warriors, while the number belonging to the whole nation is not estimated at more than 3,500.[1]

Seven separate Kasihta settlements are enumerated in the census of 1832, as follows:

On little Euchee Creek, 211, besides 105 slaves; on Tolarnulkar Hatchee, 486, and 4 slaves; on Opillikee Hatchee, Tallassee town, 171; on Chowwokolohatchee, 118; at Secharlitcha ["under black-jack trees"], 214; on Osenubba Hatchee, or Tuckabatchee Harjo's town, 269, and 8 slaves; near West Point, or Tuskehenehaw Chooley's town, 399; total, 1,868 Indians and 117 slaves.[2]

The principal chiefs and their households are omitted from the enumeration. Gatschet mentions another branch called "Tusilgis tco'ko or clapboard house."[3] After their removal they settled in the northern part of the Creek Nation in the west with the other Lower Creeks, where their descendants for the most part still are.

The Coweta[4]

The Coweta were the second great Muskogee tribe among the Lower Creeks, and they headed the war side as Kasihta headed the peace side. Their honorary title in the confederacy was Kawita maʽma'yi, "tall Coweta." Although as a definitely identified tribe they appear later in history and in the migration legends which have been preserved to us the Kasihta are given precedence, the Coweta were and still are commonly accounted the leaders of the Lower Creeks and often of the entire nation. By many early writers all of the Lower Creeks are called Coweta, and the Spaniards and French both speak of the Coweta chief as "emperor" of the Creeks. An anonymous French writer of the eighteenth century draws the following picture of his power at the time of the Yamasee uprising:

The nation of the Caoüita is governed by an emperor, who in 1714 [1715] caused to be killed all the English there were, not only in his nation, but also among the Abeca, Talapouches, Alibamons, and Cheraqui. Not content with that he went to commit depredations as far as the gates of Carolina. The English were excited and wanted to destroy them by making them drag pieces of ordinance loaded with grape-shot, by tying two ropes to the collar of the tube, on each one of which they put sixty savages, whom they killed in the midst of their labors by putting fire to the cannon; but as they saw they would take vengeance with interest, they made very great presents to the emperor to regain his friendship and that of his nation. The French do the same thing, and also the Spaniards, which makes him very rich, for the French who go to visit him are served in a silver dish. He is a man of a good appearance and good character. He has numbers of slaves who are busy night and day cooking food for those going and coming to visit him. He seldom goes on foot, always [riding on] well harnessed horses, and followed by many of his village. He is absolute in his nation. He

[1] Hodgson, Remarks during Jour. through N. Am., pp. 265–266.

[2] Senate Doc. 512, 23d Cong., 1st sess.; Schoolcraft, Ind. Tribes, IV, p. 578. In the sheets as published one figure is too large by 2 and one too small by 1. I have corrected these mistakes.

[3] Marginal note in Creek Mig. Leg., I, MS.

[4] On the maps I have spelled this phonetically, Kawita. The above is the form which has been adopted into popular usage.

has a quantity of cattle and kills them sometimes to feast his friends. No one has ever been able to make him take sides with one of the three European nations who know him, he alleging that he wishes to see everyone, to be neutral, and not to espouse any of the quarrels which the French, English, and Spaniards have with one another.[1]

Traditionally the name is supposed to have had some connection with the eastward migration of this tribe, and it is associated with the word *ayeta*, to go. No reliance can be placed upon this, however, any more than on Gatschet's derivation from the Yuchi word meaning "man."[2]

As the principal body of Muskogee in Georgia, aside from the Kasihta, it is possible that these are the Chisi, Ichisi, or Achese of the De Soto chroniclers,[3] since Ochisi (Otcī'si) is a name applied to the Muskogee by Hitchiti-speaking peoples.[4] Spanish dealings with them in the seventeenth century have already been recounted.[5] In the period between 1670 and 1700 we find them placed on maps, along with the Kasihta, about the headwaters of the Chattahoochee and Coosa, but when they are first clearly localized they are on the upper course of the Ocmulgee not far from Indian Springs, Butts County, Georgia. On French maps the Altamaha and Ocmulgee together are often called "Rivière des Caouitas." After the general westward movement, which took place after the Yamasee war, they settled on the west bank of the Chattahoochee River between the Yuchi on the south and a town known as Chattahoochee.

This last-mentioned place was the first Muskogee settlement on Chattahoochee River and is said to have been established to enable its occupants to open trade with the Spaniards. Bartram says that the people of this town spoke the true Muskogee language, and it is probable that it branched off from the Coweta, though it may have been made up from several settlements. It was in Troup or Heard Counties, Georgia, and was abandoned before Hawkins's time, 1798–99.

The first Coweta settlement on the Chattahoochee was probably at a place afterwards called Coweta Tallahassee, though at the period last mentioned it was occupied by people from Łikatcka, itself a branch of Coweta.[6] D. I. Bushnell, Jr., has published parts of a journal kept by a member of General Oglethorpe's expedition to the Creek towns in 1740, in which he gives some account of the people of Coweta.[7] In 1761 they had 130 hunters and their trader was George Galpin.[8] In 1797 Hawkins gives the names of five traders, Thomas

[1] MS in Ayer Coll., Newberry Lib. The story about slaughtering Indians who were pulling a cannon crops up in connection with the Popham colony (see Coll. Mass. Hist. Soc., 1st ser., I, p. 252).

[2] Gatschet, Creek Mig. Leg., I, p. 19.

[3] Bourne, Narr. of De Soto, I, p. 10; II, p. 54.

[4] Hence the name "Ocheese River" (p. 215). See Hawkins in Ga. Hist. Soc. Colls., IX, p. 209; and p. 148.

[5] See pp. 220–222.

[6] Ga. Hist. Soc. Colls., IX, p. 63.

[7] Amer. Anthrop., n. s., vol. X, pp. 572–574, 1908.

[8] Ga. Col. Docs., VIII, p. 522.

Marshall, John Tarvin, James Darouzeaux, Hardy Read, and Christian Russel, the last a Silesian.[1] Adair enumerates Coweta as one of the six principal towns of the Muskogee confederacy but does not mention Kasihta.[2] Hawkins furnishes the following accounts of Coweta, Coweta Tallahassee, and a branch of the latter known as Wetumpka, as they appeared in 1799:

Cow-e-tuh, on the right bank of Chat-to-ho-che, three miles below the falls, on a flat extending back one mile. The land is fine for corn; the settlements extend up the river for two miles on the river flats. These are bordered with broken pine land; the fields of the settlers who reside in the town, are on a point of land formed by a bend of the river, a part of them adjoining the point, are low, then a rise of fifteen feet, spreading back for half a mile, then another rise of fifteen feet, and flat a half mile to a swamp adjoining the highlands; the fields are below the town.

The river is one hundred and twenty yards wide, with a deep steady current from the fall; these are over a rough coarse rock, forming some islands of rock, which force the water into two narrow channels, in time of low water. One is on each side of the river, in the whole about ninety feet wide; that on the right is sixty feet wide, with a perpendicular fall of twelve feet; the other of thirty feet wide, is a long sloping curve very rapid, the fall fifteen feet in one hundred and fifty feet; fish may ascend in this channel, but it is too swift and strong for boats; here are two fisheries; one on the right belongs to this town; that on the left, to the Cussetuhs; they are at the termination of the falls; and the fish are taken with scoop nets; the fish taken are the hickory shad, rock, trout, perch, catfish, and suckers; there is sturgeon in the river, but no white shad or herring; during spring and summer, they catch the perch and rock with hooks. As soon as the fish make their appearance, the chiefs send out the women, and make them fish for the square. This expression includes all the chiefs and warriors of the town.

The land on the right bank of the river at the falls is a poor pine barren, to the water's edge; the pines are small; the falls continue three or four miles nearly of the same width, about one hundred and twenty yards; the river then expands to thrice that width, the bottom being gravelly, shoal and rocky. There are several small islands within this scope; one at the part where the expansion commences is rich and some part of it under cultivation; it is half a mile in length, but narrow; here the river is fordable; enter the left bank one hundred yards above the upper end of the island and cross over to it, and down to the fields, thence across the other channel; at the termination of the falls, a creek twenty feet wide, (O-cow-ocuh-hat-che, falls creek), joins the right side of the river. Just below this creek, and above the last reef of rocks, is another ford. The current is rapid, and the bottom even.

On the left bank of the river at the falls, the land is level; and in approaching them one is surprised to find them where there is no alteration in the trees or unevenness of land. This level continues back one mile to the poor pine barren, and is fine for corn or cotton; the timber is red oak, hickory, and pine; the banks of the river on this side below the falls are fifty feet high, and continue so, down below the town house; the flat of good land continues still lower to Hat-che thluc-co (big creek).

Ascending the river on this bank, above the falls, the following stages are noted in miles:

2½ miles, the flat land terminates; thence 3½ miles, to Chis-se Hul-cuh running to the left; thence 4 miles, to Chusse thluc-co twenty feet wide, a rocky bottom.

5 miles to Ke-tā-le, thirty feet wide, a bold, shoally rocky creek, abounding in moss. Four miles up this creek there is a village of ten families at Hat-che Uxau

---

[1] Ga. Hist. Soc. Colls., IX, pp. 170–171.

[2] Adair, Hist. Am. Inds., p. 257.

(head of a creek). The land is broken with hickory, pine, and chestnut; there is cane on the borders of the creek and reed on the branches; there are some settlements of Cowetuh people made on these creeks; all who have settled out from the town have fenced their fields and begin to be attentive to their stock.

The town has a temporary fence of three poles, the first on forks, the other two on stakes, good against cattle only; the town fields are fenced in like manner; a few of the neighboring fields, detached from the town, have good fences; the temporary, three pole fences of the town are made every spring, or repaired in a slovenly manner.

Cow-e-tuh Tal-lau-has-see; from Cow-e-tuh, Tal-lo-fau, a town, and hasse, old. It is two and a half miles below Cowetuh, on the right bank of the river. In going down the path between the two towns, in half a mile cross Kotes-ke-le-jau, ten feet wide, running to the left is a fine little creek sufficiently large for a mill, in all but the dry seasons. On the right bank enter the flat lands between the towns. These are good, with oak, hard-shelled hickory and pine: they extend two miles to Che-luc-in-ti-ge-tuh, a small creek five feet wide, bordering on the town. The town is half a mile from the river, on the right bank of the creek; it is on a high flat, bordered on the east by the flats of the river, and west by high broken hills; they have but a few settlers in the town; the fields are on a point of land three-quarters of a mile below the town, which is very rich and has been long under cultivation; they have no fence around their fields.

Here is the public establishment for the Lower Creeks, and here the agent resides. He has a garden well cultivated and planted, with a great variety of vegetables, fruits, and vines, and an orchard of peach trees. Arrangements have been made to fence two hundred acres of land fit for cultivation, and to introduce a regular husbandry to serve as a model and stimulus, for the neighborhood towns who crowd the public shops here, at all seasons, when the hunters are not in the woods.

The agent entertains doubts, already, of succeeding here in establishing a regular husbandry, from the difficulty of changing the old habits of indolence, and sitting daily in the squares, which seem peculiarly attractive to the residenters of the towns. In the event of not succeeding, he intends to move the establishment out from the town, and aid the villagers where success seems to be infallible.

They estimate their number of gun men at one hundred; but the agent has ascertained, by actual enumeration, that they have but sixty-six, including all who reside here, and in the villages belonging to the town.

They have a fine body of land below, and adjoining the town, nearly two thousand acres, all well timbered; and including the whole above and below, they have more than is sufficient for the accommodation of the whole town; they have one village belonging to the town, We-tumcau.

We-tum-cau; from We-wau, water; and tum-cau, rumbling. It is on the main branch of U-chee creek and is twelve miles northwest from the town. These people have a small town house on a poor pine ridge on the left bank of the creek below the falls; the settlers extend up the creek for three miles, and they cultivate the rich bends in the creek; there is cane on the creek and fine reed on its branches; the land higher up the creek, and on its branches is waving, with pine, oak, and hickory, fine for cultivation, on the flats and out from the branches; the range is good for stock, and some of the settlers have cattle and hogs, and begin to be attentive to them; they have been advised to spread out their settlements on the waters of this creek, and to increase their attention to stock of every kind.[1]

The trader in 1797 was James Lovet.[2] Wetumpka is probably the Wituncara of the Popple map (pl. 4).

The census of 1832 enumerated five bands of Coweta Indians, as follows: Koochkalecha town, 276 besides 12 slaves; on Toosilkstor-

[1] Ga. Hist. Soc. Colls., III, pp. 52-57.

[2] Ibid., IX, p. 63.

koo Hatchee, 85 and 15 slaves; on Warkooche Hatchee, 30; on Hallewokke Yoaxarhatchee, 191; at Cho-lose-parp Kar, or Kotchar, Tus-tun-nuckee's town, 275 and 24 slaves; total 857 Indians and 51 slaves.[1] Chiefs' families are not included.

The inferiority of this town in numbers to Kasihta was perhaps due to the fact that it had given off another settlement which afterwards constituted an independent town with its own busk ground. This was Łikatcka, or "Broken Arrow" as the name has been rudely translated into English. It is said to have been founded by some families who went off by themselves to a place where they could break reeds with which to make arrows. According to William Berryhill, an old Coweta, however, it was not so much on account of the place where they had settled as because they considered themselves to have "broken away" from the parent band in much the same manner as a reed is broken. This town is said to have been situated on a trail and ford 12 miles below Kasihta. It appears to be noted first by Swan (1791).[2] Hawkins in his Sketch of the Creek Country does not speak of it, but in a journal dated 1797 says that the people of Coweta Tallahassee had come from it.[3] In the American State Papers[4] he mentions it as having been destroyed in 1814, but it was soon restored, for it was represented at the treaty of November 15, 1827,[5] and in the census of 1832. In this latter five settlements belonging to the town are enumerated, but it is probable that only the first two of these are correctly designated. One of these latter was on Uchee Creek; the situation of the other is not specified. Together they numbered 418 inhabitants, not counting slaves and free negroes.[6]

Coweta and its chief, McIntosh, played a conspicuous part in the removal of the Creek Indians to the west. McIntosh was the leader of that party which favored removal and was killed by the conservative element in consequence. After the emigration Coweta and its branches settled in the northern part of the new country on the Arkansas, where most of their descendants still live. Their square ground was first located about 2 miles west of the present town of Coweta. After that site was fenced in and plowed up they moved it to some low-lying land close to Coweta, and later busks of a rather irregular character were held in other places, but the observance soon died out. Nevertheless the busk medicines are, or until recently were, still taken in an informal manner by the Coweta men four times a year, corresponding to the times of the three "stomp" dances and the busk. According to one informant, shortly before the Civil War, Coweta,

---

[1] Senate Doc. 512, 23d Cong., 1st sess., IV, pp. 379–386. A mistake in addition has been made on one sheet, which I have rectified.

[2] Schoolcraft, Ind. Tribes, V, p. 262.

[3] Ga. Hist. Soc. Colls., IX, p. 63.

[4] Am. State Papers, Ind. Affairs, I, 858, 1832.

[5] Indian Treaties, 1826, pp. 561–564.

[6] Senate Doc. 512, 23d Cong., 1st sess., IV, pp. 386–394.

Kasihta, Tukabahchee, and Yuchi planned to come together in one big town, but the war put an end to the project. In late times the Coweta and Chiaha were such close friends that it is said "a man of one town would not whip a dog belonging to the other." This friendship also extended to the Osochi.

The Coosa and Their Descendants

In De Soto's time the most powerful Upper Creek town was Coosa. The first news of this seems to have been obtained in Patofa (or Tatofa), a province in southern Georgia, where the natives said "that toward the northwest there was a province called Coça, a plentiful country having very large towns."[1]

The expedition reached Coça after leaving Tali and Tasqui, and after passing through several villages which according to Elvas were "subject to the cacique of Coça."[2] On Friday, July 16, 1540, they entered the town. The chief of Coosa came out to meet them in a litter borne on the shoulders of his principal men, and with many attendants playing on flutes and singing.[3] "In the barbacoas," says Elvas, "was a great quantity of maize and beans; the country, thickly settled in numerous and large towns, with fields between, extending from one to another, was pleasant, and had a rich soil with fair river margins. In the woods were many *ameixas* [plums and persimmons], as well those of Spain as of the country; and wild grapes on vines growing up into the trees, near the streams; likewise a kind that grew on low vines elsewhere, the berry being large and sweet, but, for want of hoeing and dressing, had large stones."[4]

After a slight difference with the natives, who naturally objected to having their chief virtually held captive by De Soto, the Spaniards secured the bearers and women they desired and started on again toward the south or southwest on Friday, August 20.[5] It would appear that the influence of the Coosa chief extended over a large number of the towns later called Upper Creeks, although this was probably due rather to ties of alliance and respect than to any actual overlordship on his part. At a town called Tallise, perhaps identical with the later Tulsa, this authority seems to have come to an end, and farther on were the Mobile quite beyond the sphere of his influence.

In 1559 a gigantic effort was made on the part of the Spaniards to colonize the region of our Gulf States. An expedition, led by Tristan de Luna, started from Mexico with that object in view. We have already mentioned the landing of this colony in Pensacola Harbor, or Mobile Bay, and their subsequent removal northward to a town called

[1] Bourne, Narr. of De Soto, I, p. 60.
[2] Ibid., p. 81.
[3] Ibid., p. 81; II, pp. 16, 112.
[4] Ibid., I, p. 82.
[5] Ibid., II, p. 113.

Nanipacna. Being threatened with starvation here, De Luna sent a sergeant major with six captains and 200 soldiers northward in search of Coosa, whither some of his companions had accompanied De Soto 20 years before, and which they extolled highly. They came first to a place called Olibahali, of which we shall speak again, and after a short stay there continued still farther toward the north. The narrative continues as follows:

The whole province was called Coza, taking its name from the most famous city within its boundaries. It was God's will that they should soon get within sight of that place which had been so far famed and so much thought about and, yet, it did not have above thirty houses, or a few more. There were seven little hamlets in its district, five of them smaller and two larger than Coza itself, which name prevailed for the fame it had enjoyed in its antiquity. It looked so much worse to the Spaniards for having been depicted so grandly, and they had thought it to be so much better. Its inhabitants had been said to be innumerable, the site itself as being wider and more level than Mexico, the springs had been said to be many and of very clear water, food plentiful and gold and silver in abundance, which, without judging rashly, was that which the Spaniards desired most. Truly the land was fertile, but it lacked cultivation. There was much forest, but little fruit, because as it was not cultivated the land was all unimproved and full of thistles and weeds. Those they had brought along as guides, being people who had been there before, declared that they must have been bewitched when this country seemed to them so rich and populated as they had stated. The arrival of the Spaniards in former years had driven the Indians up into the forests, where they preferred to live among the wild beasts who did no harm to them, but whom they could master, than among the Spaniards at whose hands they received injuries, although they were good to them. Those from Coza received the guests well, liberally, and with kindness, and the Spaniards appreciated this, the more so as the actions of their predecessors did not call for it. They gave them each day four fanegas[1] of corn for their men and their horses, of which latter they had fifty and none of which, even during their worst sufferings from hunger, they had wanted to kill and eat, well knowing that the Indians were more afraid of horses, and that one horse gave them a more warlike appearance, than the fists of two men together. But the soldiers did not look for maize; they asked most diligently where the gold could be found and where the silver, because only for the hopes of this as a dessert had they endured the fasts of the painful journey. Every day little groups of them went searching through the country and they found it all deserted and without news of gold. From only two tribes were there news about gold—one was the Oliuahali which they had just left; the others were the Napochies, who lived farther on. Those were enemies to those of Coza, and they had very stubborn warfare with each other, the Napochies avenging some offense they had received at the hands of the people of Coza. The latter Indians showed themselves such good friends of the Spaniards that our men did not know what recompense to give them nor what favor to do them. The wish to favor those who humiliate themselves goes hand in hand with ambition. The Spaniards have the fame of not being very humble and the people of Coza who had surrendered themselves experienced now their favors. Not only were they careful not to cause them any damage or injury, but gave them many things they had brought along, outside of what they gave in the regular exchange for maize. Their gratitude went even so far that the sergeant major, who accompanied the expedition as captain of the 200 men, told the Indians that if they wanted his favor and the strength of his men to make war on their enemies, they could have them readily, just as they had been ready

[1] About the same number of English bushels.

to receive him and his men and favor them with food. Those of Coza thought very highly of this offer, and in the hope of its fulfillment kept the Spaniards such a long time with them, giving them as much maize each day as was possible, the land being so poor and the villages few and small. The Spaniards were nearly 300 men between small and big [young and old] ones, masters and servants, and the time they all ate there was three months, the Indians making great efforts to sustain such a heavy expense for the sake of their companionship as well as for the favors they expected from them later. All the deeds in this life are done for some interested reason and, just as the Spaniards showed friendship for them that they might not shorten their provisions and perhaps escape to the forests, so the Indians showed their friendship, hoping that with their aid they could take full vengeance of their enemies. And the friars were watching, hoping that a greater population might be discovered to convert and maintain in the Christian creed. Those small hamlets had until then neither seen friars nor did they have any commodities to allow monks to live and preach among them; neither could they embrace and maintain the Christian faith without their assistance. . . .

Very bitter battles did the Napochies have with those from Coza, but justice was greatly at variance with success. Those from Coza were in the right, but the Napochies were victorious. In ancient times the Napochies were tributaries of the Coza people, because this place (Coza) was always recognized as head of the kingdom and its lord was considered to stand above the one of the Napochies. Then the people from Coza began to decrease while the Napochies were increasing until they refused to be their vassals, finding themselves strong enough to maintain their liberty which they abused. Then those of Coza took to arms to reduce the rebels to their former servitude, but the most victories were on the side of the Napochies. Those from Coza remained greatly affronted as well from seeing their ancient tribute broken off, as because they found themselves without strength to restore it. On that account they had lately stopped their fights, although their sentiments remained the same and for several months they had not gone into the battlefield, for fear lest they return vanquished, as before. When the Spaniards, grateful for good treatment, offered their assistance against their enemies, they accepted immediately, in view of their rabid thirst for vengeance. All the love they showed to the Spaniards was in the interest that they should not forget their promise. Fifteen days had passed, when, after a consultation among themselves, the principal men went before the captain and thus spoke:

"Sir, we are ashamed not to be able to serve you better, and as we would wish, but this is only because we are afflicted with wars and trouble with some Indians who are our neighbors and are called Napochies. Those have always been our tributaries acknowledging the nobility of our superiors, but a few years ago they rebelled and stopped their tribute and they killed our relatives and friends. And when they can not insult us with their deeds, they do so with words. Now, it seems only reasonable, that you, who have so much knowledge, should favor and increase ours. Thou, Señor, hast given us thy word when thou knowest our wish to help us if we should need thy assistance against our enemies. This promise we, thy servants, beg of thee humbly now to fulfill and we promise to gather the greatest army of our men [people], and with thy good order and efforts helping us, we can assure our victory. And when once reinstated in our former rights, we can serve thee ever so much better."

When the captain had listened to the well concerted reasoning of those of Coza, he replied to them with a glad countenance, that, aside from the fact that it had always been his wish to help and assist them, it was a common cause now, and he considered it convenient or even necessary to communicate with all the men, especially with the friars, who were the ministers of God, and the spiritual fathers of the army; that he would treat the matter with eagerness, procuring that their wishes be attended to and that the following day he would give them the answer, according to the resolutions taken in the matter.

He [the captain] called to council the friars, the captains, and all the others, who, according to custom had a right to be there, and, the case being proposed and explained, it was agreed that only two captains with their men should go, one of cavalry, the other of infantry, and the other four bodies of their little army remain in camp with the rest of the people. Then they likewise divided the monks, Fray Domingo de la Anunciacion going with the new army and Fray Domingo de Salazar remaining with the others in Coza. The next day, those who wished so very dearly that it be in their favor, came for the answer. The captain gave them an account of what had been decided, ordering them to get ready, because he in person desired to accompany them with the two Spanish regiments and would take along, if necessary, the rest of the Spanish army, which would readily come to their assistance. The people from Coza were very glad and thanked the captain very much, offering to dispose everything quickly for the expedition. Within six days they were all ready. The Spaniards did not want to take more than fifty men, twenty-five horsemen and twenty-five on foot. The Indians got together almost three hundred archers, very skillful and certain in the use of that arm, in which, the fact that it is the only one they have has afforded them remarkable training. Every Indian uses a bow as tall as his body; the string is not made of hemp but of animal nerve sinew well twisted and tanned. They all use a quiver full of arrows made of long, thin, and very straight rods, the points of which are of flint, curiously cut in triangular form, the wings very sharp and mostly dipped in some very poisonous and deadly substance.[1] They also use three or four feathers tied on their arrows to insure straight flying, and they are so skilled in shooting them that they can hit a flying bird. The force of the flint arrowheads is such that at a moderate distance they can pierce a coat of mail.

The Indians set forward, and it was beautiful to see them divided up in eight different groups, two of which marched together in the four directions of the earth (north, south, east, and west), which is the style in which the children of Israel used to march, three tribes together in the four directions of the world to signify that they would occupy it all. They were well disposed, and in order to fight their enemies, the Napochies, better, they lifted their bows, arranged the arrows gracefully and shifted the band of the quiver as if they wanted to beseech it to give up new shafts quickly; others examined the necklace [collar] to which the arrow points were fastened and which hung down upon their shoulders, and they all brandished their arms and stamped with their feet on the ground, all showing how great was their wish to fight and how badly they felt about the delay. Each group had its captain, whose emblem was a long stave of two brazas [2] in height and which the Indians call Otatl [3] and which has at its upper end several white feathers. These were used like banners, which everyone had to respect and obey. This was also the custom among the heathens who affixed on such a stave the head of some wild animal they had killed on a hunt, or the one of some prominent enemy whom they had killed in battle. To carry the white feathers was a mystery, for they insisted that they did not wish war with the Napochies, but to reduce them to the former condition of tributaries to them, the Coza people, and pay all since the time they had refused obedience. In order to give the Indian army more power and importance the captain had ordered a horse to be fixed with all its trappings for the lord or cacique of the Indians, and as the poor Indian had never seen much less used one, he ordered a negro to guide the animal. The Indians in those parts had seen horses very rarely, or only at a great distance and to their sorrow, nor were there any in New Spain before the arrival of the Spaniards. The caçique went or rather rode in the rear guard, not less flattered by the obsequiousness of the captain than afraid of his riding feat. Our Spaniards also left Coza, always

[1] This statement is probably erroneous, as the use of poisoned arrows among our southern Indians is denied by all other writers.

[2] One braza is 6 feet.

[3] Or *otatli*, a Nahuatl word.

being careful to put up their tents or lodgings apart from the Indians so that the latter could not commit any treachery if they so intended. One day, after they had all left Coza at a distance of about eight leagues, eight Indians, who appeared to be chiefs, entered the camp of the Spaniards, running and without uttering a word; they also passed the Indian camp and, arriving at the rear guard where their caçique was, took him down from his horse, and the one who seemed to be the highest in rank among the eight, put him on his shoulders, and the others caught him, both by his feet and arms, and they ran with great impetuosity back the same way they had come. These runners emitted very loud howlings, continuing them as long as their breath lasted, and when their wind gave out they barked like big dogs until they had recovered it in order to continue the howls and prolonged shouts. The Spaniards, though tired from the sun and hungry, observing the ceremonious superstitions of the Indians, upon seeing and hearing the mad music with which they honored their lord, could not contain their laughter in spite of their sufferings. The Indians continued their run to a distance of about half a league from where the camp was, until they arrived on a little plain near the road which had been carefully swept and cleaned for the purpose. There had been constructed in the center of that plain a shed or theatre nine cubits in height with a few rough steps to mount. Upon arriving near the theatre the Indians first carried their lord around the plain once on their shoulders, then they lowered him at the foot of the steps, which he mounted alone. He remained standing while all the Indians were seated on the plain, waiting to see what their master would do. The Spaniards were on their guard about these wonderful and quite new ceremonies and desirous to know their mysteries and understand their object and meaning. The caçique began to promenade with great majesty on the theatre, looking with severity over the world. Then they gave him a most beautiful fly flap which they had ready, made of showy birds' plumes of great value. As soon as he held it in his hand he pointed it towards the land of the Napochies in the same fashion as would the astrologer the alidade [cross-staff], or the pilot the sextant in order to take the altitude at sea. After having done this three or four times they gave him some little seeds like fern seeds, and he put them into his mouth and began to grind and pulverize them with his teeth and molars, pointing again three or four times towards the land of the Napochies as he had done before. When the seeds were all ground he began to throw them from his mouth around the plain in very small pieces. Then he turned towards his captains with a glad countenance and he said to them: "Console yourselves, my friends; our journey will have a prosperous outcome; our enemies will be conquered and their strength broken, like those seeds which I ground between my teeth." After pronouncing these few words, he descended from the scaffold and mounted his horse, continuing his way, as he had done hitherto. The Spaniards were discussing what they had seen, and laughing about this grotesque ceremony, but the blessed father, Fray Domingo de la Anunciacion, mourned over it, for it seemed sacrilege to him and a pact with the demon, those ceremonials which those poor people used in their blind idolatry. They all arrived, already late, at the banks of a river, and they decided to rest there in order to enjoy the coolness of the water to relieve the heat of the earth. When the Spaniards wanted to prepare something to eat they did not find anything. There had been a mistake, greatly to the detriment of all. The Indians had understood that the Spaniards carried food for being so much more dainty and delicate people, and the Spaniards thought the Indians had provided it, since they (the Spaniards) had gone along for their benefit. Both were to blame, and they all suffered the penalty. They remained without eating a mouthful that night and until the following one, putting down that privation more on the list of those of the past. They put up the two camps at a stone's throw, being thus always on guard by this division, for, although the Indians were at present very much their friends, they are people who make the laws of friendship doubtful and they had once been greatly offended with the Spaniards, and were now their reconciled friends.

With more precaution than satiety the Spaniards procured repose that night, when, at the tenth hour, our camp being at rest, a great noise was heard from that of the Indians, with much singing, and dances after their fashion, in the luxury of big fires which they had started in abundance, there being much firewood in that place. Our men were on their guard until briefly told by the interpreter, whom they had taken along, that there was no occasion for fear on the part of the Spaniards, but a feasting and occasion of rejoicing on that of the Indians. They felt more assured yet when they saw that the Indians did not move from their place and they now watched most attentively to enjoy their ceremonials as they had done in the past, asking the interpreter what they were saying to one another. After they had sung and danced for a long while the cacique seated himself on an elevated place, the six captains drawing near him, and he began to speak to them admonishing the whole army to be brave, restore the glory of their ancestors, and avenge the injuries they had received. "Not one of you," he said, "can help considering as particularly his this enterprise, besides being that of all in common. Remember your relatives and you will see that not one among you has been exempt from mourning those who have been killed at the hands of the Napochies. Renew the dominion of your ancestors and detest the audacity of the tributaries who have tried to violate it. If we came alone, we might be obliged to see the loss of life, but not of our honor; how much more now, that we have in our company the brave and vigorous Spaniards, sons of the sun and relatives of the gods." The captains had been listening very attentively and humbly to the reasoning of their lord, and as he finished they approached him one by one in order, repeating to him in more or fewer words this sentence: "Señor, the more than sufficient reason for what thou hast told us is known to us all; many are the damages the Napochies have done us, who besides having denied us the obedience they have inherited from their ancestors, have shed the blood of those of our kin and country. For many a day have we wished for this occasion to show our courage and serve thee, especially now, that thy great prudence has won us the favor and endeavor of the brave Spaniards. I swear to thee, Señor, before our gods, to serve thee with all my men in this battle and not turn our backs on these enemies the Napochies, until we have taken revenge." These words the captain accompanied by threats and warlike gestures, desirous (and as if calling for the occasion) to show by actions the truth of his words. All this was repeated by the second captain and the others in their order, and this homage finished, they retired for the rest of the night. The Spaniards were greatly surprised to find such obeisance used to their princes by people of such retired regions, usages which the Romans and other republics of considerable civilization practiced before they entered a war. Besides the oath the Romans made every first of January before their Emperor, the soldiers made another one to the captain under whose orders they served, promising never to desert his banner, nor evade the meeting of the enemy, but to injure him in every way. Many such examples are repeated since the time of Herodianus, Cornelius Tacitus, and Suetonius Tranquilus, with a particular reminiscence in the life of Galba. And it is well worth consideration that the power of nature should have created a similarity in the ceremonials among Indians and Romans in cases of war where good reasoning rules so that all be under the orders of the superiors and personal grievances be set aside for the common welfare. This oath the captains swore on the hands of their lord on that night because they expected to see their enemies on the following day very near by, or even be with them, and the same oath remained to be made by the soldiers to their captains. At daybreak hunger made them rise early, hoping to reach the first village of the Napochies in order to get something to eat, for they needed it very much. They traveled all that day, making their night's rest near a big river which was at a distance of two leagues from the first village of the enemy. There it seemed most convenient for the army to rest, in order to fall upon the village by surprise in the dead of night and kill them all, this being the intention of those from Coza. In order to attain better their intentions, they begged of the captain not to have the trumpet sounded that evening, which was the signal to all for prayer, greeting the queen of the Angels with the Ave Maria, which is the custom in all Christendom at nightfall. "The Napochies" said the people of Coza, "are ensnarers and always have their spies around those fields, and upon hearing the trumpet they would retire into the woods and we would remain without the victory we desire; and therefore the trumpet should not be sounded." Thus the signal remained unsounded for that one night, but the blessed father Fray Domingo de la Anunciacion, with his pious devotion, went around to all the soldiers telling them to say the Ave Maria, and he who was bugler of the evangile now had become bugler of war in the service of the Holy Virgin Mary. That night those of Coza sent their spies into the village of the Napochies to see what they were doing and if they were careless on account of their ignorance of the coming of the enemy; or, if knowing it, they were on the warpath. At midnight the spies came back, well content, for they had noticed great silence and lack of watchfulness in that village, where, not only was there no sound of arms, but even the ordinary noises of inhabited places were not heard. "They all sleep," they said, "and are entirely ignorant of our coming, and as a testimonial that we have made our investigation of the enemies' village carefully and faithfully, we bring these ears of green corn, these beans, and calabashes, taken from the gardens which the Napochies have near their own houses." With those news the Coza people recovered new life and animation, and on that night all the soldiers made their oath to their captains, just as the captains had done on the previous one to their cacique. And our Spaniards enjoyed those ceremonies at closer quarters, since they had seen from the first ceremony that this was really war against Indians which was intended, and not craft against themselves. The Indians were now very ferocious, with a great desire to come in contact with their enemies. . . .

All of the Napochies had left their town, because without it being clear who had given them warning, they had received it, and the silence the spies had noticed in the village was not due to their carelessness but to their absence. The people of Coza went marching towards the village of the Napochies in good order, spreading over the country in small companies, each keeping to one road, thus covering all the exits from the village in order to kill all of their enemies, for they thought they were quiet and unprepared in their houses. When they entered the village they were astonished at the too great quiet and, finding the houses abandoned, they saw upon entering that their enemies had left them in a hurry, for they left even their food and in several houses they found it cooking on the fire, where now those poor men found it ready to season. They found in that village, which was quite complete, a quantity of maize, beans, and many pots filled with bear fat, bears abounding in that country and their fat being greatly prized. The highest priced riches which they could carry off as spoils were skins of deer and bear, which those Indians tanned in a diligent manner very nicely and with which they covered themselves or which they used as beds. The people of Coza were desirous of finding some Indians on whom to demonstrate the fury of their wrath and vengeance and they went looking for them very diligently, but soon they saw what increased their wrath. In a square situated in the center of the village they found a pole of about three estados in height[1] which served as gallows or pillory where they affronted or insulted their enemies and also criminals. As in the past wars had been in favour of the Napochies, that pole was full of scalps of people from Coza. It was an Indian custom that the scalp of the fallen enemy was taken and hung on that pole. The dead had been numerous and the pole was quite peopled with scalps. It was a very great sorrow for the Coza people to see that testimonial of their ignominy which at once recalled the memory

[1] Three times the height of a man.

of past injuries. They all raised their voices in a furious wail, bemoaning the deaths of their relatives and friends. They shed many tears as well for the loss of their dead as for the affront to the living. Moved to compassion, the Spaniards tried to console them, but for a very long time the demonstrations of mourning did not give them a chance for a single word, nor could they do more than go around the square with extraordinary signs of compassion or sorrow for their friends or of wrath against their enemies Then they [the Indians] got hold of one of the hatchets which the Spaniards had brought with them, and they cut down the dried out tree close to the ground, taking the scalps to bury them with the superstitious practices of their kind. With all this they became so furious and filled with vengeance, that everyone of them wished to have many hands and to be able to lay them all on the Napochies. They went from house to house looking for someone like enfuriated lions and they found only a poor strange Indian [from another tribe] who was ill and very innocent of those things, but as blind vengeance does not stop to consider, they tortured the poor Indian till they left him dying. Before he expired though, the good father Fray Domingo reached his side and told him, through the interpreter he had brought along, that if he wished to enjoy the eternal blessings of heaven, he should receive the blessed water of baptism and thereby become a Christian. He further gave him a few reasonings, the shortest possible as the occasion demanded, but the unfortunate Indian, with inherent idolatry and suffering from his fresh wounds, did not pay any attention to such good council, but delivered his soul to the demon as his ancestors before him had done. This greatly pained the blessed Father Domingo, because, as his greatest aim was to save souls, their loss was his greatest sorrow.

When the vindictive fury of the Coza people could not find any hostile Napochies on whom to vent itself, they wanted to burn the whole village and they started to do so. This cruelty caused much grief to the merciful Fray Domingo de la Anunciacion, and upon his plea the captain told the people of Coza to put out the fires, and the same friar, through his interpreter, condemned their action, telling them that it was cowardice to take vengeance in the absence of the enemies whose flight, if it meant avowal of their deficiency, was so much more glory for the victors. All the courage which the Athenians and the Lacedemonians showed in their wars was nullified by the cruelty which they showed the vanquished. "How can we know," said the good father to the Spaniards, "whether the Indians of this village are not perhaps hidden in these forests, awaiting us in some narrow pass to strike us all down with their arrows? Don't allow, brethren, this cruel destruction by fire, so that God may not permit your own deaths at the hands of the inhabitants of this place [these houses]." The captain urged the cacique to have the fire stopped; and as he was tardy in ordering it, the captain told him in the name of Fray Domingo, that if the village was really to be burnt down, the Spaniards would all return because they considered this war of the fire as waged directly against them by burning down the houses, where was the food which they all needed so greatly at all times. Following this menace, the cacique ordered the Indians to put out the fire which had already made great headway and to subdue which required the efforts of the whole army. When the Indians were all quieted, the cacique took possession of the village in company with his principal men and with much singing and dancing, accompanied by the music of badly tuned flutes, they celebrated their victories.

The abundance of maize in that village was greater than had been supposed and the cacique ordered much of it to be taken to Coza [1] so that the Spaniards who had remained there should not lack food. His main intention was to reach or find the enemy, leaving enough people in that village [of the Napochies] to prove his possession and a garrison of Spanish soldiers, which the captain asked for greater security. He then left to pursue the fugitives. They left in great confusion, because they did not

[1] Acoça in the original MS.

know where to find a trace of the flight which a whole village had taken and although the people of Coza endeavored diligently to find out whether they had hidden in the forests, they could not obtain any news more certain than their own conjectures. "It can not be otherwise," they said, "than that the enemy, knowing that we were coming with the Spaniards became suspicious of the security of their forests and went to hide on the great water." When the Spaniards heard the name of great water, they thought it might be the sea, but it was only a great river, which we call the River of the Holy Spirit, the source of which is in some big forests of the country called La Florida. It is very deep and of the width of two harquebuse-shots. In a certain place which the Indians knew, it became very wide, losing its depth, so that it could be forded and it is there where the Napochies of the first village had passed, and also those who lived on the bank of that river, who, upon hearing the news, also abandoned their village, passing the waters of the Oquechiton, which is the name the Indians give that river and which means in our language the great water (la grande agua).[1] Before the Spaniards arrived at this little hamlet however, they saw on the flat roof (azotea) of an Indian house, two Indians who were on the lookout to see whether the Spaniards were pursuing the people of the two villages who had fled across the river. The horsemen spurred their horses and, when the Indians on guard saw them, they were so surprised by their monstrosity [on horseback] that they threw themselves down the embankment towards the river, without the Spaniards being able to reach them, because the bank was very steep and the Indians very swift. One of them was in such a great hurry that he left a great number of arrows behind which he had tied up in a skin, in the fashion of a quiver.

All the Spaniards arrived at the village but found it deserted, containing a great amount of food, such as maize and beans. The inhabitants of both villages were on the riverbank on the other side, quite confident that the Spaniards would not be able to ford it. They ridiculed and made angry vociferations against the people from Coza. Their mirth was short lived, however, for, as the Coza people knew that country, they found the ford in the river and they started crossing it, the water reaching the chests of those on foot and the saddles of the riders. Fray Domingo de la Anunciacion remained on this side of the water with the cacique, because as he was not of the war party it did not seem well that he should get wet. When our soldiers had reached about the middle of the river, one of them fired his flint lock which he had charged with two balls, and he felled one of the Napochies who was on the other side. When the others saw him on the ground dead, they were greatly astonished at the kind of Spanish weapon, which at such a distance could at one shot kill men. They put him on their shoulders and hurriedly carried him off, afraid that other shots might follow against their own persons. All the Napochies fled, and the people of Coza upon passing the river pursued them until the fugitives gathered on the other side of an arm of the same stream, and when those from Coza were about to pass that the Napochies called out to them and said that they would fight no longer, but that they would be friends, because they [the Coza people] brought with them the power of the Spaniards; that they were ready to return to their former tributes and acknowledgment of what they owed them [the Coza people]. Those from Coza were glad and they called to them that they should come in peace and present themselves to their cacique. They all came to present their obedience, the captain of the Spaniards requesting that the vanquished be treated benignly. The cacique received them with severity, reproaching them harshly for their past rebellion and justifying any death he might choose to give them, as well for their refusal to pay their tributes as for the lives of so many Coza people which they had taken, but that the intervention of the Spaniards was so highly appreciated that he admitted them into his reconciliation and grace, restoring former

[1] This is pure Choctaw, from oka, water, and the objective form of chito, big. This river was not the Mississippi, as Padilla supposes, but probably the Black Warrior.

conditions. The vanquished were very grateful, throwing the blame on bad counselors, as if it were not just as bad to listen to the bad which is advised as to advise it. They capitulated and peace was made.

The Napochies pledged themselves to pay as tributes, thrice a year, game, or fruits, chestnuts, and nuts, in confirmation of their [the Coza people's] superiority, which had been recognized by their forefathers. This done, the whole army returned to the first village of the Napochies, where they had left in garrison Spanish soldiers and Coza people. As this village was convenient they rested there three days, until it seemed time to return to Coza where the 150 Spanish soldiers were waiting for them. The journey was short and they arrived soon, and although they found them all in good health, including Father Fray Domingo de Salazar who had remained with them, all had suffered great hunger and want, because there were many people and they had been there a long time. They began to talk of returning to Nanipacna, where they had left their general, not having found in this land what had been claimed and hoped for. As it means valor in war sometimes to flee and temerity to attack, thus is it prudence on some occasions to retrace one's steps, when the going ahead does not bring any benefit.[1]

Barcia's account of this expedition is much shorter and contains little not given in the narrative of Padilla. He says that Father Domingo de la Anunciacion "asked the Indians about a man called Falco Herrado,[2] a soldier of low rank, who remained voluntarily at Coza when Hernando de Soto passed through there; and he also asked about a negro, by the name of Robles, whom De Soto left behind sick,[3] and he was informed that they had lived for 11 or 12 years among those Indians, who treated them very well, and that 8 or 9 years before they died from sickness."[4]

After consultation the Spaniards determined to send messengers back to De Luna, the bulk of the force remaining where it was until they learned whether he would join them. They found that the Spanish settlers had withdrawn to the port where they had originally landed, and, arrived there, they received orders to return to the Spaniards in Coza and direct them to abandon the country and unite with the rest of the colony. As soon as the messengers reached them they set out "to the great grief of the Indians who accompanied them two or three days' journey weeping, with great demonstrations of love, but not for their religion, since only one dying Indian asked for baptism, which Father Salazar administered to him. In the beginning of November they reached the port after having been seven months on this exploration."[5]

We learn from this narrative that the nucleus of the Coosa River Creeks and the Tallapoosa River Creeks was already in existence, and that the Coosa and Hoḷiwahali tribes were then most prominent

[1] Davila Padilla, Historia, pp. 205–217. Translation by Mrs. F. Bandelier.

[2] Ranjel in Bourne, Narr. of De Soto, II, p. 113; he gives this man's name as Feryada, and calls him a Levantine.

[3] Ibid., p. 114.

[4] Barcia, La Florida, p. 35.

[5] Ibid., pp. 37–39.

in the respective groups. It is probable that most of the other tribes afterwards found upon Tallapoosa River were at this time in Georgia, and it is likely that the Abihka had not yet come to settle beside the Coosa. In spite of an evident confusion in the minds of the Spaniards of Indian and feudal institutions there must have been some basis for the overlordship said to have been enjoyed by the Indians of Coosa. The Napochies seem to have been a Choctaw-speaking people on the Black Warrior and Tombigbee Rivers. Mr. Grayson informs me that the name was preserved until recent years as a war title among the Creeks. They were probably identical with the Napissa, whom Iberville notes as having already in his time (1699) united with the Chickasaw.[1]

In 1567 Juan Pardo came toward this country, advancing beyond Chiaha on the Tennessee to a place called Satapo, from which some Indians and a soldier proceeded to Coosa. On the authority of the soldier, Vandera gives the following description of Coosa town:

> Coosa is a large village, the largest to be met after leaving Santa Elena on the road we took from there. It may contain about 150 people—that is, judging by the size of the village. It seems to be a wealthier place than all the others; there are generally a great many Indians in it. It is situated in a valley at the foot of a mountain. All around it at one-quarter, one-half, and one league there are very many big places. It is a very fertile country; its situation is at midday's sun or perhaps a little less than midday.(?)[2]

Fear of this tribe, allied with the "Chisca, Carrosa, and Costehe," was what decided Pardo to turn back to Santa Elena.[3] While Vandera seems to say that Coosa had 150 inhabitants, he must mean neighborhoods, otherwise it certainly would not be the largest place the Spaniards had discovered. Garcilasso says that in Coosa there were 500 houses, but he is wont to exaggerate.[4] At the same time, if Vandera means 150 neighborhoods and Garcilasso counted all classes of buildings, the two statements could be reconciled very well.

And now, after enjoying such early prominence, the Coosa tribe slips entirely from view, and when we next catch a glimpse of it its ancient importance has gone. Adair, the first writer to notice the town particularly, says:

> In the upper or most western part of the country of the Muskohge there was an old beloved town, now reduced to a small ruinous village, called *Koosah*, which is still a place of safety to those who kill undesignedly. It stands on commanding ground, overlooking a bold river.[5]

The name appears in the enumerations of 1738,[6] 1750,[6] and 1760,[7] and a part at least in the enumeration of 1761.[8] In 1796 John O'Kelly, a half-breed, was trader there, having succeeded his father.[9]

---

1 Margry, Déc., IV, p. 180.
2 Vandera in Ruidiaz, II, pp. 485–486.
3 Ibid., p. 471.
4 Garcilasso in Shipp, De Soto and Florida, p. 374.
5 Adair, Hist. Am. Inds., p. 159.
6 MS., Ayer Coll.
7 Miss. Prov. Arch., I, pp. 94–95.
8 Col. Docs. Ga., VIII, p. 512.
9 Ga. Hist. Soc. Colls., IX, pp. 34, 169.

Hawkins describes the town as follows, as it existed in 1799:

Coo-sau; on the left bank of Coo-sau, between two creeks, Eu-fau-lau and Nau-chee. The town borders on the first, above; and on the other river. The town is on a high and beautiful hill; the land on the river is rich and flat for two hundred yards, then waving and rich, fine for wheat and corn. It is a limestone country, with fine springs, and a very desirable one; there is reed on the branches, and pea-vine in the rich bottoms and hill sides, moss in the river and on the rock beds of the creek.

They get fish plentifully in the spring season, near the mouth of Eu-fau-lau-hat-che; they are rock, trout, buffalo, red horse and perch. They have fine stocks of horses, hogs and cattle; the town gives name to the river, and is sixty miles above Tus-kee-gee.[1]

Coosa had evidently fallen off very much from its ancient grandeur and its name does not appear in the census enumeration of 1832. Those who lived there abandoned their town some years after 1799, and settled a few miles higher up on the east side of the river near what is now East Bend.[2] It is not now represented by any existing town among the Creeks, but the name is well known and still appears in war titles. From the census list of 1761 one might judge that part of the Coosa had moved down on Tallapoosa River and settled with the Fus-hatchee people, with whom they would have gone to Florida and afterwards, in part at least, to the southern part of the Seminole Nation, Oklahoma.[3] The French census of about 1760 associates them rather with the Kan-hatki, but the fate of Kan-hatki and Fus-hatchee was the same.[4] What happened to the greater portion of them will be told presently.

Besides Coosa proper we find a town placed on several maps between Tuskegee and Koasati and called "Old Coosa," or "Coussas old village." From the resemblance of the name to that of the Koasati as usually spelled, and the proximity of the two places, Gatschet thought it was another term applied to the latter.[5] But on the other hand we often find Coosa-old-town and Koasati on the same map, and both are mentioned separately in the enumerations of 1760 and 1761.[6] The fact that, according to the same lists, there were Coosa on Tallapoosa River not far away, associated with the Fus-hatchee and Kan-hatki, would strengthen the belief that there were really some Coosa Indians at this place. Even if there were not, the name itself clearly implies that the site had once been occupied by Coosa Indians, and by inference at a time anterior to the settlement of the Coosa already considered. Without traceable connection with any of these bodies is "a Small Settlement of Indians called the Cousah old Fields"

---

[1] Ga. Hist. Soc. Colls., III, p. 41.

[2] Plate 8; Royce in 18th Ann. Rept. Bur. Amer. Ethn., pt. 2, pl. CVIII, map of Alabama.

[3] Ga. Col. Docs., VIII, p. 523.

[4] Miss. Prov. Arch., I, p. 94.

[5] Creek Mig. Leg., I, p. 137.

[6] Miss. Prov. Arch., I, p. 94; Ga. Col. Docs., VIII, p. 524.

148061°—22——16

encountered in 1778 between the Choctawhatchee and Apalachicola Rivers by a British expedition under David Holmes sent into East Florida from Pensacola.[1]

Still another branch of this tribe was in all probability the Coosa of South Carolina which has been elsewhere considered.[2]

By common tradition and the busk expression, "We are Kos-istagi," still used by them, we know that there are several other towns descended from Coosa, though no longer bearing the name. The most important of these was Otciapofa, commonly called "Hickory Ground," whose people came from Little Tulsa. Little Tulsa was the seat of the famous Alexander McGillivray and was located on the east bank of Coosa River 3 miles above the falls. After his death the inhabitants all moved to the Hickory Ground, Otciapofa, which was on the same side of the river just below the falls.[3] The condition of this latter town in 1799 is thus described by Hawkins:

> O-che-au-po-fau; from Oche-ub, a hickory tree, and po-fau, in or among, called by the traders, hickory ground. It is on the left bank of the Coosau, two miles above the fork of the river, and one mile below the falls, on a flat of poor land, just below a small stream; the fields are on the right side of the river, on rich flat land; and this flat extends back for two miles, with oak and hickory, then pine forest; the range out in this forest is fine for cattle; reed is abundant in all the branches.
>
> The falls can be easily passed in canoes, either up or down; the rock is very different from that of Tallapoosa; here it is ragged and very coarse granite; the land bordering on the left side of the falls is broken or waving, gravelly, not rich. At the termination of the falls there is a fine little stream, large enough for a small mill, called, from the clearness of the water, We-hemt-le, *good water*.[4] Three and a half miles above the town are ten apple trees, planted by the late General McGillivray; half a mile further up are the remains of Old Tal-e-see,[5] formerly the residence of Mr. Lochlan[6] and his son, the general. Here are ten apple trees, planted by the father, and a stone chimney, the remains of a house built by the son, and these are all the improvements left by the father and son.
>
> These people are, some of them, industrious. They have forty gunmen, nearly three hundred cattle, and some horses and hogs; the family of the general belong to this town; he left one son and two daughters; the son is in Scotland, with his grandfather, and the daughters with Sam Macnack [Moniac], a half-breed, their uncle; the property is much of it wasted. The chiefs have requested tho agent for Indian affairs to take charge of the property for the son, to prevent its being wasted by the sisters of the general or by their children. Mrs. Durant, the oldest sister, has eight children. She is industrious, but has no economy or management. In possession of fourteen working negroes, she seldom makes bread enough, and they live poorly. She can spin and weave, and is making some feeble efforts to obtain clothing for her family. The other sister, Sehoi, has about thirty negroes, is extravagant and heedless, neither spins nor weaves, and has no government of her family. She has one son, David Tale [Tate?] who has been educated in Philadelphia and Scotland. He promises to do better.[7]

---

[1] Copy of MS., Lib. Cong.

[2] See p. 25.

[3] Hawkins in Ga. Hist. Soc. Colls., IX, p. 44.

[4] Wī hili="good water."

[5] Little Tulsa.

[6] The Lib. Cong. MS. has "Mr. Lochlan McGillivray."

[7] Ga. Hist. Soc. Colls., III, pp. 39–40.

The town is given in the lists of 1760 and 1761, by Bartram, by Swan, and in the census of 1832,[1] and, probably in a distorted form, in 1750.[2]

Big Tulsa, which separated from the town last mentioned, may be identical with that which appears in the De Soto chronicles under the synonymous terms Talisi, Tallise, and Talisse.[3] Biedma does not mention it. The other three chroniclers describe it as a large town by a great river, having plenty of corn. Elvas states that "other towns and many fields of maize were on the opposite shore."[4] Garcilasso says that this place was "the key of the country," and that it was "palisaded, invested with very good terraces, and almost surrounded by a river." He adds that "it did not heartily acknowledge the cacique [of Coosa], because of a neighboring chief, who endeavored to make the people revolt against him."[5] We may gather from this that Tulsa had at that time become such a large and strong town that it no longer leaned on the mother town of Coosa, as would be the case with a new or weak offshoot. There may indeed be some question whether this was the Tulsa of later history, but there does not appear to be a really valid reason to deny this, although the name from which it is thought to have been derived is a very common one. Spanish documents of 1597–98 speak, for instance, of a town called Talaxe (or Talashe) in Guale and a river so called, evidently the Altamaha. Woodward says that "the Tallasses never settled on the Tallapoosa River before 1756; they were moved to that place by James McQueen" from the Talladega country,[6] but the name occurs here on the earliest maps available, at a date far back of any period of which Woodward could have had information. Probably his statement applies to an independent body of Tulsa entered in the list dating from 1750,[2] as in the Abihka country, and appearing on the Purcell map (pl. 7) as "Tallassehase," Tulsa old town. The history of this settlement is otherwise unknown. In De Soto's time the several towns may not have become separated, but of that we have no knowledge. My opinion is that in either case the town entered by De Soto was farther toward the southwest than the position in which Big Tulsa was later found, somewhere, in fact, between the site of Holiwahali and that of the present St. Clair, in Lowndes County, Alabama.[7]

The name of this town occurs frequently in later documents, and it is given in the lists of 1750, 1760, and 1761, by Bartram, Swan, and

1 Miss. Prov. Arch., I, p. 95; Ga. Col. Docs., VIII, p. 523; Bartram, Travels, p. 461; Schoolcraft, Ind. Tribes, V, p. 262; Sen. Doc. 512, 23d Cong., 1st sess., IV, pp. 280–281.

2 MS., Ayer Coll.

3 Bourne, Narr. of De Soto, I, p. 86; II, pp. 115–116; Garcilasso in Shipp, De Soto and Florida, p. 375.

4 Bourne, op. cit., I, p. 86.

5 Garcilasso in Shipp, De Soto and Florida, p. 375.

6 Woodward, Reminiscences, p. 77.

7 In plate 2 the positions of Tulsa (1) and Tawasa (1) should be transposed.

Hawkins, and in the census of 1832.[1] In the great squares of this town and Tukabahchee Tecumseh met the Creeks in council. In 1797 the traders here were James McQueen, the oldest white man in the Creek Nation, who had come to Georgia as a soldier under Oglethorpe in 1733,[2] and William Powell. Hawkins gives the following description of it as it existed in 1799:

Tal-e-see, from *Tal-o-fau*, a town, and *e-see*, taken.[3] Situated in the fork of Eu-fau-be on the left bank of Tal-la-poo-sa, opposite Took-au-bat-che. Eu-fau-be has its source in the ridge dividing the waters of Chat-to-ho-che from Tal-la-poo-sa, and runs nearly west to the junction with the river; here it is sixty feet wide. The land on it is poor for some miles up, then rich flats, bordered with pine land with reedy branches; a fine range for cattle and horses.

The Indians have mostly left the town, and settled up the creek, or on its waters, for twenty miles.[4] The settlements are some of them well chosen, and fenced with worm fences. The land bordering on the streams of the right side of the creek, is better than that of the left; and here the settlements are mostly made. Twelve miles up the creek from its mouth it forks; the large fork of the left side has some rich flat swamp, large white oak, poplar, ash, and white pine. The trading path from Cus-se-tuh to the Upper Creeks crosses this fork twice. Here it is called big swamp (opil-thluc-co). The waving land to its source is stiff. The growth is post oak, pine, and hard-shelled hickory.[5]

The Indians who have settled out on the margins and branches of the creek have, several of them, cattle, hogs, and horses, and begin to be attentive to them. The head warrior of the town, Peter McQueen, a half-breed, is a snug trader, has a valuable property in negroes and stock, and begins to know their value.

These Indians were very friendly to the United States during the Revolutionary War, and their old chief, Ho-bo-ith-le Mic-co, of the halfway house (improperly called the Tal-e-see king), could not be prevailed on by any offers from the agents of Great Britain to take part with them. On the return of peace, and the establishment of friendly arrangements between the Indians and citizens of the United States, this chief felt himself neglected by Mr. Seagrove, which resenting, he robbed and insulted that gentleman, compelled him to leave his house near Took-au-bat-che, and fly into a swamp. He has since then, as from a spirit of contradiction, formed a party in opposition to the will of the nation, which has given much trouble and difficulty to the chiefs of the land. His principal assistants were the leaders of the banditti who insulted the commissioners of Spain and the United States, on the 17th September, 1799, at the confluence of Flint and Chat-to-ho-che. The exemplary punishment inflicted on them by the warriors of the nation, has effectually checked their mischief-making and silenced them. And this chief has had a solemn warning from the national council, to respect the laws of the nation, or he should meet the punishment ordained by the law. He is one of the great medal chiefs.

This spirit of party or opposition prevails not only here, but more or less in every town in the nation. The plainest proposition for ameliorating their condition, is immediately opposed; and this opposition continues as long as there is hope to obtain presents, the infallible mode heretofore in use, to gain a point.[6]

---

[1] Miss. Prov. Arch., I, p. 95; Ga. Col. Docs., VIII, p. 523; Bartram, Travels, p. 461; Schoolcraft, Ind. Tribes, V, p. 262; Ga. Hist. Soc. Colls., III, p. 25; Senate Doc. 512, 23d Cong., 1st sess., IV, pp. 260–264.

[2] Ga. Hist. Soc. Colls., IX, p. 168.

[3] There is a Creek tradition to the effect that this town was once "captured" by the Tukabahchee, but I am inclined to think that it was invented to account for the name. It is more likely that Gatschet is right in deriving the name from *tálwa*, town, and, *ahasi*, old, although it is now so much abbreviated that its original meaning is totally obscured.

[4] The Lib. Cong. MS. has "25 miles."

[5] The Lib. Cong. MS. adds the name of the magnolia.

[6] Ga. Hist. Soc. Colls., III, pp. 26–27.

Tulsa had several branch towns. Mention has already been made of one of these.[1] On the French list of 1760 and several early maps is a place called Nafape, or Nafabe, which was evidently a Tulsa out-village on a creek of the same name flowing into Ufaupee Creek.[2] Near, and possibly identical with this, was Chatukchufaula, although on some maps it appears on Tallapoosa River itself. It is evidently the "Challacpauley" of Swan,[3] and I give it as a branch of Tulsa on the authority of Woodward.[4] It was destroyed in the war of 1813–14 by Indians friendly to the United States Government and the people probably migrated to Florida.[5]

The "Halfway House," of which the "Ho-bo-ith-le Mic-co" of Hawkins was chief, is frequently mentioned by travelers. Taitt gives its Creek name as "Chavucleyhatchie." He says:

> I took the bearings and distance of the path to this place which is twenty-five miles ENE. from the Tuckabatchie, situated on a creek called Chavucleyhatchie being the north branch of Nufabee Creek, which emptys itself into the Tallapuse River at the great Tallassies. In this village which belongs to the Tallasies are about 20 gunmen and one trader.[6]

In Bartram's list (1777) it appears as "Ghuaclahatche."[7] Although given as a town distinct from the Halfway house the "Chawelatchie" of the Purcell map (pl. 7) is evidently intended for this, especially since Hawkins calls it "Chowolle Hatche."[8] The name is perpetuated in the "Chewockeleehatchee Creek" of modern maps.

Another branch was Saoga-hatchee, "Rattle Creek," which appears as early as 1760.[2] Hawkins has the following to say regarding it:

> Sou-go-hat-che; from sou-go, a cymbal, and hat-che, a creek. This joins on the left side of Tallapoosa, ten miles below Eu-fau-lau. It is a large creek, and the land on the forks and to their sources is stiff in places, and stony. The timber is red oak and small hickory; the flats on the streams are rich, covered with reed; among the branches the land is waving and fit for cultivation.
>
> They have thirty gunmen in this village, who have lately joined Tal-e-see. One of the chiefs, O-fau-mul-gau, has some cattle, others have a few, as they have only paid attention to their stock within two years, and their means for acquiring them were slender.
>
> Above this creek, on the waters of Eu-fau-lau-hat-che, there are some settlements well chosen. The upland is stiff and stony or gravelly; the timber is post and red oak, pine and hickory; the trees are small; the soil apparently rich enough, and well suited for wheat, and the streams have some rich flats.[9]

Another branch, Lutcapoga, "terrapin resort," "place where terrapins are gathered," appears only in Hawkins's Letters[10] and in

[1] See p. 243.
[2] Miss. Prov. Arch., I, p. 95.
[3] Schoolcraft, Ind. Tribes, V, p. 262.
[4] Woodward, Reminiscences, p. 35.
[5] See pp. 409–410.
[6] Mereness, Trav. Am. Col., p. 545.
[7] Bartram, Travels, p. 461.
[8] Ga. Hist. Soc. Colls., IX, p. 50.
[9] Ibid., III, p. 49.
[10] As "Luchaossoguh."—Ga. Hist. Soc. Colls., IX, p. 33.

the census of 1832.[1] There is to-day a place called Loachapoka in Lee County, Alabama, about halfway between Montgomery and West Point. The name was also given to a western tributary of the Chattahoochee.[1] After the Creek removal this town settled in the northernmost part of the nation, where the flourishing modern city of Tulsa has grown up, named for its mother town. The main town of Tulsa also split into two parts in Oklahoma, called after their respective locations Tulsa Canadian and Tulsa Little River. The last is the only one which in 1912 maintained a square ground.

The Okfuskee [Akfąski] towns constituted the largest group descended from Coosa. Like the Tulsa, these people referred to themselves in busk speeches as Kos-istâgi, "Coosa people." The name, which signifies "point between rivers," nowhere appears in the De Soto narratives, but is in evidence very early in the maps and documents of the late seventeenth and early eighteenth centuries. On the Lamhatty map it is given in the form "Oufusky," apparently as far east as the east bank of Flint River.[2] Not much reliance can be placed on the geography of this map, though it is not unlikely that Lamhatty was attempting to place the eastern Okfuskee settlements on the upper Chattahoochee River. On the De Crenay map of 1733 two Okfuskee towns appear—one, "Oefasquets," between the Coosa and Tallapoosa Rivers well down toward the point where they come together; the other, "Les grands Oefasqué," a considerable distance up the Tallapoosa.[3] They occur again in the Spanish census of 1738, in which the latter is called "Oefasque Talajase," showing it to have been the original town.[4] The same pair are repeated in the census of 1750.[5] The former appears in the list of 1760 as "Akfeechkoutchis" (i. e., Little Okfuskee); the latter as "Akfaches" (i. e., the Okfuskee proper).[6] This last is "the great Okwhuske town" which Adair mentions and locates on the west bank of Tallapoosa River. He calls the Tallapoosa River after it.[7]

In 1754 the French of Fort Toulouse almost persuaded the Okfuskee Creeks to cut off those English traders who were among them, but they were prevented by the opposition of a young chief.[8] In 1760 such a massacre did take place at Okfuskee and its branch town, Sukaispoga, as also at Okchai and Kealedji.[9] The name of Okfuskee appears in the list of 1761, and in the lists of Bartram, Swan, and Hawkins.[10] Bartram mentions an upper and a lower town of

---

1 Senate Doc. 512, 23d Cong. 1st sess., IV, pp. 270–274.

2 Plate 9.

3 Amer. Anthrop., n. s. vol. x, p. 51

4 Hamilton, Col. Mobile, p. 190.

5 MS., Ayer Lib.

6 Miss. Prov. Arch., I, p. 95.

7 Adair, Hist. Am. Inds., pp. 258, 262

8 Ga. Col. Docs., VII, pp. 41–42.

9 Ibid., pp. 261–266.

10 Ga. Col. Docs., VIII, p. 523; Bartram, Travels, p. 461; Schoolcraft, Ind. Tribes, V, p. 262; Ga. Hist. Soc. Colls., III, p. 25.

the name, perhaps the two distinguished by the French.[1] In 1797 the trader was Patrick Donnally.[2] In the census rolls of 1832 no such town appears, but by that time the main settlement seems to have adopted the name Tcatoksofka, "deep rock," i. e., one where there was a considerable fall of water, or "rock deep down," and this does occur.[3] After the removal to Oklahoma, Tcatoksofka was still the principal town. The old name Okfuskee was revived somewhat later by a chief named Fushatcutci (Little Fus-hatchee) who moved into the western part of the nation with part of the Tcatoksofka people and gave the old name to his new settlement. From this circumstance his people afterwards called him Tal-mutca's mi'ko, "New town chief."

Another branch is called Abihkutci [Abi'kutci]. The name signifies "Little Abihka" and it might naturally be supposed that the people so designating themselves belonged to the Abihka Creeks. In fact, the principal Abihka town before the emigration was known as Abihkutci, whereas, after their removal, the diminutive ending was dropped and the name Abihka resumed. Two stories were given me of the way in which this name "Abihkutci" came to be used for an Okfuskee town. According to one, the town was founded by a few Abihka Indians, but it was later filled up with Okfuskee. According to the other, some Abihka joined the Okfuskee before the Civil War and afterwards left them. Then they formed a town apart and said "We will be called Little Abihkas." But since they had at one time lived with the Okfuskee the latter adopted the name Abihkutci for use among themselves. In any case the occurrence does not seem to have preceded the westward emigration of the Creeks, and the town did not have a very long separate existence. At the present day it has no square ground of its own.

Another branch was known as Tukabahchee Tallahassee, probably because it occupied a place where the Tukabahchee had formerly lived. It appears in the lists of Swan and Hawkins,[4] and the latter states that in 1797 it received the name of Talmutcasi (New Town). We find it under this latter designation in the census list of 1832.[5] It follows from its recent origin that it is distinct from the Talimachusy[6] or Tallimuchase[7] of De Soto's time, though the names mean the same thing. After removal these people settled in the southwestern part of the nation and appear to have changed from the White to the Red side, being sometimes treated as a branch of Atasi. Their square ground was given up so long ago that very little is remembered regarding it.

---

1 Bartram, Travels, p. 461.
2 Hawkins in Ga. Hist. Soc. Colls., IX, p. 169.
3 Sen. Doc. 512, 23d Cong., 1st sess., IV, pp. 331–343.
4 Schoolcraft, Ind. Tribes, V, p. 262; Ga. Hist. Soc. Colls., II, p. 46.
5 Senate Doc. 512, 23d Cong. 1st sess., IV, pp. 254–255.
6 Bourne, Narr. of De Soto, II, p. 113.
7 Ibid., I, p. 84.

One of the oldest branches of Okfuskee was Sukaispoga, "place for getting hogs," called by Hawkins "Sooc-he-ah," and known to the traders as "Hog Range." It appears in the censuses of 1760 and 1761, and in the lists of Bartram, Swan, and Hawkins.[1] In 1772 it had about 45 gunmen.[2] From Hawkins's description, given below, it appears that the town united with Imukfa about 1799, and therefore the name does not appear in the census rolls of 1832. Imukfa was, according to Hawkins, made up of settlers from "Thu-le-oc-who-cat-lau" and the people of the town just referred to. "Thu-le-oc-who-cat-lau" is evidently the "Chuleocwhooatlee" which he mentions in 1797 in his letter and which was "on the left bank of Tallapoosa, 11 miles below Newyaucau.[3] Tohtogagi [To'togagi] is noted by Swan[4] and described (see below) by Hawkins. It preserved a separate existence after its removal west of the Mississippi down to the Civil War and was located east of the Canadian. Sometimes it was known as Hitcisihogi, after the name of its ball ground, though in the census of 1832 Hitcisihogi appears as an independent town. Perhaps two originally independent towns were later united.

While giving Atcina-ulga as an Okfuskee town, Hawkins says it was settled from Lutcapoga.[5] These two statements can not be reconciled, unless we suppose that some Okfuskee Indians were settled at Lutcapoga. Another branch village given by Hawkins is Epesaugee (Ipisagi).[6]

At a very early day several Okfuskee settlements were made on the upper course of the Chattahoochee. One was called Tukpafka, "punk," a name applied in later times to an entirely distinct town, originating from Wakokai. The name of this particular settlement occurs in Bartram's list and is referred to by Hawkins, as will be seen below.[7] In 1777 (see below) they moved over to the Tallapoosa, where their new settlement was called Nuyaka, an attempt at modifying the name of New York City to accord with the requirements of Creek harmonic feeling. According to Swan the name Nuyaka was bestowed by a Colonel Ray, a New York British loyalist,[4] while Gatschet says it was so named after the treaty of New York, concluded between the United States Government and the Creek Indians August 7, 1790.[8] It appears in the lists of Swan and Hawkins, but not on the census rolls of 1832.[9] After the removal this town continued to preserve its identity and in 1912 it was the only Okfuskee division that still maintained a square ground.

---

[1] Miss. Prov. Arch. I, 95; Ga. Col. Docs., VIII, p. 523; Bartram, Travels, p. 461; Schoolcraft, Ind. Tribes, V, p. 262; Ga. Hist. Soc. Colls., II, p. 48.

[2] Mereness, Trav. Am. Col., p. 529.

[3] Ga. Hist Soc. Colls., IX, p. 169.

[4] Schoolcraft, Ind. Tribes, V, p. 262.

[5] Ga. Hist. Soc. Colls., III, p. 45.

[6] Ibid., p. 47.

[7] Bartram, Travels, p. 462; Ga. Hist. Soc. Colls., III, p. 45.

[8] Misc. Coll. Ala. Hist. Soc., 1, p. 404.

[9] Schoolcraft, Ind. Tribes, V, p. 262; Ga. Hist. Soc. Colls., III, p. 45.

There were three Okfuskee settlements on the Chattahoochee River which existed for a longer time. These were Tcułå'ko-nini (Horse Trail), Hołi-taiga (War Ford), and Tca'hki łåko (Big Shoal). They appear in the lists of Bartram and Hawkins, and, with the possible exception of the last, in that of Swan.[1] The census of 1832 includes a town of the same name as the last, but omits the others. September 27, 1793, they were attacked by Georgians and so severely handled that the inhabitants abandoned them and located on the east side of Tallapoosa River, opposite the mother town, Big Okfuskee.[2] "Wichagoes" and "Illahatchee," given in the traders' census of 1761, were probably Okfuskee towns.[3] Kohamutkikatska, "place where blowgun canes are broken off," was a comparatively late branch of Okfuskee. The name, in an excessively corrupted form ("Nohunt, the Gartsnar town"), appears in the census list of 1832.[4] Hawkins has the following information regarding Okfuskee and its branches:

Oc-fus-kee; from Oc, in, and fuskee, a point. The name is expressive of the position of the old town, and where the town house now stands on the right bank of Tal-lapoo-sa. The town spreads out on both sides of the river and is about thirty-five miles above Took-au-bat-che. The settlers on the left side of the river are from Chat-to-ho-che. They once formed three well-settled villages on that river—Che-luc-co ne-ne, Ho-ith-le-ti-gau, and Chau-ke thluc-co.

Oc-fus-kee, with its villages, is the largest town in the nation. They estimate the number of gun men of the old town at one hundred and eighty and two hundred and seventy in the villages or small towns. The land is flat for half a mile on the river, and fit for culture; back of this there are sharp, stoney hills; the growth is pine, and the branches all have reed.

They have no fences around the town; they have some cattle, hogs, and horses, and their range is a good one; the shoals in the river afford a great supply of moss, called by the traders salt grass, and the cows which frequent these shoals, are the largest and finest in the nation; they have some peach trees in the town, and the cassine yupon, in clumps. The Indians have lately moved out and settled in villages and the town will soon be an old field; the settling out in villages has been repeatedly pressed by the agent for Indian affairs, and with considerable success; they have seven villages belonging to this town.

1st. New-yau-cau; named after New York. It is on the left bank of Tallapoosa, twenty miles above Oc-fus-kee;[5] these people lived formerly at Tote-pauf-cau, (spunk-knot) on Chat-to-ho-che, and moved from thence in 1777.[6] They would not take part in the war between the United States and Great Britian and determined to retire from their settlements, which, through the rage of war, might feel the effects of the resentment of the people of the United States when roused by the conduct of the red people, as they were placed between the combatants. The town is on a flat, bordering on the river; the adjoining lands are broken or waving and stony; on the opposite side they are broken, stony; the growth is pine, oak and hickory. The flat strips of land on the river, above and below, are generally narrow; the adjoining land is broken,

[1] Bartram, Travels, p. 462; Ga. Hist. Soc. Colls., III, p. 45; Schoolcraft, Ind. Tribes, V, p. 262.
[2] Hawkins, op. cit.; also Early map, pl. 9.
[3] Ga. Col. Docs., VIII, p. 523.
[4] Senate Doc. 512, 23d Cong., 1st sess., IV, p. 323.
[5] In notes made in 1797 he says "eighteen miles."—Ga. Hist. Soc. Colls., IX, p. 169.
[6] The Lib. Cong. MS. says "after the year 1777."

with oak, hickory, and pine. The branches all have reed; they have a fine ford at the upper end of the town; the river is one hundred and twenty yards wide. Some of the people have settled out from the town, and they have good land on Im-mook-fau Creek, which joins the right side of the river, two miles below the town.[1]

2d. Took-au-bat-che tal-lau-has-see; this village received in part a new name in 1797, Tal-lo-wau moo-chas-see (new town). It is on the right bank of the river, four miles above New-yau-cau;[2] the land around it is broken and stony; off the river the hills are waving; and post oak, hard shelled hickory, pine, and on the ridges, chestnut is the growth.

3d. Im-mook-fau (a gorget made of a conch). This village is four miles west from Tookaubatche [Tal-lauhas-see], on Immookfau Creek, which joins the right side of Tallapoosa, two miles below New-yau-cau. The settlers are from Chu-le-oc-who-cat-lau and Sooc-he-ah; they have fine rich flats on the creek, and good range for their cattle; they possess some hogs, cattle, and horses, and begin to be attentive to them.

4th. Tooh-to-cau-gee, from tooh-to, a corn house, and cau-gee, fixed or standing.[3] The Indians of Oc-fus-kee formerly built a corn house here for the convenience of their hunters and put their corn there for their support during the hunting season. It is on the right bank of Tallapoosa, twenty miles above New-yau-cau;[4] the settlements are on the narrow flat margins of the river on both sides. On the left side the mountains terminate here, the uplands are too poor and broken for cultivation; the path from E-tow-wah, in the Cherokee country, over the tops of these mountains, is a pretty good one. It winds down the mountains to this village; the river is here one hundred and twenty yards wide, a beautiful clear stream. On the right side, off from the river flats, the land is waving, with oak, hickory and pine, gravelly, and in some places large sheets of rock which wave as the land. The grit is coarse, but some of it is fit for mill stones; the land is good for corn, the trees are all small, with some chesnut on the ridges; the range is a good one for stock; reed is found on all the branches; on the path to New-yau-cau there is some large rock, the vein lies southwest; they are in two rows parallel with each other and the land good in their neighborhood.

5th. Au-che-nau-ul-gau; from Au-che-nau, cedar, and ul-gau, all; a cedar grove. These settlers are from Loo-chau-po-gau (the resort of terrapin). It is on a creek, near the old town, forty miles above New-yau-cau. This settlement is the farthest north of all the Creeks; the land is very broken in the neighborhood. West of this village, post and black oak, all small; the soil is dark and stiff with coarse gravel and in some places stone; from the color of the earth in places there must be iron ore; the streams from the glades form fine little creeks, branches of the Tallapoosa. The land on their borders is broken, stiff, stony and rich, affording fine mill seats, and on the whole it is a country where the Indians might have desirable settlements; the path from E-tow-woh to Hill-au-bee passes through these glades.

6th. E-pe-sau-gee; this village is on a large creek which gives name to it and enters the Tallapoosa opposite Oc-fus-kee. The creek has its source in the ridge, dividing the waters of this river from Chat-to-ho-che; it is thirty yards wide and has a rocky bottom; they have forty settlers in the village, who have fenced their fields this season for the benefit of their stock, and they have all of them cattle, hogs, and horses. They have some good land on the creek, but generally it is broken, the

---

[1] Near this town is Horse Shoe Bend, the scene of Jackson's decisive victory over the Creeks, March 27, 1814.

[2] In notes taken in 1797 he says "6 miles."—Ga Hist. Soc. Colls., IX, p. 170.

[3] Jackson Lewis, one of the writer's informants, says it means "two corncribs," and this has the sanction of Hawkins (Ga. Hist. Soc. Colls., IX, p. 33). It seems to be composed of tohto, corncrib, and kagi, to be or to set up. See Gatschet, Creek Mig. Leg., I, p. 148.

[4] In notes taken in 1797 he says "15 miles."—Ga. Hist. Soc. Colls., IX, p. 169.

strips of flat land are narrow; the broken is gravelly, with oak, hickory and pine, not very inviting. Four of these villages have valuable stocks of cattle. McCartney has one hundred; E-cun-chā-te E-maut-lau, one hundred; Tote-cuh Haujo, one hundred, and Took[aubatche] Micco, two hundred.

7th. Sooc-he-ah; from Sooc-cau, a hog, and he-ah, here,[1] called by the traders, hog range. It is situated on the right bank of Tallapoosa, twelve miles above Oc-fus-kee. It is a small settlement, the land is very broken, the flats on the river are narrow, the river broad and shoally. These settlers have moved, and joined Im-mook-fau, with a few exceptions.[2]

To these must be added:

Oc-fus-coo-che (little Oc-fus-kee) is a part of the small village, four miles above New-yau-cau. Some of these people lived at Oc-fus-kee nene, on the Chat-to-ho-che, from whence they were driven by an enterprising volunteer party from Georgia, the 27th September, 1793.[3]

During the Green Peach war many Okfuskee settled in the edge of the Cherokee Nation, near Braggs, Oklahoma, and afterwards some of them remained there along with a number of the Okchai Indians.

The Abihka

The Abihka constituted one of the most ancient divisions of the true Muskogee, appearing in the oldest migration legends, and are reckoned one of the four "foundation towns" of the confederacy. In ceremonial speeches they were called Abihka-nâgi, though what nâgi signifies no one at the present time knows. They were also called "the door shutters" because they guarded the northern border of the confederacy against attack. Hawkins says that among the oldest chiefs the name of this tribe was sometimes extended to the entire Creek Nation.[4] Du Pratz, who, like Iberville, distinguishes most of the true Muskogee as Conchacs, says that he believed the terms Abihka and Conchac applied to one people.[5] The relations of this tribe were naturally most intimate with the Coosa Indians. Hamilton quotes a Spanish manuscript of 1806 in which it is said that the Abihka and Coosa were as one pueblo divided into two by swift rivers.[6] Later they adopted a large portion of the refugee Natchez, who ultimately became completely absorbed. Stiggins, himself a Natchez, has the following to say regarding the Abihka and the people of their adoption:

The Au bih ka tribe reside indiscriminately in the Talladega valley with the Natche tribe, who they admitted to locate and assimilate with their tribe as one people indivisible a little more than a century ago. They at this day only pretend to know and

[1] Hawkins seems to have gotten hold of a mongrel expression, half Creek, half English. The proper Creek designation was Suka-ispoga.

[2] Ga. Hist. Soc. Colls., III, pp. 45–48; IX, p. 170.

[3] Ibid., p. 51.

[4] Ibid., p. 52.

[5] Du Pratz, La Louisiane, II, p. 208.

[6] Hamilton, Col. Mobile, 1910, p. 572.

distinguish their tribes from the mother's side of descent, but they are as one people with the Natches at this time, ... and why may they not by conjecture be entitled to the claim of the primitive Muscogee more than any other of the tribes, for they are not discriminated by any antient denomination that is known of. For their present appellation is derived from their manner of approveing or acquiescing a proposition. Tho' the national tongue is spoken by the tribe in all its purity, yet most notorious they assent or approbate what you may say to them in conversation with the long aspiration *āw̄* whereas the rest of the nation approbate or answer short *c̄āw̄*. From their singular manner of answering or approbating they got the name of *āw̄ b̄īw̄ kā*. Moreover, the rest of the Indians in talking of them and their tongue aptly call it the *aw bih ka* tongue, and never resort to the appelation of Ispocoga except in a national way.... A brass drum that was in their possession not a half century ago is kept as a trophy. And it is said by them to have been got by their ancestors in times of old from a people who invaded or past in a hostile manner through their country comeing from up the river, that they were not like any people they ever saw before, that they were ferocious, proud, and impudent in their manners. From the traditional circumstance of the brass drum it would lead to the inference that the proud people alluded to was the escort of Ferdinand Soto, and that the Indians came in possession of one of his drums by some means.[1]

Another native explanation for the tribal name is the following, originally obtained from a former Creek head chief, Spahi'tci, and related to me by the late Creek chief, Mr. G. W. Grayson: At a certain time there was a contest for supremacy between the Kasihta, Coweta, Chickasaw, and Abihka, and this consisted in seeing which tribe could bring in the most scalps and heap them highest around the ball post. Kasihta brought in the most, Coweta the next, the Chickasaw still fewer, and Abihka brought in only a very small number, which were thrown about the base of the post in a careless manner. From this circumstance they came to be called Abihka because abi'ka i'djita means "to heap up in a careless manner." Practically the same story is told by Hawkins.[2] Of course this is not related by the Abihka themselves and is simply a folk explanation. The interpretation given by Stiggins appears very plausible, but so far I have not been able to identify the linguistic fact on which it is based, and perhaps it is no longer possible to do so.[3]

I have spoken of the confusion which has resulted from the existence of an Abihkutci town occupied by Abihka Indians and another occupied by Okfuskee Indians.[4] Although Abihka sometimes appears on maps, it is curious that as soon as we have a specific town it is called Abihkutci. This appears first, so far as I am aware,[5] on the De Crenay map of 1733. It is also on the Bowen and Gibson and Mitchell maps of 1755, on the Evans map of 1777, the D'Anville map of 1790, and many others of the period. We find it in the

[1] Stiggins, MS. Nevertheless from what Swan says regarding the number of British drums in Creek towns and the esteem in which they were held it is possible that this Abihka specimen was of much more recent introduction. See Schoolcraft, Ind. Tribes, v, p. 275.

[2] Ga. Hist. Soc. Colls., III, p. 82.

[3] Mr. H. S. Halbert suggests a possible derivation from the Choctaw aiabika, "unhealthful place."

[4] See p. 247.

[5] Plate 5; Hamilton, Col. Mobile, p. 190.

census lists of 1738,[1] 1750,[1] 1760, and 1761, in the lists of Bartram, Swan, and Hawkins, and in the census list of 1832.[2] Few events of importance are connected with the history of this tribe. In 1716, according to the South Carolina documents, they suffered a severe defeat from the Cherokee,[3] and this was perhaps the beginning of those Cherokee aggressions on Creek territory which forced the Creeks out of the Tennessee Valley. If we may believe some Cherokee legends, however, that tribe had occupied much of the same country at an earlier date.[4]

The following is Hawkins's description of the Abihka town as it appeared in 1799:

> Au-be-coo-che, is on Nau-chee creek, five miles from the river, on the right bank of the creek, on a flat one mile wide. The growth is hard-shelled hickory. The town spreads itself out and is scattered on both sides of the creek, in the neighborhood of very high hills, which descend back into waving, rich land, fine for wheat or corn; the bottoms all rich; the neighborhood abounds in limestone, and large limestone springs; they have one above, and one below the town; the timber on the rich lands is oak, hickory, walnut, poplar, and mulberry.
>
> There is a very large cave north of the town, the entrance of which is small, on the side of a hill. It is much divided, and some of the rooms appear as the work of art; the doors regular; in several parts of the cave saltpetre is to be seen in crystals. On We-wo-cau creek there is a fine mill seat; the water is contracted by two hills; the fall twenty feet; and the land in the neighborhood very rich; cane is found on the creeks, and reed grows well on these lands.
>
> This town is one of the oldest in the nation; and sometimes, among the oldest chiefs, it gives name to the nation Au-be-cuh. Here some of the oldest customs had their origin. The law against adultery was passed here, and that to regulate marriages. To constitute legal marriage a man must build a house, make his crop and gather it in; then make his hunt and bring home the meat; putting all this in the possession of his wife ends the ceremony and they are married, or, as the Indians express it, the woman is bound, and not till then. This information is obtained from Co-tau-lau (Tus-se-ki-ah Mic-co of Coosau), an old and respectable chief, descended from Nau-che. He lives near We-o-coof-ke, has accumulated a handsome property, owns a fine stock, is a man of much information, and of great influence among the Indians of the towns in the neighborhood of this.
>
> They have no fences, and but a few hogs, horses, and cattle; they are attentive to white people who live among them, and particularly so to white women.[5]

The Abihka took practically no part in the Creek uprising of 1813. After their removal to Oklahoma they established their first square ground a few miles from Eufaula. Later many of them moved farther west, following the game, and they established another square, sometimes called "Abihka-in-the-west." Both of these have been long abandoned.

Before they left the old country two branch towns had arisen—Talladega [Taladigi] and Kan-tcati [Kȧn tcáti] (Red ground). They

[1] MSS., Ayer Coll.

[2] Miss. Prov. Arch., I, p. 95; Ga. Col. Docs., VIII, p. 523; Bartram, Travels, p. 461; Schoolcraft, Ind. Tribes, V, p. 262; Ga. Hist. Soc. Colls., III, p. 25; Senate Doc. 512, 23d Cong., 1st sess., pp. 315–318.

[3] S. C. Docs., MS.

[4] See p. 213.

[5] Ga. Hist. Soc. Colls., III, pp. 41–42; IX, p. 170.

were perhaps late in forming, since they do not appear separately listed before the census of 1832.[1] There is a place called "Conchardee" a few miles northwest of Talladega, in the county of the same name, Alabama. After their removal the Kan-tcati busk ground was soon given up, but that of Talladega has persisted down to the present day (1912).

Gatschet enumerates two other Abihka towns, Tcahki łåko or Big Shoal and Kayomalgi.[2] The former was on Choccolocco ("Big Shoal") Creek in Calhoun or Talladega County, Ala., and is to be distingnished carefully from the Okfuskee town so called.[3] There is some reason for thinking that Kayomalgi may have been settled by Shawnee,[4] though in 1772 a Chickasaw settlement was made on the creek which bore this name.[5] "The Lun-ham-ga Town in the Abecas" is mentioned by Tobias Fitch in 1725.[6]

On the Lamhatty map is a town called "Apeicah," located apparently on the east bank of the lower Chattahoochee.[7] This may perhaps be intended for Abihka, but if so it is badly misplaced. We have no knowledge of any portion of the Abihka people living so far to the south and east.

THE HOŁIWAHALI

The first of all red or war towns among the Upper Creeks to appear in history is Łiwahali, or, in the ancient form of the word, Hołiwahali, a name which signifies "to share out or divide war" (*hoŀi*, war, *awahaŀi*, to divide out). The explanation of this is given below. At the present time some Creeks say that Hołiwahali, Atasi, and Kealedji separated from Tukabahchee in the order given, but this story rather typifies the terms of friendship between them than explains their real origin, though there may be more substantial grounds for the belief in a common origin in the cases of the two latter. Hołiwahali, however, goes back to a remote historical period, for there can be little doubt that it is the Ulibahali of Ranjel[8] and the Ullibahali of Elvas.[9] This word might be given an interpretation in the Alabama language, but it is unlikely that any Alabama other than the Tawasa were on Tallapoosa River in De Soto's time. At any rate the town described by Ranjel and Elvas was on a river and in much the same position as that in which we later find Hołiwahali. It was fenced about with palisades, erected and loopholed in the usual Indian manner.

1 Sen. Doc. 512, 23d Cong., 1st sess., IV, pp. 304-307.
2 Ala. Hist. Soc., Misc. Colls., I, p. 391.
3 See p. 249.
4 See p. 319.
5 Taitt in Mereness, Trav. in Amer. Col., pp. 531-532.
6 Ibid., p. 189.
7 Amer. Anthrop., n. s. vol. X, p. 569.
8 Bourne, Narr. of De Soto, II, p. 113.
9 Ibid., I, p. 84.

Ranjel speaks of the grapes of this place as of particular excellence, better than any the Spaniards had tasted in Coosa, or farther north. Here it was learned the Indians had planned to attempt to rescue the chief of Coosa, whom De Soto carried along as prisoner, but the Coosa chief commanded them to lay aside their arms, which they did.[1] Of course the Spaniards interpreted this action as that of vassals obeying the commands of their lord, but the relations between the two towns were probably merely of alliance and friendship.

The sergeant major and 200 soldiers sent in search of Coosa by De Luna in 1560 reached this place after a long and toilsome journey. Padilla says:

. . . On the fiftieth day after their departure from Nanipacna, they discovered, on the banks of a river, several little Indian houses, the sight of which was a very great consolation to those, who in the immense solitude and almost facing starvation, had not seen a human inhabitant of those parts. The biggest river there was called Olibahali and had a more numerous population, which, even so, was quite small. In those hamlets they had corn, beans, and calabashes, but their abundance meant almost famine to the state of starvation the Spaniards were in. When the Indians perceived armed Spaniards they feared ill treatment as they had received it in the past, but being reassured, they returned to their houses, and the Spaniards retired outside the villages, thus avoiding frightening them. Through interpreters they communicated with them, giving them clothes in exchange for corn, which to both parties meant a great deal. The Spaniards needed food and found bread by means of these exchanges; the Indians did not wish any money, as they did not know it nor had they appreciated its value at any time since their remotest antiquity. What they value most are clothes and they treasured on this occasion the ribbons and the trinkets of colored beads which the Spaniards gave them. The soldiers were very glad for a rest at that place, although not free from misgivings concerning the Indians. They put out sentinels at night, as much in order to prevent the Indians from harming them, as their own men from going over among the Indians. At least they were all fed and it was necessary to remain at that place for several days, waiting for some of their companions who had remained behind, partly for lack of food and partly on account of illness, and those were the first days since they had left Nanipacna that they really ceased walking. . . .

Although the Indians of Olibahali showed themselves to be friends of the Spaniards, and were at peace with them, they may not have wished so many on account of the impairment to their food staples which they gathered to last them a whole year, and which their guests consumed within a few days. The corn was beginning to give out, and fearing still greater need, which was sure to come at that pace, they resorted to a wary invention to get the Spaniards out of their country. He who says that the Indians are barbarians and lack cunning, does not know them. They have cunning, and the vexations inflicted upon them by the Spaniards have made them more and more skilled with the many opportunities afforded them by the Spaniards. One day just after sunset, the dark of night fast approaching, an Indian arrived at the camp of the Spaniards, who, to judge from his appearance and demeanor, seemed to be a chief; he was accompanied by four other Indians. He carried the emblems of an ambassador, and he stated that he was such, and came from the great province of Coza. He carried in his hand a cane of six palmos[2] in length, adorned at the top with white feathers, which appeared to be those of a heron. It was the custom of the Indians to

[1] Bourne, Narr. of De Soto, I, pp. 84–85; II, pp. 113–114.

[2] One "palmo" is about 8 inches.

emphasize their messages of peace by wearing white feathers, their declaration of war by red ones. When the ambassador arrived within sight of the Spaniards, he made his obeisance after his fashion and said that the lord of Coza had sent him in the name of the whole province, offering it to them and thanking them in advance for their inclination to use it, and entreating them that his desires to receive them should not remain unfulfilled; that they should hurry to go there as he offered them those who would guide them and serve them. This Indian was a neighbour of those of Olibahali, and between them they had invented this miserable lie to get the Spaniards, whose main intention was to reach the province of Coza, out of their own territory. As the captains and priests were quite innocent of cunning they were overjoyed by this embassy, although their prudence told them that it might be artfulness on the part of those of Coza to ensnare them some way or other. For that reason their gratefulness, which in the opinion of some was due to such generous offerings, was quite guarded. At first they wished to send a captain with twelve soldiers to thank the lord of Coza for his offerings, but they finally agreed they ought not to separate, but travel all together, moving slowly towards the province of Coza; and upon asking the sham ambassador how many leagues there were to his province, he told them there were twenty. They told him to go and offer their thanks and appreciation for his coming and carry the news that the camp would break up immediately from Olibahali, in answer to the summons received, and soon go to see the lord of Coza.

The ambassador thereupon said that he had orders to guide and serve them, and in order to fulfill all his duties and do likewise what they should order him, he would accompany them one day's journey and that he would precede them. Thus they all left Olibahali together, and as soon as the ambassador had attained his intention to get them away from that place, he suddenly disappeared, showing himself to be a true Indian, who did not know how to carry to the end the plot he commenced, by bidding good-bye to the Spaniards on his way to Coza, although he was returning to his own country. As we have explained one side of the Indian character, we might just as well explain the other, namely, that although they are ingenious and ready schemers, they lack prudence and perseverance in carrying out the plot. This envoy commenced his scheme quite well, but he was too easily satisfied at merely putting them on the road, and he caused himself to be suspected in their eyes by his sudden disappearance. The prudent Spaniards discovered the truth by making a few investigations. They were not taken aback by the fact that the Indians wished to get rid of them; they were only astonished at having received the invitation that man had brought. Then they continued their journey in search of the land of promise which had been so celebrated by all who had spoken about it.[1]

On their return they probably passed through the same place, but nothing is said about it.

On the Lamhatty map is a town called "Cheeawoole," west of a river which appears to be the Flint, and from the spelling this town was probably identical with the one under discussion.[2] It appears in the census list of 1738 as "Yuguale,"[3] in that of 1750 as "Ycouale,"[3] in that of 1760 under the name "Telouales,"[4] and in that of 1761 as "Chewallee," where it is credited with 35 hunters, and is assigned to the trader James Germany along with Fus-hatchee and Kolomi.[5] In 1797 the traders were James Russel and Abraham M. Mordecai,

[1] Padilla, Historia, pp. 202-205. Translated by Mrs. F. Bandelier.
[2] Amer. Anthrop., n. s. vol. x, p. 570.
[3] MSS., Ayer Coll.
[4] Miss. Prov. Arch., I, p. 95.
[5] Ga. Col. Docs., VIII, p. 523.

the latter a Jew.[1] Bartram calls it "Cluale," Swan "Clewauleys,"[2] while in the census enumeration of 1832 it appears as "Clewalla."[3] Hawkins describes it as follows:

Ho-ith-le-wau-le, from Ho-ith-le, war, and wau-le, to share out or divide. This town had, formerly, the right to declare war;[4] the declaration was sent first to Took-au-bat-che, and thence throughout the nation, and they appointed the rendezvous of the warriors. It is on the right bank of the Tallapoosa, five miles below Aut-tos-see. In descending the river on the left side from Aut-tos-see, is two miles across Ke-bi-hat-che; thence one mile and a half O-fuck-she, and enter the fields of the town; the fields extend down the river for one and one-half miles; the town is on the right bank, on a narrow strip of good land; and back of it, under high red cliffs, are cypress ponds. It borders west on Autoshatche twenty-five feet wide.

These people have some cattle, and a few hogs and horses; they have some settlements up O-fuck-she; the increase of property among them, and the inconvenience attendant on their situation, their settlement being on the right side of the river, and their fields and stock on the left, brought the well-disposed to listen with attention to the plan of civilization, and to comment freely on their bad management. The town divided against itself; the idlers and the ill-disposed remained in the town, and the others moved over the river and fenced their fields. On this side the land is good and level, and the range out from the river good to the sources of O-fuc-she. On the other side, the high broken land comes close to the river. It is broken pine barren, back of that. The situation of the town is low and unhealthy; and this remark applies to all the towns on Tallapoosa, below the falls.

O-fuc-she has its source near Ko-e-ne-cuh, thirty miles from the river, and runs north. It has eight or nine forks, and the land is good on all of them. The growth is oak, hickory, poplar, cherry, persimmon, with cane brakes on the flats and hills. It is a delightful range for stock, and was preserved by the Indians for bears and called the beloved bear-ground. Every town had a reserve of this sort exclusively; but as the cattle increase and the bears decrease, they are hunted in common. This creek is sixty[5] feet wide, has steep banks, and is difficult to cross, when the waters are high.

Kebihatche has its source to the east, and is parallel with Ca-le-be-hat-che; the margins of the creek have rich flats bordering pine forest or post oak hills.[6]

If our identification of Ulibahali with this town is correct, the name which it bears would indicate that the Creek confederacy was in existence as far back as the period of De Soto. The fission in the town described by Hawkins was evidently that which resulted in the formation of Łapłako, since it is only after this time—namely, in the census list of 1832[7]—that we find Łapłako mentioned. According to the story now related a quarrel broke out among the Hołiwahali while they were drinking, and afterwards part of them moved away to a creek where a kind of cane grew called *ława*. From this they received their present name, a contraction of ława łåko, big ława. Łapłako comprised the more thrifty and energetic part of the popu-

1 Ga. Hist. Soc. Colls., IX, p. 168.

2 Bartram, Travels, p. 461; Schoolcraft, Ind. Tribes, V, p. 262.

3 Senate Doc. 512, 23d Cong., 1st sess., IV, pp. 315–318.

4 This fact is still remembered by some of the older Creek Indians.

5 The Lib. Cong. MS. has "20."

6 Ga. Hist. Soc. Colls., III, pp. 32–33.

7 Senate Doc. 512, 23d Cong., 1st sess., IV, pp. 268–270.

lation, and they have maintained a dance ground down to the present time, although not a regular square. The Hołiwahali proper have maintained neither dance ground nor square.

The Hilibi

We now come to three towns or groups of towns—Hilibi, Eufaula, and Wakokai—which, while they have had a long separate existence, claim and in recent years have maintained terms of the closest intimacy. Their square grounds are much the same and they generally agree in selecting their chief from the Aktayatçi clan. It is possible that this points to a common origin at some time in the remote past, but it would be hazardous to suggest it in stronger terms. From one of the best-informed Hilibi Indians I obtained the following tradition regarding the origin of his town. It was, he said, founded by a Tukpafka Indian belonging to the Aktayatci clan. Having suffered defeat in a ball game he determined to leave his own people, so he went away and founded another, gathering about him persons from many towns, but especially from Tukabahchee. When the people began to discuss what name they should give to their settlement their leader said "Quick shall be my name," and that is what Hilibi (*hilikbi*) signifies. It was because it grew up so rapidly. This story was confirmed independently by another of the best-informed old men, except that he represented the town as built up entirely of Tukpafka Indians. Tukpafka was, however, only a branch, and probably a late branch, of Wakokai, therefore we should have to look for an origin from the latter town. The historical value of this tradition may well be doubted, even with such emendation, but it serves to show the mental association between the places mentioned.

After De Soto had arrived at Cofitachequi, Ranjel states that "on Friday, May 7, Baltasar de Gallegos, with the most of the soldiers of the army, arrived at Ilapi to eat seven barbacoas of corn that they said were stored for the woman chief."[1] If Cofitachequi was Kasihta it is quite possible that other Muskogee settlements were in the neighborhood and that Ilapi was the town later called Hilibi. It is true that Hilibi is known to us almost entirely as a town of the Upper Creeks, but several of the well-known Upper Creek towns of later times were once as far east as the Ocmulgee. In northwestern Georgia is a creek called Hilibi Creek, which may mark a former town site of this tribe while on its way west. When we first get a clear historic view of the town it is on the creek which still bears the name in Alabama. On the De Crenay map the name is spelled "Ilapé," which suggests the form given by Ranjel.[2] The *p* form is used by the Lower Creeks. It appears in the census lists of 1738 and 1750 as

[1] Bourne, Narr. of De Soto, II, p. 100.

[2] Plate 5; also Hamilton, Col. Mobile, p. 190.

"Ylapé,"[1] and in those of 1760[2] and 1761.[3] In the third of these there is also a "Little Hilibi."[2] In 1761 it was assigned, along with its outsettlements, to Crook & Co.[3] Bartram places it among the Coosa towns,[4] and Swan gives it as one of the towns "central, inland, in the high country, between the Coosa and Tallapoosee Rivers, in the district called the Hillabees."[5] The town and its branches are thus described by Hawkins:

Hill-au-bee; on Col-luf-fa-dee [kålofti="bluff"], which joins Hill-au-bee Creek, on the right side, one mile below the town. Hill-au-bee joins the Tallapoosa on its right bank, eight miles below New-yau-cau. One chief only, Ene-hau-thluc-co Hau-jo [Heniha łåko Hadjo], resides in the town; the people are settled out in the four following villages:

1st. Thlā-noo-che au-bau-lau; from thlenne [łini], a mountain, oo-che [utci], little, and au-bau-lau [abåla], over. The name is expressive of its position. It is situated over a little mountain, fifteen miles above the town, on the northwest branch of Hill-au-bee Creek; the town house of this village is on the left side of the creek.

2nd. Au-net-te chap-co; from au-net-te, a swamp, and chapco, long.[6] It is situated on Choo-fun-tau-lau-hat-che [tcufi itålwa håtci, Rabbit Town Creek], which joins Hill-au-bee Creek three miles north from the town; the village is ten miles above the town.

3d. E-chuse-is-li-gau (where a young thing was found). A young child was found here, and that circumstance gives it the name. This village is four miles below the town, on the left side of Hill-au-bee Creek.

4th. Ook-tau-hau-zau-see; from ook-tau-hau [oktaha], sand, and zau-see [sasi], a great deal. It is two miles from the town, on a creek of that name, a branch of Hill-au-bee, which it joins a quarter of a mile below Col-luf-fa-dee, at a great shoal.

The land on these creeks, within the scope of the four villages, is broken and stoney, with coarse gravel; the bottoms and small bends of the creeks and branches are rich. The upland is generally stiff, rich, and fit for culture. Post oak, black oak, pine, and hickory, all small, are the growth. The whole abounds in veins of reeds and reedy branches. They call this the winter reed, as it clusters like the cane.

The villages are badly fenced, the Indians are attentive to their traders, and several of them are careful of stock and have cattle and hogs, and some few have horses. Four half-breeds have fine stocks of cattle. Thomas has one hundred and thirty cattle and ten horses. Au-wil-lau-gee,[7] the wife of O-pi-o-che-tus-tun-nug-gee,[8] has seventy[9] cattle. These Indians promised the agent, in 1799, to begin and fence their fields; they have one hundred and seventy gunmen in the four villages.

Robert Grierson,[10] the trader, a native of Scotland, has, by a steady conduct, contributed to mend the manners of these people. He has five children, half breeds, and governs them as Indians, and makes them and his whole family respect him, and is

1 MSS., Ayer Coll.

2 Miss. Prov. Arch., I, p. 95.

3 Ga. Col. Docs., VIII, p. 523.

4 Bartram, Travels, p. 462.

5 Schoolcraft, Ind. Tribes, V, p. 262.

6 Au-net-te really means a grassy thicket that one can hardly get through; a swamp is piłofa. A battle was fought here on Jan. 24, 1814.

7 Awûlgi, "they came out."

8 Abohiyutci tåstånagi, "Putting-something-down warrior."

9 The published edition has "seven."

10 In notes taken in 1797 Hawkins adds that "David Hay was his hireling," and that another white man in Hilibi, evidently a trader, was "Stephen Hawkins, an active man of weak mind; fond of drink, and much of a savage when drunk."—Ga. Hist. Soc. Colls., IX, p. 169. Robert Grierson was the direct ancestor of the late G. W. Grayson, chief of the Creek Nation.

the only man who does so in the Upper Creeks. He has three hundred cattle and thirty horses; he has, on the recommendation of the agent for Indian affairs, set up a manufactury of cotton cloth; he plants the green-seed cotton, it being too cold for the blackseed. He has raised a quantity for market, but finds it more profitable to manufacture it; he has employed an active girl of Georgia, Rachael Spillard, who was in the Cherokee department, to superintend, and allows her two hundred dollars per annum. He employs eleven hands, red, white, and black, in spinning and weaving, and the other part of his family in raising and preparing the cotton for them. His wife, an Indian woman, spins, and is fond of it; and he has a little daughter who spins well. He employs the Indian women to gather in the cotton from the fields, and has expectations of prevailing on them to take an active part in spinning.

Hill-au-bee creek has a rocky bottom, covered in many places with moss. In the spring of the year the cattle of the villages crowd after it, and are fond of it. From thence they are collected together by their owners, to mark and brand the young ones.

The climate is mild; the water seldom freezes; they have mast every other year, and peaches for the three last years. The range is a good one for stock. The owners of horses have a place called a stomp. They select a place of good food, cut down a tree or two, and make salt logs. Here the horses gather of themselves in the fly season. They have in the village a few thriving peach trees, and there is much gravelly land, which would be fine for them.[1]

A battle was fought near Hilibi town on November 18, 1813.

Another village which separated from Hilibi was known as Kitcopataki, "a wooden mortar spread out," perhaps referring to an old rotten mortar. It may have originated after Hawkins's time, since it is first mentioned in the census rolls of 1832.[2] It is the only branch clearly remembered at the present day. Of the older villages the most prominent was Oktahasasi, which appears to have maintained a separate existence for a considerable period. It is not to be confused with a modern settlement known as Oktaha, "Sand town," composed of families which had fled from the other villages to avoid being involved in the Creek-American war. After their removal to Oklahoma the latter lived for a time upon the Verdigris River, but subsequently appear to have separated. Kitcopataki does not have a distinct busk ground at the present time, but that of Hilibi is (1912) kept up near Hanna, Oklahoma.

The Eufaula

The Eufaula tribe was an independent body as far back as history takes us. According to one of my informants they branched off from Kealedji, while another seemed to think that they originated from Hilibi. Practically no confidence can be placed in these opinions. Not even a plausible guess can be furnished by the living Indians regarding the origin of the name. It is an interesting commentary on the reliability of name interpretation that a story is told to account for the designation of this place, the point of which depends on its resemblance to the English "you fall."

[1] Ga. Hist. Soc. Colls., III, pp. 43–45.

[2] Senate Doc. 512, 23d Cong., 1st sess., IV, pp. 318–319.

In Bartow County, Georgia, is a creek called Euharlee, corrupted from Cherokee Yuhali. According to the Cherokee, *fide* Mooney, this in turn is a corruption of the Creek tribal name Eufaula.[1] There is every reason to credit this and to suppose that the Eufaula were once located in the neighborhood. Perhaps it was their seat before the Yamasee war, in 1715. As the Kasihta and Kawita were in this region there is no reason why the Eufaula may not have been there as well. Their next location known to us was on Talladega Creek, a few miles south of the present Talladega, Alabama. It was afterwards known as Eufaula Old Town, but Hawkins calls it "Eu-fau-lau-hat-che" (Eufaula Creek or River), and describes it as follows:

Eau-fau-lau-hat-che, is fifteen miles up that creek [Eufaula or Talladega], on a flat of half a mile, bordering on a branch. On the left side of the creek the land is rich and waving; on the right sides are steep hills sloping off waving, rich land; hickory, oak, poplar and walnut. It is well watered, and the whole a desirable limestone country; they have fine stocks of cattle, horses, and hogs.[2]

This description dates from a time long after the Eufaula settlements next to be considered had been made, but it is probable that its inhabitants were also Eufaulas, some who had remained behind after the removal of the bulk of the population. James Lesley was the trader stationed there in 1796. He died in the spring of 1799.[3] Bartram and Swan mention this town, which they call Upper Eufaula, Swan describing it as "the Creek town farthest up Coosa River."[4]

At a comparatively early date in the eighteenth century, as appears from the maps, particularly that of De Crenay,[5] a large part of the Eufaula Indians moved southeast and settled on the middle course of the Tallapoosa. These are the "Lower Yufale" of Bartram, and the "Eu-fau-lau" of Hawkins.[6] Swan mentions two settlements here, "Big Ufala" and "Little Ufala."[7] It is the Eufaula of the censuses of 1738, 1750, 1760, and 1761.[8] The following is Hawkins's description of this town.

Eu-fau-lau; on the right bank of Tallapoosa, five miles below Oc-fus-kee, on that side of the river, and but two in a direct line; the lands on the river are fit for culture; but the flats are narrow, joined to pine hills and reedy branches.

They have hogs and cattle, and the range is a good one; they have moss in the shoals of the river; there are belonging to this town, seventy gun men, and they have begun to settle out for the benefit of their stock. This season, some of the villagers have fenced their fields. They have some fine land on Hat-che-lus-te [Hátci lásti] and several settlements there, but no fences; this creek joins the right side of the river, two

---

1 19th Ann. Rept. Bur. Amer. Ethn., p. 547.

2 Ga. Hist. Soc. Colls., III, pp. 42–43.

3 Ibid., IX, pp. 34, 169.

4 Bartram, Travels, p. 461; Schoolcraft, Ind. Tribes, V, p. 262.

5 Plate 5; Hamilton, Col. Mobile, p. 190.

6 Bartram, op. cit.; Ga. Hist. Soc. Colls., III, p. 25.

7 Schoolcraft, op. cit.

8 MSS., Ayer Coll.; Miss. Prov. Arch. I, p. 95; Ga. Col. Docs, VIII, p. 523.

miles below the town. On Woc-cau E-hoo-te [Waka ihuti, "cow yard"], this year, 1799, the villages, five families in all, have fenced their fields, and they have promised the agent to use the plough the next season. On black creek, Co-no-fix-ico [Kono fiksiko; kono="skunk"] has one hundred cattle, and makes butter and cheese. John Townshend, the trader of the town, is an honest Englishman, who has resided many years in the nation, and raised a numerous family, who conduct themselves well. His daughters, who are married, conduct themselves well, have stocks of cattle, are attentive to them, make butter and cheese, and promise to raise cotton and learn to spin. The principal cattle holders are Conofixico, who has one hundred; Choc-lo Emautlau's stock is on the decline, thirty; Will Geddis Taupixa Micco [Tapiksi miko; tapiksi="flat"], one hundred; Co Emautlau [Kowai imala; kowai=quail,] four hundred under careful management. John Townshend, one hundred and forty, and Sally, his daughter, fifty.[1]

This is the only Upper Creek town of the name represented in the census list of 1832,[2] and the only one now recognized among the Creeks in Oklahoma. It is, and since the removal always has been, located in the extreme southeastern part of the nation near the modern town of Eufaula, Oklahoma, which bears its name.

A Eufaula settlement was also made among the Lower Creeks, and although this appears on very few maps before the end of the eighteenth century, we know that it antedates 1733, because it occurs on the De Crenay map of that year.[3]

November 20, 1752, Thomas Bosomworth visited the Eufaula town among the Lower Creeks in search of some horses which had been stolen from the English. He describes it as "the Lowest in the Nation but two" and "about forty five miles from the Cowetas, and as it is chiefly composed of Runagados from all other Towns of the Nation, it is reckoned one of the most unrully, as they all Command and none obey." [4]

The name of this town appears in the census lists of 1760 and 1761,[5] but it is wanting from the lists of Bartram and Swan. The official trader there in 1761 was James Cussings.[5] Hawkins gives the following description:

Eu-fau-lau; is fifteen miles below Sau-woog-e-lo, on the left bank of the river, on a pine flat; the fields are on both sides of the river, on rich flats; below the town the land is good.

These people are very poor, but generally well behaved and very friendly to white people; they are not given to horse-stealing, have some stock, are attentive to it; they have some land fenced, and are preparing for more; they have spread out their settlements down the river; about eight miles below the town, counting on the river path, there is a little village on good land, O-ke-teyoc-en-ne.[6] Some of the village is well fenced; they raise plenty of corn and rice, and the range is a good one for stock.

From this village they have settlements down as low as the forks of the river; and they are generally on sites well chosen, some of them well cultivated; they raise plenty

[1] Ga. Hist. Soc. Colls., III, p. 48; cf. Taitt in Mereness, Trav. Am. Col., p. 528.
[2] Senate Doc. 512, 23d Cong., 1st sess., pp. 275-278.
[3] Plate 5; Hamilton, Col. Mobile, p. 190.
[4] Bosomworth's MS. Journal, in S. C. Archives.
[5] Miss. Prov. Arch., I, p. 96; Ga. Col. Docs., VIII, p. 522.
[6] This was a branch of Sawokli; see p. 143.

of corn and rice, and have cattle, horses, and hogs. Several of these Indians have Negroes, taken during the Revolutionary War, and where they are there is more industry and better farms. These Negroes were, many of them, given by the agents of Great Britain to the Indians, in payment for their services, and they generally call themselves "King's gifts." The Negroes are all of them attentive and friendly to white people, particularly so to those in authority.[1]

Lower Eufaula appears again in the census rolls of 1832, which also mention a branch village on a creek called "Chowokolohatches."[2] Among the Creeks in Oklahoma the town is known as "Yufā'la hopai', "the far-away Eufaula," and it maintained its own square ground for some time after the emigration, but this has now been given up. Part of the Eufaula went to Florida in 1761 and made a settlement afterwards known as Tcuko tcati, "Red house."[3]

The Wakokai

The readily interpretable nature of this name, which signifies "heron breeding place," suggests that the Wakokai were not an ancient Creek division; but not sufficient evidence has been found, traditional or other, to suggest an origin from any one of the remaining groups. Notice might be taken in this connection of the river Guacuca (Wakuka) crossed by the De Soto expedition just after leaving the Apalachee country.[4] Their first historical appearance is probably on the De Crenay map of 1733, which represents them on Coosa River below the Pakan tallahassee Indians.[5] Wakokai is now reckoned as a White town, but was formerly, according to the best informants, on the Red side like Hilibi and Eufaula. The name appears in the lists of 1738, 1750, 1760, and 1761, and in those of Bartram, Swan, and Hawkins.[6] The last mentioned gives the following account of its condition in 1799:

Woc-co-coie; from woc-co, a blow-horn, and coie, a nest;[7] these birds formerly had their young here. It is on Tote-pauf-cau [Tukpafka, punk used in lighting a fire] creek, a branch of Po-chuse-hat-che, which joins the Coo-sau, below Puc-cun-tal-lau-has-see. The land is very broken, sharp-hilly, and stoney; the bottoms and the fields are on the small bends and narrow strips of the creek; the country, off from the town, is broken.

These people have some horses, hogs, and cattle; the range good; moss, plenty in the creeks, and reed in the branches. Such is the attachment of horses to this moss, or as the traders call it, salt grass, that when they are removed they retain so great a fondness for it that they will attempt, from any distance within the neighboring nations, to return to it.[8]

---

[1] Ga. Hist. Soc. Colls., III, p. 66.

[2] Senate Doc. 512, 23d Cong., 1st sess., IV, pp. 337–342, 378–379.

[3] See p. 403.

[4] Bourne, Narr. of De Soto, II, p. 82.

[5] Plate 5; Hamilton, Col. Mobile, p. 190.

[6] MSS., Ayer Lib.; Miss. Prov. Arch., I, p. 95; Ga. Col. Docs., VIII, p. 523; Bartram, Travels, p. 462; Schoolcraft, Ind. Tribes, V, p. 262; Ga. Hist. Soc. Colls., III, p. 25.

[7] See above.

[8] Hawkins in Ga. Hist. Soc. Colls., III, p. 43.

Yet in an earlier list of towns, dated 1796, Hawkins does not mention this town, but only its branches, Wiogufki and Tukpafka, of which Wakokai is always said to be the "mother." The traders are given as John Clark, a Scotchman, and George Smith, an Englishman, respectively.[1] There is evidently some confusion, however, since a year later Hawkins gives James Clark as trader at Wakokai and George Smith trader at Wiogufki; the name of James Simmons is added as that of a trader at Wakokai.[2] Wiogufki and Tukpafka appear again in the census rolls of 1832,[3] from which the older name is wanting for the first time. A very good Hilibi informant told me that the Wiogufki, "muddy stream," people separated from the Wakokai first and received their name from a creek on which they had established themselves. A log lay across this, which was used by the people as a footlog, and after a time another town grew up on the side of the creek reached by it. In time this log decayed and fell away until it was nothing but punk, but the people of the new village said that, although it had fallen into punk, yet they had crossed upon it, so they took to themselves the name of Tukpafka. Regarding the main fact of relationship between the three, there can be no doubt, however the separation may have taken place. The Tukpafka mentioned here are not to be confounded with those Okfuskee Indians afterwards called Nuyaka.[4]

Some of my very best informants among the modern Creek Indians, including Jackson Lewis, now dead but in his lifetime one of the most intelligent among the older men, have told me that Sakapadai was a branch of Eufaula, although later associated with Wiogufki and Tukpafka. One even maintained that Wiogufki itself was a branch of Eufaula. Others, however, assured me with equal emphasis that it had separated from the Wakokai towns, and probability is in their favor, since Benjamin Hawkins, writing in 1797, says that Sakapadai and Wiogufki were "one fire with Woccocoie."[5] It is, of course, possible that a more remote relationship existed, as suggested above, between the Wakokai towns and Eufaula, and perhaps Hilibi, but the information so far available rather points to relationship having been assumed on the ground of an intimate association in later times between the towns concerned. Jackson Lewis told the following story regarding the origin of this town:

Some Eufaula left their town and tried to establish one of their own, but they were a shiftless people and failed. Afterwards those who passed the place where they had started their village could see old baskets lying about torn to pieces and flattened out. From this circumstance the people of the place came to be called Sakapadai (from *saka*, a basket like a hamper, and *padai*, "flattened out"). On account of the

[1] Ga. Hist. Soc. Colls., IX, p. 34.
[2] Ibid., p. 169.
[3] Senate Doc. 512, 23d Cong., 1st sess., IV, pp. 286–292.
[4] See p. 248.
[5] Ga. Hist. Soc. Colls., IX, p. 170.

failure of their attempt they also came to be called Tallahassee ("Old town" people), and later on Tallahasutci ("Little Old town" people).

Gatschet, however, says that the name "probably refers to water lilies covering the surface of a pond," the seeds of which were eaten by the natives.[1]

THE ATASI

Atasi, in its later years, was on close terms of intimacy with Tukabahchee, of which it was said to be a branch. While this may have been the case, its independent history extends back to very early times. Spanish documents of the last decade of the sixteenth century mention a town called Otaxe (Otashe), in the northernmost parts of the province of Guale. On a few maps, representing conditions before the Yamasee war, Atasi appears among the towns on Ocmulgee River. It is perhaps the "Awhissie" of Lamhatty, laid down midway between the Chattahoochee and Flint Rivers.[2] On later maps it appears on the Chattahoochee between the Kolomi and Tuskegee, but this position was probably occupied for only a few years before a permanent retirement was effected to the Tallapoosa. Another location is, however, given by Hawkins on the authority of an old Kasihta chief, Tussikaia miko, as on a creek bearing its name, near the village of Apatai (see p. 223).[3] A French writer of the middle of the eighteenth century declares that the Creeks on Tallapoosa River were formerly under absolute monarchs who resided at Atasi "and bore the same name" as the town. He adds: "After the death of the last of these princes there was no particular chief in this village, but the chief of war commands. They say that this chief has gone into the sky to see his ancestors, and that he has assured them that he will return."[4] This perhaps marks nothing more than a shift of the chieftainship from a peace to a war clan.

At least three successive places were occupied by the Atasi on Tallapoosa River. The first was some miles above the sharp bend in the river at Tukabahchee, where Bartram found them in 1777–78.[5] The second was five miles below Tukabahchee on the south side of the river,[6] and the third a few miles higher on the north side near the mouth of Calebee Creek. The name appears in the census lists of 1738, 1750, 1760, and 1761.[7] On the last mentioned date James McQueen and T. Perryman were the officially recognized traders.[7]

---

1 Gatschet in Misc. Colls. Ala. Hist. Soc., I, p. 408.

2 Amer. Anthrop., n. s. vol. X, p. 569.

3 Ga. Hist. Soc. Colls., IX, p. 70.

4 MS., Ayer Lib.

5 Bartram, Travels, p. 448 et seq.

6 Ga. Hist. Soc. Colls., IX, pp. 40, 46. "On the opposite bank [from Mr. Bailey's house] formerly stood the old town Ohassee [Ottassee], a beautifui rich level plane surrounded with hills, to the north, it was formerly a canebrake, the river, makes a curve round it to the south, so that a small fence on the hill side across would enclose it."—p. 40.

7 MSS., Ayer Lib.; Miss Prov. Arch., I, p. 95; Ga. Col. Docs., VIII, p. 523.

Bartram in 1777–78 described the square of this town at some length; his account will be given when we come to consider the social organization of the confederacy. The name appears also in the lists of Hawkins and on the census rolls of 1832, but is omitted by Swan.[1] In 1797 the traders stationed there were Richard Bailey, a native of England, and Josiah Fisher.[2] The following is what Hawkins has to say of it:

Aut-tos-see, on the left side of Tallapoosa, below and adjoining Ca-le-be-hat-che. A poor, miserable looking place, fenced with small poles; the first on forks in a line and two others on stakes hardly sufficient to keep out cattle. They have some plum and peach trees; a swamp back of the town and some good land back of that, a flat of oak, hickory and pine. On the right bank of the river, just below the town, they have a fine rich cove of land which was formerly a cane brake, and has been cultivated.

There is, [5 miles] below the town, one good farm made by the late Richard Bailey, and an orchard of peach trees. Mrs. Bailey, the widow, is neat, clean, and industrious, and very attentive to the interests of her family; qualities rarely to be met with in an Indian woman.[3] Her example has no effect on the Indians, even her own family, with the exception of her own children. She has fifty bee-hives and a great supply of honey every year; has a fine stock of hogs, cattle and horses, and they all do well. Her son, Richard Bailey, was educated in Philadelphia by the Government, and he has brought with him into the nation so much contempt for the Indian mode of life, that he has got himself into discredit with them. His young brother is under the direction of the Quakers in Philadelphia. His three sisters promise to do well, they are industrious and can spin. Some of the Indians have cattle; but in general, they are destitute of property.

In the year 1766 there were forty-three gun men, and lately they were estimated at eighty. This is a much greater increase of population than is to be met with in other towns; they appear to be stationary generally, and in some towns are on the decrease; the apparent difference here, or increase, may be greater than the real; as formerly men grown were rated as gun men, and now boys of fifteen, who are hunters, are rated as gun men; they have for two years past been on the decline; are very sickly, and have lost many of their inhabitants; they are now rated at fifty gun men only.[4]

One outsettlement is mentioned by Hawkins, on "Caloebee" Creek, although at the time he wrote (December 27, 1797)[5] it was abandoned. It appears on the Purcell map (pl. 7) as "Callobe."

Atasi was the seat of a leading camp of hostile Indians during the Creek War and the site of one of its principal battles, November 29, 1813. It suffered severely in consequence, and, whether on account of that struggle or for other causes, the number of Atasi Indians has been reduced to a mere handful.

---

[1] Ga. Hist. Soc. Colls., III, p. 25; Senate Doc. 512, 23d Cong., 1st sess., IV, pp. 252–254.

[2] Ga. Hist. Soc. Colls., IX, p. 168.

[3] She belonged to the Hotálgalgi, or Wind Clan.—Hawkins in Ga. Hist. Soc. Colls., IX, p. 39. Misprinted "Otalla (wine) family."

[4] Ga. Hist. Soc. Colls., III, pp. 31–32.

[5] Ibid., IX, p. 49.

The Kolomi

The earliest mention of Kolomi town is contained in a letter of the Spanish lieutenant at Apalachee, Antonio Mateos, in 1686.[1] A translation of this has been given in considering the history of the Kasihta.[2] The town was then probably on Ocmulgee River, where it appears on some of the very early maps, placed close to Atasi. From the failure of Mateos to mention Atasi it is possible that that town was not yet in existence. From later maps we learn that after the Yamasee war the Kolomi settled on the Chattahoochee. The maps show them in what is now Stewart County, Ga., but Colomokee Creek in Clay County may perhaps mark a former settlement of Kolomi people farther south. The name is often given on maps in the form "Colomino."[3] Still later they removed to the Tallapoosa, where, as appears from Bartram, they first settled upon the east bank but later moved across.[4] In all these changes they seem to have kept company with the Atasi. Their name appears in the lists of 1738, 1750, 1760, and 1761. In 1761 their officially recognized trader was James Germany.[5] Bartram thus describes the town in 1777:

Here are very extensive old fields, the abandoned plantations and commons of the old town, on the east side of the river; but the settlement is removed, and the new town now stands on the opposite shore, in a charming fruitful plain, under an elevated ridge of hills, the swelling beds or bases of which are covered with a pleasing verdure of grass; but the last ascent is steeper, and towards the summit discovers shelving rocky cliffs, which appear to be continually splitting and bursting to pieces, scattering their thin exfoliations over the tops of the grassy knolls beneath. The plain is narrow where the town is built; their houses are neat commodious buildings, a wooden frame with plastered walls, and roofed with Cypress bark or shingles; every habitation consists of four oblong square houses, of one story, of the same form and dimensions, and so situated as to form an exact square, encompassing an area or court yard of about a quarter of an acre of ground, leaving an entrance into it at each corner. Here is a beautiful new square or areopagus, in the centre of the new town; but the stores of the principal trader, and two or three Indian habitations, stand near the banks of the opposite shore on the site of the old Coolome town. The Tallapoose River is here three hundred yards over, and about fifteen or twenty feet deep; the water is very clear, agreeable to the taste, esteemed salubrious, and runs with a steady, active current.[6]

A little later Bartram called again and has the following to say regarding the trader, James Germany, mentioned above:

[I] called by the way at the beautiful town of Coolome, where I tarried some time with Mr. Germany the chief trader of the town, an elderly gentleman, but active, cheerful and very agreeable, who received and treated me with the utmost civility and friendship; his wife is a Creek woman, of a very amiable and worthy character

---

[1] Serrano y Sanz, Doc. Hist., pp. 194–195.

[2] See p. 221.

[3] This form of the name suggests a derivation from kulo, a kind of oak with large acorns, and omin, "where there are."

[4] Bartram, Travels, p. 394.

[5] MSS., Ayer Lib.; Miss. Prov. Arch., I, p. 94; Ga. Col. Docs., VIII, p. 523.

[6] Bartram, Travels, pp. 394–395.

and disposition, industrious, prudent and affectionate; and by her he has several children, whom he is desirous to send to Savanna or Charleston, for their education, but can not prevail on his wife to consent to it.[1]

In May, 1797, according to a list compiled by Hawkins, there was no trader in this town, but in a subsequent list, dated September of the same year, he gives William Gregory, who was formerly a hireling of Nicholas White at Fus-hatchee.[2] Swan (1791) mentions the place,[3] and Hawkins (1799) thus describes it:

Coo-loo-me is below and near to Foosce-hat-che, on the right side of the river; the town is small and compact, on a flat much too low, and subject to be overflowed in the seasons of floods, which is once in fifteen or sixteen years, always in the winter season, and mostly in March; they have, within two years, begun to settle back, next to the broken lands; the cornfields are on the opposite side, joining those of Foosce-hat-che, and extend together near four miles down the river, from one hundred to two hundred yards wide. Back of these hills there is a rich swamp of from four to six hundred yards wide, which, when reclaimed, must be valuable for corn and rice and could be easily drained into the river, which seldom overflows its banks, in spring or summer.

They have no fences; they have huts in the fields to shelter the laborers in the summer season from rain, and for the guards set to watch the crops while they are growing. At this season some families move over and reside in their fields, and return with their crops into the town. There are two paths, one through the fields on the river bank, and the other back of the swamp. In the season for melons the Indians of this town and Foosce-hat-che show in a particular manner their hospitality to all travellers, by calling to them, introducing them to their huts or the shade of their trees, and giving them excellent melons, and the best fare they possess. Opposite the town house, in the fields, is a conical mound of earth thirty feet in diameter, ten feet high, with large peach trees on several places. At the lower end of the fields, on the left bank of a fine little creek, Le-cau-suh, is a pretty little village of Coo-loo-me people, finely situated on a rising ground; the land up this creek is waving pine forest.[4]

The name of this town is wanting from the census rolls of 1832, and there is little doubt that the tradition is correct which states that it was one of those which went to Florida after the Creek war of 1813.[5] A part of the Kolomi people were already in that country, since they are noted in papers of John Stuart, the British Indian agent, dated 1778.[6] According to a very old Creek Indian, now dead, Kolomi decreased so much in numbers that it united with Fus-hatchee, and Fus-hatchee decreased so much that it united with Atasi, with which the town of Kan-hatki, to be mentioned below, also combined. But, as we shall see, this can not have been altogether true, though it is an undoubted fact that the towns mentioned were closely united in terms of friendship. While Kolomi is still preserved as a war name very few of the Creeks in Oklahoma remember it as a town.

[1] Bartram, Travels, pp. 447–448.
[2] Ga. Hist. Soc. Colls., IX, pp. 168–195.
[3] Schoolcraft, Ind. Tribes, V, p. 262.
[4] Ga. Hist. Soc. Colls., III, pp. 33–34.
[5] See Gatschet in Misc. Colls. Ala. Hist. Soc., I, p. 401.
[6] Copy of MS. in Lib Cong.

The Fus-hatchee

The descriptive name of the Fus-hatchee and their intimate relations with Kolomi, Kan-hatki, and Atasi lead me to believe that they were a comparatively late branch of one of these. They appear first on the De Crenay map of 1733, in which they are placed on the south side of the Tallapoosa.[1] They are also in the lists of 1738, 1750, 1760, and 1761.[2] James Germany was their trader in the last mentioned year. In 1797 the trader was Nicholas White.[3] The name is in the lists of Bartram[4] and Hawkins,[5] and is evidently the "Coosahatchies" of Swan.[6] In his list of Creek traders, made in May, 1797, Hawkins assigns none to this town; but in a second, dated the following September, he gives the name of William McCart, who had formerly been a hireling of Abraham M. Mordecai at Hołiwahali.[7] Hawkins describes the town as follows:

> Foosce-hŏt-che; from foo-so-wau, a bird, and hot-che, tail.[8] It is two miles below Ho-ith-le-wau-le [Hołiwahali] on the right bank of Tal-la-poo-sa, on a narrow strip of flat land; the broken lands are just back of the town; the cornfields are on the opposite side of the river, and are divided from those of Ho-ith-le-wau-le by a small creek, Noo-coose-che-po. On the right bank of this little creek, half a mile from the river, is the remains of a ditch which surrounded a fortification, and back of this for a mile is the appearance of old settlements, and back of these, pine slashes.
>
> The cornfields are narrow, and extend down, bordering on the river.[9]

This was one of those towns which went to Florida after the Creek-American war, and consequently we find no mention of it in the census list of 1832. A small band is noted in northern Florida as early as 1778.[10] It was accompanied by Kan-hatki, and after the Seminole war the two moved westward together and formed a single settlement in the southern part of the Seminole Nation. There they constituted one district, known as Fus-hatchee, and were so represented in the Seminole council. Their square ground was, however, known as Łiwahali, because the leaders in forming it are said to have been Hołiwahali Indians.

The Kan-hatki

The history of the Kan-hatki or Ikan-hatki ("White ground") is parallel with that of the Fus-hatchee. They appear on the De Crenay map, in the lists of 1738, 1750, 1760, and 1761, and in those

[1] Plate 5; also Hamilton, Col. Mobile, p. 190.
[2] MSS., Ayer Lib.; Miss. Prov. Arch., I, p. 94; Ga. Col. Docs., VIII, p. 523.
[3] Ga. Hist. Soc. Colls., IX, p. 168.
[4] Bartram, Travels, p. 461.
[5] Ga. Hist. Soc. Colls., III, p. 25.
[6] Schoolcraft, Ind. Tribes, V, p. 262.
[7] Ga. Hist. Soc. Colls., IX, pp. 168, 195.
[8] This is erroneous. It should be fuswa, bird, and hàtci, river or stream.
[9] Ga. Hist. Soc. Colls., III, p. 33.
[10] Copy of MS. in Lib. Cong.

of Bartram, Swan, and Hawkins.[1] In 1761 their officially recognized traders were Crook & Co. Swan gives Kan-hatki as one of two towns occupied by Shawnee refugees, but this statement was probably due to the presence of some Shawnee from the neighboring settlement of Sawanogi. In September, 1797, Hawkins states that the trader here was a man named Copinger.[2] He gives the following account of the town:

E-cun-hut-ke; from e-cun-nā, earth, and hut-ke, white, called by the traders white ground. This little town is just below Coo-loo-me, on the same side of the river, and five or six miles above Sam-bul-loh, a large fine creek which has its source in the pine hills to the north and its whole course through broken pine hills. It appears to be a never-failing stream, and fine for mills; the fields belonging to this town are on both sides of the river.[3]

In the census list of 1832 is a town called "Ekun-duts-ke," which may be intended for this, but we know that a large part of the Kan-hatki went to Florida after 1813, and the name above given may have belonged to an entirely different settlement, since it could be translated "a section line" or "a boundary line." The later history of the Kan-hatki is bound up with that of the Fus-hatchee, to which the reader is referred.

The Wiwohka

According to tradition, Wiwohka was a made-up or "stray" town, formed of fugitives from other settlements, or those who found it pleasanter to live at some distance from the places of their birth. One excellent informant stated that anciently it was called Witumpka, but the names mean nearly the same thing, "roaring water" and "tumbling water." Both designations are said to have arisen from the nature of the place of origin of these people, near falls, and these may have been the falls of the Coosa. From the preservation of a purely descriptive name and their comparatively recent appearance in Creek history it may be fairly assumed that they had not had a long existence. Their name appears on the De Crenay map, in the lists of 1738, 1750, 1760, and 1761.[4] It is wanting from Bartram's list, but reappears in those of Swan and Hawkins and in the census rolls of 1832.[5] The census of 1761 couples it with "New Town," and gives the traders as William Struthers and J. Morgan.[6] The irregular nature of its origin may perhaps be associated with its later responsibility for the Creek war of 1813 and the

[1] MSS., Ayer Lib.; Hamilton, Col. Mobile, p. 190; Miss. Prov. Arch., I, p. 94; Ga. Col. Docs., VIII, p. 523; Bartram, Travels, p. 461; Schoolcraft, Ind. Tribes, V, p. 262; Ga. Hist. Soc. Colls., III, p. 25.

[2] Ga. Hist. Soc. Colls., IX, pp. 168, 195.

[3] Ibid., III, p. 34.

[4] Plate 5; MSS., Ayer Lib.; Miss. Prov. Arch., I, p. 95; Ga. Col. Docs., VIII, p. 523.

[5] Schoolcraft, Ind. Tribes, V, p. 262; Ga. Hist. Soc. Colls., III, p. 25; Senate Doc. 512, 23d Cong., 1st sess., IV, pp. 282–283.

[6] Ga. Col. Docs., op. cit.

Green Peach war in Oklahoma, both of which are laid to its charge. At the present time it has so far died away that but few real Wiwohka Indians remain. Its later relations were closest with the Okchai Indians with whom the survivors now busk.

The following is Hawkins's description of this town as it was in 1799:

We-wo-cau; from we-wau, water, and wo-cau, barking or roaring, as the sound of water at high falls. It lies on a creek of the same name, which joins Puc-cun-tal-lau-has-see, on its left bank, sixteen miles below that town. We-wo-cau is fifteen miles[1] above O-che-au-po-fau and four miles from Coosau, on the left side; the land is broken, oak and hickory, with coarse gravel; the settlements are spread out, on several small streams, for the advantage of the rich flats bordering on them and for their stock; they have cattle, horses, and hogs. Here commences the moss, in the beds of the creeks, which the cattle are very fond of; horses and cattle fatten very soon on it, with a little salt; it is of quick growth, found only in the rocky beds of the creeks and rivers north from this.

The hills which surround the town are stony, and unfit for culture; the streams all have reed, and there are some fine licks near the town, where it is conjectured salt might be made. The land on the right side of the creeks is poor, pine, barren hills to the falls. The number of gun men is estimated at forty.[2]

The Kealedji

According to native tradition this was a branch of Tukabahchee, but, if so, it must have separated at a very early date. Gatschet says that the name appears to refer to a warrior's headdress, containing the words *ika*, his head, and a verb meaning to kill (iłäidshäs, I kill).[3] This seems probable. At any rate the name evidently is not old enough to be worn down much by age and suggests a comparatively recent origin for the group. This is also confirmed to a considerable extent by the absence of its name from the earliest documents. Probably it is the "Gowalege" placed on a southern affluent of the Ocmulgee on the Moll map of 1720,[4] and perhaps the "Calalek" of the De Crenay map,[5] since in the French census of 1760 we find a town "Kalalekis"[6] which looks like a misprinted form of the name of this town. In the Spanish list of Creek towns made up in 1738 the name is spelled "Caialeche" and in that of 1750 "Kalechy."[7] It is certainly the "Coillegees near Oakchoy" of the census of 1761, the traders of which were Crook & Co.[8] In 1797 the traders were John O'Riley, an Irishman, and Townlay Bruce, of Maryland, formerly a clerk in the Indian Department, "removed for improper conduct."[9] It is in the list of Bartram[10] and in that of Swan,[11] and is thus described by Hawkins:

[1] The Lib. Cong. MS. has "17."
[2] Ga. Hist. Soc. Colls., III, pp. 40–41.
[3] Also on plate 3.
[4] Gatschet, Creek Mig. Leg., I, p. 133.
[5] Plate 5; also Hamilton, Col. Mobile, p. 190.
[6] Miss. Prov. Arch., I, p. 95.
[7] MSS., Ayer Lib.
[8] Ga. Col. Docs., VIII, p. 523.
[9] Ga. Hist. Soc. Colls., IX, p. 169.
[10] Bartram, Travels, p. 462.
[11] Schoolcraft, Ind. Tribes, V, p. 262.

Ki-a-li-jee; on the right side of Kialijee Creek, two and a half miles below the junction with Hook-choie. This creek joins the right side of Tallapoosa, above the falls; all the rich flats of the creek are settled; the land about the town is poor and broken; the fields are on the narrow flats and in the bends of the creek; the broken land is gravelly or stony; the range for cattle, hogs, and horses is the poorest in the nation; the neighborhood of the town and the town itself has nothing to recommend it. The timber is pine, oak, and small hickory; the creek is fifteen [1] feet wide, and joins Tallapoosa fifteen [1] miles above Took-au-bat-che. They have two villages belonging to this town.

1st. Au-che-nau-hat-che; from *au-che-nau*, cedar; and *hat-che*, a creek. They have a few settlements on this creek, and some fine, thriving peach trees; the land on the creek is broken, but good.[2]

2d. Hat-che-chub-bau; from *hat-che*, a creek; and *chub-bau*, the middle, or halfway. This is in the pine forest, a poor, ill-chosen site, and there are but a few people.[3]

The last-mentioned settlement and the main town were burned by hostile Creeks in 1813. The name Kealedji occurs in the list of 1832.[4] After their removal west these people settled in the southeastern part of the Creek Nation, where they still (1912) have a dance ground but no regular square.

Hatcheetcaba (Håtci tcåbå), the second village of Hawkins, appears as far back as the census of 1760.[5] It is also in those of 1761,[6] and 1832,[7] but not in the lists of Bartram and Swan. It preserved its identity after removal to Oklahoma, where it maintained a dance ground, but it is not certain that it ever had a regular square.

The Pakana

We now come to peoples incorporated in the Muskhogean confederation which were probably distinct bodies and yet not certainly possessed of a peculiar dialect like the Hitchiti, Alabama, and other tribes of foreign origin already considered. The Pakana are given by Adair as one of those people which the Muskogee had "artfully" induced to incorporate with them, and he is confirmed as to the main fact by Stiggins, whose account of them is as follows:

The Puccunnas at this day are only known by tradition to have been a distinct people and their antient town or habitation is called *Puccun Tal ahassee* which is *Puccun old town.* This antient town is in the present Coosa County of this State [Alabama]. The Au-bih-kas have a tradition that they were a distinct people and that they in old times were very numerous, but do not say whether they were immigrants or not, or at what time they became one of the national body. But they say as they belonged to the national body one and inseparable there was no distinction made so that by continual intermarriage with the other tribes they at length became absorbed and assimilated with their neighbors without distinction and no other knowledge is left regarding them but the name of their antient habitation. Whether in conversation they had a separate tongue of their own or not tradition is silent.[8]

---

1 The Lib. Cong. MS. has "20" in each of these places.

2 In his "Letters" he says this village consisted of "6 habitations and a small town house."—Ga. Hist. Soc. Colls., IX, p. 34.

3 Ga. Hist. Soc. Colls., III, pp. 48–49.

4 Senate Doc. 512, 23d Cong., 1st sess., IV, pp. 327–330.

5 Miss. Prov. Arch., I, p. 95.

6 Ga. Col. Docs., VIII, p. 523.

7 Senate Doc. 512, 23d Cong., 1st sess., IV, pp. 278–280.

8 Stiggins, MS., p. 5.

Not much can be added to this. There is a tradition among the modern Creeks that the Pakana separated from the Abihka, but it is evidently due to the proximity of the two peoples in ancient times and the number of intermarriages which took place between them. Again, an old Hilibi man told me that this town was founded by a Wiogufki Indian named Bakna, who held the first busk in his own yard, and whose name became attached to the new town. But Pakana was in existence long before Wiogufki. Wakokai, the mother town of Wiogufki, and the Pakana town were, however, located near each other, and to the close relations thence arising we may attribute the tradition. It is confusing to find the name Pakan tallahassee [Påkån talahasi] ("Pakana old town") used for these people in the very earliest mention of them, the De Crenay map of 1733.[1] Since we hear shortly afterwards of a Pakana tribe—distinct from the Pakan tallahassee, which first settled near Fort Toulouse and later migrated to Louisiana—a suggestion is raised whether the Pakan tallahassee may not have been Muskogee or other Indians who had occupied a site abandoned by the Pakana proper. We have something similar in the case of the Tukabahchee tallahassee, who were really an outsettlement of Okfuskee Indians.[2] While such an interpretation is possible I think the real fact was that a single tribe split in two after Fort Toulouse was established, one part locating near it as a convenient market. At that time the original body may have received the name "old town Pakana" to distinguish them from the emigrants. It is indeed strange that on the De Crenay map we find "old town Pakana" (Pakanatalaché), but no Pakana.[1] Still, this is not conclusive, for Fort Toulouse had probably been in existence 18 years when the map was prepared and the Pakana in its neighborhood may well have been overlooked. Both bodies appear in the lists of 1750, 1760,[3] and 1761, in which last year William Struthers and J. Morgan were the officially recognized traders.[4] In 1797 the trader was "John Proctor, a half-breed."[5] The division known as Pakan tallahassee appears also in the list of 1738[6] and those of Bartram, Swan, and Hawkins, and on the census rolls of 1832.[7] In 1768, or shortly before, it was burned by the Choctaw.[8] Hawkins derives the name "from E-puc-cun-nau, a may apple, and tal-lau-has-see, old town." The first word signifies properly "a peach"—*katabuya* is May apple—but it

[1] Plate 5; also Hamilton, Col. Mobile, p. 190.
[2] See p. 247.
[3] MSS., Ayer Lib.; Miss. Col. Arch., I, p. 95.
[4] Ga. Col. Docs., VIII, p. 523.
[5] Hawkins in Ga. Hist. Soc. Colls., IX, p. 169.
[6] MS., Ayer Lib.
[7] Bartram, Travels, p. 461; Schoolcraft, Ind. Tribes, IV, p. 578; V, p. 262; Ga. Hist. Soc. Colls., III, p. 25; Senate Doc. 512, 23d Cong., 2d sess., IV, pp 285–286.
[8] Eng. Trans., MS., Lib. Cong.

is doubtful whether its original meaning was related to either. The name Pakana may have a long antecedent history and a totally different origin. Hawkins adds:

It is in the fork of a creek which gives name to the town; the creek joins on the left side of Coosau, forty miles below Coo-sau town.[1]

After the removal they settled in the southern part of the Creek Nation near Hanna, Oklahoma, and have maintained their square ground in the same place ever since.

The Pakana who settled near Fort Toulouse probably never rejoined their kindred. From a letter written by M. d'Abbadie, governor of Louisiana, April 10, 1764, we know that they emigrated to Red River at the same time as the Taensa and Apalachee.[2] He calls them "Pakanas des Alibamons," either from the name of the French post or from the fact that they were supposed to be related to the Alabama Indians. The former supposition is, I believe, correct, since in the census of 1760 we find them classed as "Alybamons," not merely with the Koasati and Tuskegee, but also with the Okchai, some Coosa Indians, and some Indians called "Thomapas"; while, on the other hand, the Muklasa, Tawasa, and part of the Coosa are put among the "Talapouches," [3] Indians on Tallapoosa River. Evidently the classification is geographical, not linguistic. Later these Pakana settled upon Calcasieu River in southwestern Louisiana, as shown in the following account given by Sibley:

Pacanas, are a small tribe of about thirty men, who live on the Quelqueshoe [Calcasieu] River, which falls into the bay between Attakapa and Sabine, which heads in a prairie, called Cooko prairie, about forty miles southwest of Natchitoches. These people are likewise emigrants from West Florida, about forty years ago. Their village is about fifty miles southeast of the Conchattas; are said to be increasing a little in number; quiet, peaceable, and friendly people. Their own language differs from any other, but speak Mobilian. [4]

Still later some or all of these Pakana united with the Alabama living in Texas, where they are still remembered. The last survivor was an old woman who died many years ago. Her language was said to be distinct from Alabama, which would naturally be the case if it was Muskogee.

The Okchai

Like the Pakana, Adair includes the Okchai among those tribes which had been "artfully decoyed" to unite with the Muskogee,[5] and Milfort says that the Okchai and Tuskegee had sought the protection of the Muskogee after having suffered severely at the hands of hostile Indians. He adds that the former "mounted ten leagues toward

[1] Ga. Hist. Soc. Colls., III, p. 41.

[2] Amer. Antiq., XIII, pp. 252–253.

[3] Miss. Prov. Arch. I, p. 94.

[4] Sibley in Annals of Congress, 9th Cong., 2d sess., 1086 (1806–07).

[5] Adair, Hist. Am. Inds., p. 257.

the north [of the confluence of the Coosa and Tallapoosa Rivers] and fixed their dwelling in a beautiful plain on the bank of a little river."[1] Among some of the living Okchai there seems to be a tradition of this foreign origin, but nowhere do we find evidence that they spoke a diverse language. Their tongue may have been a dialect of Muskogee assimilated to the current speech in very ancient times.

This tribe appears on some of the earliest maps which locate Creek towns, such as that of Popple.[2] Their original seats were, as described by Milfort, on the western side of the Coosa some miles above its junction with the Tallapoosa. By 1738, however, a part of them had left that region and moved over upon a branch of Kialaga Creek, an affluent of the Tallapoosa.[3] Another portion evidently remained for a time near their old country, since the census of 1761 mentions "Oakchoys opposite the said [i. e., the French] fort."[4]

After the cession of Mobile and its dependencies to Great Britain these probably reunited with the main body. Okchai are indeed afterwards spoken of in the neighborhood of the old fort, but they appear to have been in reality Okchaiutci, part of the Alabama, whose history has been given elsewhere.[5] The last were probably those "Okchai" who accompanied the Koasati to the Tombigbee shortly after 1763.[6]

The Okchai proper are not noted by Bartram except under the general term "Fish Pond" Indians,[7] but appear in the lists of Swan[8] and Hawkins[9] and in the census rolls of 1832.[10] Hawkins has the following description:

> Hook-choie; on a creek of that name which joins on the left side of Ki-a-li-jee, three miles below the town and seven miles south of Thlo-tlo-gul-gau. The settlements extend along the creeks; on the margins of which and the hill sides are good oak and hickory, with coarse gravel, all surrounded with pine forest.[11]

After the emigration they established their square ground on the southern border of the Creek Nation, where it has remained ever since.

A small band is recorded among the Seminoles of northern Florida in 1778.[12]

Besides Okchaiutci, which was not properly a branch at all, several settlements were given out by this town. The most prominent and probably the most ancient of these was Łåłogålga ("Fish Place"), from which the traders' name of "Fish Pond" is derived.

[1] Milfort, Mémoire, p. 267.
[2] Plate 4.
[3] MS., Ayer Lib.
[4] Ga. Col. Docs., III, pp. 521-523.
[5] See pp. 200-201.
[6] See p. 203.
[7] Bartram, Travels, p. 462.
[8] Schoolcraft, Ind. Tribes, V, p. 262.
[9] Ga. Hist. Soc. Colls., III, p. 25.
[10] Senate Doc. 512, 23d Cong., 1st sess., IV, pp. 297-298.
[11] Ga. Hist. Soc. Colls., III, p. 37.
[12] Copy of MS. in Lib. Cong.

"Fish Pond" occurs first in Bartram,[1] but it was often applied to the Okchai Indians generally, and Łåłogålga appears first as a distinct settlement in Swan's list, 1791.[2] Hawkins (1799) describes it thus:

Thlot-lo-gul-gau; from thlot-lo, fish; and ulgau, all; called by the traders fishponds. It is on a small pond-like creek, a branch of Ul-kau-hat-che, which joins Tallapoosa four miles above Oc-fus-kee, on the right side. The town is fourteen miles up the creek; the land about it is open and waving; the soil is dark and gravelly; the general growth of trees is the small hickory; they have reed in the branches.

Hannah Hale resides here. She was taken prisoner from Georgia when about eleven or twelve years old, and married the head man of this town, by whom she has five children. This woman spins and weaves, and has taught two of her daughters to spin; she has labored under many difficulties, yet by her industry has acquired some property. She has one negro boy, a horse or two, sixty cattle, and some hogs; she received the friendly attention of the agent for Indian affairs as soon as he came into the nation. He furnished her with a wheel, loom, and cards; she has an orchard of peach and apple trees. Having made her election at the national council in 1799 to reside in the nation, the agent appointed Hopoithle Haujo to look out for a suitable place for her, to help her to remove to it with her stock, and take care that she receives no insults from the Indians.[3]

In 1796 the traders stationed there were "John Shirley and Isaac Thomas, the first an American, the latter of German parents."[4]

Evidently this is one of the two Fish Pond towns mentioned in the census list of 1832.[5] There is a square ground of the name in Oklahoma at the present time, but those who formed it were not direct descendants of the people who formed the old Łåłogålga town. When the removal took place all of the Okchai Indians came together and established one square ground near the present Hanna, Okla. Later, as the result of a fission in the tribe brought about by the Civil War, part moved away and settled near Okemah sometime after 1870. There they revived the old term Łåłogålga, which they have since employed.

Asilanabi was founded later than the first Łåłogålga and was so named because it was first located in a place where *Ilex vomitoria* was to be gathered. We do not find the name in print until we come to the census rolls of 1832.[5] There is a square ground in Oklahoma so called, but, as in the case of Łåłogålga, it has no historical continuity with the older settlement. It is the result of a later fission.

The Okchai living in Oklahoma claim that Potcas hatchee (Hatchet Creek) was a former settlement of theirs which was "lost." It was in existence in Hawkins's time and appears in the census list of 1832.[6] The following is Hawkins's description of it:

Po-chuse-hat-che; from po-chu-so-wau, a hatchet, and hat-che, a creek. This creek joins Coosau, four miles below Puc-cun-tal-lau-has-see, on its right bank; this

---

1 Bartram, Travels, p. 462.

2 Schoolcraft, Ind. Tribes, v, p. 262.

3 Ga. Hist. Soc. Colls., III, pp. 49–50; IX, p. 170.

4 Ga. Hist. Soc. Colls., IX, p. 34.

5 Senate Doc. 512, 23d Cong., 1st sess., IV, pp. 297–298.

6 Ga. Hist. Soc. Colls., III, p. 50; Senate Doc. 512, 23d Cong., 1st sess., IV, pp. 284–285.

village is high up the creek, nearly forty miles from its mouth, on a flat bend on the right side of the creek; the settlements extend up and down the creek for a mile. A mile and a half above the settlements there is a large canebrake, three-quarters of a mile through and three or four miles in length.

The land adjoining the settlement is waving and rich, with oak, hickory, and poplar. The branches all have reed; the neighboring lands above these settlements are fine; those below are high, broken hills. It is situated between Hill-au-bee and Woc-co-coie, about ten miles from each town; three miles west of the town there is a small mountain; they have some hogs.[1]

Probably the remnants of this town finally reunited with the main body. Two other "lost" settlements are also remembered—Tålså håtchi (Tulsa Creek) and Tcahki łåko (broad shallow ford). This last, however, may have been the Okfuskee village of that name, at one time on Chattahoochee River.[2]

The Tukabahchee

Tukabahchee was not only considered one of the four "foundation sticks" of the Creek Confederacy, but as the leading town among the Upper Creeks, and many add the leading town of the whole nation. During later historic times it was the most populous of all the upper towns, and is to-day the most populous without any exception. Like the other head towns, it has a special ceremonial title, Spokogi, or Ispokogi. Jackson Lewis thought this meant that Tukabahchee brooded over the other towns like a hen over her chickens. Another old Creek was of the opinion that it meant "to hold something firmly," since it was this town that held the confederacy together. Gatschet interprets it as "town of survivors," or "surviving town, remnant of a town." [3] It can not be said, however, that any of the suggested interpretations has great probability in its favor. As some early writers give the second consonant as *t* instead of *k*, the initial word in the name may have been *tutka*, fire. The original Spokogi were supposed to be certain beings who descended from the upper world to the Tukabahchee and brought them their medicine. From the intimacy which long subsisted between the Tukabahchee and Shawnee I am inclined to think that the resemblance between this word and that of one of the Shawnee bands, Kispokotha, or Kispogogi, is more than accidental.

It would certainly be a shock to almost any Creek to be told that this reputed capital of the confederacy, from which, according to some of them, the busk ceremonial was derived, was not originally a true Muskogee town at all. This, however, is the conclusion to which we are brought by a study of the facts concerning its early

---

[1] Ga. Hist. Soc. Colls., III, pp. 50–51.

[2] See p. 249.

[3] Gatschet, Creek Mig. Leg., I, p. 148.

history. It is the statement of Milfort, who probably derived his information from Alexander McGillivray, and who says:

About the same time [as that in which the Muskogee and Alabama finally made peace with each other] an Indian tribe which was on the point of being destroyed by the Iroquois and the Hurons, came to ask the protection of the Moskoquis, whom I will now call Crëcks. The latter received them among themselves and assigned them a region in the center of the nation. They built a town, which is now rather large, which is named Tuket-Batchet, from the name of the Indian tribe. The great assemblies of the Crëck Nation, of which it forms an integral part, are sometimes held within its walls.[1]

Alone this would not amount to proof, Milfort not being the most trustworthy authority, but Adair confirms it in the one important point. He quotes a Tukabahchee Indian of his time named "Old Bracket" to the effect that the people of this town "were a different people from the Creeks."[2] Their origin myth also appears to have varied considerably from that of the Creeks proper. This appears from some confused notes furnished by Gatschet,[3] but still more from the following legend preserved in the Tuggle collection, though that differs not so much in general plan as in the line of march, south instead of east.

The Took-a-batchees say that a long time ago their people had a great trouble and moved away. They came to water they could not cross. They built boats and crossed the water and marched south. They decided their course of march by a pole. They stood the pole perpendicularly and let it fall and in whatever direction it fell they marched in that direction. This pole was entrusted to a prophet. They continued marching south until the pole would not fall in any definite direction, but would wabble as it fell. Here they stopped and lived a long time. After a while another great trouble came and they resumed their march until they came to water, which was too wide to cross in boats, so they marched along the coast. They followed their pole going east till they came to Georgia, where they lived when the white people came to America.

A difference is possibly indicated in the claim made by the Tukabahchee that they are "a stray" (town). This is explained, however, on the ground that they could do as they pleased, and this again may have been on account of their superiority. They were also called Itålwa fåtca, "town deviating from strictness," a title said to have been shared by the Abihka.[4]

The migration legend just quoted is borne out in this particular, that when the Spaniards first heard of the Tukabahchee they appear to have been in Georgia, but it is improbable that they reached that country by marching along the coast. The earliest notice I have of them is in a letter of Antonio Mateos, lieutenant of the Apalachee province, of May 19, 1686, already several times mentioned, in

[1] Milfort, Mémoire, pp. 265-266.

[2] Adair, Hist. Am. Inds., p. 179.

[3] Gatschet, Creek Mig. Leg., I, p. 147.

[4] Ibid., p. 148.

which he says that Indians reported the English to have visited "the province of Ticopache."[1] From the description it would appear that Coweta lay between this "province" and Carolina. In 1695, in retaliation for attacks upon the Apalachee, an expedition consisting of 400 Apalachee Indians and 7 Spaniards visited the towns of Coweta, Kasihta, Oconee, and Tukabahchee ("Tiquipache"). In one—the narrative does not say which—they captured 50 persons, but they found the other places burned and abandoned.[2] The Oconee were on the Oconee River at this time and the Coweta and Kasihta on the Ocmulgee, so that it seems probable the Tukabahchee were then in the same general region. They perhaps removed as a result of the attack. Tukabahchee Tallahassee, noticed above as an Okfuskee town and located on the upper course of Tallapoosa River,[3] was probably so named because it occupied a site formerly held by the Tukabahchee, and it is likely that this was after their removal from Georgia.

It is to be noted that in most Tukabahchee traditions the Shawnee play a leading part, and Gatschet says that some Tukabahchee claimed they were Shawnee. This statement may, however, be accounted for by the metaphorical term employed to designate certain Tukabahchee clans. This association and their tradition of a northern origin lead to the suggestion that the Tukabahchee may have been those mysterious Kaskinampo discussed elsewhere who in the seventeenth century are frequently connected with the Shawnee Indians.[4]

In the South Carolina records under date of 1712 mention is made of two "Tukabugga" slaves.[5] The Tukabahchee appear among the Upper Creeks, but at an indeterminate place, on the De Crenay map of 1733.[6] Here the word is spelled "Totipaches," in the list of 1738 "Tiquipaxche," in that of 1750 "Totipache," and on the census list of 1760 "Totepaches."[7] In 1761 James McQueen and T. Perryman were officially recognized traders at this town, "including Pea Creek and other Plantations, Chactaw Hatchee Euchees, &c."[8] In 1797 the traders there were Christopher Heickle, a German, and Obadiah Lowe.[9] Bartram[10] and Swan[11] mention it, and Hawkins gives the following description of the town as it existed in 1799:

> Took-au-bat-che. The ancient name of this town is Is-po-co-gee; its derivation uncertain; it is situated on the right bank of the Tallapoosa, opposite the junction of

---

1 Serrano y Sanz, Doc. Hist., p. 195.

2 Ibid., p. 225.

3 See p. 247. Cf. "Tukabatchee old Fields," of plate 8.

4 See pp. 213–214.

5 Proc. of Board Dealing with Ind. Trade, p. 59, MS.

6 Plate 5; also Hamilton, Col. Mobile, p. 190.

7 MSS., Ayer Lib.; Miss. Prov. Arch., I, p. 95.

8 Ga. Col. Docs., VIII, p. 523.

9 Ga. Hist. Soc. Colls., IX, p. 168.

10 Bartram, Travels, p. 461.

11 Schoolcraft, Ind. Tribes, V, p. 262.

Eu-fau-be, two and a half miles below the falls of the river, on a beautiful level. The course of the river from the falls to the town is south; it then turns east three-quarters of a mile, and short round a point opposite Eu-fau-be, thence west and west-by-north to its confluence with Coosau, about thirty miles. It is one hundred [1] yards wide opposite the town house to the south, and here are two good fords during the summer,[2] one just below the point of a small island, the other one hundred yards still lower.

The water of the falls, after tumbling over a bed of rock for half a mile, is forced into two channels; one thirty, the other fifteen feet wide. The fall is forty feet in fifty yards. The channel on the right side, which is the widest, falls nearly twenty feet in ten feet. The fish are obstructed here in their attempts to ascend the river. From appearances, they might be easily taken in the season of the ascending the rivers, but no attempts have hitherto been made to do so.

The rock is a light gray, very much divided in square blocks of various sizes for building. It requires very little labor to reduce it to form, for plain walls. Large masses of it are so nicely fitted, and so regular, as to imitate the wall of an ancient building, where the stone had passed through the hands of a mason. The quantity of this description at the falls and in the hill sides adjoining them, is great; sufficient for the building of a large city.

The falls above spread out, and the river widens to half a mile within that distance, and continues that width for four miles. Within this scope are four islands, which were formerly cultivated, but are now old fields margined with cane. The bed of the river is here rocky, shoally, and covered with moss. It is frequented in summer by cattle, horses, and deer; and in the winter, by swans, geese, and ducks.

On the right bank opposite the falls, the land is broken, stony, and gravelly. The hill sides fronting the river, exhibit this building rock. The timber is post oak, hickory, and pine, all small. From the hills the land spreads off level. The narrow flat margin between the hills and the river is convenient for a canal for mills on an extensive scale, and to supply a large extent of flat land around the town with water. Below the falls a small distance, there is a spring and branch, and within five hundred yards a small creek; thence within half a mile the land becomes level and spreads out on this side two miles, including the flats of Wol-lau-hat-che, a creek ten feet wide which rises seventeen miles from its junction with the river, in the high pine forest, and running south-southeast enters the river three miles below the town house. The whole of this flat, between the creek and the river, bordering on the town, is covered with oak and the small hard shelled hickory. The trees are all small; the land is light, and fine for corn, cotton, or melons. The creek has a little cane on its margins and reed on the small branches; but the range is much exhausted by the stock of the town.

On the left bank of the river, at the falls, the land is broken pine forest. Half a mile below there is a small creek which has its source seven miles from the river, its margins covered with reed or cane. Below the creek the land becomes flat, and continues so to Talesee on the Eu-fau-bee, and half a mile still lower, to the hills between this creek and Ca-le-be-hat-che. The hills extend nearly two miles, are intersected by one small creek and two branches, and terminate on the river in two high bluffs; from whence is an extensive view of the town, the river, the flat lands on the opposite shore, and the range of hills to the northwest; near one of the bluffs there is a fine spring, and near it a beautiful elevated situation for a settlement. The hills are bounded to the west by a small branch. Below this, the flat land spreads out for one mile. It is a quarter of a mile from the branch on this flat to the residence of Mr. Cornells (Oche

[1] The Lib. Cong. MS. has "120".

[2] The town house was opposite the mouth of the Eu-fau-be.—Ga. Hist. Soc. Colls., IX, p. 38.

Haujo [Hickory Hadjo]), thence half a mile to the public establishment, thence two miles to the mouth of Ca-le-be-hat-che. This creek has its source thirty miles to the east in waving, post oak, hickory, and pine land; in some places the swamp is wide, the beach and white oak large, with poplar, cypress, red bay, sassafras, Florida magnolia, and white pine. Broken piny woods and reedy branches on its right side, oak flats, red and post oak, willow leaved hickory, long and short leaf pine, and reedy branches on its left side. The creek at its mouth is twenty-five feet wide. The flat between it and the river is fine for corn, cotton, and melons, oak, hickory, and short-leaf pine. From this flat to its source, it is margined with cane, reed, and palmetto. Ten miles up the creek, between it and Kebihatche, the next creek below and parallel with this, are some licks in post and red oak saplin flats; the range on these creeks is apparently fine for cattle; yet from the want of salt or moss, the large ones appear poor in the fall, while other cattle, where moss is to be had, or they are regularly salted, are fat.

They have 116 gun men belonging to this town; they were formerly more numerous, but they have been unfortunate in their wars. In the last they had with the Chickasaws they lost thirty-five gun men; they have begun to settle out in villages for the conveniency of stock raising and having firewood; the stock which frequent the mossy shoals above the town, look well and appear healthy; the Indians begin to be attentive to them, and are increasing them by all the means in their power. Several of them have from fifty to one hundred, and the town furnished seventy good beef cattle in 1799. One chief, Toolk-au-bat-che Haujo [Tukaba'tci Hadjo], has five hundred, and although apparently very indigent, he never sells any; while he seems to deny himself the comforts of life, he gives continued proofs of unbounded hospitality; he seldom kills less than two large beeves a fortnight for his friends and acquaintances.

The town is on the decline. Its appearance proves the inattention of the inhabitants. It is badly fenced; thay have but a few plum trees and several clumps of cassine yupon; the land is much exhausted with continued culture, and the wood for fuel is at a great and inconvenient distance, unless boats or land carriages were in use, it could then be easily supplied; the river is navigable for boats drawing two and a half feet in the dry season from just above the town to Alabama. From the point just above the town to the falls, the river spreads over a bed of flat rock in several places, where the depth of water is something less than two feet.

This is the residence of Efau Haujo [Dog Hadjo], one of the great medal chiefs, the speaker for the nation at the national council. He is one of the best informed men of the land, faithful to his national engagements. He has five black slaves and a stock of cattle and horses; but they are of little use to him; the ancient habits instilled in him by French and British agents, that the red chiefs are to live on presents from their white friends, is so rivited, that he claims it as a tribute due to him, and one that never must be dispensed with.

At the public establishment there is a smith's shop, a dwelling house and kitchen built of logs, and a field well fenced. And it is in the contemplation of the agent to have a public garden and nursery.

The assistant and interpreter, Mr. [Alexander] Cornells (Oche Haujo [Hickory Hadjo]), one of the chiefs of the Creek Nation, has a farm well fenced and cultivated with the plough. He is a half-breed, of a strong mind, and fulfills the duties enjoined on him by his appointment, with zeal and fidelity. He has nine negroes under good government. Some of his family have good farms, and one of them, Zachariah McGive is a careful, snug farmer, has good fences, a fine young orchard, and a stock of hogs, horses, and cattle. His wife has the neatness and economy of a white woman. This family and Sullivan's, in the neighborhood, are spinning.[1]

---

[1] Ga. Hist. Soc. Colls., III, pp. 27-31.

Hawkins mentions a village belonging to Tukabahchee called Wehuarthly [Wī hili] (sweet water) from a little creek of that name near which it stood.[1]

Tecumseh held most of his councils with the Creeks in this town. The name appears in the census of 1832 [2] and often in later history. After the removal the Tukabahchee settled in the southeastern corner of their new territory, but later drifted westward, following the game, and at the present time their square ground is just north of Holdenville. This is still the most populous town in the nation and has the largest square.

Other Muskogee Towns and Villages

Besides the recognized tribes or towns of major importance and such of their offshoots as can be identified, the literature of this region contains many names of towns or villages which can not be definitely connected with any of those given. In some cases it may be that we have to deal with ancient divisions in process of decline which were never connected with the rest, but in at least nine-tenths of the cases they are nothing more than temporary offshoots of the larger bodies.

Opiłłåko ("Big Swamp") seems to have been one of the most ancient and important of these. It appears as far back as 1733, on the De Crenay map.[3] It appears also in the census lists of 1750 and 1760,[4] but not in that of 1761. The trader located there in 1797 was Hendrik Dargin.[5] Swan spells the name "Pinclatchas,"[6] and Hawkins has the following description:

> O-pil-thluc-co; from O-pil-lo-wau, a swamp; and thluc-co, big. It is situated on a creek of that name, which joins Puc-cun-tal-lau-has-see on the left side. It is 20 miles from Coosau River; the land about this village is round, flat hills, thickets of hickory saplings, and on the hillsides and their tops, hickory grub and grapevines. The land bordering on the creek is rich, and here are their fields.[7]

The town does not appear in the census list of 1832, and seems to have vanished out of the memories of the living Indians. By his classification of Opiłłåko, Hawkins clearly indicates that he considered it a branch of one of the other towns. It is probably the Weypulco of the Mitchell map (pl. 6).

Hawkins thus describes another branch village:

> Pin-e-hoo-te; from pin-e-wau [pinwa], a turkey, and ehoo-te [huti], house. It is on the right side of a fine little creek, a branch of E-pe-sau-gee. The land is stiff and

[1] Ga. Hist. Soc. Colls., IX, p. 46.
[2] Senate Doc. 512, 23d Cong., 1st sess., IV, pp. 243-252.
[3] Plate 5; also Hamilton, Col. Mobile, p. 190.
[4] MS., Ayer Lib.; Miss. Prov. Arch., I. p. 95.
[5] Ga. Hist. Soc. Colls., IX, p. 170.
[6] Schoolcraft, Ind. Tribes, V, p. 262.
[7] Ga. Hist. Soc. Colls., III, p. 50.

rich, and lies well; the timber is red oak and hickory, the branches all have reed, and the land on them, above the settlement, is good black oak, sapling, and hickory. This and the neighboring land is fine for settlement; they have here three or four houses only, some peach trees and hogs, and their fields are fenced. The path from New-yau-cau to Cow-e-tuh-tal-lau-has-see passes by these houses.[1]

Another town of the same name was in Bibb County, Alabama, east of Cahaba River, opposite the mouth of Shuts Creek.[2]

There is very much less information regarding the other villages, and I will arrange them alphabetically with the few facts we have concerning them appended:

Acpactaniche. A town in the De l'Isle map of 1703, located on the headwaters of Coosa River. The name may be intended for that of the Pakana.

Alkehatchee or Alkohatchi. De Brahm, writing in the eighteenth century, gave this as the name of an Upper Creek town.[3] It perhaps refers to Łałogálga on Elkhatchee Creek.

Atchasapa. Given on the Purcell map (pl. 7) as a town on Tallapoosa River not far below Tulsa. It may be intended for Hatcheechubba, but if so, it is not properly located.

Aucheucaula. Royce [4] gives this as a town in the northwestern part of Coosa County, Alabama. The first part of the name is probably atcina, cedar. It is evidently the Cedar Creek Village of Owen [5] and may be the Authinohatche of the Popple map (pl. 4).

Auhoba. Swan has this in his list of Creek towns immediately after Autauga.[6] It is possible that it was merely a synonym of Autauga.

Breed Camp. The census of 1761 mentions this, but states that it was already said to be broken up.[7] See, however, note 1 on page 418.

Cauwaoulau. Given by Brannon as a Lower Creek village in Russell County, Alabama, "west of Uchee P. O., south of the old Federal road." [5]

Chachane. A town which appears in the Spanish enumeration of 1738 placed among the Lower Creek towns, farther downstream than any other except Old Tamałi. It is mentioned in some other Spanish documents.[8]

Chanahunrege. On the Popple map (pl. 4). Perhaps the Clamahumgey of Taitt (see p. 418).

Chananagi ("Long ridge"). A Creek town which Brannon places "in Bullock County, just south of the Central of Georgia Railroad, near Suspension." [9] Woodward represents the people of this town as being allied with the Tukabahchee when the Creek-American war broke out. There is a modern village of this name east of Montgomery, in Russell County, Alabama.

Chichoufkee. "An Upper Creek town, in Elmore County, east of Coosa River, and near Wiwoka Creek." [10]

---

1 Ga. Hist. Soc. Colls., III, p. 50.

2 Handbook Ala. Anth. Soc. for 1920, p. 50.

3 Gatschet, Creek Mig. Leg., II, p. 182 [214]; Misc. Colls. Ala. Hist. Soc., I, p. 391.

4 Eighteenth Ann. Rept. Bur. Amer. Ethn., map of Alabama.

5 Handbook Ala. Anth. Soc. for 1920, p. 43.

6 Schoolcraft, Ind. Tribes, V, p. 262.

7 Ga. Col. Docs., VIII, p. 523.

8 MSS., Ayer Lib.

9 Jefferys, French Dom., I, p. 134, map, 1761; Handbook Ala. Anth. Soc. for 1920, p. 44; Woodward Reminiscences, p. 37.

10 Handbook Ala. Anth. Soc. for 1920, p. 44.

Chinnaby's Fort. In 1813 a Creek chief named Chinnaby, friendly to the Americans, had a kind of fort at Ten Islands, on the Coosa River, known as Chinnaby's fort.[1] Perhaps it was identical with Oti palin (q. v.).

Chiscalage. On the Popple map (pl. 4).

Cholocco Litabixee. Brannon[2] locates this in the Horseshoe Bend of Tallapoosa River, the scene of Jackson's famous victory. The first word is from Itcu łako, horse.

Chuahla. "An early Indian town, location not positive, just below White Oak Creek, south of the Alabama River."[2]

Cofa. On the Popple map (pl. 4); perhaps another form of "Coosa."

Cohatchie. Given by Royce as a town in the southwestern part of Talladega County, Alabama, on the bank of Coosa River. If correctly transcribed the name may mean "Cane River."[3]

Conaliga. Woodward mentions an Upper Creek town of this name. It is said to have been "in western Russell County, or eastern Macon, somewhere near the present Warrior Stand."[4]

Cooccohapofe. Site of an old town, apparently on Chattahoochee River. It stood on the right bank and the fields were cultivated on the left bank.[5]

Cotohautustenuggee. Royce[6] gives this as a Lower Creek settlement on the right bank of Upatoie Creek, in Muscogee County, Georgia. The last part is tástánági, "warrior," and the whole is evidently a man's name.

Cow Towns. Finnelson speaks of towns so called.[7]

Donnally's Town. Milton[8] mentions this as a settlement on Flint River, Georgia, in 1793. The trader Panton calls it "Patrick Donnelly's Town on the Chatehoochie," and says it was burned by horsemen from Georgia, September 21, 1793, 6 Indians being killed and 11 taken prisoner.[9]

Ekun-duts-ke. Given in the census enumeration of 1832.[10] Ikân tátska means "boundary line" and hence this may be identical with "Line Creek Village," said to have been on the south bank of Line Creek, in Montgomery County, Alabama. This town may have been on a boundary line between two others.[11]

Emarhe or Hemanhie Town. This is given in the census of 1832.[12] It was probably named for a man (Imahe).

Eto-husse-wakkes (Itahasiwaki) ("Old Log"). Young mentions it as a Lower Creek town on the Chattahoochee River, 3 miles above Fort Gaines, Georgia, having 100 inhabitants in 1820.[13]

Fife's Village. Given by Royce as an Upper Creek village a few miles east of Talladega, Alabama.[14]

Fin'halui ("High Log").[15] A Lower Creek settlement, perhaps the Yuchi town called High Log which appears in the census list of 1832.[16] There is a swamp of this name in Wayne County, Georgia.

---

1 Gatschet in Misc. Colls. Ala. Hist. Soc., I, p. 395, quoting Drake, Book of Indians (1848), IV, p. 55.
2 Handbook Ala. Anth. Soc. for 1920, p. 44.
3 Royce in Eighteenth Ann. Rept. Bur. Amer. Ethn., pl. CVIII, 1899.
4 Woodward, Reminiscences, p. 37, 1859; Handbook Ala. Anth. Soc. for 1920, p. 45.
5 Hawkins in Ga. Hist. Soc. Colls., IX, p. 173.
6 Thirteenth Ann. Rept. Bur. Amer. Ethn., map of Alabama.
7 Amer. State Papers, Ind. Aff., I, p. 289.
8 Ibid., II, p. 372.
9 Copy of MS in Ayer Coll., Newberry Lib., Chicago, vols. on Indian Trade, II, p. 35.
10 Senate Doc. 512, 23d Cong., 1st sess., IV, pp. 319–320.
11 See p. 270; Handbook Ala. Anth. Soc. for 1920, p. 48.
12 Senate Doc. 512, 23d Cong., 1st sess., IV, pp. 301–302.
13 Morse, Rept. to Sec. of War, p. 364.
14 Royce in Eighteenth Ann. Rept. Bur. Amer. Ethn., pl. CVIII, 1899.
15 Gatschet, Creek Mig. Leg., I, p. 130.
16 Senate Doc. 512, 23d Cong., 1st sess., IV, pp. 359–363.

HABIQUACHE. On the Popple map (pl. 4).

IKAN ATCHAKA, "Holy Ground," a temporary settlement on the south side of Alabama River, occupied by the Creek leaders, Weatherford and Hilis hadjo, during the Creek-American war, until it was destroyed, December 23, 1813. It is said to have contained 200 houses at the time. Brannon locates it in Lowndes County 2½ miles due north of White Hall, just below the mouth of Holy Ground Creek on Old Sprott Plantation.[1]

ISTAPOGA ("Where people live"). Gatschet gives this as an Upper Creek settlement, and Brannon says it was "in Talladega County, near the influx of Estaboga Creek into Choccolocco Creek; about 10 miles from the Coosa River." There is a modern place so called in Talladega County, Alabama.[2]

KEHATCHES. On the Popple map (pl. 4).

KEROFF. Given in H. R. Ex. Doc. 276, 24th Cong., 1st sess., p. 162, 1836, as a Creek settlement, apparently on the upper Coosa.

LITAFATCHI, LITTEFUTCHI. The name is said by Gatschet to refer to the manufacture of arrows, łi.[3] This was an Upper Creek town at the head of Canoe Creek, St. Clair County, Alabama. It was burned by Colonel Dyer October 29, 1813.[4] It was probably the same as, or on the same site as, the Olitifar mentioned in the Pardo narratives, although Olitifar was a "destroyed town" when Pardo heard of it.[5]

LUSTUHATCHEE. A town above the second cataract of the Tallapoosa River; *łustu*, perhaps from *làsti*, black, *hatchee*, river.

MELTON'S VILLAGE. "An Upper Creek town, in Marshall County, Alabama, on Town Creek, at the site of the present 'Old Village Ford.' Meltonsville perpetuates the name." [6]

NINNIPASKULGEE. Woodward [7] mentions a band of Upper Creek Indians of this name. They seem to have been located near Tukabahchee.

NIPKY. McCall [8] mentions this. It would appear to have been a Lower Creek town.

OAKCHINAWA VILLAGE (okchan, "salt"). Given by Owen as an Upper Creek town "In Talladega County, on both sides of Salt Creek, near the point where it flows into Big Shoal Creek." [9] There may have been some connection between this town and the Creek Oktcànàlgi or Salt Clan.

OLD OSONEE TOWN. Given by Royce as a village probably belonging to the Upper Creeks, on Cahawba River, in Shelby County, Alabama.[10]

OTI PALIN ("Ten islands"). A town on the west bank of Coosa River, just below the junction of Canoe Creek. Fort Strother was just below.[11] See Chinnaby's Fort.

OTI TUTCINA ("Oteetoocheenas, Three Islands"). Swan gives this in his list of Creek towns.[12] It seems to have been between Coosa and Opiłłako or Pakan Tallahassee, and the name probably referred to three islands in Coosa River.

PEA CREEK. A settlement mentioned along with Tukabahchee in the census of 1761.[13] It may have been an outsettlement of Tukabahchee.

---

1 Handbook Ala. Anth. Soc. for 1920, p. 46.

2 Gatschet, Creek Mig. Leg., I, p. 133; Misc. Coll. Ala. Hist. Soc., I, p. 399; Handbook Ala. Anth. Soc. for 1920, p. 47.

3 Misc. Colls. Ala. Hist. Soc., I, p. 403.

4 Pickett, Hist. Ala., II, p. 294.

5 Ruidiaz, La Florida, II, p. 485. See plate 8.

6 Handbook Ala. Anth. Soc. for 1920, p. 48.

7 Woodward, Reminiscenses, p. 37, 1859.

8 Hist. Ga., I, p. 367.

9 Handbook Ala. Anth. Soc. for 1920, p. 49.

10 Eighteenth Ann. Rept. Bur. Amer. Ethn., pl. CVIII.

11 Gatschet in Misc. Colls. Ala. Hist. Soc., I, p. 407.

12 Schoolcraft, Ind. Tribes, V, p. 262.

13 Ga. Col. Docs., VIII, p. 523.

RABBIT TOWN. Given as an Upper Creek town in the census enumeration of 1832.[1] As the rabbit is always a subject for jest among the Creeks it was suggested to me that this may have been nothing more than a nickname.

SATAPO. In the report by Vandera of Pardo's expedition into the interior this appears as a settlement, probably Creek, on Tennessee River.[2]

SECHARLECHA ("Under a blackjack tree"). A Lower Creek settlement mentioned frequently in early documents, probably a branch of Kasihta.

ST. TAFFERY'S. Given in the Ga. Col. Docs. as a small Creek town.[3]

TALWA HADJO ("Crazy Town"). An Upper Creek town on Cahawba River, far to the northwest of the other Creek towns.[4]

TALIPSEHOGY ("Two talewa plants standing together," the talewa being used in making dyes). This appears in the census enumeration of 1832 and also in Schoolcraft.[5]

TALISHATCHIE TOWN. "An Upper Creek town, in Calhoun County, Alabama, east of a branch of Tallasehatchee Creek, 3 miles southwest of Jacksonville." [6]

TALLAPOOSA. Several early maps give a town of this name, and Adair in one place, and only one, refers to a "Tallapoose town" within a day's journey of Fort Toulouse.[7] It is possible that it was an Alabama town, for the name is either Alabama or Choctaw, and the town may have given its name to the river. It seems to mean "pulverized stones," or "sand." In some maps this town seems to be placed on the Coosa (see pl. 4).

TCHUKO ŁAKO ("Big house," i. e., square ground). Gatschet has mistakenly entered two towns of this name in one of his lists of Creek towns.[8] The proper name of each of these is Tcahki łáko, "Big ford."

TOHOWOGLY. Given along with Coweta as a Lower Creek town 8 to 10 miles below the falls of the Chattahoochee.[9] Perhaps it is intended for Sawokli.

TURKEY CREEK. "An Indian town, in Jefferson County, on Turkey Creek, north of Trussville." [10] This was in territory dominated by the Creek Indians and hence was probably settled by people of that nation.

UNCUAULA. An Upper Creek town in the western part of Coosa County, on Coosa River.[11]

WALLHAL. On the Purcell map (pl. 7). The name may be intended for Eufaula, or this may have been a settlement on Wallahatchee Creek, Elmore County, Alabama.

WEYOLLA. On the Popple map (pl. 4) and some later maps; probably a very much distorted form of the name of some well-known town.

THE YUCHI

Our history of those tribes constituting the Creek Confederacy will not be complete without some mention of three alien peoples which were incorporated with it at a comparatively recent period. These are the Yuchi, the Natchez, and the Shawnee.

The Yuchi have attracted considerable attention owing to the fact that they were one of the very few small groups in the eastern part

---

1 Senate Doc. 512, 23d Cong., 1st sess., IV, pp. 313–315.

2 Ruidiaz, La Florida, II, p. 484.

3 Ga. Col. Docs., VII, p. 427.

4 Gatschet in Misc. Colls. Ala. Hist. Soc., I, p. 410.

5 Senate Doc. 512, 23d Cong., 1st sess., IV, p. 334; Schoolcraft, Ind. Tribes, IV, p. 578.

6 Handbook Ala. Anth. Soc. for 1920, p. 51.

7 Adair, Hist. Am. Inds., p. 242.

8 Gatschet, Creek Mig. Leg., I, p. 146; Misc. Colls. Ala. Hist. Soc., I, p. 411.

9 De Brahm, Hist. Prov. of Ga., p. 54.

10 Handbook Ala. Anth. Soc. for 1920, p. 52.

11 Royce in Eighteenth Ann. Rept. Bur. Amer. Ethn., pl. CVIII.

of North America having an independent stock language. Their isolation in this respect, added to the absence of a migration legend among them and their own claims, have led to a belief that they were the most ancient inhabitants of the extreme southeastern parts of the present United States. The conclusion was natural, almost inevitable, but the event proves how little the most plausible theory may amount to in the absence of adequate information. Strong evidence has now come to light that these people, far from being aboriginal inhabitants of the country later associated with them, had occupied it within the historic period.

Dr. F. G. Speck has contributed to the study of southern tribes an invaluable paper on "The Ethnology of the Yuchi Indians,"[1] but he made no special investigation into their history from documentary sources. However, he noted an apparent absence of Yuchi names—with one possible exception—in the narratives of the De Soto expedition, and particularly called attention to the non-Yuchean character of the name of Cofitachequi, which up to that time had generally been considered a Yuchi town.[2] I have touched upon this particular point more at length in another place.[3]

One reason for the general misunderstanding of the place of the Yuchi in aboriginal American history was the fact that the language was generally considered very difficult by other peoples and few learned it, and, although not necessarily resulting from that circumstance, it so happened that they were known to different tribes by different names, never apparently by the term Tsoyahá, "Offspring of the sun," which they apply to themselves. Regarding the name Yuchi, Speck says:

> It is presumably a demonstrative signifying "being far away" or "at a distance" in reference to human beings in a state of settlement (*yū*, "at a distance," *tcī*, "sitting down").
>
> It is possible, in attempting an explanation of the origin of the name, that the reply "*Yū'tcī*" was given by some Indian of the tribe in answer to a stranger's inquiry, "Where do you come from?" which is a common mode of salutation in the southeast. The reply may then have been mistaken for a tribal name and retained as such. Similar instances of mistaken analogy have occurred at various times in connection with the Indians of this continent, and as the Yuchi interpreters themselves favor this explanation it has seemed advisable at least to make note of it.[4]

I can add nothing except to say that the Creeks have no explanation of the name to offer, and that it appears rather late, little if any before the opening of the eighteenth century. In the South Carolina archives reference is made to "the Uche or Round Town people," but the second term is probably not intended as a translation of the first.[5]

---

[1] Univ. of Penn., Anth. Pub., I, no. 1.

[2] Ibid., p. 7.

[3] See pp. 216–217.

[4] Speck, op. cit., p. 13.

[5] Proc. Board of Comm. dealing with Ind. Trade, MS., p. 34.

Gatschet gives Tahogaléwi as the Delaware equivalent of Yuchi,[1] and from early maps, where it appears in the forms Tahogale, Tahogaria, Taogria, Tongaria, Tohogalegas, etc., it is evident that it was applied by other Algonquian peoples also. It was used most persistently for a band of Yuchi on Tennessee River, but on the maps of Moll and some other cartographers the Tahogale are placed along Savannah River—a fact which serves to confirm the identification of the term (see pl. 3).

Tohogalega was sometimes abbreviated to Hogologe or Hog Logee. A legend on a map in Jefferys's Atlas at a point on Savannah River several miles above Augusta reads: "Hughchees or Hogoleges Old Town deserted in 1715,"[2] and an island in the river at this point is called "Huhgchee I." The form Hughchee is somewhat unusual, but is confirmed as actually intended for Yuchi by numerous references to this island as "Uchee Island" in the Georgia Colonial Documents and elswehere, as well as the existence of a "Uchee Creek" which flows into the Savannah at this point.

The earliest historical name for the Yuchi was Chiska or Chisca. I assert this confidently on the basis of information contained in very early Spanish documents, both published and unpublished, and on the very strongest of circumstantial evidence, although as yet no categorical statement of the identity has been found. The circumstantial evidence is as follows: First, the term Chiska occurs in the same list, or on the same map, as the term Yuchi very rarely, and then when we know, or have good reason to believe, that more than one band of Yuchi were in the region covered. Secondly, the Spaniards, who use it principally, apply the term not to an obscure tribe but to a powerful people, and they mention in the same connection all of the leading tribes of the Southeast with the conspicuous exception of the Yuchi. Thirdly, the term occurs persistently in three different areas, in the region of the Upper Tennessee, on the Savannah,[3] and near the Choctawhatchee, where we know on independent evidence that just so many Yuchi bands had settled.

Some time ago I attempted a further identification of this tribe with a people settled upon the Savannah River at the time when South Carolina was colonized by the whites, and called by the latter Westo.[4] Prof. Verner W. Crane, who has made some important

[1] Gatschet, Creek Mig. Leg., I, p. 19.

[2] Jefferys's Am. Atlas, map 24.

[3] There is but one application to Savannah River, it is true, but this is of considerable importance as tending to settle an otherwise puzzling problem. It is in the version of the Creek migration legend given by Hawkins in which his native informant says that after they had crossed what is now the Chattahoochee River the Creeks spread out eastward to the Ocmulgee, Oconee, and Ogechee Rivers, and to "Chis-ke-tol-lo-fau-hatche" ("Chiska town river"). In the published version (Ga. Hist. Soc. Colls., III, p. 83) this is spelled "Chic-ko-tallo-fau-hat-che," but the original in the Library of Congress has it in the form just given.

[4] See article "Westo" in Handbook of American Indians, Bull. 30, Bur. Amer. Ethn., part 2. I did not, however, make an elaborate exposition of my views at the time when this article was written.

historical discoveries in this region, to be mentioned presently, has, however, taken strong exception to it. The resulting discussion between Professor Crane and myself has appeared in the American Anthropologist, which the reader may consult,[1] but it will not be profitable to cover the same ground again. I will merely incorporate a short statement of my present views on the subject and the reasons which lead me still to adhere to my original opinion.

My studies of southeastern tribes have clearly demonstrated that the Yuchi once inhabited some territory in the neighborhood of the southern Appalachian Mountains, from which a large part of them moved during the seventeenth and the early part of the eighteenth centuries, invading the low countries to the south of them and settling in several different places. Two or three such waves of migration can be made out with certainty, the first resulting in a settlement on Choctawhatchee River, in the western part of the present State of Florida; a second giving birth to the Yuchi settlement on Savananh River above the site of the present Augusta, later removed to the Chattahoochee River and then to the Tallapoosa; and a third, probably subsequent to the Yamasee war, which brought about a Yuchean colonization of the lower Savannah, and later became consolidated into the well-known Yuchi town among the Lower Creeks. Furthermore, distinct names are often applied to these several bands, and sometimes they appear upon the same map under the distinct names. The first name appears in history as "Chisca," but later we find them called, successively, Hogologe and Yuchi; the second are called both Hogologe and Yuchi; while the last appears as Yuchi almost invariably. On numerous maps we find the Hogologe (or Hogolege) and Yuchi entered as if they were distinct tribes, and Romans includes the two in his enumeration of the principal Lower Creek towns.[2]

So far as the Yuchi are concerned, then, the concurrent use of two or more distinct names does not prove that the people so called were unrelated. There can be no question that the Westo constituted for a long period a body of Indians distinct from those just mentioned. They were not a part of the same tribal organization. The question is, Were they or were they not a Yuchean tribe? Did they speak a Yuchean dialect?

In the first place, attention should be called to the fact that in the immediate neighborhood of the southern Appalachians the Yuchi are the only people known to have moved southward in any considerable numbers in the early historic period. Again, after the Yamassee war and the later removal of those people to whom

[1] Amer. Anthrop, n. s. vol. xx, pp. 331–337; vol. xxi, pp. 213–216, 463–465.

[2] Plates 4 and 6; Romans, Con. Nat. Hist. E. and W. Fla., p. 280.

the term Yuchi is commonly applied to the Chattahoochee River, the Yuchi and Westo towns were established a very few miles apart, where the two may readily have united. It is evident that a sufficiently large body of Westo Indians continued to exist in this neighborhood to have attracted the attention of those traders and explorers from whom accounts have come down to us if they were as different from the Creeks generally as there is every reason to believe, unless they were confused with another people which did attract such attention. And it is a matter of record that practically all earlier writers upon the Lower Creeks make particular mention of the Yuchi and comment upon their distinct language and peculiar customs.

In his last communication Professor Crane cites a new piece of evidence which he thinks renders it necessary for us to reject the Yuchean connection of the Westo. This is the reference in Woodward's Westo Narrative[1] to a report brought by two Shawnee Indians to the effect that "ye Cussetaws, Checsaws, and Chiskers were intended to come downe and fight ye Westoes." If the Chiska and Westo were both Yuchi, Professor Crane argues that they would not be fighting each other. This, however, by no means follows. Many instances may be cited of tribes related by language at bitter enmity with one another and allied on each side with peoples having no connection with them whatever. Besides, Woodward says regarding these Shawnee, "There was none here y^t understood them, but by signes they intreated freindship of ye Westoes showeing," and so on as above. One may well hesitate to place entire confidence in information obtained in this manner.

On the other hand, there is one bit of documentary evidence which tends to identify the Indians under discussion with the Chiska. This is given on page 296, and it will not be necessary to quote it at length, but the gist of it is that about 1682 La Salle encountered some Indians called "Cisca" and learned that the Indians of "English Florida" had burned one of their villages, "aided by the English," after which they had abandoned their easternmost villages and moved into the neighborhood of La Salle's fort. Now, English Florida must certainly refer to Carolina, not Virginia, and the Carolina settlers engaged in no war of consequence up to that time—certainly none resulting in the expulsion of a tribe—except that against the Westo, who had been driven out the year before.

As opposed to the Yuchean theory, Professor Crane can only suggest a possible Iroquoian connection for these otherwise enigmatic Westo, and he has but two direct arguments to offer, both of the slenderest. One of these is the superficial resemblance between the

[1] See pp. 306-307.

name Rickohockans, which, as we shall presently see, he identifies with the Westo, and the native name of the old Erie tribe Riquehronnons; the other an excerpt from the South Carolina archives to be noted presently.[1] Regarding the first point it is to be remarked that Mr. J. N. B. Hewitt, who has a profound knowledge of the languages of the Five Nations and a very considerable knowledge of Algonquian, considers the resemblance only superficial and the former word plainly Algonquian. His researches also indicate another direction of migration for the defeated Erie.

The excerpt referred to is a commentary appended to the South Carolina Commons House address of 1693 mentioned above to the effect that "the Mawhawkes are a numerous, warlike nation of Indians, and strictly aleyd to the Westos. . . ."[1] As Professor Crane says, "much depends on the interpretation of the expression 'strictly aleyd'"; but I believe that the adverb would hardly have been used if the connection between the Mohawk and Westo were merely linguistic. While that *might* have been intended as one of the bonds between them, some kind of political or military coordination appears to be hinted at also, and this was extremely improbable between sworn foes like the Erie and Iroquois, while, on the other hand, we know that the Iroquois and Yuchi were both bitter enemies of the eastern Siouan tribes.

My conclusion is that, in the present state of this question, the Yuchean connection of the Westo has greater probability in its favor than any other theory, and I shall treat their history along with that of the better identified Yuchean bands, leaving the reader to draw his own conclusions from the material available, all of which will be presented.

On taking this position, however, we are immediately confronted by a further identification, mentioned above, between the Westo and the Rickohockans or Rechahecrians, a mysterious tribe which appears in early Virginia history. Professor Crane, to whom we owe this identification, bases it on material contained in the colonial archives of the State of South Carolina, which is as follows. On January 13, 1693, the upper house of the colony of South Carolina laid before the commons house of Assembly information to the effect that some northern Indians had come to establish themselves among the Tuskegee, and others were coming the summer following to settle among the Coweta and Kasihta. The reply of the lower house, drawn up by a committee of which James Moore, a leading Indian trader, was chairman, declared "that all possible means be used to prevent the settlem[t] of any Northern nation of Indians amongst our Friends, more Espe-

[1] Crane in Amer. Anthrop., n. s. vol. xx, pp. 336–337.

cially ye Rickohogo's or Westos, a people which formerly when well used made an attempt to Destroy us. . . ." And Professor Crane well adds: "The 'Hickauhaugau' of Woodward's relation was, then, simply a variant of 'Rickohogo' or Rickahockan."[1] This identification appears to me satisfactory and very illuminating. It is to be observed, too, that the mountain habitat of these Rickohockans falls very near to, if it is not identical with, the habitat of the northern band of Chiska to be described presently. As the name Rickohockan seems, *fide* Hewitt, to be an Algonquian term signifying "cave-landers," we must not lose sight of the possibility that it may have been applied to more than one people, and that they were identical, at least in part, with the Westo of South Carolina history. Singularly enough Professor Crane, even in this identification, is confronted by the same difficulty which we note so frequently in dealing with the Yuchi—the application of synonymous terms to different bands. Thus Lederer meets in one town Rickohockans whose home was "not far westward of the Apalataean mountains" and later hears of the "Oustack," a fierce tribe at war with the Catawba.[2] These Oustack must certainly have been the Westo then living in the same region and known by a name almost identical, allowing for an ending which we may reasonably attribute to Lederer's Algonquian interpreter.

Still one more term may prove to have been applied to these people of many names, the term Tamahita. A full statement of the arguments in this case has already been given.[3] Let us now take up the history of these various Yuchi, or supposedly Yuchi, bands.

As I have already explained, there is no evidence that the Yuchi were on Savannah River in De Soto's time. In fact, there is no proof that he himself met them at all. When he was passing down the Tennessee River, however, he heard of them under the name "Chisca," the "province" so called lying across the mountains to the north. They were evidently in the rough country in the eastern part of the present State of Tennessee,[4] and De Soto sent two soldiers to visit them. The Fidalgo of Elvas says:

> In three days [after the arrival of the expedition at Coste] they that went to Chisca got back, and related that they had been taken through a country so scant of maize, and with such high mountains, that it was impossible the army should march in that direction; and finding the distance was becoming long, and that they should be back late, upon consultation they agreed to return, coming from a poor little town where there was nothing of value, bringing a cow-hide as delicate as a calfskin the people had given them, the hair being like the soft wool on the cross of the merino with the common sheep.[5]

[1] Crane, op. cit., p. 336.

[2] Lederer, in Alvord and Bidgood, First Exp. Trans-Allegheny Region, pp. 135–171.

[3] Pp. 188–191.

[4] Mr. William E. Myer, who for years has made a careful study of the archeology of Tennessee, believes that these Chiska were at the "stone fort" near Manchester, the county seat of Coffee County, Tennessee.

[5] Bourne, Narr. of De Soto, I, pp. 79–80.

Ranjel says simply that the messengers "brought good news,"[1] and Garcilasso speaks as if they actually reached the province they were in search of.[2] On account of some slip in the memories of the latter's informants he applies the name Chisca to a town near the Mississippi which the other chroniclers call Quizquiz, or Quizqui.[3] Biedma makes no mention either of the province or the expedition. It will be noticed that Elvas says nothing of any metal seen by the explorers. Garcilasso, on the other hand, states that they "reported that the mines were of a very highly colored copper".[4] The success of the expedition as reported by Garcilasso and Ranjel and this mention of copper mines accord ill with what Elvas says. Is it possible that some facts regarding the expedition were kept secret within official circles, but leaked out into the camp through the messengers? After the explorers had crossed the Mississippi Elvas tells us they "marched in quest of a province called Pacaha, which he had been informed was nigh Chisca,"[5] and, after he had arrived at the former place, he sent out an expedition to see if they could turn back toward the latter.[6] It is possible that they had learned of another band of Yuchi who are known to have been living near the Mussel Shoals about 1700 (pl. 3).

The next we hear of this province is in the Pardo narratives. In November, 1566, as we have seen, Juan Pardo left the new port of Santa Elena and marched northward to the province of Juada, probably the country of the Siouan Cheraw. There he built a fort, which he left in charge of a sergeant named Moyano (or Boyano). The following January (1567), after Pardo's return to Santa Elena, a letter reached him from Moyano informing him that his sergeant had been at war with a chief named "Chisca," that with 15 soldiers he had killed over 1,000 Indians and burned 50 huts. Later Moyano received a threatening letter from one of the mountain chiefs (un cacique de la sierra), perhaps from this same Chisca—at any rate from one of his allies. Determined to be the first to attack, Moyano

went out from the fort of San Juan with twenty soldiers, marched four days through the sierra, and reached the enemies one morning and found them so well fortified that it was a marvel, because they were surrounded with a very high wooden wall and having a small gate with its defences; and the sergeant seeing that there was no way to enter but by the gate, made a shelter by means of which they entered with great danger, because they wounded the sergeant in the mouth and nine other soldiers in different places, but none of them dangerously. When they finally gained the fort the Indians took refuge in the huts which they had inside, which were underground, from which they came out to skirmish with the Spaniards, and [the latter] killing many of the Indians, fastened the doors of the said huts and set fire to them and burned them all, so that there were killed and burned 1,500 Indians.[7]

---

1 Bourne, Narr. of De Soto, II, p. 110.

2 Garcilasso in Shipp, De Soto and Fla., pp. 372–373.

3 Ibid., p. 404 et seq.

4 Ibid., p. 372.

5 Bourne, Narr. of De Soto, I, p. 117.

6 Ibid., p. 128.

7 Ruidiaz, La Florida, II, pp. 477–480.

In contemplating this feat of Moyano's I can not help repeating Lowery's reference to a Spanish proverb, "Distant countries, big tales." It is sad to relate that the hero of the expedition was afterwards cut off, along with all of the force accompanying him except one man, by a comparatively insignificant tribe near Port Royal.[1] And yet it is possible that Moyano's narrative is true if he was accompanied by a large body of friendly Indians not mentioned in the text.

Later the Chiska chief, in alliance with those of "Carrosa, Costehe, and Coza," was reported to be lying in wait with several thousand Indians, intending to attack Pardo, and this was why Pardo turned back to Santa Elena from his second expedition that same year (1567).[2]

As we shall presently see, the Yuchi later came to be called Chichimecs by the Spaniards through a fancied resemblance in character to the wild tribes north of Mexico. A reference to "Chichimecas" far to the north of Florida in a Spanish document dating from the last quarter of the sixteenth century may possibly have reference to the tribe we are discussing.[3]

The course of Yuchi history now separates into several distinct channels, corresponding to a similar division among the people themselves. A portion of them remained in the north, a second body settled not far from Choctawhatchee River in western Florida, and two or three others established themselves on and near the Savannah River. Each will be considered in turn, beginning with that band mentioned first, which remained nearest to the original Yuchi home.

In 1656, if we accept Professor Crane's identification and my own inferences from it, the Yuchi made a sudden and spectacular appearance on and disappearance from the stage of Virginia history. John Burk has the following account of it:

> Whilst the assembly were employed in these wise and benevolent projects, information was received that a body of inland or mountain Indians, to the number of six or seven hundred, had seated themselves near the falls of James River, apparently with the intention of forming a regular settlement. Some movements were at this time noticed among the neighboring tribes which seemed to indicate something like a concert and correspondence with these strangers; and the minds of the colonists, always alive to, and apprehensive of, Indian treachery, were unusually agitated on this occasion. The place these Indians had made choice of was another source of disquiet. It was strong and difficult of access, alike calculated for offensive and defensive operations; and they recollected the immense trouble and expence that had been incurred in extirpating the tribes which formerly dwelt in that place. At the conclusion of the last peace with the Indians this station was considered so important, that its cession was insisted on, as the main pledge and security of peace; and it had hitherto continued unoccupied as a sort of barrier to the frontiers in that direction. Under all these circumstances they could not see it, without anxiety, occupied

[1] Serrano y Sanz, Doc. Hist., p. 147.
[2] Ruidiaz, op. cit., p. 471.
[3] Lowery, MSS.

by a powerful band of hardy warriors, who perhaps were only the advance guard of a more formidable and extensive emigration.

The measures of the assembly in removing this ground of alarm, were prompt and vigorous. One hundred men were dispatched under the command of Edward Hill, to dislodge the intruders. His instructions were to use peaceable means only, unless compelled by necessity; and to require the assistance of all the neighboring Indians, according to the articles of the late treaty. The governor was at the same time directed to send an account of this invasion to Totopotomoi [principal chief of the Pamunkey Indians], and desire that his influence should be exerted in procuring the immediate cooperation of the friendly tribes.

It is difficult to form any satisfactory conjecture as to the motives of this extraordinary movement directly against the stream and tide of emigration. It was certainly a bold step to descend into the plain, in the face of an enemy, whose power they must have heard of, and which could scarcely fail of inspiring astonishment and awe; and to take the place of warlike tribes, whom the skill and destructive weapons of the whites had lately exterminated and swept away.

The scanty materials which the state records have preserved of Indian affairs throw little light on this subject. But though they do not present this people in all the various relations of peace and war, we generally see them in one point of view at least; and are often able by induction, to supply a considerable range of incident and reflection. In the second session of [the] assembly, Colonel Edward Hill was cashiered, and declared incapable of holding any office, civil or military, within the colony, for improper conduct in his expedition against the Rechahecrians. We are not told whether the offence of Hill was cowardice or a wilful disobedienee of the instructions he had received. There is however reason to believe that he was defeated, and that the Rechahecrians maintained themselves in their position at the falls by force; for the governor and council were directed by the assembly to make a peace with this people, and they farther directed that the monies which were expended for this purpose should be levied on the proper estate of Hill.

From other sources almost equally authentic we learn that the aid demanded of the Indians was granted without hesitation. Totopotomoi marched at the head of an hundred warriors of the tribe of Pamunkey and fell with the greater part of his followers, gallantly fighting in this obstinate and bloody encounter.[1]

The site of this battle was at the falls of the James. It is evident that we have here the migration of a tribe, and hence the probability that this settlement was occupied by Yuchi rather than Cherokee becomes so much the stronger. Why the newcomers disappeared after having won a decisive victory over both whites and Indians, and made a treaty of peace by which their right to inhabit part of the country must have been recognized, is a mystery. The historians appear to be silent both as to the time and the manner of their going. The chances are that, having been forced or induced to abandon their original seats, they had small attachment to any new spot and were easily prevailed upon to establish themselves elsewhere. Perhaps reports filtering back to them from their kinsmen in the south led them to believe that there they should find an easier existence or less hostile neighbors. On the other hand, they may merely have returned

[1] Burk, Hist. of Va., II, pp. 104–107.

into the interior, for we know that there were Yuchi in Tennessee until a comparatively late period, but among the Florida records is one which points to a new influx of Yuchi into the south shortly after the date of the great battle on the James. This will be considered presently.

Whether these latter Indians were Rickohockans or not, there were Rickohockans still in the north. In 1670, during his second expedition into the province of Carolina, Lederer was informed by several Indians "that the nation of Rickohockans, who dwell not far to the westward of the Apalataean Mountains, are seated upon a land, as they term it, of great waves," from which Lederer infers that they meant the seashore.[1] It is more likely, as Mooney suggests, that they had reference to the mountains.[2] A tragedy of which Rickohockans were the victims was witnessed by Lederer at the town of Occaneechee. He says:

> The next day after my arrival at Akenatzy, a Rickohockan ambassadour, attended by five Indians, whose faces were coloured with auripigmentum (in which mineral these parts do much abound), was received and that night invited to a ball of their fashion; but in the height of their mirth and dancing, by a smoke contrived for that purpose, the room was suddenly darkened and, for what cause I know not, the Rickohockan and his retinue barbarously murthered.[3]

The next reference to the northern Yuchi is in a document printed in the Margry collection under the heading "Rivières et Peuplades des Pays Découverts," apparently written by La Salle shortly after his descent of the Mississippi in 1682. Unfortunately the first part is wanting. The fragment preserved begins by speaking of some people who were "neighbors of the Cisca and their allies as well as the Cicaca."[4] On the next page, in speaking of the upper Ohio region, he says:

> The Apalatchites, people of English Florida, are not far from some one of its most eastern branches, because they have war with the Tchataké [Cherokee] and the Cisca, one of whose villages they burned, aided by the English. The Ciscas then abandoned their former villages, which were much further to the east than those from which they have come here."[5]

In a letter written to M. de La Barre somewhat later La Salle refers to the Illinois, Shawnee, and "Cisca" whom he had assembled about Fort St. Louis, near the present Utica, Illinois.[6] It is also possible that they are the Chaskpe mentioned in another place in connection with the Shawnee and "Oabano,"[7] but still more probable that the Chaskpe (or Cheskape) were a part of the Shawnee, since they appear on early maps farther north than the Chiska, near the Cumberland.

---

[1] Alvord and Bidgood, First Expl. Trans-Allegheny Region, p. 155.

[2] Nineteenth Ann. Rept. Bur. Amer. Ethn., p. 183.

[3] Alvord and Bidgood, op. cit., pp. 155–156.

[4] Margry, Déc., II, p. 196.

[5] Ibid., p. 197.

[6] Ibid., p. 318.

[7] Ibid., p. 314.

Probably these Yuchi did not remain long at La Salle's fort, but from this time on the tribe appears on numerous maps under several variants of its Algonquian name—Tahogalegas, Taogaria, Tongeria, Taharea. Covens and Mortier place it on the south side of the Ohio just above its junction with the Wabash. Coxe gives it as one of four small tribes located on an island of the same name in Tennessee River.[1] Sauvole in a letter of 1701 mentions it, though the name has been misprinted "Coongalees."[2] Coxe and most of the remaining authorities represent the tribe as located lower down the Tennessee than any others except the Chickasaw, who at that time had a settlement a few leagues above its mouth. In the fall of the year 1700 Father Gravier, of the Society of Jesus, descended the Mississippi to the newly established French post in Louisiana, and some distance below the mouth of the Ohio he encounted "a pirogue of Taögria." He has the following to say regarding this adventure:

These belong to the loup nation, and carry on a considerable trade with the English. There were only 6 men in it [the pirogue] with a woman and a child; they were coming from the Akansea. He who seemed the most notable among them could speak a few words of Illinois and spoke the Chaouanoua tongue. He made me sit in front of his traveling cabin, and offered me some sagamité to eat. He afterward told me, as news, that Father de Limoges (whom he called Captain Pauiongha) had upset while in his canoe, and had lost everything; and that the Kappa akansea had supplied him with provisions and a canoe, to continue his voyage. I gave him a knife and half a box of vermilion; he made me a present of a very large piece of meat, the produce of his hunting.[3]

Gravier naturally classified these people with the Algonquians, since they were able to speak the language of their neighbors, the Shawnee, and had themselves an adopted Algonquian name.

Five Canadians who reached South Carolina via the Tennessee River in the summer of 1701 found this town above a town of the Chickasaw and below that of the Tali. They estimated the number of their men at "about 200."[4] It is probable that soon after this time the Yuchi moved higher up the Tennessee, for the next we hear of them they were living close to the Cherokee country. Through the South Carolina archives we learn that they had a town there named Chestowee or Chestowa. This is a Cherokee word which Mooney spells Tsistu'yĭ, and interprets "Rabbit place."[5] May 14, 1712, the South Carolina board dealing with Indian trade was informed that a band of "Uche or Round Town people" were on the point of abandoning their town, and this is probably the band intended.[6] We learn from the same source that in 1714 this town was "cut off" by

[1] French, Hist. Colls. La., 1856, p. 230.
[2] Ibid., 1851, p. 238.
[3] Jes. Rel., Thwaites ed., pp. 65, 115.
[4] MS., Lib. La. Hist. Soc.; Correspondence Générale, pp. 403–404.
[5] Nineteenth Ann. Rept. Bur. Amer. Ethn., p. 538.
[6] Proc. Board Dealing with Indian Trade, MS., p. 34.

the Cherokee in retaliation for the murder of a Cherokee Indian.[1] The documents add that the murder had been committed at the instigation of some English traders. The tradition of the event remained in the country for a long time, as is evident by the following statements of Ramsey. In recounting the various tribes which formerly inhabited Tennessee he says:

> A small tribe of Uchees once occupied the country near the mouth of Hiwassee. Their warriors were exterminated in a desperate battle with the Cherokees.[2]

In another place he adds that this conflict occurred at "the Uchee Old Fields, in what is now Rhea County." The site is now in Meigs County.[3] He also says that the survivors were compelled to retreat to Florida, where they became incorporated with the Seminole, but he has evidently brought together two widely separated fragments of Yuchi history. It is apparent that the extermination was not as complete as he represents, nor did the whole tribe leave the country. Mr. Mooney quotes testimony from a Cherokee mixed blood named Gansĕ'' tĭ, or Rattling-gourd, who was born on Hiwassee River in 1820 and went west with his people in 1838, to the effect that "a number of Yuchi lived, before the removal, scattered among the Cherokee near the present Cleveland, Tenn., and on Chickamauga, Cohutta, and Pinelog Creeks in the adjacent section of Georgia. They had no separate settlements, but spoke their own language, which he described as 'hard and grunting.' Some of them spoke also Cherokee and Creek."[4] As the existence of the northern band of Yuchi was not suspected when Mr. Mooney penned the above he naturally assumed that they had drifted north from the Creek country before a boundary had been fixed between the tribes. It is now apparent that they were descendants of the Yuchi whose history we have been tracing. On Mitchell's map (pl. 6) and several others we find "Chestoi O. T." (i. e., Chestowee old town) laid down upon the Hiwassee a short distance above its mouth. After the removal some of these Yuchi probably reunited with the main part of their tribe in the Creek Nation; a few are said to be still living in Tennessee,[5] and there is a modern town named "Euchee" on Tennessee River, near the northern end of Meigs County.

Before taking up the largest Yuchi divisions, those on Savannah River, it will be convenient to consider the third branch of the tribe, since it did not have the permanency of the Savannah bands, and historical information regarding it goes back to an earlier date. This third branch was located when we first learn of it in what is now the State of Florida, a short distance west of the Choctawhatchee River, for which reason the people are called Choctawhatchee Yuchi.

---

[1] Proc. Board Dealing with Indian Trade, MS., p. 87.

[2] Ramsey, Annals of Tenn., p. 81.

[3] Ibid., p. 84.

[4] Nineteenth Ann. Rept. Bur. Amer. Ethn., p. 385.

[5] Information, from T. Michelson.

The following probably refers specifically to the band under consideration. It is part of a letter written from St. Augustine, August 22, 1639, to the court by Gov. Damian de la Vega Castro y Pardo about various matters connected with the administration of his province.

A number of Indians called Ysicas or Chiscas, a warlike people and who take pride in this fact, roam through those provinces, free, originating from New Mexico. I have tried to gather them, and get them away from the trails, assigning to them a place where they could settle, ten leagues from this garrison beyond a river called Rio Blanco, near another village of Catholics. It seemed to me that taking them off the trails they could no longer molest the Christian Indians, but would spread out and multiply, making a livelihood by hunting and trying to work and cultivate the ground with the end of making of them vassals of your Majesty and converting them. Having them close by and under supervision it would be easy to punish any excesses and they could be used in helping to search for fugitive Indians, who run away from their doctrinas, which is causing great damage, for the reason that, running away this way loose, they join bands of heathens and may apostatize. Furthermore these Ysicas are friends of the Spaniards, courageous, and ready to go against any enemies. These Indians are good by land and by water, as well as several other tribes who have come to yield their obedience to your Majesty two hundred leagues from here. . . [1]

These Yuchi are again mentioned in connection with the irruption of a new horde of "barbarians" from the north to be described presently. They are represented as perpetual trouble makers for the Spaniards, and in 1674 three of them threatened to interfere with the labors of the missionaries among the Chatot. They are accused of complicity in the outbreak in that tribe one year later, being described as "a rebellious people, mountaineers (montaras), reared in license without the control of culture or other conventions, attentive solely to game, which is their means of livelihood and with which those lands abound." [2]

Their meddlesome propensities brought on a war with the Apalachee Indians in 1677, of which the following is an account. It is contained in a letter written to the King of Spain by Gov. D. Pablo de Hita Salazar, and is dated St. Augustine, November 10, 1678.

Report given to Captain Juan Fernandez de Florencia by the principal military chiefs who made war on the Chisca Indians and whose names are: Juan Mendoza, Matheo Chuba, the Cacique of Cupayca, Bernardo and Ventura de Ynija,[3] of San Luis. This report tells how the war against the Chiscas originated, which is in the following way: Many years ago those Indians used to come on the trails. It was not quite certain whether they were Chiscas or Chichutecas, but they would assault and kill the Christians or would carry them off, men, women, and children, and make slaves of them. Not until last year, which was 1676, did it become clear that they were Chiscas by the deaths they caused at Huistachuco; and by the killing among the Chines at Chachariz and at Cupayca we knew they were Chiscas, and although it is

[1] Serrano y Sanz, Doc. Hist., p. 199. Translated by Mrs. F. Bandelier.

[2] Lowery, MSS.

[3] In reality Ynija is probably a native word identical with the Creek heniha. The heniha was an assistant to a chief or other leading officer.

true that they went immediately in pursuit they could never catch them, because their assaults were made at night. It has been possible to take away from them only twice the female slaves which they had taken as well in San Luis as elsewhere, and that winter and part of the summer were spent in great anxiety and alarm until they had finished their digging. The digging being once finished, and being on armed night watch in the cabin of San Luis the said chiefs, Juan Mendoza and Matheo and Benito Ynija, discussing the case with other leading men of the settlement of San Luis, they proposed to go out and hunt for the enemy. Some of them said, "We need not be given leave to go," while others said, "It could not be denied us, since every day the enemy alarms us, and we are without tranquillity, and every day they kill our relatives, and what is more they enslave some of them and carry them off and commit all kinds of mockery with them; and we are all Christians and vassals of the king whom may God protect for many years, and we are unanimous and agree in this matter."

They all went and asked leave of the said Captain Juan Fernandez as of their lieutenant and war captain and the head of said province. Upon being told of their resolution, he gladly gave them said leave, and he furthermore comforted and animated them and promised to help them in every way possible, and they all came into this cabin.[1] The chiefs, the caciques, and other leading men were very well satisfied and joyous, and they began instantly to prepare their arms, their provisions, and bundles, and they sent out messengers to the people of the other places, telling their caciques and leading men, that, in case they should want to go and join them, they might be able to make their preparations. From San Luis there went 85 men with their arms; from the place called San Damian went its cacique, Don Bernardo with seventy men; from la Chine, which is a settlement in the district of San Luis, 8 men; from los Chacatos, which also lies within the boundaries of San Luis, 10 men; from Ayubale, came 2 men, and 3 from Tomole; also 1 from Azpalaga. These latter came without being sent by their caciques, who for some reasons which they gave excused themselves. When everything was prepared and in readiness the lieutenant reported it to the governor and his excellency approved of it and thanked the said Indians for their good intentions. The captain, Juan Fernandez, all being gathered in this cabin (bujio), provided ammunition for all the harquebusiers, and he likewise gave us a small jar of powder and a "sucuche"[2] of bullets, and we left on the 2nd of September, 1677, after the captain, Juan Fernandez, at the meeting in the cabin, had appointed as principal chiefs, Juan Mendoza, captain of San Luis; Mateo Chubas, Maese del Campo, chief of the camp, or in the field; and Don Bernardo, cacique and captain of the settlement of San Damian de Cupayca, and Ventura Ynija of this place, admonishing them to behave like united brothers, as well on the journey as on the battlefield. When the necessary orders had been given, we departed and went to sleep at the River Lagino, which is at a distance of two leagues from here, and where we arrived early. When all the people were together, we counted the men, finding that we had thirty firearms—15 from this place, San Luis, and 15 from San Damian, and between harquebusiers and archers there were 190. The chiefs made speeches to their men, telling them that they were men who could defend their homes, their wives, and children, and that with the help of God our wishes would be fulfilled and we would see our enemies. As Christians, God and His Blessed Mother would favour us. Then they arranged that 12 men should explore the country inland as spies, 12 should remain behind, each group being protected by several harquebusiers.

As it seemed early yet, we went to sleep on the banks of a small stream two leagues distant, called Lapache, which are studded with canes or reed. We placed our watches and night patrol, a precaution which was taken at all the places where we arrived. This place (Lapache) we left when the sun was high and arrived at noon at

[1] This may mean the guardhouse.

[2] This is now a nautical term and means a storeroom of a ship.

a little stream called Ystobalaga and went to sleep near another one called Ytaechato and there our watches and patrols said they had heard a noise which kept them in arms, and the next day we saw tracks of two persons away from the road. We took our noonday-rest [1] at a rivulet, wooded on both banks and from there we sent out spies to go as far as the river Santa Cruz. These returned to tell us that there were no other tracks but those of the people of Santa Cruz, which lies on the bank of the stream, where the cacique Baltasar awaited with about twenty men with canoes to ferry us across the river. We arrived at that river and went to the place mentioned, which is on the other bank, and there we remained for two days provisioning ourselves. From there we despatched twenty-four men to go ahead as spies. When we were ready to leave the cacique Baltasar came with six of his men, saying that he was a vassal of His Majesty, and that although he was but a new Christian, his heart was in God and His Blessed Mother, and that he gladly was coming along to die for God, our Lord, for his king, and for his country. We thanked him, telling him that it was a great joy to die for God. We went to sleep near a lagoon, to one side of the road and about four leagues from Santa Cruz on a plain. The spies came back, telling us they had seen a trail which, although it was not fresh, seemed to show that it was of bad people. The next day we departed and arrived at a spring which is called Calutoble,[2] from which flows a river toward the south. From here we went to sleep in a great forest [3] which is called Chapole. The next morning we prayed and recommended ourselves to Our Lady, it being her day, that she might help us in everything, for she was our patroness and our guide.

Then we journeyed on and for rest arrived at the deserted site of San Nicolas de los Chacatos. From there we went to San Carlos, which is also abandoned by the said Chacatos, and where we slept to one side of it [the settlement]. The next morning early we surrounded the whole place in order to find out whether there were any Chiscas in it, since it was their stopping place. We did not take the road which heads toward the west because it goes to the region in which the Chiscas are settled, who naturally had their sentinels everywhere, so we went southward without taking to a road until we found one which led from the sea to the village of the Chiscas and which the Chacatos and Panzacolas had opened (built), who had settled by the sea and on which we traveled with our spies ahead and behind us, exploring the country about. That night we slept by a rivulet with a small growth of wood and the next day we departed without food, because our provisions had given out. All we had that morning was a handful of "tolocomo," which is made of parched corn, and we did not eat till the next day. In the evening we arrived at the river Gurani and we passed on to Bipar, leaving sentinels, arms in hand, on either bank of the stream. On the next day, which was the tenth of the journey since we had left Apalache, we lost our way, very soon after starting and without any determined road we traveled westward, passing small streams with a big growth of reed, small creeks with many obstacles, narrow but very deep. The spies who had gone ahead returned and told us that they had seen many tracks and footpaths of bison and therefore we determined to rest for the night where they had seen them, trying to kill some with which to make our shields and still our hunger, since our provisions had entirely given out. The next morning the Chacatos who went with us killed a cow and we dried the skin. One of the men fell ill with fever and pain in his side, and some said that several of us ought to return with the sick man; others said no, and the patient himself said no, that he would prefer that they should carry him, in order that he might die seeing his enemies.

---

[1] "Sestear" is properly "to take a nap."

[2] Kali, spring.

[3] "Monte grande" could also mean a great mountain, but it is evidently a great forest.

The next day's travel brought us to a dense forest which we traversed and we slept on the other side of it. The next day we traveled in the rain and slept by a spring and the day following, after about one league's traveling, we arrived at a big river called Napa Ubab, which was as thickly wooded on one bank as on the other; we crossed it that day and, as our provisions had given out, we slept on the opposite bank. While there we heard the Chacatos, who were in our company, say that they suffered a great many hardships and privations (hunger), that the Apalachinos although great in number, did not know how to fight, and, upon seeing the palisades of the Chiscas, they most assuredly would run away, while they themselves would perish. Therefore they wished to return, but that of course, they would not be allowed to return, if they showed themselves on the roads. We, the said chiefs, called them and together we said to them, "Children, we are Christians and we bear all those sufferings with great patience, so you also have patience. We all will have to have it until we see our enemies. And should you try to return, we would take you on by force until you take us to the place where the palisade of the Chiscas is and you shall guide us. Once there, then, you may fight if you so wish to, and if not you can stand aside," which they really did, for only three of them fought beside us. The next morning we despatched spies on two different sides, and we traveled all day, night overtaking us on a little river, called Oclacasquis, which is Rio Colorado. That night some spies came back, telling us that they had seen tracks of bison and people who followed them (the bison). We were very anxious, because twelve of the spies whom we had sent out did not return all that night. In the morning we called those who had seen the tracks and ordered them to go ahead and see if they saw more tracks, and we followed them. Very soon they came running back, telling us that they had seen the Chiscas curing meat in smoke. We at once distributed our men on two wings in order to catch them between our forces and see if we could get them alive, but they defended themselves so that it became necessary to kill them. There were two. We remained there and on that day at about eight o'clock, the twelve men who had been missing fired a shot. We answered with another, and upon arriving where we were, they told us that they had lost their way, and they were greatly consoled at the sight of ears of corn which we had taken from the two Chiscas, considering them (the Chiscas) to be near by.

We continued our journey and on the seventeenth day after our departure from Apalache we rested for the night near a small lagoon, traveling the next day, always in a westerly direction. We despatched three men ahead to look for the road which led to the Chiscas, because the Chacatos had been overheard to say that we must be near to judge from the forests (or mountains) which they recognized. A short while afterwards the spies came back, telling us that they had found the road which led to the Chiscas, and we traveled until at about sunset we were on the said road. Some were of the opinion that we ought to pass the night where we had been when told about this place, others that we ought to sleep right here in order to reach the palisade early in the morning, but when we were all together the chiefs decided that we were not to sleep at all, but to keep right on advancing, and with the help of God reach the said palisade, because this was the eve of Saint Matthew, the Apostle. After having traveled about one league we heard noises and a drum and saw big fires, and we noticed that the road was a track greatly beaten by people who returned to the palisades of the Chacatos, Panzacolas, and Chiscas who lived near the sea, and we retired to a height to prepare ourselves, examine our arms, and fit ourselves up. Then all the chiefs gathered and we held a consultation about what was to be done. Some proposed to wait until sunrise, others to strike at midnight, still others shortly before sunrise. Finally we all agreed to make it a quarter before sunrise. Thus it was ordered, and we admonished our men. Then we sent two men ahead of us and most courageously followed them, and very soon we reached them, and they told us to look inside [the palisade], and that there were a great many people; that the inclosure was very big and spacious, the extent of each wall being over three hundred paces. They said the Chiscas were not sleeping; on the contrary there was much noise and they kept up big fires within and without. When we had all reached the place we sat down to watch the palisades and the great fires, and we entered into consultation whether it would be advisable to surround the inclosure, but as it was so big and we had few men, we did not dare do that, but determined to attack along one wall, and that this attack would be at three o'clock in the morning. Two captains and the Maese de Campo, Matheo Chuba, were to attack in the center, carrying the banner with the crucifix on one side and on the other Our Lady of the Rosary; the captain Don Bernardo on the east side with his drum and fife; Captain Juan Mendoza on the west side. About the time we got up to make the attack we saw a great light of the size of a man flame up behind us and then consume itself. In its center it had a blue spot. We saw about thirty persons,[1] and at this instant a Chacato who was on sentinel duty cried out that we were there.

We all attacked at once, giving them a whole charge of harquebus and archery and pulling out the sticks [from the palisade], and through the openings the captains threw themselves in upon the enemy with their harquebusiers, killing our enemies. Within the palisades there were three big houses with their embrasures, where so many of the Chiscas retired and shot so many arrows at us from their shelter that it looked like a dense smoke. As we carried with us small levers, we destroyed, helped by our firearms, many boards, and we killed and wounded so many that the wounded began fleeing and threw themselves into the river to drown themselves. Our cartridges set fire to the houses. They killed five of our men and wounded forty. There was a tree which had caught fire from our firearms and its burning leaves set fire to many houses, and the fact that although it was green it should have caught fire and should burn like tinder greatly excited our attention. When the Chiscas saw that wonder they threw themselves into the river which is in a ravine there, as well men as women with their small babies clasped to their bosoms. Although we wished to save them and keep them alive, they were almost dead and drowned. We found others alive under the corn cribs (barbacoas), and we pulled them out, separating the dead from the burned (or wounded) ones, and in so doing covered ourselves with blood from head to foot. Putting out the fire of the several houses that were burning, we found eighteen men and one boy dead. We did not count the women and children, for as they had hidden in sentry boxes and behind or under boarding many of them were consumed by the fire. All this lasted from three o'clock in the morning until sunrise, when we saw that the Chiscas had all fled and had crossed the river swimming.

We cured our wounded and reinforced our position with the sticks of the palisade which had remained, building a small inclosure to guard ourselves against those of our enemies still alive, whose loud shrieking on the other side of the river we heard. Although within the palisades we had found provisions, they were but scarce, and in our chiefs' council we decided to send out thirty men to search the plains for food and also to search the forests, for throughout that day we had been shot upon with arrows from the river bank, and as the river was but narrow they reached us. But we did not allow our men to cross the river, because so many of our men were wounded. Thus, our men were to remain on land on this side. As we were sallying forth in a little troop, one of the Chiscas shot an arrow from a sentry box and wounded one of our men after he had got some provisions. One of our men said he wanted to go back to the palisade, and, although he was admonished against it, he did not listen, and, traversing the forest, he found some Chiscas in ambush, who killed him. The rest

[1] There is evidently something lacking or the published version is poorly copied from the original.

of us went back to our palisade with our provisions, and we spent two days and two nights there, taking great precautions, keeping constant watches, and beating our war drums morning and night. All that time we heard many screams and shouts, and after a consultation among the chiefs we agreed to leave on the third day, setting fire to all that had remained. When the Chiscas saw the fire, heard the drums, and, besides, saw us come forth in two bodies, carrying our wounded in the center, a troop of them came to encounter us in the same road. Captain Bernardo de Cupayca discharged his gun, and with one shot hit a Chisca so fairly that he fell dead, and the Enija [1] from San Luis, Ventura, fired and killed another one, and our men wanted to go and scalp them, which, however, the chiefs did not allow. The Chiscas fled, and we continued on our way, enduring great suffering. After about half a league we reached a clearing, where we found four shells and several pots in which were boiled herbs. We asked the Chacatos what this might signify, and they told us it was witchcraft, in order that we might lose our way and not be able to reach our country, so that we might fall into their hands and be killed by them. But it pleased God that after eight days we entered the deserted country of the Chacatos very glad, carrying our wounded on litters, and on the ninth day we met a troop of people who came from Apalache to bring us provisions, which comforted us greatly, and we continued very happily, entering Apalache on the fifth day of October of the year 1677, by the favor of God and the Virgin of the Rosary.

I give my oath and true testimony, I, Captain Juan Fernandez de Florencia, lieutenant of this province of Apalache, that there appeared before me the said Juan Mendoza, Matheo Chuba, and Don Bernardo, the cacique of Cupayca, and Ventura, Ynija, of this place of San Luis, who, in their own language, declared the above stated and all that is written down, which I remit in the original to the governor, Don Pablo de Hita Salazar, governor and captain general of the garrison of San Agustin and its provinces by His Majesty. Made (written) in San Luis de Talimali on the 30th of August, 1678.

JUAN FERNANDEZ DE FLORENCIA.[2]

Later the same incorrigible people are held responsible, jointly with the English, for having prevented the establishment of a mission among the Apalachicola.

On the Lamhatty map (1707) these Yuchi appear in approximately the same position under the name Ogolaúghoo [Hogologe].[3] In 1718 we hear of a "Rio de los Chiscas," 5 leagues from Pensacola.[4] In the census taken in 1761 we find the "Choctaw Hatchee Euchees" included with the Tukabahchee and "Pea Creek and other plantations" under the traders James McQueen and T. Perryman,[5] and these are probably the Yuchi of the French census of the same period located close to the Tukabahchee and said to number 15 men.[6] We are to infer from this that they had then settled among the Upper Creeks. Their possible connection with the Yuchi reported by Hawkins to have united with the Shawnee on Tallapoosa River has already been mentioned.[7] We hear nothing more about them from this time on, but their name is preserved in Euchee anna, a village in Walton County, Florida.

[1] See p. 299. Enija is another spelling of Ynija.
[2] Serrano y Sanz, Doc. Hist., pp. 207-216.
[3] Amer. Anthrop., n. s. vol. x, p. 571.
[4] See p. 126.
[5] Ga. Col. Docs., VIII, p. 523.
[6] Miss. Prov. Arch., I, p. 95.
[7] See p 190.

In 1603 some old soldiers reported to Gov. Ibarra, of Florida, "that 20 leagues from Orista [in this case probably Santa Elena] is a rich people so civilized that they have their houses of hewn stone—that is, toward the northeast from whence they came, conquering those [Indians] of our lands."[1] This may refer to Yuchi, although the mention of "hewn stone" houses tends to place the account under suspicion. Another possible reference to the influx of this band appears in a letter to the king from Gov. D. Alonso de Aranguiz y Cotes, dated September 8, 1662. He says:

In a letter of Nov. 8, of the past year, 1661, I recounted to Y. M. how in the province of Goale, near this presidio, there had entered some Indians who were said to be Chichumecos which ate human flesh, and if I had not assisted in opposing their design they would have destroyed it, as I had had news regarding others from infidel Indians who came fleeing from them, and as I saw that they would retire by the way they came I made examinations and inquiries in different directions until I took four prisoners near the province of Apalachecole which is a hundred and eighty leagues distant from this presidio. Having sent infantry for the purpose I took some Indians of the Chisca Nation to serve as interpreters of their language because there was no one in these provinces who could understand them, and they said they were from Jacan, that when they retired from the province of Goale they went to that of Tama and to that of Catufa, and that there they wandered about in different bands, and the said Chisca Indians, after having explained what people they were said that very near the lands of those people there was only one very large river, on the middle course of which had fortified themselves a nation of white people who warred with them continually and were approaching these provinces, and they do not know whether they are Spaniards or English.[1]

The position which the Indians describe as that of their former home, along with their proximity to the white people, strongly suggests that occupied by the Rechahecrians on the James, yet it is strange that they should be unable to state whether their white neighbors were or were not English. These new arrivals are spoken of as if distinct from the "Chisca"—a fact tending to throw doubt on their Yuchean affinities; but it is probable that the term Chisca was limited by the governer to that band of Yuchi with which the Spaniards were familiar until then, those who had made their home on Choctawhatchee River. These invading "Chichumecos" may have been the Indians who appear soon afterwards in the narratives of the early English explorers of the Carolina coast and the accounts of the South Carolina colonists, under the name of Westo. The members of the expedition which in 1670 made the first permanent settlement learned that these Westo had attacked and destroyed the Cusabo towns at St. Helena and Kiawa. They found that the coast Indians were mortally afraid of them and accused them of being cannibals, an accusation for which there appears to have been no justification.[2]

[1] Lowery, MSS.

[2] See p. 66.

In the summer of this same year (1670) John Lederer, exploring southwest from Virginia on his own recognizance, heard of this tribe through their neighbors and enemies, the Catawba, whom he calls Ushery. He says:

This prince [i. e., the prince of the Ushery Indians], though his dominions are large and populous, is in continual fear of the Oustack Indians on the opposite side of the lake—a people so addicted to arms that even their women come into the field and shoot arrows over their husbands' shoulders, who shield them with leathern targets. The men it seems should fight with silver-hatchets; for one of the Usheryes told me that they were of the same metal with the pomel of my sword. They are a cruel generation, and prey upon people whom they either steal or force away from the Usheryes in Periago's, to sacrifice to their idols.[1]

That the Westo were then at war with the Iswa (Lederer's Ushery), a branch of the Catawba, is plainly indicated in the South Carolina archives.[2]

In 1672–73 they attacked the South Carolina settlers.[3] In 1674 Henry Woodward, the interpreter of the colony, visited a Westo town on Savannah River somewhere below the present Augusta. He describes his visit thus:

Haveing paddled about a league upp [the Savannah] wee came in sight of ye Westoe towne, alias ye Hickauhaugau which stands uppon a poynt of ye river (which is undoubtedly ye river May) uppon ye Westerne side soe y[t] ye river encompasseth two-thirds thereof. When we came w[th]in [sight] of the towne I fired my fowling piece & pistol w[ch] was answered with a hollow & imediately thereuppon they gave mee a vollew of fifty or sixty small arms. Here was a concourse of some hundred of Indians drest up in their anticke fighting garbe. Through ye midst of whom being conducted to their cheiftaines house ye which not being capable to containe ye crowd y[t] came to see me, ye smaller fry got up & uncouvered the top of ye house to satisfy their curiosity. Ye cheife of ye Indians made long speeches intimateing their own strength (& as I judged their desire of Freindship wth us). This night first haveing oyled my eyes and joynts with beares oyl, they presented mee divers deare skins setting before me sufficient of their food to satisfy at least half a dozen of their owne appetites. Here takeing my first nights repose, ye next day I viewed ye Towne which is built in a confused manner, consisting of many long houses whose sides and tops are both artifitially done wth barke uppon ye tops of most whereof fastened to ye ends of long poles hang ye locks of haire of Indians that they have slaine. Ye inland side of ye towne being duble Pallisadoed, & y[t] part which fronts ye river haveing only a single one, under whose steep banks seldom ly less then one hundred faire canoes ready uppon all occasions. They are well provided with arms, amunition, tradeing cloath & other trade from ye northward for which at set times of ye year they truck drest deare skins furrs & young Indian Slaves. In ten daies time y[t] I tarried here I viewed ye adjacent part of ye Country, they are Seated uppon a most fruitfull soyl. Ye earth is intermingled wth a sparkling substance like Antimony, finding severall flakes of Isinglass in ye paths. Ye soales of my Indian shooes in which I travelled glistened like sylver. Ye clay of which their pots & pipes are made is intermingled wth ye like substance ye wood land is abounding wth various sorts of very large straite timber. Eight dais journey from ye towne ye River hath it first falls West. N. West were it

---

[1]Lederer, Discoveries, pp. 20–21.
[2]S. C. Hist. Soc. Colls., v, p. 428.
[3]Ibid., pp. 406, 427–428, 461.

divides it selfe into three branches, amongst which dividing branches inhabit ye Cowatoe and Chorakae Indians wth whom they are at continual warrs. Forty miles distant from the towne northward they say lye ye head of Ædistaw river being a great meer or lake. Two days before my departure arrived two Savana Indians living as they said twenty days journey West Southwardly from them. There was none here y^t^ understood them but by signes they intreated freindship of ye Westoes showeing y^t^ ye Cussetaws, Chaesaws & Chiskers[1] were intended to come downe and fight ye Westoes. At which news they expeditiously repaired their pallisadoes, keeping watch all night. In the time of my abode here they gave me a young Indian boy taken from ye falls of y^t^ River. The Savana Indians brought Spanish beeds & other trade as presents makeing signes y^t^ they had comerce wth white people like unto mee, whom were not good. These they civilly treated & dismissed before my departure ten of them prepared to accompany mee in my journey home.[2]

As pointed out by Professor Crane, "Hickauhaugau" is probably miscopied from "Rickauhaugau" and is a synonym for Rickohockan.

In April, 1680, the governor of South Carolina had a conference with certain of the Westo chiefs, but later the Westo attacked some coast Indians, friendly to the colonists. War followed between them and the English, and, according to the colonial historians, it would have been disastrous to the new settlements had not a body of Shawnee fallen upon their enemies and driven them away from the Savannah.[3] This happened in 1681, and the Indians thus dispossessed appear to have settled on Ocmulgee River near the Coweta, then living in the neighborhood of the present Butts County, Georgia. At any rate Fray Francisco Gutierrez de Vera states, in a letter dated May 19, 1681, largely concerned with the Chatot mission, that the Coweta chief had arrived and reported that "many Chuchumecas" had come to live at his town.[4] There was certainly a settlement of Westo near there, numbering 15 men at the outbreak of the Yamasee war. But from the note discovered by Professor Crane it is probable that their numbers had been augmented by other Yuchi from the north.[5] Individuals, as we have seen, strayed far enough westward to meet the French under La Salle.[6]

During or immediately after the Yamasee war they retired beyond the Chattahoochee, where they are located on maps of the eighteenth century for a long time afterwards. They appear to have lived close to the mouth of Little Uchee Creek, Russell County, Alabama. They probably united with the main Yuchi town after its removal to Alabama, but we have no direct evidence regarding the time or manner in which this event took place. On the Purcell map, however, we find a town called Woristo, between Kasihta and

---

[1] This seems to be the original spelling of these names, which I have restored. The editor of the narrative gave them as Cussetaws, Checsaws, and Chiokees.

[2] S. C. Hist. Soc. Colls., v, pp. 459–461.

[3] Hewat, Hist. Acct. S. C. and Ga., pp. 63–64.

[4] Lowery, MSS.

[5] See p. 291.

[6] See p. 296.

Okmulgee (pl. 7). As the large Yuchi town and the Westo town were both here it seems probable that Woristo is meant for Westo, and that it was used for all of the Yuchi, especially since there is every reason to believe that the Westo town proper had already been given up.

In 1708 a rough Indian census made on behalf of the State of South Carolina makes no mention of Yuchi Indians, though they may be included in the eleven Lower Creek towns referred to,[1] but the detailed census of 1715 gives two Yuchi towns 180 miles W. N. W. of Charleston.[2] They were probably north of the Shawnee on Savannah River between Augusta, Georgia, and the Cherokee, and constituted the band which moved over to the Chattahoochee after the Yamasee war. This band is the one to which the term Hogologe is attached more particularly. They were accompanied by a part of the Shawnee and the Apalachicola Indians, the latter under Cherokee leechee.[3]

As nearly as can be made out from the maps they settled near the mouth of Cowikee Creek in Barbour County, Alabama, but before many years they accompanied the Shawnee to Tallapoosa River. Their name is mentioned by Romans when enumerating the Creek tribes,[4] and their town is probably the Chisketaloofa of the census of 1761, which had 30 hunters and was assigned, along with Weupkees (Okitiyagana), to the traders Macartan and Campbell.[5] Morse enumerates "Cheskitalowas" among the Seminole villages.[6] The name Chiska also appears in much later documents associated with a point near the lower Chattahoochee. In a letter from the Secretary of the Treasury transmitting copies of the report of the Commissioners of Land Claims in East and West Florida, February 22, 1825 (pub., Washington, 1825), Cheeskatalofa is mentioned as a town in which a meeting was held (p. 18). But while the name preserved a memory of them, the greater part of the Yuchi had probably moved even before 1761, since we know that their Shawnee friends had already done so. For a conjecture as to their subsequent fortunes see my discussion of the Tamahita, pages 188–191.

Shortly after the Yamasee war another influx of Yuchee into the Savannah country took place, though little specific information regarding this seems to be preserved. The new arrivals settled at or near Silver Bluff, at Mount Pleasant, and as far down the river as Ebenezer Creek.

Hawkins says that there were villages at Ponpon and Saltkechers, in South Carolina,[7] but this is the sole evidence we have regarding

---

[1] S. C. Pub. Docs., v., pp. 207–209.

[2] Rivers, Hist. S. C., p. 94.

[3] Brinton, The Floridian Peninsula, p. 141; see also p. 131.

[4] Romans, Nat. Hist. E. and W. Fla., p. 280.

[5] Ga. Col. Docs., VIII, p. 523.

[6] Page 409; Morse, Rept. to Sec. of War, p. 364.

[7] See p. 309.

settlements so far to the east of the Savannah. Possibly some Coosa Indians of South Carolina afterwards combined with them. After the establishment of a Yuchi settlement on the Chattahoochee by Chief Ellick of the Kasihta, in the year 1729, as will be detailed below, they began to make their permanent residence more and more among the Creeks, using their old territories principally for hunting. Although the white settlers naturally coveted these lands, left vacant for so much of the time, Governor Oglethorpe restrained them and preserved the territory inviolate until after 1740. Not many years later they had been practically given over by the Yuchi themselves. Two very good descriptions of the Yuchi town on the Chattahoochee have been preserved to us—one by Bartram and one by Hawkins. It stood at the mouth of the present Big Uchee Creek. Bartram, who passed through the place in 1778, says of it:

The Uche town is situated in a low ground immediately bordering on the river; it is the largest, most compact, and best situated Indian town I ever saw; the habitations are large and neatly built; the walls of the houses are constructed of a wooden frame, then lathed and plastered inside and out with a reddish well-tempered clay or mortar, which gives them the appearance of red brick walls; and these houses are neatly covered or roofed with Cypress bark or shingles of that tree. The town appeared to be populous and thriving, full of youth and young children. I suppose the number of inhabitants, men, women and children, might amount to one thousand or fifteen hundred, as it is said they are able to muster five hundred gunmen or warriors. Their own national language is altogether or radically different from the Creek or Muscogulge tongue, and is called the Savanna or Savanuca tongue; I was told by the traders it was the same with, or a dialect of the Shawanese. They are in confederacy with the Creeks, but do not mix with them; and on account of their numbers and strength, are of importance enough to excite and draw upon them the jealousy of the whole Muscogulge confederacy, and are usually at variance, yet are wise enough to unite against a common enemy, to support the interest and glory of the general Creek confederacy.[1]

Of course the Shawnee and Yuchi languages are radically distinct. Bartram was led into the error of supposing a relation to subsist between them by the fact that the two tribes were on very intimate terms, were mixed together, and both spoke languages quite different from Creek.[2]

Hawkins's description follows:

U-chee: is on the right bank of Chat-to-ho-che, ten and a half miles below Cow-e-tuh tal-lau-has-see, on a flat of rich land, with hickory, oak, blackjack, and long-leaf pine; the flat extends from one to two miles back from the river. Above the town, and bordering on it, Uchee Creek, eighty-five[3] feet wide, joins the river. Opposite the town house, on the left bank of the river, there is a narrow strip of flat land from fifty to one hundred yards wide, then high pine barren hills; these people speak a tongue different from the Creeks; they were formerly settled in small villages at Ponpon, Saltketchers (Sol-ke-chuh), Silver Bluff, and O-ge-chee, and were continually at war with the Cherokees, Ca-tau-bau, and Creeks.

[1] Bartram, Travels, pp. 386-387.

[2] See p. 190.

[3] The Lib. Cong. MS. has "45."

In the year 1729, an old chief of Cussetuh, called by the white people Captain Ellick, married three Uchee women, and brought them to Cussetuh, which was greatly disliked by his towns people; their opposition determined him to move from Cussetuh; he went down opposite where the town now is, and settled with his three brothers; two of whom had Uchee wives; he, after this, collected all the Uchees, gave them the land where their town now is, and there they settled.

These people are more civil and orderly than their neighbors; their women are more chaste, and the men better hunters; they retain all their original customs and laws, and have adopted none of the Creeks; they have some worm fences in and about their town, but very few peach trees.

They have lately begun to settle out in villages, and are industrious, compared with their neighbors; the men take part in the labors of the women, and are more constant in their attachment to their women than is usual among red people.

The number of gun men is variously estimated; they do not exceed two hundred and fifty, including all who are settled in villages, of which they have three.

1st. In-tuch-cul-gau; from in-tuch-ke, a dam across water [a "cut off"]; and ul-gau, all; applied to beaver dams. This is on Opil-thluc-co, twenty-eight miles from its junction with Flint River. This creek is sixty feet wide at its mouth, one and a half miles above Timothy Barnard's; the land bordering on the creek, up to the village, is good. Eight miles below the village the good land spreads out for four or five miles on both sides of the creek, with oaky woods (Tuck-au-mau-pa-fau); the range is fine for cattle; cane grows on the creeks, and reeds on all the branches.

They have fourteen families in the village; their industry is increasing; they built a square in 1798, which serves for their town house; they have a few cattle, hogs, and horses.[1]

2d. Pad-gee-li-gau [padjilaiga]; from pad-jee, a pidgeon; and ligau, sit; pidgeon roost. This was formerly a large town, but broken up by Benjamin Harrison and his associates, who murdered sixteen of their gun men in Georgia; it is on the right bank of Flint River, and this creek, adjoining the river; the village takes its name from the creek; it is nine miles below the second falls of the river;[2] these falls are at the island's ford, where the path now crosses from Cussetuh to Fort Wilkinson; the village is advantageoulsy situated; the land is rich, the range good for cattle and hogs; the swamp is more than three miles through, on the left bank of the river, and is high and good canebrake; on the right bank, it is one mile through, low and flat; the cane, sassafras, and sumach, are large; this extensive and valuable swamp extends down on one side or the other of the river for twelve miles.

They have but a few families there, notwithstanding it is one of the best situations the Indians possess, for stock, farming, and fish. Being a frontier, the great loss they sustained in having sixteen of their gun men murdered discourages them from returning.[3]

3d. Toc-co-gul-egau (tad pole) [tóki ûlga, tadpole place]; a small settlement on Kit-cho-foo-ne Creek, near some beaver dams on branches of that creek; the land is good, but broken; fine range, small canes, and pea vines on the hills, and reeds on the branches; they have eight or ten families; this establishment is of two years only, and they have worm fences. U-che Will, the head of the village has some cattle, and they have promised to attend to hogs, and to follow the direction of the agent for Indian affairs, as soon as they can get into stock.

---

[1] Also see Hawkins in Ga. Hist. Soc. Colls., IX, pp. 171–172.

[2] "18 miles above Timothy Barnard's and 9 miles below the old horse path, the first rock falls in the river."—Hawkins, in Ga. Hist. Soc. Colls., IX, p. 171.

[3] Another description by the same writer, largely parallel, is in Ga. Hist. Soc. Colls., IX, p. 171.

Some of the Uchees have settled with the Shaw-a-ne, at Sau-va-no-gee, among the Creeks of the upper towns.[1]

I will also add what Hawkins has to say regarding the settlement of Timothy Barnard, who plays a prominent part in Creek history, both before and after this time:

This gentleman lives on the right bank of Flint River, fifteen miles below Pad-jee-li-gau. He has eleven children by a U-chee woman, and they are settled with and around him, and have fine stocks of cattle in an excellent range. He has a valuable property, but not productive; his farm is well fenced on both sides of the river; he has a peach orchard of fine fruit, and some fine nectarines, a garden well stored with vegetables, and some grape vines presented to him by the agent. He is an assistant and interpreter, and a man who has uniformly supported an honest character, friendly to peace during the revolutionary war, and to man. He has 40 sheep, some goats, and stock of every description, and keeps a very hospitable house. He is not much acquainted with farming, and receives light slowly on this subject, as is the case with all the Indian countrymen, without exception."[2]

The trader located at the main Yuchi town in 1797 is given by Hawkins as James Smithmoor.[3]

The Yuchi also appear in the enumerations of 1760,[4] 1761,[5] that of Swan,[6] and in the census of 1832, when they were credited with one main town and with a branch village called High Log.[7] During the latter part of the eighteenth century and the first of the nineteenth, settlements of Yuchi were probably scattered through southern Georgia at many places. Imlay says "The Uchees Indians occupy four different places of residence, at the head of St. John's, the Fork of St. Mary's, the head of Cannuchee, and the head of St. Tillis (Satilla)."[8]

After their removal to the new Creek territories west of the Mississippi they settled in the northwestern part of the nation, where they continued an almost distinct tribal life, although represented in the Creek national assembly. The reader is referred to Dr. Speck's admirable paper for an account of their later condition.[9]

Besides the Savannah, the Yuchi also occupied at least the upper portion of Ogeechee River. This is indicated by Hawkins in his account of the Yuchi town just given and also by several maps of the eighteenth century, in which the Ogeechee is called "Great Ogeechee or Hughchee River,"[10] the latter being one spelling of the

---

[1] Ga. Hist. Soc. Colls., III, pp. 61–63.
[2] Ibid., pp. 66–67.
[3] Ibid., IX, p. 171.
[4] Miss Prov. Arch., I, p. 96.
[5] Ga. Col. Docs., VIII, p. 522.
[6] Schoolcraft, Ind. Tribes, V, p. 262.
[7] Senate Doc. 512, 23d Cong., 1st sess., IV, pp. 356–363; Schoolcraft, op. cit., p. 578.
[8] Imlay, Top. Descr. of N. A., p. 369.
[9] Univ. of Pa., Anthrop. Publ., I, No. 1.
[10] Jefferys, Am. Atlas, map 24.

name Yuchi. On many maps we find "Ogeechee Old Town" laid down near the upper course of Ogeechee River and on the trading path from Augusta to Ocmulgee old fields and the Creek country. The way in which this appears indicates that the town had removed at the time of the Yamasee war, when it may have united with those Yuchi known as Westo, the larger body of Yuchi not migrating until some years later. Their fate is somewhat confused by the following reference in Bartram:

> Mr. Egan politely rode with me over a great part of the island (Amelia). On Egmont estate are several very large Indian tumuli, which are called Ogeeche mounts, so named from that nation of Indians who took shelter here, after being driven from their native settlements on the main near Ogeeche River. Here they were constantly harrassed by the Carolinians and Creeks, and at length slain by their conquerors, and their bones entombed in these heaps of earth and shells.[1]

If there is any truth in this legend at all it is probable that the people referred to were Yamasee, or at least Indians of the province of Guale who had perhaps lived about the mouth of the Ogeechee, but not the Ogeechee tribe we have been considering.

As noted above, a portion of the Yuchi went to Florida. They appear first in west Florida near the Mikasuki,[2] but later they moved across the peninsula and settled at Spring Garden, east of Dexters Lake, in Volusia County. Afterwards they were involved in the long Seminole war with the whites. All of them did not go in the first emigrations, a special census taken in the year 1847 giving four Yuchi warriors among the Seminole left in the peninsula.[3]

THE NATCHEZ

The Natchez having been made the subject of a special study by the writer,[4] no extended notice need be given here. Their earliest known home was on St. Catharines Creek, Mississippi, close to the present city which bears their name. After Louisiana was colonized by the French the latter established a post among them, which was in a very flourishing condition when, in the year 1729, it was suddenly cut off by a native uprising. Subsequently the French attacked these Indians, killed many, captured some, whom they sent to Santo Domingo as slaves, and forced the rest to abandon their old country and settle among the Chickasaw. When the French turned their attacks against the Chickasaw the Natchez found it necessary to move again, and some went to the Cherokee, some to the Catawba,

---

[1] Bartram, Travels, pp. 63-64.

[2] See pp. 406, 409, 412.

[3] Schoolcraft, Ind. Tribes, I, p. 522.

[4] Indian Tribes of the Lower Miss. Valley and Adj. Coast of the Gulf of Mex., Bull. 43, Bur. Amer. Ethn., pp. 45-257.

and some to the Creeks. Those who went to the Cherokee and Creeks subsequently followed their fortunes, and the latter band was taken in by the Abihka. They seem to have conformed in most particulars to the usages of their neighbors. Taitt thus describes his visit to them on March 27, 1772:

I went this morning to black drink to the Square, where I was very kindley received by the head men of the town who told me to look on myself as being amongst my friends and not to be affraid of any thing, for their fire was the same as Charlestown fire and they never had Spilt the blood of any white Man;[1] after that I had Smoked Tobacco and drinked black drink with them they desired that I might Stay in their Town all day as they were building a hot house and Should have a dance in the Evening which they wanted me to see. In the Evening I went to the Square where thirteen Chickasaws had joined the Natchies and Creeks for the dance. . . The women being dressed like Warriours with bows, hatchets, and other weapons in their hands, came into the Square and danced round the fire, the pole Cat dance, two men Singing and ratling their Callabashes all the time.[2]

Although having separate towns, the Natchez and Abihka are said to have intermarried to such an extent as to become completely fused. Since descent was reckoned in the female line the Natchez were still distinguished from the Abihka through their mothers, and the language was transmitted thus for many years, but it is now extinct. Among the Cherokee the Natchez preserved their identity longer, and a few Indians remain who can speak the old tongue. Among the Creeks some stories are still told regarding them. Jackson Lewis repeated a tradition to the effect that the Natchez were at one time hemmed in by the French, but all that could move, men, women, and children, escaped by wading through water. Then they went to the Chickasaw to live, but after a time they found some of their children who had gone out berrying run through with canes. This was done by the Chickasaw, who did not want the Natchez among them, so the latter moved on and came to where the Abihka lived. They asked the Abihka to take them in and the Abihka told them to "enter the gates" and confer with the chiefs, the Abihka being the "door shutters" of the confederacy. The Natchez did this and were adopted. They were allowed to settle with the Abihka, according to one story, because the Abihka were a very small people, perhaps having been reduced in wars with the Cherokee. According to Adair, some Chickasaw moved with the Natchez and the two occupied a town called Ooe-asa, somewhere near the upper course of Coosa River.[3]

To these few notes I will add the account which Stiggins gives of this tribe which was not included in my bulletin above mentioned.

---

[1] A notable prevarication, except on the supposition that the speaker meant *English* white men.

[2] Mereness, Trav. Am. Col., pp. 531-532.

[3] Adair, Hist. Am. Inds., p. 319.

It is of particular interest inasmuch as Stiggins himself was a Natchez Indian.[1] It has not before been published.

The Natches.—The men of that tribe almost all converse in the Creek tongue, with their families or not. Tho' the women can speak it fluently yet most generally in their own common concerns and to their children they use their own native tongue. Frequently in one house they use both tongues without any detriment to their conversation or business. The tradition they relate as the cause of their removal from the seat of their nativity to their final settlement in the Taladega Valley I will relate as I heard it. That about one century ago that the tribe lived in one large body or tribe on the bank of the Mississippi where the present city of Natches now stands and extended above it, that their government was monarchical, and that all cases both civil and political were determined by the king and his suite, for he was attended by both men and women in great state. The throne was hereditary and the king was supreme head of the tribe. His person was sacred and his mandates inviolable. He lived in a retired manner in the suburbs of the town, secluded from the society of all persons but his own near relations, who officiated about his person both men and women as attendants and guards, about one-third of his connection at a time, and such as were not in attendance on his person were in the forest in search of game for his subsistance. During the hunting excursion the party was headed by one of his near relatives to direct and take care of the party. But it must be noticed that all earthly institutions tho' made for lasting happiness for ages, are delusive and visionary. So it happened to them. For while they were living under their peaceable and happy institution of government, a government familiarized to them by time, and consonant to their habits of life, they received a visit from a detachment of French who went up the river Mississippi to explore the country and fix on an eligible spot to erect a garrison, and without a previous compact with the natives to insure their good will. They pitched on a site in the vicinity of the town. Tho' much against the will of the Indians, they disguised their chagrin and seemingly were careless and not opposed to the encroachment of their unwelcome visitants and neighbors, who had fortified themselves in the suburb below the town.

The French, by their gallantry, pursued the destructive course said to have been in Sodom of olden time. As tho' danger was not imbruing nor destruction awfully pending over their ill-fated heads they made free with the men and married their women. They were tolerated in their love to their women with seeming good will by the natives for they saw the advantage that would ultimately result through their blind devotion to love, for it would make them unsuspicious and unguarded against a design they had in contemplation to effect through that means. As was expected their lewd practices soon caused a relaxation of their vigilance and discipline, for they frequented the town at night in a careless manner and unguardedly admitted the women into the fortress at night and made them welcome visitants at all times. The Indians saw how remiss and negligent the French were getting in their manner of living, as was expected, and they for revenge secretly and exultingly proceeded to put their scheme into execution, which was to exterminate their gallant and unwelcome neighbors. Therefore the Indian men concerted a plan with their women as though without design for the women to make their appointments with the Frenchmen to be and stay within the fortress on such a night, which appointment was accordingly made and the garrison overreached. For when the time arrived, instead of the expected women, the fortress was entered by men in disguise and armed, who on entrance instantly fell to work and exterminated the whole garrison of men. One man escaped because his loving wife, wishing to save him, had prevailed on him to stay with her

[1] Probably a son of Joseph Stiggins, trader in the Natchez town in 1796.—Hawkins in Ga. Hist. Soc. Colls., IX, p. 34.

in the town that night, and after the above catastrophe she effected his escape down the river Mississippi. So he carried the news of the disaster to his comrades to his countrymen.

The Indians were very much elated with the successful event of their plan, which had even exceeded their most sanguine expectations, getting clear of their intruders so quickly and easily without the loss of any of their own blood. But their joy was of short duration. They equipt themselves with the spoils of their vanquished neighbors, in arms, clothing, provisions, and hats, which last they particularly admired, and they did not suppose there were any more to revenge their horrid deed. In their enthusiasm to take possession of their empty garrison that they so easily attained they unanimously concluded and even prompted his majesty and all his suite, and all that could get quarters to remove therein as the buildings were more commodious than those of the town. Then, after they had arranged their new habitation and gotten all snug and secure, the king sent out the usual hunting party headed by one of his nephews. But after their hunting excursion was over and they returned, behold their surprise at seeing a number of shipping moored in front of the fort and apparently the whole of their tribe in the act of embarking on board of the shipping under the guard and control of two rows of white men with hats on similar to those worn by the people that they destroyed. From the following circumstance I expect the whole of the tribe were not captured, as there is a people on the south waters of the Missouri who call themselves Natchez, who probably made their escape when those in the fortress were surrounded and captured. All that were shipped off by the French were insulated and settled in the island of St? Domingo where their progeny now remain. Their arms offensive and defensive were bows and arrows pointed with either sharpened bone or pieces of flint. With these weapons they attacked their enemy or killed their game for subsistence. When those that had been a hunting returned and saw their tribe on the ships and saw them disappear down the river, they could not imagine what would be their destination and fate, so in their incertitude and perplexity of mind they concluded to leave their forlorn case with the seat of their ancestors forever, and in the scenes of a new and untried home forget the wreck of their tribe who they expected were doomed to slavery and wretchedness. Having had intercourse and friendship with the Chickasaws they moved to them first where some took up their abode, and some with the Cherokees, but the greater part headed by the royal family, made a compact of assimilation with the *Au bih kas* or Creek tribe and settled in the Tallidega Valley. They remained thus sequestered for about twenty-five years, when, at the instance of their chief, they all made a final exit and settled in the Valley and by their compact became a member of the Ispocoga body, which they have remained down to this period.

This remnant of the Natche tribe to this distant day are unfriendly to the French people. Their antient manners and customs it is said were similar to those of the *Au bih kas*, so they had to make no change in their habits of life by their removal. These statements were handed down to the most antient of the present day by their forefathers, who were spectators, though in their infancy, of what had happened to and in their tribe. They have a belief in a supreme being but no worship or adoration. Though they generally talk about good and bad actions in this life I never could understand that they had any idea of rewards or punishments in future, for they generally believe in another life here on a place they can not describe. They keep the Busk festival in a very devout and sacred manner. Near one of the towns in the Valley not very far from Soto's fortification there is a cavern said to be near a quarter of a mile long and much dissected. Such Indians as have been in it say that it is peopled by fairies. They have never seen any because they have the power of making themselves imperceptible, but they have seen their tracks and know that they live on the innumerable bats and swallows that stay in there. It was entered by some men many years since, that is a half century ago. They found the bones of a human being in the first room and right by him carved in a rock, "I. W. Wright, 1723"

In the beginning of my narrative I said as a prelude I would intersperce an occasional tradition, therefore I will relate one retained by the Natche tribe and related by them as a matter handed down through successive generations for their information. I insert it to show in its connection and inference that in olden times their patriarch knew or heard in some way of the deluge and that the primary information or knowledge he had of it had got blended with traditional fiction. It is said that speech and rational power was given to man alone and he by his knowledge and understanding is enabled to make the other creatures subservient to him, so that he rules and manages them in a way most conducive to his will and their comfort in life, but when the gift of speech is imparted to a dumb creature it is to be observed as a matter of inspiration to the beast purposed by the great spirit to be words of sacred truth from himself through said creature. As a manifest proof of the foregoing remarks it is said that there was a large assemblage of the antients on some particular occasion, in times of yore, when to their surprise they were accosted by a little dog, who, having gaped and yawned in a particular whining manner, began in articulate words to bemoan their sudden fate. He called on them individually to look between his ears first toward sunset and then in every other direction and see their fate. They looked accordingly as he said. They could see nothing, but on a second bidding they could see mountains of water rolling toward them. He bade him who could fly to the mountains for safety and escape death, so they fled. Only a few of them reached the mountains, however, most being overtaken and overwhelmed by the waving torrent of water. Among them the "old man of sorrow" was one who escaped by his flight to the mountains. He is called in their tongue *Tam seal hous hous opah*.[1] He uttered his wailings and lamentations continually, and in tears of sorrow he mourned for all that perished, and his sorrow likewise extended to the living whom he took under his care and instructed them by good words how best to live in future in order to shun the paths of destruction. The earth was overwhelmed by the billows of water and no one survived that did not attain the summit of the mountains. From these was the earth repeopled. Who this old man of lamentation or sorrow was may be a question but as I never heard any more of him I shall leave him as I heard of him, without any conjecture relative to him, to be solved by the inquisitive, and the antient of days.[2]

In 1796 the trader in this town was Joseph Stiggins, as above noted; in 1797 the traders were "James Quarls," who had "the character of an honest man," and "Thomas Wilson, a saddler." [3]

It is not generally known that John Stuart, Indian agent under the British Government, at one time formulated a proposition to restore these Indians to their old home near Natchez, Mississippi. His suggestion is outlined in a letter dated December 2, 1766, in the following terms:

This consideration [that the Choctaw might at any time obstruct the navigation of the Mississippi] suggested to me the advantage which might arise to His Majesty's Service from collecting the Scatter'd Remains of the Natchez and giving them a Settlement in their own Country again. There may be from 150 to 200 Gun Men of them remaining, in the Cherokee, Creek, and Chickasaw Nations; they still retain their Language and Customs, as well as the strongest Resentment for the Expulsion and in a great Measure the Destruction of their Nation by the French.[4]

---

[1] *Tam* =*dom*', person; *seal*=*sīl*, big; *hous hous opah* may be from the stem *hō*, duplicated, meaning to howl, or from *hac*, old, perhaps in the form *hachactipa*, "is very old," though I do not have this form in my material.

[2] Stiggins, MS., pp. 7-11.

[3] Ga. Hist. Soc. Colls., IX, pp. 34, 169.

[4] English Transcriptions, Lib. Cong.

THE SHAWNEE

The earliest known home of the Shawnee was on Cumberland River. From there some of them moved across to the Tennessee and established settlements about the Big Bend. As we have seen, Henry Woodward was a witness, in 1674, to what was probably the first appearance of members of the tribe on Savannah River.[1] Although he represents them as settled southwest of that stream near the Spaniards, it is more likely that the individuals whom he met belonged on the Cumberland, had been to St. Augustine to trade with the Spaniards, and were on their return home. Shortly afterwards a Shawnee band settled near what is now Augusta, and, as already stated, in 1681 [1] they drove the Westo Indians from that neighborhood. In 1708 they had three towns on Savannah River, and the number of their men was estimated at 150,[2] but in 1715 a more detailed census gives three towns, 67 men, and 233 souls.[3]

Before even the first of these enumerations, however, a part of the Shawnee had moved north to join their relatives from the Ohio and Cumberland who had settled in Lancaster County, Pennsylvania, about 15 years before.[4] These latter belonged to the Piqua band, and the association of the southern Shawnee Indians with them led Mooney to state that the Shawnee in Carolina belonged to both the Piqua and Hathewekela,[5] but there is no absolute proof of this, and it is more likely that all the Piqua came directly from the Cumberland. There is some doubt as to the time when the first Shawnee moved from Carolina into Pennsylvania, yet we are able to fix upon the probable period. In the first place, Lawson, in his History of Carolina, published in 1709, says that the "Savannas Indians" had formerly lived on the banks of the Mississippi "and removed thence to the head of one of the rivers of South Carolina [the Savannah], since which, for some dislike, most of them are removed to live in the quarters of the Iroquois or Sinnagars [Seneca], which are on the heads of the rivers that disgorge themselves into the bay of Chesapeak."[6]

In June, 1707, Gov. John Evans of Pennsylvania visited the Shawnee Indians on the Susquehanna and states that, while he was at their village—

> several of the Shawnee Indians from the southward came to settle here, and were admitted to so do by Opessah, with the governor's consent; at the same time an Indian from a Shawnee town near Carolina came in, and gave an account that 450 of the Flat Head (Catawba) Indians had besieged them, and that in all probability the same was taken. Bezallion (a Trader, who acted as interpreter) informed the Governor

[1] See p. 307.

[2] S. C. Pub. Docs., v, pp. 207-209, MS.

[3] Rivers, Hist. S. C., p. 94.

[4] Hanna, The Wilderness Trail, I, pp. 119-160.

[5] Handbook of Amer. Inds., Bull. 30, Bur. Amer. Ethn., pt. 2, Article "Shawnee."

[6] Lawson, Hist. Car., pp. 279-270.

that the Shawnees of Carolina, he was told, had killed several Christians; whereupon the government of that province had raised the said Flat Head Indians, and joined some Christians to them, besieged, and have taken, as it is thought, the said Shawnee town.[1]

It is probable that the numbers of those Carolina Shawnee who had migrated to Pennsylvania were constantly swollen. In 1715, as a result of the Yamasee war, a part of the Shawnee on Savannah River moved to the Chattahoochee, settling apparently near where Fort Gaines is now located. The rest either remained in their old towns until about 1731 or began moving north immediately. All we know with certainty is that they were in Pennsylvania by October of the latter year, as the following testimony demonstrates:

On October 29, 1731, two traders, named Jonah Davenport and James Le Tort, furnished detailed information to the governor of Pennsylvania regarding the number of Indians in the Alleghany country, and this testimony contains the following item:

Assiwikales: 50 families; lately from S. Carolina to Ptowmack, and from thence thither; making 100 men. Aqueloma, their chief, true to the English.[2]

On an earlier page he enumerates these people as if they were distinct from the Shawnee. As a matter of fact they were the principal Shawnee division in the south, and according to recent information gathered by Doctor Michelson would seem to have been considered first in rank.

In order to reach Pennsylvania the Piqua seem, as Hanna suggests, to have ascended the Ohio or Cumberland and then to have crossed to the headwaters of the Potomac by "the Virginia Valley, the Kanawha, or the Youghiogheny,"[3] Part of them occupied towns on the upper course of the Potomac for a time, while the remainder kept on eastward to the Susquehanna. As these upper Potomac towns appear to be apart from and to one side of the Shawnee towns reported near Winchester, Va., the latter may have marked a stage in the northward movement of the Carolina Shawnee. The following information regarding the Winchester settlements is contained in Kercheval's History of the Valley of Virginia:

The Shawnee tribe, it is well known, were settled about the neighborhood of Winchester. What are called the "Shawnee cabins" and "Shawnee springs" immediately adjoining the town is well known. It is also equally certain that this tribe had a considerable village, on Babb's marsh, some three or four miles northwest of Winchester.[4]

Of course, which band of Shawnee was actually settled here can not as yet be demonstrated. Those who went to the Chattahoochee probably remained there very few years, since we soon hear of them among the Upper Creeks. Another band of Shawnee came from the

[1] Hanna, The Wilderness Trail, I, pp. 150–151; Day, Hist. Coll. State of Pa., p. 391.

[2] Hanna, The Wilderness Trail, I, p. 296.

[3] Ibid., p. 158.

[4] Kercheval, Hist. Val. of Va., p. 58.

north about this time, but whether the two belonged to the same Shawnee subdivision we do not know. These were evidently the Indians encountered by Adair in the year 1747 on their way south.[1] According to Draper these Shawnee made a settlement in the northern part of the Creek Nation, and after a few years returned to the Ohio without going farther south.[2] Adair himself speaks of the Shawnee "who settled between the Ooe-asa and Koosah towns."[3] Some Chickasaw legends regarding the movement of these people to the Creeks and back is given in another place.[4]

At any rate several distinct Shawnee settlements existed among the Upper Creeks at the same time. In 1752 and the year following there was a Shawnee town not far from Coosa River, apparently in the country of the Abihka Indians. In fact, some maps show two settlements of the tribe here, one of which is called "Cayomulgi," which is evidently the "Kiamulgatown" of the census list of 1832.[5] No town of the name is now remembered; perhaps it was the Creek name for the Shawnee town, which had by the whites been applied to a later Creek settlement. Hawkins gives "Kiomulgee" as the name of the upper part of Natchez or Tallasee Hatchee Creek, which extends toward Sylacauga.[6] This would agree well with the location of a town on the Purcell map (pl. 7) called Mulberry Tree, not otherwise identified. It should be noted that the Creek word for mulberry is *kĭ* while *omulga* signifies all.

In the French census of 1760 there appear among the Creeks two Shawnee towns of 50 men each. One was evidently the settlement just mentioned, which is called Chalakagay, perhaps intended for Sylacauga, a name which indicates in Creek a place where buzzards are plentiful—and the other is meant for "Little Shawnee." The latter is placed within 3 leagues of Fort Toulouse.[7] In the census of 1761 we find only the latter settlement, "Savanalis opposite to Muck-lassee or shaircula savanalis." "Shaircula" is probably intended for Hathawekela. It then numbered 30 hunters and had as agents William Trewin and Crook & Co.[8] Bartram includes this in his list of Creek towns, but confounds its inhabitants with the Yuchi.[9] Swan gives a town bearing the Shawnee name and states that Kan-hatki was also occupied by Indians of this tribe.[10] I have elsewhere shown that, on this latter point, he is in error.

In 1797 Hawkins states that the trader here was "John Haigue, commonly called Savannah Jack," evidently a mixed blood.[11] In his sketch he has the following to say regarding it:

---

[1] Adair, Hist. Am. Inds., pp. 2–3.

[2] Hanna, The Wilderness Trail, II, pp. 240–242.

[3] Adair, Hist. Am. Inds., pp. 155–156.

[4] See pp. 414–416.

[5] Senate Doc. 512, 23d Cong., 1st sess., pp. 302–309; Schoolcraft, Ind. Tribes, IV, p. 578.

[6] Ga. Hist. Soc., Colls. IX, p. 34.

[7] Miss. Prov. Arch., p. 96.

[8] Ga. Col. Docs., VIII, p. 523.

[9] Bartram, Travels, pp. 462, 464.

[10] Schoolcraft, Ind. Tribes, V, p. 262.

[11] Ga. Hist. Soc. Colls., IX, p. 169.

Sau-wa-no-gee is on a pine flat,[1] three miles below Le-cau-suh, and back from a swamp bordering on the river; their fields are on both sides of the river, but mostly on the left bank, between the swamp and the river, on a vein of rich canebreak land; they are the Shaw-a-ne, and retain the language and customs of their countrymen to the northwest, and aided them in their late war with the United States. Some Uchees have settled with them; they are industrious, work with their women, and make plenty of corn; they have no cattle, and but few horses and hogs; the town house is an oblong square cabin, roof eight feet pitch, the sides and roof covered with the bark of the pine; on the left of the river.[2]

The tribe does not appear in the census list of 1832 unless it may be concealed under the appellation "Kiamulgatown" above mentioned.[3] At what time the Shawnee separated definitely from the Creeks I do not know, but it was as early as the time of the removal, although their reservations in the west adjoined and the Shawnee and Creeks retained their old-time intimacy.

THE ANCIENT INHABITANTS OF FLORIDA

History

Most of the tribes considered hitherto had had very intimate relations with the Creek Confederacy, the central object of our investigation. We now come to peoples who remained for the most part distinct from the Creeks, but whose history nevertheless occupies an important place in the background of this study—first, because they were near neighbors and had dealings with them, usually of a hostile character, for a long period, and, secondly, because their country was later the home of the Seminole, an important Creek offshoot which must presently receive consideration. These were the ancient inhabitants of Florida. I have already called attention to the distinction which existed between the Timucua of northern and central Florida and the south Florida tribes below Tampa Bay and Cape Canaveral,[4] and I will discuss the geographical distribution and subdivisions of each separately before proceeding to their history proper.

When we first become acquainted with the Timucua Indians through the medium of French explorers we find a great number of towns combined into groups under certain powerful chiefs. It is probable that all of these groups, like the "empire" of Powhatan, were by no means permanent, yet some of the tribes remained dominant throughout Timucua history and gave their names to missionary provinces. The French speak of about five of these associations or confederacies. That of Saturiwa, or that headed by Saturiwa—for it is uncertain whether the name belonged properly to a tribe or a chief—was on both sides of the lower St. Johns and seems to have included Cumberland Island. The Timucua proper, or Utina,

[1] The published edition has "forest."

[2] Hawkins in Ga. Hist. Soc. Colls., III, pp. 34–35; IX, p. 41.

[3] Senate Doc. 512, 23d Cong., 1st sess., IV, pp. 302–303.

[4] See pp 27–31.

centered about Santa Fe Lake, but extended eastward across the St. Johns. The Potano were apparently on the Alachua plains, but sometimes Potano province is made to reach eastward to the Atlantic, and to include the "Fresh Water" province. Northwest of the Potano, and bordering on the Apalachee country, were the provinces of Onatheaqua and Hostaqua (or Yustaga).

In the Spanish period our information becomes more detailed, owing largely to the labors of the Franciscan missionaries. Utina, Potano, and Hostaqua or Yustaga, are still recognized as important provinces, but Onatheaqua has disappeared, and it is difficult to tell just what province corresponds to the old overlordship of Saturiwa. Yustaga is mentioned in one letter as though it were independent of and coordinate with Timucua. Tacatacuru, or Cumberland Island, is certainly independent. The mission field to the south is divided between San Juan del Puerto at the mouth of St. Johns River and St. Augustine. However, according to one account, Doña Maria, chieftainess of Nombre de Dios de Florida, close to the latter place, was ruler over San Juan del Puerto, so that the territory governed by her may have been the old domain of Saturiwa. Inland from Tacatacuru, known to the Spaniards as San Pedro, were two independent Timucua provinces called Yui (Ibi, Iuy) and Icafi or Icafui. There is some confusion about this last, because the missionaries seem to speak of it as identical with Cascangue or Cascange, while this latter is often referred to as a Guale tribe, and it took part in the uprising of 1597. Probably we have to deal with two peoples, one Timucua, the other Guale, living close together.

South of St. Augustine was a group of towns classed together in what the Spaniards called the Fresh Water district, which seems to have been placed by some in the Potano province. It was long and narrow; Maiaca, the farthest town, was 8 leagues from Tocoy, the nearest. In the minds of some there was a doubt as to whether this last belonged properly to the province or not. Toward Cape Canaveral was a tribe called Surruque, Curruque, or by some similar name. It is probably the Serropé mentioned by Laudonnière, although he places it on a large lake inland. By the large lake we must understand the lagoons back of Canaveral. Surruque may be classed provisionally as Timucua, though there is no certainty. Tocobaga was a province between Tampa Bay and Withlacoochee River, Ocale a province north of the Withlacoochee, and Acuera inland to the east of the latter. In De Soto's time there seems to have been a town or province of considerable importance called Aguacaleyquen between the Santa Fe and the upper Suwanee.

Below is a practically complete list of Florida missions and Timucua provinces, tribes, towns, and chiefs, so far as they have been revealed to us by the early writers

FLORIDA MISSIONS

List of 1655	List of 1680
PROVINCIA DE GUALE Y MOCAMO	
Nuestra Señora de Guadalupe.	Nuestra Señora de Guadalupe de Tolomato.
San Juan del Puerto, en la costa	Señor San Juan del Puerto.
San Pedro Mocama.	
	Señor San Felipe de Athuluteca (given in 1643 as San Pedro Atuluteca).
San Buenaventura de Boadalquiví.	Señor San Buenaventura de Ovadalquini.
Santo Domingo de Talaje.	Señor Santo Domingo de Assaho.
San Josef de Zapala.	Señor San Joseph de Capala.
Santiago de Ocone, isla.	
Santa Catarina de Guale, y es la principal de esta provincia de Guale.	Señora Santa Cathalina de Guale.
San Felipe.	
Chatuache, y es la última por la costa del Norte.	
PROVINCIA DE TIMUCUA	
La doctrina del pueblo de Nombre de Dios.	Nombre de Dios de Amacarisse.
	Señor San Diego de Eçalamototo.
San Salvador de Macaya.	Señor Salvador de Maiaca, converssion nueva.
San Antonio de Nacape.	Señor San Antonio de Anacape, converssion nueva.
San Francisco Patano [Potano].	Señor San Francisco de Potano.
Santa Fe de Toloco.	Señor Santo Thomas de Santa Fee.
	Señora Santa Cathalina de Ahoica.
Santa Cruz de Tarica.	Santa Cruz de Tharihica.
	Señor San Juan de Guacara.
San Pedro y San Pablo de Poturiba.	Señor San Pedro de Pothohiriva.
Santa Elena de Machaba.	Señora Santa Helena de Machava.
	Señor San Matheo de Tolapatafi.
San Miguel de Asile.	Señor San Miguel de Assile.
San Agustín de Urica.	
Santa María de los Angeles de Arapaja.	
Santa Cruz de Cachipile.	
San Francisco de Chuaquín.	
San Ildefonso de Chamini.	
San Martín de Ayaocuto.	
San Luis, de la provincia de Acuera, al Sur.	
Santa Lucía, idem.	
San Diego de Laca.	

PROVINCIA DE APALACHE

San Lorenzo de Apalache.	Señor San Lorenço de Ybithachucu.
La Concepción de Apalache.	Nuestra Señora de La Purissima Conçepçion de Ajubali.
San Francisco de Apalache.	Señor San Françisco de Oconi.
San Juan de Apalache.	Señor San Joan de Ospalaga.
San Josef de Apalache.	Señor San Joseph de Ocuia.
San Pedro y San Pablo de Kpal [evidently Apal].	Señores San Pedro y San Pablo de Patali.
	Señor San Antonio de Bacuqua.
San Cosme y San Damian.	Señores San Cosme y San Damian de Yecambi.
	Señor San Carlos de los Chacatos, conversion nueva.
San Luis de Apalache.	Señor San Luis de Talimali.
	Nuestra Señora de la Candelaria de la Tama, conversion nueva.
	Señor San Pedro de los Chines, conversion nueva.
San Martín de Apalache.	Señor San Martin de Tomoli.
	Santa Cruz y San Pedro de Alcantara de Ychutafun.
Coaba, en la cordillera de Apalache.	

TIMUCUA PROVINCES, TRIBES, TOWNS, AND CHIEFS

ABINO. This town and two others named Tucuro and Utiaca were said to be 40 leagues inland from St. Augustine, four days' journey, and to be 1½ to 2 leagues apart. Their country is mentioned as a good agricultural region.

ACAHONO. One of the chiefs living inland from San Pedro, who met Ibarra in 1604.

ACASSA. A town inland from Tampa Bay.

ACELA. *See* Vicela.

ACUERA, AQUERA, ACQUERA, AGUERA. An important province somewhere near the upper course of the Ocklawaha River. In 1655 it was the seat of a Franciscan mission called San Luis, and there was another mission there known as Santa Lucia.

AGILE. *See* Assile.

AGUACALECUEN, AGUACALEYQUEN, CALIQUEN. A town and province visited by De Soto. It seems to have lain between the Suwanee and its branch, the Santa Fe.

AHOICA. A town which gave its name to the mission of Santa Cathalina de Ahoica, which seems to have been somewhere near the Santa Fe River.

ALACHEPOYO. A town inland from Tampa Bay.

ALATICO, OLATAYCO. A town belonging to the province of San Pedro or Tacatacuru. The name is probably from holata, chief, and hica, town settlement.

ALIMACANI, ALLIMACANY, HALMACANIR, ALIMACANY. An island and town not far to the north of the mouth of St. Johns River.

AMACA. A town inland from Tampa Bay.

AMACARISSE. A mission of the province of Timucua existing in 1655 is called Nombre de Dios de Amacarisse. This was settled by Yamasee, and its name is probably the original of the name Yamacraw.

ANACAPE, NACAPE, ANACABILA. A town in the Fresh Water province which gave its name to the mission of San Antonio de Anacape (1655). It was 20 leagues south of St. Augustine. Reckoning them in their order from St. Augustine southward the Fresh Water towns were: Tocoy, Antonico(?), St. Julian, Filache, Equale, Anacape, Maiaca. Yamasee were settled here in 1680.

ANACHARAQUA. A place mentioned by Laudonnière.

ANTONICO, ATONICO, possibly also called TUNSA. One of the Fresh Water towns. The name is probably Spanish. (See Anacape.)

APALU, APALOU, HAPALUYA. A town mentioned by the De Soto chroniclers and Laudonnière. It was in the northwestern part of the Timucua country near Oçachile and in the province of Hostaqua. The name means "fort" in Timucua.

AQUERA. *See* Acuera.

ARAPAJA, HARPAHA. This place gave its name to the mission of Santa María de los Angeles de Arapaja, which was 70 leagues from St. Augustine, probably northwest.

ARAYA. A place in Florida south of the Withlacoochee.

ARCHAHA. A place mentioned by Laudonnière.

ASSILE, AGILE, AXILLE, AGUIL, OCHILE, OCILLA, ASILE. An important town in the westernmost part of the Timucua country. It gave its name to the mission of San Miguel de Assile and to the River Ocilla.

ASTINA. Given by Laudonnière as the name of a chief and town.

ATULUTECA. A town which gave its name to the mission of San Felipe de Athuluteca. This is called in another place San Pedro de Atuluteca. It was probably near San Pedro or Cumberland Island.

AYACAMALE. There is a single reference to this town in one of the Lowery MSS.

AYAOCUTO. It gave its name to the mission of San Martín de Ayaocuto. The chief of this town was leader in the Timucua insurrection of 1656.

AYBE. *See* Yui.

AYOTORE, ATHORE. Governor Ibarra gives this town as one of those in the country inland from San Pedro but subject to the chieftainess of Nombre de Dios. Laudonnière seems to place it nearer the St. Johns.

BECA, VECA. Mentioned among the towns whose chiefs came to "give their obedience" to Governor de Canço.

BECAO. Mentioned in the same connection as the last.

BEJESI. Mentioned once in the Lowery MSS. Possibly the Apalachee town of Wacissa.

CACHIPILE. This town gave its name to a mission, Santa Cruz de Cachipile, in 1655.

ÇACOROY, ZACOROY. A town south of St. Augustine, 1½ leagues from Nocoroco.

CADECHA. One of the towns reported to the French in 1565 as allied with Utina.

CALABAY. *See* Sarauahi.

CALANY. A town reported to the French in 1565 to be allied with Utina.

CALE. *See* Ocale.

CALIQUEN. *See* Aguacalecuen.

CAÑOGACOLA. A warlike tribe near the Suwanee mentioned by Fontaneda. I believe these were the Potano. (See pp. 29–30.)

CAPALOEY. Ranjel records this as the name of a chief near Tampa Bay.

CAPARACA, CAPOACA, XAPUICA(?). A town southwest of Nocoroco and south of St. Augustine.

CASCANGUE. *See* Icafi.

CASTI. Given by Laudonnière as a Timucua town.

CAYUCO. A town near Tampa Bay.

CHAMINI. A town that gave its name to the mission of San Ildefonso de Chamini.

CHILILI. *See* Çilili.

CHIMAUCAYO. A town south of St. Augustine.

CHINICA, CHINISCA. A town 1½ leagues from San Juan del Puerto, and attached to it as a mission station.

CHOLUPAHA. A Florida town reached by De Soto just before he came to Aguacaleyquen.

CHUAQUÍN. A town which gave its name to the mission of San Francisco de Chuaquín.

Çicale, Cicale, Çical, Sicale. A town south of St. Augustine and 3 leagues south of Nocoroco.

Ciguache. *See* Siyagueche.

Çilili, Chilili, Chilily. A town mentioned by Laudonnière and by one of the older Spanish chroniclers.

Colucuchia, Colcuhia. A town several leagues south of Nocoroco.

Corruque, Corrouque, Curruche, Curruquey, Curruque. See Surruque.

Coya. A Florida town mentioned by Laudonnière.

Disnica. A town given in the Lowery MSS. and probably south of St. Augustine. It may be miscopied as *d* is rarely found in Timucua names.

Dulchanchellin. A chief met by Narvaez in the western Timucua country. (See p. 334.)

Eçalamototo. A town which gave its name to the mission of San Diego de Eçalamototo (1680).

Eçita. Given by Ranjel as a chief and perhaps town near Tampa Bay, in 1539. It may be a variant of Oçita (q. v.).

Eclauou. A town mentioned by Laudonnière, 1565.

Edelano, Lano. An island in St. Johns River and a town on the same.

Elajay. An old field. It may have been the site of Elafay. (See next list, p. 332.)

Elanogue. A town in the Fresh Water province, near Antonico.

Emola. A town mentioned by Laudonnière.

Enecaque, Enacappe, Eneguape. A town mentioned by Laudonnière.

Equale, Loguale. A town in the Fresh Water country, fifth in order from St. Augustine.

Ereze. A town inland from Tampa Bay.

Esquega. A chief whose province, according to an early Spanish document, lay on the west coast of Florida between those of Pebe and Osigubede.

Etocale. *See* Ocale.

Exangue. A town in the neighborhood of San Pedro (Tacatacuru).

Filache. A town in the Fresh Water province, the fourth in order from St. Augustine.

Guacara. A town which gave its name to the mission of San Juan de Guacara. It took part in the Timucua rising of 1656; subsequently it was occupied by Apalachee.

Guaçoco. A plain, and probably a town, in the Tocobaga country. Recorded by Ranjel.

Guatutima. An Indian of rank belonging to Aguacalecuen. Mentioned by Ranjel.

Halmacanir. *See* Alimacani.

Hapaluya. *See* Apalu.

Harpaha. *See* Arapaja.

Heliocopile. A chief and town mentioned by Laudonnière.

Helmacape. A chief and town mentioned by Laudonnière.

Hicachirico. A town 1 league from San Juan del Puerto, the missionary at which point visited it.

Hiocaia. A chief, and probably a town, mentioned by Laudonnière.

Homoloa, Homolona. *See* Moloa.

Horruque. *See* Surruque.

Hostaqua, Hostaque, Houstaqua, Yustaga, Yustaqua, Ustaga, Ustaqua, Ostaga. A province in the northwestern part of the Timucua country bordering on the Apalachee. It seems to have consisted of a number of towns or small tribes, probably not always under one government. That there were some differences between these people and the rest of the Timucua appears to be indicated by one of the early writers who speaks of "the provinces of Ustaqua and Timuqua."

HUARA. A town inland from San Pedro. The chief was summoned by Ibarra to meet him in San Pedro.

HURRIPACUXI. *See* Orriparacogi.

ICAFI, ICAFUI, YCAFUI. A Timucua province identical with or confused with Cascangue. It lay on the border between the Timucua and Guale provinces, apparently on the mainland, and comprised seven or eight towns. It was visited by the missionary at San Pedro.

ITARAHOLATA, YTARA. A small town abounding in corn which De Soto entered one day before he reached Potano. (For the meaning of holata see Alatico.)

JURAYA. A rancheria in Florida, about 7 leagues from Utina Paja hacienda.

LACA. A town which gave its name to the mission of San Diego de Laca (1655), 7 leagues from St. Augustine.

LAMALE. A town inland from San Pedro. The chief came to see Ibarra in 1604.

LANO. *See* Edelano.

LOQUALE. *See* Equale.

LUCA. A town visited by De Soto. It was between Tampa Bay and the Withlacoochee River.

MACHABA, MACHAVA, MACHAGUA. A town which gave its name to the mission of Santa Elena de Machaba. It was inland near the northern border of the Timucua country.

MAIACA. A town which gave its name to the mission of San Salvador de Maiaca (1680). What is probably the same town appears in the mission list of 1655 as San Salvador de Macaya. We also find a town the name of which is spelled Maycoya or Mayguia. Either two towns have been confused or the letters in one name transposed. Maiaca was the most distant from St. Augustine of all the Fresh Water towns. It was a few leagues north of Cape Canaveral, on St. Johns River. Laudonnière also spells the name Mayarque and Maquarqua.

MAIERA. *See* Mayara.

MALACA, MALICA. A town south of St. Augustine and Nocoroco. Evidently the Malica of Laudonnière.

MALAND. *See* Perquymaland.

MARRACOU. A chief and town mentioned by Laudonnière.

MATHIAQUA, OMITIAQUA. A chief and town mentioned by Laudonnière.

MAYACA. *See* Maiaca.

MAYAJUACA, MAYJUACA. A town near Maiacà, for which Fontaneda is the principal authority.

MAYARA, MAYRRA, MAIERA. A town and chief of the lower St. Johns River mentioned by Laudonnière.

MOCAMA. The mission on Cumberland Island was called San Pedro Mocama, and Mocama may have been the native name of the town, but the name may also have been transferred from the religious province which was called the province of Mocama. The word means "on the sea."

MOCOÇO, MOQUOSO, MOGOSO. A province of considerable importance north of Tampa Bay and apparently on Hillsborough River. It is mentioned by the De Soto chroniclers, Laudonnière, and other explorers.

MOGOTE. A town south of St. Augustine in the region of Nocoroco.

MOLOA, MOLOUA, MOLO, MOLONA, MOLLONA, HOMOLOA, HOMOLOUS, OMOLOA, MOTOA. A town mentioned by Laudonnière and some early Spanish writers, on the south side of St. Johns River, near its mouth. De Gourgues places one of similar name 60 leagues inland on the same river. It is probably identical with the Motoa mentioned by Ibarra as a chief and town near San Juan del Puerto at the mouth of the St. Johns River. An early Spanish document speaks of this town, or its chief, as "Moloa the brave." It was later a mission station 5 leagues from San Juan del Puerto.

NACAI E. *See* Anacape.

NAGUARETE. A chief in the country between Tampa Bay and the Withlacoochee River, mentioned by Ranjel.

NAPA, NAPUICA, NAPUYCA (*hica* means town or settlement). An island, village, and mission station 1 league from San Pedro. A mission station called Santo Domingo was in this island and in or near it Santa Maria de Sena.

NAPITUCA, NAPETACA. A village apparently in the province of Aguacalecuen, between the Suwanee and Santa Fe Rivers. Ranjel describes it as "a very pleasant village, in a pretty spot, with plenty of food." It was here that the people of Aguacalecuen endeavored to recover their chief.

NATOBO (or RATOBO). A mission station 2½ leagues from San Juan del Puerto.

NIA CUBACANI. A chieftainess mentioned by Laudonnière. *Nia* is the Timucua word meaning "woman." No town bore this name.

NOCOROCO. A town at the mouth of a river (Halifax River ?) bearing the same name which was one day's journey south of Matanzas Inlet.

OCALE, OCALY, CALE, ETOCALE, OLOGALE. A province and town which De Soto passed through. It was north of the Withlacoochee, not far from the present Ocala.

OCHILE, OCILLA. *See* Assile.

OÇITA, UCITA. A town at or near the head of Hillsborough Bay, where De Soto landed.

OLATA OUAE UTINA. Full name of the head chief of Utina or Timucua, according to Laudonnière.

OLATAYCO. *See* Alatico.

OLOGALE. *See* Ocale.

OLOTACARA. A Florida chief prominent in the account of the De Gourgues expedition.

OMITIAQUA. *See* Mathiaqua.

OMOLOA. *See* Moloa.

ONATHAQUA. Mentioned by Laudonnière as a tribe or town near Cape Canaveral.

ONATHEAQUA. Given by Laudonnière as the name of a province in the northwestern part of Florida bordering on the Apalachee.

ORIBIA, ORIBE. *See* Urubia.

ORRIPARACOGI, ORRIPARAGI, URRIPARACOXI, PARACOXI, HURRIPACUXI, URRIBARACUXI, URRIPACOXIT. A chief and province spoken of by the De Soto chroniclers. It was inland, northeast of Tampa Bay.

ORRIYGUA. Given by Ranjel as the name of a chief living north of Tampa Bay.

OSIQUEVEDE, OSIGUBEDE. A province mentioned by Fontaneda south of Apalachee (see p. 30).

OSSACHILE. *See* Uçachile.

OSTAGA. *See* Hostaqua.

PANARA. One of the towns lying inland from San Pedro; the chief came to meet Ibarra in 1604.

PARACOXI. *See* Orriparacogi.

PARCA. This town name appears in one document. The spelling is somewhat in doubt.

PATICA. A town mentioned by Laudonnière, on the seacoast 8 leagues south of St. Johns River. Another town of the same name was on the west bank of the St. Johns in the territory of the Timucua tribe. Le Moyne spells the latter Patchica. An early Spanish document spells the name Palica.

PEBE. Given in an early Spanish manuscript as the name of a chief on the west coast of Florida between Cañogacola and Esquega.

PENTOAYA. Name of a town at the head of the River of Ais.

PERQUYMALAND. This seems to be given as a town south of St. Augustine and Nocoroco, but it is doubtful whether the name has been copied correctly. There may be two names here, the original being "Perqui y Maland."

PIA. A town on the east coast south of St. Augustine and Nocoroco.

PITANO. A mission station a league or half a league from San Pablo (Puturiba).

PIYAYA. Given in an early Spanish manuscript as the name of a chief on the west coast of Florida between Osigubede and Tanpacaste.

POOY, POJOY. Mentioned in a Spanish document of 1612 as a town or province situated on a certain bay. The document says: "The best bay [on the southwestern coast of Florida] is the bay of Pooy, which is where the Indians say Hernando de Soto disembarked." This is Tampa Bay or that part of it known as Hillsborough Bay. A letter of 1625 mentions a province called Posoy, which is probably identical with this. In 1680 a Calusa province is referred to called Rojoi, said to contain a population of non-Christian Indians numbering 300. Rojoi is probably a misspelling of Pojoi (=Pojoy).

POTANO, POTANOU, PATANO. One of the most important provinces or tribes in Florida and seemingly the most warlike. It was in the Alachua plains and was later the seat of the mission of San Francisco de Potano.

POTAYA. A town and mission station 4 leagues from San Juan del Puerto.

POTOYOTOYA. A carry back of Cape Canaveral, where the Indians moved their canoes across from one lagoon to another.

PUALA. A town in the neighborhood of San Pedro, whose chief came to see Gov. Ibarra in 1604.

PUNHURI. A town inland from San Pedro, whose chief came to see Ibarra in 1604.

PUTURIBA, POTURIBA, POTORIBA, POTHOHIRIVA, POTOGIRIBIA. A town and missionary seat which seems to have been located on San Pedro (Cumberland) Island near its northern end. The river which separated the provinces of Timucua and Guale, and which was probably the Satilla, bore its name. The chief of this town was among the insurgents of 1656. The mission was called San Pedro y San Pablo de Puturiba.

RATOBO. *See* Natobo.

SABOBCHE, SAVOVOCHEQUEYA. A town near the east coast south of St. Augustine and Nocoroco.

[ST. JULIAN.] One of the Fresh Water towns, the third from St. Augustine. The native name is not preserved, or at least not identified.

SALINACANI. Given by Laudonnière as the name of a Florida river; probably a misprint of Halimacani (*see* Alimacani).

[SAN MATEO.] A village about 2 leagues from San Juan del Puerto.

[SAN PABLO.] A village about 1½ leagues from San Juan del Puerto. To be distinguished from San Pedro y San Pablo de Poturiba (see Puturiba).

[SAN SEBASTIAN.] A town on an arm of the sea near St. Augustine, destroyed about 1600 by a flood.

SARAUAHI, SARAURAHI, SARACARY, SERRANAY, SARABAY, CARABAY, CALABAY. Apparently the name of Nassau River and a town a quarter of a league from San Juan del Puerto.

SATURIWA, SATURIUA, SATURIONA, SATURIBA, SATORIVA, SOTORIBA. One of the leading chiefs in Laudonnière's time, and his province. It is scarcely mentioned by the Spaniards. The province lay on both sides of the St. Johns at its mouth. Doña Maria, a leading supporter of the Spaniards, whose town was close to St. Augustine, probably ruled over the Saturiwa territories in later times.

SELOY. *See* Soloy.

SENA. I do not know whether this is a native or a Spanish word. A mission not appearing in the regular lists was known as Santa Maria de Sena. Possibly this is intended for Sienna. It was on an inlet north of the mouth of the St. Johns, perhaps Amelia River.

SICALE. *See* Çicale.

SIYAGUECHE, CIGUACHE. A town near Cape Canaveral.

SOCOCHUNO. A town mentioned in one of the early Spanish documents.

SOLOY. A town not far from St. Augustine. It was probably on the river called by the French Seloy and Seloy is probably a variant form of the word.

SURRUQUE, SURRUCHE, SURRUCLE, SERRALLI, CORRUQUE, CORROUQUE, CURRUCHE, CURBUQUEY, SURUDE, CURRUQUE, URRUCLE, HORRUQUE, ZORRUQUE. A town or tribe at Cape Canaveral. It is probably the Sorrochos of Le Moyne's map and I believe also the original of his Sarropé. Lake Sarropé is probably placed too far to the south and too far inland. The French knew of it only by hearsay.

TACATACURU, TACADOCOROU, TACATACOURU, TECATACOUROU, TACURURU. The native name for Cumberland Island, later known to the Spaniards as San Pedro. It may also have been the ancient name of the chief town, the seat of the mission of San Pedro Mocamo, which was situated on the inner side of Cumberland Island near the southern end and 2 leagues from the Barra of San Pedro.

TAFOCOLE. A town inland from Tampa Bay.

TAHUPA. A town inland from San Pedro, whose chief came to visit Ibarra in 1604.

TANPACASTE. Given in an old Spanish document as a chief between Piyaya on the north and Pooy on the south.

TARIHICA, TARIXICA, THARIHICA, TARICA. A town 54 leagues from St. Augustine which gave its name to the mission of Santa Cruz de Tarihica. It was one of the 11 towns which rebelled in 1656.

TIMUCUA, THIMOGOA. Name of the largest confederacy or tribe in Florida, also called Utina. It has given its name to a group of tribes speaking similar dialects, the Timuquanan linguistic stock. With the possible exception of the Potano it was the most powerful tribe as well as the largest. The center of its domain was about Santa Fe Lake and its overlordship or dominance extended to the eastern shores of the St. Johns.

TOCASTE. A village which De Soto passed through. It was on a large lake some distance south of the Withlacoochee.

TOCOAYA, TOCOHAYA, TOCOYA. A town very close to San Pedro, Cumberland Island. Its chief was one of those who met Ibarra at the latter place in 1604.

TOCOBAGA, TOCOVAGA, TOCOBAA, TOCOPACA, TOPOBAGA. A chief and province frequently mentioned in Spanish documents but not by De Soto or the later writers. It was on the west coast and one old document places it, probably erroneously, between the province of Mogoso on the north and that of Cañogacola on the south. The chief town was at the head of one of the arms of Tampa Bay.

TOCOY, TOCOI. A town of the Fresh Water district, the nearest of all to St. Augustine, from which it was 5 leagues distant, according to one writer, and 24 according to another.

TOLAPATAFI. A town which gave its name to one of the later Florida missions, San Matheo de Tolapatafi. It seems to have been in the western part of the Timucua country, near Assile.

TOLOCO. A town from which the mission of Santa Fe de Toloco received its name. It is perhaps the Santo Thomas de Santa Fee of the mission list of 1680.

TOMEO. A town apparently in the neighborhood of the Fresh Water province.

TUCURA. A town apparently in the same province as the above.

TUCURO. One of three towns 40 leagues from St. Augustine. *See* Abino. This may be identical with the above, though the distance seems to be against such a supposition.

TUNSA. *See* Antonico.

UÇACHILE, UZACHIL, OSSACHILE, VEACHILE. This has been discussed in full in dealing with the Osochi tribe. (See p. 165.)

UCITA. *See* Oçita.

UFERA. *See* Yufera.

ULUMAY. A province and town just south of Cape Canaveral. There is reason to think that it belonged to the province of Ais rather than to the Timucua country.

UQUETEN. Ranjel gives this as the name of the first village of the province of Ocale.

URICA. A town which gave its name to the mission of San Augustin de Urica (1655).

URIUTINA. Ranjel describes this as "a village of pleasant aspect and abundant food." It was passed by De Soto just after crossing the river of Aguacalecuen.

URRIPACOXIT, URRIBARACUXI, URRIPARACOXI. *See* Orriparacogi.

URRUCLE. *See* Surruque.

URUBIA, URRUYA, ORIBIA, ORIBE. A town near Cape Canaveral, 1½ leagues from the town of Surruque.

USTAGA, USTAQUA. *See* Hostaqua.

UTAYNE. A town inland from San Pedro, whose chief came to see Ibarra in 1604.

UTIACA. A town 40 leagues from St. Augustine. *See* Abino.

UTICHINI. A place evidently situated inland from San Pedro, and within a league or half a league of San Pablo (Puturiba).

UTINA. A synonym for Timucua, q. v.

UTINA PAJA. Timucua name of a Spanish hacienda.

UTINAMOCHARRA, UTINAMA. A town passed by De Soto one day's journey north of Potano.

UZACHIL. *See* Oçachile.

VEACHILE. *See* Oçachile.

VECA. *See* Beca.

[VERA CRUZ.] A village half a league from San Juan del Puerto.

VICELA, ACELA. A small town passed through by De Soto a short distance south of the Withlacoochee.

XAPUICA. This occurs in connection with some Guale towns, but the word appears to be rather Timucua. It may be a synonym for Caparaca, q. v.

XATALALANO. A town inland from San Pedro, whose chief came to see Ibarra in 1604.

YAOCAY. A town in the Fresh Water province, near Antonico.

YCAFUI. *See* Icafi.

YCAPALANO. A town inland from San Pedro and said to be within a league or half a league of the mission of San Pablo, presumably the mission of San Pedro y San Pablo de Poturiba.

YTARA. *See* Itaraholata.

YUA. A town whose chief came "to give obedience" to Méndez de Canço in 1598 or shortly before. Perhaps this is really Yui.

YUFERA, UFERA. A town inland from San Pedro, apparently toward the northwest, for it was passed through by some missionaries returning to San Pedro from the upper Altamaha. Its chief was one of those inland chiefs who came to visit Ibarra in 1604.

YUI, YBI, YBY, AYBI (?). The name of this province should probably be pronounced Ewe in English. It was a small province on the mainland, consisting of five towns, and was 14 leagues from San Pedro. It was visited by the missionary at San Pedro.

YUSTAGA, YUSTAQUA. *See* Hostaqua.

ZACOROY. *See* Çacoroy.

ZORRUQUE. *See* Surruque.

All of the Indians of southern Florida on the western side of the peninsula, from the Timucua territories as far as and including the Florida Keys, belonged to a confederacy or overlordship called Calusa or Calos. On the eastern coast were a number of small independent tribes, each usually occupying only one settlement. The most important of these appears to have been Ais, located close to what is now Indian River Inlet. The next in prominence, if not in power, were the Tekesta, at or near the present Miami, and between these were the Jeaga, or Jega, in Jupiter Inlet, and the Guacata and Santa Lucia Indians, probably identical, who lived about St. Lucie River. The province of Ais is said to have extended northward almost to Cape Canaveral, but the authority of its chief was probably not very great along the northern edge of this area, where we are told of a province called Ulumay.

We will consider first the towns of Calusa. Two lists of Calusa towns have come to my notice; one in Fontaneda's Memoir, the other—possibly from him also, but containing many more names and some variants of the names in his Memoir—in the Lowery manuscripts. From the fact that Tampa is given by Fontaneda as a Calusa town, it has been quite generally assumed that the Calusa extended as far north as the bay of that name, but in the Lowery manuscripts I find very strong evidence that the original Tampa Bay was farther south than the inlet now so called, and was probably identical with what is now Charlotte Harbor. The principal Calusa town was farther south on San Carlos Bay. Fontaneda classifies the Calusa towns into three groups, those on the west coast of the peninsula, those about Lake Mayaimi, now Okeechobee, and those on the Florida Keys. The following list is as complete as I can furnish. In the list from the Lowery manuscripts the towns, or, as the document gives it, their caciques—since town and chief were called by the same name by the Spaniards—are given from north to south, and I indicate in each case the town above and below the one named, mentioning the one to the north first. In the case of towns from Fontaneda's list I give the group to which each belongs:

ABIR. Between Ñeguitun and Cutespa.

ALCOLA (or CHOSA). Mentioned in the narrative of an expedition into the Calusa country in 1680, and said to have 300 people.

APOJOLA NEGRA. This is given in an account of an expedition into the Calusa country in 1680. The expedition was accompanied by Timucua interpreters and this name seems to contain the Spanish word black and the Timucua word for buzzard. It contained 20 people.

CALAOBE. Belongs to the seacoast division (see p. 29).

CARAGARA. Between Namuguya and Henhenguepa.

CASITOA, CASITUA. Seacoast division. Between Muspa and Cotebo.

CAYOVEA. Seacoast division.

CAYUCAR. Between Tonco and Ñeguitun.

CHIPI. Between Tomçobe and Taguagemae (or Taguagemue).

COMACHICA. Seacoast division.

CONONOGUAY. Between Cutespa and Estegue.

COTEBO. Between Casitua and Coyobia.

COYOBIA. Between Cotebo and Tequemapo.

CUCHIYAGA, CUCHIAGA, CUCLYYAGA. A town of the Florida keys. It was said to be southwest from Bahia Honda and 40 leagues northeast of Guarungube. Probably it was on Big Pine Key.

CUSTAVUI. South of Jutun.

CUTESPA. Inland division. Between Abir and Cononoguay.

ELAFAY. In the report of an expedition to Calusa in 1680. It had 40 people. The word may be in the Timucua language.

ENEMPA. In interior division.

ESTAME. Seacoast division. Between Metamapo and Sacaspada.

ESTANTAPACA. Between Yagua and Queÿhicha.

ESTEGUE. Between Cononoguay and Tomsobe.

EXCURU. Between Janar and Metamapo.

GUARUNGUBE, GUARUGUMBE, GARUNGUNVE. The outermost town on the Florida keys, "on the point of the Martyrs," and thus probably near Key West.

GUEVU. Seacoast division.

HENHENGUEPA. Between Caragara and Ocapataga.

JANAR. Between Ocapataga and Escuru.

JUDYI. Between Satucuava and Soco.

JUESTOCOBAGA. Between Queyhicha and Sinapa.

JUTUN. Seacoast division. Between Tequemapo and Custavui.

METAMAPO. Seacoast division. Between Escuru and Estame.

MUSPA. Seacoast division. Between Teyo and Casitua.

NAMUGUYA. Between Taguagemae and Caragara.

ÑEGUITUN. Between Cayucar and Abir.

ÑO (or NON). Seacoast division. The word is said to mean "town beloved." (See p. 30.)

OCAPATAGA. Between Henhenguepa and Janar.

QUEYHICHA. Between Estantapaca and Juestocobaga.

QUISIYOVE. Seacoast division.

SACASPADA, ÇACASPADA. Seacoast division. Between Estame and Satucuava.

SATUCUAVA. Between Sacaspada and Judyi.

SINAESTA. Seacoast division.

SINAPA. Seacoast division. Between Juestocobaga and Tonco.

SOCO. Seacoast division. Between Judyi and Vuebe.

TAGUAGEMAE (*or* Taguagemue). Between Chipi and Namuguya.

TAMPA, TANPA. Seacoast division. The northernmost town of the Calusa country, followed on the south by Yagua. It was probably on Charlotte Harbor. According to one Spanish writer the Indians at the mouth of the present Tampa Bay were called by some people Tampas, by others "Vantabales."

TATESTA, TESTA. Seacoast division. It is given as a town between Tekesta and Cuchiaga, according to one writer, about 80 leagues north of the latter town. A "key of Tachista" is also mentioned in one place, and still another document places it on the Florida Keys. It may have been near their inner end.

TAVAGUEMUE. Interior division.

TEQUEMAPO. Seacoast division. Between Coyobia and Jutun.

TEYO. Between Vuebe and Muspa.

TIQUIJAGUA. From the narrative of a Calusa expedition undertaken in 1680. Population of town, 300.

TOMO. Seacoast division.

TOMSOBE, TOMÇOBE. Interior division. Between Estegue and Chipi. Perhaps the Sonsobe of Fontaneda, who in one place speaks of it as a province distinct from Calusa.

TONCO. Between Sinapa and Cayucar.

TUCHI. Seacoast division.

VANTABALES. *See* Tampa.

VUEBE. Between Soco and Teyo. Possibly the Guevu of Fontaneda.

YAGUA. Seacoast division. Between Tampa and Estantapaca.

As stated above, the settlements on the east coast did not belong to a single province, although there is reason to consider them as having constituted one linguistic group with the Calusa.[1] The following settlements are mentioned, beginning at the southern end of this strip of coast:

TEKESTA, TEGESTA, TEQUESTA. Situated close to the present Miami.

TAVUACIO.

JANAR. As the writer who gives this is the same who records a town Janar among the Calusa we may assume that they are not identical.

CABISTA.

CUSTEGIYO.

JEAGA, GEAGA, JEGA, GEGA, GUEGA. This was located in the present Jupiter Inlet. According to Spanish writers it was 10 leagues north of Tekesta and 18 leagues south-southeast of Ais.

GUACATA, CUACATA. In one place Fontaneda speaks of this as a town on Lake Mayaimi (Okeechobee) and elsewhere as one of the provinces of the east coast. A Spanish document in the Lowery collection gives it as a place "in the land of Ays." It is possible that these people lived on St. Lucie River and camped farther inland than most of the coast people. In that case they would probably be identical with the people of the town afterwards known as Santa Lucia from a missionary establishment started among them.

TUNSA. Given as a town or province "in the land of Ays." But see TUNSA in the Timucua list.

AIS, AYS, AIZ, HAYZ, JECE. The chief of this town or province was the most powerful on the eastern coast. From Dickenson it appears that he was able to overawe all of the chiefs to the south of him as far as the Jeaga, and the "province of Ais" is made by the Spaniards to extend in the other direction nearly to Cape Canaveral. The capital town itself was near Indian River Inlet, and Indian River itself was known as "the river of Ais." This is sometimes called San Agustin de Ais from an abortive missionary attempt made there.

ULUMAY (given in one place as COLOMAS). This is spoken of as a "province" and at the same time placed in the territory of Ais. It was near Cape Canaveral and on the borders of the south Florida linguistic area or areas. Fontaneda makes the language of Ais extend as far as Maiaca and Maiajuaca, but the first of these was Timucua, and there is reason to think that the Timucua tribes extended even farther south. *See* Surruque in the Timucua list.

ORDONOY. A town in the province of Ulumay.

BOVOCHE. A town in the province of Ulumay.

REA. A land or town of the province of Ais. (See p. 342.) It is doubtful whether this word has been correctly copied.

Harrisse has shown that the peninsula of Florida was almost certainly discovered and mapped with an approximation to accuracy late in the fifteenth or early in the sixteenth century, a dozen years at least before the supposed discovery by Ponce de Leon in 1512 or 1513.[2] Still, if Florida does not owe her entry into European history to the last-mentioned navigator, she unquestionably

[1] See p. 31.

[2] Harrisse, Disc. of N. A., pp. 77-109, 142-153.

does her name, which afterwards displaced all previous appellations. Ponce de Leon ranged the coasts seemingly for many miles, on both the eastern and western sides, and then returned to Porto Rico, where he had outfitted. In 1521 he undertook a second expedition, coasting the western side of the peninsula and making a landing, perhaps in Apalachee Bay, as suggested by Harrisse.[1] Here, however, he was defeated by the Indians and badly wounded. He returned to Cuba to be cured, but soon died. Meantime, in 1519, Francisco de Garay sent an expedition into the Gulf of Mexico, which traced the northern coast of the Gulf from Florida to the River Panuco. In 1524 Verrazano is supposed to have followed the coast of North America from Florida northward. All of these navigators simply touched upon the shores of the peninsula. We now come to expeditions which penetrated some distance into the interior. The first of these was led by the unfortunate Narvaez, who landed in Florida April 11, 1528, probably at or near Tampa Bay. From there the Spaniards marched inland, meeting very few Indians and apparently only one or two Indian villages. They crossed two rivers, which we may surmise to have been the Withlacoochee and Suwanee, and finally came to the country of the Apalachee. No tribal names are mentioned in the territory traversed before reaching these people; merely the name of a chief, Dulchanchellin, whose village seems to have been in that province which the De Soto narratives call Ocale.[2] What happened to the Spaniards among the Apalachee has been related in giving the history of the Apalachee tribe.[3]

The expedition of De Soto reached Tampa Bay May 25, 1539. On Tuesday, July 15, it set out from the town of Oçita, or Ucita, which was evidently near the head of the bay, passed through the territory of Mocoço, and then through a number of places which seem to have been under a chief named Urriparacogi. Afterwards the explorers crossed the Withlacoochee River and came into the province of Ocale, and from there, leaving the province of Acuera to one side, reached the important province of Potano on or near the Alachua plains. Then they passed northward through Potano, crossed another river, perhaps the Santa Fe, and came into still another important province known as Aguacalecuen, or Caliquen. It is uncertain whether the places entered by them, beyond the capital of this province, all belonged to it or not. At any rate the next great chief mentioned was Uçachile, Uzachil, or Ossachile, a name which I have sought to identify with the later Osochi, and from his territory they traveled into the province of Apalachee northward of Ocilla River.[4] All of the people living in

[1] Harrisse, Disc. of N. A., p. 152.

[2] Bandelier, Jour. of Cabeza de Vaca, pp. 9-23; Oviedo, Hist. Gen., III, pp. 579-581; Doc. Ined., XIV, pp. 269-271.

[3] See pp. 112-115.

[4] Bourne, Narr. of De Soto, I, pp. 21-46; II, pp. 4-6, 51-71

these places probably belonged to the great Timucua group. The De Soto chroniclers are of particular service in giving us an early picture of the tribes of this stock toward the western side of the peninsula, the later settlements all having been made from the east.

The next important chapter in the history of Florida is its settlement by French Huguenots. The first expedition sailed in February, 1562, under Jean Ribault, and sighted land on the east coast near where St. Augustine now stands. There Ribault opened communications with the natives, entered the River St. Johns, and afterwards sailed on up the coasts of Florida and Georgia until he arrived at what is now Broad River, South Carolina. There he established a small colony in the neighborhood of the present Beaufort and then returned to France. The party left by him succeeded very well for a time, but, becoming impatient at his long absence and despairing of his return, they finally built a small vessel in which a few of them at length reached France after incredible hardships. In 1564 three vessels were sent out from Havre under the command of Réné Goulaine de Laudonnière and came in sight of Florida at a point about 30 leagues south of the entrance to the River St. Johns, which had already been named by Ribault the River May. They opened communications with the Indians almost immediately, and after exploring the country in search of a suitable site for an establishment, finally picked out a place on the south bank of the St. Johns River and built a fort there, which they named Fort Caroline. This fort was occupied by the French from some time in July, 1564, to September 19, 1565, when it was captured by the Spaniards under Pedro Menendez de Aviles, and the brief French colonial period in Florida and Carolina was brought to an end.[1]

During the time of their occupancy the Frenchmen explored the country in all directions, and the accounts which they have left, supplemented by the drawings of Le Moyne, a member of the second expedition, give us more ethnological information regarding the ancient Floridians—outside the domain of language—than is preserved from the entire Spanish period. An expedition to avenge those Frenchmen who had been put to death by Menendez was undertaken in the year 1567 by Dominique de Gourgues and was eminently successful, but the Spaniards remained in possession of the country and continued to occupy it, with one brief interruption, until 1821.

The Spanish conquest of Florida—both civil and spiritual—starting from St. Augustine, proceeded slowly in all directions. The Indians were at first hostile, for no nation secured the attachment of the natives so quickly as the French; but as the French refugees

[1] Laudonnière, Hist. Not. de La Floride; Le Moyne, Narrative.

were gradually weeded out from among the Indians and the latter became used to their new neighbors the opposition died down. A letter dated 1568 states that there had recently been a massacre of Spaniards at Tocobaga. In 1576 or 1577 Pedro de Andrada was sent at the head of 80 soldiers to support Autina (Utina) against Saturiwa, Nocoroco, Potano, and other chiefs.[1] In 1583 Governor Pedro Menendez Marques writes that all of the Indians in the interior, as well as on the coast, had come to see him and yield their obedience. He declares that the Indians were being converted rapidly.[2]

In 1584 war broke out again with the Potano and Captain Andrada, who had been sent against the tribe as before, was killed along with 19 of his men.[1] In retaliation a body of troops under Gutierrez de Miranda, alcaide of Santa Elena, was sent against these people, many were killed, and they were driven from their town.[3] In 1585 there was considerable mortality among the Indians.[3] These events do not seem to have interfered with the conversion of the natives, however, which contemporary documents speak of as proceeding very rapidly. The work was assisted particularly by two native leaders, Doña Maria, chieftainess of a town within two gunshots of St. Augustine, and Don Juan, chief of the island of Tacatacuru or San Pedro, the present Cumberland Island. The former, whose husband was a Spaniard, was of material assistance, receiving and entertaining those Indians who came to St. Augustine from a distance. A letter written, or rather dictated, to the King of Spain by her, is preserved in the Spanish archives. Don Juan is the chief who, although a Timucua, desired to be made mico mayor of the province of Guale.[4] This chief was of great assistance in driving back the rebellious inhabitants of Guale in 1597.[5] In the eastern Timucua districts alone, including Nombre de Dios, San Pedro, San Antonio, and the Fresh Water district to the south, there were said to be more than 1,500 Christian Indians in 1597. They came from all quarters, however, to be baptized.[1]

About the time of the Guale outbreak trouble arose with a tribe in the neighborhood of Cape Canaveral, whose name is spelled Curruque, Surruque, Zorruque, Horruque, Surreche, and in various other ways. According to some of the missionaries the governor made an unprovoked attack upon this tribe, but he himself says that these people had killed a Spaniard named Juan Ramirez de Contreras and two Indian interpreters, besides several persons who had been shipwrecked among them. At any rate he sent a force which fell suddenly upon a town of this province where he believed the chief to be living and 60 persons were killed and 54 taken prisoner.

---

[1] Lowery, MSS.

[2] Brooks and Lowery, MSS.

[3] Brooks, MSS.

[4] Brooks and Lowery, MSS. See p. 84.

[5] See p. 87.

It is said in one account that Ais Indians were among those slain, and this province and Ais are certainly frequently spoken of together, yet it is probable that they belonged to different linguistic groups and were associated only geographically as also in their manner of living.[1] Don Juan, the chief of San Pedro and intimate friend of the Spaniards, died June 16, 1600. He was succeeded by his niece (his sister's daughter), in accordance with the custom of the country.[1] During the same year, or shortly before, the Indian town of San Sebastian, which lay on an arm of the sea back of St. Augustine, was overwhelmed by an unusual high water and many of its inhabitants drowned.[1] In 1601 the Potano Indians asked to be allowed to return to their town which they had vacated in the war of 1584.[2] In 1602 valuable letters from the missionaries Fray Baltazar Lopez, who was stationed at San Pedro, and Fray Francisco de Pareja, at San Juan del Puerto, at the mouth of the St. Johns River, give us minute information regarding the mission stations within their districts and the number of Christianized Indians in each. In the former there were 8 settlements and nearly 800 Christians. In the latter Pareja mentions 10 settlements and about 500 Christians, "big and little."

These friars also speak of several other provinces which they visited or where there were Christians, including Ybi with 5 towns and more than 1,000 Indians, Cascangui or Ycafui with 7 or 8 towns and 700–800 Indians, Timucua with 1,500 Indians, Potano with 5 towns and where as many as 1,100 Indians were being catechised, and the Fresh Water province where were said to be six or more towns of Christian Indians, besides the Mayaca Indians, who had not been visited by monks.[2] Pareja is the well-known author of Timucua catechisms and manuals and a grammar of the language. A letter from a third friar written the same month states that there were about 200 Christians in the Fresh Water towns and in Mayaca perhaps 100 more to be baptized.[2] Governor Canço estimates about 1,200 Christians in the four visitas of San Pedro, San Antonio, San Juan, and Nombre de Dios.[2] Pedro Ruiz seems to have been the missionary at San Pedro in 1604.[2] In 1606 these various missions, along with those in the province of Guale, were visited by the Bishop of Cuba, who confirmed 2,075 Indians and 370 Spaniards.[2] Letters of Alonso de Peñaranda and Francisco Pareja, of November 20, 1607, complain of attacks made by wild Indians on those who had been Christianized. They state that between November, 1606, and October, 1607, 1,000 Indians had been Christianized, and that in all there were over 6,000 Christian Indians.[2] In 1608 Governor Ibarra

[1] Lowery and Brooks, MSS.

[2] Lowery, MSS.

claims that 4,000 Indians had been converted in a year and a half and that 1,000 more were under instruction by the missionaries. He says that the church in San Pedro was as big as that in St. Augustine; that it had cost the Indians more than 300 ducats, and had they not worked on it themselves it would have cost them more than 2,000 ducats.[1] In 1609 the chief of Timucua (Utina) with his heir and the leading men of his tribe were baptized in St. Augustine; and later we are told that 28 Timucua and Apalachee chiefs begged for baptism.[2] A letter from the missionaries dated January 17, 1617, informs us, however, that in the preceding four years more than half of the Indians had died of pestilence. Yet they claim 8,000 Christianized Indians still living.[2] It is stated that many missionaries died of the pest in 1649 and 1650; yet in the latter year there were 70 in Florida.[2] It is not said whether this pestilence extended to the natives. The number and names of the Timucua missions existing in the years 1655 and 1680 have already been given.[3]

In the year 1656 a rebellion broke out among the Timucua and lasted eight months, even spreading to the Apalachee. Governor Robelledo says that it was directed against the friars, but the letter of a missionary lays the blame upon the governor himself, because he had tried to compel the Indians to bring corn on their backs into St. Augustine. The leader of this revolt is said to have been the chief of St. Martin, evidently the town known as San Martín de Ayaocuto, and was participated in by 10 others, including the chiefs of Santa Fe de Toloco, San Francisco de Potano, San Pedro y San Pablo de Puturiba, Santa Elena de Machaba, San Francisco de Chuaquin, Santa Cruz de Tarixica, San Matheo de Tolapatafi, San Juan del Puerto, and San Juan de Guacara. The Sergeant Major Adrian de Cañiçares was sent to the disturbed area by Governor Robelledo with 60 infantry, the rebellion was put down, and 11 Indians garroted.[2] This appears to have been the only uprising of any consequence in which the Timucua Indians were involved. A letter from Capt. Juan Francisco de Florencia to the then governor of Florida, dated 1670, states that in November, 1659, he had been ordered to go to the provinces of Ustaqua and Timucua to people and rebuild the towns of San Francisco, Santa Fe, San Martin, and San Juan de Guacara, which had been depopulated because some natives had died in the pestilences they had had and others had gone to the forests (montes), "because these places formed the passageway and means of communication to the said provinces from the presidio of St. Augustine."[1] This depopulation was probably due immediately to the great rebellion.

In 1672 there is said to have been another great mortality among the Indians.[1] A memorial by Fray Alonso del Moral, dated September

---

[1] Lowery, MSS. [2] Lowery and Brooks, MSS. [3] See p. 322.

24, 1676, states that there were then 70 places for missionaries but usually only about 40 to fill them; in 1681 the number of missionaries is given as 34.[1] The list of missions drawn up in 1680, while showing more in the Apalachee province and practically the same number in Guale, exhibits a distinct decrease among the Timucua missions and it is evident that some former Timucua missions are largely concerned with different peoples. In 1688 a letter was written to the then King of Spain, Charles II, by several Timucua chiefs, with the assistance, of course, of the missionaries. It was a companion letter to that sent by the Apalachee already mentioned.[2] It was signed by Don Francisco, chief of San Matheo; Don Pedro, chief of San Pedro; Don Ventura, chief of Asile; Don Diego, chief of Machaua; Gregorio, chief of San Juan de Guacara; and Francisco Martinez, residente in San Matheo.[3] These are given in the Spanish version. In the Timucua some of these and some parts of the letter do not appear. We may assume that the towns mentioned were the chief remaining towns of the Timucua. Utina, Potano, Acuera, and the Fresh Water district are not represented. In 1697 it is said that the missionary, Fray Luis Sanchez, was murdered in Maiaca, which is spoken of as a new conversion; and, although this mission bears a Timucua name, it is evident that it was then settled largely by Yamasee.[1]

The destruction of the Timucua missions by the Creeks and English, along with those of the Apalachee and other Florida Indians, now followed rapidly, so rapidly that one writer declares the destruction of the provinces of Timucua, Apalachee, and Guale took place within four or five months. He places the event in the year 1704, which is only approximately correct.[4] A royal officer, Juan de Pueyo, writing November 10, 1707, says that the province of Florida was then being rapidly depopulated by the English and infidel Indians, who were extending their depredations southward of St. Augustine. He states that 32 settlements of Indians had been destroyed, a number almost as great as that of the missions.[4] It is possible that some Timucua had revolted along with the Guale Indians and the Yamasee, but probably not many did so. The following general account of the destruction of the missions, along with some information regarding the last Indian villages in Florida before the arrival of the Seminole, is contained in a letter by Governor Dionisio de la Vega, written August 27, 1728:

> Up to the year 1703, when the English made their first invasion from Carolina assisted by the Indians in their interest into the provinces of Apalache and Guale, the Indians thereof lived in perfect peace and tranquility; and from time to time some infidel Indians would come and join them, desirous of pledging their obedience. But the said provinces having been destroyed by virtue of said invasions, and all the

[1] Lowery, MSS.
[2] See. pp. 12, 120.
[3] Gatschet in Proc. Am. Phil. Soc., XVIII, pp. 495-497.
[4] Brooks, MSS.

towns deserted and many of the Indians, converted as well as infidels, killed or made prisoners, while the majority of them revolted and joined the English, enjoying the freedom under which they were allowed to live. The few who then preferred to remain under the protection of the arms of Y. M., settled down upon other lands where they could consider themselves free and secured from the attacks of the revolted Indians and formed their huts and settlements under the name of towns, where they were assisted by the missionary fathers with that love and zeal which was required of them.

After the destruction of these provinces and their towns, war continued to rage between the converted and infidel Indians, the latter assisted and fomented by the English. All around their [i. e., the English] towns are settlements, where they have congregated a large number of Caribe Indians, allowing them those liberties to which they are accustomed, and in this manner they have succeeded in annihilating over four-fifths of the number of Indians who had sought refuge. The rest of them remaining in their settlements, the largest of which hardly had a population of sixty souls, males, females, children, and Indians all told. In each of those settlements resided a clergyman, this being indispensable owing to the diversity of languages, which requires their separate instruction in the doctrine, and in some of those settlements it was necessary to have two clergymen because of the population being composed of Indians of distinct nationalities.

In none of these settlements was it ever possible to have a church where the holy sacrament of the Eucharist could be offered, notwithstanding they were distant only seven, five, and three leagues from this city (St. Augustine); so great was the fear they had of the infidels, that for the slightest cause they would move from one place to another without ever having a permanent residence.

For this reason, and because the churches dedicated for mass to be said in them, were not decent, it was decided to administer the Viaticum to the sick Indians during the hour of its celebration only.

But seeing themselves every day more and more harrassed by the infidel Indians, they sought refuge under the guns of the fort of this city, where they have formed their settlements, the farthest being within gunshot distance, the names of the said settlements or towns being Mores, Nombre de Dios, El Nuevo, Tolemato, La Costa, Palica, and Casapuyas. The first one was composed of twenty men, eighteen women, and ten children, and among them there were only one man and one woman infidels. The second was composed of eighteen men, fourteen women, and eight children, all Christians. The third one was composed of twenty-three men, twenty-two women, and twenty children, all Christians, except one of the men who was an infidel. The fourth one has no fixed number; sometimes it has thirty or forty, and at other times only four or six, owing to its inhabitants being fond of moving about, similar to those from the keys. The women who generally reside there are seven, and about twelve children, all [the latter] Christians. The men [of the last town] are mostly infidels, and of the women three. The fifth had fourteen men, ten women, of whom some are infidels, and possibly had about four or five children. Chiqueto, which is also called Nombre de Dios, had about fifteen men, and twenty women, all Christians, and finally Casapuyas had fourteen men, and as many women, of whom the majority were infidels, and was composed of two different nations.[1]

There is an evident mistake in the last paragraph quoted, but as it has occurred in the Spanish transcription and possibly was made by the author himself, it can not be entirely rectified here. The principal trouble is that, while the writer professes to give the popu-

[1] Brooks, MSS.

lation of the several towns in the order in which their names appear, one of them, Nombre de Dios, is second in the list of names and sixth in the statistical list. This leaves it uncertain whether the other names and figures correspond, especially since the word "fifth" in the translation has been substituted for "sixth" in the original on the probable, but not necessarily correct, supposition that the writer had made a mistake. It is also possible that the Spanish text names six towns instead of seven. It runs as follows: "meres nombre de Dios Tolemato el nuevo la costa Palica y Casapuyas," and it is impossible to say whether the name of the third is Tolemato or Tolemato el nuevo. I have assumed the former provisionally in order to make the seven towns which the statistics call for. In the English translation accompanying this text matters have been made worse by the entire omission of Mores, El Nuevo, and La Costa. Nevertheless, with the exception just noted, we have no reason to doubt the correctness of the town names given and the statistical information is borne out by a comparison with that on pages 105–106, although the number of the towns themselves does not precisely correspond.

Following the above, De la Vega adds the information regarding the Apalachee towns which I have quoted elsewhere. Then he continues:

> The aforesaid was the condition of the religious settlements in the provinces subject to the jurisdiction of San Agustin de la Florida, whose churches were built of palmetto, both the walls and roof, except the one at Holomacos [Tolomato], which was built of lumber board, and the one at Nombre de Dios, which was the best and contained the image of Our Lady of the Milk, the walls of which, through private donations of the faithful, had been built of stone and mortar, although the roof was of palmetto like the others. But a body of two hundred English having penetrated into that town on the aforesaid day, the twentieth of March [1728], together with as many Indians, they plundered and pillaged it and set the whole town on fire. They robbed the church and the convent and profaned the images, killing six and wounding eight Indians, a lieutenant and a soldier of infantry. They also took several prisoners with them and withdrew without further action. In view of this the governor had the church blown up by means of powder, withdrawing the Indians who had remained there to the shelter of this city, leaving only the town of Pocotabaco [Pocotalaco] under the protection of the guns of this fort.[1]

As I have pointed out elsewhere, the Yamasee or Guale element was evidently predominant in these villages, and how many of them were occupied by Timucua we do not know, although that called "Pueblo de Timucua"[2] probably contained most of them. A few may have emigrated to southern Florida and joined the Indians there, and a few were probably absorbed into the Yamasee. Those who retained their tribal identity withdrew to the Mosquito Lagoon and Halifax River, Volusia County, where Tomoka River keeps

---

[1] Brooks, MSS.

[2] See p. 105.

their name alive. Ultimately, even these must have been absorbed by the invading Seminole.

It is somewhat singular that during this period of intense missionary activity in northern Florida the Indians in the southern part of the peninsula had been left for the most part to their own devices. They would perhaps have been left entirely alone had it not been for the numerous shipwrecks on their coast and the necessity of protecting the lives and property of those cast away among them. Shortly after founding St. Augustine, Menendez visited the head chiefs of Calos and Tocobaga, the latter probably Timucua, however.[1] In 1566 we learn that the Takesta protected some Spaniards from the chief of Calos,[2] and in the legend on an early Spanish map it is stated that the Indians in that neighborhood had been converted by Pedro Menendez Marques. They afterwards abandoned their spiritual but retained their political allegiance.[3] During or just before 1570 there was war between the Spaniards and the people of Ais, for we read in an early manuscript that, in accordance with the terms of a treaty of peace made with Ais in 1570, 40 reales were given to the chief of Colomas [Ulumay], "a land of the Cacique of Ays," and 80 to the chief of Rea in the same province. It is probable that the last name has been miscopied.[4] In 1597 Governor Mendez de Canço traveled from the head of the Florida Keys to St. Augustine. The chief of Ais met him with 15 canoes and more than 80 Indians.[5] In a letter written the year following Canco says that this chief had more Indians than any other between those two points.[5] The Ais are mentioned in connection with the Curruque expedition about the same time but they were only incidentally concerned in it.[6]

In 1605 an Ais Indian called Chico, or the Little Captain, evidently a subordinate chief, came to St. Augustine with 24 warriors to offer his services to Governor Ibarra, who, he had heard, was at war with the French and English. Complaint was made that the Indians of Nocoroco had bewitched the cousin of the grand chief of Ais. A messenger was sent to confer with the grand chief and promise was made that some young Spaniards would be sent to learn the Ais language.[5] In 1607 Governor Ibarra states that during Holy Week he had received visits from the chief of Santa Lucia, Don Luis, the Little Captain of Ais, Don Juan Gega, and others, "who are the principal lords of the mouth of the Miguel Mora."[3] This name was given to the opening between the Florida mainland and the keys on the eastern side. From a letter written the following year it appears

[1] Lowery, Span. Settl., II, pp. 228–243, 277–280; Barcia, Florida, pp. 94–98, 125–129.
[2] Barcia, Florida, p. 124.
[3] Brooks, MSS.
[4] Copy of MS. in Ayer Coll., Newberry Library.
[5] Lowery, MSS.
[6] See pp. 336–337.

that Don Luis, chief of the mouths of Miguel Mora, and the chief of Guega [Jeaga] had been at war, and that the governor had made peace between them.[1] In 1609 the chief of Ais visited St. Augustine and several chiefs living on the southeast coast were baptized in that city.[1]

In 1612 an expedition was sent to the southwest coast of Florida to punish the chiefs of Pooy and Tocopaca (Tocobaga) because they had attacked Christian Indians. This expedition also pushed on farther south until it came to the town of Calos, from which more than 60 canoes came out to meet it. The chief of Calos is said to have had more than 70 towns under him, not counting the very great number which paid him tribute because they feared him.[1] The same year Indians came from beyond Calos asking for missionaries.[1] A missionary letter of 1618 states, however, that the Indians of Jeaga and Santa Lucia were "rebellious," and Christianity seems not to have affected them permanently.[1] A decade later we hear that hostile English and Dutch vessels were using this territory, particularly that between the bar of Ais and Jeaga, as an anchorage ground.[1] In 1680 the clergy of Florida desired to enter upon the conversion of the natives of the southern part of the peninsula, and in consequence the governor of Florida, Don Pablo de Hita Salazar, sent an interpreter to reconnoiter that region. The latter entered several Calos towns, but was finally turned back by the natives, who feared that they should be held responsible by the chief of Calos if they allowed him to proceed to that place. He reported that the Calusa Indians dominated all others in that part of the peninsula and forced them to pay tribute to their chief, who was known as "No he querido" ("Not loved").[1] A letter written in 1681 states that many Indians fleeing from Guale had settled in the towns of Calos.[1] Another effort to missionize the Calusa in 1697 also failed, but it is said that the Indians then living on Matacumbe Island were "Catholics."[2]

An intimate picture of the Indians of the southeastern coast is given by the Quaker Dickenson, who was cast away there with a party from Pennsylvania in 1699.[3] An attempt was made to "reduce" the Ais Indians to the Catholic faith in 1703,[4] but there is no evidence that any success was attained, and both they and the Calusa apparently remained unconverted to the very end of Spanish rule. Romans states that in 1763, the year when Florida passed from Spanish to British control, the last of the Calusa people, consisting of 80 families, crossed to Havana.[5] Not all of the Calusa left the country, however, and indeed the emigrants may have been Tekesta and

---

[1] Lowery, MSS.
[2] Barcia, Florida, p. 316.
[3] See pages 92–93, 389 et seq.
[4] Barcia, Florida, p. 322.
[5] Romans, Concise Nat. Hist. Fla., p. 29.

other occupants of the eastern shore, who were always rather better inclined toward the Spanish Government than were the Calusa. Until recently this fate of the old Florida tribes was remembered by some of the oldest Creek Indians.[1] Possibly the Calusa may have emigrated in the year mentioned and returned with the return of the Spaniards 20 years later, but it is improbable that southern Florida was ever entirely abandoned. At any rate some of these people were in occupancy of the territory about Charlotte Harbor and the Caloosahatchie River in the period of the Seminole war. They took no part in this contest during its earlier stages. They made no treaties with the Americans and at no time agreed to remove to the west. Comparatively unnoticed, they remained in their old haunts, carrying on a considerable commerce with Havana, and looking to that city as their trading point. Williams describes their condition in the first half of the nineteenth century as follows:

> The inhabitants of several large settlements around the Caximba Inlet, the heads of the Hujelos, St. Mary's, and other southern streams, never appeared at the agency to draw annuities, but lived by cultivating their fields, hunting, trading at the Spanish ranchos, bartering skins, mocking birds, and pet squirrels, for guns, ammunition and clothing, and sometimes assisting in the fisheries. This race of Indians would have remained peaceable to this day had not an order been issued from the agency requiring them all to remove. They never agreed to remove, either personally or by their representatives; and they were easily excited to fight rather than leave the homes of their ancestors. Their knowledge of the country and their long connection with the Spanish traders and fishermen afforded perfect facilities for supplying the Seminoles with arms and munitions of war, and those facilities are at this time improved to our great injury.[2]

They were first seriously disturbed when the Seminole, hard pressed in their seats near the center of the State, moved southward into the Everglades. There they intrenched themselves and induced the Calusa, or "Spanish Indians," as they are called in the documents of the time, to take up arms in their interest. In 1839 Colonel Harney had gone to Charlotte Harbor to establish a trading post for the Indians, when his camp, consisting of 30 men, was attacked by 250 Indians and 18 were killed.[3] In retaliation for this injury Colonel Harney fell upon the Spanish Indians, under their chief Chekika, July 23, 1839, killed Chekika and hung six of his followers.[4] The next year Doctor Perrine, a botanist living on Indian Key, who was devoting himself to the culture of tropical plants, was killed by Chekika's band. This happened on the 7th of May, 1840.[5] Other depredations were also committed by them. If they are the

---

[1] See p. 188.
[2] John Lee Williams, The Territory of Florida, 1837, p. 242.
[3] Fairbanks, Hist. of Florida, p. 191.
[4] Ibid., p. 194. But Fairbanks dates the event too late.
[5] Ibid., p. 191

Florida "Choctaw," as I have supposed, we can trace them down to 1847 when "four Choctaw warriors" are enumerated in the peninsula.[1] In 1850 seventy-six more Seminole were sent west,[1] but we do not know whether the remnant in question was among them or remained in its ancient home. The latter would be the more likely supposition, but the reverse is indicated by an old Seminole Indian in Oklahoma, who declared that he knew of these Florida Choctaw, asserting that one youth descended from them is still living among the Seminole of Oklahoma. He added that when the Seminole reached Fort Smith during their removal west the Choctaw who were with them wanted to remain with the Choctaw who had emigrated from Mississippi, but the Indian agent would not allow it. He knew nothing regarding the origin of this band of Choctaw, but thought they had emigrated to Florida from Mississippi about the time when the other Seminole settled there.

Ethnology

From what has been said regarding the history of the Florida Indians it is evident that it is no longer possible to add to their ethnology, except as new manuscripts come to light from time to time, particularly in the Spanish archives. It is probable, however, that such supplementary information will be comparatively small. We must rely principally on the narratives of Laudonnière and his companions, assisted by the illustrations of Le Moyne, on such information as may be extracted from the writings of the Franciscan fathers, Pareja and Mouilla, and on a few notes in the works of other Spaniards. It has not been thought best to reproduce Le Moyne's drawings in the present volume, although his text has been freely drawn upon, because the former contain so many errors that Le Moyne must have intrusted the execution to some one entirely unfamiliar with his subject, or else extreme liberties must have been taken with the originals.

Ribault describes the Timucua as "of good stature, well shaped of body as any people in the world; very gentle, courteous, and good-natured, of tawny color, hawked nose, and of pleasant countenance."[2] They were good swimmers and could climb trees with agility.

The only invariable article of apparel worn by males was the breechclout, which we are informed consisted of a painted deerskin. Le Moyne represents this as if it were in one piece, passed about the privates, and carried round and tied at the back. If his representation might be relied upon the Florida Indians would be set off in this

[1] Schoolcraft, Ind. Tribes, I, p 522.

[2] French, Hist. Colls. La., 1875, pp. 171, 172.

particular from all Indian tribes known to us, but there is every reason to believe he is wrong. As worn elsewhere, the breechclout consisted of a belt about the waist and a skin or piece of cloth passed between the legs and between the belt and the body, the ends being allowed to fall down in front and behind. That the natives did have belts is proved by Ribault's narrative, for he says that when he was at the mouth of the St. Johns River a chief sent him a girdle of red leather in token of friendship.[1] The warm climate of Florida rendered additional garments less necessary than with other southern tribes, but it is quite certain that they were worn. So far as men are concerned, the only direct evidence of this which we have, however, is contained in one of Le Moyne's drawings in which the chief Saturiwa is represented wearing a long garment,[2] and in a statement by Spark, who says:

> In their apparell the men only vse deer skinnes, wherewith some onely couer their priuy members, other some vse the same as garments to couer them before and behind; which skins are painted, some yellow and red, some blacke and russet, and euery man according to his owne fancy.[3]

He adds that the color with which these skins were adorned "neither fadeth away nor altereth color" when washed.[4] The one figured by Le Moyne is apparently a painted deerskin, but it appears to be intended rather to add to the gorgeous appearance of the chief who wears it than to protect him from the cold. Women wore a kind of short skirt made of Spanish moss.[5] If Le Moyne may be trusted, instead of being fastened around the waist, this was sometimes carried up over one shoulder.[6] An anonymous writer who accompanied Laudonnière says:

> The women have around them a certain very long white moss, covering their breasts and their private parts.[7]

Sometimes this was of skin, for Le Challeux remarks:

> The woman girds herself with a little covering of the skin of a deer or other animal, the knot saddling the left side above the thigh, in order to cover the most private parts.[8]

And Hawkins's chronicler confirms this:

> The women also for their apparell vse painted skinnes, but most of them gownes of mosse, somewhat longer than our mosse, which they sowe together artificially, and make the same surplesse wise.[3]

---

[1] French, Hist. Colls. La., 1875, p. 170.
[2] Le Moyne, Narrative, pl. 39.
[3] Hakluyt, Voyages, III, p. 613.
[4] Ibid., p. 615.
[5] Le Moyne, Narrative, plates and p. 14; French, Hist. Colls. La., 1875, p. 172.
[6] Le Moyne, Ibid.
[7] Gaffarel, Hist. Floride française, p. 405.
[8] Ibid., p. 461.

Dickenson testifies to the same effect:

The women natives of these towns clothe themselves with the moss of trees, making gowns and petticoats thereof, which at a distance, or in the night, looks very neat.[1]

Most of the people of whom he speaks were, however, refugees from Guale. In his narrative Le Moyne also mentions "many pieces of a stuff made of feathers, and most skilfully ornamented with rushes of different colors," sent in from the western Timucua by a French officer. They may have been those feather cloaks so common throughout the south. The women wore their hair long, but certainly not in the disheveled fashion represented by Le Moyne.[2] From a remark of Ribault it is evident that the men were in the habit of pulling out the hair on all parts of their bodies except the head.[3] They do not seem to have roached their heads like the Creeks. Ribault says, in describing those Indians whom he saw, "Their hair was long and trussed up, with a lace made of herbs, to the top of their heads," and this remark is confirmed by Laudonnière and in the pictures of Le Moyne.[4] In another place, where he describes the leading men who accompanied Saturiwa, Ribault states that their hair was "trussed up, gathered and worked together with great cunning, and fastened after the form of a diadem."[5] Le Challeux says:

They keep their hair long, and they truss it up neatly all around their heads, and this truss of hair serves them as a quiver in which to carry their arrows when they are at war.[6]

He also says, regarding feathers:

They esteem nothing richer or more beautiful than bird feathers of different colors.[7]

These are represented by Le Moyne on several of his subjects, used in a great variety of ways. One has a single sheaf of feathers coming straight out from the knot of hair at the back of his head. Another has a number of long, curving feathers in the same place, suggesting a fountain. Another has a kind of feather tassel tied to the top-knot by a cord or small withe. Many have feathers around the edges of the hair lower down, either alone or in addition to some of the central clumps of feathers just mentioned. Saturiwa and some of his leading men are represented on various occasions with small tufts of feathers of exceptional height over the middle of the forehead in front, with the tail of an animal hanging from the top-knot, or again with what appears to be a metallic diadem encircling

---

1 Dickenson, Narrative, p. 93.

2 Cf. Hakluyt, Voyages, III, p. 613. "Wearing theire haire downe to their shoulders, like the [East] Indians."

3 French, Hist. Colls. La., 1875, p. 172.

4 Le Moyne, Narrative, plates and p. 14; French, Hist. Colls. La., 1875, p. 173.

5 Ibid., p. 178.

6 Gaffarel, op. cit., p. 461.

7 Ibid., p. 462.

the forehead. As is well known, circlets of this last kind made of silver were in common use among our southern Indians. There must also be mentioned skins of animals with the head on, one of which appears with a kind of tassel hanging out of the mouth. The persons who wear these are evidently doctors or other principal functionaries.[1] Laudonnière says that feathers were worn particularly when they went to war.[2] Perhaps the most interesting headdress is what appears to be a basket hat.[3] We should have to go as far as the great plateaus to find anything comparable. Pareja, however, speaks of a palm-leaf hat worn by the women,[4] and this is what Le Moyne may have intended.

Turning to ornaments, we find it worthy of note that there is no evidence that these people pierced the nose or the ears except in one place, the soft lobe, where nearly all of Le Moyne's figures, both male and female, are represented with a kind of dumb-bell shaped ornament.[5] Le Moyne says of this:

> All the men and women have the ends of their ears pierced, and pass through them small oblong fish-bladders, which when inflated shine like pearls, and which, being dyed red, look like a light-colored carbuncle.[6]

In two cases men are represented with staple-shaped earrings, in one with a ring, and in another with the claws of some bird thrust through this member. The person wearing these last was probably a doctor. Says Le Challeux:

> They prize highly little beads, which they make of the bones of fishes and other animals and of green and red stones.[7]

Ornaments were also worn about the neck, wrists, and ankles, just above the elbows and biceps, just below the knees, and hanging from the breechclout. One woman is represented with a double row of pearls or beads about her waist.[8] Ribault says that the French obtained from the Indians of Florida, gold, silver, copper, lead, turquoises, "and a great abundance of pearls, which they told us they took out of oysters along the riverside; and as fair pearls as are found in any country of the world."[9] By oysters I suppose we are to understand fresh-water mussels. At least the greater part of the pearls among the southern Indians were extracted from these. Says Spark:

> The Frenchmen obteined pearles of them of great bignesse, but they were blacke, be meanes of rosting of them, for they do not fish for them as the Spanyards doe, but for their meat.[10]

---

[1] Le Moyne, Narrative, plates.
[2] Laudonnière, Hist. Not. de la Floride, p. 9; French, Hist. Colls. La., 1869, p. 172.
[3] Le Moyne, Narrative, pl. 11.
[4] See p. 387.
[5] Le Moyne, Narrative, ills.
[6] Ibid. p. 14.
[7] Gafferel, Hist. Floride française, p. 462.
[8] Le Moyne, Narrative, p. 37.
[9] French, Hist. Colls. La., 1875, p. 177.
[10] Hakluyt, Voyages, III, p. 616.

Shells, and beads worked out of shells, were also employed, and Le Moyne mentions "bracelets of fishes' teeth." [1] The gold and silver, as Laudonnière expressly states—and in this he is confirmed by Fontaneda—were obtained from wrecked Spanish vessels bound from Mexico and other parts of the "Indies" to Spain; [2] and the quantity among them speaks volumes for the number of disasters of this kind which must have taken place.

Hawkins's chronicler describes the gold and silver found in Florida at considerable length, but to much the same purport:

> Golde and siluer they want, not: for at the Frenchmens first comming thither they had the same offered them for little or nothing, for they receiued for a hatchet two pound weight of golde, because they knew not the estimation thereof: but the souldiers being greedy of the same, did take it from them, giuing them nothing for it: the which they perceiuing, that both the Frenchmen did greatly esteeme it, and also did rigorously deale with them, by taking the same away from them, at last would not be knowen they had any more, neither durst they weare the same for feare of being taken away: so that sauing at their first comming, they could get none of them: and how they came of this gold and siluer the Frenchmen know not as yet, but by gesse, who hauing trauelled to the Southwest of the cape, hauing found the same dangerous, by means of sundry banks, as we also haue found the same: and there finding masts which were wracks of Spanyards comming from Mexico, iudged that they had gotten treasure by them. For it is most true that diuers wracks haue beene made of Spanyards, hauing much treasure: for the Frenchmen hauing trauelled to the capeward an hundred and fiftie miles, did finde two Spanyards with the Floridians, which they brought afterward to their fort, whereof one was in a carauel comming from the Indies, which was cast away fourteene yeeres ago, the other twelue yeeres; of whose fellowes some escaped, othersome were slain by the inhabitants. It seemeth thay had estimation of their golde & siluer, for it is wrought flat and grauen, which they weare about their neckes; othersome made round like a pancake, with a hole in the midst, to boulster vp their breasts withall, because they thinke it a deformity to haue great breasts. As for mines either of gold or siluer, the Frenchmen can heare of none they haue vpon the Island, but of copper, whereof as yet also they haue not made the proofe, because they were but few men: but it is not unlike, but that in the maine where are high hilles, may be golde and siluer as well as in Mexico, because it is all one maine.[3]

To the same origin must be attributed the "gold alloyed with brass, and silver not thoroughly smelted" which one of Laudonnière's lieutenants sent him from the western Timucua districts.[4] The articles made of these, however, were without doubt worked over into objects such as had been manufactured out of copper already in pre-Columbian times. I have made mention of the metal diadems. Le Moyne figures round and oval metal plates strung together into bands below the knee and above the biceps. Numbers of them

---

[1] Le Moyne, Narrative, p. 2.

[2] Laudonnière, Hist. Not. de la Floride, p. 6; French, Hist. Colls. La., 1869, p. 170; Mem. Fontaneda, ed. Smith, pp. 21-24.

[3] Hakluyt, Voyages, III, pp. 615-616.

[4] Le Moyne, Narrative, p. 8.

also appear fastened to the breechclouts by separate cords in the manner of a fringe, and larger circular pieces are hung about the necks of several of the principal men.[1] We are told that the plates fastened to the breechclouts were placed there so as to produce a tinkling sound when the wearer moved, and they were particularly used in dances.[2] How they were made fast to the strings is not evident, but the large neck pieces were secured to a cord about the neck of the wearer by means of a hole in the center of the plate, through which the cord was passed and knotted on the outside so that the knot would not pull through.[3] The later southern Indian method of fastening silver ornaments to clothing was similar. All of the gorgets which Le Moyne depicts are circular, while the other plates are oval.[3] In his text he enumerates among the things sent by La Roche Ferriere from the western Timucua country "circular plates of gold and silver as large as a moderate-sized platter, such as they are accustomed to wear to protect the back and breast in war."[4] This passage suggests another use for these plates, and no doubt they actually did furnish a certain amount of protection to the wearer; but if they were consciously worn with this object in view the idea must have been secondary, for most of the warriors are represented without them, and the largest that Le Moyne figures furnish but very partial protection. Ribault mentions one Indian who had hanging about his neck "a round plate of red copper, well polished, with a small one of silver hung in the middle of it; and on his ears a small plate of copper, with which they wipe the sweat from their bodies."[5] This last was rather utilitarian than ornamental, but seems to have served both purposes. It is the only mention of a sweat scraper in America that has come to my attention. Another man had "a pearl hanging to a collar of gold about his neck, as great as an acorn."[6] If we could trust the expression used here we would have to suppose another kind of neck ornament which fitted closer than the ornaments already described, but this is the only Florida reference upon which such a conclusion can be based, and nothing of the kind is figured by Le Moyne. Nevertheless Le Moyne speaks of "girdles of silver-colored balls, some round and some oblong."[7] If the translation is correct we seem to have an ornament somewhat more difficult to manufacture than the plates elsewhere described, but here again there is no certain evidence with which to back up the inference. Silver chains mentioned as worn by the chiefs[8] were probably of Spanish origin. The beads and pearls were arranged in separate

[1] Le Moyne, Narrative, plates.
[2] Ibid., p. 14.
[3] Ibid., plates.
[4] Ibid., p. 8.
[5] French, Hist. Colls. La., 1875, p. 178.
[6] Ibid., p. 177.
[7] Le Moyne, Narrative, pp. 2, 14 (ill.).
[8] French, Hist. Colls. La., 1869, p. 350.

strings or mixed together in all the places in which metal plates could be worn, except as tinklers on the breechclout. Spark says:

The Floridians haue pieces of vnicornes hornes which they weare about their necks, whereof the Frenchmen obteined many pieces.[1]

The absolute silence of French writers on this subject is ground for suspicion that Spark misunderstood the origin of the shell gorgets, though it is quite possible that bison horns or portions of them were worn in this manner.

In one picture Le Moyne represents feather fans on the ends of poles borne by two companions of the chief and again by companions of a woman being brought to the chief as his wife.[2] A Florida chief presented Ribault with a "plume, a fan of harnshau (heron) feathers, dyed red." [3]

Like their neighbors to the north, the Timucua resorted to tattooing very extensively. Ribault says:

The forepart of their bodies and arms they also paint with pretty devices in azure, red, and black, so well and properly, that the best painters of Europe could not improve upon it.[4]

This is not given as tattooing, but Laudonnière is evidently speaking of the same designs when he remarks:

The most part of them have their bodies, arms, and thighs painted with very fair devices, the painting whereof can never be taken away, because the same is pricked into their flesh.[5]

Says Le Moyne:

The reader should be informed that all these chiefs and their wives ornament their skin with punctures arranged so as to make certain designs, as the following pictures show. Doing this sometimes makes them sick for seven or eight days. They rub the punctured places with a certain herb, which leaves an indelible color.[6]

Le Challeux also says that "for ornament they have their skin checkered (marqueté) in a strange fashion,"[7] and John Spark, chronicler of Hawkins's second voyage, adds the following testimony:

They do not omit to paint their bodies also with curious knots, or antike worke, as every man in his own fancy deuiseth, which painting, to make it continue the better, they vse with a thorne to pricke their flesh, and dent in the same, whereby the painting may have better hold.[8]

They supplemented this with temporary face paintings, particularly upon state occasions or when they went to war.

In their warres [says the writer last quoted] they vse a sleighter colour of painting their faces, thereby to make themselves shew the more fierce; which after their warres ended, they wash away againe.[8]

---

1 Hakluyt, Voyages, III, p. 616.
2 Le Moyne, Narrative, pls. 37, 39.
3 French, Hist. Colls. La., 1869, p. 180.
4 Ibid., 1875, p. 171.
5 Laudonnière, Hist. Not. de la Floride, p. 6.
6 Le Moyne, Narrative, p. 15 (ill.).
7 Gaffarel, Hist. Floride française, p. 461.
8 Hakluyt, Voyages, III, p. 613.

Farther on he states that the colors employed were "red, blacke, yellow, and russet, very perfect." [1] When Ribault and his companions crossed the St. Johns after having met the Indians on one side, he says that he found them "waiting for us quietly, and in good order, with new paintings upon their faces, and feathers upon their heads." [2] And Laudonnière states that when they went to war they painted their faces much, "and stick their hair full of feathers, or down, that they may seem more terrible." [3] Le Moyne notes that they were "in the habit of painting the skin around their mouths of a blue color." [4] Like the Creeks, their neighbors, they kept their bodies covered with bear grease, for some ceremonial reason, Laudonnière declares, and also to protect them from the sun's heat. [5]

The chiefs Onatheaqua and Houstaqua living near the Apalachee painted their faces black, while the other Timucua chiefs painted theirs red.[6] The Indians first seen by De Soto and his men at Tampa Bay were painted red.[7]

Another peculiar custom is thus described by Le Moyne:

They let their nails grow long both on fingers and toes, cutting (or scraping) the former away, however, at the sides (with a certain shell), so as to leave them very sharp, the men especially; and when they take one of the enemy they sink their nails deep in his forehead, and tear down the skin, so as to wound and blind him.[4]

There are not many special descriptions of Timucua houses. Ribault says, in speaking of the dwellings of those Indians whom he met at the mouth of the river which he called the Seine and which was probably what is now known as the St. Marys:

Their houses are made of wood, fitly and closely set up, and covered with reeds, the most part after the fashion of a pavilion. But there was one house among the rest very long and wide, with seats around about made of reeds nicely put together, which serve both for beds and seats, two feet high from the ground, set upon round pillars painted red, yellow, and blue, and neatly polished.[8]

Le Challeux describes them thus:

Their dwellings are of a round shape and in style almost like the pigeon houses of this country, the foundation and main structure being of great trees, covered over with palmetto leaves, and not fearing either wind or tempest.[9]

Says Le Moyne:

The chief's dwelling stands in the middle of the town, and is partly underground in consequence of the sun's heat. Around this are the houses of the principal men, all lightly roofed with palm branches, as they are occupied only nine months in the year; the other three, as has been related, being spent in the woods. When they

---

1 Hakluyt, Voyages, III, p. 615.
2 French, op. cit., p. 178.
3 Laudonnière, op. cit., p. 9.
4 Le Moyne, Narrative, pp. 8, 15.
5 Laudonnière, op. cit., p. 12.
6 Ibid., p. 91.
7 Bourne, Narr. of De Soto, II, p. 56.
8 French, op. cit., p. 180.
9 Gaffarel, Hist. Floride française, p. 461.

come back they occupy their houses again; and if they find that the enemy has burnt them down, they build others of similar materials. Thus magnificent are the palaces of the Indians.[1]

The description of Timucua houses given by Spark contains details not noted by the others:

Their houses are not many together, for in one house an hundred of them do lodge; they being made much like a great barne, and in strength not inferiour to ours, for they haue stanchions and rafters of whole trees, and are covered with palmito-leaues, hauing no place diuided, but one small roome for their king and queene.[2]

It is to be noticed that the houses at the mouth of the St. Marys were covered with reeds, while on those which were farther south palmetto was employed. It is probable that the frames and the rest of the construction were practically identical. The greater part of the common houses figured by Le Moyne are circular, but there is another type square or squarish in ground plan and with a pronounced gable, although the gable ends are sloping, not perpendicular. Besides these, two houses are figured square or oblong in outline, with a dome-shaped roof, and the door in one end very similar to some of the houses on the North Carolina coast.[3] The town house, the one described at most length by Ribault, is also figured by Le Moyne in one place.[4] It is represented as a long, quadrilateral building with a regular gable and perpendicular ends. This specimen appears to be thatched with palmetto like the rest. In 1699 Dickenson described the town houses in three mission stations in this region, but these were mainly occupied by Indians from the former province of Guale, and the architecture can not be set down as certainly Timucua. What he has to say regarding them will be found on pages 92–93. Cabeza de Vaca must mean one of the town houses when he speaks of a house "so large that it could hold more than 300 people." [5]

The following description of the village of Ucita on Tampa Bay may be given by way of contrast, showing as it does either a somewhat different method of arrangement on the west coast of Florida or greater variety in method than the French narratives indicate:

The town [of Ucita] was of seven or eight houses, built of timber, and covered with palm leaves. The chief's house stood near the beach, upon a very high mount, made by hand for defense; at the other end of the town was a temple, on the roof of which perched a wooden fowl with gilded eyes.[6]

In the center of the town of Uriutina was "a very large open court,"[7] and in Napetaca a "town yard" is mentioned.[8] It appears that the beds of these Indians were made on a raised platform about the sides

---

[1] Le Moyne, Narrative, p. 12 (ill.).
[2] Hakluyt, Voyages, III, p. 613.
[3] Le Moyne, Narrative, pls. 30–33.
[4] Ibid., pl. 30.
[5] Bandelier, Jour. Cabeza de Vaca, p. 10.
[6] Bourne, Narr. of De Soto, I, p. 23.
[7] Ibid., II, p. 72.
[8] Ibid., p. 44.

of the houses precisely like those of the other southern tribes. The seats illustrated by Le Moyne were probably made in an identical manner and were in fact the same thing.[1] Their openwork construction offered certain advantages, thus explained by a writer quoted by Gaffarel:

> They are often bothered by little flies, which they call in their language maringous and it is usually necessary for them to make fires in their houses, absolutely under their beds, in order to be freed from these vermin; and they say that they bite severely, and the part of the skin affected by their bite becomes like that of a leper.[2]

Spark seems to have seen a more solidly constructed bed, provided with a wooden pillow:

> In the middest of this house is a hearth, where they make great fires all night, and they sleepe vpon certeine pieces of wood hewin in for the bowing of their backs, and another place made high for their heads, which they put one by another all along the walles on both sides.[3]

The narrative of De Gourgues records that Saturiwa seated him upon "a seat of wood of lentisque, covered with moss, made of purpose like unto his own,"[4] the rest sitting upon the ground. Perhaps these seats were of the three-legged variety used in the West Indies and throughout the Southern States generally.

They made their fires in the usual Indian fashion, by means of two sticks.[3]

Le Moyne figures several different kinds of pots and baskets. Some of the former are of a size and shape suggestive of Creek sofki pots. In one picture a large pot with a round bottom is seen placed over a fire. There are also two or three earthen pots, some with short handles, a few flat dishes or pans, and in one place are two large gourds or earthen jugs which seem to be provided with strap handles and to be closed by means of small earthen jars placed over them, mouth down.[5] Laudonnière saw in the house of one of the chiefs "a great vessel of earth made after a strange fashion, full of fountain water, clear, and very excellent."[6] "A little vessel of wood," used as a cup, is spoken of in the same connection,[6] and Le Moyne mentions round bottles or wooden vessels in which they carried cassine.[7]

Among baskets we find the common southern carrying basket with a strap passing over the forehead of the bearer. Le Moyne figures sieves and fanners. In addition, however, there is a basket with two handles very much like our bushel basket, and several

---

[1] Le Moyne, Narrative, pls. 29, 38.

[2] Gaffarel, Hist. Floride française, pp. 461–462.

[3] Hakluyt, Voyages, III, p. 613.

[4] Laudonnière, La Floride, p. 209.

[5] Le Moyne, Narrative, pl. 20.

[6] Laudonnière, La Floride, p. 74; French, Hist. Colls. La., 1869, pp. 228–229.

[7] Le Moyne, op. cit., p. 12 (ill.).

baskets with one handle like European baskets.[1] These last I believe to have been based on the imagination of the illustrator. In 1562 one of the Florida chiefs presented Ribault with "a basket made of palm boughs, after the Indian fashion, and wrought very artificially."[2] Three years later one of his lieutenants received "little panniers skillfully made of palm leaves, full of gourds, red and blue."[3] Woven mats are also spoken of.[4] It appears from Pareja that shells were ordinarily used as drinking cups.[5]

Regarding skin dressing Le Moyne says:

> They know how to prepare deerskin, not with iron instruments, but with shells, in a surprisingly excellent manner; indeed I do not believe that any European could do it as well.[6]

Skins, painted and unpainted, were presented to the French; and one of those given to Ribault was "painted and drawn throughout with pictures of divers wild beasts; so lively drawn and portrayed that nothing lacked but life.[7]

Le Moyne mentions "green and blue stones, which some thought to be emeralds and sapphires, in the form of wedges, which they used, instead of axes, for cutting wood."[6] From this it appears that they probably felled trees, cleared their land, and manufactured canoes in the same manner as the other southern Indians, using stone axes and fire. At any rate they made their canoes out of single trunks of trees. Ribault says that these would hold 15 or 20 men, and he adds that they rowed, or rather paddled, standing up.[8] The canoes illustrated by Le Moyne all have blunt bows, but those at present employed by the Florida Seminole are pointed, and the canoes recovered from time to time from the marshes also have pointed bows. The use of additional pieces for the bow and stern does not seem to have been known. Le Moyne represents their paddles with rather short, wide blades.[9] That they had means of cutting very hard substances is shown by the statement in Elvas that the Indians captured by De Soto's army would file through the irons at night with a splinter of stone.[10] As elsewhere in the Southeast, cane knives were extensively employed.

The dog was the only domestic animal, and there is no evidence that it was used to assist in transportation; therefore land transportation was all on foot, berdaches being employed to carry very heavy

---

1 Le Moyne, Narrative, plates.
2 Laudonnière, La Floride, p. 17; French, Hist. Colls. La., 1869, p. 180.
3 Laudonnière, ibid., p. 75; French, ibid., p. 230.
4 Laudonnière, ibid., p. 168; French, ibid., p. 315.
5 See p. 384.
6 Le Moyne, op. cit., p. 8.
7 Laudonnière, op. cit., p. 17; French, op. cit., p. 180.
8 French, op. cit., 1875, p. 178.
9 Le Moyne, op. cit., plates.
10 Bourne, Narr. of De Soto, I, p. 46.

burdens.[1] The chiefs, chiefs' wives, and other principal persons were, on occasions of state, carried in litters, borne on the shoulders of several men. All early Spanish travelers among the southern Indians speak of these, and Le Moyne illustrates one in which a woman is being borne on the shoulders of four men.[2] She is placed on a raised seat covered with a decorated skin, and protected from the sun by a structure of green boughs. Each of the bearers carries a crotched stick in one hand. The opposite end of each of these was stuck into the ground when they made a halt and the handles of the litter were allowed to rest in the crotches. Before march two men blowing on flutes, and at the sides are two others with large feather fans on the ends of long poles. Some of these features, especially the last, seem suspiciously European, but the use of flutes before such personages is well attested. Feather fans were also employed throughout the southern area; it is rather the type of fan shown here that is doubtful.

Other animals besides the dog were perhaps reared from time to time, as one of Laudonnière's lieutenants was presented with two young eagles by a chief who had bred them in his house.[3] The statement in De Soto's letter regarding domestication of turkeys and deer is evidently a mistake.[4] Ribault says that the tools with which they made their "spades and mattocks," their bows and arrows, and short lances, and with which they "cut and polished all sorts of wood that they employed about their buildings," were "certain stones, oyster shells, and mussels."[5]

They lived partly upon the natural products of the earth, but depended principally upon the chase, fishing, and agriculture. Laudonnière says:

> They make the string of their bow of the gut of the stag, or of a stag's skin, which they know how to dress as well as any man in France, and with as different sorts of colors. They head their arrows with the teeth of fishes, which they work very finely and handsomely.[6]

Ribault states that the shafts of their arrows were of reed.[7] Spark is considerably more detailed:

> In their warres they vse bowes and arrowes, whereof their bowes are made of a kind of Yew, but blacker than ours, and for the most part passing the strength of the Negros or Indians, for it is not greatly inferior to ours: their arrowes are also of a great length, but yet of reeds like other Indians, but varying in two points, both in length and also for nocks and feathers, which the other lacke, whereby they shoot very

---

1 See p. 373.
2 Le Moyne, Narrative, pl. 37.
3 Laudonnière, La Floride, p. 75; French, Hist. Colls. La., 1875, p. 230.
4 Bourne, Narr. of De Soto, II, p. 162.
5 French, op. cit., p. 174.
6 Laudonnière, op. cit., p. 7; French, Hist. Colls. La., 1869, pp. 170–171.
7 French, Hist. Colls. La., 1875, p. 174.

stedy: the heads of the same are vipers teeth, bones of fishes, flint stones, piked points of knives, which they hauing gotten of the French men, broke the same, & put the points of them in their arrowes heads: some of them haue their heads of siluer, othersome that haue want of these, put in a kind of hard wood, notched, which pierceth as farre as any of the rest. In their fight, being in the woods, they vse a maruellous pollicie for their owne safegard, which is by clasping a tree in their armes, and yet shooting notwithstanding: this policy they vsed with the French men in their fight, whereby it appeareth that they are people of some policy.[1]

Commenting on the weapons of the Timucua farther west, Elvas says:

Their bows are very perfect; the arrows are made of certain canes, like reeds, very heavy, and so stiff that one of them, when sharpened, will pass through a target. Some are pointed with the bone of a fish, sharp, and like a chisel; others with some stone like a point of diamond; of such the greater number, when they strike upon armor, break at the place the parts are put together; those of cane split, and will enter a shirt of mail, doing more injury than when armed.[2]

Le Moyne speaks of arrows with gold heads sent in by one of the Frenchmen from the western Timucua, but these were probably copper.[3] Their arrows were not poisoned.[4] Quivers were made of skins, but from Le Challeux it appears that their hair was impressed into service as a natural receptacle for arrows (see p. 347). He adds:

It is wonderful how suddenly they take them in their hands in order to shoot to a distance and as straight as possible.[5]

A wrist guard made from bark is described and figured by Le Moyne.[6]

Deer were stalked, as we know from a picture of Le Moyne's and the following description accompanying it:

The Indians have a way of hunting deer which we never saw before. They manage to put on the skins of the largest which have been taken, in such a manner, with the heads on their own heads, so that they can see out through the eyes as through a mask. Thus accoutered they can approach close to the deer without frightening them. They take advantage of the time when the animals come to drink at the river, and, having their bow and arrows all ready, easily shoot them, as they are very plentiful in those regions.[7]

The only difference to be noticed between the method illustrated here and that known to have been used north and west is the use of the entire deerskin instead of the head only.

The spears spoken of and illustrated by Le Moyne were probably used in killing fish; probably fishhooks were also in use. The only method of fishing about which we have direct information, however, was by means of fish traps or weirs. Some are figured by Le Moyne,[8] and Ribault says that they were "built in the water with

---

1 Hakluyt, Voyages, III, p. 613.
2 Bourne, Narr. of De Soto, I, p. 26.
3 Le Moyne, Narrative, p. 8.
4 Bourne, op. cit. II, p. 69.
5 Gaffarel, Hist. Floride française, p. 461.
6 Le Moyne, op. cit., p. 10 (ill.), pl. 14.
7 Ibid., p. 10 (ill.).
8 Ibid., pl. 3.

great reeds, so well and cunningly set together after the fashion of a labyrinth, with many turns and crooks, which it was impossible to construct without much skill and industry."[1] Among the fish given to the French were "trout, great mullets, plaice, turbots, and marvelous store of other sorts of fishes, altogether different from ours."[2] Ribault mentions crabs, lobsters [?], and crawfish among the articles of diet.[3] Laudonnière received presents of "fish, deer, turkey cocks, leopards [panthers], and little brown bears."[4] An early Spanish writer says that the natives of San Pedro (Cumberland Island) "sustained themselves the greater part of the year on shellfish (marisco), acorns, and roots."[5]

Alligators formed quite an item in the Floridian bill of fare, and Le Moyne thus describes how they were hunted:

> They put up, near a river, a little hut full of cracks and holes, and in this they station a watchman, so that they can see the crocodiles [or alligators] and hear them a good way off; for, when driven by hunger, they come out of the rivers and crawl about on the islands after prey, and, if they find none, they make such a frightful noise that it can be heard for half a mile. Then the watchman calls the rest of the watch, who are in readiness; and taking a portion, ten or twelve feet long, of the stem of a tree, they go out to find the monster, who is crawling along with his mouth wide open, all ready to catch one of them if he can; and with the greatest quickness they push the pole, small end first, as deep as possible down his throat, so that the roughness and irregularity of the bark may hold it from being got out again. Then they turn the crocodile over on his back, and with clubs and arrows pound and pierce his belly, which is softer; for his back, especially if he is an old one, is impenetrable, being protected by hard scales.[6]

We must, of course, discount the man-eating proclivities attributed to this animal, but the description of the hunt may nevertheless be perfectly correct. We are also indebted to this author for the only extant account of the methods pursued in preserving game and fish:

> In order to keep these animals longer they are in the habit of preparing them as follows: They set up in the earth four stout forked stakes; and on these they lay others, so as to form a sort of grating. On this they lay their game, and then build a fire underneath, so as to harden them in the smoke. In this process they use a great deal of care to have the drying perfectly performed, to prevent the meat from spoiling, as the picture shows. I suppose this stock to be laid in for their winter's supply in the woods, as at that time we could never obtain the least provision from them.[7]

The picture to which reference is made shows such a frame surmounted by several fish, a deer, an alligator, a snake, and some quadruped about the size of a fox. This, and a statement by Le Challeux, are the only references to snake eating which the various narratives

[1] French, Hist. Colls. La., 1875, p. 172.
[2] Laudonnière, La Floride, p. 18; French, Hist. Colls. La., 1869, p. 180.
[3] French, Hist. Colls. La., 1875, p. 178. Perhaps the "lobster" was the "langosta" mentioned by Fontaneda, p. 387.
[4] Laudonnière, La Floride, p. 130; French, Hist. Colls. La., 1869, p. 279.
[5] Lowery, MSS.
[6] Le Moyne, Narrative, p. 10 (ill.) and pl. 26.
[7] Ibid., pp. 9–10 (ill.).

contain, although the last author speaks of the eating of lizards.[1] It may be suspected that this picture is drawn from the imagination of the illustrator rather than from direct observation, for it is improbable that such animals were dried without being dressed. The description of the general drying process agrees very well, however, with what we know of this process elsewhere in the South. Le Challeux says that they used fish grease in place of butter "or any other sauce."[2] The same observer thus speaks of corn: "They do not have wheat, but they have corn in abundance, and it grows to the height of 7 feet; its stem is as big as that of a cane and its grain is as large as a pea, the ear a foot in length; its color is like that of fresh wax."[2] The following statement by Laudonnière gives the best account of the method of cultivation and along with it an insight into the native economic life:

They sow their maize twice a year—to wit in March and in June—and all in one and the same soil. The said maize, from the time that it is sowed until the time that it be ready to be gathered, is but three months on the ground; the other six months, they let the earth rest. They have also fine pumpkins, and very good beans. They never dung their land, only when they would sow they set weeds on fire, which grow up the six months, and burn them all. They dig their ground with an instrument of wood, which is fashioned like a broad mattock, wherewith they dig their vines in France; they put two grains of maize together. When the land is to be sowed, the king commandeth one of his men to assemble his subjects every day to labor, during which labor the king causeth store of that drink [cassine] to be made for them whereof we have spoken. At the time when the maize is gathered, it is all carried into a common house, where it is distributed to every man, according to his quality. They sow no more but that which they think will serve their turn for six months, and that very scarcely. For, during the winter, they retire themselves for three or four months in the year, into the woods, where they make little cottages of palm boughs for their retreat, and live there of maste, of fish which they take, of disters [oysters], of stags, of turkey cocks, and other beasts which they take.[3]

Le Moyne, however, asserts that they planted toward the end of the year, allowing their seed to lie in the ground nearly all winter.

The Indians cultivate the earth diligently; and the men know how to make a kind of hoe from fish bones, which they fit to wooden handles, and with these they prepare the land well enough, as the soil is light. When the ground is sufficiently broken up and levelled, the women come with beans and millet, or maize. Some go first with a stick, and make holes, in which the others place the beans, or grains of maize. After planting they leave the fields alone, as the winter in that country, situated between the west and the north, is pretty cold for about three months, being from the 24th of December to the 15th of March; and during that time, as they go naked, they shelter themselves in the woods.[4] When the winter is over, they return to their homes to wait for their crops to ripen. After gathering in their harvest, they store the whole of it for the year's use, not employing any part of it in trade, unless, perhaps some barter is made for some little household article.[5]

---

[1] Le Moyne, Narrative, p. 2.

[2] Gaffarel, Hist. Floride française, p. 462.

[3] Laudonnière, La Floride, pp. 11-12; French, Hist. Colls. La., 1869, p. 174.

[4] In small huts; Laudonnière, op. cit., pp. 12, 144; French, op. cit., pp. 174, 294.

[5] Le Moyne, Narrative, p. 9 (ill.).

As with the more northern tribes, small outhouses were built near the fields and watchers posted in each to drive away crows.[1]

Ribault mentions among the things planted by the Floridians "beans, gourds, citrons, cucumbers, peas, and many other fruits and roots unknown to us."[2] For "citrons" and "cucumbers" we should probably understand pumpkins and squashes. Later Spanish writers tell us, however, that the Indians of the Fresh Water district lived only on fish and roots.[3] The same was true of all the Indians on the coast to the southward.[4] In later times a change may have taken place for Dickenson encountered cultivated fields north of Cape Canaveral in which pumpkins were growing.[5]

Their food was broiled on the coals, roasted, or boiled. There is every reason to believe that corn was cooked in all the numerous ways known to other southern Indians. Le Moyne enumerates "grains of maize roasted, or ground into flour, or whole ears of it" among the things which the natives brought to Laudonnière's people,[6] and at one time they were presented with "little cakes."[7] Laudonnière mentions among the articles of food carried along by the Indians when they were away from home "victuals . . . of bread, of honey, and of meal, made of maize, parched in the fire, which they keep without being marred a long while. They carry also sometimes fish, which they cause to be dressed in the smoke."[8] Le Challeux says:

> The method of using it [corn] is first to rub it and resolve it into flour; afterward they dissolve it [in water] and make of it their porridge [migan], which resembles the rice used in this country; it must be eaten as soon as it is made, because it spoils quickly and can not be kept at all.[9]

Spark gives the following naive account of the use of tobacco:

> The Floridians when they trauell, haue a kinde of herbe dried, who with a cane and an earthen cup in the end, with fire, and the dried herbs put together doe sucke thorow the cane the smoke thereof, which smoke satisfieth their hunger, and therewith they liue foure or fiue dayes without meat or drinke, and this all the Frenchmen vsed for this purpose; yet do they hold opinion withall, that it causeth water & fleame to void from their stomacks.[10]

While we do not find it stated specifically that the Timucua cultivated tobacco, the fact may probably be assumed.

The granary or storehouse has been mentioned, but the various accounts leave us in the dark as to whether all of these granaries were public or whether there were private granaries also. The reference

---

1 Laudonnière, in French, Hist. Colls. La., 1869, p. 227.
2 French, Hist. Colls. La., 1875, p. 174.
3 Lowery, MSS.
4 Brooks, MSS.
5 Dickenson, Narrative, p. 66.
6 Le Moyne, Narrative, p. 2.
7 French, Hist. Colls. La., 1875, p. 177.
8 Laudonnière, La Floride, p. 9; French, Hist. Colls. La., 1869, p. 172. The mention of honey is curious and seems to be unique so far as Florida is concerned. But see p. 202.
9 Gaffarel, Hist. Floride française, p. 462.
10 Hakluyt, Voyages, III, p. 615; see also p. 386.

in Le Moyne's account of the disposition of the corn-crop would lead one to suppose that he is speaking of family granaries,[1] and the same seems to be in some measure implied in the section in which he tells of the way in which native wild fruits were stored. He says:

There are in that region a great many islands, producing abundance of various kinds of fruits, which they gather twice a year, and carry home in canoes, and store up in roomy low granaries built of stones and earth, and roofed thickly with palm-branches and a kind of soft earth fit for the purpose. These granaries are usually erected near some mountain, or on the bank of some river, so as to be out of the sun's rays, in order that the contents may keep better. Here they also store up any other provisions which they may wish to preserve, and the remainder of their stores; and they go and get them as need may require, without any apprehensions of being defrauded. Indeed it is to be wished that, among the Christians, avarice prevailed no more than among them, and tormented no more the minds of men.[2]

This use of "stones and earth" for granaries is confined, so far as we now know, to Florida; elsewhere they were of poles. The mutual regard which they observed with reference to their stores did not prevent them from pilfering small articles from the French colonists. An anonymous writer says:

They are, however, the greatest thieves in the world, for they take as well with the foot as with the hand.[3]

But he exonerates the women from this charge. Le Challeux, however, confirms the main accusation:

They steal without conscience and claim all that they can carry away secretly.[4]

In the following section, where Le Moyne speaks of the storage of animal food, he is certainly referring to a public storehouse:

At a set time every year they gather in all sorts of wild animals, fish, and even crocodiles; these are then put in baskets, and loaded upon a sufficient number of the curly-haired hermaphrodites above mentioned, who carry them on their shoulders to the storehouse. This supply, however, they do not resort to unless in case of the last necessity. In such event, in order to preclude any dissension, full notice is given to all interested; for they live in the utmost harmony among themselves. The chief, however, is at liberty to take whatever of this supply he may choose.[5]

It does not seem very likely that all of the animal food was put into public storehouses and all of the corn and wild fruits into private ones. Evidently both kinds of granary were in existence, but our authorities are not clear regarding the relative functions of the two.

The number of natural products drawn upon in addition to the cultivated plants and animal foods must have been very large, but we have only the reference just given, and one or two others. Ribault makes a statement to the effect that the natives gave them "mulberries, raspberries, and other fruits they found in their way,"[6]

---

[1] See p. 360.
[2] Le Moyne, Narrative, p. 9 (ill.).
[3] Gaffarel, op. cit., p. 405.
[4] Ibid., p. 461.
[5] Le Moyne, Narative, p. 9 (ill.).
[6] French, Hist. Colls. La., 1875, p. 173.

and there is a reference to the use of chinquapins in one of the De Soto narratives.[1] Laudonnière speaks of "mulberries, both red and white," also of grapes.[2] The last are also mentioned by Le Challeux [3] and Spark.[4] From Utina the French received upon one occasion two baskets of "pinocks, which are a kind of little green fruit, which grow among the weeds, in the river, and are as big as cherries." [5] It is evident from the context that the berries to which Ribault refers were plucked and eaten fresh. Among the roots mentioned the kunti of the Florida Seminole is perhaps to be included, though the latitude is rather high for it, or they might have had the original kunti of the Creeks, the China brier. Acorns are referred to by one writer,[6] and Spark states that the French resorted to them in their extremity, washing them several times in order to remove the bitter taste,[7] from which it may be assumed that they prepared them in the same manner as the Indians to the north. A marginal extension of the native dietary is indicated by Laudonnière and Pareja. The former says:

> In necessity they eat a thousand rifraffs, even to the swallowing down of coal, and putting sand into the pottage that they make with the meal.[8]

And from Pareja's catechism it appears that on occasion they ate coal, dirt, broken pottery, fleas, and lice, though some of these may have been taken rather as remedies than as food.[9]

Not much can be gathered from our French informants regarding the social organization of these people, but there is enough to show that they had a class of chiefs to whom great respect was paid, indicating resemblances to the oligarchic system of the Creeks. Ribault says:

> It is their manner to talk and bargain sitting; and the chief or king to be separated from the common people; with a show of great obedience to their kings, elders, and superiors.[10]

This impression is confirmed by Pareja, the Franciscan missionary, and in addition he gives us some information regarding both the caste and the clan systems, the only information of this nature accessible to us. Naturally this account leaves much to be desired, but we should rather rejoice at its completeness under the circumstances than complain on account of its omissions. This part of Pareja's catechism has been published and most of it translated

[1] Bourne, Narr. of De Soto, II, pp. 70–71.
[2] French, op. cit., 1869, pp. 181, 182, 257.
[3] Gaffarel, Hist. Floride française, p. 462.
[4] Hakluyt, Voyages, III, p. 613.
[5] Laudonnière, La Floride, p. 149; French, Hist. Colls. La., 1869, p. 298.
[6] See p. 358; also cf. pp. 359 and 383.
[7] Hakluyt, Voyages, III, p. 614.
[8] Laudonnière, op. cit., p. 9; French, op. cit., p. 172.
[9] Proc. Am. Philos. Soc., XVI, p. 683.
[10] French, Hist. Colls. La., 1875, p. 171.

by Gatschet,[1] but there are some unfortunate errors and omissions which have made it necessary to go back to the original work. A careful study of this has made the general outlines of the Timucua organization sufficiently plain.

Pareja gives the following terms of relationship and their significance along with certain grammatical forms based on them. I have arranged them for convenience under the appropriate stem words.

chirico: chirico viro, chirico nia, used by father and mother in speaking to their son and daughter, respectively.

ahono: ahono viro, ahono nia, used precisely like the above. Among terms used by males we find this given farther on again as a mode of expression "more used in the interior." The following additional examples occur: Ahono viro misoma, my elder son; ahono nia misoma, my elder daughter; ahono viro pacanoqua, my intermediate son; ahono nia pacanoqua, my intermediate daughter; ahono viro quianima, my younger son; ahono viro iubuacoli, ahono viro quianicocoma, my youngest or last son; ahono nia iubuacoli, ahono nia quianicocoma, my youngest or last daughter; ahono viro ysicora, ahono chirico, ahono ysinahoma, my very last son.

iti: itina, my father; itaye, thy father; oqe itimima, the father of that one; itinica, itinicale, itinicano, ytimile, our father; itayaque, your father; oqecare itimitilama, ytimilemala, their father; ytele, paternal uncle; yteleye, thy paternal uncle; itilemima, his uncle; itelemile, ytelenica, ytelenicano, our paternal uncle; yteleyaqe, your paternal uncle; ytilemitilama, their paternal uncle; ytemiso, name given to an uncle older than the father; ytequiany, name given to an uncle younger than the father; ytimale, father and son; ytelemele, uncle and nephew; ytemisomale, eldér uncle and nephew; ytequianimale, younger uncle and nephew.

itora (probably from the preceding stem), grandfather, father-in-law, or godfather; ytorinà, ytorana, my grandfather, etc.; ytoraye, thy grandfather; ytorimima, his grandfather; ytorimile, ytorinica, ytorinicale, ytorinicano, our grandfather; ytorayaqe, your grandfather; ytori mitilama, their grandfather; ytora naribua, coesa ytora, great-grandfather; ytora naribuana, my great-grandfather; ytora naribuaye, thy great-grandfather; ytora naribuamima, his grandfather; ytora naribuamile, our great-grandfather; ytora naribuaiaqe, your great-grandfather; ytora naribuamitilama, their great-grandfather; ytora mulu, great-great-grandfather; ytora muluna, my great-great-grandfather; ytora muleye, thy great-great-grandfather; ytora mulumima, his great-great-grandfather; ytora mulumile, ytora mulunica, ytora mulunicano, our great-great-grandfather; ytora muluyaqe, ytora muluyaqeno, your great-great-grandfather; ytora mulumitilama, ytora mulumitilale, their great-great-grandfather; ytora is the name given by children to their father, his brothers, and their mother's brothers after the death of their mother; ytorapatami, ytorapatamima, paternal uncle's wife; ytora, term given by a woman to the husband of her aunt; ytora naribua mulumale, the great-great-grandfather and great-great-grandson; ytorimale, grandfather and grandson; ytorimalema, uncle and nephew or godfather and godchild.

siqinona, nisiqisama, the one who begot me (name given to the father after his death); siqinomale, son and father.

naribuana, "my old man," name given to father's brother after his death; naribuapacano, name given to a man deprived of his children by death.

hue sipire, hue asire, the second stepfather.

isa, mother: ysona, my mother; ysaya, ysayente, is it thy mother? ysayesa, did thy mother do that or this? ysayeste, did thy mother say this or that? ysaye, iste, thy

[1] Proc. Amer. Philos. Soc., XVII, pp. 491–497.

mother does not wish; ysomima, his mother; heca ysomile, heca ysonica, our mother; ysayaqe, your mother; ysomitilama, their mother; ysale, maternal aunt; ysalena, my maternal aunt; ysaleye, thy maternal aunt; ysalemima, his maternal aunt; isalenica, lsalemile, ysalenicano, our maternal aunt; ysaleyaqe, your maternal aunt; ysalemitiiama, their maternal aunt; ysamiso, maternal aunt older than mother; ysa quianima, maternal aunt younger than mother; ysomale, ysomalema, mother and daughter; ysalemale, nephew and uncle or niece and aunt.

ule, child (name given by woman): ulena, my child; ulaya, is it thy child? ulemile, it is her child; ulemima, is it the child of that woman? Maria ulemima (or ulemila), the child of this Maria, or the child of Maria; ulenica, ulemile, it is our child; uleyaqe, your child; ulemitilama, the child of that one; Ana ulemicare, the children of Ana; ulena miso, my elder child; ulena pacanoquana, my second child; ulena quianima, the younger child; ulena quianicocoma, the fourth child; ulena yubacoli, ulena usicora, my very last child; ano-ulemama, the mother of living children; ulena, my sister's child; ulena, my child (name given by stepmother to stepchild).

yacha: yache pacano, name given to a mother without children or kindred; yacha quianima, name by which the elder brother calls his younger brother and younger sister; yacha miso, name by which the elder brother calls his elder sister, applying also to the children of the father's brother and the mother's sister; yachimale, male and female children of brothers when spoken of collectively; yachemulecoco, great-grandmother on father's side and on mother's; yachimalema, sister and brother; yachema, mother of a girl just having reached maturity (?).

yquine: yquinena, she who gave me milk (name given to mother after her death); yquyneye, the mother who gave thee milk; yquinemima, the mother who gave him milk; yquinemile, the mother who gave us milk; yquineyaqe, the mother who gave you milk; yquinemitilama, the mother who gave them milk.

nibira, grandmother, stepmother, godmother, aunt on father's and mother's side after father's death; mother after father's death; nibirina, honihe nibira, my grandmother, etc.; nibiraye, thy grandmother; nibirimima, his grandmother; nibirimile, nibirinica, our grandmother; nibirayaqe, your grandmother; nibirimitilama, their grandmother; nibirayache, ysa yache, great-grandmother; nibirayachena, ysayachena, my great-grandmother; nibira yacheye, isaiache, thy great-grandmother; nibira yachemima, ysayachemima, his great-grandmother; nibira yachemile, nibira yachenica, ysayachemile, ysayachenica, yachenicano; nibira yacheyaqe, ysayacheyaqe, your great-grandmother; nibira yachemitilama, isayachemitilama, their great-grandmother; nibirayachemulu, great-great-grandmother; nibira yachemuluna, my great-great-grandmother; nibira yachemuluye, thy great-great-grandmother; nibira yachemulumima, his great-great-grandmother; nibira yachemulunica, nibira yachemulunicano, our great-great-grandmother; nibira yachemuluyaqe, your great-great-grandmother; nibira yachemulumitilama, their great-great-grandmother; nybira yachemulumale, nibira yachemale, great-grandmother and great-grandchild; nibirimalema, godmother and godchild.

neba, uncle on mother's side; nebena, my uncle; nebaye, thy uncle; nebemima, his uncle; nebemile, nebenica, nebenicano, our uncle; nebayaqe, your uncle; nebemitilama, their uncle; nebua naribama, nebua nebemima, uncle of my uncle; nebapatani, uncle's wife; nebemale, uncle and nephew.

nibe, paternal aunt; nibina, my paternal aunt; nibaye, thy aunt; nibimima, his aunt; nibinica, nibinile, nibinicano, our aunt; nibeyaqe, your aunt; nibimitilama, their aunt; nibirimalema, aunt and nephew or niece.

nasi, son-in-law, also name given to husband of niece, probably the husband of a man's brother's daughter and the husband of a woman's sister's daughter; ano nasimitama, father-in-law, mother-in-law; ano nasimitachiqe, those with fathers- or mothers-in-law; nasimitana, my father-in-law, or mother-in-law; nasimitaye, thy father- or mother-in-law; nasimitamima, his father- or mother-in-law; nasimitanica; nasimitamile, nasimitamileno, our father- or mother-in-law; nasimitayaqe, your father- or mother-in-law; nasimita mitilama, their father- or mother-in-law; nasi, nasimileno, son-in-law; nasina, my son-in-law; nasiye, thy son-in-law; nasimima, his son-in-law; nasinica, nasimile, our son-in-law; nasimile carema, our sons-in-law; nasaye, your son-in-law; nasiyaqe, your sons-in-law; nasimitilama, their son-in-law; nasimitamale, father-in-law, and son-in-law and daughter-in-law.

nubo, nubuo, daughter-in-law, also wife of nephew, probably the wife of a man's brother's son, and a woman's sister's son: nubona, nubuona, my daughter-in-law; nuboye, thy daughter-in-law; nubomima, his daughter-in-law; nubonica, nubuomile, our daughter-in-law; nuboyaqe, your daughter-in-law; nubuomitilama, their daughter-in-law; nubuomitana, nynubemitama, ninubuomitama, my father-in-law or my mother-in-law; nubuomitamalema, daughter-in-law and father- or mother-in-law.

piliqua, name given by one parent to his or her children after the death of the other; also given by the children to each other under those circumstances; it is also given by the mother's sister and father's brother to the children when a parent has died; also used in general for a child without father or mother, or without a relative.

hiosa, elder brother of man, elder boy of father's brother and mother's sister, name which children give each other after death of one parent: name given to two chiefs of equal rank; women of the Timuqua tribe use this for the elder brother.

qui: quiena, qiena, my child (used by men only); qiena miso, my older child; quyanima, my younger child; quiani cocoma, yubuacoli, my last or latest child; quiena, name a man gives his mother's brother's child.

quisotimi, name given to third cousins, also to father's sister's child, also to a stepson or stepdaughter; quisotina (another form); niquisa, my (w. sp.) brother's wife; niquisimitana, my (w. sp.) husband's sister; qisitomale, the grandson and the grandfather, the great-grandson and great-grandfather.

ama, children of father's sister; amamale, male cousins of brother and sister.

eqeta, equeta, children of father's sister; eqetamale, male cousins of brother and sister.

aruqui, children of father's sister.

pacanoqua, the intermediate child, child born between others.

yubuacoli, last child (of man or woman); yubuaribana, name by which a man calls his younger brother after the latter's death.

isicora, isinahoma, the very last child (of man or woman).

anta, antina, name used by a man to his brother and a woman to her sister in the Timuqua dialect.

yame, a man's, and probably also a woman's, sister's husband; yamancha, yamenchu, the same in the Timuqua dialect; yamemitana, the name a man calls his wife's sister.

tafi seems to be the name applied to a man's brother's wife; tafimitana was the name given by a woman to her husband's brother.

niha, elder brother of man, in Timuqua dialect elder brother of woman also, also son of father's brother and mother's sister older than self; nihona, elder sister of woman; ano nihanibama, my sister's son (said by a woman after his death); ano nihanema, child of sister's son (said by a woman after its death).

amita, amitina, younger brother and sister of man, also the father's brother's son and daughter and mother's sisters younger than self; amitina, amita oroco, younger sister of woman; in Potano and Icafi dialects amita chirima, amita chirico.

ano ecoyana, name a man gives to his elder brother after his death.

coni, name which a man gives to his sister's childern: conina, my nephew or niece; conaye, thy nephew; conimima, his nephew; coninica, conimile, our nephew; conayaqe, your nephew; conimitilama, their nephew.

ebo, evo, a woman's brothers' and sisters' children, also her mother's brothers' children; ebona, ebuona, evona, my nephew or niece; eboya, ebuoia, thy nephew; ebuomina, her nephew.

iquilnona, name by which a man calls his wife's sister.

poy, woman's elder brother; poyna misoma, my elder brother; poyna quianima, my younger brother; poymale, brother and sister.

anetana, ano etana, my brother's son (said by a woman after his death).

inihi: inihimale, husband and wife, wife and husband, male and female. This is usually employed for wife.

inifa, the usual term for husband.

taca: tacamale, husband and wife, wife and husband, male and female of human beings only.

aymantanica, sister's son (used by a woman after his death); aymantana, name given to the deceased son of the preceding, also a deceased near relative dearly lóved; aymanino neletema, a dearly loved deceased chief (so called by both men and women).

ano quelana, or anona, "my relative," covers those of the same house, lineage, or parent by the female side.

The following terms and sentences given by Pareja also have a bearing on the social organization of the Timucua:

üti nocoromale, those who are natives or of one country.

hica nocoromale, those who are of one town.

paha nocoromale, those who are of one house.

hica niahobale, hica nicorobale, we are of one town.

paha niocoralebale, we are all of one house.

ano quela niyahobale, we are of one lineage, caste, or generation; ano quela chiyahobale, thou art of one lineage, caste, or generation; ano quela yahomale, they are of one lineage, caste, or generation.

ano quela chichaquene?, of what lineage are you?

ano chichaquene chitacochianomi (or chitaco anoya)?, who are your kindred?

ano virona, elapachana, names by which relatives and brothers and sisters call each other.

anonia male, elapacha male, brothers and sisters, and male and female kinsmen so speak to each other.

elapacha, anomalema, ano oquomi, ano oquo malema, indicate common relationship.

ubua, name given to a widow or widower by all of the relatives of the deceased.

ocorotasiqino, name given to all of those descended from two lineages.

siquita pahana, all of those descended from one lineage or parentage, if it is in the male line.

ucucanimi, distant relationship.

anocomalema, master and vassal, slave, male or female, and master, and master and male or female servant.

ano quelamalema, ano pequatamale, master and servant and master and vassal.

atemalema, lord and slave, male or female (when master is placed first the word for master is used, and when servant is placed first the term for servant is used).[1]

While the relationships expressed by the terms given above seem at first sight very complicated the majority are reducible into a few comparatively simple categories which are expressed in the following tables. Terms applied to individuals belonging to the same clan as self are italicized.

[1] Pareja, Cathecismo, en lengua Castellana y Timuquana, pp. 107–128.

SELF MALE

I

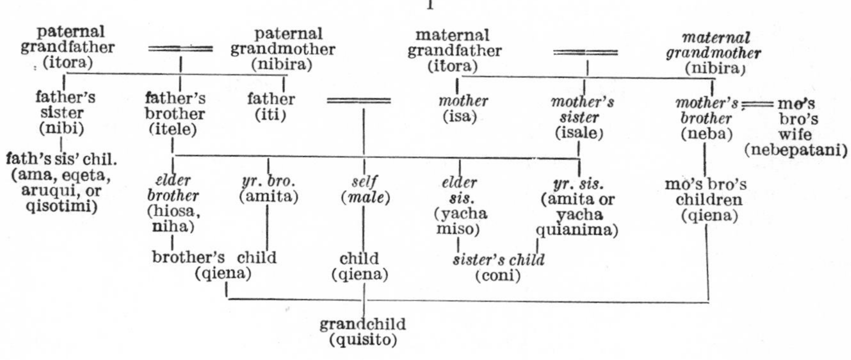

II

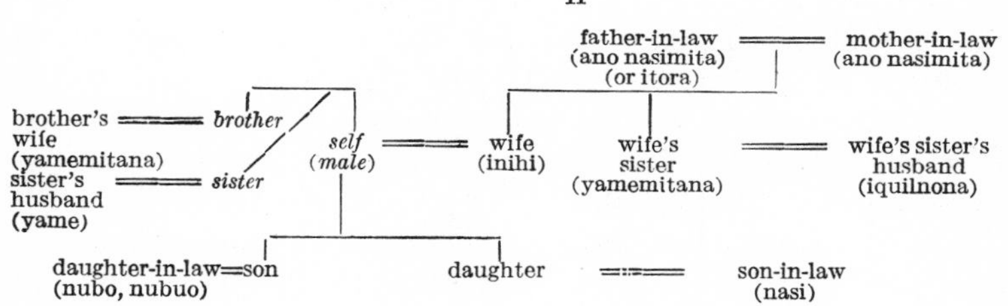

SELF FEMALE

I

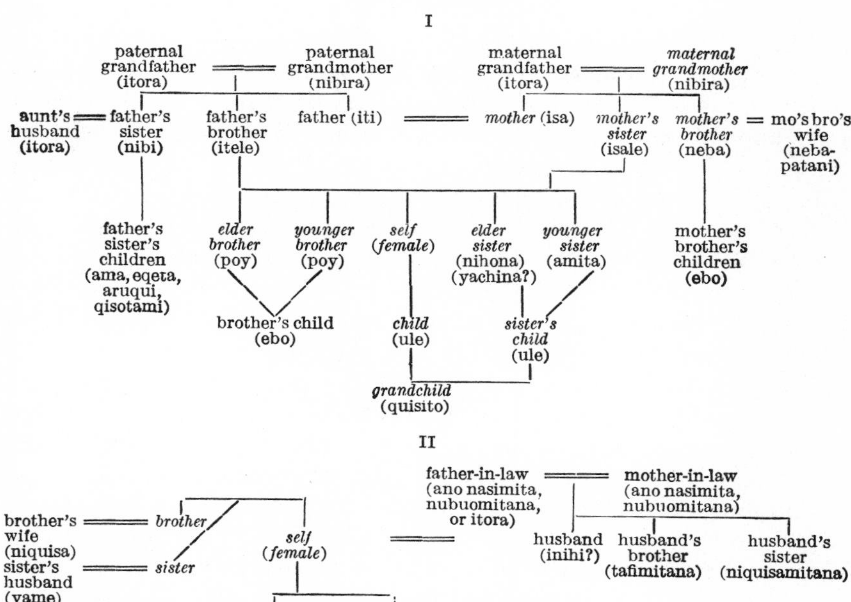

Some points are obscure but the outlines of the organization are perfectly clear. There was one term for both father's father and mother's father, and from what we know of Indian tribes elsewhere it is probable that this term was extended generally to designate the old men of the tribe. A complementary term was used for grandmother, employed in precisely the same ways. There was one term for father and one for mother, but, with the addition of a syllable, these were made to apply to the father's brothers and the mother's sisters, respectively. From experience with other types of organization we may feel sure that they were used for the men and women of the father's and mother's clans of their generation also. There was a term for mother's brother and a term for father's sister, each of which probably had similar clan extensions. While pronounced differently these two, *neba* and *nibi*, have a most suggestive similarity. There were terms for elder brother, younger brother, elder sister, and younger sister. The sister, however, made less distinction between the elder and the younger brother than did the brother between his elder and younger sister. These terms likewise included elder and younger brothers and sisters of the father's brothers and the mother's sisters. There was one term for the child of self whether male or female, and by the man this term was used for the brothers' children and for the mother's brothers' children as well. The name used for her children by a woman, however, was applied only to them and to the children of her sisters. On the other hand, she called by one term, which we may compare to our nephew or niece, the children of her brothers and of her mother's brothers, while the man's corresponding term applied only to his sisters' children. There was one term for grandchild of wide application and a term for father's sister's child. From the nature of the terms used I will hazard a guess that it was from this last group that husbands and wives were selected. Regarding in-law relationships this much is certain, that there was one distinct term for son-in-law and another for daughter-in-law. The terms for father-in-law and mother-in-law are based upon these. The terms used for brother-in-law and sister-in-law seem to have been as follows: one for the individual of the opposite sex on either side (tafi), one for the husband of a man's sister and probably for the brother of his wife, and one for the wife of a woman's brother and the sister of her husband. Most of the other terms are descriptive.

The influence of the clan system on the extension of these terms would probably be evident if Pareja had taken the trouble to give more extended information, but it is by no means necessary that it should belong to a tribe having exogamous groups. The terms for grandfather, grandmother, and grandchild probably have no connection with clans. The terms for father's brother and mother's sister, which are modifications of those for father and mother, might equally well be used by tribes with clans or without clans, and when we get to the next generation we find the children of the father's brothers and those of the mother's sisters called alike by the same terms as the own brothers and sisters. They might all belong to the same clan, it is true, but only in case there were but two exogamous groups in the tribe or in case Pareja has merely recorded the terms used in such cases. Distinction of descent as between father and mother is carefully preserved also in the generation succeeding, a man calling his brothers' children by the same terms as his own children, and a woman her sisters' children by the same names as her own children, while the sisters' children and brothers' children, respectively, receive still other terms. Of course this might indicate exogamous groups, as it is probable there would be a feeling against intermarriage between persons calling themselves brothers and sisters, but unless we suppose, as already stated, only two exogamous groups there is no reason why the children of brothers should belong to the same clan. The mother's brother's child is called by the same name as his own child by a man and by the same name as her brother's child by a woman. These two terms suggest a clan organization more strongly than any others, but do not establish it. The individuals of these classes might have been categorized together without any further extension of the terms. If we assume but two exogamous groups among the Timucua the above terms will fall in with it harmoniously, but there is every reason to suppose that there were more; and, such being the case, we find that many groups of persons receive one name not because they are of one clan but because they bear a certain blood relation to self or because their parents had received a certain name. With more than two clans the children of brothers are not necessarily of one clan. If they then call each other brothers and sisters it is evidently on account of the relationship between their fathers. I call my brothers' children by the same name as mine, although they may belong to several clans, simply because their fathers are my brothers. Precisely this classification is found among the Creeks, except that with them a term is used which distinguishes my actual children from the children of my clan brothers. Both, however, convey the significance of "my son" or "my boy," and the distinction introduced does not follow clan lines. One includes my actual children; the other children of my clansmen, whether they are of the same clan as my children or not.

We have several documentary statements regarding the existence of matrilineal descent and the inheritance of the sister's son. All beyond this that we know of the clan system of the Timucua is contained in the following paragraphs of Pareja, which I quote from Gatschet's translation with one or two small corrections. It occurs in the original immediately after the terms of relationship.

There are many other terms for degrees of kinship too prolix to be given here, and I therefore mention only the most important. In the following lines I will mention some of the principal lineages found in every part and province of the country, though sometimes occurring in a different shape, and I begin with the pedigrees of the upper chiefs and their progeny.

The upper chiefs (caciques), to whom other chiefs are subject, are called *ano parucusi holata ico* (or *olato aco;* or *utinama*). From this class comes a councillor, who leads the chief by the hand, and whose title is *inihama*. From him comes another class, that of the *anacotima*; the cacique seeks the advice of these second councillors, when he does not require that of the *inihama*. Another caste descends from the *anacotima;* it is that of the *second anacotima*, and from these the *afetamà* derive themselves. Another class (of councillors) usually accompanies the *iniha*, who forms the first degree after the head-chief; this class is the *ibitano* class. From the *ibitano* a line proceeds, that affords councillors; this line is called *toponole*, and from them spring the *ibichara*.

From the last named proceed the *amalachini*, and the last lineage that traces its origin to the head chief is *itorimitono*, to which little respect is paid. But all the other classes, mentioned before this last, are held in high consideration; they do not intermarry, and although they are now Christians, they remain observers of these caste distinctions and family pedigrees.

Of a further line derived from the upper chief all members call and consider each other as "nephews." This is the line of the White Deer, *honoso nayo*. In the provinces of the "Fresh Water" and Potano, all these lineages emanating from the chief are termed people of the Great Deer, *quibiro ano*. Families sprung from former chiefs are: *oyorano fiyo chuluquita oconi*, (or simply) *oyolano*.

The lower pedigrees of the common people are the "Dirt (or Earth) pedigree," *utihasomi enatiqi;* the Fish pedigree, *cuyuhasomi*, and its progeny, called *cuyuhasomi aroqui*, *cuyuhasomiele*, while its progenitors are termed *tucunubala*, *irihibano*, *apichi*.

Another strange lineage is that of the Buzzard, *apohola;* from it descend those of the *nuculaha*, *nuculahaquo*, *nucula-haruqui*, *chorofa*, *usinaca*, *ayahanisino*, *napoya*, *amacahuri*, *ha-uenayo*, *amusaya*. These lineages all derive themselves from the *apohola* and do not intermarry.

Still another pedigree is that of the *chulufichi;* from it is derived the *arahasomi* or Bear pedigree, the *habachaca* and others, proceeding from this last.

From the *acheha* derives itself the Lion family or *hiyaraba*, the Partridge line or *cayahasomi*, and others, as the *efaca*, *hobatine*, *quasi*, *chehelu*. In some districts these lineages are of low degree, while in others they rank among the first, and since it would be mere loss of time to give more, the above may suffice.[1]

Two different classifications seem to be represented here, of which the second is plainly along the line of clans, and the groups probably were in fact clans similar to those of the Creeks. The first, however, indicates a kind of aristocratic system which appears to have been based on male descent and recalls somewhat the special privileges accorded to children and grandchildren of "Suns" among the Natchez. Perhaps these "lineages" were actually associated with clans, just as the henihas among the Creeks were drawn from a certain clan, and among some towns the tåstenågis and imałas were largely from definite clans. Since the ending *-ma* of inihama is probably the plural, it is quite possible or even probable that the inihama were the Timucua equivalents of the Creek henihålgi. We find that linked clans

[1] Pareja, Cathecismo, pp. 130-133; Gatschet in Proc. Am. Philos. Soc., XVII, pp. 492-493.

or phratries existed among the Timucua. The word for clan appears to have been hasomi. Pareja mentions six phratries—that of the White Deer, or Great Deer, which seems to have been that to which the chief usually belonged in the provinces best known to him; the Dirt or Earth phratry; the Fish phratry; the Buzzard (or Vulture, *aura*) phratry; the Chulufichi phratry; and the Acheha phratry. Some of their subdivisions are also given by Pareja.

The aristocratic nature of Timucua government is apparent from the statements of the French already referred to as well as from the information regarding their social organization recorded by Pareja.

From Pareja's Catechism it appears that chiefs were allowed to exact tribute and labor from their subjects, and that by way of punishment they sometimes had the arms of their laborers broken.[1] From the same source we learn that just before assuming the chieftainship a man had a new fire lighted and maintained for six days in a small house or arbor which was closed up with laurels and "other things."[2] The chiefs wore at times long painted skins, the ends of which were held up from the ground by attendants. Le Moyne figures this[3] and the custom is directly confirmed by Laudonnière, whose testimony there is no reason to doubt; otherwise we might regard it as something drawn from the customs of European courts and falsely attributed to the Floridians. These skins were often presented to the French as marks of esteem.[4] In giving out drinking water the bearer observed "a certain order and reverence" to each.[5]

As intimated above, the country appears to have been divided between a limited number of head chiefs, under each of whom were a very much greater number of local chiefs. These little confederacies may have been of the nature of some of the larger Creek groups which consisted of a head town and a number of outsettlements.

From Laudonnière we learn that, like Indian tribes generally, the ancient Floridians observed taboos with reference to women at the time of their monthly periods and when a child was born. He implies that when a woman was pregnant she lived in a house apart from that of her husband. The men would not eat food touched by a menstruant woman.[6]

Of their marriages the same writer says:

They marry, and every one hath his wife, and it is lawful for the king to have two or three, yet none but the first is honored and acknowledged for queen, and none but the children of the first wife inherit the goods and authority of the father.[7]

1 Proc. Am. Philos. Soc., XVIII, pp. 489, 490.
2 Ibid., p. 490.
3 Le Moyne, Narrative, pl. 39.
4 Laudonnière, La Floride, pp. 72–73; French, Hist. Colls. La., 1869, p. 228.
5 Laudonnière, ibid., p. 74; French, ibid., p. 229.
6 Laudonnière, ibid., pp. 8–9; French, ibid., p. 172.
7 Laudonnière, ibid., p. 8; French, ibid., p. 172.

The marriage of a chief was consummated in a great ceremony, to which Le Moyne devotes two of his illustrations [1] and the following descriptions:

When a king chooses to take a wife, he directs the tallest and handsomest of the daughters of the chief men to be selected. Then a seat is made on two stout poles and covered with the skin of some rare sort of animal, while it is set off with a structure of boughs, bending over forward so as to shade the head of the sitter. The queen elect having been placed on this, four strong men take up the poles and support them on their shoulders, each carrying in one hand a forked wooden stick to support the pole at halting. Two more walk at the sides, each carrying on a staff a round screen elegantly made, to protect the queen from the sun's rays. Others go before, blowing upon trumpets made of bark, which are smaller above and larger at the farther end and having only the two orifices, one at each end. They are hung with small oval balls of gold, silver, and brass, for the sake of a finer combination of sounds. Behind follow the most beautiful girls that can be found, elegantly decorated with necklaces and armlets of pearls, each carrying in her hand a basket full of choice fruits and belted below the navel and down to the thighs with the moss of certain trees, to cover their nakedness. After them come the bodyguards.

With this display the queen is brought to the king in a place arranged for the purpose, where a good-sized platform is built up of round logs, having on either side a long bench where the chief men are seated. The king sits on the platform on the right-hand side The queen, who is placed on the left, is congratulated by him on her accession and told why he chose her for his first wife. She, with a certain modest majesty, and holding her fan in her hand, answers with as good a grace as she can. Then the young women form a circle without joining hands and with a costume differing from the usual one, for their hair is tied at the back of the neck and then left to flow over the shoulders and back; and they wear a broad girdle below the navel, having in front something like a purse, which hangs down so as to cover their nudity. To the rest of this girdle are hung ovals of gold and silver, coming down upon the thighs, so as to tinkle when they dance, while at the same time they chant the praises of the king and queen. In this dance they all raise and lower their hands together.[2]

Le Challeux says that "each has his own wife, and they protect marriage indeed very rigorously,"[3] from which it would seem that laws similar to those of the Creeks were in force among them.

Two other sketches of Le Moyne illustrate the ceremonies undergone by widows; and they are thus explained:

The wives of such as have fallen in war or died by disease are accustomed to get together on some day which they find convenient for approaching the chief. They come before him with great weeping and outcry, sit down on their heels, hide their faces in their hands, and with much clamor and lamentation require of the chief vengeance for their dead husbands, the means of living during their widowhood, and permission to marry again at the end of the time appointed by law. The chief, sympathizing with them, assents, and they go home weeping and lamenting, so as to show the strength of their love for the deceased. After some days spent in this mourning they proceed to the graves of their husbands, carrying the weapons and drinking cups of the dead, and there they mourn for them again and perform other feminine ceremonies. . . .

After coming to the graves of their husbands they cut off their hair below the ears and scatter it upon the graves, and then cast upon them the weapons and drinking

[1] Le Moyne, Narrative, pls. 37, 38.

[2] Ibid., pp. 13–14 (ill.).

[3] Gaffarel, Hist. Floride française, p. 461.

shells of the deceased, as memorials of brave men. This done they return home, but are not allowed to marry again until their hair has grown long enough to cover their shoulders.[1]

Regarding the division of labor between the sexes, there seems to have been little difference between the Timucua and Creeks. Laudonniere says that "the women do all the business at home;"[2] and Le Moyne indicates that the men prepared the ground for planting, while the women made holes and dropped in the seed.[3]

Le Moyne has the following to say of berdaches:

Hermaphrodites, partaking of the nature of each sex, are quite common in these parts, and are considered odious by the Indians themselves, who, however, employ them, as they are strong, instead of beasts of burden. When a chief goes out to war the hermaphrodites carry the provisions. When any Indian is dead of wounds or disease, two hermaphrodites take a couple of stout poles, fasten cross-pieces on them, and attach to these a mat woven of reeds. On this they place the deceased, with a skin under his head, a second bound around his body, a third around one thigh, a fourth around one leg. Why these are so used I did not ascertain; but I imagine by way of ornament, as in some cases they do not go so far, but put the skin upon one leg only. Then they take thongs of hide, three or four fingers broad, fasten the ends to the ends of the poles, and put the middle over their heads, which are remarkably hard; and in this manner they carry the deceased to the place of burial. Persons having contagious diseases are also carried to places appointed for the purpose on the shoulders of the hermaphrodites, who supply them with food, and take care of them until they get quite well again.[4]

As quoted above, he also speaks of the service rendered by these persons in bringing food to the storehouses.[5]

The following regarding burial customs is from Laudonnière:

When a king dieth, they bury him very solemnly, and, upon his grave they set the cup wherein he was wont to drink; and round about the said grave, they stick many arrows, and weep and fast three days together, without ceasing. All the kings which were his friends make the like mourning; and, in token of the love which they bear him, they cut off more than the one-half of their hair, as well men as women. During the space of six moons (so they reckon their months), there are certain women appointed which bewail the death of this king, crying, with a loud voice, thrice a day—to wit, in the morning, at noon, and at evening. All the goods of this king are put into his house, and, afterwards, they set it on fire, so that nothing is ever more after to be seen. The like is done with the goods of the priests; and, besides, they bury the bodies of their priests in their houses, and then set them on fire.[6]

The mourning rites for persons of the lower orders are not given, but from Pareja it appears that the custom of cutting off the hair was universal.[7] He also informs us that some object was placed with the body in the tomb.[7] In the narrative of De Gourgues's expedition

---

1 Le Moyne, Narrative, p. 8.

2 Laudonnière, La Floride, p. 8; French, Hist. Colls. La., 1869, p. 172.

3 Le Moyne, op. cit., p. 9 (ill.).

4 Ibid., pp. 7-8 (Ill.).

5 See p. 361.

6 Laudonnière, La Floride, pp. 10-11; French, Hist. Colls. La., 1869, pp. 173-174.

7 Pareja, Confessionario en Lengua Castellana y Timuquana, p. 127.

Olotocara, the nephew of Saturiwa, is said to have begged De Gourgues "to give unto his wife, if he escaped not, that which he had meant to bestow on him, that she might bury the same with him, that thereby he might be better welcome unto the village of the souls or spirits departed."[1] Le Moyne says:

When a chief in that province dies, he is buried with great solemnities; his drinking-cup is placed on the grave, and many arrows are planted in the earth about the mound itself. His subjects mourn for him three whole days and nights, without taking any food. All the other chiefs, his friends, mourn in like manner; and both men and women, in testimony of their love for him, cut off more than half their hair. Besides this, for six months afterwards certain chosen women three times every day, at dawn, noon, and twilight, mourn for the deceased king with a great howling. And all his household stuff is put into his house, which is set on fire, and the whole burned up together.

In like manner, when their priests die, they are buried in their own houses; which are then set on fire, and burned up with all their furniture.[2]

A manuscript, copies of which are to be found in both the Lowery and Brooks collections, contains an interesting account of the burial customs of the Tocobaga Indians. It is entitled "Notes and Annotations of the Cosmographer, Lopez de Velasco," and the part which concerns the Tocobaga runs thus:

When one of the principal caciques dies, they cut him to pieces and cook him in large pots during two days, when the flesh has entirely separated from the bones, and adjust one to another until they have formed the skeleton of the man, as he was in life. Then they carry it to a house which they call their temple. This operation lasts four days and during all this time they fast. At the end of the four days, when everything is ready, all the Indians of the town get together and come out with the skeleton in procession, and they bury it with the greatest show and reverence. Then they say that all those who have participated in the ceremonies gain indulgencies.[3]

The skill displayed by these Indians in debate is testified to by Spark.[4] Laudonnière and Le Moyne describe at considerable length their method of holding councils. Laudonnière says:

They take no enterprise in hand, but first they assemble oftentimes their council together, and they take very good advisement before they grow to a resolution. They meet together every morning in a great common house, whither their king repaireth, and setteth him down upon a seat, which is higher than the seats of the others; where all of them, one after another, come and salute him; and the most ancient begin their salutations, lifting up both their hands twice as high as their face, saying, *Ha, he, ha!* and the rest answer, *Ah, ah!* As soon as they have done their salutation, every man sitteth him down upon the seats which are round about in the house. If there be anything to entreat of, the king calleth the *lawas*, that is to say, their priests and the most ancient men, and asketh them their advice. Afterward, he commandeth *cassine* to be brewed, which is a drink made of the leaves of a certain tree. They drink this *cassine*[5] very hot; he drinketh first, then he causeth to be given thereof to all of them,

---

1 Laudonnière, La Floride, p. 216; French, Hist. Colls. La., 1869, p. 356.
2 Le Moyne, Narrative, p. 15 (Ill.).
3 Brooks MSS., Lib. Cong., translated by Miss Brooks.
4 Hakluyt, Voyages, III, p. 613.
5 Le Challeux spells the word cassinet.—Gaffarel, Hist. Floride française, p. 462.

one after another, in the same bowl, which holdeth well a quart-measure of *Paris*. They make so great account of this drink, that no man may taste thereof, in this assembly, unless he hath made proof of his valor in the war. Moreover, this drink hath such a virtue, that, as soon as they have drunk it, they become all of a sweat, which sweats being past, it taketh away hunger and thirst for twenty-four hours after.[1]

Le Moyne's account, as usual inserted to accompany a sketch, is as follows:

The chief and his nobles are accustomed during certain days of the year to meet early every morning for this express purpose in a public place, in which a long bench is constructed, having at the middle of it a projecting part laid with nine round trunks of trees for the chief's seat On this he sits by himself, for distinction's sake, and here the rest come to salute him, one at a time, the oldest first, by lifting both hands twice to the height of the head and saying, "Ha, he, ya, ha, ha." To this the rest answer, "Ha, ha." Each, as he completes his salutation, takes his seat on the bench. If any question of importance is to be discussed, the chief calls upon his *laüas* (that is, his priests) and upon the elders, one at a time, to deliver their opinions. They decide upon nothing until they have held a number of councils over it, and they deliberate very sagely before deciding. Meanwhile the chief orders the women to boil some *casina*, which is a drink prepared from the leaves of a certain root [plant], and which they afterwards pass through a strainer. The chief and his councillors being now seated in their places, one stands before him, and spreading forth his hands wide open asks a blessing upon the chief and the others who are to drink. Then the cup bearer brings the hot drink in a capacious shell, first to the chief and then, as the chief directs, to the rest in their order, in the same shell. They esteem this drink so highly that no one is allowed to drink it in council unless he has proved himself a brave warrior. Moreover, this drink has the quality of at once throwing into a sweat whoever drinks it. On this account those who can not keep it down, but whose stomachs reject it, are not intrusted with any difficult commission or any military responsibility, being considered unfit, for they often have to go three or four days without food; but one who can drink this liquor can go for twenty-four hours afterwards without eating or drinking. In military expeditions, also, the only supplies which the hermaphrodites carry consist of gourd bottles or wooden vessels full of this drink. It strengthens and nourishes the body, and yet does not fly to the head, as we have observed on occasion of these feasts of theirs.[2]

To these accounts of the regular gatherings I will add one of the ceremony attending a meeting between one of the Florida chiefs, Saturiwa, and the French. The usual form of friendly greeting consisted in rubbing the body of the visitor, seemingly a continent-wide method of salutation.[3]

The king [Saturiwa] was accompanied by seven or eight hundred men, handsome, strong, well made, and active fellows, the best trained and swiftest of his force, all under arms as if on a military expedition. Before him marched fifty youths with javelins or spears, and behind these and next to himself were twenty pipers, who produced a wild noise without musical harmony or regularity, but only blowing away with all their might, each trying to be the loudest. Their instruments were nothing but a thick sort of reed or cane, with two openings, one at the top to blow into and the other end for the wind to come out of, like organ pipes or whistles. On

[1] Laudonnière, La Floride, pp. 9–10; French, Hist. Colls. La., 1869, pp. 172–173. Strangers of note were treated to this drink and given corn to eat.—Gaffarel, Hist. Floride française, p. 407.

[2] Le Moyne, Narrative, pp. 11–12 (ill.).

[3] Anonymous writer in Gaffarel, Hist. Floride française, p. 404.

his right hand limped his soothsayer, and on the left was his chief counsellor, without which two personages he never proceeded on any matter whatever. He entered the place prepared for him alone [an arbor made of boughs] and sat down in it after the Indian manner—that is, by squatting on the ground like an ape or any other animal. Then, having looked all around and having observed our little force drawn up in line of battle, he ordered MM. de Laudonnière and d'Ottigny to be invited into his tabernacle, where he delivered to them a long oration, which they understood only in part.[1]

All of the French chroniclers relate that these chiefs were preceded by men who built arbors for them to sit in when holding council, and Ribault speaks of arbors constructed both for the Indian chief and for the French, distant two fathoms.[2] Other boughs were spread upon the ground, on which they squatted cross-legged.

Le Moyne thus describes the preparations for an ordinary social feast:

At the time of year when they are in the habit of feasting each other, they employ cooks, who are chosen on purpose for the business. These, first of all, take a great round earthen vessel (which they know how to make and to burn so that water can be boiled in it as well as in our kettles), and place it over a large wood fire, which one of them drives with a fan very effectively, holding it in the hand. The head cook now puts the things to be cooked into the great pot; others put water for washing into a hole in the ground; another brings water in a utensil that serves for a bucket; another pounds on a stone the aromatics that are to be used for seasoning; while the women are picking over or preparing the viands.[3]

The native institution with which the authorities which we depend upon had most to deal was, not unnaturally, war, and 10 of Le Moyne's 42 sketches deal with it in one way or another. Some of these do not bring in native customs and need not be referred to, but the remainder give us our best information on the subject. Timucua weapons consisted of bows and arrows, darts, and clubs, the last of a type different from the Creek átâsa, if we may trust the illustrations. "A chief who declares war against his enemy," says Le Moyne, "does not send a herald to do it, but orders some arrows, having locks of hairs fastened at the notches, to be stuck up along the public ways."[4] He gives the following account of the manner in which Saturiwa set out to war against his enemy, Utina:

He assembled his men, decorated, after the Indian manner, with feathers and other things, in a level place, the soldiers of Laudonnière being present, and the force sat down in a circle, the chief being in the middle. A fire was then lighted on his left and two great vessels full of water were set on his right. Then, the chief, after rolling his eyes as if excited by anger, uttering some sounds deep down in his throat, and making various gestures, all at once raised a horrid yell; and all his soldiers repeated this yell, striking their hips and rattling their weapons. Then the

[1] Le Moyne, Narrative, p. 3.
[2] French, Hist. Colls. La., 1875, p. 171.
[3] Le Moyne, Narrative, p. 11 (ill.).
[4] Ibid., p. 13 (ill.).

chief, taking a wooden platter of water, turned toward the sun and worshiped it, praying to it for victory over the enemy, and that, as he should now scatter the water that he had dipped up in the wooden platter, so might their blood be poured out. Then he flung the water with a great cast up into the air, and as it fell down upon his men he added, "As I have done with this water, so I pray that you may do with the blood of your enemies." Then he poured the water in the other vase upon the fire and said, "So may you be able to extinguish your enemies and bring back their scalps." Then they all arose and set off by land, up the river, upon their expedition.[1]

The following is Laudonnière's version of this ceremony:

When he [Saturiwa] was sitting down by the river's side, being compassed about with ten other *paracoussies*, he commanded water to be brought him speedily. This done, looking up into heaven, he fell to discourse of divers things, with gestures that showed him to be in exceeding great choler, which made him one while shake his head hither and thither; and, by and by, with, I wot not what fury, to turn his face toward the country of his enemies, and to threaten to kill them. He oftentimes looked upon the sun, praying him to grant him a glorious victory of his enemies; which, when he had done, by the space of half an hour, he sprinkled, with his hand, a little of the water, which he held in a vessel, upon the heads of the *paracoussies*, and cast the rest, as it were, in a rage and despite, into a fire, which was there prepared for the purpose. This done, he cried out, thrice, *He Thimogoa!* and was followed with five hundred Indians, at the least, which were there assembled, which cried, all with one voice, *He Thimogoa!* This ceremony, as a certain Indian told me, familiarly, signified nothing else but that Saturiwa besought the *Sun* to grant unto him so happy a victory, that he might shed his enemies' blood, as he had shed the water at his pleasure. Moreover, that the *paracoussies*, which were sprinkled with a part of that water, might return with the heads of their enemies, which is the only, and chief, triumph of their victories.[2]

We learn from Pareja's Catechism that before they set out on an expedition the warriors bathed in certain herbs.[3]

Provisions were carried along by women, young boys, and berdaches, but frequently it seems to have been confined to parched corn.[4]

The following descriptions of the conduct of a Florida war expedition accompany three of Le Moyne's sketches, but may very properly be run together:

When Saturiwa went to war his men preserved no order, but went along one after another, just as it happened. On the contrary, his enemy, Holata Outina, whose name, as I now remember, means "king of many kings," and who was much more powerful than he as regards both wealth and number of his subjects, used to march with regular ranks, like an organized army; himself marching alone in the middle of the whole force, painted red. On the wings, or horns, of his order of march were his young men, the swiftest of whom, also painted red, acted as advanced guards and scouts for reconnoitering the enemy. These are able to follow up the traces of the enemy by scent, as dogs do wild beasts; and, when they come upon such traces, they immediately return to the army to report. And, as we make use of trumpets and

---

1 Le Moyne, Narrative, p. 5 (ill.).

2 Laudonnière, La Floride, pp. 98–99; French, Hist. Colls. La., pp. 251–252.

3 Proc. Amer. Philos. Soc., XVI, p. 637.

4 Laudonnière, op. cit., p. 141; French, op. cit., p. 291. Spark probably means parched corn by "the head of maiz roasted" on which he says they "will travel a whole day."

drums in our armies to promulgate orders, so they have heralds, who by cries of certain sorts direct them to halt, or to advance, or to attack, or to perform any other military duty. After sunset they halt, and are never wont to give battle. For encamping, they are arranged in squads of ten each,[1] the bravest men being put in squads by themselves. When the chief has chosen the place of encampment for the night, in open fields or woods, and after he has eaten, and is established by himself, the quartermasters place ten of these squads of the bravest men in a circle around him. About ten paces outside of this circle is placed another line of twenty squads; at twenty yards farther, another of forty squads; and so on, increasing the number and distance of these lines, according to the size of the army.

At no time while the French were acting along with the great chief Holata Outina in his wars against his enemies, was there any combat which could be called a regular battle; but all their military operations consisted either in secret incursions, or in skirmishes as light troops, fresh men being constantly sent out in place of any who retired. Whichever side first slew an enemy, no matter how insignificant the person, claimed the victory, even though losing a greater number of men. In their skirmishes, any who fall are instantly dragged off by persons detailed for the purpose; who, with slips of reeds sharper than any steel blade, cut the skin of the head to the bone, from front to back, all the way round, and pull it off with the hair, more than a foot and a half long, still adhering, done up in a knot on the crown, and with that lower down round the forehead and back cut short into a ring about two fingers wide, like the rim of a hat. Then, if they have time, they dig a hole in the ground, and make a fire, kindling it with some which they keep burning in moss, done up in skins, and carry round with them at their belts; and then dry these scalps to a state as hard as parchment. They also are accustomed, after a battle, to cut off with these reed knives the arms of the dead near the shoulders, and their legs near the hips, breaking the bones, when laid bare, with a club, and then to lay these fresh broken, and still running with blood, over the same fires to be dried. Then hanging them, and the scalps also, to the ends of their spears, they carry them off home in triumph. I used to be astonished at one habit of theirs—for I was one of the party which Laudonnière sent out under M. d'Ottigny—which was, that they never left the field of battle without shooting an arrow as deep as they could into the arms of each of the corpses of the enemy, after mutilating them as above—an operation which was sometimes sufficiently dangerous, unless those engaged in it had an escort of soldiers. * * *

After returning from a military expedition they assembled in a place set apart for the purpose, to which they bring the legs, arms, and scalps which they have taken from the enemy, and with solemn formalities fix them up on tall poles set in the ground in a row. Then they all, men and women, sit down on the ground in a circle before these members; while the sorcerer, holding a small image in his hand, goes through a form of cursing the enemy, uttering in a low voice, according to their manner, a thousand imprecations. At the side of the circle opposite to him there are placed three men kneeling down, one of whom holds in both hands a club, with which he pounds on a flat stone, marking time to every word of the sorcerer. At each side of him the other two hold in each hand the fruit of a certain plant, something like a gourd or pumpkin, which has been dried, opened at each end, its marrow and seeds taken out, and then mounted on a stick, and charged with small stones or seeds of some kind. These they rattle after the fashion of a bell, accompanying the words of the sorcerer with a kind of song after their manner. They have such a celebration as this every time they take any of the enemy.[2]

In the particular case of the expedition by Saturiwa against Thimogoa Laudonnière says that after having attacked one of the enemies' towns successfully and taken 24 prisoners, they

[1] Laudonnière says they were encamped six by six.—La Floride, p. 141.

[2] Le Moyne, Narrative, pp. 6-7 (ill.).

retired themselves immediately into their boats, which waited for them. Being come thither, they began to sing praises unto the *Sun*, to whom they attributed their victory. And, afterwards, they put the skins of those heads on the ends of their javelins, and went all together toward the territories of *Paracoussy* Omoloa, one of them which was in the company. Being come thither, they divided their prisoners, equally, to each of the *paracoussies*, and left thirteen of them to Saturiwa, which straightway dispatched an Indian, his subject, to carry news before of the victory to them which stayed at home to guard their houses, which immediately began to weep. But as soon as night was come, they never left dancing, and playing a thousand gambols, in honor of the feast.

The next day the *Paracoussy* Saturiwa came home, who, before he entered into his lodging, caused all the scalps of his enemies to be set up before his door, and crowned them with branches of laurel, showing, by this glorious spectacle, the triumph of the victory which he had obtained. Straightway began lamentation and mourning, which, as soon as the night began, were turned into pleasures and dances.[1]

Some captives were probably tortured to death, as was threatened in the case of the Spaniard, Juan Ortiz, who was "bound hand and foot to four stakes, and laid upon scaffolding, beneath which a fire was kindled, that he might be burned." [2]

One of Laudonnière's lieutenants was witness of a ceremony intended to keep in mind the injuries which his people had received in times past from their enemies. It consisted in the mock killing of one of his family and subsequent wailing over him. This was performed only when they returned from a war expedition without the heads of their enemies or any captives.[3]

Le Moyne thus describes Floridian fortified towns:

A position is selected near the channel of some swift stream. They level it as even as possible, and then dig a ditch in a circle around the site, in which they set thick round pales, close together, to twice the height of a man; and they carry this paling some ways past the beginning of it, spiralwise, to make a narrow entrance admitting not more than two persons abreast. The course of the stream is also diverted to this entrance; and at each end of it they are accustomed to erect a small round building, each full of cracks and holes, and built, considering their means, with much elegance. In these they station as sentinels men who can scent the traces of an enemy at a great distance, and who, as soon as they perceive such traces, set off to discover them. As soon as they find them, they set up a cry which summons those within the town to the defence, armed with bows and arrows and clubs. The chief's dwelling stands in the middle of the town, and is partly underground, in consequence of the sun's heat. Around this are the houses of the principal men, all lightly roofed with palm branches, as they are occupied only nine months in the year; the other three, as has been related, being spent in the woods. When they come back, they occupy their houses again, and if they find that the enemy has burned them down, they build others of similar materials. . . .

For the enemy, eager for revenge, sometimes will creep up by night in the utmost silence, and reconnoiter to see if the watch be asleep. If they find everything silent, they approach the rear of the town, set fire to some dry moss from trees, which they

---

[1] Laudonnière, La Floride, pp. 100–101; French, Hist. Colls. La., 1869, pp. 253–254.

[2] Bourne, Narr. of De Soto, I, p. 28.

[3] Laudonnière, La Floride, pp. 93–97; French, Hist. Colls. La., 1869, pp. 248–249.

prepare in a particular manner, and fasten to the heads of their arrows. They then fire these into the town, so as to ignite the roofs of the houses, which are made of palm branches thoroughly dried with the summer heats. As soon as they see that the roofs are burning, they make off as fast as possible, before they are discovered, and they move so swiftly that it is a hard matter to overtake them; and meanwhile also the fire is giving the people in the town enough to do to save themselves from it and get it under. Such are the stratagems used in war by the Indians for firing the enemy's towns; but the damage done is trifling, as it amounts only to the labor required for putting up new houses.

But when the burning of a town has happened in consequence of the negligence of the watch, the penalty is as follows: The chief takes his place alone on his bench, those next to him in authority being seated on another long bench curved in a half circle; and the executioner orders the culprit to kneel down before the chief. He then sets his left foot on the delinquent's back; and, taking in both hands a club of ebony [?] or some other hard wood, worked to an edge at the sides, he strikes him on the head with it, so severely as almost to split the skull open. The same penalty is inflicted for some other crime reckoned capital among them; for we saw two persons punished in this same way.[1]

When fishing in a certain lake in their country the people of Potano set a watch to protect the fishermen.[2] News of the approach of an enemy was conveyed by means of smoke signals.[3]

The following notes regarding war are from Laudonnière:

The kings of the country make war, one against another, which is not executed except by surprise, and they kill all the men they can take; afterwards they cut off their heads, to have their hair, which, returning home, they carry away, to make thereof their triumph when they come to their houses. They save the women and children, and nourish them, and keep them always with them. Being returned home from the war, they assemble all their subjects, and, for joy, three days and three nights, they make good cheer, they dance and sing; likewise, they make the most ancient women of the country to dance, holding the hairs of their enemies in their hands, and, in dancing, they sing praises to the sun, ascribing unto him the honor of the victory. . . . When they go to war, their king marcheth first, with a club in one hand, and his bow in the other, with his quiver full of arrows. While they fight, they make great cries and exclamations.[4]

The valor and skill of Timucua warriors is also well attested by the chroniclers of the expedition of De Soto. What is said about their method of treating captives shows at once that slavery was not institutional among them. In the fight which Laudonnière's men had with Utina the Indians displayed great skill, discharging their arrows by squads and throwing themselves on the ground when the Frenchmen aimed at them.[5]

That fighting with bows and arrows was an art in itself is shown by this description of the Fidalgo of Elvas:

The Indians are exceedingly ready with their weapons, and so warlike and nimble that they have no fear of footmen; for if these charge them they flee, and when

[1] Le Moyne, Narrative, p. 12 (ill.).
[2] Laudonnière, La Floride, p. 142; French, Hist. Colls. La., 1869, p. 291.
[3] Bourne, Narr. of De Soto, I, p. 22; Le Challeux in Gaffarel, Hist. Floride française, p. 460.
[4] Laudonnière, op. cit., pp. 7-8; French, op. cit., p. 171.
[5] Laudonnière, op. cit., p. 166; French, op. cit., pp. 313-314.

they turn their backs they are presently upon them. They avoid nothing more easily than the flight of an arrow. They never remain quiet, but are continually running, traversing from place to place, so that neither crossbow nor arquebuse can be aimed at them. Before a Christian can make a single shot with either, an Indian will discharge three or four arrows; and he seldom misses of his object. Where the arrow meets with no armor, it pierces as deeply as the shaft from a crossbow.[1]

Regarding games Laudonnière says:

They exercise their young men to run well, and they make a game, among themselves, which he winneth that hath the longest breath. They also exercise themselves much in shooting. They play at the ball in this manner: They set up a tree in the midst of a place, which is eight or nine fathoms high, in the top whereof there is set a square mat, made of reeds, or bullrushes, which whosoever hitteth in playing thereat winneth the game.[2]

And Le Moyne:

Their youth are trained in running, and a prize is offered for him who can run longest without stopping; and they frequently practise with the bow. They also play a game of ball, as follows: In the middle of an open space is set up a tree some eight or nine fathoms high, with a square frame woven of twigs on the top; this is to be hit with the ball, and he who strikes it first gets a prize.[3]

To be sure Le Challeux remarks, "they never teach their children and do not correct them in any way;"[4] but he is referring to the training of young children in matters connected with morals and manners.

According to our French informants the sun and moon were the principal objects of adoration among these Indians, particularly the former.[5] This probably means that their beliefs were substantially like those of the Creeks and Chickasaw. A side light on their cult is furnished in the following account of a ceremony by Le Moyne:

The subjects of the Chief Outina were accustomed every year, a little before their spring—that is, in the end of February—to take the skin of the largest stag they could get, keeping the horns on it; to stuff it full of all the choicest sorts of roots that grow among them, and to hang long wreaths or garlands of the best fruits on the horns, neck, and other parts of the body. Thus decorated, they carried it, with music and songs, to a very large and splendid level space, where they set it up on a very high tree, with the head and breast toward the sunrise. They then offered prayers to the sun, that he would cause to grow on their lands good things such as those offered him. The chief, with his sorcerer, stands nearest the tree and offers the prayer; the common people, placed at a distance, make responses. Then the chief and all the rest, saluting the sun, depart, leaving the deer's hide there until the next year. This ceremony they repeat annually.[6]

Pareja says that there were many different ceremonies, varying from tribe to tribe, and he mentions one called "the ceremony of

---

[1] Bourne, Narr. of De Soto, I, pp. 25-26.

[2] Laudonnière, La Floride, p. 7; French, Hist. Colls. La., 1869, p. 171.

[3] Le Moyne, Narrative, p. 13 (ill.).

[4] Gaffarel, Hist. Floride française, p. 461.

[5] French, Hist. Colls. La., 1869, p. 171; Laudonnière, La Floride, p. 8.

[6] Le Moyne, op. cit.

the laurel performed to serve the Demon."[1] When passing a ledge in the ocean where surf broke, the Timucua Indian whistled to it so that he would not be upset, and he also whistled to the storm to make it stop.[2]

If we may believe Le Moyne, the high opinion in which chiefs were held had resulted in a kind of chief cult accompanied by human sacrifice.

> Their custom is to offer up the first-born son to the chief. When the day for the sacrifice is notified to the chief, he proceeds to a place set apart for the purpose, where there is a bench for him, on which he takes his seat. In the middle of the area before him is a wooden stump two feet high, and as many thick, before which the mother sits on her heels, with her face covered in her hands, lamenting the loss of her child. The principal one of her female relatives or friends now offers the child to the chief in worship, after which the women who have accompanied the mother form a circle, and dance around with demonstrations of joy, but without joining hands. She who holds the child goes and dances in the middle, singing some praises of the chief. Meanwhile, six Indians, chosen for the purpose, take their stand apart in a certain place in the open area; and midway among them the sacrificing officer, who is decorated with a sort of magnificence, and holds a club. The ceremonies being through, the sacrificer takes the child, and slays it in honor of the chief, before them all, upon the wooden stump. The offering was on one occasion performed in our presence.[3]

This suggests, in a way, the rites and customs of the Natchez Indians.

Elvas declares that human sacrifice existed also among the people of Tampa Bay:

> The Indians are worshippers of the devil, and it is their custom to make sacrifices of the blood and bodies of their people, or of those of any other they can come by; and they affirm, too, that when he would have them make an offering, he speaks, telling them that he is athirst, and that they must sacrifice to him.[4]

As an example of the reverence which they paid to particular objects may be cited their treatment of the column set up by Ribault in 1562. When Laudonnière saw it three years later it was "crowned with crowns of bay, and, at the foot thereof, many little baskets full of mill [i. e., corn], which they call in their language tapaga tapola. Then, when they came hither, they kissed the same with great reverence, and besought us to do the like."[5]

Le Moyne says of this:

> On approaching, they found that these Indians were worshipping this stone as an idol; and the chief himself, having saluted it with signs of reverence such as his subjects were in the habit of showing to himself, kissed it. His men followed his example, and we were invited to do the same. Before the monument there lay various offerings of the fruits, and edible or medicinal roots, growing thereabouts; vessels of perfumed oils; a bow, and arrows; and it was wreathed around from top to bottom with flowers of all sorts, and boughs of the trees esteemed choicest.[6]

The Spaniards speak of temples among some Timucua tribes, but it is probable that these were identical with the town houses men-

---

1 Proc. Amer. Philos. Soc., XVIII, p. 491.
2 Ibid., XVI, p. 637.
3 Le Moyne, Narrative, p. 13.
4 Bourne, Narr. of De Soto, I, pp. 29–30.
5 Laudonnière, La Floride, pp. 69–70; French, Hist. Colls. La., p. 224.
6 Le Moyne, Narrative, p. 4 (ill.).

tioned by the French, although their situation with respect to the town was not always central; and, moreover, they were sometimes placed upon mounds. Thus Elvas says that there was such a temple in the town of Ucita at the opposite end from the house of the chief. On the top was a wooden fowl with gilded eyes, "and within were found some pearls of small value, injured by fire, such as the Indians pierce for beads." [1] The temple of Tocobaga was in this section of Florida [2] and Tocobaga and Ucita may in fact have been the same place.

Pareja's Confessionario gives us considerable insight into the smaller superstitions and taboos shared by the people as a whole, which compensate in some degree for a lack of more detailed information regarding tribal beliefs and ceremonies. When a kind of owl hooted it was believed to be saying something and it was appealed to for help. If this owl or another variety called the "red owl" (mochuelo) hooted they said, "Do not interrupt it or it will do you harm." It was thought to be an omen, and usually one of evil. If a person uttered a cry when woodpeckers were making a noise it was thought he would have nosebleed. If one heard the noise made by a fawn he must put herbs into his nostrils to keep from sneezing, and if he did sneeze he must go home and bathe in an infusion of herbs or he would die. When one jay chattered to another it was a sign that a visitor was coming. In winter the small partridge (la gallina pequeña) must not be eaten. When a snake was encountered, either on a country trail or in the house, it was believed to portend misfortune. When the fire crackled it was considered a sign of war, and war was also forecasted from lightning. Belching either portended death or else was a sign that there would be much food. Dreams were believed in.

Omens were also drawn from the tremblings or twitchings of different parts of the body. Such a trembling sometimes indicated that a visitor was coming. If one's eyes trembled it portended weeping. If his mouth twitched it was a sign that something bad was going to happen to the individual, or that people were saying something about him, or that a feast was to take place.

There were many food taboos. The first acorns or fruits gathered were not eaten. The corn in a cornfield where lightning had struck was not eaten, nor the first ripened corn. The first fish caught in a new fishweir was not eaten, but laid down beside it so that a great quantity of fish would come into it with the next tide. It was thought that if the first fish caught in such a weir were thrown into hot water, no other fish would be caught. After eating bear's meat they drank from a different shell than that ordinarily used so that they would not fall sick. When a man had lost his wife, a woman her

---

[1] Bourne, Narr. of De Soto, I, p. 23.

[2] Barcia, La Florida, p. 127.

husband, or either a relative, they would not eat corn which had been sowed by the deceased or corn from land which he or she had been wont to sow, but would give it to some one else or have the crop destroyed. After attending a burial a person bathed and abstained for some time from eating fish. Before tilling a field an ancient ceremony was recited to the shaman (i. e., probably under his leadership). Prayer was offered—that is, a formula was repeated—over the first corn, and when the corncrib was opened a formula was recited over the first flour. A ceremony accompanied with formulæ was performed with laurel when chestnuts (?) and palmetto berries were gathered, nor were wild fruits eaten until formulæ had been repeated over them. Perhaps this applied only to the first wild fruits of the season. Corn from a newly broken field was not supposed to be eaten, apparently, though it is hard to believe that this regulation was absolute. Unless prayers had been offered to the "spirit" by a shaman, no one was allowed to approach or open the corncrib. Some ceremony is mentioned which took place early in the sowing season, in which six old men ate a pot of "fritters."

When a party was to go out hunting the chief had formulæ repeated over tobacco, and when the hunting ground was reached all of the arrows were laid together and the shaman repeated other formulæ over them. It was usual to give the shaman the first deer that was killed. Before fishing on a lake formulæ were also recited, and after the fish were caught the shaman prayed over them and was given half. The first fish caught, however, was, after the usual formulæ, placed in the storehouse. Pareja also mentions a kind of hunting ceremony performed by kicking with the feet, probably some form of sympathetic magic, and it appears that not a great deal of flesh was eaten immediately after hunting for fear that no more animals would be killed. It was also thought that no more game would be killed if the lungs and liver of an animal were thrown into cold water for cooking. If a hunter pierced an animal with an arrow without killing it he repeated a formula over his next arrow, believing that it was then sure to inflict a mortal wound. If the grease of partridges or other small game which had been caught with a snare or lasso was spilled it was thought that the snare would catch nothing more. Formulæ were uttered to enable hunters to find turtles. Bones of animals caught in a snare or trap were not thrown away but were hung up or placed on the roof of the house. If this ceremony were omitted it was thought that the animals would not enter the snare or trap again. When they went to hunt deer they took the antlers of another deer and repeated formulæ over them. If a man went to his fishweir immediately after having had intercourse with his wife he thought that no more fish or eels would enter it.

At the time of her monthly period and for sometime after her confinement a woman did not eat fish or venison. It was also considered wrong for her to anoint herself with bear grease or eat fish for a number of moons after having given birth. Both at that time and at the menstrual period she must not make a new fire or approach one.

A gambler rubbed his hands with certain herbs in order that he might be fortunate in play. A runner is also said to have taken an herb to make him win, and this seems to have been in the form of a drink.[1]

The only reference to a future state of existence is in the account of De Gourgues's expedition, and it has been given already.[2]

Regarding priests or shamans there is information both from Laudonnière and Le Moyne. The former says:

They have their priests, to whom they give great credit, because they are great magicians, great soothsayers, and callers upon devils. These priests serve them instead of physicians and surgeons; they carry always about with them a bag full of herbs and drugs, to cure the sick who, for the most part, are sick of the pox.[3]

Le Moyne thus describes the ceremony gone through by an aged shaman in order to forecast the fortunes of chief Utina's expedition against the Potano:

The sorcerer . . . made ready a place in the middle of the army, and, seeing the shield which D'Ottigny's page was carrying, asked to take it. On receiving it, he laid it on the ground, and drew around it a circle, upon which he inscribed various characters and signs. Then he knelt down on the shield, and sat on his heels, so that no part of him touched the earth, and began to recite some unknown words in a low tone, and to make various gestures, as if engaged in a vehement discourse. This lasted for a quarter of an hour, when he began to assume an appearance so frightful that he was hardly like a human being; for he twisted his limbs so that the bones could be heard to snap out of place, and did many other unnatural things. After going through with all this he came back all at once to his ordinary condition, but in a very fatigued state, and with an air as if astonished; and then, stepping out of his circle, he saluted the chief, and told him the number of the enemy, and where they were intending to meet him.[4]

We may add that according to both Laudonnière and Le Moyne the event verified the prediction.

Le Moyne thus describes how the sick were cared for:

Their way of curing diseases is as follows: They put up a bench or platform of sufficient length and breadth for the patient . . . and lay the sick person upon it with his face up or down, according to the nature of his complaint; and, cutting into the skin of the forehead with a sharp shell, they suck out blood with their mouths, and spit it into an earthen vessel or a gourd bottle. Women who are

[1] Pareja, Confessionario en Lengua Castellana y Timuquana, pp. 123–133; Proc. Am. Philos. Soc., XVI, pp. 635–638; XVII, pp. 500–501; XVIII, pp. 489–491.

[2] See p. 374.

[3] Laudonnière, La Floride, p. 8; French, Hist. Colls. La., 1869, pp. 171–172.

[4] Le Moyne, Narrative, pp. 5–6 (ill.).

suckling boys, or who are with child, come and drink this blood, particularly if it is that of a strong young man; as it is expected to make their milk better, and to render the children who have the benefit of it bolder and more energetic. For those who are laid on their faces they prepare fumigations by throwing certain seeds on hot coals; the smoke being made to pass through the nose and mouth into all parts of the body, and thus to act as an emetic, or to overcome and expel the cause of the disease. They have a certain plant, whose name has escaped me, which the Brazilians call *petum* [*petun*], and the Spaniards *tapaco*. The leaves of this, carefully dried, they place in the wider part of a pipe; and setting them on fire, and putting the other end in their mouths, they inhale the smoke so strongly, that it comes out at their mouths and noses, and operates powerfully to expel the humors. In particular they are extremely subject to the venereal disease, for curing which they have remedies of their own, supplied by nature.[1]

Ribault mentions among the presents which his people received from the Indians "roots like rinbabe [rhubarb], which they hold in great estimation, and make use of for medicine.[2]

Pareja sheds a great deal of light on the activities of shamans. As we have seen, the shaman prayed over the new corn. He also performed ceremonies to find a lost object, and he brought on rain and tempest. He was asked to pray over a new fishweir so that many more fish would enter. When it thundered, in order to keep back the rain, he would blow toward the sky and repeat formulæ. Pareja explains that in cases of sickness the native doctors were accustomed to place a kind of cupping glass over the affected part and then suck it, afterwards exhibiting a little piece of coal, earth, or "other unclean thing," or something alive or which appeared to be alive. This evidently quite impressed the good father, who attributed the performance to the devil. The doctor would also place white feathers, new skins ("chamois"), and the ears of an owl before a sick person and thrust arrows into the soil there, saying that he would draw out the disease as he withdrew the arrows. Sharp practice was evidently well known among these primitive physicians. We are informed that when a sick person was getting better he prepared "food of a sort of cakes or fritters or other things" and shouted out after the doctor that he had cured him. Otherwise it was thought that the disease would reappear. A shaman was also known to threaten that the people would all be killed unless they gave him something to avert a calamity which he declared was threatening. Sometimes he injured a person whom he considered had not paid him enough. He is also accused of having caused delay in childbirth at times so that he would be called in and paid well to hasten the delivery; or, when he had been called, it is alleged that he would make the patient suffer more until he was paid what he thought he ought to receive. The principle of the "hold up" was thus well recognized among Timucua doctors.

---

[1] Le Moyne, Narrative, pp. 8-9 (ill.).

[2] French, Hist. Colls. La., 1875, p. 177.

It appears that when a man fell sick a new house was built for him, probably only a temporary affair, and a new fire was also made at which his food was cooked. Perhaps part of the motive for this was to protect the principal dwelling in case of the sick man's death, for it was usual to burn the houses of chiefs and shamans at such times. Formulæ were also repeated over the sick. Some sickness was attributed to witchcraft and herbs were used to counteract the effects. When foot races were held herbs were sometimes used to cause a rival to faint. The Timucua wizard, who desired to cause the death of a person, used in his incantations the skin of a "viper" and that of a black snake, along with part of the "black guano" (a kind of palm tree) and other herbs. While he was going through his incantations he would not eat fish, cut his hair, or sleep with his wife. When the person he was trying to kill died the wizard bathed and broke his fast. If the victim did not die it seems to have been thought that the incantation would react upon the wizard himself and kill him. Instead of killing a person the wizard sometimes injured him in some particular part, such as the feet. Witchcraft was also resorted to to attract the regard of a person of the opposite sex. Sometimes this was effected by getting an herb into the person's mouth and by the use of certain songs. To bring back the affections of her husband a woman bathed in an infusion of certain herbs. For the same purpose she tinged her palm-leaf hat with the juice of an herb, or she did this to induce another person to fall in love with her. Fasting was resorted to with the same intention.[1]

Notes conveying specific information regarding the ethnology of the Calusa, Tekesta, and Ais Indians of southern Florida are few. An early Spanish writer, Gov. Mendez de Canço, writing in 1598 or 1599, says that the Indians of southern Florida did not live in settled villages because they had no corn, but wandered about in search of fish and roots. Fontaneda, whose information dates from a very early period, has the following to say about the Indians of Calos:

> These Indians possess neither gold nor silver, and still less clothing, for they go almost naked, wearing only a sort of apron. The dress of the men consists of braided palm leaves, and that of the women of moss, which grows on trees and somewhat resembles wool. Their common food consists of fish, turtles, snails, tunny fish, and whales, which they catch in their season. Some of them also eat the wolf fish, but this is not a common thing, owing to certain distinctions which they make between food proper for the chiefs and that of their subjects. On these islands is found a shell-fish known as the *langosta*, a sort of lobster, and another known in Spain as the *chapin* (trunk fish), of which they consume not less than the former. There are also on the islands a great number of animals, especially deer; and on some of them large bears are found.[2]

---

[1] Pareja, op. cit.; Proc. Am. Philos. Soc., XVII, pp. 500-501.

[2] Doc. Ined., V, pp. 532-533.

A later writer says that the Calusa Indians wore gold and other metal on their foreheads, but this was a custom general in the peninsula.[1]

The people in the interior of the country about Lake Okeechobee, which was called by them "the little ocean,"[1] were probably related to these Calusa. Fontaneda speaks of them thus:

This lake [Mayaimi] is situated in the midst of the country, and is surrounded by a great number of villages of from thirty to forty inhabitants each, who live on bread made from roots during most of the year. They can not procure it, however, when the waters of the lake rise very high. They have roots which resemble the truffles of this country [Spain], and have besides excellent fish. Whenever game is to be had, either deer or birds, they eat meat. Large numbers of very fat eels are found in the rivers, some of them as large as a man's thigh, and enormous trout, almost as large as a man's body; although smaller ones are also found. The natives eat lizards, snakes, and rats, which infest the lakes, fresh-water turtles, and many other animals which it would be tiresome to enumerate. They live in a country covered with swamps and cut up by high bluffs. They have no metals, nor anything belonging to the Old World. They go naked, except the women, who wear little aprons woven of shreds of palm. They pay tribute to Carlos, composed of all the objects of which I have spoken, such as fish, game, roots, deer skins, etc.[2]

Still less is to be learned regarding the social organization and religious beliefs of these people. From what has already been said and from what Fontaneda and others relate elsewhere it is plain that the chief of Calos was head chief either of a very large tribe or of a sort of confederacy centering about Charlotte Harbor and San Carlos Bay, that his power was similar to that of the Timucua chiefs, and that here also there was a class of nobles. The riches and consequently the power of the Calos chief ruling in the latter part of the sixteenth century were greatly enhanced by the gold and silver cast upon his coast in wrecked Spanish vessels from Mexico and Central America. In Laudonnière's time he had united spiritual with political and social power, for that adventurer learned through a Spaniard who had been a captive in the country of Calos that he made his subjects believe—

that his sorceries and charms were the causes that made the earth bring forth her fruit; and, that he might the easier persuade them that it was so he retired himself once or twice a year to a certain house, accompanied by two or three of his most familiar friends, where he used certain enchantments; and, if any man intruded himself to go to see what they did in this place, the king immediately caused him to be put to death.

Moreover, they told me, that, every year, in the time of harvest, this savage king sacrificed one man, which was kept expressly for this purpose, and taken out of the number of the Spaniards, which, by tempest, were cast away upon that coast.[3]

This sacrifice is also mentioned by Barcia, but perhaps on Laudonnière's authority.[4]

---

[1] Brooks and Lowery, MSS.

[2] Doc. Ined., v, pp. 534–535.

[3] Laudonnière, La Floride, p. 132; French, Hist. Colls. La., 1869, p. 282.

[4] Barcia, La Florida, p. 94.

It is referred to at more length in the notes of Lopez de Velasco from which we have already quoted.[1] He says:

The Indians of Carlos have the following customs:

First. Every time that the son of a cacique dies, each neighbor sacrifices (or kills) his sons or daughters who have accompanied the dead body of the cacique's son.

Second. When the cacique himself, or the caciqua [his wife] dies, every servant of his or hers, as the case may be, is put to death.

Third. Each year they kill a Christian captive to feed their idol, which they adore, and they say that it has to eat every year the eyes of a man, and then they all dance around the dead man's head.

Fourth. Every year after the summer begins they make witches, in the shape of devils with horns on their heads, howling like wolves, and many other idols of different kinds, who cry loud like wild beasts, which they remain four months. They never rest, but on the contrary, they keep on the run with fury all the time, day and night. The actions of these bestial creatures are worth relating.[2]

The following, also from the notes of Lopez de Velasco, is all that I have been able to find regarding the customs of the Tekesta Indians. This writer extends the term, however, to cover the entire southeast coast of Florida as far as Cape Canaveral.

The Indians of Tegesta, which is another province extending from the Martires to Canaveral, have a custom, when the cacique dies, of disjointing his body and taking out the largest bones. These are placed in a large box and carried to the house of the cacique, where every Indian from the town goes to see and adore them, believing them to be their gods.

In winter all the Indians go out to sea in their canoes, to hunt for sea cows. One of their number carries three stakes fastened to his girdle and a rope on his arm. When he discovers a sea cow he throws his rope around its neck, and as the animal sinks under the water, the Indian drives a stake through one of its nostrils, and no matter how much it may dive, the Indian never loses it, because he goes on its back. After it has been killed they cut open its head and take out two large bones, which they place in the coffin, with the bodies of their dead and worship them.[3]

Concerning the other east coast peoples, the Jeaga and Ais, nothing is to be had from Spanish sources, but this gap is in some degree filled by the information contained in a small work entitled "Narrative of a Shipwreck in the Gulph of Florida: Showing, God's Protecting Providence, Man's Surest Help and Defence in Times of Greatest Difficulty, and Most Imminent Danger. Faithfully Related by One of the Persons Concerned therein, Jonathan Dickenson." This describes the adventures of the passengers and crew of a vessel which sailed from Port Royal, Jamaica, June 23, 1699, and was wrecked on the east coast of Florida on July 23 following. The place where this vessel struck was a few miles northward of an inlet called Hobe, now known as Jupiter Inlet. The Indians stripped them of all of their clothing and other possessions, but spared their lives. They took them first to the town at Hobe, probably identical with Fontaneda's

[1] See p. 374.

[2] Lowery and Brooks, MSS. Translated by Miss Brooks.

[3] Brooks MSS., Lib. Cong. Translated by Miss Brooks.

Jeaga. Later they allowed them to travel northward toward St. Augustine, which they reached September 15, after very great hardships, from which a few died. After having been very well entertained by the Spanish governor they set out northward again, reached Charleston, S. C., October 26, and arrived at Philadelphia February 1. The work is in the form of a diary, and proved so popular when it first appeared that it went through a number of editions. Internal evidence shows that great reliance may be placed upon it.

In their travels along the Florida coast, after leaving Hobe, this party passed two Indian villages and came to a third called by the Spaniards Santa Lucia, where a mission station was at one time established, though there were no Spaniards there at the time. I have already given reasons for identifying this place with the Guacata of Fontaneda.[1] From this place they were hurried away at midnight of the second day, apparently at the command of the chief of Ais, who lived about 20 miles to the northward, and after passing another village they came to Ais in safety. Dickenson calls this place Jece, but there is practically no doubt of its identity with the Ais of the Spaniards. The chief of this town is said to have been chief of all the towns from Santa Lucia to Ais and northward. He was even in a position to domineer over the chief of Hobe, from whom he secured a part of the plunder the latter had collected. At Ais the fugitives found a party from another English vessel, and they remained one month, when they were rescued by a Spanish coast patrol. Between Ais and Mosquito Inlet they passed six inhabited towns and one that had been abandoned. The two last occupied towns were large and stood near together a little south of the inlet. Possibly they were the towns called Mayarca and Mayajuaca by Fontaneda, which were probably Timucua. Somewhere back of Cape Canaveral they came upon the first Indian plantation and saw some pumpkins growing there. This may have been about on the border between the Timucua Indians and those of southern Florida, for Dickenson asserts that all of those in the towns between Hobe and the place last mentioned raised nothing.

The ethnological information which this work contains applies almost entirely to the Indians of Hobe, Santa Lucia, and Ais—i. e., those called by Fontaneda Jeaga, Guacata, and Ais. It is probable that their culture and language were the same, and very likely close to those of the Calusa, and it is fortunate that from the Ais, who appear to have had the greatest individuality, the largest part of this information comes. On account of the evident likeness of these three peoples I will place the material available together.

---

[1] See p. 333.

We find the following information regarding clothing. At Santa Lucia, Dickenson writes:

In a little time some raw deer skins were brought in, and given to my wife and negro woman, and to us men, such as the Indians wear, being a piece of plaitwork of straws, wrought of divers colours, and of a triangular figure, with a belt of four fingers broad of the same, wrought together, which goes about the waist; and the angle of the other having a thing to it coming between the legs; and strings to the end of the belt, all three meeting together, are fastened behind with a horse tail, or a bunch of silk grass, exactly resembling it, of a flaxen colour; this being all the apparel or covering that the men wear.[1]

This article of male attire is, of course, the breechclout. It is described less at length as worn by the two Hobe Indians who first met our travelers after their shipwreck. Dickenson adds that "they had their hair tied in a roll behind, in which stuck two bones, shaped one like a broad arrow, the other like a spearhead." [2]

The town of Hobe is described as "being little wigwams made of small poles stuck in the ground, which they bent one to another, making an arch, and covering them with thatch of small palmetto leaves." [3] The chief's house was "about a man's height to the top," and within was a platform bed "made with sticks, about a foot high, covered with a mat." [3] The chief's house in Santa Lucia "was about forty feet long, and twenty-five feet wide, covered with palmetto leaves, both top and sides. There was a range of cabins [beds] on one side and two ends; at the entering on one side of the house, a passage was made of benches on each side, leading to the cabins." [4]

The chief of Hobe, to make a rude wind break, "got some stakes and stuck them in a row joining to his wigwam, and tied some sticks, whereon were small palmettoes tied, and fastened them to the stakes about three feet high, and laid two or three mats, made of reeds, down for shelter." [5]

The floors of the houses were the bare earth, covered, however, with filth and vermin.[6]

The beds, as has been noticed, were provided with mats, and Dickenson mentions among certain articles presented to the chief of Santa Lucia "some plaited balls stuffed with moss to lay their heads on instead of pillows." [7]

Pots, including "a deep round bowl," [8] and baskets are mentioned, also a "bag made of grass." [9] Cooked fish was served to the white people on palmetto leaves. Gourds were also used.

---

[1] Dickenson, Narrative, pp. 33–34.
[2] Ibid., pp. 9–10
[3] Ibid., p. 17.
[4] Ibid., p. 33.
[5] Ibid., p. 18.
[6] Ibid., p. 34.
[7] Ibid., p. 37.
[8] Ibid., p. 35.
[9] Ibid., p. 54.

Regarding their economic life, the following statement will hold for all of these towns:

These people neither sow nor plant any manner of thing whatsoever, nor care for any thing but what the barren sands produce. Fish they have as plenty as they please.[1]

The castaways thus describe one, and what appears to have been the most common, way of fishing:

The Cassekey [of Hobe] sent his son with his striking staff to strike fish for us, which was performed with great dexterity; for some of us walked down with him, and though we looked very earnestly when he threw his staff from him, we could not see a fish at the time he saw it, and brought it to shore on the end of his staff. Sometimes he would run swiftly pursuing a fish, and seldom missed when he darted at it; in two hours time he got as many fish as would serve twenty men.[2]

The striking staff or spear was the ordinary fishing implement; what purpose the bow and arrow served other than that of war is not apparent. One night, shortly after the fishing performance that has just been described, some Indians were seen fishing from a canoe by means of a torch.[3] The fish brought to the whites are said to have been "boiled with the scales, heads, and gills, and nothing taken from them but the guts."[4] At one place they were given oysters to eat and at another clams, and they were instructed how to roast them.[5] The vegetable food of the people of Ais consisted principally of "palm berries [species uncertain], coco-plums [*Chrysobalanus icaco*], and sea grapes [*Coccoloba uvifera*] . . . the time of these fruits bearing being over they have no other till the next spring."[6] The two latter suited the palates of the whites very well, but the palm berries they could not endure, and this is not surprising, since, according to Dickenson's testimony, they "could compare them to nothing else but rotten cheese steeped in tobacco juice."[7] They are spoken of in each of the principal towns which they visited, however, and were evidently a staple article of diet with the natives. The Indians provided water for the whites, and very likely for themselves, by scratching holes in the sand.[8]

These Indians occupied a thin strip of shore backed by swamps and dense undergrowth and do not seem to have ventured far inland. Their means of transportation and intercommunication were dugout canoes, used more often in the long narrow lagoons of that coast than on the open ocean, and often poled rather than paddled.[9] Indeed some of these were almost too small for outside work; the castaways were ferried across to Hobe in one just wide enough to sit

[1] Dickenson, Narrative, p. 51.
[2] Ibid., p. 19.
[3] Ibid., p. 29.
[4] Ibid., p. 36.
[5] Ibid., pp. 23, 36.
[6] Ibid., p. 51. For the identifications I am indebted to Lieut. W. E. Safford, of the Bureau of Plant Industry, U. S. Department of Agriculture.
[7] Ibid., pp. 37–38.
[8] Ibid., p. 17.
[9] Ibid., p. 48.

down in.[1] On certain occasions, especially when large burdens were to be carried, two canoes were lashed side by side but some distance apart, poles were laid across to make a platform, and mats were placed on top of this.[2]

Tobacco was very much valued by these people, but apparently not cultivated by them. "A leaf, or a half a leaf of tobacco, would purchase a yard of linen or woolen, or silk, from the Indians." Ambergris, found along their coast, was so little esteemed that an Indian of Ais, "having a considerable quantity of ambergris, boasted that when he went for St. Augustine with that he could purchase of the Spaniards a looking glass, an axe, a knife or two, and three or four mannocoes, which is about five or six pounds of tobacco; the quantity of ambergris might be about five pounds weight." [3]

The little that we learn regarding the private life of these people, their manners and customs, does not set them forth in a very engaging light. That they should plunder the white people of their possessions was to have been expected, and the latter were lucky to have escaped with their lives, but their treatment of them in small matters shows them to have been deceitful, overbearing, unfeeling, and cowardly. They mocked and insulted them in every manner, and upon one occasion an Indian filled the mouth of Dickenson's infant son with sand. They made fun of two of the English who were seized with fever and ague, and Dickenson goes on to remark that they treated their own unfortunates as badly.

> This we well observed, that these people had no compassion on their own aged declining people when they were past labour, nor on others of their own which lay under any declining condition; for the younger is served before the elder, and the elder people, both men and women, are slaves to the younger.[4]

This, it is to be observed, is sharply at variance with the treatment of their old men by the Creeks. Nevertheless the English did not want for some defenders and protectors in each town, and when there was more than enough food for the Indians they had plenty. As an example of primitive generosity in supplying at least the essentials of existence to all may be cited one occasion at Ais when a canoe laden with fish came in, "and it was free for those that would, to take as much as they pleased. The Indians put us to go and take, for it was a kind of scramble amongst us and the young Indian men and boys. All of us got fish enough to serve us two or three days." [5]

In spite of the extreme primitiveness and simplicity of their culture the town chief was treated with considerable respect and seems to have exerted very great influence. His house is represented as the largest in the town, and seems to have supplied the place of the public

---

1 Dickenson, Narrative, p. 17.
2 Ibid., p. 48.
3 Ibid., p. 60.
4 Ibid., p. 55.
5 Ibid., p. 56

houses of the Timucua and Creeks, with which it may indeed have been identical, since the chief among the Creeks was at the same time guardian of the town house. The house of the Santa Lucia chief has already been described. His own seat is placed "at the upper end of the cabin";[1] but from the context it is evident that the middle of the side farthest from the door is intended. The wording is in somewhat archaic English and by no means clear, but we must assume one of two arrangements as follows:

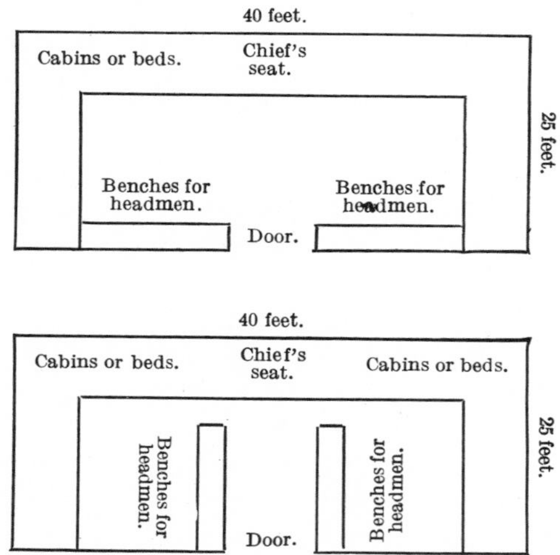

In the first plan it does not seem natural that the head men should sit on either side of the door, where in most tribes the slaves or inferior persons were placed; in the second it does not seem natural to break up the floor space, yet a similar order is met with in a Cusabo town (see p. 64), and was probably the correct one. Daily meetings were held here, in which the black drink was brewed and imbibed in quantities, the custom resembling closely in its observances that found among the Creeks. Dickenson describes it thus:

> The Indians were seated as aforesaid, the cassekey at the upper end of them, and the range of cabins was filled with men, women, and children, beholding us. At length we heard a woman or two cry, according to their manner, and that very sorrowfully, one of which I took to be the cassekey's wife; which occasioned some of us to think that something extraordinary was to be done to us; we also heard a strange sort of a noise, which was not like the noise made by a man, but we could not understand what, nor where it was; for sometimes it sounded to be in one part of the house, and sometimes in another, to which we had an ear. And indeed our ears and eyes could perceive or hear nothing but what was strange and dismal, and death seemed to surround us; but time discovered this noise to us. The occasion of it was thus:
>
> In one part of this house, where a fire was kept, was an Indian man, having a pot on the fire wherein he was making a drink of a shrub, which we understood afterwards

[1] Dickenson, Narrative, pp. 33-34.

by the Spaniards is called Casseena, boiling the said leaves, after they had parched them in a pot; then with a gourd, having a long neck, and at the top of it a small hole, which the top of one's finger could cover, and at the side of it a round hole of two inches diameter. They take the liquor out [of] the pot, and put it into a deep round bowl, which being almost filled, contains nigh three gallons; with this gourd they brew the liquor and make it froth very much; it looks of a deep brown colour. In the brewing of this liquor was this noise made, which we thought strange; for the pressing of the gourd gently down into the liquor, and the air it contained being forced out of a little hole at the top, occasioned a sound, and according to the time and motion given, would be various. The drink when made cool to sup, was in a shell first carried to the cassekey, who threw part of it on the ground and the rest he drank up, and then made a loud hem; and afterwards the cup passed to the rest of the cassekey's associates as aforesaid; but no other person must touch or taste of this sort of drink; of which they sat sipping, chattering, and smoking tobacco, or some other herb instead thereof, for the most part of the day. [1]

The evening festivities which followed were much after the same style.

In the evening we being laid on the place aforesaid [on mats on the floor], the Indians made a drum of a skin, covering therewith the deep bowl, in which they brewed their drink, beating thereon with a stick; and having a couple of rattles made of a small gourd, put on a stick with small stones in it, shaking it, they began to set up a most hideous howling, very irksome to us; and some time after came many of their young women, some singing, some dancing. This continued till midnight, after which they went to sleep.[2]

All this was at the town of Santa Lucia, and there also the Pennsylvanians had an opportunity to observe the ceremony with which an ambassador from another chief was received. In this case the emissary was from the chief of Ais, who, as has been said, seems to have been considered the superior of the chief of Santa Lucia and all other chiefs in that region. Says Dickenson:

About the tenth hour we observed the Indians to be in a sudden motion, and the principal part of them betook themselves to their houses; the cassekey went to dressing his head and painting himself, and so did all the rest; after they had done, they came into the cassekey's house and seated themselves in order. In a small time after came an Indian with some small attendance into the house making a ceremonious motion, and seated himself by the cassekey, and the persons that came with him seated themselves amongst the others; after a small pause the cassekey began a discourse which held him nigh an hour, after which, the strange Indian and his companions went forth to the water side to their canoe, lying in the sound, and returned presently with such presents as they had brought, delivering them to the cassekey and those sitting by, giving an applause. The presents were a few bunches of the herb they had made their drink of and another herb they use instead of tobacco, and some plaited balls stuffed with moss to lay their heads on instead of pillows; the ceremony being ended, they all seated themselves again and went to drinking casseena, smoking, and talking during the stranger's stay.[3]

Soon after several of the white people were themselves asked to take seats in the cabin, beside the chief—an evident mark of honor.[2]

---

[1] Dickenson, Narrative, pp. 33-36.

[2] Ibid., p. 36.

[3] Ibid., pp. 36-37.

The chief of Ais was treated with still more respect by his own people. Dickenson thus describes his return from Hobe, whither he had gone in the hope of obtaining some of the things out of the wrecked vessel:

We perceived he came in state, having his two canoes lashed together, with poles across from one to the other, making a platform, which being covered with a mat, on it stood a chest, which belonged to us, and my negro boy Cesar, that the cassekey of Hoe-bay took from me, whom he had got from the Indians; upon this chest he sat cross legged, being newly painted red, and his men with poles setting the canoe along to the shore. On seeing us, he cried "Wough," and looked very stern at us.

He was received by his people with great homage, holding out his hands, as their custom is, to be kissed, having his chest carried before him to his house, whither he went, and the house was filled with Indians: the old cassekey began, and held a discourse for some hours, giving an account, as we suppose, what he heard and saw, in which discourse he would often mention Nickaleer, which caused us to fear, that all things were not well. After he had told his story, and some of the elder Indians had expressed their sentiments thereon, they drank casseena, and smoked till evening.[1]

Some of these social customs, such, for instance, as the brewing of the black drink, contain religious elements, but, beyond these, two ceremonies are described which seem to have been primarily religious. The first took place the night after the arrival of our travelers at Hobe. It is detailed thus:

Night being come and the moon being up, an Indian, who performed their ceremonies, stood out, looking full at the moon, making a hideous noise, and crying out, acting like a mad man for the space of half an hour, all the Indians being silent till he had done; after which they made a fearful noise, some like the barking of a dog, wolf, and other strange sounds; after this, one got a log and set himself down, holding the stick or log upright on the ground, and several others got about him, making a hideous noise, singing to our amazement; at length their women joined the concert, and made the noise more terrible, which they continued till midnight.[2]

The first part was probably a shamanistic performance; the latter may have been merely a social dance, the upright log being really an extemporized drum. The second ceremonial took place at Ais between the 18th and 25th of August and the account we have of it is the only narrative in any way complete of an Ais ceremonial. From the first sentence it might be thought that this was a monthly ceremony, but there is no certainty. It strongly suggests the Creek busk and probably belonged in the same class, though these people did not raise corn and the date of celebrating it was a month or two too late for a new-corn ceremony. The account follows:

It now being the time of the moon's entering the first quarter the Indians had a ceremonious dance, which they began about 8 o'clock in the morning. In the first place came in an old man, and took a staff about 8 feet long, having a broad arrow on the head thereof, and thence halfway painted red and white, like a barber's pole. In the middle of this staff was fixed a piece of wood, shaped like unto a thigh, leg,

[1] Dickenson, Narrative, p. 48.

[2] Ibid., p. 19.

and foot of a man, and the lower part of it was painted black. This staff, being carried out of the cassekey's house, was set fast in the ground standing upright, which being done he brought out a basket containing six rattles, which were taken out thereof and placed at the foot of the staff. Another old man came in and set up a howling like unto a mighty dog, but beyond him for length of breath, withal making a proclamation. This being done and most of them having painted themselves, some red, some black, some with black and red, with their bellies girt up as tight as well they could girt themselves with ropes, having their sheaths of arrows at their backs and their bows in their hands, being gathered together about the staff, six of the chiefest men in esteem amongst them, especially one who is their doctor, took up the rattles and began an hideous noise, standing round the staff with their rattles and bowing to it without ceasing for about half an hour. Whilst these six were thus employed all the rest were staring and scratching, pointing upwards and downwards on this and the other side, every way looking like men frightened, or more like furies. Thus they behaved until the six had done shaking their rattles; then they all began to dance, violently stamping on the ground for the space of an hour or more without ceasing, in which time they sweat in a most excessive manner, so that by the time the dance was over, by their sweat and the violent stamping of their feet, the ground was trodden into furrows, and by morning the place where they danced was covered with maggots; thus, often repeating the manner, they continued till about 3 or 4 o'clock in the afternoon, by which time many were sick and faint. Being gathered into the cassekey's house they sat down, having some hot casseena ready, which they drank plentifully of, and gave greater quantities thereof to the sick and faint than to others; then they eat berries. On these days they eat not any food till night.

The next day, about the same time, they began their dance as the day before; also the third day they began at the usual time, when many Indians came from other towns and fell to dancing, without taking any notice one of another. This day they were stricter than the other two days, for no woman must look upon them, but if any of their women went out of their houses they went veiled with a mat.[1]

The fact that the castaways had an abundance of fish and berries to eat on the 25th probably had something to do with the ceremony, feasting being a constant preliminary accompaniment of fasting. The day after (i. e., the 26th) Dickenson says:

We observed that great baskets of dried berries were brought in from divers towns and delivered to the king or young cassekey, which we supposed to be a tribute to the king of this town, who is chief of all the towns from St. a Lucia to the northward of this town of Jece.[2]

These presents were probably rather to discharge social obligations or secure the good will of the chief than actual tribute, and it is to be suspected that they had some connection with the ceremony just concluded.

Altogether the culture of the people of Ais and the east Florida coast generally seems to have belonged with that of Calos. Its simplicity was partly due, without doubt, to the poverty of the country; in fact, in later times the economic condition was considerably advanced by frequent wrecks along the coast, though at the same time native industry must have been proportionately

[1] Dickenson, Narrative, pp. 52-54. [2] Ibid., p. 54.

discouraged. The rather high position of the chief is probably attributable in some degree to the influence of their neighbors on the north and west.

THE SEMINOLE

The history of the Seminole is very well known in outline, and much has been written regarding our famous Seminole war; yet it is evident that much remains to be said, on the Indian side at least, before we can have a clear understanding of the Seminole people and Seminole history. The name, as is well known, is applied by the Creeks to people who remove from populous towns and live by themselves, and it is commonly stated that the Seminole consisted of "runaways" and outlaws from the Creek Nation proper. A careful study of their history, however, shows this to be only a partial statement of the case.

Perhaps the best account we have regarding the beginnings of the Seminole is by Bartram. The destruction of the Apalachee towns in the manner elsewhere narrated [1] had partially cleared the way for settlements in Florida by Indians from the north, and in the period immediately succeeding bodies of them gradually pushed southward from the large Creek towns on Chattahoochee River. The first impulse toward Florida of any consequence began with that great upheaval we have so often mentioned—the Yamasee war. The Yamasee themselves entered Florida almost in a body, but they arrived there as friends of the Spaniards, adding their strength to the decaying forces of the original Floridian tribes, and themselves shared in large measure the fate of those peoples—extermination or expulsion from the country. At the same time a movement was started which resulted in the invasion of the peninsula on its western side, and this, indeed, marks the real beginning of the Seminole. Bartram gives an account of it in describing his journey from the Savannah River to Mobile, and it has been reproduced in detailing the history of the Oconee Indians.[2]

By consulting this it will be seen that the Oconee Indians were a nucleus about which the Seminole Nation grew up. It is evident that for a considerable period part of them remained near the Chattahoochee, for they are recorded in the census of 1761 [3] and their town is described by Hawkins in 1799.[4] It disappears in the interval between 1799 and 1832, when the government census of Creeks was taken, and probably all had then moved to Florida.[4] Brinton says that the first group of Seminole came into Florida in 1750, under a chief named Secoffee.[5] He was probably the one known to the English as

[1] See pp. 121–123.
[2] See p. 180.
[3] Ga. Col. Docs., VIII, p. 522.
[4] See p. 181.
[5] Brinton, The Floridian Peninsula, p. 145.

"the Cowkeeper," mentioned in the quotation above from Bartram. He appears in the Georgia Colonial Documents as living well toward the south and spending most of his time in warring with the Spaniards.[1] The Oconee chief who participated in Oglethorpe's first general Indian council was "Oueekachumpa," called by the English "Long King."[2] It does not appear whether Secoffee was his successor or merely the leader of those Oconee who went into Florida. I do not know on what authority Brinton places the invasion of Florida by Secoffee in 1750, but the date appears to be at least approximately correct, and is important as establishing the beginnings of the Seminole as a distinct people. Fairbanks incorrectly states—that is, if Secoffee is really the Cowkeeper of the English—that he "left two sons, head chiefs, Payne and Bowlegs."[3] This is, of course, an assumption natural to a white man, but descent was in the female line among both Creeks and Seminole, and Cohen, who knew Indian customs much better than Fairbanks, is undoubtedly correct when he says that Cowkeeper was "uncle of old Payne."[4] He adds that the former had been given a silver crown by the British Government for services during the American Revolution, from which we know that he lived at least almost to the end of that struggle. Cohen apparently contradicts himself in referring to these chiefs, but his later statement appears to be correct, and from this it seems that the Cowkeeper was succeeded by a chief known as "King Payne." Cohen says that he married a Yamasee woman.[5] The grant of land to Forbes & Co. made in 1811 in payment for debts contracted by the Indians was signed among others by Payne for all of the Alachua settlements and by Capitchy Micco [Kapitsa miko] for the Mikasuki. In 1812, in revenge for depredations committed on the Georgia settlements by these Indians, Colonel Newman, Inspector General of Florida, offered to lead a party against Payne's town, which was still in Alachua, and probably just where Bartram found it. In the fight which ensued near that place King Payne was mortally wounded, and many other Indians killed or wounded, but the invaders were forced to retreat under cover of night. King Payne was succeeded by his brother, Bowlegs, whose Indian name is given by Cohen as Islapaopaya [*opaya* meaning "far away"].[6] Cohen says that the Alachua settlements were broken up in 1814 by the Tennesseeans and Bowlegs was killed.[7] At any rate about this time the Alachuas, or part of them, moved farther south, and we presently find their head chief, Mikonopi ("Top Chief"), the nephew of King Payne and Bow-

[1] Ga. Col. Docs., VII, p. 626 et seq.
[2] Acct. Shewing the Progress of Ga., pp. 35–36.
[3] Fairbanks, Hist of Fla., p. 174.
[4] Cohen, Notices of Florida, p. 238.
[5] Ibid., p. 33.
[6] Ibid., pp. 35, 238.
[7] Ibid., p. 35.

legs, living at Okihamki, just west of Lake Harris or Astatula.[1] Mikonopi came as near being "head chief of the Seminoles" as any at the outbreak of the great Seminole war. We may therefore say that the nucleus of the Seminole Nation was not merely a body of "outcasts" as has been so often represented, but a distinct tribe, the Oconee, affiliated, it is true, with the Creeks, but always on the outer margin of the confederacy and to a considerable extent an independent body, representing not the Muskogee but the Hitchiti speaking peoples of southern Georgia—those who called themselves Atcik-hata.[2]

The Hitchiti character of this Seminole nucleus comes out still stronger when we turn to examine those towns established in the wake of the Oconee invasion. The only early lists available are those given by Bartram and Hawkins, which are as follows:

SEMINOLE TOWNS ACCORDING TO BARTRAM (1778)[3]

Suola-nocha.
Cuscowilla or Alachua.
Talahasochte.
Caloosahatche.
——— Great island.
——— Great hammock.
——— Capon. } Traders' names.
——— St. Mark's.
——— Forks.

SEMINOLE TOWNS ACCORDING TO HAWKINS (1799)[4]

Sim-e-no-le-tal-lau-has-see.
Mic-c-sooc-e.
We-cho-took-me.
Au-lot-che-wau.
Oc-le-wau thluc-co.
Tal-lau-gue chapco pop-cau.
Cull-oo-sau hat-che.

Hawkins says of the Seminole settlements enumerated by him:

> These towns are made from the towns O-co-nee, Sau-woog-e-lo, Eu-fau-lau, Tum-mault-lau, Pā-lā-chooc-le and Hitch-e-tee.[5]

Of these six towns only Eu-fau-lau is certainly known to have belonged to the Muskogee proper, and one early writer represents this as made up of outcasts from all quarters. We do not know the status of Tum-mault-lau with certainty, but the form of the name itself, the position which it occupied in very early times, and certain other

[1] His residence is often given as Pilaklakaha, which appears to have been a Negro town near Okihamki.
[2] See p. 172.
[3] Bartram, Travels, p. 462.
[4] Ga. Hist. Soc. Colls., III, p. 25. A more nearly phonetic way of rendering the fifth would be Ạklawaha łȧko, and the sixth Talaa'lgi tcȧpko popka ("a place to eat cow or stock peas").
[5] Ga. Hist. Soc. Colls., III, p. 25.

considerations, all point to a connection with the Hitchiti-speaking peoples.[1] The language of the Mikasuki in Oklahoma is so close to that of the Hitchiti that they are commonly considered to be parts of one people; and the following story regarding them was told to me by Jackson Lewis, an old Hitchiti Indian, for whose opinions I have the greatest respect. He said that the name was properly Nikasuki.

> The Nikasukis are precisely the same as the Hitchiti. In early days some Hitchiti went hunting to a point where two rivers met. They found alligators there which they ate, and when they came back they reported that they were good food. They went many times, and finally they came to like this point of land so well that a number of them settled there permanently. They had reported that alligators were as numerous and as easy to obtain as hogs (*suki* in Hitchiti), so that the parent tribe called their settlement Hog-eaters, which is what Nikasuki means.

We can not, however, concede the likelihood that *n* could so easily have been corrupted into *m*, since the latter appears in the early documents as far back as we can go. I have elsewhere quoted the opinion of the old Mikasuki chief relative to the distinction between his people and the Hitchiti, and their supposed relationship to the Chiaha. It must be remembered that the Chiaha anciently came away from the Yamasee, at a point not far from the earlier home of the Oconee, and it is quite possible that they recognized a closer connection with the Oconee Indians than with the Hitchiti proper. True, Mr. Penieres, subagent for Indian affairs in Florida, reported in 1821 that only a few straggling families of Chiaha were to be found in the peninsula;[2] but it is quite possible that these represented a much later immigration, the earlier colonists having already (by 1778) adopted the name Mikasuki. The first settlement of these "true Mikasuki," as I venture to call them, was, so far as we know, at Old Mikasuki, near the lake which bears their name, in Jefferson County, Florida. Later they, or part of them, moved to New Mikasuki, somewhere near Greenville, in Madison County. In 1823 the chief of this town was Tuskameha (Taski heniha).[3] It appears from Cohen, however, that at a somewhat earlier date the chief of the Mikasuki was named Tokos imała, called by the whites John Hicks, or Hext.[4] Tokos imała appears in a list of towns dated 1821 as chief of the town in the Alachua plains,[5] and he did not die until 1835; therefore when no town is enumerated in the Alachua plains in 1823 and no chief bearing the name,[6] we are left to guess whether the town has been omitted or whether someone else appears in his place. It is probable that the Mikasuki

[1] See p. 12.
[2] See p. 404.
[3] See p. 411.
[4] Cohen, Notices of Florida, p. 641.
[5] See p. 406.
[6] List on pp. 411-412.

were scattered among several towns, but as these, with but few exceptions, received new names from each new location, it is practically impossible to trace them.

From notes gathered by myself and the statements of early writers it is evident that this Mikasuki element was one of the most important, if not the most important, among the Seminole. It is also evident that there was before the outbreak of the final Seminole war a certain amount of friction and mutual jealousy between them and the Muskogee Seminole, founded partly, no doubt, on differences in speech and customs. Thus, in a letter written by William P. Duval to Col. Thomas L. McKenney, general superintendent of Indian affairs, and dated Tallahassee, April 5, 1826, we find the following disparaging notice:

The Mickasuky tribe I must except from this general [commendatory] remark. They are, and ever have been, the most violent and lawless Indians in all the South. They have set their own chiefs at defiance, killing their hogs and cattle, and pillaging their plantations. There are about two hundred of these Indians that never can be managed but by force. Three times have they attempted to put to death their head chief, because he has endeavored to restrain their excesses.

All the chiefs, in open council, have denounced them; and have assured me that, if the Government will afford them assistance, they will punish these outlaws of their nation and bring them into their boundary. I have seen many of them on the Suwanee and Ocilla Rivers; they are actually raising crops in the neighborhood of the whites, although I furnished them with provisions two months since, when they all promised immediately to go into the boundary. Not one has gone, nor will they move unless compelled. I have been upwards of two months in the woods, regulating and bringing the Indians to order; and have completely succeeded, except with the Mickasuky tribe. The inhabitants are greatly exasperated at the injuries they have sustained from this tribe, and the worst consequences may be expected. I acknowledge I can do nothing more without force. No confidence can be placed in this tribe, and the orderly Indians complain as much of them as the whites. They have most wantonly killed up the cattle and hogs of the nation, and will continue to do so. In fact, their own people have suffered as much from their depredations as our citizens.[1]

On the other hand, John Hicks, chief of at least a part of the Mikasuki, is represented by Cohen as the most influential and far-sighted man among the Seminole and a supporter of the emigration idea.[2] His death was followed almost immediately by the ascendency of the party opposed to emigration and the outbreak of the Seminole war. Cohen is also authority for the statement that the Ocklawaha tribe or band represented the last element of Yamasee Indians, and he is probably correct, since the Yamasee are placed near Ocklawaha River on several maps of a slightly earlier period. He adds that they were noticeably darker than the other Seminole.[3] On the list of towns given in 1823 appears one called "Yumersee," located "at the

---

[1] Am. State Papers, Indian Affairs, II, p. 694.
[2] Cohen, Notices of Florida, p. 64 et seq.
[3] Ibid., p. 33.

head of Sumulga Hatchee River, 20 miles north of St. Marks." The chief at that time was "Alac Hajo" (Ahalak hadjo, "potato hadjo").[1] I have given their history elsewhere.[2]

According to an aged Oklahoma Seminole who was born in Florida, the people of Tallahassee, where the State capital now stands, were Sawokli. It appears from the early records that this was an old Florida settlement, but I have no other evidence regarding its origin. The Cull-oo-sau hat-che (Kalusa hâtchi) town of Hawkins I believe to have been occupied by some of the earlier natives of Florida, which, as has been seen, had remained down into American times.[3]

The history of the earliest Muskogee element in Florida is rescued for us in part by Romans, who says:

> About the middle of the land, nearly in latitude 28, is a village called New Eufala, being a colony from Yufala, in the Upper Creek Nation, planted in 1767, in a beautiful and fertile plain.[4]

Although a little too far south, as given by him, there is reason to believe that this is the town later known as Tco′ko tca′ti, or "Red House," and sometimes as "Red Town," between the Big hammock and the hammock called from the name of this town "Chucoochartie hammock."

There is no way of determining whence the populations of "We-cho-took-me" and "Tallau-gue chapco pop-cau," the two remaining towns in Hawkins's list, were drawn, nor those of most of the towns mentioned by Bartram. We-cho-took-me was remembered by Jackson Lewis, the informant to whom I have so often referred. He pronounced the name Oetcotukni and interpreted it to mean "where there is a pond of water."

A few years after the date set by Romans, namely in 1778, a new Muskogee element appears in this region contributed by the towns of Kolomi, Fus-hatchee and Okchai, besides an Alabama contingent from Tawasa and Kan-tcati.[5]

After the conclusion of the Creek war of 1813–14 great numbers of Creeks, especially from the Upper Creek country, in a few cases entire towns, descended into Florida, increasing the original population by about two-thirds. And, whereas we have seen that up to this time the Hitchiti element was predominant, it now begins to be swallowed up or overshadowed by that of the true Creeks or Muskogee. The distinction between the older or true Seminole and the later comers was maintained for a time, as appears in the reports and documents of the early years of the nineteenth century relating to Indian affairs in Florida. One of the most important statements in this connection

---

[1] See p. 411.
[2] See p. 108.
[3] See p. 344.
[4] Romans, Concise Nat. Hist. Fla., p. 280.
[5] MS., Lib. Cong.

is by Mr. Penieres in a letter to General Jackson, dated July, 1821, though the estimates of population given by him are probably too high. This has been printed several times, but I here take it from Jedidiah Morse's Report on the Indian Tribes, where it seems to appear with the smallest number of typographical blemishes:

The Indian tribes known under the denomination of the *Creeks*, are divided into bands, designated to me as follows: The Mekasousky, Souhane, Moskoky, Santa-Fé, Red-stick and Echitos. I have been assured that those bands had raised, during the late war, more than twelve hundred warriors, which may lead to suppose a population of more than three thousand individuals.

The nation known under the denomination of *Seminoles*, is composed of seven bands—viz, the Larchivue, Oklêvuaha, Chockechiatte, Pyaklé-kaha, Taléhouyana and Topkélaké. Besides these are some remnants of ancient tribes, as the Houtchis, Chaas, Cana-acke, etc.; but of these there are only a few straggling families.

On the borders of Georgia is another tribe, called Cahouita. This tribe, under the orders of Mc'Intosh, raised from one hundred to one hundred and fifty warriors; who under this chief, about seven years ago, waged a civil war on the whites and Seminoles who hold them in the utmost detestation.

To this census, which would carry the Indian population to more than five thousand individuals, of both sexes, must be added five or six hundred maroon negroes, or mulattos, who live wild in the woods, or in a state of half slavery among the Indians.[1]

Mr. Penieres evidently distinguishes as "Creeks" the later comers into Florida, and as "Seminoles" the earlier occupants of the peninsula. Under the first heading he is not describing the Creek Nation in general, but only those who had settled in Florida within the seven years preceding the date of his letter. Although there at first appears to be great lack of system in this enumeration, a careful examination shows that it has a real significance and helps us to understand the Indian population of Florida, the elements which entered into it, and to some extent the distribution of those elements. Let us take the Seminole proper first. The name first given, "Latchivue," is without doubt meant for Alachua, but it is not intended to designate the Oconee who lived on the Alachua plains in Bartram's time, but evidently that portion of the Mikasuki under John Hicks or Takos imała known on independent evidence to have been there in 1821. "Oklevuaha" is, of course, Ocklawaha, and represents probably, as I have said above, the old Yamasee element. "Chockechiatte" is Tcoko tcati, the Eufaula colony.[2] Pyaklé-kaha is evidently identical with Pelaclekaha, which is given by some authorities as the residence of Mikonopi and by others as a Negro town near Okiḥamgi, his actual residence. At any rate it clearly refers to the Oconee colony in Florida, the pioneer town and the one visited by Bartram when situated on the Alachua plains. The town next mentioned, Taléhouyana, is misprinted in most of the other places where this letter has been copied. While its identity is not entirely assured there is good

[1] Morse, Rept. to the Sec. of War, p. 311.

[2] See p. 403.

reason to believe that it is none other than the town of Hotalgihuyana, settled by Chiaha and Osochi Indians. The place last mentioned is "Topkélaké," which means "fort place," "place where there is a fort." There were several localities known by the name. One appears in 1821 near the present city of Tallahassee, and there was probably another near Tohopekaliga Lake in central Florida, but I am inclined to identify this settlement with a town which occurs in the enumeration made in 1823 and which is placed 30 miles "east," by which I suppose we are to understand north, of Cape Florida.[1] It would thus seem to have been in the neighborhood of Hillsboro Inlet. The settlers were probably from the Upper Creeks.[2] While it is said that the Seminole were composed of seven bands, only six are enumerated. Perhaps Mr. Penieres classed as a seventh the "remnants of ancient tribes" to which he refers immediately afterwards. Of these the "Houtchis" are of course the Yuchi, and we know from several sources that their settlement was one called "Tallahassee or Spring Garden," in the enumeration of 1823, near a place in Volusia County called Spring Garden to-day.[1] The "Chaas" were probably the Chiaha, a settlement of whom, according to Bell, was at a place called Beech Creek, the exact location of which I have been unable to determine.[3] According to my Seminole informants there was a great fighter in Florida named Kana'ki, and they thought the name "Cana-acke" might have been derived from him, but I believe it is intended for the Kan-hatki.[4]

Turning to those bands set down as belonging to the Creeks we find some that are undoubtedly Muskogee and some of different lineage. The Mikasuki are also referred to under this head, and the name was probably used for those at New Mikasuki, who may have come from the Lower Creek towns much later than the ones already considered. The "Echitos" are, of course, Hitchiti, in this case people from the true Hitchiti town. The rest appear to have been mainly Muskogee, although there were some Alabama and Koasati among them. The "Souhane" were those Indians settled on Suwanee River, who, according to a letter written by Gen. Jackson in 1821, were from the Upper Creeks.[5] The Santa Fe band must have been the Indians on Santa Fe River. Jackson gives a Santa Fe talofa "at the east fork of the Suwanee," but does not state whether its people came from the Upper Creeks or were old inhabitants of Florida.[6] The "Red-Stick" band may have been so named merely because they belonged to the element among the Creeks recently at war with the whites, or they may have been that portion from the Red towns. In any case

[1] See p. 412.
[2] See p. 407, town No. 22.
[3] See p. 407.
[4] See p. 269.
[5] See p. 406, town No. 11.
[6] See p. 406, town No. 9.

we can not separate them from the band set down as "Moskoky"—the Muskogee. In Jackson's letter 11 towns beside two on the Suwanee are definitely identified as having come from the Creeks, and nearly all of these were from the Upper Creeks.[1] The remaining seven are either given as containing strictly Florida people or else are passed over without comment, and among them are one or two which there is reason to believe belong among the later comers. The relation of two to one, which I have already mentioned as representing probably the proportion of refugee Creeks to old Seminole, is therefore maintained roughly, even in the number of their towns. The "Spanish Indians," consisting of remnants of the ancient Florida peoples, are not included in this enumeration.

The Seminole towns moved about so frequently and their names were altered so often that it is impossible to give a complete history of the people by towns, or to identify in every case the tribes which occupied them. Two or three town lists have been preserved from the period just before the outbreak of the Seminole war and it may be of some interest to insert these. They vividly illustrate the truth of the statement I have just made. The first is contained in a letter of Capt. John H. Bell, agent for the Indians in Florida, addressed to a committee of Congress, in February, 1821, and reproduced by Jedidiah Morse in his Report on Indian Affairs.[2] It is as follows:

1. Red-town, at Tampa Bay. Number of souls unknown.
2. Oc-lack-o-na-yahe, above Tampa Bay. A number of souls.
3. O-po-nays Town, back of Tampa Bay.
4. Tots-ta-la-hoeets-ka, or Watermelon Town, on the seaboard, west side Tampa Bay; the greater part of all these fled from the Upper Creeks when peace was given to that nation.
5. A-ha-pop-ka, situated back of the Musquitoe.
6. Low-walta Village, composed of those who fled from Coosa, and followed McQueen and Francis, their prophets.
7. McQueen's Village, east side Tampa Bay.
8. A-lack-a-way-talofa, in the Alachua Plains. A great number of souls. Took-o-sa-moth-lay, the chief.
9. Santa-fee-talofa, at the east fork of Suwany. Lock-taw-me-coocky, the chief.
10. Waw-ka-sau-su, on the east side of the mouth of the Suwany, on the seaboard; these are from the Coosa River, followers of McQueen and Francis.
11. Old Suwany Town, burnt in 1818, on the Suwany River. These are from the Tallapoosa towns, and they are from the Upper Creeks.
12. A-la-pa-ha-talofa, west of Suwany and east of the Miccasuky. The chief Ock-mulgee is lately dead.
13. Wa-cissa-talofa, at the head of St. Mark's River. These are from the Chattahouchy, Upper Creeks.
14. Willa-noucha-talofa, near the head of St. Mark's River, west of Wa-cissa-talofa. Natives of Florida.

---

[1] See below.

[2] Morse, Rept. to the Sec. of War, pp. 306–308.

15. Talla-hasse, on the waters of the Miccasuky pond. These have lived there a long time, have about 100 warriors, and suppose 10 souls to a warrior; say 1,000 souls.

16. Top-ke-gal-ga, on the east side on the O-clock-ney, near Talla-hasse.

17. We-thoe-cuchy-talofa [Withla-cooche talofa], between the St. Mark's and O-clock-ney Rivers, in the fork of the latter; very few of them are natives of the land.

18. O-chuce-ulga, east of the Apalachicola, where Hambly and Blunt [Blount] live; about 250 souls. Coth-rin, the chief.

19. Cho-co-nickla Village, the chief is Nea-thoe-o-mot-la, the second chief, Mulatto-King; were raised here; have about sixty warriors on the west side of the Apalachicola.

20. Top-hulga.[1] This village and Cho-co-nick-la join each other. Raised in East Florida, and removed there.

21. Tock-to-eth-la, west of Fort Scott and Chatta-houchy, ten miles above the forks; forty or fifty warriors were raised at the O-cun-cha-ta, or Red Ground, and moved down.

22. Another town in East Florida Point, called O-chu-po-cras-sa. These moved down from the Upper Creeks. About thirty warriors, and a great many women and children settled there.

The foregoing list is extracted from a talk held by General Jackson with three Chiefs of the Florida Indians, viz, Blount, Nea-moth-la, and Mulatto King, at Pensacola, 19th September, 1821. To which may be added the following settlements in East Florida:

23. Pe-lac-le-ke-ha, the residence of Miccanopa, chief of the Seminole nations, situated about one hundred and twenty miles south of Alachua.

24. Chu-ku-chatta, about twenty miles south of Pilaclekaha.

25. Hich-a-pue-susse, about twenty miles southeast of Chukuchatta, at the same distance from the head of Tampa.

26. Big Hammock settlement, the most numerous, north of Tampa Bay and west of Hechapususse.

27. Oc-la-wa-haw, on the river of that name, west of St. John's River.

28. Mulatto Girl's Town, south of Caskawilla Lake.

29. Bucker Woman's Town, near Long Swamp, east of Big Hammock.

30. King Heijah's, south, and Payne's negro settlements in Alachua; these are slaves belonging to the Seminoles, in all about three hundred.

31. John Hicks' Town, west of Payne's Savannah, *Miccasukys.*

32. Oke-a-fenoke swamp, south side, a number of *Cowetas.*

33. Beech Creek, settlement of *Cheehaws.*[2]

34. Spring Garden, above Lake George, *Uchees.* Billy is their chief.

35. South of Tampa, near Charlotte's Bay, *Choctaws.*

It is probable that the supplementary list repeats under a different name some of those in the list quoted from Jackson. Thus Bell's "John Hicks' Town," No. 31, is evidently identical with Jackson's "A-lack-a-way-talofa," No. 8, John Hicks's Indian name having been Takos imała. Jackson's "Red Town," No. 1, may also be the same as Bell's "Chu-ku-chatta," No. 24, the latter meaning "red house;" but in that case we must suppose that Jackson has erred in classing the town with those "the greater part" of which fled from

[1] Also called Attapulgas; the Creek is Atap'halgi from the atap'ha, dogwood. (See Gatschet in Misc. Coll. Ala. Hist. Soc., I, p. 393.)

[2] Possibly this is identical with Fulemmy's Town or Pinder Town, which is placed on Suwanee River in 1817 and was inhabited by Chiaha Indians. "Pinder" is dialectic for peanut. (See Misc. Colls. Ala. Hist. Soc., I, p. 396.)

the Upper Creeks. Analyzing the composition of these towns as far as the information at hand will allow we find the following condition: Nos. 8 and 31, as just noted, represent one town, occupied by the Mikasuki, but probably by only a part of them; No. 23 represents the old Oconee; No. 24, the Eufaula Indians; No. 27, the Yamasee; No. 32, Coweta Indians; No. 33, Chiaha; No. 34, Yuchi; and Nos. 28 to 30 were probably settled almost entirely by negroes. I have already given my reasons for thinking that the "Choctaws" settled according to Bell in No. 35 were really Calusa Indians.[1] No. 21 is said to have been drawn from the Red Ground among the Upper Creeks. There were two towns of this name—one an Abihka, the other an Alabama town. I believe that the one here referred to was the Alabama town because the Abihka were little involved in the war, and it appears, moreover, that comparatively few of the Indians engaged in the fight at Horseshoe Bend emigrated to Florida. On the other hand, the Alabama were active hostiles, and Paddy Walsh, one of the ablest Creek leaders, was an Alabama of Tawasa town. The Indians of town No. 7 were probably Tulsa, because Peter McQueen, their leader, was a Tulsa Indian. The name of No. 6 is probably an attempt at Łiwahali. There is to-day in the Seminole Nation a town of this name. It is said to have consisted partly of Hołiwahali Indians, as the name implies, but also of people from Kan-hatki and Fus-hatchee.[2] Probably No. 6 is this compound town or the nucleus out of which it developed.

Nos. 1 to 4 are said by Jackson to have come for the most part from the Upper Creeks; and No. 22, apparently the settlement at Cape Florida, is assigned a similar origin. No. 13 is said to have come from the Chattahoochee and at the same time from the Upper Creek settlements. Perhaps the inhabitants were from those settlements above the falls of the Chattahoochee which were established in early times by the Okfuskee. No. 10 is given as from the Coosa, and No. 11 from the Tallapoosa, while No. 17 is merely said to have consisted of immigrants. Nos. 25 and 26 were probably from the Upper Creeks. Nos. 14, 19, and 20 are said to have been occupied by old Florida Indians, while Nos. 4, 9, 12, 16, and 18 were also probably populated from the older occupants of the peninsula. Tallahassee, No. 15, is said by some living informants to have been a Sawokli settlement. To summarize, 16 towns appear to have belonged to the old Seminoles, 15 to the immigrants from the Upper Creeks, and 3 to the Negroes settled among them. The towns of the newcomers were apparently more populous, since they seem to have outnumbered the earlier occupants.

---

[1] See p. 28.

[2] See p. 269.

In his estimates of population Morse gives a somewhat different list furnished by a Capt. Young, and dating from a slightly earlier period:[1]

Tribe.	Population.	Location.
1. Micasukeys [Mikasuki]	1,400	30 m. NNE. from Fort St. Mark, on a pond 14 miles long, 2 or 3 wide; land fertile, and of a beautiful aspect.
2. Fowl Towns [or Totalosi talofa].[2]	300	12 miles E. Fort Scott; land tolerable.
3. Oka-tiokinans [Okitiyakani].	580	Near Fort Gaines.
4. Uchees [Yuchi].	130	Near the Mikasukey.
5. Ehawho-ka-les [Sawokli].	150	On Apalachicola, 12 miles below Ocheese bluff.
6. Ocheeses	220	At the bluff of their name.
7. Tamatles [Tamałi]	220	7 miles above the Ocheeses.
8. Attapulgas [or Atap'hulga].[3]	220	On Little River, a branch of Okalokina, 15 miles above the Mikasukey path, from Fort Gadsden; fine body of lands.
9. Telmocresses [Tȧl mutcȧsi].[4]	100	W. side of Chattahoochee, 15 miles above the fork; good land.
10. Cheskitalowas [Chiska talofa].[5]	580	On the W. side of Chattahoochee, 2 miles above the line.
11. Wekivas	250	4 miles above the Cheskitalowas.
12. Emusas [Yamasee][6]	20	2 miles above the Wekivas.
13. Ufallahs [Eufaula]	670	12 miles above Fort Gaines.
14. Red grounds [Alabama Indians?].	100	2 miles above the line.
15. Eto-husse-w a k k e s [Itahasiwaki].	100	3 miles above Fort Gaines.
16. T a t t o-whe-h a l l y s [Chatukchufaula?].[7]	130	Scattered among other towns; dishonest.
17. Tallehassas[8] [Tallahassee].	15	On the road from Okalokina to Micasukey.
18. Owassissas[9]	100	On the eastern waters of St. Mark's River.
19. Chehaws [Chiaha]	670	On the Flint River, in the fork of Makulley Creek.
20. Talle-whe-anas [Hotalgihuyana].	210	E. side of Flint River, not far from Chehaws.
21. Oakmulges [Okmulgee].	220	E. of Flint River, near the Tallewheanas.
Total	6,385	

This appears to include merely the uppermost Seminole towns along with some which properly belong to the Lower Creeks. Most of them are easily identified, as has been indicated in the brackets.

[1] Morse, Rept. to Sec. of War, p. 364.

[2] A writer quoted by Gatschet gives these as Cahalli hatchi, old Tallahassi, Atap'halgi, Allik hadshi, Etatulga, Mikasuki, (Misc. Colls. Ala. Hist. Soc., I, p. 413). The second, third, and last of these occur independently in the above list. Also see p. 177.

[3] See No. 20 in Bell's list.

[4] A Tȧl mutcȧsi in this neighborhood is recorded by no one else unless it is intended by the "Sumachaches" of Manuel Garcia's diary, dated 1800 (Edward E. Ayer Coll. in Newberry Library, Chicago). The same officer mentions Tallahassey and Bruacissey (Owassissas), besides several towns properly belonging to the Lower Creeks.

[5] See p. 308.

[6] See p. 108.

[7] See p. 245.

[8] See p. 403.

[9] See p. 406.

This group of quasi-Seminole towns, along with the Lower Creeks, ceded a tract of land to Panton, Leslie & Co. in 1785 in order to extinguish debts contracted with that trading house, and confirmed it in 1806. The following chiefs affixed their signatures to the confirmation of this treaty. I have preserved the manuscript orthography.

Hopay Hacho Totolozu Talofa [Totalosi Talofa], great orator of the Seminole.
Hothepocio Justannagee of Totolose Talofa [Totalosi Talofa]
Hopay micco of Ocknuilgeeche [Okmulgee or Okmulgutci].
Tustannagee micco of the same town.
Kuneeka Thlucco of Cheeyaha [Chiaha].
Emathlee Thlucio of the same.
Mico Napamico of Cuasita [Kasihta].
Yahullo Emathla of Chiska Talofa.
Tasikaya mico of Osootchie [Osotci].
Uchee Tustannagee of Uchee [Yuchi].
Yahulla micco of Ufalles [Eufaula].
Albania Justannagee of Ufallee [Eufaula].
Tasikaya Hadjo of Ocheesces [Ochisi].
Nika mico of Achinalga [Achinaalga].
Tustannage Hadjo of Tochtouheithles.[1]
Ninnyyuageichy of Tochtouheithles.[1]
Tustannage of Palachucklie [Apalachicola].
Yahulla Ennakla or John Meally of Ocheesa [Otcisi].
Hopay Hadjo, for Copixtsy mico, of Mickacuky [Mikasuki].
Justannagee Hopay or Little Prince of Cowetas [Coweta].
Ocheesce mico of Yauollee [Iolee].[2]
Hopayok Hadjo of Yanollee [Iolee].
Mico Tecocksy or Hatas mico.
Hopayoo mico of Tauassees [Tawasa].
Totka Tustannage of Wifalutka.[3]
Efau Tustannagee of Mikasuky [Mikasuki] for Hopay Hadjo.
Pawas mico of Ocoteyokony [Okitiyagani].
Tustannage Chapo of Ennussee [Emussee or Yamasee].
Tasikaya mico of the same.
Tustannage Chupko of Tomathly [Tamałi].
Halleveccha, king of Tomathla [Tamałi].
Tuskinia, lieutenant of Chatoackchufall [Chatukchufaula].[4]

The Chatukchufaula Indians were probably on the Chattahoochee at this time above the Coweta, and were therefore included. A similar grant of land was made to Forbes & Co. in 1811.[5]

The third list of Seminole towns was made only two years after Bell's.[6] Where possible, in the subjoined reproduction of it, I have indicated by numbers in brackets the town in list 1 to which each corresponds, but the number of cases in which it has been found

[1] The town numbered 21 in list 1 and 5 in list 3, and are probably of Alabama origin.
[2] Seven of list 3.
[3] Perhaps identical with No. 13 in the third list.
[4] Copy of MS., Ayer Coll., Newberry Lib.
[5] In the Ayer collection is a statement of the debts contracted by the Indians with this firm, the amount of each debt, and the name of the debtor, but the names are mostly English nicknames.
[3] American State Papers, Indian Affairs, II, p. 439.

impossible to do this, together with the numerous changes in the names of the chiefs and in the town locations, show the difficulties encountered in tracing the history of Seminole bands.

Town.	Chief.	Situation.
1. Cohowofooche	Neamothla [Heniha imała].	23 miles N. by W. from St. Mark's.
2 [15]. Tallahassa [Talahasi].	Chefixico [Tcu fiksiko]	20 miles N. by W. from St. Mark's.
3 [23]. Okehumpkee [Okihûmga].	Miconope [Miko nàbà]	60 miles SW. from Volusia.
4 [20]. Taphulga [Atap'hulga].[1]	Ehe-mathlochee [Imałutci?].	30 miles E. of Appalachicola, and 1 mile N. of Forbes's purchase.
5 [21]. Totoawathla	Eheconhatamico [Ikànhàtki miko].	W. side of Chattahoochee, 10 miles above the forks.
6 [19]. Chokonokla ["Burnt house"?]	Mulatto King	W. side of Appalachicola, 4 m. below the fork.
7 [18]. Iolee	Blount	60 m. above the mouth of Appalachicola, on the W. bank.
8 [18]. Spanawalka ["Plenty of Spaniards there"?].	Cochrane	2 m. below Iolee, on the same side.
9. Oscillee	Latafixico [Hola'ta fiksiko].	At the mouth of Oscillee River, on the E. bank.
10. Ohathlokhouchy [Oiłàkutci].	Woxaholahta [Woksi hola'ta].	On Little River, 40 m. E. of Appalachicola.
11. Yumersee	Alac Hajo [Ahalak hadjo]	Head of Sumulga Hatchee River, 20 m. N. of St. Mark's.
12. Lochchiocha	Okoska-amathla [Okoski imała].	60 m. E. of Appalachicola, and near Ochlochne.
13 [14?]. Alouko	Tukchuslu Hajo	E. side of Sumulga Hatchee River, 20 m. N. of St. Mark's.
14. Hiamonee	Chowastic [Tcowastayi].	5 m. from the Georgia line, on the E. bank of Ochlochne River.
15. Tuckagulga	Ben Burgess	On the E. bank of Ochlochne River, between that and Hiamonee.
16. Wasupa	Toshatehismico [Koasati miko].	2 m. E. of Sumulga Hatchee River and 18 m. from St. Mark's.
17. Hatchcalamocha	Amathla Hajo [Imała hadjo].	Near Drum Swamp, 18 m. W. of New Mickasuky town.
18. Etotulga ["Fallen tree"].	Mickcooche [Mikotci]	10 m. E. of the old Mickasuky town.
19. Topananaulka [Tubenànàlga, "Place of zigzag timber"].	Obiakee	3 m. W. of New Mickasuky.
20. Seleuxa [Ironwood?]	Koamathła [Koe imała?].	Head of Oscillee River.
21. Ahosulga	Hockoknakola	5 m. S. of New Mickasuky town.
22. Mickasuky (New)	Tuskameha	30 m. W. of Suwanee River.
23. Sampala [Sàmbala]	Ehe-maltho-chee [Imałotci].	26 m. above the forks of the Appalachicola, on the W bank.
24. Oktahatku [Oktaha hàtki].	Menohomaltha Hajo [Heniha imała hadjo].	7 m. E. of W. [!] from Sampala.
25 [12]. Chohalaboohhulka [Tcu lihaboá'lga, "Place where deer tracks abound"].	Yahola Hajo	W. side of Suwanee, above its junction with Alapaha.

[1] Mentioned under the name of its chief, "Ematlochee," in U. S. Ind. Treaties (1833), p. 578, 1837, as a Creek town.

Town.	Chief.	Situation.
26. Welika..............	Lathwamaltha [Hola'ta imała].	4 m. E. of Tallahassee towns.
27 [9]. Wachitokha.......	Ho-lahta-mico [Hola'-ta miko].	E. side of Suwanee, between that and Santa Fe.
28. Talakhacha [Tȧlȧ hȧtci?].	Tullis Hajo [Hilis hadjo]	W. side of Cape Florida, on the seacoast.
29 [22]. Sohopikaliga [To-hopki lăgi, "Where sits a fort"].	Cho-kē-hip-kalana......	E. of the last town, 30 m.
30. Loksachumpa.........	Lok-po-ka, Sakoosa Hajo [Takusa Hadjo].	Head of St. John's River.
31. Ahapapka ["Place to eat potatoes"].	Ocheesetustanuka[Otcī'-si tȧstȧnȧgi].	Head of Okelawaha.
32. Apukasasoche........	Enehe-mathlochee (Hen-iha imałutci].	20 m. W. from the head of St. John's.
33. Yulaka [Wialaka, spring, or Yulaha, orange?].	Philip, or Emathla......	On the W. side of St. John's River, 35 m. from Volusia or Dexter.
34 [34]. Talahassee, or Spring Gardens.	Uchee Tustehuka, or Billy [Yutci tȧstȧnȧgi].	10 m. from Volusia.
35 Etanie	Checota Hajo...........	W. of St. John's, E. of Black Creek.
36. Tuslalahockaka........	Alac Hajo [Ahalak hadjo]	10 m. W. of Walalecooche.
37 [27]. Yalacasooche.....	Yelathaloke............	Mouth of Oklawaha.

Jackson Lewis gave me the name of one later Seminole town, Łanū'tci abā'la ("Across a little mountain"), which I have not been able to identify in the above lists.

With the Seminole war we have little to do. As an example of the possibilities of Indian warfare when opposed to European it has no parallel, having dragged through eight years, not including Jackson's first raid into northern Florida, and having cost the United States Government, it is estimated, $20,000,000, the lives of many thousand persons of both sexes, and enormous property losses besides. Mikonopi, who, as I have shown, represented the old Oconee element, was the theoretical head chief of the Indians during this contest, but the brains of native resistance were Osceola, an Indian from Tulsa, and Jumper, who is said to have come from the Upper Towns, but to have been the last survivor of "some ancient tribe." In spite of the prominence of these two Creeks, the Mikasuki and the other older elements as a whole took the most conspicuous parts in it. Although they were outnumbered, and in time nearly overwhelmed, by the later Creek refugees, to whom the popular but erroneous rendering of the term "Seminole," that of "runaways," would more particularly apply, the fact must be emphasized that the primacy in this war belonged to a non-Muskogee people who had in no way been concerned in the great Creek uprising, and that it was therefore at base a war with an entirely separate tribe.

We learn from the report of an Indian agent,[1] writing in 1846, that the year before, shortly after the removal of the Seminole to

[1] Ind. Affs. Rept. for 1846, p. 278.

the strip of Oklahoma later occupied by them, there were 27 "towns" or bands there which were in 1846 reduced to 25 by the death of two leaders, and the incorporation of their bands with others. The associations of the Creek elements in particular, in Florida, were so little sanctified by time and custom that they were easily destroyed, and progressively, with gradual losses in numbers, these 25 were still further cut down, until within the memory of the older people, only eight towns or neighborhoods supporting square grounds remained, and in 1912 these had been still further reduced to six. The Mikasuki preserve a ground near Seminole, Okla., and the Hitchiti had one near Keokuk Falls, which was given up many years ago. Of the remainder, one, located near Sasakwa, is called Łiwahali, and, as I have stated above, contains, besides persons from the Upper Creek town of that name, the descendants of those who once occupied Kan-hatki and Fus-hatchee. Eufaula may be assumed to represent the descendants of that old Seminole colony planted at Tcuko tcati. According to the people now constituting it, the only Indians other than Eufaula living there are Chiaha. The other square grounds are called Okfuskee, Chiaha, Talahasutci, and Otcisi. Okfuskee and Chiaha bear names of former Creek towns, but I learn that the appellations are quite conventional, although no doubt some of the individuals going by the name are actually descended from people belonging to the town which the name indicates. Talahasutci is probably the "Talahasochte" of Bartram. There are now no old people belonging to it, but the chief told me he thought it had broken away from Tulsa. On the other hand, some Creek informants insisted that it came either from Abihka or from Abihka through Pakan talahasi. As I have pointed out elsewhere, Pakan talahasi did not come from Abihka, and it is not likely that this town did either. If Hawkins is right in his description of the make-up of the Seminole population it would seem that originally it must have been either a Mikasuki town or a branch of Lower Eufaula.[1] Conclusive evidence is lacking. In Bartram's time the chief was known as the White King (Miko hȧtki).[2] Otcisi is a name not found among the regular town names of the Creeks proper. One of my oldest informants said that his mother explained it as derived from the custom of going out after hickory nuts (otci) with which to make oil. He thought the town was a branch of Eufaula hopai, but that into it had been gathered people from other places. Otcisi was, however, a name given by Hitchiti-speaking people to the Creeks, and in fact to any who used a language different from their own. Another informant, himself an Otcisi, said that

[1] See p. 400.

[2] Bartram, Travels, p. 224 et seq.

most of the inhabitants came from Hickory Ground, though a few were from Tälwå łåko. This is, perhaps, the most probable statement, since this man, Yonasi, was the oldest person belonging to that place. The name, as applied to a town, appears as early as 1800 in the diary of Manuel Garcia, a Spanish officer sent to receive the Apalachee fort from Bowles.[1]

But, as I have already said, the lack of permanence of most Seminole towns, and the frequent change of name which they underwent, has rendered it next to impossible to follow in any connected manner the history of more than a very few groups. At the same time the main outlines of Seminole history and the principal factors entering into it are quite evident. They were at base a portion of the Atsikhata or non-Muskogee people of southern Georgia, around whom had gathered a still more numerous body of refugee Muskogee. These latter obscured their original character to such an extent that its basal separateness was usually unrecognized, and ultimately the language of the invaders overwhelmed that of the original settlers. This fact lends coherence to several early statements like that of Swan that "the Seminoles are the original stock of the Creek, but their language has undergone so great a change that it is hardly understood by the Upper Creeks, or even by themselves in general. It is preserved by many old people, and taught by women to the children as a kind of religious duty; but as they grow to manhood, they forget and lose it by the more frequent use of the modern tongue."[2] Of course, Swan misunderstood the situation. The original Creek language of which he speaks was Mikasuki, which in his time was already being crowded out by Muskogee or Creek proper.

THE CHICKASAW

The Chickasaw have had a simple, readily traceable history since the time when they first appear in our documents, and although from the point of view of the historian proper they might be made the subject of a long memoir, a short sketch will satisfy my present purpose. Our first notice of them is in the De Soto narratives and there we learn that they then possessed those great warlike qualities for which they were afterwards noted. De Soto passed the winter of 1540–41, from about Christmas to March 4, in what appears to have been the principal Chickasaw town.[3] On the evening of March 3 the Spanish commander made a demand on the Chickasaw chief

[1] Archivo Nacional, Sevilla, copy in Edward E. Ayer Coll., Newberry Library.

[2] Swan in Schoolcraft, Ind. Tribes, v, p. 260.

[3] T. H. Lewis discusses the location of the Chickasaw towns which De Soto visited in the National Magazine, vol. 15, pp. 57–61, 1891–92, criticizing the earlier investigations of Claiborne. The last word has evidently not been said on this subject.

for carriers so that he could set out in the morning, but early on that very day the Indians suddenly fell upon the camp in four bands, got past the sentinels with fire concealed in little pots—after the manner of Gideon—set fire to the town, and attacked the Spaniards so unexpectedly that only two were able to mount their horses, most of which ran away or were killed. The men on foot were also in such confusion that, had the Indians been aware of their advantage and pressed it, the chroniclers testify that not a soul would have survived. As it was, mistaking the horses running wildly about for cavalry preparing to charge them, the Indians became frightened and fled. Next day the badly shattered European force moved to a smaller town a league away, where the Chickasaw chief himself usually lived. There they set up a forge with bellows of bear skins and began to manufacture new saddles and spears, and to retemper their weapons. Fortunately for them the Indians left them in peace until the new weapons had been completed, and eight days later, when they ventured an assault, they were easily beaten off.[1] The Chickasaw thus have the distinction of being the tribe which came nearest to putting an end to De Soto and his entire army, and the escape of the whites was due rather to a number of fortuitous and unexpected circumstances than to their own foresight or bravery. In the interest of history and ethnology we may consider ourselves fortunate that the disaster was averted.

Neither the expedition of De Luna nor that of Pardo reached this tribe, although the Napochies[2] with whom De Luna fought were probably, in part at least, identical with the Napissa, noted by Iberville in 1699 as having united with the Chickasaw.[3] Spanish documents of the seventeenth century again mention them, but they do not reemerge into clear light until the settlement of Carolina and Louisiana. Woodward, in the account of his Westo discovery, dated 1674, mentions Chickasaw in connection with the Kasihta and Chiska Indians.[4] English traders had reached the Mississippi by 1700 and their first settlements among the Chickasaw must have been made at the same period (see pl. 6). From then on the Chickasaw formed a base for the extension of British trade and British power, and they remained firmly attached to their English allies until the period of the American Revolution.

Shortly before 1715 the Chickasaw and Cherokee drove the Shawnee Indians from their long-established settlements on Cumberland River.[5] In 1745 a band of Shawnee returned to this region but were

[1] Bourne, Narr. of De Soto, I, pp. 100–108; II, pp. 22–24, 131–135.
[2] See pp. 231–240.
[3] Margry, Déc., IV, pp. 164, 180, 184.
[4] S. Car. Hist. Soc. Colls., V, p. 461; and p. 307.
[5] Hanna, The Wilderness Trail, I, p. 131.

shortly afterwards driven out and retired among the Creeks.[1] Haywood thus records the Chickasaw tradition regarding the event:

> The Chickasaws formerly claimed for their nation, exclusively, all the lands north of the Tennessee, and they have denied that the Cherokees were joined with them in the war against the Shawnees when they were driven from their settlements in Cumberland. They said that the Shawnees first came up the Tennessee in canoes, and thence up Bear Creek thirty miles; and there left their canoes, and came to war with the Chickasaws, and killed several of their nation. The Chickasaw chiefs and warriors embodied and drove them off. From thence they went to the Creeks, and lived with them for some time. They then returned and crossed at the Chickasaw Old Field, above the Muscle Shoals. From thence they went to Duck River and the Cumberland River, and settled there; and the Chickasaws discovered their settlements. Two of the chiefs of the Chickasaws who were in those days their principal leaders—the one named Opoia Matehah and the other Pinskey Matehah—raised their warriors and went against the Shawnees, and defeated them and took all their horses and brought them into the nation. The Cherokees, they said, had no share in the conquest, and that they drove the Shawnees themselves, without any assistance from any red people.

Haywood adds that "this information is contained in a public document of the nation, signed by Chenobee, the king, Maj. George Colbert, and others." [2]

This is part of a brief against the claims of the Cherokee to land north of the Tennessee and must be interpreted in the light of that fact, nor must too much confidence be placed in the particular narrative given, since the mythizing tendency always lays hold of such events, and, moreover, events belonging to several different years may be crowded together to set off one main fact.

French writers hold the Chickasaw, or the British traders through them, responsible in large part for the Natchez uprising of 1729, and from what Adair tells us there was evidently ground for the accusation.[3] At any rate, after the Natchez had been defeated and driven away by the Louisiana French, the latter turned their attention to the Chickasaw as allies of those implacable foes, and Bienville undertook to crush them by two simultaneous movements against their towns, from the north and south. The movements were not synchronized, however, and resulted in utter failure. D'Artaguette led 140 whites and about 300 Indians from his post on the Illinois, but between the Mississippi River and the Chickasaw country they were set upon by Indians and their English allies at the town of Hashuk humma,[4] their leader and a few others were captured and burned to death, and the rest of the force killed or dispersed. The army approaching from the south consisted of 500 French and numerous Choctaw allies. They attacked one of the palisaded villages of the Chickasaw, but were repulsed with heavy loss and retreated to Mobile. The Chickasaw on their side are said to have had 60 killed,

---

[1] Hanna, Wilderness Trail, II, p. 241.

[2] Haywood, Hist. of Tenn., p. 426.

[3] Adair, Hist. Am. Inds., pp. 353-354.

[4] Warren in Pub. Miss. Hist. Soc., VIII, p. 550.

but felt this so keenly that according to Andrews, a Cherokee trader, they "had quitted their lands and were drawn near to the Creeks, who received them kindly." This, however, may refer to the Natchez, because the bulk of the Chickasaw certainly remained in the same situation. Under date of June 15, 1738, the above trader informed William Stephens that the Choctaw and French had fallen out, and this news determined some Chickasaw who had come to Carolina to return.[1]

To retrieve the disaster he had suffered, Bienville, in 1740, collected a huge army on the Mississippi with which he hoped to deal his enemy a crushing blow, but, being unable adequately to provision such a force, the greater part was soon obliged to disband. A small expedition, under the Canadian Céloron, moved on toward the Chickasaw, who, believing it to be the advance guard of that huge host they had seen assembling against them, entered into a peace agreement, the terms of which on the surface were decidedly favorable to the French. Nevertheless, the Chickasaw recovered their courage as soon as the expedition had dissolved, the treaty became a dead letter, and the Indians were soon raiding French posts and intercepting canoes on the Mississippi as formerly. These wars were not undertaken without great losses on their part. Adair, who was with them in the forties, thus describes the manner in which their numbers had become reduced:

> The Chikkasah in the year 1720, had four large contiguous settlements, which lay nearly in the form of three parts of a square, only that the eastern side was five miles shorter than the western with the open part toward the Choktah. One was called *Yaneka*, about a mile wide and six miles long, at the distance of twelve miles from their present towns. Another was ten computed miles long, at the like distance from their present settlements, and from one to two miles broad. The towns were called *Shatara*, *Chookheereso*, *Hykehah*, *Tuskawillao*, and *Phalacheho*. The other square was single, began three miles from their present place of residence, and ran four miles in length, and one mile in breadth. This was called *Chookka Pharàah*, or "the long house." It was more populous than their whole nation contains at present. The remains of this once formidable people make up the northern angle of that broken square. They now scarcely consist of four hundred and fifty warriors, and are settled three miles westward from the deep creek, in a clear tract of rich land, about three miles square, running afterwards about five miles towards the N. W. where the old fields are usually a mile broad. The superior number of their enemies forced them to take into this narrow circle, for social defence; and to build their towns on commanding ground, at such a convenient distance from one another as to have their enemies, when attacked, between two fires.[2]

From the estimates of Chickasaw population given in even very early times it would seem that this decrease was not as great as Adair supposes; the matter will be taken up in another place.

Besides the towns above enumerated one or two additional Chickasaw settlements are to be mentioned. Adair speaks of a town occu-

[1] Ga. Col. Docs., IV, pp. 134, 156.

[2] Adair, Hist. Am. Inds., pp. 352, 353.

pied by them "in the upper or most western part of the Muskohge country, about 300 miles eastward of their own nation," which was known as "Ooe-ása," the latter half of the word evidently from Chickasaw *a^n^sha*, to settle, to stay.[1] This can not have lasted long, as we find David Taitt, in a letter written at Tukabachee, March 16, 1772, saying:

About Thirteen Chickasaws were at the Abicouchies lately wanting to settle in this Nation: the Head man of the Town gave them leave to settle the Ground they formerly possessed on Condition of their Continuing in this Land, they returned to their own lands and it is uncertain whether they come back.[2]

The settlement must have been attempted, however, because 11 days later he met the very same number of Chickasaw in the Natchez town, and he says of them:

These Chickasaws are making a Settlement on the side of a Creek called Caimulga, about 15 miles north from this, and falling into the Coosa River at the Chickasaw Trading path, about a mile above Clamahumgey.[3]

As a "Kiamulgatown" appears in the roll of towns taken just before the removal it is possible that these Chickasaw continued to occupy it until then, but it is more likely that they had been displaced by Creeks, or perhaps Shawnee.[4]

Another Chickasaw settlement was made at a very early date near New Windsor on the South Carolina side of Savannah River. This was not later than the third decade of the eighteenth century, for in 1737, when they moved over to the newly established post of Augusta, Georgia, it is said that they had been located at the former place "for some time past."[5] A Chickasaw band continued near Augusta probably down to the period of the American Revolution. The chief of the band in 1737 was named the "Squirrel King."[5]

In June, 1755, we find reference to 35 Chickasaw Indians "that usually reside about Augusta;"[6] and under date of November 27, 1760, the same records speak of Chickasaw settled at New Savannah, about 12 miles from Augusta.[7] In 1795 the tribe laid claim to land opposite Augusta on the basis of this early settlement, and a memorial was sent to the United States Government to substantiate it,[8] but it was probably not occupied after the Revolution. The later history of the Savannah band is thus given by Hawkins, quoting Tåsikaia miko, a Kasihta chief. It contains an interesting hint regarding the past history of the people under consideration.

---

[1] Adair, Hist. Am. Inds., p. 54. Mr. Halbert interprets it very plausibly as *wiha a^n^sha*, "home of emigrants," and identifies it with the Breed Camp mentioned in the census of 1761, perhaps because the Chickasaw Indians are known to have been called "the breed."

[2] Mereness, Trav. in Amer. Col., pp. 525–526.

[3] Ibid., pp. 531–532.

[4] See p. 319.

[5] Ga. Col. Rec., IV, p. 47.

[6] Ibid., VII, p. 206.

[7] Ibid., VIII, p. 433.

[8] Ramsey, Ann. of Tenn., p. 81.

Cussetuh and Chickasaw consider themselves as people of one fire (tote-kit-cau humgoce) from the earliest account of their origin. Cussetuh appointed the first Micco for them, directed him to sit down in the big Savanna, where they now are, and govern them. Some of the Chickasaws straggled off and settled near Augusta, from whence they returned and sat down near Cussetuh, and thence back to their nation. Cussetuh and Chickasaw have remained friends ever since their first acquaintance.[1]

Hawkins adds that on account of this friendship the Kasihta town refused to take part in the war between the Creeks and Chickasaw in 1795.[1] As Hawkins wrote in 1799 it appears that this band of Chickasaw had rejoined their own people by that date.

Still another outsettlement was on the lower course of the Tennessee River, where it is mentioned by Coxe [2] and some other very early writers, but it was soon abandoned for the main settlements. In comparatively late times a small body settled temporarily on the Ohio.

In 1752 and 1753 the Chickasaw defeated MM. Benoist and Reggio.[3] Under date of August, 1754, the Colonial Documents of Georgia inform us that the Chickasaw had been twice attacked, evidently referring to these expeditions, and reported that they could not stand a third assault without help.[4] Aid was in consequence sent to them. A little later war broke out with the Cherokee and terminated about 1768 with a decisive Chickasaw victory on the Chickasaw old fields.[5]

During this period they were harassed more by the Choctaw and other French Indians than by the French, and their numbers fell off greatly in consequence. Romans, who visited their towns in 1771, compares them with the Choctaw rather to their own disadvantage. He says that the Chickasaw towns, or "town" as he chooses to call it, "they divide into seven by the names of *Melattaw* (i. e., hat and feather); *Chatelaw* (i. e., copper town); *Chukafalaya* (i. e., long town); *Hikihaw* (i. e., stand still); *Chucalissa* (i. e., great town);[6] *Tuckahaw* (i. e., a certain weed); and *Ashuck hooma* (i. e., red grass); This was formerly inclosed in palisadoes, and thus well fortified against the attacks of small arms, but now it lays open."[7] He says that the traders nicknamed this tribe "the breed," presumably on account of the extent to which it had intermixed with others and with the whites. He himself declares that there were only two genuine Chickasaw of the old stock living—one a man named Northwest.

The fidelity which this tribe had displayed with but individual exceptions toward the English was afterwards transferred to the Americans, and few disputes arose between the two peoples. In 1786 official relations with the United States Government began

[1] Hawkins, Ga. Hist. Soc. Colls., III, p. 83.
[2] French, Hist. Colls. La., 1850, p. 229.
[3] Romans, Concise Nat. Hist. E. and W. Fla., p. 59.
[4] Ga. Col. Rec., VI, pp. 448–450.
[5] Haywood, Hist. of Tenn., pp. 446–462.
[6] The translation is wrong. It means "town deserted."
[7] Romans, op. cit., p. 63.

when, by the Hopewell treaty, their northern boundary was placed at the Ohio.[1] In 1793–1795 war broke out with the Creeks, who invaded the Chickasaw country to the number of 1,000. Here they attacked a small stockade. They were met by a mere handful of Chickasaw, but an unaccountable panic seized the invaders, who fled precipitately. This victory was won by a body of about 200 Chickasaw. Soon afterwards peace was made.[2]

Although they were at peace with the white settlers, the latter after this time began to press steadily in upon the Chickasaw, who, by a treaty signed July 23, 1805, made their first cession of territory to the United States Government. Further cessions were made September 14, 1816, October 19, 1818, and October 20, 1832. By the provisions of the treaty signed on the date last mentioned they yielded up their right to all of their lands to the east of the Mississippi [3] and accepted new homes in the territory now included in the State of Oklahoma. The actual migration began in 1822, ten years before the treaty was signed, and extended to 1838. Together with the Choctaw they occupied what is now the southeastern part of this State between the Arkansas and Canadian Rivers on the north and the Red River on the south. The two tribes mingled together rather indiscriminately at first, but were separated in 1855, the Chickasaw being assigned the westernmost part of the above area. Here a national government was established after the pattern of those of the Choctaw and the other "civilized tribes," and this lasted until the nation merged into the State of Oklahoma, of which the Chickasaw are now citizens.

THE CHOCTAW

The present work has been undertaken primarily with the object of furnishing an adequate setting for an understanding of the evolution of the Creek Confederacy and the various elements entering into it. What has been said regarding the South Carolina and Florida tribes and the Chickasaw have marginal importance in the carrying out of this purpose, though they are of less absolute concern. When we come to the Choctaw, however, we are met with a different problem. The Choctaw were always one of the largest southern tribes, and they were more numerous than the Creeks even in the palmiest days of the latter. Although of the same linguistic stock, their customs, social organization, and even their physical characteristics were very different. They never seem to have been on a footing of friendship with the Creeks, and in fact fought them on equal terms during a long period. So far as our acquaintance with them extends they appear to have been a relatively homogeneous

[1] Eighteenth Ann. Rept. Bur. Amer. Ethn., part 2, p. 650.
[2] Haywood, Hist. Tenn., p. 461; also Stiggins's MS.
[3] See Eighteenth Ann. Rept. Bur. Amer. Ethn., part 2.

people, whose history lacks the complication of that of most of the tribes so far considered. While it is capable of extended treatment, for our present purpose a few words will tell all about it that we need to know. It is probable that the Apafalaya chief and river spoken of by Ranjel and the Pafallaya province of Elvas,[1] refer to the Choctaw, or to some of them, since Adair informs us that "Long Hairs," (Pa^{n}s-falaya) was a name given to the Choctaw by their neighbors.[2] We do not hear of the tribe again until late in the seventeenth century, when they occupied the region in the southeastern part of the present State of Mississippi and the southwestern part of Alabama, which they held until their removal to Oklahoma in the fourth decade of the nineteenth century. A small portion of them have remained in their old country to the present day, while a few are to be found in Louisiana.

POPULATION OF THE SOUTHEASTERN TRIBES

The population of an Indian tribe at any early period in its history can not be determined with exactness. In the case of the Creeks we have to consider not only the Muskogee or Creeks proper, but a number of tribes afterwards permanently or temporarily incorporated with them, and the problem is proportionately complicated. Fortunately we are helped out by a considerable number of censuses, some of which were taken with more than usual care.

The Cusabo tribes were always small, even at the time of their first intercourse with the Spaniards and French, but we have no data regarding their population until the year 1715, just before the outbreak of the Yamasee war, when a careful estimate approaching an actual enumeration as closely as was possible at that time was made under the auspices of Governor Johnson of South Carolina. There were then two bands left belonging to this group. The "Corsaboys" (i. e., the Cusabo proper) are credited with five villages, 95 men, and a total population of 295, while the Itwans of Charleston Entrance had but one village, with 80 men, and a total population of 240.[3] The entire population of this group was therefore 535, and they are already described as "mixed with the English settlement." The Yamasee war depleted their numbers considerably. Most of them probably remained in the same place, where they progressively declined and disappeared, though a few retired among the inland Indians. The Coosa are not separately enumerated in this list, and it is uncertain whether they were omitted or are included among the Cusabo. According to Adair some of them later joined the Catawba, but probably not all.[4]

---

[1] Bourne, Narr. of De Soto, I, p. 99; II, pp. 129–130.

[2] Adair, Hist. Am. Inds., p. 192.

[3] S. Car. MS. Docs. at Columbia; also Rivers, Chap. in Early Hist. S. Car., p. 94.

[4] Adair, Hist. Am. Inds., p. 225.

The province of Guale, between Savannah River and St. Andrews Sound, was evidently very populous in early Spanish times; but Barcia represents the number of Indians there to have been considerably reduced as a result of the first uprising against the missionaries at the end of the sixteenth century.[1] In 1602 the missionaries claimed that there were "more than 1,200 Christians" in Guale. In 1670 Owen estimated that there were about 300 Indians under the priest at St. Catherines, and that the Indians under all of the priests upon that coast would total 700.[2] Among these may be included a few Timucua, but most were Guale Indians and Yamasee. The figures refer merely to the number of effective men, not to the total population. After these Indians had settled in South Carolina under the leadership of the Yamasee they occupied 10 towns which in 1708 were estimated to contain 500 men able to bear arms,[3] and in 1715, just before the Yamasee uprising, they were reported to have 413 men and a total population of 1,215.[4] The war which followed sadly depleted them and their losses continued after they had retired to Florida, whither they were pursued by the English and with still more effect by the Creeks. Almost immediately after they had been driven out of Carolina the English settlers learned that one of their chiefs had been made by the Spaniards general in chief over 500 Indians to be sent against Carolina, but of course only a fraction of these were Yamasee.[5] By this time they had probably become completely merged with the Indians of Guale. In 1719 a captive reported only 60 Yamasee near St. Augustine.[6] In 1728 and 1736 we have from Spanish sources detailed statements of the population of all the Indian towns near St. Augustine,[7] and these agree very closely, although a disastrous British raid had taken place between them. The first mentions seven settlements with an aggregate population of 115 to 125 men, 105 women, and upward of 55 children, the number of children in two towns not being given. The second list gives eight towns with 123 men capable of bearing arms and 295 women and children, a total of 418. Fifty or more belonged to the Timucua town and there are two or three Apalachee, but upward of 360 must have been Yamasee or Indians of Guale. While this figure is considerably higher than the total indicated in the earlier list the numbers of men reported in both agree quite closely and there is reason to think that in the earlier the numbers of children, and probably those of the women also, were considerably underestimated. In 1761 Yamasee numbering 20 men were reported living near St. Augustine,[8] but we know that several bodies were settled elsewhere. Some

---

[1] Barcia, La Florida, pp. 170–172.

[2] S. Car. Hist. Soc. Colls., v, p. 198.

[3] Pub. Rec. of S. C., MS., v, pp. 207–209.

[4] S. C. MS. Docs. at Columbia.

[5] Pub. Rec. of S. C., MS., VII, p. 186.

[6] Ibid., VIII, p. 7.

[7] See pp. 105–106, 304.

[8] A Descr. of S. C., etc., 1761, p. 63.

of them constituted the village of Yamacraw with which Oglethorpe had to deal. In Adair's time a few were with the Catawba.[1] In 1821 the "Emusas" on Chattahoochee River, whom I believe to have been descendants of the Yamasee, numbered 20 souls.[2]

It is evident that the Apalachee were a large tribe at the very earliest period, but they certainly did not number 15,000, 16,000, 30,000, or 34,000, as estimated by various Spanish missionaries.[3] Much more probable is the statement in a memorial, dated 1676, to the effect that there were then 5,000.[4] In 1702 we find it stated that Spaniards planned to fall upon the English settlements at the head of 900 Apalachee Indians.[5] From Moore's report on his destruction of the Apalachee towns in the winter of 1703–04 it appears that he and his Indian allies killed about 400 Apalachee and brought away 1,400.[6] Two towns and part of another did not come with him. He expected some of them to follow, but they fled for the most part to Mobile to place themselves under the protection of the French.[7] Bienville states that these originally numbered 500 men but by 1725 or 1726 had become reduced to 100,[8] partly from natural causes, partly through removal to Pensacola. In 1708 the Apalachee who had been carried off by the Carolinians and settled on Savannah River numbered about 250 men.[9] The census of 1715 gives their population more accurately as 275 men and 638 souls in four villages.[10] A French manuscript of a little later period estimates 600 men.[11] After the Yamasee war all of these seem to have returned to Florida, and in 1718 they started a town near Pensacola, where it is said that more than 100 settled, and they increased every day afterwards, partly from the Apalachee who had been living near Mobile.[12] According to Governor De la Vega the Apalachee in their old country had in 1728 become reduced to two villages, one of 140 persons, the other of 20.[13] In 1758 De Kerlerec gives the number of their warriors as 30, probably including both the Spanish and the French bands.[14] In 1764, after the cession of Mobile to Great Britain, the Apalachee, along with several other tribes, moved over into Louisiana and settled on Red River. In 1806 we learn from Sibley that they counted but 14 men.[15] Whether this band embraced both the Mobile and Florida Apalachee is uncertain, but probably all went together. Morse reported 150 in Louisiana in 1817, a very considerable overestimate.[16]

---

1 Adair, Hist. Am. Inds., p. 225.

2 Morse, Rept. on Ind. Affairs, p. 364.

3 See p. 118.

4 Lowery, MSS.

5 Carroll, Hist. Colls. S. C., II, p. 351.

6 See pp. 121-123.

7 See p. 123.

8 Copy of MS. in Lib. Cong.

9 Pub. Rec. of S. C., Ms., v, pp. 207–209.

10 Ibid.; also Rivers, A Chapter in the Early Hist. of S. C., p. 94.

11 Copy of MS. in Lib. Cong.

12 Barcia, La Florida, p. 341.

13 See p. 127.

14 Compte Rendu, XV sess. Internat. Cong. Am., I, p. 86.

15 Sibley, Annals of Cong., 9th Cong., 2d sess., 1085.

16 Morse, Rept. to the Sec. of War, p. 373.

Only one or two Indians of Apalachee blood are now known to be in existence in Louisiana and Texas. There are a very few among the Alabama in Oklahoma.

We have no estimate of the number of Apalachicola Indians until they were removed to the Savannah. In 1708 the number of their men was 80.[1] In the census of 1715 they are credited with 2 villages, 64 men, and 214 souls.[2] After the Yamasee war they settled upon Chattahoochee River, at first all in one town. Later several bands left, most of them going south into Florida. By the census of 1738,[3] and the French census of 1760,[4] those that remained were credited with 60 men, by the French estimate of 1750 with more than 30,[3] by the English census of 1761 with 20,[5] by the Georgia census of 1792 with 100, including the Chiaha (p. 435), and in the census of 1832 with 2 settlements and 239 persons besides 7 slaves.[6] The census of 1738 gives, however, what is probably another band of Apalachicola Indians under the name of their chief, Cherokee leechee, and credits them with 45 men.[7] At the present time there are only a few left, living near Okmulgee, Oklahoma.

The Franciscan missionaries reported 300 conversions among the Chatot in 1674. When they settled near Mobile Bienville states that they could muster 250 men, but in 1725–26 they had become reduced to 40 men.[8] Du Pratz says this tribe occupied about 40 cabins, circa 1730.[9] In 1806, after their removal to Louisiana, they numbered 30 men.[10] In 1817 there were, all told, according to Morse, 240,[11] a figure much too large. They have now disappeared, unless they are represented by some band of Choctaw and their name concealed by that of the larger tribe.

No separate enumeration of the Tawasa and Pawokti is available, except in the census of 1760, which returns about 40 Tawasa[12] men, the Georgia census of 1792, which reports about 60, and the 1832 census, where, including Autauga, 321 are given, with 21 negro slaves.[13] It is probable, however, that this last includes all of the Alabama at that time remaining in the Creek Nation.

The Sawokli united with the Lower Creeks. In 1738 the Spaniards estimated the number of their men at 20.[14] In 1750, however, four Sawokli settlements appear to be named with more than 50 men[14] and in 1760 four with a total of 190.[15] The Tamałi are perhaps

[1] Pub. Rec. of S. C., MS., pp. 207–209.
[2] Rivers, Chap. in Early Hist. S. C., p. 94.
[3] Copy of MS. in Ayer Coll., Newberry Lib.
[4] Miss. Prov. Arch., I, p. 96.
[5] Ga. Col. Rec., VIII, p. 522.
[6] Sen. Doc. 512, 23d Cong., 1st sess., pp. 345–347.
[7] Copy of MS. in Ayer Coll., Newberry Lib.
[8] Copy of MS. in Lib. Cong.
[9] Du Pratz, Hist. de la Louisiane, II, pp. 212–213.
[10] Sibley, Annals of Cong., 9th Cong., 2d sess., 1087.
[11] Morse, Rept. to the Sec. of War, p. 373.
[12] Miss. Prov. Arch., I, pp. 94–95.
[13] Sen. Doc. 512, 23d Cong., 1st sess., IV, pp. 258–260.
[14] MS., Ayer Coll.
[15] Miss. Prov. Arch., I, p. 96.

included in this last census. In 1761 they and the neighboring villages, probably of the same connection, were estimated to contain only 50 hunters.[1] Hawkins says that Sawoklutci contained 20 families, but gives no figures for Sawokli itself.[2] Young (1821) gives a town called Ehawho-ka-les, apparently intended for Sawokli, having 150 inhabitants.[4] He gives 580 in Okitiyagana.[3] The census of 1832 gives 187 Sawokli, besides 42 slaves, 157 in its branch town, Okawaigi, and 106 in another branch, Hatcheetcaba.[4] The few still living are about Okmulgee, Oklahoma.

The Pensacola Indians were so insignificant in historic times that Bienville, writing in 1725 or 1726, says there were not more than 40 men in their village and that of the neighboring Biloxi together.[5] In 1764 John Stuart places them in one group with the Biloxi, Chatot, Capinans, Washa, Chawasha, and Pascagoula, and allows them all but 241 men.[6]

From the De Soto narratives we know that the Mobile Indians were once a powerful people. The numbers lost by them when the Spaniards stormed their town—2,500 according to Elvas, over 3,000 according to Ranjel—at once testify to this fact and to the terrible blow they then suffered.[7] In 1702, when Iberville was in the Pascagoula village on the river of the same name, he was given to understand that the Mobile tribe had 300 warriors and the Tohome as many more, but two years later he visited them himself and estimated that both together comprised only about 350.[8] Du Pratz, about 1730, says that the Tohome were of approximately the same size as the Chatot, which he estimates to include about 40 cabins, but he gives nothing with reference to the population of the Mobile.[9] In 1758 De Kerlerec estimates the Mobile Tohome and Naniaba at about 100 warriors.[10]

In 1725–26 Bienville states that the Mobile numbered only 60 men, the Big Tohome 60, and the Little Tohome—probably identical with the Naniaba—30, and he adds that within his own remembrance the former had counted 500 and the latter 300.[11] This is difficult to reconcile with the statements made by his brother. Regis de Rouillet, in 1730, gives the number of warriors as 30, 60, and 50, respectively, making the Mobile the smallest of the three.[11]

---

[1] Ga. Col. Rec., VIII, p. 522.
[2] Hawkins in Ga. Hist. Soc. Colls., III, p. 66.
[3] Morse, Rept. to Sec. of War., p. 364.
[4] Sen. Doc. 512, 23d Cong., 1st sess., IV, pp. 342–344.
[5] Copy of MS. in Lib. Cong.
[6] Am. Hist. Rev., XX, p. 825.
[7] Bourne, Narr. of De Soto, I, p. 97; II, p. 128.
[8] Margry, Déc., IV, pp. 427, 514.
[9] Du Pratz, Hist. Louisiane, II, p. 213.
[10] Compte Rendu Int. Cong. Amér., 1906, I, p. 85.
[11] MS., Lib. Cong.

As we have seen, there were two distinct bands of Chiaha, one on the Tennessee and one originally near the Yamasee, later among the Lower Creeks. The first are scarcely heard of after De Soto's time until we come to the census of 1832, which mentions two towns, one of 126 and the other of 306 Indians.[1] These may have been descendants of this northern body, or a later settlement from the other Creek towns. The second body is said to have numbered 120 men in 1738,[2] 160 in 1760, and in 1761, as has already been said, together with the Osochi and Okmulgee, 120 hunters.[3] In 1792 they and the Apalachicola together were reputed to have 100 gunmen (p. 435). Hawkins states that the Chiaha and Osochi branch settlement of Hotalgihuyana contained 20 families in 1799.[4] Young (1821) enumerates 670 Chiaha proper and 210 Hotalgihuyana Indians.[5] According to the census of 1832 the Chiaha and Hotalgihuyana counted 427 Indians and 70 slaves.[6]

The enumeration of 1750 estimates the number of Osochi men at 30, but that of 1760 has 50.[7] In the English census of 1761 they and the Chiaha and Okmulgee are given together 120 men,[8] in 1792 they appear alone credited with 50 men (p. 434), while in the American census taken in 1832 are two Osochi towns with an aggregate Indian population of 539.[9]

In 1738 we find the number of Hitchiti men placed at 60,[2] in 1750 at only 15,[2] and in 1760 at 50.[10] In 1761 it was estimated that they had 40 hunters,[11] and in 1772 Taitt says there were "about 90 gunmen."[12] Young gives the population of the Fowl Towns, occupied largely by Hitchiti Indians, as 300 in 1821.[13] In 1832 they are credited, including a branch village, with a population of 381, besides 20 negro slaves.[14] Though still fairly numerous they are more or less confounded with other groups speaking a similar language.

The Okmulgee are enumerated first in 1750, when they are credited with more than 20 men, and the census of 1760 gives them 30 men.[10] In 1761 they are said to have had, together with the Chiaha and Osochi, 120 hunters.[11] Hawkins does not give their numbers, but

---

1 Sen. Doc. 512, 23d Cong., 1st sess., IV, pp. 307–309.

2 MS., Ayer Coll.

3 Miss. Prov. Arch., I, p. 96; Ga. Col. Docs., VIII, p. 522.

4 Hawkins in Ga. Hist. Soc. Colls., III, p. 64.

5 Page 409; Morse, Rept. to Sec. of War, p. 364.

6 Sen. Doc. 512, pp. 350–352.

7 MS., Ayer Coll.; Miss. Prov. Arch., I, p. 96.

8 Ga. Col. Docs., VIII, p. 522.

10 Sen. Doc. 512, 23d Cong., 1st sess., IV, p. 512.

11 Miss. Prov. Arch., op. cit.

12 Ga. Col. Docs., op. cit.

13 Trav. in Am. Col., p. 548.

14 Morse, op. cit.

15 Sen. Doc. 512, pp. 347–350.

Morse in 1822 says, on the authority of Young, that there were 220 in all.[1] They may be one of the two Osochi towns in the list of 1832 which number almost alike.[2] The omission of their name is strange since, after the removal to Oklahoma, they constituted a very important town.

In 1738, 50 men are given as belonging to the Oconee, in 1750, 30 men,[3] and in 1760, 50 men.[4] In 1761 we find "Oconees big and little" given with 50 hunters.[5] There were evidently fewer in Hawkins's time, but meanwhile many of them had gone to Florida.

The Spanish census of 1738 includes two Tamałi towns—old Tamałi (Tamaxle el viejo) and new Tamałi (Tamaxle nuevo), the first with 12 men, the second with 26.[6] The latter, however, was probably in the main a Sawokli settlement.[7] The French estimate of 1750 mentions only one town of 10 men.[3]. No further reference to the population of this town appears until we come to Young's enumeration of the Seminole towns included in Morse's report, where the total population appears as 220.[8]

The only references bearing on the population of the Tamahita tribe are in the census list of 1750, where the "Tamaita" among the Lower Creeks are set down as having more than 18 men,[3] and in that of 1761 where the "Coosawtee including Tomhetaws" are credited with 125 hunters.[9] But see pp. 188–191.

In 1702 Iberville estimated that the Alabama Indians consisted of 400 families in two villages.[10] This enumeration would, of course, not include the Tawasa, nor probably the Pawokti, but, on the other hand, may have embraced some Koasati. The same limitations would probably apply to the figures in the Carolina census of 1715, in which we find them given four villages, 214 men, and a total population of 770.[11] According to a French manuscript of the third decade of the same century there were then 6 Alabama towns and 400 men.[12] The estimate of 1750 seems to mention only two Alabama towns with 15 and 40 men, respectively. De Kerlerec places the number of Alabama warriors at 1,000 in 1758, but he includes the Talapoosa Indians and Abihka, therefore his figure is of no value.[13] The census of 1760 gives about 40 Tawasa men and 50 Mugulasha, while a town which perhaps corresponds to Okchaiutci contained 100 men.[14] The census of 1761 gives 30 hunters for Muklasa, 20 for Okchaiutci, and 70 for Wetumpka and "Red Ground," the second of which was probably also an Alabama settlement, but there is no

---

1 Morse, op. cit.
2 Sen. Doc. 512, pp. 353–356.
3 MSS., Ayer Coll.
4 Miss. Prov. Arch., op. cit.
5 Ga. Col. Docs., op. cit.
6 Copy of MSS., Ayer Coll.
7 See p. 143.
8 See p. 409.
9 Ga. Col. Docs., VIII, p. 524.
10 Margry, Déc., IV, p. 514.
11 Rivers, Chap. Early Hist. S. C., p. 94.
12 MS., Lib. Cong.
13 Compte Rendu, Int. Cong. Am., XV sess., I, p. 83.
14 Miss Prov. Arch., I, p. 94.

reference to Pawokti, Tawasa, or Autauga, though at this time they must have been among the Upper Creeks.[1] Henry Bouquet in 1764 gives 6,000 warriors[!],[2] and Marbury in 1792 has 60 Alabama Indians, 40 Okchaiutci, 30 Muklasa, and apparently 60 Tawasa (including Red Ground), though his spelling renders this uncertain. Hawkins in 1799 estimated the Alabama proper—Tawasa, Pawokti, and Autauga—to comprise about 80 gun men, but he does not give the number of those in Okchaiutci or Muklasa.[3] Stiggins places the number of Alabama in 1814 at 2,000, which is excessive.[4] In 1832 the Alabama are represented only by Tawasa and Autauga with a combined population of 321 and 21 slaves.[5] This was after the separation of those Alabama who went to Louisiana and Texas. In 1806 Sibley states that there were two Alabama villages in Louisiana, one containing about 30, the other about 40 men.[6] According to Morse, in 1817, there were 160 Alabama, all told, in Texas, but he probably overlooked some bands.[7]

In 1882 the United States Indian Office reported, or rather estimated, 290 "Alabama, Kushatta, and Muskogee" in the State of Texas,[8] and the same figure is repeated without variation in every subsequent report until 1901, when 470 are given on the authority of the census of 1900.[9] This figure is repeated until 1911. In 1910 a special agent was sent to these people from the Indian Office to inquire into their condition and make an enumeration of them, but his instructions did not cover the Koasati Indians, who were consequently ignored. The number of Alabama was found to be 192; the Koasati were estimated along with some Seminole, Isleta, and other Indians in different parts of the State.[10] These figures were repeated in the Indian Office Reports for 1912, 1913, and 1914. The census of 1910 returned 187 Alabama in Texas and 111 in Louisiana—a total of 298.[11] The number of those in Oklahoma is small, but there are enough to maintain a square ground. No separate enumeration of them has been made, so far as I am aware.

By the earliest writers the Koasati were probably included among the Alabama. The first independent enumeration of them is in the estimate of 1750, which gives 50 men. That of 1760 gives 150 men.[12]

---

[1] Ga. Col. Docs., VIII, pp. 523–524.
[2] Schoolcraft, Ind. Tribes, III, p. 559.
[3] Ga. Hist. Soc. Colls., III, p. 37.
[4] Stiggins, MS.
[5] Sen. Doc. 512, 23d Cong., 1st sess., IV, pp. 258–260.
[6] Ann. of Cong., 9th Cong., 2d sess., 1085.
[7] Morse, Rept. to Sec. of War, p. 373.
[8] Rept. Comm. Ind. Aff. for 1882 p. 340.
[9] Ibid., 1901, p. 702.
[10] Ibid., 1911, p. 67.
[11] Ind. pop. of the U. S., census of 1910, p. 17.
[12] MS., Ayer Coll.; Miss. Prov. Arch., I, p. 94.

In the census of 1761 they and the Tamahita together are reported as having had 125 hunters.[1] At least 100 of these were undoubtedly Koasati. Taitt, writing in 1772, reports 40 "Alibamons" here.[2] He probably means 40 gunmen. In 1792 Marbury credits them with 130 men (see p. 437). About 1793 some of them began to move to Louisiana and others followed from time to time. Those that were left in 1832 numbered 82 according to the census of that year.[3] In 1806 Sibley states that the Koasati in Louisiana supposed the number of men in all their settlements there to reach 200.[4] Schermerhorn estimates their number on the Sabine in 1814 at 600.[5] Morse, in 1817, gives 350 on Red River, 50 on the Neches 40 miles above its mouth, and 240 on the Trinity, a total of 640 men, women, and children.[6] In 1829 Porter gives 180 Koasati.[7] Bollaert in 1850 estimated the number of warriors among the Koasati on the lower Trinity alone at 500 in two villages.[8] After 1882 they were enumerated by the Indian Office along with the Alabama as given above. In 1910 11 were with the Alabama in Texas, 85 in Louisiana, and 2 in Nebraska—a total of 98.[9] A few more are in Oklahoma.

There were two branches of the Tuskegee, one of which united with the Cherokee. The latter was probably small and I have no data regarding it. The other is set down in the census of 1750 as containing 10 men, in that of 1760 as containing 50 men,[10] and in that of 1761 as containing, along with "Coosaw old town," 40 hunters.[11] Taitt, in 1772, gives about 25 gunmen,[12] as does Marbury in 1792 (p. 437). In 1799 Hawkins says they had 35 gunmen.[13] The census of 1832 returned 216 Indians and 35 slaves.[14]

The Spanish census of 1738 gives 111 men in Kasihta,[15] the French census of 1750 more than 80,[15] and that of 1760, 150,[16] while that of 1761 places the number of hunters belonging to it at 100.[17] With this Taitt (1772) agrees,[18] but Marbury (1792) raises it, counting in the villages, to 375 (p. 434). In 1799 Hawkins estimated the number

---

[1] Ga. Col. Rec., VIII, p. 524.
[2] Trav. in Am. Col., p. 536.
[3] Sen. Doc. 512, 23d Cong., 1st sess., IV, pp. 265–266.
[4] Sibley in Ann. Cong., 9th Cong., 2d sess., 1085.
[5] Mass. Hist. Soc. Colls., II, p. 26.
[6] Morse, Rept. to Sec. of War, p. 373.
[7] Schoolcraft, Ind. Tribes, III, p. 596.
[8] Jour. Eth. Soc. of London, 2, p. 282.
[9] Ind. Pop., Bur. of Census, p. 18.
[10] Miss. Prov. Arch., I, p. 94.
[11] Ga. Col. Rec., VIII, p. 524.
[12] Trav. in Am. Col., p. 541.
[13] Ga. Hist. Soc. Colls., III, p. 39.
[14] Sen. Doc. 512, 23d Cong., 1st sess., IV, pp. 265–266.
[15] Copy of MS., Ayer Coll.
[16] Miss. Prov. Arch., I, p. 96.
[17] Ga. Col. Rec., VIII, p. 522.
[18] Trav. in Am. Col., p. 550.

of gunmen here at 180, although they themselves placed it at 300.[1] It was then the largest town in the nation. The census of 1832 gives them seven distinct settlements and a total population of 1,918 Indians and 134 slaves.[2] They are now, of course, much reduced in numbers.

The estimate of Coweta men in 1738 was 132,[3] in 1750, 80+,[4] in 1760, 150,[5] and in 1761, 130 hunters are enumerated.[6] Taitt (1772) gives 220 gunmen in "Coweta, Little Coweta, and Bigskin Creek," [7] and Marbury (1792) puts the number of men in Coweta and its villages at 280 (p. 434). Hawkins places the number of gunmen in Coweta Tallahassee and its outvillages in 1799 at 66 by actual count against a claimed total by the people themselves of 100, but he furnishes no figure for Coweta itself.[8] The census of 1832 enumerated five Coweta settlements with a total population of 896 Indians and 67 slaves.[9] To this must be added the Indians of Broken Arrow,[10] which, if we could trust this census, would increase the Coweta Indians by 1,082 Indians and 59 slaves.[9] It is evident, however, that among the five Broken Arrow towns here enumerated two or three are really Okfuskee villages and probably only the two first mentioned towns represent this division. If this is so, the Broken Arrow population would number only 438 Indians and 31 slaves, which would raise the total Coweta population to 1,334 Indians and 99 slaves. They have since fallen off very rapidly in numbers.

The Coosa Indians were evidently powerful and numerous in De Soto's time. Pardo reported that in 1567 the Coosa town had 150 neighborhoods—i. e., small villages.[11] Garcilasso says there were 500 houses, but he is notoriously given to exaggeration when it comes to figures of any sort.[12] Those of the De Luna expedition who visited Coosa in 1559 reported that the principal town of the province had 30 houses, a figure which may be accepted as approximately correct. They add that there were seven other villages in its neighborhood, "five of them smaller and two larger," and allowing 20 houses on the average to each of these we should have about 170 houses, by which I suppose we are to understand 170 different family establishments.[13] This would furnish the amount of leeway that

1 Ga. Hist. Soc. Colls., III, p. 59.

2 Sen. Doc. 512, 23d Cong., 1st sess., IV, pp. 363–398.

3 Copy of MS., Ayer Coll.

4 MS., Ayer Coll.

5 Miss. Prov. Arch., I, p. 96.

6 Ga. Col. Rec., VIII, p. 522.

7 Trav. in Am. Col., p. 549.

8 Ga. Hist. Soc. Colls., III, p. 56.

9 Sen. Doc. 512, 23d Cong., 1st sess., IV, pp. 379–386.

10 The population of Broken Arrow is referred to by only one other writer. This is David Taitt in 1772, who gives 60 gunmen. See Mereness, Trav. in Am. Col., p. 549.

11 Ruidiaz, La Florida, II, p. 484.

12 Garcilasso, in Shipp, De Soto and Fla., p. 374.

13 Barcia, La Florida, p. 32.

Garcilasso's figuring always requires, and it is not far out of the way as compared with Pardo's, if the latter's 150 "vecinos" means family groups. When Coosa reappears in history the town is small and decayed, but, as explained elsewhere, there is every reason to believe that the Coosa tribe continued to be represented by a number of the leading towns of the Creek Confederacy.

The Spanish census of 1738 gives 100 men in Coosa and 414 in the Coosa group of towns.[1] The French estimate of 1750 gives 30+ in the town and 240+ in the group.[2] In 1760 the Coosa group of towns numbered about 430 men, and in 1761 about 270 hunters are reported in them.[3] In 1792 the "Coosa of Chickasaw Camp" were credited with 80 men, and all the Coosa offshoots together with 440.[4] According to the figures furnished by Hawkins the entire Coosa connection would number upward of 520, and by the census of 1832 the grand total was 3,792 Indians, about one-sixth of the entire Creek population.

The Abihka are treated as a distinct tribe by many early writers, but the Coosa Indians are sometimes included with them, and perhaps others. This appears to be the case, for instance, in the census of 1715 which returned 15 Abihka towns with 502 men and a total population of 1773.[5] In 1738 Abihkutci, the only Abihka town given, was estimated to contain 30 men.[1] In 1750 the same town is set down with more than 60 inhabitants,[2] in 1760 with 130 men[6] and in 1761, 50 hunters.[7] Taitt in 1772 estimates 45 gunmen,[8] and Marbury (1792) puts the figure as low as 15 (p. 435). In 1832 Talladega, Abihkutci, and Kan-tcadi are separately entered with a combined population of 905, exclusive of slaves.[9]

In 1738 the Wakokai included 100 men,[1] in 1750 60+,[2] in 1760 100 men,[10] and in 1761 60 hunters.[7] Taitt (1772) gives 100 gunmen;[11] Marbury (1792) 300 (p. 437). In 1832 the combined population of Wiogufki, Tukpafka, and Sakapadai was 942 Indians and 5 slaves.[12]

---

1 Copy of MS., Ayer Coll.

2 MS., Ayer Coll.

3 Miss. Prov. Arch., I, p. 95; Ga. Col. Rec., VIII, p. 523. David Taitt (Travels in Am. Col., pp. 502, 528) states in his diary of 1772 that some years before his time Okfuskee numbered 300 gunmen but the town had then spread out so much into branch villages that there were only about 30 gunmen in the old settlement. In the same way Great Tulsa which had once contained 100 gunmen had become reduced to "not above thirty" by the settlement of two outvillages, one 8, the other 25 miles off. The Coosa towns at about that time must have contained upward of 400 gunmen.

4 MS., Lib. Cong.

5 Rivers, Chap. Early Hist. S. Car., p. 94.

6 Miss. Prov. Arch., I, p. 95.

7 Ga. Col. Rec., VIII, p. 523.

8 Trav. in Am. Col., p. 534.

9 Sen. Doc. 512, 23d Cong., 1st sess., IV, pp. 304–307, 315–318.

10 Miss. Prov. Arch., I, p. 95.

11 Trav. in Am. Col., p. 535.

12 Sen. Doc. 512, 23d Cong., 1st sess., IV, pp. 286–293.

In 1738 the Hołiwahali were credited with 10 men,[1] in 1750 with 15,[2] in 1760 with 70,[3] and in 1761 with 35 hunters.[4] Marbury, in 1792, places the number of men as high as 110 (p. 435). In 1832 this town and its branch, Łapłåko, appear with a population of 607 Indians and 36 slaves.[5]

The number of gunmen in Hilibi and its branches is given successively as 80 in 1738,[1] 20 in 1750,[2] 80 in 1760,[6] 40 in 1761,[7] 100 in 1772,[8] 160 in 1732,[9] and in 1832 the total population was reported as 804 souls, exclusive of slaves.[10]

In 1738 there were reported 131 Eufaula men among both Upper and Lower Creeks;[1] in 1750, 25 +;[2] and in 1760, 160.[11] In 1761 they had 125 hunters,[12] and in 1792 Marbury estimates 80 men in the two towns among the Upper Creeks but does not include the one upon the Chattahoochee (pp. 436–437). Hawkins gives 70 gunmen in Upper Eufaula,[13] but ventures no estimate of the other Eufaula settlements. Young (1822) gives 670 Lower Eufaula Indians.[14] In 1832 there were 1,440 Eufaula Indians of the upper and lower towns with 21 slaves.[15]

Atasi is reported to have had 56 men in 1738,[1] 40+ in 1750,[2] 80 in 1760,[3] and 50 hunters in 1761.[4] In 1772 Taitt estimated 60 gunmen,[16] but Marbury in 1792 only half that number (p. 435). According to Hawkins they had 43 gunmen in 1766, afterwards increased to 80, and in his time, 1799, they had fallen off again to 50 gunmen.[17] The population in 1832 is given as 358.[18]

In 1738 Kolomi appears with 50 men,[1] in 1750 with 25;[2] in 1760, 1761, and 1792 with 50;[19] but no figures are given by Hawkins.

The Pakan Tallahassee Indians were estimated to have 60 men in 1738,[1] 10 in 1750,[2] 100 in 1760,[20] 75 hunters in 1761,[4] 20 gunmen in 1772,[21] and 50 in 1792 (p. 435), and are credited with a population of 288 in the census of 1832.[22] When the last enumeration was made part had gone to Louisiana. In 1806 Sibley says these comprised about 30 men.[23]

The Okchai towns are supposed to have counted, all together in 1738, 200 men;[1] in 1750, 80;[2] in 1760, 200 men;[24] and in 1761, 125 hunters.[25] In 1792 they are pyramided up to 385, including, however, the town of Opiłłåko (p. 436). In 1832 the Indian population

---

1 Copy of MS., Ayer Coll.
2 MS., Ayer Coll.
3 Miss. Prov. Arch., I, p. 95.
4 Ga. Col. Rec., VIII, p. 523.
5 Sen. Doc. 512, 23d Cong., 1st sess., IV, pp. 255–258, 268–270.
6 Miss. Prov. Arch., I, p. 95.
7 Ga. Col. Rec., VIII, p. 523.
8 Trav. in Am. Col., p. 530.
9 MS., Lib. Cong.
10 Sen. Doc. 512, op. cit., pp. 296–297, 318–323.
11 Miss. Prov. Arch., I, pp. 95–96.
12 Ga. Col. Rec., VIII, pp. 522–523.
13 Ga. Hist. Soc. Colls., III, p. 48.
14 Morse, Rept. to Sec. of War, p. 364.
15 Sen. Doc. 512, op. cit., pp. 275–278, 337–342, 378–379.
16 Trav. in Am. Col., p. 540.
17 Ga. Hist. Soc. Colls., III, p. 32.
18 Sen. Doc. 512, op. cit., pp. 252–254.
19 Miss. Prov. Arch., I, p. 94; Ga. Col. Rec., op. cit.
20 Miss. Prov. Arch., I, p. 94.
21 Mereness, Trav. in Am. Col., p. 535.
22 Sen. Doc. 512, op. cit., pp. 285–286.
23 Sibley, in Ann. Cong., 9th Cong., 2d sess., 1086.
24 Miss. Prov. Arch., I, pp. 94–95.
25 Ga. Col. Rec., VIII, pp. 523–524.

is given as 1,375.[1] At the present day their numbers proportionately are well kept up.

Although the connection is not established beyond doubt I will consider Tukabahchee and Kealedji together. In 1738 about 150 men;[2] in 1750, 75+;[3] in 1760, about 350 men;[4] and in 1761 about 130 hunters were credited to these towns and their branches.[5] Taitt (1772) has 190 gunmen, 120 in Tukabahchee and 70 in Kealedji.[6] In 1792 Tukabahchee is, curiously enough, omitted; Kealedji is estimated to contain 100 men (p. 436). In Hawkins's time, 1799, there were 116 gunmen in Tukabahchee,[7] reduced very much shortly before, he says, by misfortunes in war. He does not give the population of Kealedji. In 1832 the two towns, including Hachee tcaba, are given a total population of 2,079 Indians and 183 slaves.[8]

The census of 1715 gives two Yuchi towns with 130 men and 400 souls,[9] but this does not include the Yuchi on Choctawhatchee, the Westo, or the band on Tennessee River. About 1730 this last was supposed to count about 150 men.[10] In 1760 there were 65 men, 15 in an Upper Creek town.[11] In 1761 the Yuchi among the Lower Creeks are credited with 50 hunters,[12] and to them must be added a few Choctawhatchee Yuchi enumerated with the Tukabahchee. Bartram, in 1777, estimated their warriors at 500 and their population at from 1,000 to 1,500.[13] In 1792 Marbury reports 300 men, which would mean a population of over 1,000 (p. 434). By 1799, when Hawkins wrote, practically all of these had been gathered into one main settlement, though with outlying villages.[14] Young (1822) gives in one settlement 130 Yuchi.[15] In 1832 two Yuchi settlements appear, having a total Indian population of 1,139.[16] Dr. Speck states that their number "can hardly exceed five hundred" at the present day (1909),[17] but the official enumeration for 1910 was only 78.[18]

---

[1] Sen. Doc. 512, 23d Cong , 1st sess., IV, pp. 241–243, 284–285, 293–296, 297–299.
[2] Copy of MS., Ayer Coll.
[3] MS., Ayer Coll.
[4] Miss. Prov. Arch., I, p .95.
[5] Ga. Col. Rec., VIII, p. 523.
[6] Travels in Am. Col., pp. 502, 516.
[7] Ga. Hist. Soc. Colls., III, pp. 29–30.
[8] Sen. Doc. 512, 23d Cong., 1st sess., IV, pp. 243–252, 278–280, 327–330.
[9] Rivers, Hist. S. C., p. 94.
[10] Copy of MS. in Lib. Cong.
[11] Miss. Prov. Arch., I, pp. 95–96.
[12] Ga. Col. Rec., VIII, p. 522.
[13] Bartram, Travels, p. 386.
[14] Ga. Hist. Soc. Colls., III, p. 62.
[15] Morse, Rept. to Sec. of War, p. 364.
[16] Sen. Doc. 512, 23d Cong., 1st sess., IV, pp. 356–363.
[17] Speck, Anth. Pub. Univ. of Pa. Mus., I, p. 9.
[18] Pop. of Ind. Tribes, 1910, p. 21.

Figures and estimates for the Natchez who settled among the Creeks have been given in a separate publication.[1]

In addition, a word may be said regarding those Shawnee who for a time constituted part of the confederacy. In 1708 the South Carolina documents give three Shawnee towns in that colony and 150 men;[2] in the census of 1715 three towns with 67 men, and 233 souls.[3] In 1760 there were 100 Shawnee men in the bands among the Creeks.[4] In 1761 the united Shawnee on Tallapoosa River were estimated to have 30 hunters,[5] but Marbury (1792) raises this to 60 (p. 436). Hawkins does not give any figures, and the name Shawnee does not occur in the census list of 1832, but we find a town called "Kiamulga-town" which appears elsewhere coupled with the Shawnee and may have been occupied by them. It had a population of 175.[6]

The following table contains the population of all the above towns as well as the remaining towns of the confederacy, so far as they are known, drawn from the Spanish, French, and English trading lists of 1738, 1750, 1760, and 1761, as given by Taitt, Marbury, and Hawkins, and in the census of 1832.

COMPARATIVE TOWN CENSUS

Town.	Spanish census of 1738 (men).	French census of 1750 (men).	Census of 1760 [7] (men).	Census of 1761 [8] (hunters).	Taitt, 1772 (gunmen).	Marbury, 1792 (men).	Hawkins, 1799 [9] (gunmen).	U. S. census of 1832 [10] (souls).
New Tamałi	26	......	......	......	......	......	......	......
Coweta	132	+80	150	130	220	280	......	896
Broken Arrow	......	......	......	......	60	......	......	438
Kasihta	111	+80	150	100	100	375	180	1,918
Yuchi	......	......	50	50	......	300	[11] 250	1,139
Osochi		30	50		......	50	......	539
Chiaha	[12] 120	[13] 20	160	120	......	([14])	......	427
Okmulgee		+20	30		......	......	......	......
Hitchiti	60	15	50	40	90	......	......	381

[1] Bull. 43, Bur. Amer. Ethn. I may add that Taitt says there were 30 gunmen, "Natches and Creeks," in the Natchez town among the Upper Creeks in 1772 (Mereness, Trav. Am. Col., p. 532), and Marbury places the figure at 110 in 1792 (p. 436).

[2] S. C. Pub. Docs., MS., v, pp. 207–209.

[3] Rivers, Chap. Early Hist. S. C., p. 96.

[4] Miss. Prov. Arch., I, p. 96.

[5] Ga. Col. Rec., VIII, p. 523.

[6] Sen. Doc. 512, 23d Cong., 1st sess., IV, pp. 302–303.

[7] Miss. Prov. Arch., I, pp. 94–96.

[8] Ga. Col. Docs., VIII, pp. 522–524.

[9] Ga. Hist. Soc. Colls., III, pp. 26–66.

[10] Sen. Doc. 512, 23d Cong., 1st sess., IV, pp. 239–394. My figures often differ from those given in the document because it was found that many errors in compilation had been made.

[11] Native estimate.

[12] Including 3 towns.

[13] "Cina."

[14] With Apalachicola.

COMPARATIVE TOWN CENSUS—Continued

Town.	Spanish census of 1738 (men).	French census of 1750 (men).	Census of 1760 (men).	Census of 1761 (hunters).	Taitt, 1772 (gunmen).	Marbury, 1792 (men).	Hawkins, 1799 (gunmen).	U. S. census of 1832 (souls).
Apalachicola	60	+30	60	20	......	[1] 100	......	239
Sawokli and villages	20	+50	190	50	......	......	......	450
Oconee	50	30	50	50	......	......	......	......
Eufaula, Lower	111	+15	60	90	......	......	......	981
Chiska talofa	......	......	......	30	......	......	......	......
Weupkees (?) (Okitiyagena)	......	......	30	90	......	......	......	......
Cherokeeleechee	45	......	......	......	......	......	......	......
Chachaue	10	......	......	......	......	......	......	......
Old Tamałi	12	10	......	......	......	......	......	......
Tamahita	......	+18	......	......	......	......	......	......
Total of Lower towns	757	398	1,030	770	470	1,105	430	7,408
Tulsa	100	{ 25 +30 }	[2] 200	80	30	250	......	610
Saogahatchee	......	......	15	......	......	......	30	240
Lutcapoga	......	......	......	......	......	......	......	564
Tukabahchee	100	+50	200	[3] 90	120	......	116	1,287
Yuchi	......	......	15	([4])	......	......	......	......
Atasi	56	+40	80	50	60	30	[5] 80	358
Hołiwahali	10	15	70	35	......	110	......	427
Łapłåko	......	......	......	......	......	......	......	180
Fus-hatchee	20	+30	[6] 60	[7] 50	......	50	......	......
Kolomi	50	25	50	50	......	50	......	......
Kan-hatki	12	15	[8] 40	30	......	30	......	......
Muklasa	......	......	50	30	......	30	......	......
Otciapofa }	......	15(?)	{ 40	} 20	......	30	{ 40	216
Hatchee tcaba }			([9]) }				......	201
Wiwohka	100	+40	[10] 100	35	......	70	40	301
Tal mutcasi	......	......	......	......	......	......	......	144
Pakan tallahassee	60	10	......	45	20	50	......	288
Pakana (at Fort Toulouse)	......	30	50	30	......	......	......	......
Abihkutci	30	+60	130	50	45	15	......	378

[1] With Chiaha.
[2] With Nafape.
[3] Including outsettlements and some Yuchi.
[4] See above.
[5] 43 in 1766.
[6] With some Tawasa.
[7] Including some Coosa.
[8] With some Coosa.
[9] See Wiwohka.
[10] Including Tcatoksofka and Hatchee tcaba.

COMPARATIVE TOWN CENSUS—Continued

Town.	Spanish census of 1738 (men).	French census of 1750 (men).	Census of 1760 (men).	Census of 1761 (hunters).	Taitt, 1772 (gunmen).	Marbury, 1792 (men).	Hawkins, 1799 (gunmen).	U. S. census of 1832 (souls).
Kan-tcati								191
Talladega								334
Breed Camp				[1] 60				
Pilłåko		10	40			([2])		
Hilibi	80	20	[3] 80	40	100	150	170 (Hilibi and Oktahasasi)	485
Oktahasasi								131
Kitcopataki								188
Sukaispoga				20	45	10		
Okfuskee	[4] 200	+100	300	[5] 130	30	80 [7] 60	180 [7] 270	[6] 493 [8] 1,162
Okfuskutci	14	10	15					
Kealedji	50	+25	130	40	70	100		591
Coosa	100	+30	20			80		
Eufaula, Upper	20	10	100	[9] 35		40	70	459
Natchez			20		30	110		
Okchai (2 towns)	200	+80	130	125		200		493
Łåłogålga						140		313
Asilanabi						[10] 30		181
Potcas hatchee						15		[11] 388
Wakokai	100	+60	100	60	100	300		
Wiogufki								353
Tukpafka								391
Sakapadai								198
Sawanogi (Shawnee)			[11] 100	30		60		
Kiamulgatown								175
Thomapas			70					
Okchaiutci		40	100	20		40		
Tawasa		20	10			[11] 60		[12] 108 [13] 213

[1] Said to have been broken up soon afterwards.
[2] See Asilanabi.
[3] With Little Hilibi.
[4] Okfuskee old town.
[5] With some outvillages.
[6] Tcatoksofka.
[7] In the villages, including Nuyaka.
[8] Outvillages, including Kohamutkikatska with a population of 405, Tohtogagi with 113, Hołitaiga with 93, Tcułåko-nini with 339, and Hitcisihogi with 212.
[9] Including Black Creek village.
[10] Including Pilłåko.
[11] Two towns.
[12] Tawasa.
[13] Autauga.

COMPARATIVE TOWN CENSUS—Continued

Town.	Spanish census of 1738 (men).	French census of 1750 (men).	Census of 1760 (men).	Census of 1761 (hunters).	Taitt, 1772 (gunmen).	Marbury, 1792 (men).	Hawkins, 1799 (gunmen).	U. S. census of 1832 (souls).
Alabama	......	[1] 15	[1] 150	[2] 70	......	60	80	......
Coosa old town	......	......	20	......	......	......	......	......
Tuskegee	......	10	50	[3] 40	25	25	35	216
Koasati	......	......	......	[4] 125	......	130	......	82
Chickasaw (a stray band)	......	50	40	......	40	......	......	......
Chiaha (Upper)	......	......	......	......	......	......	......	[5] 432
Cubihatcha	......	......	......	......	......	......	......	128
Talipsehogy	......	......	......	......	......	......	......	72
Emarhetown (or Hemanhie Town)	......	......	......	......	......	......	......	210
Chockolocko [Tcahki łåko]	......	......	......	......	......	10	......	456
Tallase-hatchee	......	......	......	......	......	......	......	298
Rabbit	......	......	......	......	......	......	......	243
Ekun-duts-ke	......	......	......	......	......	......	......	147
Aubasé	4	......	......	......	......	......	......	......
Eufaula hatchee	......	......	......	......	......	40	......	......
Three Islands	......	......	......	......	......	25	......	......
Atchina hatchee	......	......	......	......	......	20	......	......
Total of Upper towns	1,306	865	2,575	1,390	[5] 715	2,500	[6] 1,111	14,325
Lower towns	757	398	1,030	770	[7] 470	1,105	[8] 430	7,408
Grand total	2,063	1,263	3,605	2,160	[9] 1,185	3,605	[10] 1,541	21,733

In addition to the town enumerations already given we have many general estimates of Creek population which, though they may not in all cases be so accurate, yet tell a more connected story.

In 1702 Iberville places the total number of Creek and Alabama families at 2,000.[11] In 1708 an early South Carolina estimate gives 600 men among the "Ochesee" (i. e., the Lower Creeks), in 11 towns, and 1,300 men among the Upper Creeks, in "many towns," besides

[1] Kan-tcati.
[2] Witumpka and Red Ground.
[3] Including Coosa old town.
[4] Including Tamahita.
[5] 13 towns.
[6] 11 towns.
[7] 4 towns.
[8] 2 towns.
[9] 17 towns.
[10] 13 towns.
[11] Margry, Déc., IV, p. 602.

the people of Chattahoochee town not enumerated.[1] The census of 1715 gives for the "Ochesees or Creeks," 10 towns, 731 men, and 2,406 souls; for the "Abikaws," 15 towns, 502 men, and 1,773 souls; and for the "Talliboosas," 13 towns, 636 men, and 2,343 souls; or in all 38 towns, 1,869 men, and 6,522 souls.[2] This is exclusive of the Alabama, Yuchi, Shawnee, Apalachicola, and Yamasee. An estimate made in 1739 gives 1,500 warriors for the Creeks,[3] and one of 1747–48, "not much over 2,500 men."[4] Adair says that "this nation is generally computed to consist of about 3,500 men fit to bear arms"; and adds, on the authority of a "gentleman of distinguished character," that they had doubled their numbers "within the space of thirty years past," which would be perhaps from 1720 to 1750 or 1730 to 1760.[5] In De Brahm's "History of the Province of Georgia" the entire Creek population about 1753 is estimated at 15,000 and the number of their warriors at 3,000.[6] De Kerlerec, in 1758, estimated the Alabama, Tallapoosa, and Abihka Indians at 1,000 warriors, and the "Kaouitas" (i. e., Lower Creeks), at 2,000.[7] A French manuscript from the third decade of the eighteenth century seems to give 3,500 men, exclusive of 400 Alabama, although the material is somewhat confused.[8] An estimate dated in the year 1761 gives 2,500 gunmen.[9] In 1764 John Stuart places the total number of Creek gunmen, exclusive of the Natchez, Yuchi, Shawnee, and some Alabama, at 3,600.[10] Romans estimates 3,500 gunmen in 1771,[11] and Bartram, about the same time, a total population of 11,000.[12] The latter arrives at his conclusion by allowing 200 persons to each of the 55 Creek towns known to him.

Swan, 1791, says "the smallest of their towns have from 20 to 30 houses in them, and some of the largest contain from 150 to 200, that are tolerably compact";[13] and further on Gen. M'Gillivray estimates the number of gunmen to be between 5,000 and 6,000, exclusive of marauders, acting independent of the general interest of the others. The "useless" old men and the women and children were reckoned as three times the number of gunmen, making the total about 25,000 or 26,000 souls.[14] These figures are perhaps a little high, as the census of 1832, taken just before the removal of the Creeks to the other side of the Mississippi, yielded a grand total of 21,759.[15] The figures given out by the U. S. Indian Office and

[1] Pub. Rec. S. C., MS., v, pp. 207–209.
[2] Rivers, Chap. Early Hist. of S. C., p. 94.
[3] Ga. Col. Rec., v, p. 191.
[4] Pub. Rec. S. C., MS., xxiii, pp. 74–75
[5] Adair, Hist. Am. Inds., pp. 257–259.
[6] De Brahm, Hist. Prov. Ga., p. 55.
[7] Compte Rendu, Int. Cong. Am., 1906, i, pp. 83, 84.
[8] Copy of MS., Lib. Cong.
[9] A Descr. of the Prov. of S. C., pp. 60–61.
[10] Am. Hist. Rev., xx, 4, p. 825.
[11] Romans, E. and W. Fla., p. 91.
[12] Bartram, Travels, pp. 462–463.
[13] Schoolcraft, Ind. Tribes, v, p. 262.
[14] Ibid., p. 263.
[15] Sen. Doc. 512, 23d Cong., 1st sess., iv, pp. 334–394.

from other sources between this date and 1857 vary between 20,000 and 25,000, but it is probable that the Creek population was actually shrinking during the period, for a more accurate census taken by the Indian Office in 1857 gave only 14,888. Since then they have shrunk slowly, even in the official enumerations, and more rapidly if we take into consideration the actual amount of Indian blood which these figures represent. This latter element probably accounts in a measure for the fact that the U. S. Official Census of 1910 gives only 6,945 Creeks as against 11,911 in the Report of the U. S. Indian Office issued the same year.

The difficulty with the foregoing figures is the fact that during most of this period the population was both receiving accessions from outside and giving out part of its population in various directions. Some of the accessions were received so far back that all of our figures include them. The Apalachicola, Yuchi, Natchez, Yamasee, Oconee, and Shawnee, however, also some of the Alabama, were taken in after certain of the estimates and counts had been made. On the other hand, from comparatively early in the eighteenth century, bands of Indians began to move into the Florida peninsula, and thither went also some tribes like the Yamasee and Oconee, which would otherwise have united with the Creeks permanently. After the Creek war still greater numbers went to Florida, including several entire towns.

There are no figures on which an accurate estimate of the Indian population of Florida before the Seminole intrusion may be based. A document dated 1597 claims more than 1,400 to 1,500 Christian Indians in the territory attached to Nombre de Dios, San Pedro, the Fresh Water district, and that of San Antonio.[1] In 1602 792 Christian Indians were reported from the "vicaria of San Pedro," 500 in that of San Juan del Puerto, and about 200 in the Fresh Water district. In addition, 100 were under instruction in the province last mentioned and 1,100 in the province of Icafi. The same manuscript gives a total population of 700 to 800 in the province of Yui, 1,500 in Timucua or Utina, and 1,000 in Potano.[1] In 1606 the Bishop of Cuba visited the Florida missions and confirmed 2,074 Indians.[1] In 1608 it is claimed that 5,000 Indians were converted or being catechised.[1] A letter written February 2, 1635, claims 30,000 Christian Indians were connected with the 44 missions.[1] As the Apalachee field had but just been opened this includes principally Timucua and Guale Indians. It is probably much too high. In 1728 the town of Nombre De Dios or Chiquito, which seems to have contained most of the surviving Timucua, had about 15 men and 20 women; eight years later the number of men was 17.

---

[1] Lowery, MSS.

From southern Florida we have only the most general statements. All agree that the most populous tribe by far was the Calusa, and several say that the Ais were the most numerous of all on the Atlantic seaboard. But in details there is no approximation to uniformity. Thus one writer states that there were more than 70 Calusa towns,[1] and another "more than 600," not including tributaries.[1] In any case these "towns" were nothing more than small hunting and fishing camps, the south Florida Indians not having been addicted to agriculture. In another place I have given a list of 56 Calusa towns with their names.[2] An expedition sent into the Calusa country in 1680 passed through five villages said to have a total population of 960. From about this time on the population would probably show a steady decline had we the means of registering it.

In 1778 Bartram says of the Seminole:

> All of them, I suppose, would not be sufficient to people one of the towns in the Muscogulge; for instance, the Uches on the main branch of the Apalachucla River, which alone contains near two thousand inhabitants.[3]

He probably much exaggerated the number of Yuchi, but there is reason to believe that his estimate for the Seminole was not far wrong. Upon the whole, it appears likely that the older Seminole with whom Bartram had to deal, those living in the peninsula before the Creek-American war, constituted about one-third of the total number after the refugees from the Upper Creeks had been incorporated, and this would make them 1,500 or a little more. The Seminole seem to have been underestimated in most of the reports made of them. Joseph M. White, secretary to the Commission for Land Titles in Florida, and Mr. Penieres, subagent for Indian affairs, estimated them at about 3,000,[4] and figures are given as low as 2,000. In 1823, however, an actual count was furnished by the Indians themselves, in which 4,883 were returned, exclusive of Negroes.[5] Later, as various bands of Seminole were captured and sent west, the numbers of the bands are given, and we find a total of about 4,000. When we allow for those who had been killed or who had died from other causes, and those who escaped enumeration in one way or another, the correctness of the Indian figure appears to be indicated. Another estimate by Mr. Penieres to the effect that there were about 1,200 warriors would agree with this very well.[6] In 1836 the United States Indian Office reported 3,765 Seminole in the west,[7] and in

[1] Lowery, MSS.

[2] See pp. 331–333.

[3] Bartram, Travels, p. 209.

[4] Am. State Papers, Ind. Aff., II, pp. 411, 413–414.

[5] Ibid., p. 439.

[6] Ibid., p. 411.

[7] Rept. Comm. Ind. Aff. for 1846, p. 397.

1837, 5,400.[1] Between 1838 and 1843 the figures are a little over 3,500, and between 1844 and 1856 between 2,500 and 3,000, or a trifle more. Most of these were based on the preceding enumerations, and when, in 1857, an actual census was taken only 1,907 were returned.[2] During the next 15 years the number increased slowly until it reached about 2,500, and it has continued to vary between this figure and 3,000 down to the present time. Nevertheless this includes the Seminole Negroes or freedmen, and in 1905 it was found that they constituted about one-third of the nation, a proportion they have maintained ever since. In 1908 an attempt was made to secure separate figures for the full and mixed bloods, and 1,399 were returned for the former and 739 for the latter.[3] It is probable that this separation was only relative and that the actual full bloods, could the truth be known, would be found to number a mere handful. The census of 1910 gives 1,729 Seminole Indians, of whom 1,503 were in Oklahoma and 226 in Florida.[4] The last number is evidently an underestimate.

Until 1893 no figures were given by the United States Indian Office for those Seminole who had remained in Florida. MacCaulay, however, attempted an exact enumeration of them in 1880 and found 208 individuals.[5] In 1893 the Indian Office reported, or rather estimated, 450,[6] and the same figure was repeated in 1894.[7] In the report of 1895 we find 565 entered and the same number in 1896 and 1897.[8] In 1898, 1899, and 1900 the number given is 575.[9] In 1902 it is reduced to 358[10] and so appears until 1911, when it jumps to 446.[11] In 1912 this is repeated, but in 1913 it is increased to 600,[12] and in 1914 reduced to 562.[13] There is known to be a considerable admixture of Negro blood in the band, but the amount of white blood is practically negligible. No separate enumeration of mixed bloods has been made.

The following tables contain the earlier estimates of Creek and Seminole population in a more compact form and all of the important censuses taken of them in later times.

---

[1] Rept. Comm. Ind. Aff. for 1847, p. 592, including Apalachicola Indians.

[2] Ibid. for 1847, p. 229.

[3] Ibid. for 1908, p. 185.

[4] Ind. Pop., Census 1910, p. 20.

[5] Fifth Ann. Rept. Bur. Amer. Ethn., pp. 476–480.

[6] Rept. Comm. Ind. Aff. for 1893, p. 696.

[7] Ibid. for 1894, p. 570.

[8] Ibid. for 1895, p. 566; 1896, p. 532; 1897, p. 484.

[9] Ibid. for 1898, p. 600; 1899, p. 564; 1900, p. 640.

[10] Ibid. for 1902, p. 632.

[11] Ibid. for 1911, p. 59.

[12] Ibid. for 1912, p. 136; 1913, p. 50.

[13] Ibid. for 1914, p. 78.

Creek and Seminole Population at Various Periods Prior to 1834[1]

[The figures are for the Creeks unless otherwise specified.]

Authority.	Year.	Warriors.	Total population.[2]
Iberville	1702	[3] 2,000	7,000
South Carolina records	1708	[3] 2,000	7,000
Do	1715	[3] 2,083	7,292
Bienville	1725–26	2,200	7,700
Spanish manuscript	1738	[4] 2,063	7,220
Georgia records	1739	[5] 1,500	5,250
South Carolina records	1747–48	+2,500	8,750
Adair	1750(?)	3,500	12,250
An anonymous French estimate	1750(?)	[6] 1,258	4,403
De Brahm	1753	3,000	[7] 10,500
De Kerlerec	1758	3,000	10,500
French census	1760	3,655	12,792
Anonymous description of South Carolina	1761	2,500	8,750
Georgia Colonial Documents	1761	[8] 2,160	7,560
John Stuart	1764	3,600	12,600
Col. Henry Bouquet	1764	[9] 2,950	10,325
Elam Potter	1768	1,600	5,600
Romans	1771	3,500	12,250
Bartram	1778	....	11,000
Purcell	1780	[10] 5,860	17,280
Morse	1786	5,860	17,280
H. Knox, Secretary of War	1789	4,000–6,000	14,000 to 21,000

[1] Authorities: Iberville in Margry, Déc., IV, pp. 601–602; S. C. Pub. Rec., MS., V, pp. 207–209; Rivers, A Chapter in the Early Histroy of South Carolina, p. 94; Copy of Spanish MS. in Ayer Coll.; Ga. Col. Rec., V, p. 191; S. C. Public Records, MS., XXIII, p. 75; Adair, Hist. Am. Inds., p. 257; Anonymous French Memoir, MS., Ayer Coll.; De Brahm, History of the Province of Georgia, p. 55; DeKerlérec in Compte Rendu, Int. Cong. Americanists, 1906, I, pp. 83–84; French Census in Miss. Prov. Arch., I, pp. 94–97; A Description of S. C., pp. 60–61; Ga. Col. Rec., VIII, pp. 522–524; Bouquet in Schoolcraft, Ind. Tribes, III, p. 559; Am. Hist. Rev., XX, 4, p. 825; Potter in Mass. Hist. Soc. Colls., 1st ser., X, p. 121; Romans, A Concise Nat. Hist. of E. and W. Florida, p. 91; Bartram, Travels, pp. 462–463; Purcell in Mass. Hist. Soc. Colls., 1st ser., IV, p. 99; Morse in Rept. to Sec. of War, p. 146; Knox in American State Papers, Ind. Aff., I, p. 60; Swan in Schoolcraft, Ind. Tribes, V, p. 263; Schermerhorn in Mass. Hist. Soc. Colls., 2d ser., II, p. 20; Penieres in Am. State Papers, Ind. Aff., II, pp. 411–413; Am. State Papers, II, p. 439; Schoolcraft, Ind. Tribes, III, p. 584; U. S. Census in Schoolcraft, Ind. Tribes, IV, p. 578; MSS., Lib. Cong.

[2] Obtained, where number of warriors is given, by multiplying by 3½.

[3] Exclusive of Yamasee, Apalachicola, Shawnee, and Yuchi, but including Alabama. The last was an actual census.

[4] Excludes Alabama and neighboring towns.

[5] From this time on the Apalachicola, some Shawnee, a few Yamasee, and nearly all of the Yuchi are included.

[6] Evidently incomplete.

[7] Given as 15,000.

[8] From about this time the nation lost many to Florida.

[9] With 600 Alabama.

[10] Creeks and Seminole.

CREEK AND SEMINOLE POPULATION AT VARIOUS PERIODS PRIOR TO 1834—Con.

Authority.	Year.	Warriors.	Total population.
Swan	1791	5,000–6,000	[1] 17,500 to [1] 21,000
Marbury	1792	[2] 3,605	12,618
		1,399	4,882
Schermerhorn	1814	5,000	[3] 17,750
Andrew Jackson	1821	[2] 1,200	[2] 3,000
Do	1821		[2] 2,000
Penieres	1821		[2] +5,000
White	1821		[2] 3,000
Report to American Commissioners	1823		[4] 4,883
In Schoolcraft	1825		20,000
			[2] 5,000
Porter	1829		20,000
			[2] 4,000
United States Census	1832		21,759

CREEK AND SEMINOLE POPULATION SUBSEQUENT TO 1834

	Total population.
United States Indian Office:	
1835—Creeks	22,000
1836—Creeks	22,000
Seminole	3,765
1837—Creeks	21,437
Seminole	5,072
1838—Creeks	25,293
Seminole	3,565
1841—Creeks	25,338
Seminole	3,765
1842—Creeks	25,338
Seminole (in west; and so with following figures)	3,612
1843—Creeks	25,338
Seminole	3,824
1844—Creeks	25,338
Seminole	3,136
1845—Creeks	24,754
Seminole	3,136
Schoolcraft:	
1846 [5]—Seminole	3,250
1847 [6]—Creeks	25,000
Seminole	1,500
1847 [7]—Seminole in Florida	370
1850 [7]—Seminole in Florida	348

[1] Given as 25,000 to 26,000.
[2] Seminole.
[3] Given as 20,000.
[4] Seminole, exclusive of Negroes.
[5] Schoolcraft, Ind. Tribes, III, p. 621.
[6] Ibid., I, pp. 6–24.
[7] Ibid., I, p. 522.

	Total population.
United States Indian Office:	
1851—Seminole	2,500
1853—Creeks	25,000
Seminole (including 500in Florida)	3,000
1855—(Same).	
Schoolcraft:	
1855—Seminole	2,500
1857—Seminole	2,500
United States Indian Office (new census):	
1857—Creeks	14,888
Seminole[1]	1,907
Schoolcraft:	
1857—Creeks	28,214
Seminole	1,870
United States Indian Office:	
1858—Seminole	2,060
1859—Creeks	13,550
Seminole	2,253
1861—Creeks	13,550
Seminole	2,267
1865–66—Creeks	14,396
Seminole	2,000
1867—Creeks	12,294
Seminole	2,236
1868—Creeks	12,003
Seminole	1,950
1869—Creeks	12,294
Seminole	2,136
1870—Creeks	12,294
Seminole	2,136
1871—Creeks	13,000
Seminole	2,300
1872—Creeks	13,000
Seminole	2,398
1873—Creeks	13,000
Seminole	2,438
1874—Creeks (including 2,000 freedmen)	13,000
Seminole	2,438
1875—(Same).	
1876—Creeks (including 3,000 mixed bloods)	14,000
Seminole (100 mixed bloods)	2,553
1877—Creeks (1,200 mixed bloods)	14,000
Seminole (200 mixed bloods)	2,443
1878—(Same).	
1879—Creeks	14,500
Seminole	2,560
1880—Creeks	15,000
Seminole	2,667
1881—Creeks	15,000
Seminole	2,667
1882—Creeks	15,000
Seminole	2,700
Alabama, Koasati, and Muskogee in Texas	290

[1] From here on the Seminole removed to the west are meant unless otherwise specified.

United States Indian Office—Continued.

	Total population.
1883—Creeks	14,000
Seminole	3,000
Alabama, Koasati, and Muskogee in Texas	290
1884—(Same).	
1885—Creeks	14,000
Seminole	3,000
Alabama, Koasati, and Muskogee in Texas	290
1886—(Same).	
1887—(Same).	
1888—Creeks	14,200
Seminole	3,050
Alabama, Koasati, and Muskogee in Texas	290
1889—Creeks	14,200
Seminole	2,600
Alabama, Koasati, and Muskogee in Texas	290
1890—Creeks	15,000
Seminole	2,600
Alabama, Koasati, and Muskogee in Texas	290
1891—Creeks	15,000
Seminole	2,600
Alabama, Koasati, and Muskogee in Texas	290
1892—Creeks	15,000
Seminole	3,000
Alabama, Koasati, and Muskogee in Texas	290
1893—(Same and).	
Florida Seminole	450
1894—(Same and).	
Florida Seminole	450
1895—Creeks: full blood Indians	9,447
Creek freedmen	4,416
Seminole	2,900
Florida Seminole	565
Alabama, Koasati, and Muskogee in Texas	290
1896—Creeks	13,863
Seminole	2,000
Florida Seminole	565
Alabama, Koasati, and Muskogee in Texas	290
1897—Creeks	13,863
Seminole	2,900
Florida Seminole	565
Alabama, Koasati, and Muskogee in Texas	290
1898—Creeks: by blood	10,014
Creek freedmen	4,757
Seminole	2,900
Florida Seminole	575
Alabama, Koasati, and Muskogee in Texas	290
1899—Creeks	14,771
Seminole	2,900
Florida Seminole	575
Alabama, Koasati, and Muskogee in Texas	290
1900—Creeks by blood	10,000
Creek freedmen	6,000
Seminole	3,000

United States Indian Office—Continued.

		Total population.
1900—	Seminole freedmen	575
	Alabama, Koasati, and Muskogee in Texas	290
1901—	Creeks by blood	10,000
	Creek freedmen	5,000
	Seminole	2,757
	Florida Seminole	358
	Alabama, Koasati, and Muskogee in Texas	470
1902—	Creeks	15,000
	Seminole	2,750
	Florida Seminole	358
	Alabama, Koasati, and Muskogee	470
1903—	Creeks by blood	9,624
	Creek freedmen	4,954
	Seminole	2,750
	Florida Seminole	358
	Alabama, Koasati, and Muskogee	470
1904—	Creeks by blood	9,905
	Creek freedmen	5,473
	Florida Seminole	358
	Alabama, Koasati, and Muskogee	470
1905—	Creeks by blood	10,185
	Creek freedmen	5,738
	Seminole by blood	2,099
	Seminole freedmen	950
	Florida Seminole	358
	Alabama, Koasati, and Muskogee	470
1906—	Creeks by blood	11,081
	Creek freedmen	6,265
	Seminole by blood	2,132
	Seminole freedmen	979
	Florida Seminole	358
	Alabama, Koasati, and Muskogee	470
1907—	Creeks by blood	11,895
	Creek freedmen	6,807
	Seminole by blood	2,138
	Seminole freedmen	986
	Florida Seminole	358
	Alabama, Koasati, and Muskogee	470
1908—	Creek full bloods	6,812
	Creek mixed bloods	5,083
	Creek freedmen	6,807
	Seminole full bloods	1,399
	Seminole mixed bloods	739
	Seminole freedmen	986
	Florida Seminole	358
	Alabama, Koasati, and Muskogee	420
1909—	Creek full bloods	6,816
	Creek mixed bloods	5,091
	Creek freedmen	6,807
	Seminole full bloods	1,399
	Seminole mixed bloods	739

United States Indian Office—Continued.	Total population.
Seminole freedmen	986
1909—Florida Seminole	358
Alabama, Koasati, and Muskogee	470
1910—Creeks by blood	11,911
Creek freedmen	6,806
Seminole by blood	2,137
Seminole freedmen	986
Florida Seminole	358
Alabama, Koasati, and Muskogee	470
Census of 1910—	
Creeks (full bloods?)	6,945
Seminole (full bloods?)	1,729
Alabama	298
Koasati	98
United States Indian Office:	
1911—Creeks by blood	11,911
Creek freedmen	6,806
Seminole by blood	2,137
Seminole freedmen	986
Florida Seminole	446
Alabama in Texas	192
1912—Creeks by blood	11,911
Creek freedmen	6,806
Seminole by blood	2,137
Seminole freedmen	986
Florida Seminole	446
Alabama in Texas	192
1913—Creeks by blood	11,893
Creek freedmen	6,807
Seminole by blood	2,133
Seminole freedmen	986
Florida Seminole	600
Alabama in Texas	192
1914—Creeks by blood	11,905
Creek freedmen	6,807
Seminole by blood	2,133
Seminole freedmen	986
Florida Seminole	562
Alabama in Texas	192
1915—Creeks by blood (full blood, 6,873; half blood or more, 1,698; less than half blood, 3,396)	11,967
Creek freedmen	6,809
Seminole by blood (full, 1,254; one-half or more, 478; less than one-half, 409)	2,141
Seminole freedmen	986
Seminole in Florida	578
Alabama in Texas	192
1916—Creeks by blood	11,965
Creek freedmen	6,809
Seminole by blood	2,141

United States Indian Office—Continued.

	Total population.
1916—Seminole freedmen	986
Florida Seminole	574
Alabama in Texas	192
1917—Creeks by blood	11,952
Creek freedmen	6,809
Seminole by blood	2,141
Seminole freedmen	986
Florida Seminole	586
Alabama in Texas	192
1918—Creeks by blood	11,952
Creek freedmen	6,809
Seminole by blood	2,141
Seminole freedmen	986
Florida Seminole	585
Alabama in Texas	192
1919—Creeks and Seminole	(same as in 1918)
Florida Seminole	573
Alabama and Koasati in Polk County, Texas	206

To the figures since 1910 must be added about 100 for the Koasati and 100 for the Alabama Indians in Louisiana.

The earlier figures for the Chickasaw are so discordant that not much satisfaction can be obtained from them. Particularly it is hard to reconcile them with the size of the later figures. Either we must suppose that the earlier figures are too low or that there was a considerable increase in population during the latter part of the eighteenth century and the first part of the nineteenth. For about 20 years after their removal west of the Mississippi the Chickasaw and Choctaw were much mingled together, and some addition to the population may have come from the latter tribe. The slaves were also reckoned in and later as freedmen account for much of the increase shown, but they do not account for all of it in the period under consideration. Early in the eighteenth century we hear that the tribe had lost so heavily in its wars with the French and their Indian allies that it had become "reduced to 200–300 warriors," which would indicate a population of not much over 1,000 at the outside,[1] yet Morse's Report shows what appears to have been an exact enumeration of 3,625 in 1821;[2] and 15 years later the United States Indian Office estimates 5,400.[3] For the period from about 1800 to 1840 I think we must assume an actual increase, but it is probable that the earlier estimates of population were sometimes too low, and I venture to place the population in 1700 at from 3,000 to 3,500.

[1] S. C. Pub. Rec., XXIII, p. 75.

[2] Morse, Rept. to Sec. of War, p. 364.

[3] Rept. Comm. Ind. Aff. for 1836, p. 402.

Chickasaw Population at Various Periods Prior to 1834[1]

1699. M. de Montigny, 350 cabins.
1702. Iberville, 2,000 families.
1704. De La Vente, "as numerous as the Choctaw," i. e., 700 to 800 cabins.
1708. South Carolina documents, at least 600 warriors.
1715. South Carolina census, 6 villages, 700 men, 1,900 population.
1722–23. Bienville, 6–7 villages, 800 men.
1739. Georgia records, 500 warriors.
1747. South Carolina public documents, reduced to 200 to 300 warriors.
1750. Adair, barely 450 warriors.
1750. An anonymous French memoir, 560 warriors.
1764. Capt. Thos. Hutchins, 750 warriors.
1764. Col. Bouquet, 750 warriors.
1764. John Stuart, 500 gunmen.
1768. Rev. Elam Potter, estimated at 300 to 400 warriors.
1771. Romans, 250 warriors.
1780. Purcell, 575 warriors, 2,290 population.
1814. Schermerhorn, 1,000 warriors, 35,000 population.
1817. Morse, 3,625 population.
1829. Gen. Peter B. Porter, 3,600.
1833. Report in Schoolcraft, 4,715.

Chickasaw Population Subsequent to 1834

1836. United States Indian Office, 5,400.
1838. United States Indian Office, 4,176 (in west).
1839. United States Indian Office, 5,000.
1841. United States Indian Office, 5,000.
1842. United States Indian Office, 5,010.
1843. United States Indian Office, 5,010.
1844. United States Indian Office, 4,130.
1845. United States Indian Office, 4,211.
1847. United States Indian Office (in Schoolcraft), 1,166 families, 4,260.
1847. Another entry in Schoolcraft, 6,500.
1853. United States Indian Office, 4,709.
1855. United States Indian Office, 4,787.
1861. United States Indian Office, 5,000.
1865–1870. United States Indian Office, 4,500.
1871. United States Indian Office, 5,000.
1872–1875. United States Indian Office, 6,000.
1876. United States Indian Office, 5,800.
1877–1878. United States Indian Office, 5,600.
1879. United States Indian Office, 7,000.
1880–1889. United States Indian Office, 6,000.
1890–1891. United States Indian Office, 6,400.

[1] Authorities: Compte Rendu, Int. Cong. Am., 15th sess., I, p. 35; Iberville in Margry, Déc., IV, pp. 601–602; S. C. Pub. Rec., MS., V, pp. 207–209; Rivers, A Chapter in the Early Hist. of S. Car., p. 94; Ga. Col. Rec., V, p. 191; S. C. Pub. Rec., XXIII, p. 75, MS.; Adair, Hist. Am. Inds., p. 353; Hutchins in Schoolcraft, Ind. Tribes, III, p. 555; Bouquet, ibid., p. 559; Potter in Mass. Hist. Soc. Colls., 1st ser., X, p. 121; Am. Hist. Rev., XX, 4, p. 825; Romans, Concise Nat. Hist. of E. and W. Fla., p. 69; Purcell in Mass. Hist. Soc. Colls., 1st ser., IV, p. 100; Schermerhorn in Mass. Hist. Soc. Colls., 2d ser., II, p. 16; Morse, Rept. to Sec. of War, p. 364; Porter in Schoolcraft, Ind. Tribes, III, p. 597; Schoolcraft, Ind. Tribes (1833); Reports U. S. Indian Office: Ind. Pop. in U. S., U. S. Census of 1910, p. 15; MS., Lib. Cong.

1892. United States Indian Office, 6,800.
1893–1897. United States Indian Office, 6,000.
1898. United States Indian Office, 8,730.
1899. United States Indian Office, 9,048.
1900. United States Indian Office, 10,500.
1901. United States Indian Office, 6,000 Indians, 3,500 freedmen.
1902. United States Indian Office, 11,500.
1903. United States Indian Office, 4,659 by blood, 198 by intermarriage, 4,211 freedmen.
1904. United States Indian Office, 4,826 by blood, 348 intermarried, 4,471 freedmen.
1905. United States Indian Office, 5,474 by blood, 598 intermarried, 4,695 freedmen.
1906. United States Indian Office, 5,558 by blood, 623 intermarried, 4,730 freedmen.
1907. United States Indian Office, 5,684 by blood, 635 intermarried, 4,670 freedmen.
1908. United States Indian Office, 1,538 full bloods, 4,146 mixed bloods, 635 intermarried, 4,670 freedmen.
1909. United States Indian Office, 1,550 full bloods, 4,185 mixed bloods, 647 intermarried, 4,673 freedmen.
1910. United States Census, 4,204.
1910–1912. United States Indian Office, 5,688 by blood, 645 intermarried, 4,651 freedmen.
1913. United States Indian Office, 5,674 by blood, 645 by intermarriage, 4,670 freedmen.
1914. United States Indian Office, 10,955 total population.
1915. United States Indian Office, 1,515 full bloods, 966 one-half or more, 3,823 less than half (including 645 by intermarriage), 4,662 freedmen.
1916–1919. United States Indian Office, 5,659 by blood, 645 intermarried, 4,652 freedmen.

The only attempt to give the Chickasaw population by towns, so far as I am aware, is contained in an anonymous French memoir of about 1750,[1] from which I quote the following:

	Men.
Ayanaqua	40
Falatché	50
Goulat chitou	60
Acquina	40
Concquafala	50
Outanquatle	30
Achouqueouma	30
Coüi loussa	60
Tasca oullon	80
Apeonné	120
	560

The figures for the Choctaw appear to tell a simple story. Setting aside two or three early estimates, which are evidently too small or too large, there is practical unanimity. It would seem from the figures given us by travelers and officials that during the eighteenth century the tribe had a population of about 15,000. Only a few small tribes were added to it during the historic period. Toward

[1] MS., Ayer Lib.

the end of that century and during the first three decades of the nineteenth the population appears to have increased gradually, for the census of 1831, taken just before the removal, shows 19,554.[1] Allowing for the 1,000 or 2,000 Choctaw who remained in Mississippi and are not always enumerated in the later returns, we seem to have a surprising constancy in Choctaw population. Thus in 1904, when a careful census was made in which the Indians, intermarried whites, freedmen, and Mississippi Choctaw were carefully distinguished, we find 15,550 Indians belonging to the old emigration to Oklahoma to whom the 2,255 "Mississippi Choctaws" must be added.[2] These last were not, however, the Choctaw then living in Mississippi, but those who had emigrated recently from that State to share in the Choctaw allotment. As in 1910 there were 1,366 in Mississippi, Alabama, Louisiana, and other States,[3] we must also add at least that number, making a total of 18,539. This shows a decrease of only about 1,000 since 1831, but to the earlier figures something like 1,200 must be added for those Choctáw who had left the nation previous to the census of 1831 and settled in Louisiana and Texas. An actual decline of about 2,200 is thus indicated. It must, however, be remembered that the amount of Indian blood represented by the 18,539 Choctaw listed in 1904 was much smaller in quantity, relatively as well as absolutely, than that in the 19,554 of 1831, the quantity of white and Negro blood having been continually on the increase. From 1903 to 1914 the figures of the Indian Office show an apparent increase, so that, including the older emigrants to Oklahoma, the later emigrants, and the Indians in other States, there is a total of 20,451. But when one considers the premium placed upon Indian blood during the period of allotment and the constant lowering of the bars it will at once be suspected that all of this is not a legitimate Indian growth, and that these 20,451 are for the most part not ethnic Indians but legal Indians. The true state of affairs is probably approached much closer in the census returns of 1910, in which we find 14,551 given in Oklahoma, 1,162 in Mississippi, 115 in Louisiana, 57 in Alabama, and 32 in other States—a total of 15,917.[3] There had thus been an actual decrease in the numbers of the tribe since 1831, and a still greater decrease in its blood, though this latter must be corrected in turn by the addition of a certain amount which has passed out among the whites and Negroes and is no longer recognized as Choctaw, or even as Indian, and by allowing for certain individuals who have left the Indian country and now live the lives of ordinary white citizens.

---

[1] Sen. Doc. 512, 23d Cong., 1st sess., III, p. 149.

[2] Rept. Comm. Ind. Aff. for 1904, p. 598.

[3] Ind. Pop. in the U. S., Census of 1910, p. 17.

The following table contains the figures upon which this discussion is based:

POPULATION OF THE CHOCTAW AT VARIOUS PERIODS PRIOR TO 1834 [1]

Authority.	Year.	Warriors.	Total population.
Iberville	1702	3, 800–4, 000	[2] [13, 300–14, 000]
De la Vente	1704	....	[3] 7, 000–8, 000
Moll map	1715	700	[2, 450]
Bienville	1725–26	8, 000	[28, 000]
Regis du Roullet	1730	+3, 000	[+10, 500]
Père Baudoin	1732	1, 466	[5, 131]
Colonial Records of Georgia	1738	16, 000	[56, 000]
Colonial Records of Georgia	1739	5, 000	[4] [17, 500]
Anonymous French MS	1750(?)	+3, 610	[5] +12, 635
Adair	1750(?)	[6] 4, 500	[15, 750]
De Kerlerec	1758	3, 500–4, 000	[7] [12, 250–14, 000]
Bouquet	1764	4, 500	[15, 750]
Hutchins	1764	....	21, 500
Letter of John Stuart	1764	5, 000	[17, 500]
Potter	1768	800–900	[2, 800–3, 150]
Romans	1771	2, 600	9, 100
Ramsey	1780	4, 141	13, 423
Smith	1785	4, 500	[15, 750]
Schermerhorn	1814	4, 000	15, 000
Hodgson	1820	....	15, 000–20, 000
Morse	1822	....	25, 000
Armstrong (a census)	[8] 1831	....	19, 554

[1] Authorities: Iberville in Margry, Déc., IV, pp. 601–602; Compte Rendu, Int. Cong. Am., XV sess., I, p. 35; Moll map; Ga. Col. Rec., V, p. 56; Ibid., p. 191; Mem. Am. Anth. Ass'n, V, No. 2, pp. 71–72; Adair, Hist. Am. Inds., p. 282; De Kerlerec in Compte Rendu, Int. Cong. Am., XV sess., I, p. 76; Bouquet in Schoolcraft, Ind. Tribes, III, p. 559; Hutchins, ibid., p. 555; Am. Hist. Mag., vol. XX, 4, p. 825; Potter in Mass. Hist. Soc. Colls., 1st ser., X, p. 121; Romans, Concise Nat. Hist. of E. and W. Fla., p. 74; Ramsey in Mass. Hist. Soc. Colls., 1st ser., IV, p. 99; Smith in Schoolcraft, Ind. Tribes, III, p. 555; Schermerhorn in Mass. Hist. Soc. Colls., 2d ser., II, p. 17; Hodgson, Journ. N. Amer., pp. 274–275; Morse, Rept. to Sec. of War, p. 364; Reports U. S. Ind. Office; Ind. Pop. in U. S., U. S. Census of 1910, p. 15.

[2] Figures in brackets are derived by multiplying the number of warriors by 3½; the rest are as given in the originals.

[3] More than 700–800 cabins.

[4] 46 towns.

[5] 45 towns.

[6] Not above this figure.

[7] 52 towns.

[8] Correspondence on the subject of the Emigration of Indians, &c., Senate Document No. 512, 1833, Washington, 1835, III, p. 149

Choctaw Population Subsequent to 1834

1835. United States Indian Office, 18,500.
1838–1843. United States Indian Office, 18,500.
1844. United States Indian Office, 19,410.
1845. United States Indian Office, 19,392.
1847. United States Indian Office, 16,000.
1850. United States Indian Office, 12,760.
1853. Schoolcraft (from census rolls), 15,767.
1854. United States Indian Office, 15,767.
1855. United States Indian Office, 16,000.
1856. United States Indian Office, 22,707.
1857. United States Indian Office, 19,707.
1861. United States Indian Office, 18,000.
1865–1870. United States Indian Office, 12,500.
1871. United States Indian Office, 15,000.
1872–1878. United States Indian Office, 16,000.
1879. United States Indian Office, 16,500.
1880. United States Indian Office, 15,800.
1881. United States Indian Office, 15,890.
1882. United States Indian Office, 16,000.
1883–1885. United States Indian Office, 18,000.
1886. United States Indian Office, 16,000.
1887. United States Indian Office, 18,000.
1888. United States Indian Office, 18,200.
1889–1892. United States Indian Office, 18,000.
1893–94. United States Indian Office, 20,000.
1895–1897. United States Indian Office, 17,819.
1898. United States Indian Office, 18,456, including freedmen but excluding intermarried whites.
1898. United States Indian Office, 19,406, including freedmen and intermarried whites.
1900. United States Indian Office, 20,250.
1901. United States Indian Office, 16,000, not counting 4,250 freedmen.
1902. United States Indian Office, 20,250, including freedmen.
1903. United States Indian Office, 14,918, besides 205 intermarried whites and 2,983 freedmen.
1904. United States Indian Office, 15,550, besides 954 intermarried whites, 4,722 freedmen, and 2,255 Mississippi Choctaws.[1]
1905. United States Indian Office, 17,160, besides 1,467 intermarried whites, 5,254 freedmen, and 1,235 Mississippi Choctaws.
1906. United States Indian Office, 17,529, besides 1,550 intermarried whites, 5,378 freedmen, and 1,356 Mississippi Choctaws.
1907. United States Indian Office, 19,036, besides 1,585 intermarried whites and 5,994 freedmen.
1908. United States Indian Office, 19,036, including 10,717 mixed bloods, but not including 1,585 intermarried whites and 5,994 freedmen.
1909. United States Indian Office, 19,106, including 10,769 mixed bloods, but not including 1,671 intermarried whites and 5,994 freedmen.
1910. Census returns (including 1,162 in Mississippi, 14,551 in Oklahoma, 115 in Louisiana, 57 in Alabama, and 32 in other States), 15,911.

---

[1] By Mississippi Choctaws are meant Indians in the Choctaw Nation who had recently arrived from Mississippi; those remaining in the latter State are spoken of as Choctaws in Mississippi.

1910. United States Indian Office, 17,489, besides 1,651 intermarried whites, 5,985 freedmen, and 1,637 Mississippi Choctaws.

1911–12. United States Indian Office, 17,479, besides 1,651 intermarried whites, 5,985 freedmen and 1,672 Mississippi Choctaws.

1913. United States Indian Office, 17,328, besides 1,651 intermarried whites, 5,994 freedmen, and 1,639 Mississippi Choctaws.

1914. United States Indian Office, 17,446, besides 1,651 intermarried whites, 5,994 freedmen, and 1,639 Mississippi Choctaws.

1915. United States Indian Office, 20,799 (8,444 full bloods, 2,473 half bloods or more, 10,822 less than half blood, including 1,651 by intermarriage); freedmen 6,029; in Mississippi 1,253; in Louisiana, a few.

1916–1919. United States Indian Office, 17,488 by blood, 1,651 intermarried, 6,029 freedmen, 1,660 "Mississippi Choctaw," and 1,253 in the State of Mississippi.

To the last figures must be added about 200 for the Choctaw in Louisiana, Alabama, and elsewhere.

The only early town-by-town censuses of the Choctaw Nation which have come to my attention are contained in two manuscripts, the one in the French archives, a copy being in the Library of Congress, the other in a manuscript preserved in the Edward E. Ayer collection at the Newberry Library, Chicago,[1] the same from which the Chickasaw census on page 450 was taken. The first is dated 1730 and is by Regis du Roullet, a French officer sent among the Choctaw in order to enlist their aid against the Natchez Indians; the author of the second is unknown and its date uncertain, that provisionally set for it, 1750, being more likely too late than too early.

The following table embodies the material contained in these two lists, the subdivisions being given in accordance with the census of 1750, and the orthography of the town names in accordance with the same census except in the case of those towns which do not appear in it:

NUMBER OF MEN IN THE CHOCTAW TOWNS

	1730[2]	1750
Those of the east:		
Chicachae	160	150
Osquæ alagna	[3]200	400
Tala	60	60
Nachoubaoüenya	50	40
Nacchoubanfouny	20	......
Bouctouloutchy	30	30
Youanny	50	30
Those of the south.		
Conchats	100	[4]150
Yanabé	60	100
Oqué loüsa	100	80
Coït chitou	80	80

[1] Mem. Am. Anth. Assn., v, No. 2, pp. 71–72.

[2] The number of men in a few of these towns is given in a communication by the same writer the year before. These are Coit Chitou 400, Bouctoulōuchy (?) 20, Yanabé 30, Oqueloüsa 60, Coucha 200, and 30 youths, Nachoubaoüenya 30, Osquea alagna 500, Tala 30, Youanny 60, Chicachaé 150.

[3] Including Cheniacha.

[4] Adair, however, reports "Coosah," the Conchats of the above list, to have been the largest town in his time.—Hist. Am. Inds., p. 283.

Those of the west:

	1730	1750
Bouctoucoulou	....	60
Pinté	70	50
Abissa	30	40
Boucfalaya	15	70
Stéchipouta [Itéchipouta]	60	40
Filitamon	....	60
Conchaboulouncta	....	100
Louscouchetacanlé [Pouscouchetacanlé]	80	50
Ectchanqué	20	30
Ougoulabalbaa	....	100
Oqué oülloü	20	60
Mongoulacha	100	150
Otouc falayá	....	100
Boucfouca	130	80
Faniakné	20	....
Castacha	120	80
Yachou	60	40
Abeca	50	200
Cafétalaya	130	70
Outapacha	....	40
Toüalé	....	40
Achouqouma[1]	20	30
Bisacha	15	80
Scanapa	180	30
Ebitoupougoula	100	60
Bouctoucoüloü	130	90
Alibamons-chouga-lougolé	40	....
Abeca	100	60
Oulitacha	50	40
Loucféatá	60	50
Choukelissa	30	....
Mongoulacha	20	60
Yachoü or Achouq loüá	70	70
Itéopchaqüo [Itéokchaqüo]	100	100
Rouctacanté	10	....
Osapaissa	....	50
Ouatonaoülá	30	80
Boucchito	30	....
Epitoupougoula	....	80
Ougoulatanap	....	150

While the number of southern tribes progressively decreased from early times until many of them became wholly or nearly extinct, the surviving groups, the Creeks, Seminole, Chickasaw, and Choctaw, appear at first rather to have increased. Owing to their numerous wars the Chickasaw decreased in the first half of the eighteenth century, but after that time there is evidence that they grew rapidly, until they reached about 5,000, where their population remained stationary down to the present day. In appearance they continued

[1] Spelled Atchouchouga by Regis du Roullet.

to mount up much beyond that point, but later figures show that this was due to the inclusion of an almost equal number of Negro freedmen among them. Actually we find that the proportion of full bloods has decreased and that the maintenance of their numbers exclusive of freedmen has been due to an extensive contribution of white and Negro blood. Like the Chickasaw, the Creeks show a considerable increase during the last part of the eighteenth century and the first part of the nineteenth, in spite of the many Indians who removed to Florida. This growth may have been in part fictitious since, when a census was taken in 1857, both Creeks and Seminole were found much less numerous than had been supposed. Nevertheless the figures for the Seminole which can be checked show that before these tribes were removed to the West they were populous. Their losses during the emigration and in the period during which they were trying to adapt themselves to their new surroundings may account in part for the discrepancy, although in the case of the Creeks there may have been some frauds due to the intrigues of designing contractors. Still the Creeks can hardly have been less than 15,000, and 20,000 would not be an excessive estimate for the mother tribe of a people of 5,000 like the Seminole. From time to time these tribes have undergone periods of increase and decrease. As in the case of the Chickasaw, their apparent strength has been augmented by including Negro freedmen, descendants of those slaves formerly held by the Indians. In the case of the Creeks, Seminole, and Choctaw, however, the Negroes were not so numerous, being a little more than one-third instead of a little less than one-half. The number of Creek and Seminole full bloods has also declined progressively. In 1908 rather more than half of both were returned as full-blood Indians, but I am confident that the actual number is very much smaller, so small as to be barely a handful. In short the Indian blood in all of these tribes appears to be spreading out continually, but it is spreading over a body of white and Negro blood ever greater in amount, while the Indian blood becomes less and less.

Perhaps we shall not be far wrong if we assume a Creek population of about 7,000 in 1700, 12,000 in 1750–1760, 20,000 in 1832, 15,000 in 1857, 10,000 in 1898 (exclusive of freedmen), and 7,000 in 1910. For the Seminole we may give the following estimates: 1,500 in 1780, 4,750 in 1821, 2,500 in 1857, 3,500 in 1892, 2,500 in 1906 (including freedmen), and down to the present time, with the same increase of white and Negro blood. For the Chickasaw: 3,000 to 3,500 in 1700, 2,000 in 1715, 1,500 in 1750–1770, 3,600 in 1821, 5,000 in 1836, 4,000 in 1910. For the Choctaw: 15,000 in 1700, 21,000 in 1831, 16,000 in 1910, with the reservations above made.

BIBLIOGRAPHY

ACCOUNT SHEWING THE PROGRESS OF THE COLONY OF GEORGIA FROM ITS FIRST ESTABLISHMENT. Published by order of the Honorable Trustees [for establishing the Colony of Georgia in America], London, 1741.

ADAIR, JAS. The history of the American Indians. London, 1775.

ALABAMA ANTHROPOLOGICAL SOCIETY, Handbook, 1920. Montgomery, Ala., 1920.

ALABAMA HISTORICAL SOCIETY, Transactions of the. Tuscaloosa, Ala., 1896–1900.

ALVORD, CLARENCE W., and BIDGOOD, LEE. First explorations of the Trans-Allegheny region by the Virginians, 1650–1674. Cleveland, 1912.

AMERICAN ANTIQUARIAN AND ORIENTAL JOURNAL. Vols. I–XXXII, Chicago [and elsewhere], 1878–1910.

AMERICAN STATE PAPERS. Documents, legislative and executive, of the Congress of the United States. Class II, Indian Affairs. Vols. I–II. Washington, 1832–34. Public Lands. Vols. I–VIII. Washington, 1832–1861.

AYER LIBRARY OF AMERICANA, in Newberry Library, Chicago, Ill. Original Span ish and French MSS. and copies of such MSS.

BANDELIER, AD. F., *ed.* The journey of Alvar Nunez Cabeza de Vaca. Trans. by F. Bandelier. New York, 1905.

BARCIA CARBALLIDO Y ZUÑIGA, ANDRÉS G. Ensayo cronológico para la historia general de la Florida, 1512–1722, por Gabriel de Cardenas Z. Cano [*pseud.*]. Madrid, 1723.

BARTRAM, JOHN. Description of East Florida. London, 1769.

BARTRAM, WM. Travels through North and South Carolina, Georgia, East and West Florida, the Cherokee country, the extensive territories of the Muscogulges or Creek Confederacy, and the country of the Chactaws. Philadelphia, 1791. London, 1792.

BIDGOOD, LEE. See Alvord, Clarence W., and Bidgood.

BOLLAERT, WM. Observations on the Indian tribes in Texas. (Jour. Ethnol. Soc. London, vol. II, 1850.)

BOSOMWORTH, THOMAS. Journal of 1752. [MS. in South Carolina Archives; copy in Archives Bur. Amer. Ethnol.]

BOSSU, M. Nouveaux Voyages aux Indes Occidentales; Contenant une Relation des différens Peuples qui habitent les environs du grand Fleuve Saint-Louis, appellé vulgairement le Mississipi; leur Religion; leur gouvernement; leurs moeurs; leurs guerres & leur commerce. Vols. I–II. Paris, 1768.

BOURNE, E. G., *ed.* Narratives of the career of Hernando de Soto. Vols. I–II. New York, 1904.

BRINTON, DANIEL G. Notes on the Floridian peninsula, its literary history, Indian tribes and antiquities. Philadelphia, 1859.

BURK, JOHN. The history of Virginia from its first settlement to the present day. Vols. I–III. Petersburg, Va., 1805.

BUSHNELL, DAVID I., Jr. The account of Lamhatty. Amer. Anthrop., n. s. vol. 10, No. 4, pp. 568–574, Lancaster, 1908.

CANDLER, ALLEN D. *See* COLONIAL RECORDS OF THE STATE OF GEORGIA.

CARROLL, B. R. Historical collections of South Carolina; embracing many rare and valuable pamphlets, and other documents, relating to the history of that state, from its first discovery to its independence, in the year 1776. Vols. I–II. New York, 1836.

COHEN, M. M. Notices of Florida and the Campaigns. New York, 1836.

COLECCIÓN DE DOCUMENTOS INÉDITOS, relativos al descubrimiento, conquista y colonización de las posesiones Españolas en América y Oceanía. Tomos I–XLI. Madrid, 1864–84.

COLLOT, LE GENERAL VICTOR. Voyage dans l'Amérique Septentrionale, etc. Vols. I–II and atlas. Paris, 1826.

COLONIAL RECORDS OF THE STATE OF GEORGIA (THE). Compiled and published under authority of the Legislature, by Allen D. Candler. Atlanta, Ga., 1904–1909.

CONGRÈS INTERNATIONAL DES AMÉRICANISTES. Compte-rendu. Quinzième session, Québec, 1906. Quebec, 1907.

CORRESPONDENCE ON THE SUBJECT OF THE EMIGRATION OF INDIANS. Vols. I–V. (Sen. Doc. 512, 23rd Cong., 1st sess., Washington, 1834–1835.)

COXE, DANIEL. A description of the English province of Carolana. By the Spaniards call'd Florida, and by the French, La Louisiane. London, 1741. (*Same*, in FRENCH, B. F., Historical collections of Louisiana, 2d ed., pt. 2, Philadelphia, 1850.)

DAVIES, JNO. History of the Carribbee islands. Translated from the French. London, 1666.

DAVILA PADILLA, FRAY AUGUSTIN. Historia de la fundacion y discurso de la provincia de Santiago de Mexico de la Orden de Predicadores por los vidas de sus varones insignes y casos notables de Nueva España. Brussels, 1625.

DE BRAHM, JOHN GERAR WILLIAMS. History of the Province of Georgia. Wormsloe, 1899.

DESCRIPTION OF SOUTH CAROLINA. (Anonymous.) 1761.

DICKENSON, JONATHAN. Narrative of a shipwreck in the Gulph of Florida. 6th ed. Stanford, N. Y., 1803.

DORSEY, JAMES OWEN, *and* SWANTON, JOHN R. A dictionary of the Biloxi and Ofo languages. Bull. 47, Bur. Amer. Ethn., Washington, 1912.

ETHNOLOGICAL SOCIETY OF LONDON. Journal, vols. I–IV, Edinburgh and London, 1848–56. New series, vols. I–II, London, 1869–71.

——— Transactions, vols. I–VIII, London, 1861–69.

FAIRBANKS, G. R. History of St. Augustine. New York, 1858.

——— History of Florida, 1512–1842. Philadelphia, 1871.

FONTANEDA, HERNANDO DE ESCALANTE. Memoria de las cosas y costa y Indios de la Florida. (Documentos Inéditos, tomo V, 532–548, Madrid, 1866. *Same*, in Smith, B., Letter of Hernando de Soto, and Memoir of Hernando de Escalante Fontaneda, Washington, 1854. *Same*, French trans., in Ternaux-Compans, Voyages, tome XX, 9–42, Paris, 1841.)

FRENCH, B. F. Historical collections of Louisiana, embracing many rare and valuable documents relating to the natural, civil, and political history of that state. Parts I–V. New York, 1846–53. (*Same*, New ser., New York, 1869. *Same*, Second ser., New York, 1875.)

GAFFAREL, PAUL LOUIS JACQUES. Histoire de la Floride française. Paris, 1875.

GATSCHET, ALBERT S. The Timucua language. (Proc. Am. Philos. Soc., vols. XVI–XVIII, Philadelphia, 1877–1880.)

——— A migration legend of the Creek Indians. Vol. I, Philadelphia, 1884 [Brinton's Library of Aboriginal American Literature, No. 4]. Vol. II, St. Louis, 1888 [Trans. Acad. Sci. St. Louis, vol. V, nos. 1 and 2].

GEORGIA HISTORICAL SOCIETY. Collections. Vols. I–IV. Savannah, 1840–78.

GOMARA, FRANCISCO LOPEZ DE. Historia de las Indias. Antwerp, 1554. (French trans., Paris, 1606.)

GREGG, ALEXANDER. History of the old Cheraws, containing an account of aborigines of the Pedee, 1730–1810. New York, 1867.

HAKLUYT, RICHARD. Collection of the early voyages, travels, and discoveries of the English nation. Vols. I–III. London, 1810.

HAMILTON, PETER J. Colonial Mobile, an historical study largely from original sources, of the Alabama-Tombigbee basin from the discovery of Mobile bay in 1519 until the demolition of Fort Charlotte in 1820. Boston and New York, 1910.

HANNA, C. A. The wilderness trail, or the ventures and adventures of the Pennsylvania traders on the Allegheny Path with some new annals of the old West, and the records of some strong men and some bad ones. Vols. I–II. New York and London, 1911.

HARRISSE, HENRY. The discovery of North America. A critical documentary and historic investigation. London and Paris, 1892.

HAWKINS, BENJ. A sketch of the Creek country, in 1798 and 99. (Georgia Hist. Soc. Colls., vol. III, Savannah, 1848.) Besides the original of this work in the possession of the Georgia Historical Society there is a copy, also in Hawkins's handwriting, in the Manuscripts Division of the Library of Congress, Washington, D. C. There are few differences of consequence between this and the published version, but a number of minor points, and where the Library of Congress MS. seems to be superior I have followed it. I have not attempted to point out these changes separately, but the more material divergencies are indicated in footnotes.

——— Letters of Benjamin Hawkins 1796–1806. (Georgia Hist. Soc. Colls., vol. IX, Savannah, 1916.)

HAYWOOD, JNO. The natural and aboriginal history of Tennessee, up to the first settlements therein by the white people, in the year 1768. Nashville, 1823.

HERRERA, ANTONIO DE. Historia general de los hechos de los Castellanos en las islas i tierra firme del mar oceano. Tomos I–V. Madrid, 1720.

HEWAT, ALEX. Historical account of the rise and progress of the colonies of South Carolina and Georgia. Vols. I–II. London, 1779.

HODGSON, ADAM. Remarks during a Journey through North America in the years 1819, 1820, and 1821. New York, 1823.

IMLAY, GILBERT. A topographical description of the western territory of North America. London, 1797.

INDIAN AFFAIRS (U. S.). Office of Indian Affairs (War Department). Reports, 1825–1848. Report of the Commissioner (Department of the Interior), 1849–1914.

INDIAN TREATIES and laws and regulations relating to Indian affairs. Washington, 1826.

——— Treaties between the United States of America and the several Indian tribes from 1778 to 1837. Washington, 1837.

INDIAN POPULATION IN THE UNITED STATES AND ALASKA, 1910. (Department of Commerce, Bureau of the Census, Washington, 1915.)

JEFFERYS, THOS. The natural and civil history of the French dominions in North and South America. Parts I–II. London, 1761.

——— The American atlas or a geographical description of the whole continent of America. London, 1776.

JESUIT RELATIONS and allied documents. Travels and explorations of the Jesuit missionaries in New France, 1610–1791. Reuben Gold Thwaites, *ed.* Vols. I–LXXIII. Cleveland, 1896–1901.

——— Relations des Jesuites contenant ce qui s'est passé de plus remarquable dans les missions des pères de la Compagnie de Jesus dans la Nouvelle-France. Embrassant les années 1611–1672. Tomes I–III. Quebec, 1858.

JONES, CHAS. C. Historical sketch of Tomo-chi-chi. Albany, 1868.

KERCHEVAL, SAMUEL. A History of the Valley of Virginia. Winchester, 1833.

LA HARPE, BERNARD DE. Journal historique de l'éstablissement des Français à la Louisiane. Nouvelle Orléans, 1831. (*Same*, trans. in French, B. F., Hist. Coll. La., vol. III, New York, 1851.)

LAUDONNIÈRE, RENÉ. L'Histoire notable de la Floride située ès Indes Occidentales, contenant les trois voyages faits en icelle par certains Capitaines et Pilotes françois, qui y a commandé l'espace d'un an trois moys: a laquelle a esté adjousté un quatriesme voyage fait par le Capitaine Gourgues, mise en lumière par M. Basnier. Paris, 1586. (*Same*, Paris, 1853.)

—— History of the first attempt of the French (The Huguenots) to colonize the newly discovered country of Florida. (A translation of the above in French, B. F., Hist. Colls. of La. and Fla., n. s., pp. 165–175, New York, 1869.)

LAWSON, JNO. History of Carolina, containing the exact description and natural history of that country. London, 1714. (*Reprint*, Raleigh, 1860.)

LEDERER, JOHN. The discoveries of John Lederer in three several marches from Virginia to the west of Carolina and other parts of this continent; begun in March, 1669 and ended September, 1670. Together with a general map of the whole territory which he traversed. Collected and translated by Sir William Talbot, Baronet. London, 1672. Reprinted, Rochester, N. Y., 1902.

LE MOYNE, JACQUES. Narrative of Le Moyne, an artist who accompanied the French expedition to Florida under Laudonnière, 1564. Translated from the Latin of De Bry. Boston, 1875.

LE PAGE DU PRATZ, ANTOINE S. Histoire de la Louisiane. Tomes I–III. Paris, 1758. (*Same*, English trans., London, 1763, 1774.)

LIBRARY OF CONGRESS, MANUSCRIPTS DIVISION. One of the greatest single sources of information, rich in original documents and in copies of such documents.

LOGAN, JNO. H. A history of the upper country of South Carolina, from the earliest period to the close of the War of Independence. Vol. I. Charleston and Columbia, 1859.

LOUISIANA HISTORICAL SOCIETY MSS.

LOWERY, WOODBURY. The Spanish settlements within the present limits of the United States. 1513–1561. New York and London, 1901.

—— Spanish settlements within the present limits of the United States: Florida, 1564–1574. New York and London, 1905.

—— Florida Manuscripts. (Library of Congress.)

MACCAULEY, CLAY. The Seminole Indians of Florida. Fifth Ann. Rept. Bur. Ethn., pp. 469–531.

M'CALL, HUGH. The history of Georgia, containing brief sketches of the most remarkable events, up to the present day. Vols. I–II. Savannah, 1811–16.

MARGRY, PIERRE. Découvertes et établissements des Français dans l'ouest et dans le sud de l'Amérique Septentrionale (1614–1754). Mémoires et documents originaux, Pts. I–VI. Paris, 1875–86.

MARTYR, PETER (D'ANGHIERA). De Orbe Novo. English trans. by F. A. MacNutt. Vols. I–II. New York, 1912.

MASSACHUSETTS HISTORICAL SOCIETY. Collections. Vols. I–X, Boston, 1792–1809 (vol. I reprinted in 1806 and 1859; vol. V in 1816 and 1835). 2d ser., I–X, Boston, 1814–23 (reprinted 1838–43). 3d ser., I–X, Boston, 1825–49 (vol. I reprinted 1846). 4th ser., I–X, Boston, 1852–71.

MERENESS, NEWTON D., *ed.* Travels in the American Colonies. New York, 1916.

MILFORT, LE CLERC. Mémoire ou coup-d'œil rapide sur mes différens voyages et mon séjour dans la nation Crëck. Paris, 1802.

MISSISSIPPI PROVINCIAL ARCHIVES, 1763–1766. English Dominion. Compiled and edited by Dunbar Rowland. Vol. I. Nashville, Tenn., 1911.

MOONEY, JAMES. The Siouan Tribes of the East. Bull. 22, Bur. Amer. Ethn., Washington, 1894.

—— Myths of the Cherokee. Nineteenth Rept. Bur. Amer. Ethn., pt. 1, Washington, 1900.

MORSE, JEDIDIAH. A report to the Secretary of War of the United States, on Indian affairs, comprising a narrative of a tour performed in the summer of 1820. New Haven, 1822.

NAVARRETE, MARTIN FERNANDEZ DE. Coleccion de los viages y descubrimientos que hicieron por mar los Españoles desde fines del siglo XV. Madrid, 1825 [-1837].

OVIEDO Y VALDEZ, GONZALO FERNÁNDEZ DE. Historia general y natural de las Indias. Primera parte. Madrid, 1851.

PAREJA, FRANCISCO. Cathecismo, en lengva Castellana, y Timuquana. Mexico, 1612.

——— Confessionario, en lengua Castellana, y Timuquana. Mexico, 1613.

——— Arte de la lengva Timvqvana compvesta en 1614. (Bibliothèque Linguistique Américaine, tome XI, Paris, 1886.)

——— *See* GATSCHET, A. S. (Timucua language, 1878.)

PICKETT, ALBERT J. History of Alabama, and incidentally of Georgia and Mississippi, from the earliest period. 3d ed. Vols. I–II. Charleston, 1851.

PROCEEDINGS OF THE BOARD DEALING WITH INDIAN TRADE. (MS. in State Archives of S. Car.)

PUBLIC RECORDS OF SOUTH CAROLINA. [MSS.]

RAMSEY, J. G. M. The annals of Tennessee to the end of the eighteenth century. Philadelphia, 1853.

RIVERS, W. S. A chapter in the early history of South Carolina. Charleston, 1874.

ROMANS, BERNARD. A concise natural history of East and West Florida. Vol. I (Vol. II unpublished). New York, 1775.

ROYCE, CHARLES C. Indian Land Cessions in the United States. Eighteenth Ann. Rept. Bur. Amer. Ethn., part 2, Washington, 1899.

RUIDIAZ Y CARAVIA, EUGENIO. La Florida su conquista y colonización por Pedro Menéndez de Avilés. Vols. I–II. Madrid, 1894.

SCHOOLCRAFT, HENRY R. Historical and statistical information, respecting the history, condition and prospects of the Indian tribes of the United States. Parts I–VI. Philadelphia, 1851–57.

SENATE DOCUMENT 512. See Correspondence on emigration of Indians.

[SERRANO Y SANZ, MANUEL, *ed.*] Documentos historicos de la Florida y la Luisiana siglos XVI al XVIII. Madrid, 1913.

SHIPP, BARNARD. The history of Hernando de Soto and Florida; or, record of the events of fifty-six years, from 1512 to 1568. Philadelphia, 1881.

SIBLEY, JNO. Historical sketches of the several Indian tribes in Louisiana, south of the Arkansa river, and between the Mississippi and River Grand. Message from the President communicating discoveries made by Captains Lewis and Clark, Washington, 1806. *Same*, in Am. State Papers, Indian Affairs, vol. I, 1832. *Same*, in Annals of Congress, 9th Cong., 2d sess., 1076–1088.

SMITH, BUCKINGHAM. Two documents in two of the early tongues of Florida, Apalachian and Timuquan. Washington, 1860.

———, *tr.* Letter of Hernando de Soto and Memoir of Hernando de Escalante Fontaneda. Washington, 1854.

SOUTH CAROLINA HISTORICAL AND GENEALOGICAL MAGAZINE. Vols. I–XVIII. Charleston, S. C., 1900–1912.

SOUTH CAROLINA HISTORICAL SOCIETY. Collections. Vols. I–V. Charleston and Richmond, 1857–1897.

SPECK, FRANK G. The Creek Indians of Taskigi town. (Mem. Am. Anthr. Asso., vol. II, pt. 2, Lancaster, Pa., 1907.)

——— Ethnology of the Yuchi Indians. (Anthr. Pub. Univ. Mus., Univ. Pa., vol. I, no. 1, Philadelphia, 1909.)

Stiggins, George. A historical narration of the genealogy, traditions, and downfall of the Ispocoga or Creek tribe of Indians writ by one of the tribe. (MS. in possession of the Wisconsin Historical Society.)

Swan, Caleb. Position and state of manners and arts in the Creek, or Muscogee Nation in 1791. (*In* Schoolcraft, Indian Tribes, vol. v, pp. 251–283, Philadelphia, 1855.)

Swanton, John R. Indian tribes of the lower Mississippi Valley and adjacent coast of the Gulf of Mexico. (Bull. 43, Bur. Amer. Ethn., Washington, 1911.)

——— De Soto's line of march from the viewpoint of an ethnologist. (Proc. Miss. Valley Hist. Asso. for 1911–1912, vol. v, pp. 147–157, Cedar Rapids, Iowa, 1912.)

——— *See* Dorsey, J. O.

Tailfer, Patrick T., Anderson, H., Douglas, D., and others. A true and historical narrative of the colony of Georgia. Charles Town, S. Car., 1741. (Reprinted in Ga. Hist. Soc. Colls., vol. ii, pp. 163–263, Savannah, 1842.)

Thomas, Cyrus. Introduction to Indian Land Cessions in the United States. By Charles C. Royce. (Eighteenth Ann. Rept. Bur. Amer. Ethn., pt. 2, Washington, 1902.)

True (A) and Historical Narrative of the colony of Georgia in America, &c. (Anonymous.) Charles Town, S. C., 1741.

Tuggle, W. O. Myths of the Creeks. (MS. in archives of the Bureau of American Ethnology.)

Williams, Jno. Lee. The Territory of Florida; or sketches of the topography, civil and natural history, of the country. New York, 1837.

Winsor, Justin. Narrative and critical history of America. Vols. i–viii. Boston and New York, 1884–89.

Woodward, Thos. S. Woodward's reminiscences of the Creek, or Muscogee Indians, contained in letters to friends in Georgia and Alabama. Montgomery, 1859.

INDEX